D1513902

OXFORD MEDICAL PUBLICATIONS

HENDERSON AND GILLESPIE'S
TEXTBOOK
OF PSYCHIATRY

HENDERSON AND GILLESPIE'S
TEXTBOOK
OF PSYCHIATRY

FOR
STUDENTS AND PRACTITIONERS

TENTH EDITION

Revised by

IVOR R. C. BATCHELOR
M.B., Ch.B., F.R.C.P.E., F.R.S.E., D.P.M.
Professor of Psychiatry, University of Dundee

LONDON
OXFORD UNIVERSITY PRESS
NEW YORK   TORONTO

Oxford University Press, Ely House, London W. 1

GLASGOW NEW YORK TORONTO MELBOURNE WELLINGTON
CAPE TOWN IBADAN NAIROBI DAR ES SALAAM LUSAKA ADDIS ABABA
DELHI BOMBAY CALCUTTA MADRAS KARACHI LAHORE DACCA
KUALA LUMPUR SINGAPORE HONG KONG TOKYO

Hardback Edition ISBN 0 19 264412 2
Paperback Edition ISBN 0 19 264413 0

© Oxford University Press 1962, 1969

First Edition 1927
Tenth Edition 1969
Second impression 1973

Printed in Great Britain
by R. & R. Clark, Ltd., Edinburgh

In respectful and affectionate remembrance
of
ADOLF MEYER (1866–1950), M.D., LL.D.
Professor of Psychiatry and Director of the
Henry Phipps Psychiatric Clinic
Johns Hopkins Hospital, Baltimore

★

His imaginative leadership instituted a new era
in psychiatric thought and practice

CONTENTS

PREFACE TO THE TENTH EDITION

Sir David Henderson was born on April 24, 1884, and died on April 20, 1965. He had written the greater part of the first edition of this textbook and of its subsequent eight editions over a period of 35 years. It embodied eloquently the wide range of his interests and erudition, his clinical teaching and humanity. A sensitive understanding of the personal psychological problems of each patient was for him of central importance. He thought in terms of sick people rather than of disease entities, and his use of a classification by reaction-types and of detailed case-histories expressed his abiding concern for the needs of the individual patient. In seeking to meet these needs he was practical, constructive and optimistic, and his broad-minded eclectciism gave him great flexibility of approach.

For this tenth edition much of the text has been reordered and rewritten and chapters have been added, to deal more fully with current interests and problems and the new data from research. It is my hope that these changes will ensure for this textbook a continued useful life, without the loss of too much of its original character.

Dundee
August 1968

I. R. C. B.

PREFACE TO THE FIRST EDITION

Our aim in this book has been to present psychiatry as a living subject, with important relations not only to general medicine, but to the social problems of everyday life. Recent work in psychopathology has given to the study of mental disorders a human and a scientific interest which was too often lacking before. Most of all, the biological viewpoint of Adolf Meyer and his followers of the American school has seemed to us to shed fresh light on the nature of mental illness, and to offer new hope in its prevention and treatment. This biological hypothesis regards mental illness as the cumulative result of unhealthy reactions of the individual mind to its environment, and seeks to trace in a given case all the factors that go to the production of these reactions. We hope to have shown to some extent in the following pages how much of understanding and interest these and other recent researches have added to psychiatry.

Nomenclature we have sought to make as simple as possible, as we believe that the facts are best expressed in ordinary language, and that the use of technical terms should be restricted to occasions where brevity and convenience demand them. One thing will be apparent to the reader; namely, how much regarding the nature of mental disorder remains unknown. We have presented the facts and the chief interpretations of them, indicating what among the latter seems most likely to be verified. We believe the time has come when mental illness need no longer be regarded as the mysterious preserve of a few specialists now that a working knowledge of psychiatry is within easy reach of the general practitioner, with all that that implies in the way of early recognition, prevention and treatment.

We have made a point of quoting at length clinical records of cases in our own practice, so far as space permits; and this for several reasons. Mental illness is an individual affair. Its symptoms have little meaning apart from the setting in which they occur. This setting includes not only the general mental and physical condition at the time, but the individual's personality, circumstances and history from his earliest days. Hence general descriptions of clinical syndromes, while interesting, are not of the first importance. What is wanted always is an understanding of the patient as a human being, and of the problems which he is meeting in a morbid way with his 'symptoms'. It is in accordance with these principles, and with what is called the 'dynamic' view, that we have utilized clinical records so extensively.

The clinical material upon which the book is largely based was observed at the Glasgow Royal Mental Hospital; the Henry Phipps Psychiatric Clinic of the Johns Hopkins Hospital, Baltimore; the Psychiatric Institute of the New York State Hospital, Ward's Island, New York; the Cassel Hospital, Penshurst, Kent; and Guy's Hospital.

We have appended only a brief bibliography. To have furnished a comprehensive list of references would have meant much additional space. We must therefore content ourselves with acknowledging our indebtedness to many of the standard textbooks and to monographs dealing with special topics. Throughout the text we refer to a number of these, but where we have failed to make acknowledgement we now do so.

D. K. H.
R. D. G.

May 1927

1

HISTORICAL REVIEW OF THE CARE
AND TREATMENT OF MENTAL ILLNESS

Mental disorder, in one form or another, has been recognized from time immemorial, but it is only in comparatively recent years that serious attempts have been made to study and understand it. Progress in this branch of medicine has been slow, but the difficulties to be contended with—professional apathy, public prejudice and the inherent complexity of the subject—have been very great, and the advance which has actually taken place has not been sufficiently recognized. To give perspective to modern psychiatric problems, therefore, we have thought it wise to mention some of the more important landmarks in the social history of psychiatry.

Writers on the history of psychiatry have habitually referred to records, in Greek poetry and mythology, of episodes of frenzy affecting the Heroes, but it is quite impossible at this date to form a definite opinion of the relationship of these states to mental disorder as it is understood to-day. Early Egyptian papyri contain references to mental disturbances. Thus, about 1500 B.C., it was written of senility that 'The heart grows heavy, and remembers not yesterday.' This statement may have had a basis, even at that time, in anatomical as well as in psychological observations; Elliot Smith has demonstrated arteriosclerosis in his dissections of mummies. The first authentic cases of mental disorder are recorded in the Books of the Old Testament, where Saul, David and Nebuchadnezzar are famous examples. Epilepsy was the type of mental illness with which the ancients were specially familiar. It was long known to them as the 'sacred disease', but Hippocrates, with his customary insight, stated that 'The sacred disease (epilepsy) appears to me to be nowise more divine nor more sacred than other diseases, but has a natural cause from which it originates like other affections. Men regard its nature and cause as divine from ignorance, and wonder because it is not like other diseases.' Cambyses, the King of Persia, is a much-quoted example.

An early reference, perhaps the first, to the treatment of the insane is contained in Plato's *Republic* (Bk. xi. c. 13). 'If anyone is insane let him not be seen openly in the city, but let the relatives of such a person watch over him at home in the best manner they know of, and if they are negligent let them pay a fine.' In the time of Hippocrates, it was the custom for the mentally afflicted to visit the temple of Aesculapius, where sacrifices and prayer were offered. Incantations and purifications seem to have been specially recommended for epilepsy. Hippocrates himself, however, believed that the brain was the organ of mind, and he denied that there was anything occult or mysterious about the occurrence of a mental disorder. Democritus, in his correspondence with Hippocrates, made the curious statement that 'Hellebore when given to the sane pours darkness over the mind, but to the insane is very profitable'! Haemorrhoids and varicose veins were alleged to relieve a disturbed mind. The treatment attributed traditionally to Asclepiades (who flourished in the first century B.C.) was later described in the Christian era by Celsus, who advocated two widely divergent methods. On the one hand, he had a use for such methods as starving, chains and flogging; because under such treatment, it was said, those who had refused food started to eat, and in certain cases the memory was refreshed. On the other hand, he deprecated venesection and the use of fomentations of poppy and hyoscyamus, maintaining that everything possible should be done to divert the melancholic, and commenting favourably on sports, music, reading aloud, rocking in a hammock and the sound of a waterfall as methods of treatment. Themison, another disciple of Asclepiades, recommended a liberal diet, baths and fomentations. Titus has the invidious distinction of recommending stripes. Caelius Aurelianus is worthy of much praise, for he placed his patients under the best conditions of light, temperature and quiet, and recommended that everything of an exciting character should be excluded. Of particular interest are his references to tactfulness in attendants for the avoidance of antagonism, and to the limited and cautious use of physical restraint. The physician, he said, should not see the patient too frequently, lest his authority be undermined. Theatrical entertainments, riding, walking and work were all recommended, particularly during the period of convalescence. Topics of conversation were to be such as would suit the patient's condition. Later, excursions by land and water, and various other distractions, were to be used. He denounced semi-starvation, bleeding, chains and excessive drug therapy. Galen, basing his treatment on humoral pathology, recommended a just balance between 'moisture' and 'dryness'. Aretaeus, probably a contemporary of Galen, advised bleeding to relieve the liver in melancholy, purging by means of aloes, and baths; and, in convalescence, natural hot baths for their sulphur and bitumen.

Mediaeval Europe left the treatment of mental illness to priests, and superstitious beliefs in witchcraft and the like flourished. Special reference may be made to contemporary customs in the British Isles. Treatment by herbs, and binding in chains and fetters, are mentioned in old Saxon chronicles. Certain wells were considered to have special virtue. Of these, the most famous were St. Fillans, St. Ronans, Struthill, and a well on a small island on Loch Maree, in Scotland; St. Winifred's Well in Wales; and some in England, particularly in Cornwall. The Valley of Glen-na-Galt in Ireland had more than a local reputation.

Lunacy legislation in England dates from 1320 when it was enacted during the reign of Edward II that the property of lunatics should be vested in the Crown. Bethlem, which had been founded in London in 1247 as a priory of the Order of the Star of Bethlem, was the first hospital in the British Isles to care for the insane. It is recorded that in 1403 six lunatics were confined there. In 1546 Henry VIII granted St. Bartholomew's Hospital and Bethlem to the laity; in 1618 Dr. Helkiah Crooke was appointed Keeper and Physician to Bethlem.

In the seventeenth century the great Sydenham prescribed for 'mania' after long agues a cordial, generous indeed, consisting of Venice treacle (which contained the flesh and blood of vipers, and sixty-one more ingredients), canary wine and honey. This was given three times a day, with rest in bed; even pregnancy was no contra-indication. In addition Sydenham strongly recommended bleeding in the treatment of 'mania', saying, 'Young subjects, if of a sanguine habit, are to be bled to the extent of nine ounces on two or three occasions, with three days between each bleeding.' A caution was given not to exceed this amount of bleeding, 'otherwise idiocy and not recovery will result'. The bleeding was followed by a course of purgative pills. In place of venesection, Denis, of Paris, in 1667, introduced the transfusion of blood. This he employed in the case of a love-sick youth, with fatal results, and an ensuing action for damages.

In the next century the treatment of King George III, who suffered from recurrent attacks of maniacal excitement, served to arouse much public interest and controversy. His physician was a Dr. Willis, who had acquired a high reputation for his skill in dealing with such cases through his experience derived from the management of a private mental home in Lincolnshire which provided accommodation for twenty patients. Willis allowed his maniacal patients much freedom. If they escaped, the wages of the delinquent attendant were withheld until the patient returned. The Royal patient was treated with singularly little respect. No hesitation was evinced in knocking him down, and one attendant was even heard to boast that he had knocked him 'as flat as a flounder'. Willis ascribed great value in the King's case to the use of Peruvian bark, but other physicians who were consulted did not agree with him. In consequence of the rivalry, jealousy and differences of opinion which were revealed, the House of Lords decided to appoint a Committee to institute a detailed inquiry. This served a most useful purpose not only by directing greater attention to the King's treatment, but also to the medical and nursing care of all mentally afflicted throughout the whole country.

The modern era of the treatment of mental illness dates from the end of the eighteenth century, and may be divided into four periods:

1. The period of humane reform with which are associated the names of Pinel, Esquirol and Daquin in France; Tuke in England; Fricke in Germany; Morgagni and Chiarugi in Italy; Andrew Duncan in Scotland.
2. The introduction of non-restraint by Gardiner Hill, Charlesworth and Conolly in England, and by Bond, Kirkbride and Rush in the United States of America.
3. The hospital period.
4. The social and community period.

These periods will be discussed separately even although there is considerable overlapping.

HUMANE REFORM

It was in 1794 that Philippe Pinel was appointed to the medical staff of the Bicêtre Hospital, Paris. For several years he had shown great interest in the care and treatment of those who were mentally ill, and wrote a number of papers in which he discussed 'moral' treatment; one of his papers was entitled 'The most efficacious means of treating Mental Diseases occurring before Old Age'. It has been said that Thouret, an influential member of the Assembly, was impressed by Pinel's dissertation, and supported his candidature for the vacant post at Bicêtre Hospital. Pinel was a shy, timid, self-conscious man, but like many other sensitive people he had great tenacity of purpose, and it was not long before he was able to institute the beneficent and humanitarian reforms which were so close to his heart, and which have become so indissolubly associated with his name. At that time Bicêtre housed upwards of 200 male patients who were regarded not only as incurable but also as extremely dangerous. Some had been chained and fettered and confined in dungeons for many years, and yet Pinel was convinced that they were only unmanageable because they had been robbed of air and liberty, and freedom of action. His highest hopes were amply justified; the happy results proved the correctness of his opinions. Instead of blows and chains he introduced light and fresh air, cleanliness, workshops and promenades, but above all kindliness and understanding. The reforms which had proved so successful at Bicêtre were duplicated at the Salpêtrière, a mental hospital for women, where at a later date Esquirol became the physician in charge. A great epoch in the treatment of the mentally ill had been ushered in, which was acclaimed and had its reverberations in every country where psychiatry was practised.

Pinel was much more than a mental hospital administrator and physician. He set a high standard of medical care and practice, insisted on good case-taking, and made outstanding contributions to psychiatric literature. He taught by his writing and character more than by word of mouth.

Jean Étienne Dominique Esquirol, who may be described as Pinel's most distinguished pupil and interpreter, was appointed in 1812 to the medical staff of the Salpêtrière. He also managed a small private mental hospital at 23 Rue de Buffon, Paris, and in 1825 was appointed Chief Physician of the Charenton Mental Hospital. He became recognized as an authority on mental hospital construction—he founded no less than ten—but he was especially famous for instituting the first clinical lecture course on psychological medicine. He became known as a great teacher, and attracted students and doctors from all over the world. For instance, Sir Alexander Morison's lectures on psychiatry, and his textbook on mental diseases, were based on Esquirol's teaching; Dr. Andrew Combe and Sir Robert Christison were other distinguished Edinburgh physicians who attended Esquirol's lectures. Esquirol may be regarded as one of the first, if not the first, to establish a school of psychiatry.

After Esquirol came Ferrus, who received the new title, 'Inspecteur-Général du Service des Aliénés'. He had the distinction of starting a farm worked by patients who were being cared for at Bicêtre hospital. From his advocacy resulted the law of 1838 for the establishment of new mental hospitals in every department of France, and the improvement of the existing ones.

Almost simultaneously with these epoch-making reforms in France, the humanitarian efforts of William Tuke and Lindley Murray resulted in the opening in 1796 of the York Retreat in England. In Scotland, in 1792, Dr.

Andrew Duncan, who was Professor of Medicine, Edinburgh University, and President of the Royal College of Physicians, Edinburgh, sponsored an appeal for funds to establish the Royal Edinburgh Mental Hospital, which was opened in 1813.

In Germany the modern era began with Fricke, who in Brunswick in 1793 applied humane medical treatment and greatly reduced mechanical restraint. In 1803 Reil published a volume entitled *Rhapsodies on the Use of Psychic Treatment in Mental Disorder*, and in 1805 the first journal devoted to the study of mental disorders—the *Magazin für Nervenheilkunde*—was edited by Reil and Kayssler.

The reforms begun in England by Tuke, which resulted in the establishment of the York Retreat, were followed by the introduction of a Bill into Parliament for the better treatment of the insane. This became known as 'Wynn's Act', and was introduced in 1808 with the purpose of providing 'better care and maintenance of lunatics being paupers or criminals in England'. Amending Acts were introduced in 1811, 1815, 1819 and 1824 which laid the basis for the ensuing lunacy administration of this country. The Lunacy Commission, which was established in 1845, became reorganized in 1913 as the Board of Control, England, which now in terms of the 1959 Mental Health Act has been merged in the Ministry of Health.

In 1815 a Committee was appointed to investigate the conditions in 'madhouses' in England. The Report stated that keepers of houses for the insane admitted a greater number of persons than they were calculated for, there was an insufficient staff, too much restraint was used, the certificates on which the patients were received were often faulty and the visitation and inspection of private madhouses was inefficient. The Report drew attention to the flagrant abuses which existed, but no immediate action was taken. For instance, at the York Lunatic Asylum it was found that there had been great neglect and cruelty. Of 365 patients who had died, the deaths of only 221 had been reported; a patient had been killed and his body disposed of so as to avoid an inquest; and two sets of books had been kept. When Dr. Munro, the Superintendent of Bethlem, was questioned about the treatment of his patients, he said: 'Patients are ordered to be bled about the latter end of May, according to the weather. After they have been bled they take vomits once a week for a certain number of weeks. After that we purge the patients. That has been the practice for years, long before my time.' It is true there were no strait-jackets—irons were held in more esteem! Patients were chained in a state of nudity to tables. A female patient in a hospital at Bethnal Green was confined in a quondam pigsty. Male attendants not infrequently had charge of female wards (the practice appears to be returning) and the immorality and depravity which existed beggar description. In 1828 an Act (9 Geo. IV, c. 40) was passed appointing fifteen Metropolitan Commissioners to visit Homes in which the insane were detained.

It is obvious from what has been said that there was urgent need for the introduction of courses of instruction in psychiatry. In 1753 Dr. William Battie

B

attained the distinction of being the first psychiatrist in the British Isles to give clinical instruction at St. Luke's Hospital, London; 'young physicians well-recommended' visited the hospital with Dr. Battie, and were able to observe the treatment of the patients. Robertson (1928) states that Battie 'gave occasional clinical lectures to a few pupils'. In 1823 in Edinburgh, Sir Alexander Morison, who, as stated previously, had been a pupil of Esquirol, instituted a course of nine systematic lectures in psychiatry; in 1826 these lectures were duplicated in London, and this dual arrangement was maintained until 1852—a truly remarkable and unique performance. It can be claimed, therefore, with considerable justification, that Morison was the first teacher of systematic psychiatry in this country.

In the United States of America, Bond, Kirkbride and Rush were all responsible for instituting reforms which were very much in line with what was happening in France and Great Britain. The otherwise enlightened Rush (he was a graduate of Edinburgh University) published *Observations on the Human Mind*, in which he advocated copious bleeding, low diet, purges, calomel and opium. These methods came to be discarded by his successors, who were more in favour of 'supporting treatment'.

While the above changes, indicative of a more humanitarian outlook in regard to the treatment of the mentally disordered, were being engendered and spread over the civilized world, it is of interest to recall that even in 1731 Jonathan Swift, the famous Dean of St. Patrick's, Dublin, had foreshadowed the changes which might occur. It was in that year that he wrote his ode entitled *Verses on the Death of Dr. Swift*, the concluding lines of which consisted of the well-known quip or jest:

> He gave the little wealth he had
> To build a house for fools and mad;
> And show'd, by one satiric touch,
> No nation wanted it so much.

In 1745, at the time of his death, it was found that he had bequeathed a sum of between ten and eleven thousand pounds to found a hospital for the treatment of the insane. St. Patrick's Hospital was the first to be established in Ireland. The charter for erecting and endowing it was obtained in 1746, and in 1757 the first patients were admitted. It continues to maintain the great tradition of its past.

ABOLITION OF RESTRAINT

This period was initiated in 1837 by Gardiner Hill and Charlesworth at the Lincoln Asylum. In 1827, in the asylum, there were 72 patients. Of these, 39 were constantly in restraint and the total number of hours of restraint per annum amounted to 20,424. Under the regime of Hill and Charlesworth a revolution was effected; out of 130 patients only two were under restraint for a total period of 28 hours per annum. Subsequently mechanical restraint was entirely abolished. The patients showed a great improvement in their physical and mental health, their conduct was more controlled and the numbers of accidents and suicides was greatly decreased. Conolly in 1838 at Hanwell Asylum became an enthusiastic advocate of non-restraint, and in one of his reports he wrote: 'There is no asylum in the world in which all mechanical restraints may not be abolished, not only with perfect safety, but with incalculable advantage.' In 1856 he embodied his wide experience and his wisdom in a book entitled *The Treatment of the Insane without Mechanical Restraint.* The *Edinburgh Review* in 1870, commenting on Conolly's remarkable achievement, wrote as follows: 'To Conolly belongs a still higher crown, not merely for his courage in carrying out a beneficent conception on a large scale and in a conspicuous theatre, but for his genius in extending it. To him, hobbles and chains, handcuffs and muffs, were but material impediments that merely confined the limbs; to get rid of these he spent the best years of his life; but beyond these mechanical fetters he saw there were a hundred fetters to the spirit which human sympathy, courage and time only could remove.'

One of the most outstanding and courageous personalities among the early pioneers was the American school teacher Dorothea Lynde Dix. This remarkable woman, handicapped as she was by her upbringing and poor physical health, showed a spirit and an enterprise in relation to the welfare of the mentally disordered which has reverberated throughout the world. In America she was not only responsible for effecting great improvements but also founded approximately thirty-two institutions. 'Could all the prisons on new and better plans she carried Bills for, and all the almshouses she caused to be thoroughly reconstructed be added to these, and then all brought vividly before the mind's eye, the impressions would be amazing indeed.' Here in Scotland we are under a particular debt of gratitude to her. She had come to Great Britain to recuperate from a serious physical illness. She came to Edinburgh and visited a number of houses and hospitals where mentally ill patients were being cared for. Some were reasonably well-conducted but in others she discovered the most serious abuses. She tried to interest the local authorities, lawyers and doctors in what she felt was wrong but her protestations were received with coldness and contempt. She was dubbed 'the American invader', an interfering busybody. She was, however, a woman of great determination, and irrespective of all obstacles and local antagonism she journeyed to London, and was successful in obtaining an interview with the Home Secretary. The evidence which she presented so impressed him that in a few weeks a Royal Commission was appointed to inquire into the condition of lunatic asylums in Scotland, and the existing state of the law of that country in reference to lunatics and lunatic asylums. The Commission was appointed on April 3, 1855, and it was largely as a result of its findings that public mental hospitals were established throughout Scotland. She had accomplished in a few months what others during many years had striven to do.

It was due to the lack of suitable hospital organizations for the care and treatment of mental patients that a system of colony care arose which met with gratifying success. The colonies of Gheel and Lierneux in Belgium, of Clairmont (Oise) near Paris, and of those in Hanover and Moravia deserve special mention.

The one at Gheel is the best known. Its fame as a place of cure for the mentally ill arose from the legend of Dymphna, the beautiful daughter of an Irish king, who had made incestuous proposals to her. She refused, fled in a state of alarm to Belgium, but was followed, captured and beheaded by her father. Among those who witnessed this dreadful crime were some mentally afflicted persons who were stated to have, immediately, recovered their sanity. The scene of the crime became hallowed ground, pilgrimages were organized for the mentally sick and many remained to live among the inhabitants, so forming the first 'colony'. As organized at present it consists of a central psychiatric hospital of 200 beds, and in addition more than 2000 patients live, under supervision, in private homes and are employed, principally, in agricultural work. The patient lives as one of the family, and has no restrictions placed upon his freedom, except that he must be home by eight o'clock in the summer and by four o'clock in the winter. He is not allowed to enter an inn, or be served with alcohol, without special permission. On admission to the colony the patient is placed in an observation hospital and after his mental state has been carefully determined he is transferred to a family residence where he is likely to be suitably cared for. This system ensures a good degree of personal liberty, it is economical and promotes recovery through individualization and association with other persons who are able to behave and think in a normal manner.

Boarding Out. This is the term used in Scotland to describe the system of care and treatment whereby certain easily managed, long-continued-treatment cases can be maintained under guardianship in private homes. The patients are not segregated in one colony, as at Gheel, but are placed in those parts of the country where the most suitable guardians and houses are available. Minute inquiries are made beforehand as to the domestic arrangements, the amount of accommodation available, the facilities for occupation, recreation, social activities and, most important of all, the experience of the guardians. The possible exploitation of the patients requires to be safeguarded. Some patients may be 'boarded out' direct from their own homes, but the majority are transferred from a mental hospital or hospital for the subnormal where they have been under treatment. The sanction of the Mental Welfare Commission must be obtained in all cases. If, for any reason, the arrangements do not prove satisfactory the patient may be re-transferred to the mental organization from which he was 'boarded out'. During the period he is under private care his welfare is safeguarded by visits of inspection, four times a year by the district medical officer, twice a year by a public assistance employee, and once a year by a deputy medical commissioner or Commissioner of the Mental Welfare Commission. A record of visits requires to be kept. Patients under private care are either placed singly or in numbers not exceeding four of the same sex in any one house; the more usual arrangement is for one patient only. The above system has been in operation since the middle of the last century, and has much to commend it. It provides, under sheltered conditions, an approximation to home life which is not only beneficent and humanitarian but also much more economic than continued residence in a mental hospital organization. In 1968 in Scotland there were 861 subnormal patients formally boarded out, but very few mental patients. In Scandinavia, Canada and the United States, similar schemes have been put into operation.

THE HOSPITAL PERIOD

Since the beginning of the century the modernization and up-grading of mental hospitals has been a continuing process which has resulted in numerous beneficial changes. Their administration, medical and nursing staffing, the employment of psychiatric social workers, occupational therapists, psychologists, chiropodists and hairdressers, have raised the standard of care and treatment to a level of which we can be proud. The introduction of the National Health Service Act (1948) acted as a spur to our efforts and government funds became available whereby old hospitals could be renovated, and extensive reconstruction programmes could be undertaken. Our object is to develop the preventive and curative side of mental hospital work, and, *pari passu*, to educate our professional brethren and the public so that they may regard the mental hospital as an asset to the medical service of the community. The Mental Health Acts (1959 and 1960) whereby patients can be admitted to such hospitals 'informally' just as to general hospitals, have greatly facilitated the disappearance of the shades of the prison-house.

In order to gain a proper perspective it is of interest and value to recapitulate, summarily, some of the more important changes which have been effected.

After the period of 'non-restraint' had run its course, a system of 'seclusion' for dangerous impulsive patients who could not be trusted was introduced. This consisted of the use of single rooms—sometimes referred to as strong rooms— and of padded rooms which were locked, and in which patients might be confined both during the day and at night. Those in favour of the above system argued that it prevented struggling with the patient, it obviated serious accidents and there was much less necessity to use powerful sedatives. Furthermore it eased the burden and responsibility of a small, often sorely-tried medical and nursing staff. As the medical and nursing staffs became increased, both in quantity and quality, it soon became evident that the vast majority—if not all—of the so-called single room cases responded more co-operatively when cared for and nursed in open wards where they could be adequately supervised. The single rooms and padded rooms of the past have now been converted into comfortable bed-sitting rooms which are appreciated by those who are accustomed to privacy. We believe that the above-mentioned changes received a considerable impetus when as long ago as 1841 Dr. Samuel Hitch, who founded the Royal Medico-Psychological Association, suggested that much benefit might result from the employment of female nurses in the male wards of mental hospitals. At the Gloucester General Lunatic Asylum (as it was then called) he employed the wives of his married male nurses, to assist their husbands. In 1854 Dr. Browne, the Medical Superintendent of the Crichton Royal, Dumfries, instituted classes for the training of nurses, and in 1877 a similar systematic course of instruction was put into effect at the McLean Hospital, Boston, Massachusetts. In 1880 Dr. Campbell Clark conceived the idea that the standard of mental hospital nursing could be advanced to a higher level by the appointment of a general hospital trained nurse as matron of the Lanarkshire Mental Hospital at Bothwell; he was also responsible for the publication of a *Handbook for Attendants on the Insane* which has been greatly extended and brought up to date. As the *Handbook for Psychiatric Nurses* (9th ed.) it is still in use by mental hospital nurses who are preparing for the examinations conducted by the General Nursing Councils.

Clouston, Turnbull and Robertson were a few of the distinguished Scottish psychiatrists who were ardent protagonists of the introduction of general hospital nurses to positions of high responsibility, *e.g.* matrons, and assistant matrons, and of female nurses in the male wards. It has been our experience that male patients respond more naturally and politely to female nurses. But at the same time we appreciate that well-trained male nurses (many of whom now combine general and mental hospital training) are an indispensable and essential part of any mental hospital organization. Indeed the pendulum has been swinging in the contrary direction, and in some mental hospitals and psychiatric units male nurses are being appointed to senior posts on the female wards. That such an arrangement can now be generally applicable and successful has yet to be proven.

The care of patients in mental hospitals has been made easier by the establishment of smaller ward units, and by making special arrangements for attractive admission wards, hospital units for those requiring special nursing, *e.g.* acute mental states, convalescent cases, and those requiring more prolonged care. A special department for geriatric patients is to be desired.

The medical staffs of mental hospitals have been greatly increased. The post of Medical Superintendent has lost its administrative and clinical importance; the duties formerly undertaken by one person are now shared by lay administrators, by medical committees, and by consultant psychiatrists (whole and part-time) who assume clinical responsibility for departments or wards under their particular direction. Whether or not these are steps in the right direction remains to be seen. There are some who believe that a mental hospital with all its special activities which require co-ordination should be under unitary control, and that the splitting of authority is apt to lead to discordance not only in the care and treatment of the patients—which is the main issue—but also in the control of the nursing, domestic and artisan staff.

However that may be, the fact remains that the mental hospital to-day has established outside contacts and interests which, previously, did not exist. The medical staff are not only engaged in indoor duties, but their experience and training has been broadened by their participation in out-patient clinics, child-guidance clinics, domiciliary consultations, medico-legal work and university departments of psychiatry. The scope and training of the young psychiatrist have been developed so much that he has every opportunity to become familiar with preventive medico-social aspects of psychiatry which were not in the purview of his predecessors. Instead of locked doors and high walls we are developing anew the open door system where the wards are unlocked, and where the patients are given the freedom of the grounds and of the adjoining city or countryside. Following the lead of Professor Ewen Cameron, McGill University, Montreal, we have established Day and Night hospitals which can be of practical advantage in the convalescence and rehabilitation of those patients who may require additional help before they are fully able to resume their previous positions either at home or at work. In addition, in a large number of areas in Great Britain, Holland, Canada and the United States, determined attempts are being made to treat larger numbers of patients in their own homes. This is made possible through the co-operation of Public Health officials, out-patient departments, family practice units, psychiatrists, psychiatric social workers and health visitors. Our aim is to diminish our mental hospital admission rates and to maintain patients at work so long as it is compatible with their well-being.

We should stress particularly the advantages to be gained by establishing closer liaison with general practitioners, and with medical, surgical and other specialists. Such teamwork is not only of enormous benefit to the psychiatrist but serves the dual purpose of familiarizing the other members of our profession with the significance of the psychological factors in all forms of illness. It is by such co-ordinated methods that the prejudice and stigma so traditionally associated with mental illness will be eliminated.

A prerequisite for the extension of psychiatric work and service revolves round a comprehensive development of undergraduate and postgraduate psychiatric education. Psychiatry has earned a more prominent place in the medical curriculum. We advocate the establishment of chairs of psychiatry in every medical school, and the incorporation of a professional examination in psychiatry in the final medical examination. A medical student should be as adequately trained in psychological as in physiological principles, and we believe that this can be effected by blending these disciplines throughout his undergraduate career. There is still a place for systematic lectures as well as for seminars, and from the angle of clinical instruction there is no better training ground than the psychiatric out-patient department of a large general hospital. We meet there a good cross-section of the medico-social problems which occur in general practice; we can demonstrate methods of examination; we can emphasize the salient features which will require further investigation under more private conditions. Our experience has convinced us that patients who are tactfully dealt with become most co-operative, and gain a sense of pride and prestige from the interest, understanding and sympathy which is shown them; and successful treatment can be more readily accomplished.

From the postgraduate angle much has been done to extend the training and experience of the psychiatric specialist. The University of Edinburgh in 1912 set up regulations governing examination for the Diploma of Psychiatry. In the examination for Membership of the Royal College of Physicians of Edinburgh the candidate, in addition to his examination in general medicine, is allowed to choose a selected subject of which psychiatry is one. This scheme ensures that the successful candidate not only has to reach a very high standard in general medicine, but also a more than usually good knowledge of psychiatry.

While therefore we must continue to increase the efficiency of the medical, nursing, research and administrative aspects of every mental hospital, yet our ability to keep people out of mental hospitals, and to build up the preventive and curative side of our work, will be the ultimate tokens of our success. We recommend the even more widespread establishment of psychiatric clinics as an integral part of every teaching general hospital. The necessary out-patient departments, social service and other ancillaries such as research laboratories would be indispensable adjuncts. Where it may not be possible to establish a separate unit it is quite feasible to reserve certain wards in the general hospital for psychiatric cases. In our opinion every large general hospital would benefit by providing 5–10 per cent. of its beds for that purpose. Modern methods of treatment by means of drugs, electric convulsion therapy and appropriate psychotherapy have made it possible to treat a wide variety of nervous and mental illness without disturbing the amenity of the general hospital. Psychiatry will thus assume an equal status with general medicine to the advantage of both.

To ensure the success of our preventive work we must constantly remind ourselves that the seeds of many nervous and mental disorders are sown in childhood. For this reason we advocate that departments of child psychiatry should be integrated with paediatric hospitals. This has been done in many places and countries, in the United States, Canada, Scandinavia, Great Britain and Germany. Such departments widen the scope of Child Guidance Clinics, where the resources of psychiatrist, psychologist, educationist and social worker can be utilized as a team. Childhood constitutes the golden period for the inculcation of mental hygiene; it is the plastic period of development, the time when prophylactic work should have its greatest reward. A modification of environment and social circumstances can work wonders, and the vast majority of personal emotional difficulties can be dealt with at an objective level; relatively few—but they can be important and difficult—may require prolonged investigation at a subjective and subconscious level. Again we require to have the complete co-operation of parents, schoolmasters, the law courts, employers of labour, and social organizations concerned with the problems of children. Emotional and social security is the greatest safeguard against all subsequent disorder of life and conduct (Henderson, 1955).

While we note the changes which have occurred in psychiatric work and practice we would remind the psychiatrists of to-day that it has been an evolutionary process rather than a revolutionary one. It is salutory to remember the work of our predecessors, and to disabuse our minds of the idea that the real study of psychiatry stemmed from Kraepelin, Freud, the World Wars or the introduction of physical methods of treatment. For instance, in the middle of the nineteenth century Thomas Laycock held the joint appointment of Professor of Medicine of Edinburgh University and Lecturer in Medical Psychology and Mental Diseases. In 1840 he published a book entitled *Nervous Diseases of*

Women to be followed in 1860 by *Mind and Brain*. As an example of his imaginative foresight he stressed the reciprocal action of body and mind and stated that 'a practical knowledge of mental science is essential to parents, jurists and legislators, governors of jails, schoolmasters, and teachers, ministers (gospel), naval and military officers, and employers of labour'. In Laycock's estimation psychiatry was not a narrow specialty but a discipline for general application in studying the conduct of man. Laycock combined his lecture course with clinical demonstrations by Skae at the Royal Edinburgh Hospital for Mental Disorders. In 1879 Clouston was appointed to the Lectureship of Mental Diseases in Edinburgh University.

As regards research it was in 1866 that the West Riding Mental Hospital Reports (Crichton Browne) were published. They incorporated the work of Ferrier on the *Localisation of Brain Function* and inspired much of the subsequent work of the British school of neurology.

In 1895–96 Pathological Laboratories for the development of research were inaugurated almost contemporaneously in Edinburgh (by Clouston), in London (Mott) and in New York (van Giesen). Observation wards for the study and treatment of acute psychiatric disorders were under the charge of Griesinger in 1865 at the Royal Charité (general hospital), Berlin. Similar wards were in 1889 inaugurated by Dr. John Carswell in Barnhill Parochial Hospital, Glasgow. Such pioneer efforts were the forerunners of the psychiatric clinics and out-patient departments which are so indispensable.

COMMUNITY PERIOD

The establishment of Departments or Institutes of Social Medicine in every university illustrates the changed outlook on the prevention of illness in preference to its cure. In the past Public Health Departments had an objective, mechanistic approach, confined for the most part to the betterment of physical and environmental conditions, to vital statistics, sanitary problems, the purity of water and milk supplies, the control of infectious diseases and epidemics. Now we seek to promote measures which will protect the individual and the community so that man's mental and physical capacity can be maintained at its peak. For this purpose investigations into the social, genetic, environmental and domestic factors are being undertaken in the hope that we may acquire greater knowledge in relation to the epidemiology of human disease, and of those more subtle influences which produce nervous and mental instability. The whole personality of man has to be studied in relation to his social setting. Psychiatrists were doing just that, applying the psychobiological principles formulated by Adolf Meyer, long before Institutes of Social Medicine had been inaugurated, but that is not gainsaying the most valuable contributions which they are making. The fact that of every 100 children born 8 will have a nervous breakdown and 3 will spend some part of their lives in a mental hospital is alarming enough, but it completely fails to express the anxiety, distress and unhappiness of sorrowing relatives. The fact, too, that the combined number of mentally ill and defective is closely approximate to all those under treatment in general hospitals is indicative of the social and economic burdens for which the healthier members of the community have to assume responsibility. A more concrete example has been reported by Canby Robinson (1942), who in a study of 174 patients admitted to the medical wards of Johns Hopkins Hospital, Baltimore, found that no less than 66 per cent. presented social problems that were related to their illness, and in 36 per cent. social and emotional factors were the chief precipitating cause of illness. More specifically still Aubrey Lewis (1951) wrote as follows: 'Of all the studies in this field, I think those called "ecological" have been the most promising and informative. . . . The chief of them was carried out by E. L. Faris and Warren Dunham. They examined the origin of nearly 35,000 patients admitted to Chicago mental hospitals between 1932 and 1934, and they found that those areas which had the highest rate of incidence of mental disorder had the highest indices of social disorganization: suicide, venereal disease, family disruption, juvenile and adult crime, high mobility in the population, poverty, demoralization, cultural heterogeneity were also at a high level in these areas.' At another point he commented: 'And in his daily work the psychiatrist, even more than other physicians, is incessantly forced to consider the social relations of his patients.'

It is evident from what has been said that further important developments in the medico-social field lie ahead of us. But while we look forward, a glance to the past will help us to keep our ideas in reasonable perspective. No history of psychiatry would be complete without reference to that remarkable American humanitarian Clifford W. Beers, who in 1907 wrote an autobiographical study entitled *A Mind That Found Itself*. Therein he described his experiences while he had been a patient in mental hospitals, and made constructive suggestions as to the improvements which might be effected. In furtherance of his ideas, in 1908 he founded the Connecticut Society for Mental Hygiene, and soon every State in the Union had its own Mental Hygiene Society. Other civilized countries soon followed the example which had been set, and in 1930 the First International Congress of Mental Hygiene was held in Washington: representatives attended from all over the world. The International Association of Mental Hygiene has now been superseded by the World Federation of Mental Health. In addition, the World Health Organization with its headquarters in Geneva has a highly efficient psychiatric department. The expressed objects of these organizations are to enlist the co-operation of the public in developing those preventive measures which may lead to greater social solidarity and individual well-being. If we are successful in our efforts we may be able to effect a substantial reduction in those seeking admission to psychiatric clinics and mental hospitals, and with the aid of civic organizations, education authorities, trained social workers and general practitioners, build up an effective community health service. Querido in Amsterdam has established a Psychiatric Consultative Bureau where psychiatrists and social workers maintain a 24-hour service. The Bureau assists the family doctor in the treatment of the patient in his own home, or may arrange for his admission to a psychiatric clinic or mental hospital, depending on the particular nature and acuteness of the illness. In addition the Bureau works in close association with the public assistance department and the labour exchange, and may take an active part in rehabilitation. Such a type of organization serves the dual purpose of preventing the admission of patients to hospital and of facilitating their discharge by means of a well-organized after-care service.

REFERENCES AND FURTHER READING

Beers, C. W. (1908) *A Mind That Found Itself*, New York.
Bucknill, J. C., and Tuke, D. H. (1858) *Psychological Medicine*, Philadelphia.
Ciba Symposium (1950) *French Psychiatry*.
Conolly, John (1849) *On Some Forms of Insanity*. Reprinted by St. Bernard's Hospital Management Committee, July 1960.
Deutsch, Albert (1937) *The Mentally Ill in America*, New York.
Guthrie, D. (1957) *Med. Hist.*, **1**, 307.
Harms, E. (1960) *Amer. J. Psychiat.*, **116**, 1037.
Henderson, D. (1955) *Brit. med. J.*, **2**, 519.
Janet, P. (1925) *Psychological Healing*, London.
Jones, E. (1953–55) *Sigmund Freud; Life and Work*, London.
Lewis, A. (1951) *Edinb. med. J.*, **58**, 214, 231.
Robertson, G. M. (1928) *Edinb. med. J.*, **35**, 192.
Robinson, G. C. (1942) *Clinics*, **1**, 842.
Tiffany, F. (1890) *Dorothea Lynde Dix*, Boston.
Tuke, T. H. (1882) *History of the Insane*, London.
Tuke, T. H. (1892) *Dictionary of Psychological Medicine*, London.
Whitwell, J. R. (1943) *Historical Notes on Psychiatry*, 2nd ed., London.
Zilboorg, G., and Henry, G. W. (1941) *A History of Medical Psychology*. New York.

2
PSYCHIATRY AND GENERAL MEDICINE

It is not so long ago since a wide gap separated psychiatry from general medicine. It was not until the twentieth century that psychiatry became a compulsory subject in the medical curriculum, and even then the amount of teaching was meagre, and was confined almost entirely to the psychoses, so that the young graduate entered into the practice of his profession with a very limited knowledge and understanding of the implications of psychiatric work. Psychiatry was a minor specialty practised almost entirely in mental hospitals; the neuroses—when recognized as such—were the particular province of the neurologists—and were treated by galvanism, faradism, hypnotism and a Weir-Mitchell regime.

As time has gone on great changes have been effected—professorial chairs of psychiatry have been established in most of our medical schools; a professional examination in psychiatry forms part of the final examination in medicine; the teaching of psychiatry has come to occupy an increasing part of the medical curriculum; the extramural, social and community aspects of psychiatry have been enormously increased; the crippling legal enactments which differentiated mental illness from physical illness have been abolished. The gap, therefore, between psychiatry and general medicine is being bridged, and it may be hoped that, in the not too distant future, psychiatry in its preventive aspects will become a part of general medical practice. It has, of course, its important specialist aspects but our aim is to train the general practitioners of the future so that they may become as interested in and as able to treat their psychiatric patients as those who are physically involved; the psychic and somatic constantly react on one another and cannot be completely separated. That is why we stress the treatment of the whole man, and not merely the particular disease from which he may be suffering. To do so effectively we must know his background, his personality structure plus his environmental situation, and the biological manner in which he has been able to adapt to the various exigencies of a physical or psychological nature which he has been called upon to meet. The general practioner, therefore, must be as expert in conducting a psychological examination of his patient as a physical one, and in the long run he can rest assured that he will save much more time than he wastes. He will acquire a more comprehensive viewpoint, he will inspire greater confidence, he will be able to exercise a stronger influence, he will be able to go to the core of the situation. Among other things he will find that many of the bodily states which have not responded to surgery or pharmacology will disappear, miraculously, once the underlying psychological factors have been disclosed. It is for such reasons that we believe that all medical students at the beginning of their training should be informed that there is a mind as well as a body, that the two work in harmony, are delicately balanced and must be handled with the greatest care; the one is complementary to the other. All good doctors in general practice recognize those things, their success in practice depends on them, but there are others who say that they are too busy to listen to the complaints of their nervous patients, who dismiss them summarily, tell them 'there is nothing wrong', 'forget it', 'it is all imagination', 'take a long sea trip to Africa', etc., but our view is that it is implicit in the doctor's calling and his obligation to relieve distress wherever he finds it irrespective of its psychological or physical nature; and it is his failure to do so which renders so many patients disappointed with orthodox medicine so that they turn, in despair, to the arts of the unqualified. There may have been an excuse in the past, but now that the Faculties of Medicine of our great universities are becoming better orientated towards the teaching of psychiatry and the part it should occupy in the medical curriculum, it should not be long before all practitioners of medicine will deal more expertly with the preventive and curative sides of nervous and mental illness. We may need more psychiatric specialists, but our particular and most urgent need is an increase of general practitioners with psychological insight. They will acquire the confidence to treat more patients in their own homes, to keep them at work while treating them as outpatients, and to diminish the admission rate to mental hospitals and to psychiatric clinics. All such things have become more possible due to our greater knowledge of psychotherapy, and potent pharmacological and physical remedies; but for these agents to act to the best advantage it is essential that a good rapport, an empathy, should have been established between doctor and patient. A good doctor will not be hasty and impatient in his judgement; he will take time, he will not dismiss the subjective complaints of his patients as sheer nonsense but will consider them worthy of investigation. If his careful physical examination has failed to disclose an objective organic cause, he will at once extend his inquiries into the possibility of constitutional anomalies and emotional problems as being the causative agents.

What are the particular nervous and mental states which the general practitioner is most commonly called upon to deal with? We would suggest the following which have been more fully discussed under the general heading of the neuroses and psychosomatic states, *e.g.* anxiety states with a fear of impending death (*angor animi*); conversion hysterical symptoms (which are much less common than they used to be); obsessive thinking with compulsive tendencies; the asthmatic, duodenal ulcer, and dermatological conditions which so often reflect emotional immaturity; depressive states with suicidal impulses; and certain cases of sexual anomaly.

While the above states can be discriminated by the different forms they assume the root factor which is common to all is fear. Most of us at one time or another have experienced a quick beating of the heart, a cold sweat, hurried breathing, dryness of the mouth, a tendency to yawn, a catch in the throat, fluttering in the abdomen, which are the accompaniments of fear. Montaigne exclaimed: 'The thing in the world I am most afraid of is fear; that passion in the trouble of it exceeding all other accidents.' The physiologists in their investigation of such distressing and painful bodily phenomena have correlated them with an oversensitization of the autonomic nervous system, which may be sparked off by causes which seem trivial and insignificant, so that Ernest Jones came to define morbid fear as 'a disproportion between the intensity of the emotion and the occasion of its occurrence'. He regarded fear as the most frequent single symptom in psychopathology and perhaps in all medicine. 'It is', he said, 'the Alpha and Omega of practical psychiatry.' (Jones, 1911.) In his elaboration of the above opinion Jones accepted the Freudian hypotheses that morbid fears of external objects or situations are projections of internal mental processes; that every fear is the obverse of a wish, that fear and desire are intimately associated; and that fears have their origin on a sexual basis. According to that theory there is a never-ending struggle between Eros and Death with fear as a fundamental component.

We believe that a much broader interpretation is more satisfying and agree with Suttie's criticism of the Freudian doctrine when he lays the emphasis on love as a protective mechanism, giving rise to a sense of security. According to Suttie, the source of love is dependent on the mechanism of self-preservation, on the need of food, and not sexual desires and sensations; the original object of love is the mother, and it is the innate need for companionship which is the infant's only way for self-preservation. The infant's mind, from the beginning, is dominated by the need to retain the mother, a need which, if not satisfied, may produce intense emotional distress such as anger, rage, terror, as the loss of the mother may symbolize death itself (Henderson, 1939). Emancipation, therefore, may prove to be a highly traumatic event not only at birth, but later in life as well. Anxious fears, indecision, a lack of emotional maturity may come to dominate the person's life, and it is because of those facts that all doctors and intelligent parents should study the psychic needs of the developing child as much as its physical hygiene, and should minimize their impact as much as possible. We have seen how the wrong choice of a school, of a career, of a wife or a husband may produce the most disastrous results, and we believe that the family doctor with his intimate knowledge of family resources and potentialities could be an infinitely better guide if he took time to consider that he would be doing valuable preventive work in dealing with the difficulties and disharmonies of everyday life. That point of view was envisaged at the time when the National Health Act was introduced and sentiments were expressed then which even yet contain an important message. For instance, it was stated: 'Health is a way of living, it is not a negative state, it involves more than the mere absence of disease'; and, 'the medical practitioner and the medical services should view the individual as a living organism in relation to his whole environment'; and again: 'In the future the doctor's work will be more and more educational and less and less curative. He will deal more with physiology and psychology and less with pathology. This re-orientation of his education and his work is overdue.'

We have stressed the above points because we believe that they form the background of most of the cases of nervous illness with which the family doctor should be familiar. If he does not have them in mind, and does not realize how much they mean to his patient, he is likely to fail in coping with the presenting symptoms which are merely the symbols of strong underlying conflicts and resentments. And it is important to deal with the symptoms in the first place, even although a much longer time may be required to straighten out the personality disturbance. Like the surgeon we require to let the acute inflammatory symptoms subside before a radical operation is undertaken. The fact that painful, crippling symptoms have been cured helps to establish a good jumping-off ground for more detailed investigations. The change may be brought about simply enough. It may be a change in the environment, an easement of tension, better sleep at night-time, a readjustment of habits, rather than the employment of any highly specialized technique, which will make the position more acceptable. Kindness, consideration, encouragement, a transitory rest in hospital or nursing home, a careful case-history, taking into consideration the adequacy or failure of biological adjustment, can work wonders. Medical students in their training appreciate that point of view, it interests them, they want much more of it, it gives them something to work with in the treatment of their patients, which is far more important than coming to a formal diagnosis. They are warned that they are not likely to see or effect the quick results which occur in other branches of medical work, but if they have patience they may experience the great satisfaction of contributing to the art of living, to harmonious relationships, to the prevention of illness rather than to the mere dispensing of medicine for intractable complaints which have never been traced to their source. That is why we maintain that psychiatry is hardly a 'specialty' at all—it is not like brain surgery, ophthalmology, otology—but it may be part and parcel of all forms of medical work. That is the reason why we will welcome the day when all teachers of medicine, surgery and the special subjects will regard it as imperative to draw attention to the personality of the patient, to his environment, and to the influence of the psychological factors. Such advice coming from the physician, the surgeon, the gynaecologist will be more impressive and carry more weight than if uttered by the psychiatrist; the psychiatrist, however, can supply the ammunition. The whole theme and endeavour of this book has been to broaden the education of the medical student so that he may become a better informed medical practitioner equally conversant with the management of physiological and psychological anomalies. Whitehorn expressed the same idea in this way: 'to prepare the medical student to deal intelligently and skilfully with patients as persons, and to provide him with the basic knowledge of psychological and social problems and resources in relation to health and disease'. The idea inherent in such attempts at definition is surely to widen our horizons and to recognize that medicine (all forms of medicine) is concerned not only with the treatment of the ill but with the wider task of the welfare of society.

From a more detailed and practical angle the new Mental Health Acts which have been introduced into England and Scotland are likely to make it much easier for general practitioners to make arrangements for the treatment of acute psychiatric emergencies. It is now possible for any patient in need of treatment for mental disorder to be admitted to any hospital or nursing home and receive treatment there without any legal formalities, and in the same informal way as patients suffering from physical conditions. No doubt there will always be a certain number of patients who are so unco-operative that compulsory measures may be required, but the majority will be glad to avail themselves of the informal provisions. This should result in earlier treatment and in better prospects of recovery, and the doctor will be relieved of legal responsibilities which often appeared to be formidable.

Acute psychiatric cases, however, have never assumed a large proportion of the general practitioner's work, and when they have occurred they have usually necessitated treatment and care in clinic or hospital. But even a considerable number of these cases may be successfully treated in their own homes by their own doctors with the specialist assistance provided by domiciliary consultations, psychiatric social workers and health visitors. The build-up of a community health service has much to be said for it, both in regard to the treatment of the patient and the education of the medical profession.

The real problem of general practice centres round the treatment of the large numbers of neurotic and psychosomatic patients who congregate in the out-patient departments of every large general hospital, who are regular visitors to health centres and private consulting rooms. Many of them must consume a fortune in the form of sedatives, tranquillizers and tonics, and their numbers seem to increase, rather than to lessen. What is responsible for this? Are we becoming too health-conscious? What has been the effect of documentary and commercial television with its seductive advertising? Is it just sheer bad doctoring due to our one-sided training and inability to understand the whole-man aspect? Is it the discontent which seems to permeate all ranks of society leading to futile, silly strikes or threats of strikes on the basis of larger pay claims and shorter hours of work? Whatever it may be, the result is tending towards a selfish, individualistic society without much thought of family, business, profession or patriotic obligations. It breeds unhappiness and inefficiency and domestic disharmony, and it is these medico-social phenomena which require to be put right if we are to make much progress in dealing with the many neurotic, dissatisfied persons we have to treat. Psychotherapy in its various forms can accomplish much—but the real secret is for a better mental hygiene of childhood, better homes to live in and a more contented, philosophical outlook on life's problems.

Sleeplessness, carrying in its train a variety of other symptoms, is the most frequent premonitory indication of a nervous system which is becoming over-strained. Sometimes it may be helped by simple measures such as a frank discussion of possible causes, a readjustment of the environment, e.g. home, work, etc., an appropriate sedative. If, however, the sleeplessness becomes more intractable, fails to respond adequately to sedatives and is accompanied by anxiety, fear, fatigue, hypochondriasis, a decision may require to be taken as to whether it would be advisable to 'down tools' completely, and seek treatment in hospital or nursing home. It is not an easy decision to make—it is not wise to be arbitrary —and the sensitivity and reactions of the person should always be taken into careful consideration. Some people do not like hospitals or nursing homes, they are afraid of them, they feel they may be influenced by the condition of others, they miss the privacy of their own homes, and not infrequently a patient's condition may be aggravated rather than helped. Sometimes, although a risk is being taken, it is wiser to treat the patient as an out-patient, to keep him at work even although he may require the aid of drugs, because work is often a good remedy and allows the patient to retain his prestige. We have known many patients whom we have been able to assist by keeping in touch with them, advising and encouraging them, and using sedatives and hypnotics as stabilizers. It is impossible to state what the best drugs are, they vary according to the person, and can be changed as the occasion may arise. There are a considerable number of patients who are ambivalent in regard to sleep. They may long for it but are afraid of it, afraid of sinking into unconsciousness, of the unknown, of death. Such patients fight against sedatives, they are not willing to be dominated, they waken with a start if they should fall asleep, and more and more sedatives confuse and befuddle them rather than produce the desired effect. Sleep, it should be understood, is a symbol of death. W. H. Hudson records (*Far Away and Long Ago*) his feelings when he was present at the burial of a favourite dog. It was Mr. Trigg, the schoolmaster, who made the grave-side address: 'That's the end. Every dog has its day and so has every man; and the end is the same for both. We die like old Caesar, and are put into the ground, and have the earth shovelled over us.' Hudson, when he heard those words, recalls: 'Now these simple, common words affected me more than any other words I have heard in my life. They pierced me to the heart. I had heard something terrible— too terrible to think of, incredible, and yet if it was not so why had he said it.' It was only when Hudson realized that the part 'that really mattered, the myself, the I am I, which knew and considered things would never perish', that sudden immense relief was obtained. That short extract exemplifies the intensity of the fear reaction and illustrates how relief can come, almost miraculously, once faith and confidence and insight are attained. Sensitive people cannot be bludgeoned out of their fears and forebodings, they require more delicate measures, especially the tense and anxious patients who suffer from the tormenting distressing feeling that they 'will fall down dead'.

We would like to emphasize once more that the general practitioner should bring the same interested attitude to bear whether he is dealing with bodily or psychological symptoms. He should have patience to investigate, the ability to see the position as it appears to the patient, to establish confidence so that time will be available in which to come to a true estimate of the symptoms. This approach may be sufficient to instil a feeling of reassurance, optimism and security. It puts the patient at his ease, allows him to talk naturally, so that the physician becomes a sort of father-confessor. In that rôle he is able to gather together the besetting problems of a personal, domestic or business nature which have influenced his patient's life, and may be able to direct them into healthier channels. The ability to keep in touch with the patient, even although the practitioner may feel that he is not contributing anything, may accomplish far more than he thinks. It is by working together, by co-operation and mutual trust that the patient may be led gradually to acquire that greater insight and

C

self-knowledge whereby he gains confidence and independence. And that is the very best type of psychotherapy which can be utilized. It is not abstruse, mystical nor concerned with symbolic interpretation (which can be dangerous), but deals with the patient's reactions, of a bodily or psychological nature, from the point of view of a dynamic psychobiology. If by any chance the general practitioner should feel out of his depth, or if the patient himself is dissatisfied with his progress, then there should be no delay in referring the patient to a suitable consultant, or to a specialized hospital where more expert and prolonged treatment is available. Under the National Health Service there is no one in Great Britain who cannot have the benefit of the best advice available whenever or wherever it may be desired.

REFERENCES

Henderson, D. K. (1939) *Psychopathic States*, London.
Jones, E. (1911) *J. abnorm. soc. Psychol.*, 6, 81.
Suttie, I. D. (1935) *Origins of Love and Hate*, London.

3

CLASSIFICATION

In the time of Hippocrates a few comprehensive types of mental disorder were recognized, so-called 'mania', 'melancholia' and 'dementia', but their significance was ill-defined, and for two thousand years little advance was made. It could hardly be otherwise, so long as supernatural agency was invoked to account for mental disorder, and so long as physiologists believed in humours, spirits and bizarre localization of function, and had no constant recognition of the interrelation of mind and brain.

With the beginning of pathological investigation and its correlation with clinical symptoms by Willis in the seventeenth century, by Haslam towards the end of the eighteenth, and by Bayle in his classical description of general paralysis which appeared in 1820, the foundations were laid for a more fruitful psychiatric classification.

The principles adopted for subdivision have been symptomatological, aetiological, psychological and physiological. Often two or more of these have been simultaneously used in the same classification.

PSYCHOLOGICAL CLASSIFICATIONS

In this method, *a priori* formulations have been made usually from current academic psychology, and an attempt made to fit all cases into the rack thus constructed. Linnaeus (1763) was early in this field, and divided his cases into Ideales, Imaginarii and Pathetici. Arnold (1782) had two main divisions, Ideal and Notional, or as we should say, disorders of perception and imagination, and conceptual disorders. Crichton (1798) described insanity under the headings of Faculties (including attention, etc.), Principles (including volition and consciousness) and Passions. Pritchard's two divisions (1822) were Moral Insanity and Intellectual Insanity. His 'moral insanity' was corrupted into 'moral imbecility' or 'moral defectiveness' and now is recognized by the term 'psychopathic state'; it will be considered separately and in detail in another chapter. Heinroth's analysis was more searching, and included disorders of the understanding, disorders of the will or propensities, and mixtures of these. Bucknill and Tuke, following the Scots metaphysicians, had two main divisions, Intellectual and Affective, the latter being subdivided into the moral sentiments and the animal propensities. Ziehen classified mental disorders into those without and those with intellectual defect, and the former into affective and intellectual forms, while the latter are subdivided into congenital and acquired.

The disadvantages of psychological classifications have been chiefly these: they have been derived from speculation remote from the field of psychopathology;

disorders have been forced into one psychological category, when they may more correctly belong to several; and they bring together in one group psychoses essentially different (Kraepelin).

PHYSIOLOGICAL CLASSIFICATIONS

The primary and damning disadvantage of this method is that so little is known of the physiology of normal mental processes, and still less of abnormal ones. Further, the method often involves ill-established hypotheses of localization. Conolly's is an early example. 'All forms of mental disorder are dependent on one of three states of the nervous system: a state of increased or diminished or unequal excitement.' Laycock made much use of a hypothetical localization, e.g. he wrote of 'disorders of encephalic centres subservient to emotions and sentiments'—'the ideogenic or sensorial substances' of the cerebellum and hemispheres, but he stressed especially the reciprocal influence of body and mind. Tuke (1892) based his classification on the divisions of sensory, motor and ideational centres, with their corresponding disordered manifestations of hallucinations, paralysis and dementia. Meynert's scheme (1884) was partly dependent on physiological assumptions. His groups were: 1. clinical forms arising from anatomical changes; 2. disorders of nutrition involving (a) cortical excitement, mania and melancholia, (b) subcortical irritation or feebleness (e.g. delusions and hallucinations), and (c) disorders of subcortical vascular centres (e.g. epilepsy); and 3. intoxications. Wernicke made several sweeping psychophysiological assumptions which were fundamental for his grouping. Making use of the doctrine of specific nerve-energies, he first of all assumed that every content of consciousness was dependent on a definite set of nervous elements. Further, he took his aphasic scheme as the paradigm for mental processes in general, which consisted for him in a chain containing a psychosensory, an intrapsychic and a psychomotor element. In mental disorders interruption might occur at any point ('sejunction'), and the function of any element might be either increased or diminished. Accordingly he arranged the disorders of the associative chain as follows:

PSYCHOSENSORY SPHERE	INTRAPSYCHIC SPHERE	PSYCHOMOTOR SPHERE
Anaesthesia	Afunction	Akinesis
Hyperaesthesia	Hyperfunction	Hyperkinesis
Paraesthesia	Parafunction	Parakinesis

Wernicke believed in the localization of memories, and that hallucinations were caused by irritation of the memory-image centres and irradiation thence to perception-cells. His classification depended equally on the above assumptions and on his division of concepts into those of the outside world, of the personality, and of the body—'allopsychic', 'autopsychic' and 'somatopsychic'. Neither his rigid application of the doctrine of specific nerve-energies nor his theories of localization and sejunction were valid.

AETIOLOGICAL CLASSIFICATIONS

Classification according to cause has obvious disadvantages—the multiplicity of causes and imperfect knowledge of most of them, and the fact that one cause may produce vastly different clinical pictures in different persons, and, conversely, that very various clinical pictures may arise from the same apparent cause. Jacobi was a pioneer in this method, and, in 1830, boldly declared that insanity existed solely as the result of disease in the bodily system.

Morel (1860) described hereditary, toxic, idiopathic and sympathetic insanity, and insanity 'from transformation of other diseases'. Skae went much further, and his classification had a type of mental disturbance for almost every common physical disorder—gout, phthisis, uterine, ovarian, etc.

Clouston followed Skae's example, and had a number of 'more or less important clinical varieties'—anaemic, diabetic, metastatic and a dozen others.

Tuke made classification easy by enumerating, like Skae, all disorders associated with known organic conditions, and by throwing all the rest into a group covered by 'disease of the generative system'—a sweeping aetiological theory which had no more than a coincidental foundation at that time.

SYMPTOMATOLOGICAL CLASSIFICATIONS

Kraepelin has been the outstanding exponent of this method, and he obtained his most valuable inductions from it. Yet even his method involves much aetiology as well. The symptomatological method is essentially the method of clinical psychiatry, and if only for that reason is to be commended; for it stimulates observation, and, if broadly used, has valuable consequences. It includes the principles of other methods without falling into their errors and becoming involved in their unnecessary assumptions. It is true, of course, that in this method, as in Nature generally, there are no hard and fast boundaries, and that a given symptom will appear in several symptom groups; but 'the agreement of a great number of cases in certain signs', as Griesinger puts it, is the justification for the construction of an empirical division. If further, not simply a 'cross-section' of each case is taken, but a 'longitudinal section' also, so that the evolution of the psychosis is taken into account in the symptomatology, a more comprehensive foundation is obtained for classification.

A distinction, first made by Kahlbaum, arises here—that between the fundamental underlying disease and the temporary symptom-complex which it displays. The method of observation which has just been commended enables this distinction to be made, and allows us to speak of episodes arising in the course of a disorder, such as hysterical symptoms in a schizophrenic psychosis, and depressive periods in the course of general paralysis. This distinction of Kahlbaum's was carried further, so that the mental disorder itself was regarded as the expression of a fundamental innate disposition (e.g. Bleuler's 'schizoid' disposition).

It was Kraepelin who first furnished a systematic symptomatological grouping with special attention to the course and outcome of the various types of disorder. This he accomplished by following them over a long period of years.

ADOLF MEYER'S CLASSIFICATION

Meyer constructed a classification round the root word 'ergasia', meaning function, or the total behaviour of the individual. The appropriate descriptive prefix is added, *e.g.* merergasia—the usual neurotic reactions.

Thymergasia—the primary affective disorders, divided into hyperergastic or other active manic states and hypoergastic or depressive retarded states.

Parergasia—the fantastic, incongruous schizophrenic states.

Dysergasia—the toxic delirious states.

Anergasia—with defect traits characteristic of the organic group.

Oligergasia—the group of constitutionally defective states.

The truth is that no attempt at psychiatric classification is entirely satisfactory, and consequently that 'diagnosis', or the placing of the patient in the appropriate class, is on an unstable foundation. But, fortunately, it is not diagnosis only that matters, but the understanding of the disorder, and of the patient who suffers from it—under what circumstances it arose, how it is related to the patient's normal condition, what the disorder means, what light is shed on his problems, and what can be done to help towards a favourable outcome. In Adolf Meyer's words, it is not the patients we are to sort out, but the facts; and while in the following pages the case records will be arranged in groups for the sake of more or less systematic description, the disorders exhibited will be considered as the individual reactions of a specifically endowed, and often constitutionally loaded, organism to the environment.

Nevertheless, classification is useful and necessary; first, for the student, that he may more readily grasp and arrange his cases; and second, for the compilation of a uniform set of statistics by institutions and administrative authorities, in order to make comparison possible, both within and between countries. Epidemiological research depends upon classification.

Following Meyer, in this book, we speak of different types of mental disorder as different types of reaction. We use the term 'reaction-types' instead of referring to mental diseases, as expressing the point of view which concentrates upon the study of the individual as a psychobiological organism perpetually called upon to adapt to a social environment. We recognize that in many instances the constitutional element is the important factor, that the environmental influences in a number of cases are of relatively minor importance and that there are all degrees of relative participation of these two factors. But we also recognize that there is an internal environment and that what is regarded as a 'constitutional' type of mental disorder may often be the reaction of the mind to inner stimuli to which it finds difficulty in maintaining a healthy adjustment.

CURRENT CLASSIFICATIONS

The two classifications currently most widely.used are, in this country, that of the *International Classification of Diseases*, 1965, published by the World Health Organization (1967); and, in the U.S.A., the American Psychiatric Association's *Standard Classification* (1952).

Section V of the *International Classification of Diseases* comprises 'Mental Disorders', and 'includes all forms of mental disorder, even though associated with or secondary to physical conditions'. The classification is as follows (the detailed subheadings are not given):

PSYCHOSES

    Senile and pre-senile dementia
    Alcoholic psychosis
    Psychosis associated with intracranial infection
    Psychosis associated with other cerebral condition
    Psychosis associated with other physical condition
    Schizophrenia
    Affective psychoses
    Paranoid states
    Other psychoses
    Unspecified psychosis

NEUROSES, PERSONALITY DISORDERS AND OTHER NON-PSYCHOTIC MENTAL DISORDERS

    Neuroses
    Personality disorders
    Sexual deviation
    Alcoholism
    Drug dependence
    Physical disorders of presumably psychogenic origin
    Special symptoms not elsewhere classified
    Transient situational disturbances
    Behaviour disorders of childhood
    Mental disorders not specified as psychotic associated with physical conditions

MENTAL RETARDATION

    Borderline mental retardation
    Mild mental retardation
    Moderate mental retardation
    Severe mental retardation
    Profound mental retardation
    Unspecified mental retardation

This Eighth Revision of the *International Classification*, which came into operation in this country in 1968, improves upon the Seventh Revision which had been used in the previous decade. Practically all psychiatric disorders are now included in Section V; and a valuable complementary Glossary for use in Britain, which has been compiled by the Registrar General's Advisory Committee on Medical Nomenclature and Statistics, has been issued from the General Register Office (1968). This glossary should help considerably to achieve consistency in the use of the new classification. Not all psychiatrists will agree with the details of this new classification, but all can use it conscientiously and its use does not exclude the development of more elaborate classifications for the purposes of individual interest or research.

The following points, some of which may cause difficulty or argument, may be noted. Depression cannot be diagnosed without qualification. In the group of Affective Psychoses both manic-depressive psychosis and involutional melancholia are recognized: also, amongst the Other Psychoses a reactive depressive psychosis—surely an unnecessary addition. A paranoid type of Schizophrenia is described; while Paranoid States (a separate category) include paraphrenia and the paranoid reactions of old age but exclude paranoid schizophrenia and, less understandably, acute paranoid reactions—the latter are to be classified in the group of Other Psychoses. Infantile autism is classified with schizophrenia. Delirium is not given a separate category: it is to be classified as a psychosis associated with a certain underlying physical condition. Puerperal psychoses are not to be diagnosed as such, but assigned to the reaction-type.

Amongst the Neuroses are included anxiety neurosis, hysterical neurosis, phobic neurosis, obsessive compulsive neurosis, depressive neurosis (neurotic depression), neurasthenia, depersonalization syndrome and hypochondriacal neurosis. Anorexia nervosa is classified separately, as a feeding disturbance under the heading Special Symptoms not elsewhere classified. Amongst the Personality Disorders the psychopath is classified as an antisocial personality, if he offends against society: he could also sometimes more properly be included under the alternative headings of explosive or asthenic personality.

The grades or degrees of Mental Retardation are given precise I.Q. limits: e.g. mild mental retardation has an I.Q. range from 52 to 67, severe mental retardation from 20 to 35. Fourth-digit sub-divisions may be used with these categories, to indicate aetiological groups (e.g. chromosomal abnormalities, disorders of metabolism).

Under the Behavioural Disorders of Childhood only jealousy, masturbation, tantrum and truancy are included, since it is intended that most of the conditions which occur in infancy and childhood can be classified elsewhere.

The American Psychiatric Association's *Standard Classification* is as follows (the detailed subheadings are not given):

DISORDERS CAUSED BY OR ASSOCIATED WITH IMPAIRMENT OF BRAIN TISSUE
FUNCTIONS

ACUTE BRAIN DISORDERS

Disorders due to or associated with infection
Disorders due to or associated with intoxication

Disorders due to or associated with trauma

Disorders due to or associated with circulatory disturbance

Disorders due to or associated with disturbance of innervation or of psychic control

Disorders due to or associated with disturbance of metabolism, growth or nutrition

Disorders due to or associated with new growth

Disorders due to unknown or uncertain cause

Disorders due to unknown or uncertain cause with the functional reaction alone manifest

CHRONIC BRAIN DISORDERS

Disorders due to parental (constitutional) influence

Disorders due to or associated with infection

Disorders associated with intoxication

Disorders associated with trauma

Disorders associated with circulatory disturbances

Disorders associated with disturbances of innervation or of psychic control

Disorders associated with disturbance of metabolism, growth or nutrition

Disorders associated with new growth

Disorders associated with unknown or uncertain cause

Disorders due to unknown or uncertain cause with the functional reaction alone manifest

MENTAL DEFICIENCY

Disorders due to unknown or uncertain cause with the functional reaction alone manifest; hereditary and familial diseases of this nature

DISORDERS OF PSYCHOGENIC ORIGIN OR WITHOUT CLEARLY DEFINED PHYSICAL CAUSE OR STRUCTURAL CHANGE IN THE BRAIN

PSYCHOTIC DISORDERS

Disorders due to disturbance of metabolism, growth, nutrition or endocrine function

Disorders of psychogenic origin or without clearly defined tangible cause or structural change

Affective reactions

Schizophrenic reactions

Paranoid reactions

Psychotic reaction without clearly defined structural change, other than above

PSYCHOPHYSIOLOGIC AUTONOMIC AND VISCERAL DISORDERS

Disorders due to disturbance of innervation or of psychic control

PSYCHONEUROTIC DISORDERS

Disorders of psychogenic origin or without clearly defined tangible cause or structural change

PERSONALITY DISORDERS
>   Disorders of psychogenic origin or without clearly defined tangible cause
>   or structural change
>   Personality pattern disturbance
>   Personality trait disturbance
>   Sociopathic personality disturbance
>   Special symptom reactions

TRANSIENT SITUATIONAL PERSONALITY DISORDERS

This classification is based on aetiological groupings, so far as the data seem
to allow. The basic division is into 'mental disorders associated with organic
brain disturbance, and those occurring without such primary disturbance of
brain function, and NOT into psychoses, psychoneuroses and personality
disorders'. Psychosomatic syndromes are classified under the heading 'Psychophysiologic Autonomic and Visceral Disorders'. Hysteria is not classified as
such, but can be placed under the heads of 'Dissociative Reaction' or 'Conversion Reaction'.

There are perhaps two main areas of this classification which are open to
criticism. Subnormality (Mental Deficiency) comes rather awkwardly under two
heads—'Chronic Brain Disorders' and 'Mental Deficiency' itself: the subnormal
(feeble-minded) will mostly come into the latter category. (The terms idiot,
imbecile and moron have been abandoned.) The groupings suggested for the Personality Disorders also seem rather arbitrary and uncertain. While Schizoid
Personality is classified under the 'Personality Pattern Disturbances', Compulsive
Personality is classified as a 'Personality Trait Disturbance'. The term Sociopathic Personality is preferred to Psychopathic Personality, and the category
includes both sexual deviation and addiction. Speech disturbances and enuresis
are classified under Personality Disorders, though the latter certainly would
seem to come more readily under the Psychophysiologic Autonomic and Visceral Disorders. Somnambulism is also listed under the Personality Disorders.

The A.P.A. classification is backed by a *Diagnostic and Statistical Manual*,
which defines terms and gives guidance about the recording of psychiatric
conditions.

FUTURE DEVELOPMENTS

In general, psychiatrists agree fairly well in their diagnoses of the major
psychoses. It is in the field of the neuroses, personality anomalies and psychopathic states that diagnoses are so frequently discordant that statisticians have
been inclined to think them haphazard. While our knowledge of aetiology
remains partial, a classification which is based both on symptomatic and aetiological factors is inevitable. Classifications of the future will have a more comprehensive aetiological basis, but we must accept that they will always clearly
reflect the limitations of our clinical knowledge. While we need to classify the
phenomena of mental illness for purposes of research, to compare for example

the incidence, prevalence and response to treatment of the various reaction-types, we should also remember that to tidy clinical data into the neat pigeon-holes of a consistent classification can be premature if not arbitrary. What was written in another connection is perhaps relevant here: 'in the present state of our faculties, any system which is without its paradoxes, is by the same token as suspicious as an exact correspondence of several witnesses in a trial at the Old Bailey'.

REFERENCES

A Glossary of Mental Disorders: Studies on Medical and Population Subjects, No. 22 (1968), London, H.M.S.O.
American Psychiatric Association Diagnostic and Statistical Manual for Mental Disorders (1952), Washington, D.C.
International Classification of Diseases (1967), Geneva, World Health Organization.

4

AETIOLOGY

ITS IMPORTANCE

The relative importance of the various causative factors of nervous and mental illness is most difficult to evaluate. Our inability to do so constitutes one of the fundamental problems of psychiatry. There is no specific relationship between cause and effect such as exists in physical illness, but rather are we called upon to deal with a constellation of causes of an hereditary, constitutional or personality nature plus an almost bewildering variety of environmental stresses. That is why in the organization of preventive and remedial psychiatry it is always so necessary, in every case, to consider the man in the setting of his environment, and not as a mere disease entity.

The economic burden involved in providing care and treatment for those who are incapacitated by some form of nervous or mental disease is enormous, but the accompanying individual, family and social problems are even more distressing and alarming. New laws, new drugs, other new methods of treatment, and greatly improved hospital conditions are all having a beneficial impact, but the statistics which we are about to quote indicate the urgent need for more intensive efforts entailing greater research.

About 40 per cent. of the hospital beds in this country are occupied by patients suffering from mental illness: and the number of admissions to these beds (though not the number of individual patients admitted) is rising annually. In Scotland, a country with a population of approximately 5,000,000 persons, there was in 1966 a total of 19,437 patients in mental hospitals. In addition there were 6882 subnormal (mentally defective) individuals in institutions, and a further 973 were under guardianship. Apart from those who are being cared for in hospitals or under guardianship it has been estimated that 10 per cent. of the total population of school age are so dull and backward that special schools, special classes, occupation centres and sheltered workshops are required for their training and happiness.

In England and Wales in 1966 the total number of patients in mental hospitals amounted to 123,615. During that year there were 164,153 admissions to mental hospitals compared with 91,558 in 1958 and 55,856 in 1950. In addition the total number of subnormal or mentally defective persons in hospitals amounted to 64,628. Furthermore, 9511 were admitted to hospitals in 1966.

Both in Scotland and in England and Wales there has been a gratifying increase in the number of patients who seek treatment on an informal basis, while the number of compulsory patients has been showing a steady decrease. In Scotland in 1966, 91 per cent. of the total admissions to mental hospitals were on an informal basis: in England and Wales 80.2 per cent. were. The percentage of subnormal patients admitted on an informal basis was 88.

The high admission rate of so many informal patients has been accompanied by a considerably increased discharge rate, due to early and improved methods of treatment, but it is disquieting to find out that there is also a high readmission rate. It is a reminder that therapeutic success may be more apparent than real, and more transient than had been anticipated. Of the 20,181 admissions to Scottish mental hospitals in 1966, 54 per cent. had been admitted previously: the percentage of readmissions to the mental hospitals of England and Wales was 48 per cent. in that year. This compares with 32 per cent. readmissions to the Scottish hospitals in 1949, and 43.5 per cent. in 1956.

Between 1954 and 1963 the number of patients in the mental hospitals in England and Wales decreased by 20,000: but this decrease represents not only therapeutic successes but the burden also of individuals with persistent mental ill health which has fallen upon the community and its inadequate medical and social services. In the younger age groups schizophrenia still accounts for much chronic disability, social estrangement and unemployment—and for some crime: and the affective psychoses are at all ages relatively common illnesses. A survey of mental illness in general practice (Watts *et al.*, 1964) has suggested that there may be twice as many mentally disabled persons in the community as in the mental hospitals.

Current population trends also heighten the seriousness of the problem with which we have to deal. Six and a half million of the population of Britain, 12 per cent. of it, are now over the age of 65: and the numbers in this age group are expected to increase by a third by 1980. And it is, of course, well known that with the increase of the life span there is a greater liability to bodily and mental incapacity. Already in 1963 in England and Wales (Brooke, 1967) there were 51,616 patients, aged 65 or over, in psychiatric units, 39 per cent. of all resident patients and almost 1 per cent. of this age group in the general population.

In many other countries it may be taken for granted that an almost similar state of affairs exists. Everywhere mental hospitals are crowded with patients, and the numbers of subnormal individuals and epileptics, for whom hospital accommodation is an urgent necessity, are increasing. To develop constructive measures whereby this social and economic burden of caring for and rehabilitating the increasing number of the unfit is a pressing challenge of our times. Perhaps we are going about it in the wrong way, and would attain better results if we placed even greater emphasis on the positive aspect of ensuring the birth of healthy children. We will do well to remember the slogan: 'To make the unfit fit is a noble task, but to make the fit fitter is a higher and finer achievement'.

Our story is still incomplete. In addition to those who require hospital and institutional care we must direct attention to: 1. neurotics; and 2. social misfits for whom special arrangements require to be made. In the case of the former, accounting for approximately 10 per cent. of all consultations in general practice annually, a small number may require in-patient treatment, preferably in the psychiatric units of general hospitals, but the vast majority can be treated, to the best advantage, as out-patients.

The social misfit group comprise the inefficient, shiftless, unemployable, morally twisted, delinquents, criminals and prostitutes. Many of them are the recidivists, the 'ins and outs' of the prison system. When their particular disability is combined with mental illness or subnormality or stems from such disabilities then arrangements may be made for care and treatment in our special State organizations, *e.g.* Broadmoor and Rampton in England, and Carstairs in Scotland.

Sufficient has been said to indicate that our task of elucidating the aetiology of disorders of the mind with a view to treatment is one of great magnitude which requires to be tackled with all the measures which modern medical concepts provide. The work may prove most rewarding. Our hospital clinics, examination techniques and treatment facilities require even greater development. At the risk of being redundant the question may be asked again as to whether we are tackling our problem in the right way: is it not steadily growing greater because the proper measures are being taken too late? It would be no small reward for our labours if it could be shown that by beginning further back, by treating the causes of mental disorder and of its companions and consequences, criminality, vice, alcoholism, poverty, unemployment and the like, we could render unnecessary much of the misery, money-spending and machinery which these disasters entail. This desirable goal can only be reached by an intense and systematic study throughout the country in well-conceived schemes, and with all the means at one's command, of the causation of mental disorders. To obtain co-operation between all individuals and authorities interested in human betterment the issues have to be clearly defined so that the public can be fully informed of the principles of mental hygiene.

AETIOLOGICAL INVESTIGATIONS

It is customary to discuss aetiology under a series of headings—as to sex, age, race, and what not. This does no harm, so long as it is remembered that such items have no necessarily specific aetiological connection with a given case. A mental disorder is the sum of many conditions, and the end-result of a long chain of processes. The earliest of these may have begun in the unfertilized germ-plasm, another may have operated *in utero*, and the rest may be the reactions of an organism thus handicapped to the aids and obstacles which it subsequently meets in the environment in which it finds itself—the influence of parents and teachers, the difficulties in the path of ambition and the ease as well as the hardness of innumerable situations in life. The first of these factors falls, in the usual scheme, under 'heredity', the second under 'congenital' and the next under the headings of age, sex, family, etc. But it is the ensemble of all such factors that is the 'cause'. An examination of our case-records shows that there is very rarely, in a given case, one single aetiological factor, but nearly always a constellation of them. Moreover, the cause is not a bolt from the blue, nor a mysterious entity destined to implant itself at a certain epoch on unprepared soil; the 'cause' is a process—something that moves and shapes itself in the passage of time.

So long as these conceptions are remembered it does no harm, and it is con-

venient, to consider separately some of the commoner and more easily categorized factors in the production of mental disorder.

HEREDITY

The rôle of heredity in relation to mental disorders is of fundamental importance and demands the closest study. That we do not know more about this aspect
of aetiology is probably due to two main causes: first, psychiatrists have tended
in recent years to pay greater attention to environmental than to constitutional
factors, since the former are in general more easily modified, and there has been
a tendency also to equate hereditary determination of an illness with incurability
and even untreatability; and second, the facts about human inheritance are not
easily obtained.

Experimental human breeding is impossible, and human families with their
long intervals between generations and the small numbers of their members do
not lend themselves to studies in heredity. Moreover, the members of a family
may become widely scattered, and it is often necessary to collect data about
ancestors on a hearsay basis only. People dissemble about themselves and their
relatives, and even when information is freely given such descriptive terms as
nervousness, irritability and the like, so often used by lay persons, make it of
little value. However, as Penrose (1950) has pointed out, the genetical study of
human beings has the advantages of being the study of a natural population,
and 'there are excellent opportunities for examining gene frequencies, modification of genetical characters by environment, mutation rates, changes due to
natural selection and the effects of different mating systems'; while 'the length of
human life enables medical science, psychology and social investigation to study
both the internal physiology and pathology as well as the external environment
to an extent unknown elsewhere in the natural history of the animal kingdom'.

In the case of any single individual there is no point in asking which is the
more important—nature or nurture, heredity or environment. Both heredity and
environment are essential factors for the development of practically every human
character, and both are potent factors in causing human beings to differ. There
are in fact only three or four inherited human traits which are known to be
uninfluenced by environment. When therefore we raise the question of the relative importance of heredity and environment, we are comparing one individual
with another and inquiring what has made them different. From the genetic
standpoint, 'the term hereditary applies to any mental disorder that would not
originate without the presence of a certain gene combination'.

The Mode of Inheritance

Genetics has now become a complex science, and it is impossible here to give
an adequate account of its basic data. These facts should be sought in a textbook
such as Fraser Roberts' *An Introduction to Medical Genetics*. The following
statements will assume some slight background knowledge, and stress what has
clinical applications.

In general it is not completely developed traits or abnormal characters which are inherited, but predispositions to them. The hereditary factor in the genesis of abnormal mental states is not a general predisposition to all or many mental illnesses, but a specific predisposition to one or other or to more than one particular illness. The fact that more than one abnormal predisposition may be inherited by the same individual may account in part for the great variety and admixture of clinical syndromes which are encountered.

Classification of a trait as inherited does not imply that all possessors of the gene or genes responsible for the trait will develop it. The genes have a range of variability in their manifestation which is called their expressivity and which is due to their several effects being subject to the background influences of other genes and modified also usually by the environment. Thus in the psychiatric field it is possible that the possessor of an abnormal gene or genes may be clinically (phenotypically) normal, or show a certain type of personality, or in unfavourable circumstances develop a psychosis, according to how completely his abnormal genotype is expressed. It is probable also that clinically similar or apparently identical illnesses may be due in some cases to the effects of different genes.

There seem to be two main modes of hereditary transmission: *single-factor inheritance*, where the trait or character is more or less completely determined by the presence of one gene; and *multifactor inheritance*, where it is determined by the combined action of many genes. Where they are inherited, most gross abnormalities and defects are due probably to the action of single genes. Dominant, recessive and sex-linked types of inheritance depend upon single factors.

Dominant Inheritance. The gene produces its effect in single or heterozygous form, and whether it is present upon one or upon both chromosomes of the pair concerned. Clinically, the features of complete dominance are:

1. The affected individual has an affected parent. Inheritance is usually from one parent only.
2. One-half of the children are affected where there is a parent affected.
3. Normals related to affected individuals are wholly normal and will produce, when mated with normals, normal children.
4. A pedigree covering three generations of an affected family is often sufficient to reveal the mode of inheritance. Direct transmission of an abnormal, inherited trait through three generations is almost pathognomonic of dominant inheritance.

The classical example in psychiatry of dominant inheritance is Huntington's chorea [see p. 387]. But such a clear clinical demonstration of this type of inheritance is unusual, since in the majority of cases the expression of dominant genes is irregular and incomplete. Occasionally a dominantly inherited defect appears sporadically, and it is assumed that there has been a mutation.

Recessive Inheritance. The gene produces its effect only in double or homozygous form, and when it is present upon both chromosomes of the pair concerned. Clinically, the features of complete recessivity are:

1. The affected individual has usually outwardly (phenotypically) normal parents, who are heterozygous carriers of the gene.

2. Among the children of such heterozygous parents, the expected proportion of affecteds is one-quarter.

3. The parents are more frequently blood relatives than is the case in the general population, *i.e.* they show a higher incidence of consanguineous matings.

4. The pedigree of one affected family is not sufficient to reveal the mode of inheritance. Pedigrees must be pooled. Though the abnormality is frequently manifested in more than one sibling, the gene responsible may be transmitted undetected through many generations.

Recessive inheritance is the most common type of transmission of human abnormalities: and diseases recessively inherited show usually less variation and are usually more severe than those inherited as dominants. A typical example of recessive inheritance is phenylketonuria [see p. 456].

Sex-linked Inheritance. This is nearly always X-linked. A woman who is the heterozygous carrier (on one of her two X chromosomes) of the abnormal gene does not herself manifest the abnormal trait: but the risk that she will transmit the trait to a son or the carrier state to a daughter is one in two. An affected man cannot transmit the abnormal trait to a son, but his daughters will be heterozygous and liable to transmit the trait to their offspring.

Sex-linked inheritance is of little importance in the psychiatric field where the conditions it causes are very rare. An example is nephrogenic diabetes insipidus, which may be associated with subnormality [see p. 459].

Multifactor Inheritance. Here many genes are involved: their individual effects are small, non-specific and additive, and are combined to produce at least in part those traits or graded characters which distinguish normal people. These traits do not segregate but display a continuous range of variation. It is believed that the greater part of the variability of stature (about 80 per cent.) and intelligence (60–80 per cent.) in the normal population is due to multifactor or polygenic inheritance. Qualities of temperament and personality are probably also to a considerable degree multifactorially determined, but our knowledge in this area is very scanty.

Multifactor inheritance is detected by biometrical methods of some complexity. Mendelian methods of analysis, concerned with genes of large effect which produce discontinuous variation, cannot be applied.

Chromosome Abnormalities. Only since 1956 has it become possible to count accurately human chromosomes, to identify individual pairs of chromosomes, and to ascertain the nuclear sex. In normal men and women the diploid number of chromosomes is 46: 22 pairs of autosomes and one sex chromosome pair. Males and females have different numbers of X chromosomes, and the male has a Y chromosome which is absent in the female. In man this Y chromosome appears to be the male determinant: males are XY, females XX. The nuclei of chromosomal females possess sex chromatin (are chromatin-positive), those of chromosomal males lack it.

As a result of researches which have used new techniques of arresting cell division in cells from bone marrow, skin or peripheral blood, and of separating,

D

spreading and staining the chromosomes, it is now known that there may be abnormalities either in the number (most often, an additional chromosome) or in the structure of the chromosomes (with loss or rearrangement of chromosome material).

While autosomal aberrations produce mental defect, sex chromosome abnormalities are associated more with alterations in personality and behaviour and defect if it occurs tends to be of slight degree. Down's syndrome (mongolism) is an example of the former; the male criminal with a XYY chromosome complex, of the latter.

Methods of Genetical Investigation

It must be emphasized that genetical investigations are pointless unless diagnosis of the trait or character under investigation is precise, and unless it is a biological entity. Much of the psychiatric field is not yet sufficiently clearly delineated for this type of research.

The high familial incidence of a rare character strongly suggests that it is inherited, but the familial occurrence of a disease does not of course prove that the disease is inherited. Members of a family may develop similar illnesses because they have been subject to similar environmental influences. Further research is therefore required to separate genetic and environmental factors, and three main methods are employed—pedigree, twin and statistical studies.

Pedigree Studies. Relatives of the affected individual (the propositus) are studied for the presence of similar traits. All near relatives should if possible be examined personally by the investigator, and a family tree constructed. If the pedigree shows that the distribution of an abnormal trait in a family has a Mendelian pattern, the possibility of a genetic aetiology of the trait is raised and must be further tested in investigations of other families with affected members. Single and small pedigrees are often misleading, variation in the clinical expression of genes may make interpretation difficult, and statistical corrections must be made for bias in sampling. The classical example of this method has been the elucidation of the genetic nature of Huntington's chorea. Pedigree studies will also become of considerable importance in investigations of the genetic linkage of heritable traits, which are becoming possible with the recognition of 'marker' genes (e.g. genes for the blood groups) for certain chromosome pairs. These more easily recognizable genes may in the future be used to trace the inheritance of genes responsible for mental illness and thus perhaps to predict the occurrence of breakdown.

Twin Studies. Francis Galton (1883) pioneered this approach, and notable contributions have been made amongst others by Lange and Conrad in Germany, by Rosanoff and Kallmann in U.S.A., by Slater in England, and by Sjögren and fellow Scandinavian workers. The method allows a rough assessment to be made of the relative importance of hereditary and environmental factors in the genesis of specific nervous and mental illnesses. It does not, however, provide a quantitative measurement of the hereditary influences, and it gives no information about the mode of inheritance.

The method depends on the recognition and separation of the two main types of human twins, and upon their detailed comparison. Uniovular (monozygotic) twins, which constitute about one-quarter of all twin pairs, are thought to develop from a single fertilized ovum: they have the same genetical make-up (genotype), and for this reason are frequently called 'identical'. Binovular (dizygotic) or fraternal twins, which develop from two separate fertilized ova, are genetically no more alike than other brothers and sisters of a family. Any difference between uniovular twins must be due to effects of the environment, pre- or post-natal. Uniovular twins reared apart are of the greatest interest. Comparison between binovular twin pairs and their siblings can give some measure of the minimum effects of the environment. In assessing the extent of the hereditary influence in the genesis of some abnormal condition, the proportion of uniovular twin pairs in which the condition has become manifest in both members of a pair (*i.e.* in which the twins are concordant for the abnormality) is compared with the proportion of binovular pairs concordantly affected. Pairs of like sex must be selected for comparison, if the condition shows any differential sex incidence.

It is obvious that the comparison of uniovular and binovular twin pairs can only be revealing if the ovularity of the twins is correctly diagnosed. Unlike sexed pairs are of course binovular. Like sexed pairs must be scrutinized for similarities in characteristics which are determined genetically and whose expression is known to be little influenced by environment. Close resemblances in general appearance and stature are of importance in this discrimination, as is a history of great similarity of the twins when younger: uniovular twins may be easily mistaken for each other when children. More detailed criteria must also be satisfied before a twin pair is accepted as uniovular: there must be close similarity in colour of eyes, in colour and texture of hair, in structure of the ears, in finger, palm and foot prints, and in the ability or inability to taste phenylthiourea. The blood groups of uniovular twin pairs are identical. The minimal criteria for the diagnosis of uniovularity have not yet been laid down. The greater the number of detailed resemblances, the more certain becomes the diagnosis; and qualitative and quantitative analyses of the hand- and foot-prints (dermatoglyphics), together with examination of the various blood group systems and typing for serum proteins, are usually now considered necessary.

Where comparison is being made between uniovular and binovular twin pairs, sufficient numbers of cases must be found to allow statistically valid conclusions to be drawn, and care must be taken to avoid biased sampling of the twin population. Single case reports, though often inconclusive, may give fruitful leads for research into aetiology. The study of discordant uniovular twin pairs should be particularly profitable.

Kallmann expanded the twin method of research to include detailed study of the full sibs, half sibs and step sibs of the twins, and this extended 'twin family method' is to be preferred, as giving a more adequate picture of family constellations and as revealing the responses of genetically dissimilar individuals to similar environments.

Recent research has shown that the situation is not quite as simple as has been outlined above. There are now known to be more than two types of twin: twins intermediate between monozygotic and dizygotic may occur rarely. A mosaic with some cells with a male and some with a female complement of chromosomes may result from two sperms fertilizing one egg. Even more unusual, monozygotic twins may not be of the same apparent sex, due perhaps to non-disjunction of the sex chromosomes at the second cleavage division: cases have been reported where one monozygotic twin had an X and a Y chromosome, the other only a single X chromosome. Allen (1965) has discussed in a critical review this multiplicity of twin types, the question of how far twins are atypical members of the general population, and the problems of sampling and of the analysis of data in twin studies.

Statistical Investigations. Statistical methods are employed particularly in genetical studies of the general population: for example, in the analysis of multifactor inheritance, of problems of gene frequency and mutation rates, and in investigation of the results in a community of departures from random mating. In-breeding, particularly the marriage of cousins, is of importance in fostering the appearance of rare recessive defects: and assortative mating, which is the tendency of individuals to choose marital partners who are in certain respects similar to themselves, may pose serious social problems when those who marry are mentally backward or delinquent.

The Genetics of Mental Illness and Defect

Here only a brief summary of the present position will be attempted. Further details will be found in later pages where the various reaction-types are discussed.

Nervous and Mental Illness. The most clear-cut example of single-factor inheritance is Huntington's chorea, which is transmitted as a simple dominant. Amongst other conditions in which single-factor dominant inheritance is known or suspected, the most important appears to be manic-depressive psychosis, where the penetrance of the gene is notably incomplete. It is possible also that Pick's pre-senile dementia is inherited as a dominant.

Twin studies have provided evidence of the importance of heredity in schizophrenia, and some authorities (Luxemburger, Kallmann) have believed that it is recessively inherited and due to a single gene. Others have favoured a polygenic explanation; and Book suggested that the gene responsible might be an intermediate one, neither dominant nor recessive. A major difficulty in this research has been, of course, the delimitation of schizophrenia. Even when the reaction-type is strictly defined clinically, it may be the product of a number of different genotypes.

Though the evidence is as yet very incomplete, multifactor inheritance is thought to play some rôle in the aetiology of the neuroses. The protagonists of this theory conceive the neurotic to be a normal variant.

There is considerable disagreement about the genetic background of the epilepsies. Recent studies seem to support the distinction between idiopathic and symptomatic epilepsy, and to demonstrate the importance of heredity in cases of *petit mal* (*i.e.* those which show a three per second wave and spike pattern in the E.E.G.).

Other conditions in which the importance of genetic factors has been demonstrated are senescence and overt homosexuality.

Subnormality or Mental Defect. In the field of subnormality a broad distinction may be made between subnormal and severely subnormal cases.

In the aetiology of many cases of subnormality (previously designated feebleminded), constituting probably at least one-third of the total defective population, multiple genes (polygenes) play an important and perhaps predominant rôle, as they do in the aetiology of normal intelligence. These 'sub-cultural', defective individuals occupy the lower part of the normal frequency distribution curve of intelligence, and subnormality is common amongst their relatives. Polygenes probably also play a part in determining some cases of severe subnormality.

Severe subnormality (which includes cases previously designated idiots and imbeciles) comprises a large number of clinical entities, many still not satisfactorily differentiated, of very various aetiology. Amongst these an as yet undetermined but important number are due mainly or wholly to the effects of single genes. Amongst such conditions believed to be dominantly inherited are tuberous sclerosis (epiloia), neurofibromatosis, naevoid amentia and hypertelorism. Recessively inherited defects tend to be even more sharply demarcated, and include amaurotic family idiocy, phenylketonuria, gargoylism, 'true' microcephaly, hepatolenticular degeneration, and some forms of diffuse sclerosis (Schilder's disease).

The associations between subnormality and chromosome abnormalities are described on pages 460–2. Down's syndrome (mongolism) is much the most important of these conditions, accounting as it does for about 10 per cent. of the patients who have to be cared for in mental deficiency hospitals.

EUGENICS

By dictionary definition eugenics is the science of the production of fine offspring. In practice, eugenics has usually a wider connotation, and the humanitarian spirit which has inspired this movement for human betterment is more fitly expressed in Francis Galton's own statement (1908): 'Man is gifted with pity and other kindly feelings; he has also the power of preventing many kinds of suffering. I conceive it to fall well within his province to replace Natural Selection by other processes that are more merciful and not less effective.'

Galton's work on *Hereditary Genius*, his study (along with Schuster) of *Noteworthy Families*, and the book of F. A. Woods on *Mental and Moral Heredity in Royalty* all demonstrate that 'a considerable proportion of the noteworthy members in a population spring from comparatively few families'. Furthermore, Galton's investigations in relation to the kinship of the Fellows of the Royal Society, of English judges, and of groups of illustrious men from every walk of life showed that eminent men tend to have eminent relatives, and that this is not dependent on special environmental advantages. Terman, in U.S.A., found among gifted children with an I.Q. of 130 or better that in 53 per cent. the fathers were of the professional class; 37 per cent. were clerical workers; and 10 per cent. were skilled artisans: that is, while the professional class constituted about 2 per cent. of the whole population of a State, this class produced 50 per cent. of the children of high natural endowment.

In Great Britain the evidence of differential reproductive rates has caused some speculation that less valuable stocks may be multiplying at the expense of the good (Thomson *et al.*, 1947). The most highly endowed individuals, irrespective of social or economic class, have been producing the smallest families: and it has been found that there is a negative association of size of family with intelligence test scores—the individual child's test score tends to go down as the number of his siblings goes up. So one might expect as a result of this population trend that, if tested intelligence is, as it appears to be, largely inherited and if the tests applied have been as valid and reliable as has been thought, the average intelligence of our population might show a decline. In fact, however, there is as yet no evidence that this expected decline in intelligence is taking place. For example, in Scotland in 1932, 90,000 11-year-olds had their intelligence tested, and in 1947 a similar sample of the school population was similarly tested: and in 1947 the mean score of those tested was found to be slightly higher than it was in 1932. Yet, despite these figures, adverse selection may be proceeding unobserved, temporarily masked by favourable environmental factors.

The matter is one of which every responsible person must take cognizance, and the situation must continue to be watched closely. Burt has expressed the problem this way: 'As a nation we should know our resources in mind-power as accurately as we do in man-power, iron and coal'.

Other dysgenic influences can be detected, more or less certainly, in our Western civilization. Its wars have led to the mutilation and death of some of its fittest citizens: the advances of preventive and therapeutic medicine and surgery have mitigated the pressures of natural selection and have preserved the lives of many who are constitutionally frail or damaged: the increasing exposure of the population to radiation may produce harmful mutations.

It is of course to combat prejudicial population trends that eugenic movements and societies have taken the field and call for and merit our support. But it is necessary also that we should be broad-minded and somewhat sceptical in our approach to this subject. Natural selection is infinitely more potent than selection by deliberate human agency is ever likely to be, and the general population is a great reservoir, not only of definite good and bad, but of that variety and potentiality without which the healthy development of a society fails. Eugenics is wholly dependent upon our knowledge of genetics, and genetics is still a young science, operating in an area where a great deal is unknown. Also, before we can select effectively we must know clearly what products we desire. We do know in a very general way the kinds of individual whose birth and growth we wish to encourage, but we cannot yet be categorical: while we have had some success in measuring intelligence, the measurement of personality and temperament and of all the subtler qualities of human beings eludes us. It would be quite arbitrary to proceed to measure human beings in terms of some current standard of behaviour or concepts of mental hygiene, and to ignore the contributions which have been made, and will be made, to any society by many who are technically unstable. Again, an emphasis on eugenics must not lead to any undervaluation of environmental factors or to any *laissez-faire* attitude towards economic and social betterment. Finally, we should remember that the ultimate arbiter of our recommendations will be that public opinion which it is always better to seek to educate than to coerce, and which for long has been firmly convinced, with much justice, that it takes all kinds to make a world.

Negative and Positive Eugenic Programmes

Negative Eugenics. By negative eugenics is meant the method whereby a reduction can be effected in those below average, and the measures advocated may be grouped as follows:

1. Celibacy and sexual abstinence.
2. Marriage regulations.
3. Segregation.
4. Contraception.
5. Sterilization.
6. Abortion.

All reasonable people are coming to appreciate that there are certain persons who as a result of hereditary or environmental factors, or both, are either so subnormal (mentally defective) or so temperamentally unstable that they should be discouraged from parenthood, both for their own sake and that of their progeny. In consequence of this it has been advocated that a law should be introduced forbidding the marriage of those likely to transmit undesirable traits. In practice this would mean the establishment of a bureau with the power to grant or withhold marriage certificates. That would inevitably be a cumbrous, costly and ineffective procedure, and in our opinion the emphasis should be placed more on health education and propaganda than on legislation.

Segregation. In colonies for the subnormal or in mental hospitals segregation is an accepted and beneficent mode of caring for the majority of those who are so mentally incapacitated as to be unable to fit into the social *milieu*. In many instances, particularly in cases of severe subnormality (mental defect), it means the continuous care of the individual throughout his life, but in others treatment may be of a temporary nature resulting in complete recovery medically and socially. Segregation, however, is considerably limited in its application, and for the most part cannot be utilized for the so-called 'social problem' or psychopathic group—a group which constitutes the greatest danger to society.

Contraception or Birth-control. The establishment of birth-control clinics and the widespread use of contraception are proving one of the most useful of modern health developments. The public have been informed why, for certain medical, psychological and sociological reasons, pregnancy should be avoided, and on the positive side how pregnancies may be spaced so as to ensure adequate health for both mother and child. The efficiency of contraception, however, depends on careful and intelligent application and, unfortunately, these are just the qualities which are lacking in the subnormal, psychopathic and unstable members of the community. However, there is evidence that the negative correlation of social class and fertility is decreasing in this country.

Sterilization. Sterilization laws were promulgated in the United States of America in 1910, and are effective in 27 States of the Union. In 1948, for example, 2322 official sterilizations were performed. Similar laws are in force in Scandinavian countries and in Switzerland. In general it may be said that the provisions are aimed mainly against the propagation of mental disease, subnormality and epilepsy, and that the sterilization is on a voluntary basis.

In Britain a Departmental Committee on Sterilization (Brock Report, 1934) advocated that, subject to certain safeguards, voluntary sterilization should be legalized in the case of:

1. A person who is mentally defective or who has suffered from mental disorder.
2. A person who suffers from or is believed to be a carrier of a grave physical disability which has been shown to be transmissible.
3. A person who is believed to be likely to transmit mental disorder or defect.

These proposals, which have not been embodied in law, were both wide and vague. There is no justification whatever for advocating sterilization in a wholesale way as a means of improving the quality of a population: but if the measure is kept on an individual basis, if each case is judged on its merits, particular families may be helped and few people would raise any objection to its application. Sterilization of women is practised quite frequently in this country to protect their health and to prevent the birth of abnormal babies. The patient must of course give her, or his, full and valid consent to the operation.

Therapeutic Abortion. Social and moral attitudes in this society are changing rapidly: capital punishment, homosexuality, divorce, abortion, in fact the whole structure of our social mores has recently been under review. It has been due more to pressures from the community than from the medical profession that the law on abortion has been altered. Certainly some doctors, under the previously existing law in England, had felt inhibited in advising on or carrying out termination of pregnancy: but more had felt constrained by the absence of agreed opinion about the indications for and effects of this procedure and by a disinclination to encourage abortion on demand.

Under the terms of the Abortion Act 1967, a pregnancy may be terminated if two registered medical practitioners are of the opinion:

(*a*) that the continuance of the pregnancy would involve risk to the life of the pregnant woman, or of injury to the physical or mental health of the pregnant woman or any existing children of her family, greater than if the pregnancy were terminated; or

(*b*) that there is a substantial risk that if the child were born it would suffer from such physical or mental abnormalities as to be seriously handicapped.

In determining whether the continuance of a pregnancy would involve risk of injury to health, account may be taken of the pregnant woman's actual or reasonably foreseeable environment.

The provisions of this Act clearly allow the doctor full freedom to exercise his professional judgement, in taking into account the physical, psychiatric and social aspects of the pregnant woman's situation. Termination of pregnancy on psychiatric grounds can be undertaken without reference to a psychiatrist: and there is furthermore no indication in the Act that psychiatrists are to be considered more competent to judge the possibly mentally harmful effects of the social environment than any other doctor.

Most of the scientifically significant research into the effects of therapeutic abortion has been done in Scandinavia, where legal enactments have been different from those in this country. Ekblad (1955), following up 479 cases of therapeutic abortion, found no ill effects in 75 per cent. Twenty-five per cent. of these women expressed significant self-reproach or regret: but though in 11 per cent. of the whole sample this self-reproach was considered serious, generally the symptoms of it were mild, rarely requiring medical treatment and only exceptionally disabling. Höök (1963) reported the status on follow-up of 249 women whose application for legal abortion had been refused by the National Board of Health in Sweden in 1948. No suicides or suicidal attempts occurred after the refusal: but 11 per cent. procured an abortion. Sixty-nine per cent. of the women who had given birth to a child had adjusted themselves and were content with the situation. Thirty-one per cent. were dissatisfied or poorly adjusted, these were mainly women of unstable personality and they were thought likely to be providing an unfavourable environment for the child. As might be expected, amongst the temperamentally unstable rejection of the pregnancy is liable to be followed by rejection of the child. Jansson (1965), writing also from Sweden, confirms that serious mental disorders following abortion arise predominantly in women already predisposed to them; and draws attention to the paradoxical situation that it is in those cases in which a therapeutic abortion can best be justified on psychiatric grounds that the risk of abnormal mental sequelae is greatest. Jansson's conclusion is as follows: 'It may be said, perhaps, that legal abortion stands out as a fairly ineffective therapeutic means. Women who are psychically vulnerable risk a deterioration in their condition through an unwelcome pregnancy and the extra load this involves, whatever course is adopted; while those who are mentally stable get over an abortion, or a rejection of their application for an abortion, considerably better.'

There has been only one recent substantial study in Britain of the effects of therapeutic abortion: that carried out by Anderson (1961) in Manchester. He recommended termination of pregnancy on psychiatric grounds in 39 of the 95 (41 per cent.) cases referred to him. Reviewing these cases in retrospect and after follow-up, he could find no clear-cut indications for the operation, and admitted that looking at the figures of its results in his series it was 'hard to see any convincing case for the efficacy of abortion as a therapeutic procedure'. He summarized his views as follows: 'There is a growing body of evidence that abortion undertaken on psychiatric grounds is often an unsound and meddlesome, or at any rate unnecessary procedure. Yet there remains pretty certainly a handful of cases where it seems to be beneficial.'

Because of this paucity of follow-up studies of the effects of termination of pregnancy on psychiatric grounds, opinions and responsible practice have varied widely in this country, extending from those who maintain that there are no psychiatric grounds for terminating a pregnancy, though Anderson's opinion that termination is practically never indicated in depressions, to the practice in Aberdeen (Baird, 1965) where termination of pregnancy has been on psychiatric or psychiatric plus social grounds in 70 per cent. of cases and the psychiatric conditions most commonly calling for termination have been considered to be depression and anxiety.

No doctor is required to participate in the treatment authorized by the Abortion Act if he has a conscientious objection to it: and those doctors who because of their religions or ethical beliefs will not advise abortion in any case may be expected to declare to their medical colleagues the fact and grounds of their opposition. Their objections are entirely proper and must be respected. All those other doctors who may have to advise and act in the new circumstances created by this Act, will have to proceed with their traditional integrity and on the basis of the most careful evaluation of the particular circumstances of each individual case. It may be suggested that the psychiatrist should reach a conclusion to recommend termination only after a full discussion with the family doctor and with the gynaecologist: and whenever possible the family doctor should be the person who refers the patient to a psychiatrist, not a doctor to whom she is a stranger.

A more satisfactory appraisal of the patient's mental state can often be made if she is admitted for at least a few days to the psychiatric unit of a general hospital, or to wherever else detailed observation and investigation can be undertaken.

In cases of schizophrenia or paranoid psychosis, or severe subnormality, conditions which relatively rarely have to be considered in this connection, termination of the pregnancy will usually be considered advisable.

Cases of affective psychosis present more complex problems. The presence of a psychosis provides clearly stronger grounds for termination of pregnancy than the possibility of a psychosis developing later in the pregnancy or in the puerperium. Most puerperal psychoses are affective and the prognosis is generally very favourable. Furthermore, if a woman has had a puerperal psychosis it is difficult, if not impossible, to forecast accurately whether or not she will suffer a further psychosis following another pregnancy. Again, a depressive psychosis in pregnancy usually responds well to treatment with E.C.T. The risk of suicide must also be considered. While a pregnant woman may attempt suicide, few in fact commit suicide. All these considerations must be borne in mind and weighed before coming to a decision.

The chief difficulties arise in cases of neurotic or allied disturbances of the personality. Therapeutic abortion could easily be justified in the case of a woman suffering from a severe obsessional illness, but this is an exceptional situation.

The cases which give rise to most debate and differences of opinion are those in which the emotional reaction has closely followed the realization of pregnancy, where the pregnancy is unwanted or illegitimate, where the woman is unsupported by a stable husband or paramour, and when she is threatening suicide. Such states are usually to be classified as neurotic or situational depressions or in Anderson's term 'distress reactions'. Though the pregnancy is obviously unwelcome and rejected, the distress may be rather superficial and if abortion is refused the individual often settles down fairly soon to accept the pregnancy. Probably the majority of such reactions do not provide grounds for recommending therapeutic abortion.

Pregnancy as a result of rape or incest constitutes obviously a severe psychological trauma, with an evident risk to mental health in most cases should the pregnancy be allowed to continue.

The severely psychopathic woman who becomes pregnant is likely to be so inadequate and irresponsible a mother as to increase the risk of the health of existing children of the family (if she is caring for them) being prejudiced, so that termination in such circumstances may properly be recommended.

In every case all aspects of the situation must be reviewed, not only the current circumstances but the previous health of the pregnant woman: and it will often be useful to have a report from a psychiatric or medical social worker about the family and domestic background.

Should it be decided that the pregnancy of an emotionally unstable woman should not be terminated, other medical help is usually required, psychotherapeutic support or drugs or E.C.T.: and in many cases, since domestic or social stress is so frequently a factor, the rôle of the social worker or health visitor is a key one, in bringing practical domestic help and guidance. Whether one is a psychiatrist or a general practitioner, the decision whether or not to advise abortion is only one part of one's medical responsibilities, and these responsibilities may extend throughout the pregnancy into the puerperium.

In most cases in which therapeutic abortion is carried out the woman is relieved and satisfied. The operation may, however, precipitate a severe reaction of guilt, with morbid depression and even suicide—though such a tragedy is exceptional. Fearing such a reaction in an obsessional personality, one may advise against abortion and condemn a woman to what in retrospect may seem indefensible mental suffering. There are no rules of thumb: there can not be, since the aetiology is multiple and the individual circumstances are so various. The doctor is faced frequently with an anxious and perplexing situation, and it is perhaps best that it should remain in most cases a difficult decision.

Therapeutic abortion may also now be carried out on eugenic grounds, if there is substantial risk of the birth of a seriously physically or mentally handicapped child. Here usually one has only the probabilities of an abnormal birth, upon which to base a recommendation. Abortion would, for example, clearly be permissible in the case of a woman who had already given birth to a mongol or a phenylketonuric child.

How successful can these negative eugenic measures be, which have been described? Deliberate negative selection against traits determined by many genes is very difficult: for example, in the control of subnormality it would entail prevention of the assortative mating and reproduction of subnormal individuals, most of whom are at liberty and employed in the community. More perhaps can be effected in the case of traits determined by single genes, but here too our powers are very considerably limited, especially where the inheritance is recessive.

Natural selection acts to modify or eliminate dominant defects rather rapidly. If the inherited disability is very severe and is developed early in life, the natural rate of elimination is high. A high mutation rate (*e.g.* in epiloia) may, however, balance this loss of genes by early death. It is the severe dominant defects which are not manifested until later in life that are perpetuated by transmission to offspring, and it is against these that we would seek to employ negative eugenic measures. Huntington's chorea is an example of such a defect, and it may be used to illustrate the eugenic possibilities. If all the children of parents with Huntington's chorea were sterilized or otherwise remained childless, the incidence of the condition would rapidly diminish. Two major difficulties, however, arise; first, one-half of the children of a parent with Huntington's chorea will be unaffected, and childlessness would be for many of them a severe privation; and second, the average age of onset of the illness is around 35 years, and we know no way of identifying, before he develops it, the individual who is going to be its victim, and it is likely that in many cases the affected individual will have reproduced before his illness displays itself. Progress in eugenic control of this severe disease is likely to be made, therefore, only when we have found a means of recognizing the heterozygote at an early age. Moreover, it must be remembered that the occurrence of new mutations makes the disease ineradicable.

Natural selection acts exceedingly slowly against recessive defects. Single genes which cause rare recessive diseases or defects in humans do not usually give rise to any disability in the carriers (heterozygotes). We can rarely detect these carriers: and most of the parents of those who develop recessive disabilities are clinically normal. Negative selective measures such as sterilization can therefore very rarely be applied. Furthermore, it may be said in general that from the eugenic point of view the sufferer from, or carrier of, a recessive abnormality should not be discouraged from marrying, if he does not wish to marry a blood relative or into a family in which the same abnormality has appeared.

The association of trisomy of chromosome 21 with advanced maternal age is well recognized, it is by far the commonest cause of Down's syndrome (mongolism) and the risk of the woman having a further mongol child is slight. In a very small number of cases a translocation is inherited, and the 15/21 translocation carrier woman has a much increased risk of having a mongol child. The chance of giving birth to a mongol may in these cases be as high as 1 in 5 in each pregnancy. Genetic counselling can be given with confidence if the ages and chromosomal constitutions of the parents are known.

With regard to epilepsy, the genetic background of the symptom is by no means clear, and it seems that there are no good grounds for forbidding most epileptics to marry and to have children.

Positive Eugenics. A positive eugenic policy aims at increasing the numbers of those above average. This may be effected in the following ways:

1. Family allowances.
2. Relief from taxation.
3. Educational opportunities.
4. Contraception.
5. Marriage certificates.

The objectives are to encourage those individuals with noteworthy heritable qualities to produce bigger families. Much has been done in this country and elsewhere by means of bursaries and scholarships to increase educational opportunities for children and young people showing exceptional aptitudes.

One method of encouraging the growth and development of healthy families is by making 'family allowances' to parents. This has become national policy in Italy, for example, and in France and Great Britain. In Britain it is being used to an increasing extent to ease the social problems of the larger families—those with 3 or more children. The highest fertility ratios are in our economically poorest areas. Large families tend to be associated with low parental earnings and low socio-economic status. The children of these large families suffer often from overcrowding, defective care in childhood and reduced educational opportunities. It is right that they should be helped: but increased financial aid for these families will in the short term do nothing to reduce but may tend to increase their size. Greater benefit is likely to come from raising incomes, improving education and providing a domiciliary service of contraceptive advice and materials in these impoverished homes.

All measures encouraging the production of larger families must now be scrutinized against the rapid rate of population growth throughout the world and the immense problems which this is already creating, especially in the economically less developed countries. The emphasis will have to be placed increasingly on small families, born of healthy stock and given the best environmental circumstances for their upbringing and individual development.

In conclusion, it may be said that in most cases of nervous and mental illness the aetiology is multiple, that genetic and environmental factors interact, and that with our present knowledge we are likely to gain more by seeking to control the environmental factors.

Marriage and Motherhood

Marriage. An unhappy marriage is one of the most potent factors in the production of mental distress. It may cause suspicion and jealousy which can lead to mental and physical cruelty, to alcoholism, divorce and a broken home.

There are people who do ask for help and genetic advice in regard to marriage, but the advice given is usually acted upon only when it coincides with the applicant's own ideas. In order to give a reasoned opinion, we must ascertain the facts about the family history both of the man and of the woman and obtain as complete a record as possible of the health of their relatives. It is in fact rare to find a family tree devoid of all trace of nervous or mental disease, and a positive family history of mental illness does not necessarily indicate a bad heredity; the very salt of the earth may spring from such a stock. Furthermore a family stock may be improved by mating with a healthier stock. There has been a tendency for enthusiasts for eugenics to be too arbitrary in advising against the marriage of people with a family history of psychiatric disabilities. As regards cousin marriages, if the cousins come from healthy families there is no medical bar against marriage: but it must be remembered that recessive defects may become manifest.

The ages and personal medical histories of those who seek advice about marriage must also be considered. With few important exceptions (for example, Huntington's chorea), the person who has attained the age of twenty-five years with a clean bill of mental health and marries a person equally healthy, is likely to have healthy children.

More specifically, a family history of manic-depressive psychosis cannot be considered a bar to marriage: the manic-depressive genotype is very widely distributed in the community and is very often associated with admirable traits of character and with high intelligence and achievement. A personal history of manic-depressive illness must be assessed according to the facts of each individual case; the age of onset, and the frequency and duration of the attacks.

In schizophrenia the position is rather different. The marriage and fertility rates are low. Nature thus tends to act eugenically by limiting the birth of schizophrenics. Kallmann's investigations have shown that of 1087 probands, 562 had no children: the highest degree of childlessness occurred among male hebephrenics and male and female catatonics. It is only after the most careful consideration that a recovered schizophrenic should be advised to marry, and always with the proviso that parenthood is inadvisable.

In addition to the psychoses which have been mentioned, the possible consequences of hereditary predisposition may seriously perturb members of those families who have suffered from neuroses, psychopathic states, organic brain disease, or criminal conduct. Often it is impossible to give the complete reassurance which is so anxiously sought. But we can make sure that each case is carefully investigated, and that an arbitrary and categorical opinion is not expressed. Much may depend on the opinion given and on how it is given. We must take both heredity and environment into account, and we should not be unduly pessimistic. We should always urge the contracting parties to be frank with each other: want of frankness may lead to much unhappiness later, if one or other partner has a breakdown. Ultimately these are matters which we should leave to the individual conscience, while, as our knowledge of genetics deepens, we attempt to mould public opinion to the appreciation of their vast importance. The public must be enlightened to realize for themselves the difficulties, the trials and the sorrow which the birth of mentally handicapped children means both to the parents and to the offspring.

It may appear that we are putting a great deal of emphasis on hereditary predisposition and its possible consequences. We make no excuse for doing so. We believe that a healthy constitution is of paramount importance for the welfare of the individual and the race. The application of genetic knowledge may make a valuable contribution to the health of the nation and should be the subject of intensive study in the medical departments of our universities.

Motherhood. This is a matter which, psychiatrically, has never had the attention it deserves. Motherhood is the time, above all others, when the interrelationship between the physiological and the psychological functions requires earnest and thoughtful consideration; they may reverberate on each other to an extreme degree, and may constitute the best example of the concept of psychosomatic medicine. Needless to say, at such a critical period in a woman's life everything possible must be done to conserve her strength—physical and mental—and to ensure her welfare. While we do so we must likewise safeguard the prospects of the unborn child so that the child may be born healthy, and be brought up in a good environment. That means that the mother throughout her pregnancy should have been under skilled medical guidance, and that all the possible physical and psychological complications which might occur would have had adequate consideration. Some of the more common factors which may be present are the worry, anxiety and fear associated with the possible transmission of deleterious hereditary tendencies, previous attacks of nervous or mental instability, too frequent pregnancies, difficult social and economic conditions. Furthermore, the unwanted child, the illegitimate one, and the broken-home child may give rise to emotional situations which may seriously complicate married life, and may operate with disastrous consequences throughout pregnancy, at the time of childbirth, or subsequently. 'It may be said that any condition which gives rise to a conflict about childbirth resulting in an increase of the mental strain may operate as a precipitating factor and may, provided other predisposing conditions exist, result in psychotic reactions.' Many patients, while conscious of their psychological difficulties may never voice them, and it comes as a great shock and surprise when they become aware of their aversion to marital intercourse let alone childbirth. This aversion may amount to antagonism and hostility, and sometimes may be traced to experiences which have been present in the parental home. When the hostility to the husband is projected on to the child, which is by no means uncommon, serious consequences, *e.g.* infanticide, may result. Fortunately, however, psychotic reactions are comparatively rare. An endless variety of neurotic reactions are seen which may prove difficult to treat, but usually respond to psychological interpretation and analysis. The somatic symptoms may be in the ascendant and may present as nausea, persistent vomiting, abortion and stillbirth. Sometimes the above symptoms are the result of physiological dysfunction, but in other instances they appear to symbolize the rejection of the unborn child. Such phenomena are usually indicative of anxiety, or a hysterical conversion state, or depression, or even a feeling of unreality which may raise the possibility of a schizophrenic involvement. Even the entire character of a pregnant woman may change. For the time being she may be unreliable and untrustworthy: thieving, lying, having unfounded likes and dislikes, craving for food and drink to which she has never been accustomed, may all prove difficult to treat. Such disorders of conduct seem to point to deep-seated complex factors, *e.g.* a young married woman, five months pregnant, when shopping returned home with bags of apples which she always placed on the floor under a particular chair. Sometimes an illegitimate pregnancy will be concealed and the woman may continue in her employment up until the moment of her delivery. These cases may have serious repercussions, resulting in dangerous attempts to dispose of the unwanted child; the act is determined by a sense of guilt. The state of conflicting emotions was demonstrated in a woman 42 years old, who, when pregnant, described how, alternately, she was surprised, delighted, and afraid. The conflict would resolve itself into one of: 'I shall have a baby' with the opposing negative: 'I shall have no child—I have no right to one—I shall lose it—I shall pay for it with my death'.

Motherhood, then, may be a very complex and difficult problem, one which requires the greatest care and most considerate management. To effect such a purpose it would seem essential to establish the closest possible working arrangements between obstetrical, psychiatric and paediatric departments.

ALCOHOLISM

The Influence of Alcohol on the Normal Man. It is generally agreed that alcohol is a depressant and not a stimulant, from the very beginning of its direct action on the central nervous system; and that it reduces both mental and muscular efficiency. The deceptive early appearance of stimulation, and the euphoria which misleads the subject into a too favourable view of his performance after he has taken alcohol, arise from the release of the lower nervous centres from control by the higher, by depression of the functions of the latter. In a dose such as is contained in 2–3 ounces of whisky (alcohol 40 per cent. of volume), alcohol causes a disorder of attention, concentration, memory and powers of reasoning; sensory acuity in all fields and the sense of time are impaired; and sensory-motor co-ordination is disturbed. His inhibitions lowered, his self-criticism blurred, his sense of well-being and confidence usually enhanced, the individual is obviously less able to assess risks and to deal with any situation calling for judgement and discriminating response. There is wide variation in the susceptibility and reactions of different individuals to the same amount of alcohol, so that a quantitative estimate of the amount of alcohol in the individual's body cannot give an accurate measure of the degree of disorder in his behaviour. It has been stated that if the percentage of alcohol in the blood is under 0·1 per cent. the individual's faculties are unlikely to be impaired. In larger doses, alcohol produces all the well-known symptoms of intoxication. Under the provisions of the Road Safety Act, 1967, it is an offence for a motorist to drive or attempt to drive or be in charge of a vehicle if his blood alcohol is over 80 mg./100 ml.: and the ability of most drivers to drive safely is impaired when the blood alcohol is well below this level. A tolerance for alcohol may be acquired by regular drinking. A heavy drinker may have to drink more than twice as much to produce a given degree of intoxication as an abstainer.

Alcohol then is not only a beverage but a narcotic drug, whose toxic effects lead to clumsy, inappropriate and finally completely disordered responses to the environment. It has, of course, also positive and helpful effects. Alcohol facilitates social contacts and warms festive occasions; it can promote generosity and courage. 'It brings its votary from the chill periphery of things to the radiant core', reducing feelings of shyness, inferiority and loneliness, and is highly effective (if only transiently so) in relieving tensions and easing guilt, drowning the nagging voices of duty and conscience: so that it is not surprising that so many abuse it.

Alcohol, supplying calories, ranks as a food but cannot of course provide an adequate diet. The more that alcohol displaces other foods in the individual's daily consumption the greater is the risk of vitamin deficiency resulting. Not only does the vitamin content of the diet decrease absolutely, relatively the balance of vitamin and caloric intake is also disturbed; and the progressively disordered function of the stomach, liver and other organs causes defective absorption and utilization of these essential food factors.

Trends of abnormality and instability in the personality are very apt to be aggravated by alcohol, and alcohol readily reveals the defective control which may follow head injury and accompany epilepsy, or indeed almost any kind of nervous or mental illness or defect.

The Setting and Individual Effects of Chronically Excessive Consumption of Alcohol. Research into the problems of alcoholism has been hindered not only by a frequent lack of precision in the use of such terms as 'abnormal drinkers', 'alcoholic addicts' and 'chronic alcoholics', but also by the considerable difficulties which arise in trying to estimate the extent of the problem. We agree with Lemert (1951) that 'there is no one index which can serve as a measure of the total number of intemperate users of alcohol. The methods which have been employed to throw light upon the quantitative aspect of the alcoholic "problems" include surveys of insurance policy holders, absenteeism records in factories, arrests for drunkenness, death rates caused by alcoholism and admissions to mental hospitals of alcoholics with or without psychosis. All these methods individually suffer from one defect or another so that they cannot be relied upon alone as measures of alcoholism.' Jellinek (1960) pointed out that alcoholism is a genus with many species and only two factors common to all of them, namely drinking and the damage resulting from it. Any research aiming at an adequate coverage of the problem must investigate in detail both these aspects. Some of the epidemiological problems have been discussed critically by Keller (1962).

The prevalence of alcoholism varies from country to country according to the prevailing culture, as it does amongst the individuals and groups comprising each community. Certain generalizations are, however, possible. Of the ethnic groups, the Irish and North American Negroes show a high prevalence of alcoholism, the Jews a markedly low one. The rates are higher in urban than in rural areas. Alcoholism in all societies is commoner amongst men than amongst women: in 1962, for example, in England and Wales the male/female ratio for mental hospital admission was 4·3:1. All social classes are involved: in this

E

country the upper two and lower two mainly, it is probable, though the admission rates to psychiatric units are not very reliable indices. It must be added that in England and Wales there is an excess mortality from hepatic cirrhosis in Social Class I. Those who handle alcohol as part of their jobs (brewers, publicans, barmen) are more apt to become alcoholic than the average man. The customs of the individual's social set may also have an important influence. Week-end boozing is less damaging in the long run than steady, excessive daily drinking.

We do not know accurately the prevalence of alcoholism in any country. A survey carried out in 1962–63 by the Joseph Rowntree Social Service Trust (1965) in 5 areas in England, in which information was obtained from family doctors, health visitors and probation officers, suggested that there are at least 70,000 chronic alcoholics in England and Wales. This estimated rate of 2·2 per 1000 corresponds with that of about 2 per 1000 reported by Shepherd and his colleagues (1966) in a study in London of psychiatric morbidity in general practice. The Rowntree survey also suggested that there may be a further 200,000 individuals in England and Wales at serious risk of becoming chronic alcoholics.

There has in recent years been an increase in social drinking in this country, with the inevitable result that more people have been found to be vulnerable to the effects of alcohol and have become addicted to it. Convictions for drunkenness have risen, as have the number of admissions for alcoholism to mental hospitals and deaths from cirrhosis of the liver.

The position is more serious in Scotland than in England and Wales (Scottish Home and Health Department Report, 1965). First admission rates to mental hospitals in Scotland for alcoholism are approximately 6 times as high as those for England and Wales; and cases of alcoholism now constitute 10–12 per cent. of the total mental hospital admissions in Scotland. Earlier this century the proportion of 'alcoholic psychoses' to total admissions to mental hospitals was recorded at from 10–15 per cent. In England and Wales, where the percentage of admissions for alcoholism in 1962 was 2·4, it had decreased from 15·99 in 1902 to 1·66 in 1956.

The rate of mental hospital admissions for alcoholic psychoses does not give a complete picture of their incidence. Delirium tremens, the most characteristic alcoholic psychosis, being of brief duration is usually treated outwith the mental hospitals.

Other Antisocial Effects of the Consumption of Alcohol. Alcohol's disinhibiting effects very frequently have seriously antisocial results, not only for those who persistently abuse alcohol. Surly, rowdy and aggressive behaviour, sexual promiscuity, assaults and other crimes, dangerous driving leading to road accidents, hang-overs affecting efficiency at work, may all result.

All authorities agree that alcoholism is an important factor in the genesis particularly of sexual and aggressive crimes. Planned crimes, *e.g.* thefts and house-breaking, can be carried out usually only in the early stages of drunkenness. As intoxication increases, violent outbursts may precede the stage of 'drunk and incapable'.

Alcoholism, though rarely wholly or mainly the cause of a suicidal attempt, is a significant factor in about one-third of these acts, and in men about twice as often as women. Many of these individuals have alcoholic forebears, come from homes 'broken' by parental alcoholism, and themselves have a history of excessive drinking. The suicidal attempt itself may be made after drinking. A relatively small amount of alcohol seems to be more potent than a large excess in releasing this type of abnormal behaviour; and it is unusual for there to be an amnesia for a suicidal attempt made under its influence. This is what one would expect, since enough alcohol must have been taken to produce disinhibition but not enough to cause insensibility. Investigation of aggressive crimes directed against other persons reveals parallel findings. There is rarely a true amnesia for a crime committed when the individual is drunk.

EXOGENOUS CHEMICAL POISONS

Of the chemical poisons producing mental disturbance, alcohol has already been discussed. There are many others, metallic and gaseous poisons, and drugs. New processes in industry bring yearly new risks of poisoning, and it is a tribute to the increasing care taken of the workers that the incidence of serious illness is relatively slight. Psychosis due to a chemical poison is a rare cause of admission to a psychiatric unit. The mental symptoms in these cases result from direct toxic action on the nervous system.

Metallic Poisons. Lead, mercury, arsenic, silver and thallium have all produced mental disturbance, the first not uncommonly and the remainder rarely. The effects of lead poisoning are described on page 366.

Gaseous Poisons. The commonest is carbon monoxide, a most dangerous constituent of coal-gas and exhaust gas, and found in mines, blast furnaces, etc. Carbon monoxide poisoning, which may be accidental or suicidal, produces acute transient symptoms, and, if its action is prolonged, a chronic, irrecoverable organic disorder. The latter is rare; but it is probable that as a cause of organic dementia it is sometimes overlooked. A fuller description is given on page 367. Amongst other gaseous poisons which may affect the nervous system, mention may be made of arseniuretted and sulphuretted hydrogen, methyl bromide and methyl chloride, carbon tetrachloride and carbon disulphide.

Drugs. The chief psychiatric problems here are overdoses of drugs taken with suicidal intent [see p. 72 and Chapter 18], and the personality deterioration which may develop through addiction to certain drugs, which is discussed in detail in Chapter 16.

INFECTION

Almost any infection may produce mental disturbance. The occurrence of the latter depends not only on toxaemia, or on actual brain lesions, but on the make-up of the individual infected. Some people become mentally ill much more readily than others as the result of infection, and children and old people are more prone to react in this way than those in the middle years. The mental reactions occurring in the acute stage of infection (*e.g.* in pneumonia or typhoid fever) are most commonly of the acute type—delirium. Rarely there occur other syndromes. We have seen simply extreme talkativeness—'pressure' or 'push' of talk—in the acute stage of epidemic encephalitis. The mental after-effects of infection can be very varied. There is no exact correspondence between infecting agent and type of mental illness resulting; the same specific fever may precipitate any one of the ordinary mental syndromes. The influence of the infection is in lowering the general resistance, giving mental instability or predisposition a chance to show itself, and not in any particularity in the reaction. Moreover, no novel mental disorder is produced by any specific infective agent (except, perhaps, the virus of epidemic encephalitis). Thus a depressive or manic reaction may follow an infection, or an irritable, suspicious deluded state, according to the individual's constitutional or genetic make-up.

PHYSICAL DISEASES OTHER THAN INFECTION

As with the acute infections, so with metabolic and systemic diseases; there is no specificity in the mental syndrome associated with a given physical agent. Certain systemic physical diseases play a part, not always well defined, in the production of mental symptoms. Some of them affect the circulation in, and the nutrition of, the brain, and may do so sufficiently to produce an organic type of mental disturbance, *e.g.* the delirium of heart failure. Arteriosclerosis is, however, the commonest cause of circulatory deficiency in the brain, and it can produce both the acute and chronic types of organic mental reaction.

Other chronic systemic diseases produce, in a more subtle, psychological way, slighter mental changes, which are partly a reaction to the victim's knowledge of the presence of the disease, and partly a result of his physical weakness and discomfort. The rôle of endocrinopathies in the aetiology of mental disorder will be discussed separately.

FATIGUE AND EXHAUSTION

The term fatigue has been applied to things as far apart as a weakness in metals induced by repeated blows, and the extra-professional duties of a soldier. As a phenomenon of human activity much about it remains vague or unknown. Little of the basic physiology even of the fatigue which follows prolonged exercise has been worked out: while in psychology it has no precise meaning and 'is applied to any of a series of states running all the way from true physiological exhaustion to psychological frustration uncomplicated by any detectable somatic disorder' (Russell Davis). Yet it is a daily experience common to us all, and probably one of the body's most important defensive regulations.

The more obvious signs and symptoms of fatigue are now well known, as the result of the work of pioneers which include Mosso, McDougall and Kraepelin, and from observations made upon factory workers by Vernon and others. Fatigue causes decreased quantity and quality of work; an increase in accidents and errors; bodily disturbances, such as eyestrain, digestive upset and muscle pains and cramps; and psychological changes both in the intellectual and affective spheres. It is most inimical to learning: memory is impaired, and powers of concentration and association are reduced. Fatigue tends also to weaken emotional control, to disinhibit, so that the tired individual is emotionally unduly labile or irritable, stubborn and less than normally self-critical. Furthermore, it may bring on feelings of depersonalization and hallucinations in the form of revived perceptual experiences (after-sensations).

Bartlett, dissatisfied with the limited results of tests involving the repetition of elementary mental operations, chose, during the Second World War, to study the fatigue following highly skilled work, and to observe not only what the fatigued man does but also how he does it. This research was carried out at Cambridge, mostly on Royal Air Force pilots, who in the laboratory (in the so-called Cambridge cockpit) were given a stringent exercise in instrument flying. Prolonged effort at this difficult task, which may also have produced some degree of mental conflict, resulted in disorganization of their skilled activities: the main factor in this disorganization was considered to be the fatiguing conditions.

Bartlett himself in his Ferrier Lecture (1943) described particularly the perceptual aspects of this disorganization, and stressed the importance of three phenomena: the raising of the threshold of range of sensitivity to stimuli calling for compensatory activity, the loss of accurate timing, and the splitting up of stimulus and response patterns. In skill-fatigue there is failure to maintain organized, co-ordinated and timed responses. As fatigue develops there is progressive inefficiency: though the skill-tired man may in fact be doing not less work but more, his performance becomes irregular and the rhythm of sequence of the activity is lost.

Russell Davis (1946) studied further the motor and emotional aspects of this disorganization of behaviour as fatigue developed in the test situation. The effects differed from one individual to another, and three-quarters of the fit men tested showed slight or no changes. But in certain individuals, two distinct responses to the test conditions could be described: an 'overactivity' reaction and a 'withdrawal' reaction. The 'overactivity' reaction was characterized by manifest emotional disturbance, the individual became dissatisfied, irritable and agitated as he made restless and inappropriate movements: he also showed bodily changes, flushing of the face, sweating and increased muscle tonus. In the 'withdrawal' reaction errors were less frequent but greater, and correction was tardy, concentration and interest failed, and there was a tendency to apathy and discouragement. Davis has claimed that the degree and type of the disorganization of behaviour he observed in the test depended on the grade and type of the neurotic predisposition of the individuals he tested: and he has suggested that the disorganization of activity shown by some individuals in the test was essentially similar to that occurring in the neurotic reactions of air-crew personnel to flying stresses; the 'overactivity' reaction, found particularly in individuals of obsessional personality, being similar to acute anxiety, and the 'withdrawal' reaction in some ways being similar to hysteria. These findings, which should be confirmed and extended, have obvious relevance to clinical problems in psychiatry:

they demonstrate the significance of fatigue as a factor in the development of nervous symptoms, and how important it is in studying behaviour to take into full account the personality of the individual.

Fatigue, of which exhaustion is the extreme case, was formerly considered to be an important cause of mental illness. 'Overwork', especially mental over-work, was thought to lead to fatigue, and fatigue to mental symptoms; whereas more recently it has become customary to regard both overwork and fatigue as themselves symptoms, the outcome of mental instability or actual mental disease. There is no doubt at all that fatigue or actual exhaustion are very frequently complained of, especially by neurotic and by depressed patients. Fatigue is the classical symptom of 'neurasthenia' and it may appear as a conversion pheno-menon in hysterical reactions. The fatigue of depression is typically worst in the mornings and rest does not dispel it. Abnormal fatigability is also a com-mon complaint after head injury, and it may, of course, be a symptom of other physical diseases which give rise to differential diagnostic problems in the psy-chiatric field, for example, myasthenia gravis and vitamin deficiency. A tendency to overwork himself is characteristic of the anxious person who is not actually ill; and when his anxiety attains morbid intensity the symptom of overwork is exalted into a cause. It is a consoling thought that one's breakdown is the result of too earnest and too continuous effort.

Russell Fraser (1947) has stated that working over 75 hours of industrial duty per week is one of the circumstances associated with more than the usual inci-dence of neurosis. Such long hours of work are, of course, exceptional, and simple physical over-exertion probably rarely produces significant nervous symptoms, for the sensation of fatigue is itself a safeguard, limiting activity. It is not in uncomplicated work that sensations of this kind are frequently disregarded, but usually only in work plus emotional stress, where they are noticed either too much or too little. In peace-time, it is perhaps especially the housewife and mother of a young family who willy-nilly is chronically overworked, and amongst this group fatigue is more often a precipitant of nervous illness than has usually been suspected.

In war-time, cases of extreme fatigue are more often encountered. Sargant and Slater (1940) reported on the acute psychiatric casualties of the evacuation from Dunkirk. These men had been subjected to exceptional physical and mental stress, and exhaustion combined with loss of weight had been important factors in their breakdown. But in war-time, as in peace-time, the importance of fatigue can be exaggerated: and most psychiatrists who had experience in the Second World War would corroborate Henderson's comment made about the First World War, that he was impressed by the excellent physical condition of the majority of mental and nervous cases examined from the various seats of war, and that he had not seen a case which could be labelled 'exhaustion psychosis'. During the Second World War the label 'effort syndrome', affixed to neurotic cases with prominent fatigue and effort intolerance, gave a misleading impression that the neurotic symptoms in these cases were mainly due to activity: and Grinker and Spiegel wrote in protest, 'Operational fatigue is the euphemism by which neuroses are designated in the (U.S.) Army Air Force.'

Some individuals are undeniably more prone to fatigue than others, and we know little about the constitutional reasons for this. Sheldon considered that cerebrotonia is characterized by ready fatigability. It has also often been speculated that some endocrine anomaly might underlie a tendency to develop neurasthenic symptoms, and comparisons have been made with the fatigue which is so characteristic of Addison's disease and which may be a presenting symptom in cases of spontaneous hypoglycaemia. Probably neurotic individuals with autonomic instability are more than usually prone to hypoglycaemic symptoms, and this may in some cases be the physical basis for their complaints of tiredness.

In short, emotional conflict and perturbation lead to fatigue; while fatigue allows emotional disturbances to appear, such as anxiety symptoms, irritability and depression, especially in people of obsessional temperament.

TRAUMA

Trauma may produce mental symptoms in one of two ways. Either it causes structural injury to the brain, or it causes emotional disturbances which in one form or another are prolonged. In the first instance the mental reaction is of the organic type, often with certain more subtle changes of personality; in the second the result is usually a neurosis. In the first group the injury is directly or indirectly to the head; in the second, the seat of injury may be anywhere—or nowhere. The first group have been called 'traumatic psychoses', when organic personality change or dementia has resulted from the head injury. Clinically, the difficulty arises in determining to what extent in any patient the symptoms are due to organic lesion. Wars and the increasing use of motor vehicles in this century have caused a higher incidence of these traumatic psychoses, particularly amongst younger men. Neuroses following trauma are much more frequent than traumatic psychoses. It seems indisputable that their incidence has increased in Britain since the introduction of the Insurance and other Compensation Acts. Miller (1961) found that neuroses following industrial accidents are twice as frequent as those following road accidents, and more than twice as frequent in men as in women. They are commoner after slight than after severe head injuries: and commoner when compensation issues are involved. There is no doubt that in compensation cases the desire for financial recompense plays a part, more or less consciously, in aggravating the symptoms: and that the often considerable delay before there is a settlement in court, with the attendant uncertainty, unemployment and need for self-justification, prolongs the disability. Settlement of the claim usually leads to resolution of the neurosis. Of the 50 cases followed up by Miller two years after settlement, only two were still disabled by psychiatric symptoms.

MENTAL FACTORS

These may be divided into two classes, social and intrinsic. The latter are more subtle, being compounded of inner desires and the mental precipitates, as it were, of environmental influences. They will be described under 'Psychopathology'. The commonest immediate social factors are financial and business worries, domestic difficulties, dissatisfactions of all kinds, disappointments and worries in the sexual sphere and deaths of relatives. It is such situations as these that the individual, especially the susceptible individual, finds it difficult to face. He may surmount one difficulty successfully, only to go down before an accumulation of troubles. It is not the situation itself that matters, but what the subject feels about it.

SOCIAL FACTORS AND ASPECTS

There are certain social factors of a general and pervasive kind which are of particular significance in favouring mental illness, more especially of the so-called minor sort, that is to say the neurotic conditions which depend so largely on the existence of anxiety.

Emotional Deprivation and Insecurity in Childhood. The first and possibly the most universally operative of these is emotional insecurity in early life. This can arise especially from an unsatisfactory emotional relationship between parents and child, which again is naturally influenced by unsatisfactory relationships between the parents themselves. In early life this may produce a nervous child, and the effects can persist into adult life. A feeling on the child's part of a lack of affection from his parents or their substitutes, and a feeling of being unwanted, can produce not only morbid anxiety, but a desire for recompense, or even for revenge, of which the result may be delinquency. Indiscriminate affection, on the other hand, induces a sheltered attitude which is apt to persist as a habit and produce a neurotic or unstable adolescence.

One of the more obvious sources of emotional insecurity of early origin is the so-called 'broken home'. This term 'broken home' is of wide reference and is often used much too vaguely and even without operative definition. It implies that the children in a home have been deprived, physically, mentally or morally, of a normal life with their parents. The deprivation may not only have many causes but may take many forms. Amongst the causes one may list illegitimacy; the temporary or permanent loss of one or other or both parents due to separation, divorce or death; alcoholism in a parent; persistent parental quarrelling; and adoption, evacuation during war-time, or rearing in a foster-home or institution. The absence of a parent, besides producing a general sense of insecurity from lack of one source of affection, means the absence of an important figure with whom a child can identify himself, as well as — what is sometimes overlooked in theoretical discussions—the absence of a source of training in sound habits. There is also the attitude and personality of the remaining parent to be considered, who may in such circumstances be unhappy or neurotic or unstable.

Bowlby in England, and Goldfarb, Spitz, Bender, Levy and others in the U.S.A., have investigated the adverse effects of early maternal deprivation. Bowlby's general thesis, stated first in his book *Maternal Care and Mental Health* (1951) was that 'mother-love in infancy and childhood is as important for mental health as are vitamins and proteins for physical health', and that 'the prolonged deprivation of the young child of maternal care may have grave and far-reaching effects on his character and so on the whole of his future life'. In a study of 44 juvenile thieves (1944), he linked early maternal deprivation with the later development of psychopathic states; and he considered that the first three or four years of life are of critical importance.

Goldfarb (1955), investigating older children who had spent the first three years of their lives in an institution, found in them not only a tendency to psychopathic traits—impaired ability to form close personal relationships, low frustration tolerance and lack of anxiety and guilt about antisocial behaviour; but also disturbances in learning and concept formation. Institutional environments vary of course greatly in quality; and separation from the mother is only one of the many traumata which the child reared there may suffer. The worst institutions may deprive the child both of maternal and other personal care and of the sensory, educational and social stimulation which are necessary for normal development.

In later studies Bowlby and his colleagues, amongst others, have drawn attention to the great variation in outcome which may follow a prolonged separation experience starting before the child's fourth birthday: some children appear to suffer much damage, others none. In a follow-up investigation of 60 children aged 6–14 years who had been hospitalized for tuberculosis in their first three years, they found that 63 per cent. were maladjusted (with a tendency to withdrawal or aggressiveness) as compared with 40 per cent. of the controls. The hospitalized children had, however, suffered no intellectual impairment and only a very small minority were seriously disturbed. The outcomes were obviously very variable and unpredictable: and many factors besides the after-effects of separation from the mother had determined these outcomes. Bowlby commented (1958): 'statements implying that children who are brought up in institutions or who suffer other forms of serious privation and deprivation in early life *commonly* develop psychopathic or affectionless characters are seen to be mistaken'.

The more acute reactions of children to hospitalization have also been studied: and similar findings have been reported by Spitz, Prugh and Shaffer in the U.S.A. and by Robertson and Bowlby in England. As one could predict, not all children react similarly or to the same degree to this experience; much depends upon the age and personality of the child and upon how sympathetically and understandingly his reactions are handled by others. In the 2–3-year-old there is quite commonly this sequence of responses: a period initially of crying and protest, in which the child seems to be trying to regain the mother; and then a phase of detachment, with an emotional withdrawal resembling despair or resignation, during which the child may show little obvious feeling towards his parents during their visits. After return home, the child may show regressive behaviour, becoming enuretic again at night for example, and be for some time both hostile towards the mother and unduly clinging. Bowlby described the earlier phases of this reaction as those of protest, despair and detachment: and in a provocative and still speculative excursion likened the infant or young child's reaction after separation from the mother to pathological mourning in the adult, detecting in both similar emotions of anxiety, grief and aggression (Bowlby, 1961).

Inferences about the long-term effects which may follow separation from the mother in early life have mostly been based on retrospective studies, there have been few statistically validated investigations making use of control groups, and it has often been impossible to separate the effects of maternal deprivation *per se* from its surrounding circumstances and sequelae. There are obviously many different varieties of separation and deprivation experiences, varying in their age of impact, duration, degree and quality; and the rôle of the father has been too often neglected. The effects of separation bear differently on boys and girls, and certainly have different meanings for each child, according to his or her psychological make-up. The outcome will depend both on the relationships existing before the separation and on those after it—particularly upon whether or not the child finds an adequate substitute mother-figure. Repeated separations tend to be the most damaging with cumulative effects upon personality development. For a fuller review, reference should be made to Yarrow (1964).

The rôle of the father, too, requires attention. In a patriarchal society the father is the figure in the home probably of chief importance for the child's super-ego development. His absence, ineffectiveness or hostility, as well as the mother's, may prejudice the child's upbringing. Andry (1957), in a controlled study of 80 male juvenile delinquents who were recidivist thieves, reported that the paternal affective relationships of the boys were less adequate than the maternal affective relationships and that the boys often felt rejected by both parents, but especially by their fathers. He concluded: 'Some form of parental rejection over a period of years rather than separation from a mother at an early age would appear to be one of the main mechanisms at work in the majority of cases in the development of delinquent behaviour.' He did not find any relationship between father-absence during early childhood and later delinquent behaviour.

The effects of separation are not always injurious: the child may thrive better away from hostile or feckless parents. Lewis (1954) in her study of deprived children admitted to a reception centre, demonstrated very clearly that separation from a very adverse family environment may promote mental health. 'Some children long exposed to the dislike or indifference of their natural mothers gained rather than lost by separation, provided they passed into kind and sensible hands.'

These studies of childhood experiences have prompted numerous investigators to look at the incidence of 'broken homes' in the previous histories of those who have later developed mental illnesses. It appears that the incidence of loss of one or other parent in childhood may be higher in the case of adult psychiatric patients than in the general population (Dennehy, 1966): but no relationship has been definitely established between parental loss and any particular mental reaction-type. The effects of childhood parental loss, in so far as they persist into adult life, appear not to be specific. It should be emphasized also that parental deprivation and loss in childhood are common. Munro (1965) found that 47 per cent. of 210 out-patients of non-psychiatric clinics at a general hospital reported that they had suffered from some form of parental deprivation in their first 16 years: 30 had prematurely lost a parent by death.

There is more substantial evidence that childhood deprivation may predispose to suicidal acts in later life. Batchelor and Napier (1953b) reported that 58 per cent. of 200 consecutive cases of attempted suicide came from broken homes: among the 42 psychopaths in this series the incidence was 74 per cent. While it appeared that the loss of a parent or parents at any time in childhood might be traumatic, 20 per cent. of the 200 cases had suffered parental deprivation in their first 4 years, and 16 per cent. between 5 and 9 years. Walton (1958) also, in a carefully controlled study, found that parental deprivation during childhood was very significantly associated with suicidal behaviour in depressive illness. Greer *et al.* (1966), on the basis of a study of 156 attempted suicides and controls, reported that attempted suicides had a greater incidence of childhood parental loss; in this series the loss more commonly than in the controls involved both parents, occurred earlier and was more likely to be permanent (due to death or divorce).

In summary, we may say that while childhood deprivations may play an important part in predisposing to or causing nervous symptoms and delinquency both in the child and in the adult, it remains true that the aetiology of nervous and mental illness is usually complex, and that one cannot safely neglect or minimize either endogenous or exogenous influences. A 'broken home' in many cases is only one adverse factor among many, and is frequently of less importance than, for example, a morbid inheritance. Looking at the figures of the incidence of broken homes in the histories of those who have become maladjusted, one may legitimately ask—were these homes not broken often because the parents were themselves temperamentally abnormal? Do these figures not demonstrate a genetic rather than an environmental effect? There is, however, now a good deal of evidence that parental deprivation in childhood may lead to distortions of personality development, and predispose to delinquent [see also p. 526] and suicidal behaviour. More research is required. We do not yet know whether an absence or distortion of parental influences (*e.g.* parental alcoholism) is the more important, nor at what time the greatest damage may be done to the child, nor which parent is the more essential to certain years of the child's development, nor whether boys and girls differ in these respects.

Whatever criticisms may be made of the still provisional nature of the findings and theory in this field of psychiatric research, it must be recognized that the methodological problems of research in this area are considerable and granted freely that the pioneering studies of Bowlby and others have had valuable practical effects. It is largely as a result of them that frequent visiting by parents of children in hospital has been established, that the need for stable foster-home care for the previously deprived has been more fully recognized, and that there has been a widespread improvement in the quality of the institutional care of children.

Bereavement in Adult Life. There is no doubt that bereavement in adult life may affect both mental and physical health profoundly.

Lindemann (1944) has described the symptomatology of acute grief following bereavement. There is somatic distress, recurring in waves precipitated and aggravated by reminders of the deceased person—feelings of tension, choking sensations, shortness of breath, sighing, loss of appetite, empty feelings in the abdomen, and exhaustion. The bereaved person is restless, often irritable, does not wish to be bothered, is understandably depressed in his spirits and sleeps badly. He may have feelings of panic, unreality and guilt. He is preoccupied with the image of and yearns for the dead person. This is a normal process, lasting acutely for 4–6 weeks and resolving, with emotional and social readjustment, within about 6 months.

The duration and intensity of the grief reaction are subject understandably to great variations, depending upon factors which include the personality and age of the bereaved person, the closeness and quality of the previous relationship with the deceased, whether the death had been sudden and unexpected, the quality of other potentially supporting relationships and the individual's social and economic circumstances. Readjustment is quicker if the grief reaction is accepted, ventilated and worked through. Lindemann described also two main kinds of pathological variants: delayed and distorted reactions. Grief reactions may be delayed for weeks, months and exceptionally years; and are then apt to be more severe and disabling. They may also be distorted: the bereaved person may show social withdrawal or become overactive, or become hostile towards others (blaming them for the death), or identify herself with the dead person showing some of his personality traits or complaining of some of his symptoms: furthermore, a psychosomatic disorder or agitated depression may in some cases be precipitated. Parkes (1965) states that people developing a mental illness after bereavement commonly exhibit symptoms which differ in intensity and duration but not in kind from the features of typical grief. Certainly, it is very important to recognize that a grief reaction may shade over into a depressive illness, with a considerable suicidal risk. Such features as intense feelings of guilt, early morning wakening, retardation and a consistent diurnal variation in the mood would of course suggest that a depression had developed.

Parkes (1964) has drawn attention to the importance of bereavement as a cause of mental illness. Examining patients admitted to the Bethlem Royal and Maudsley Hospitals, he found that the number of patients whose illness had followed the loss of a spouse was six times greater than expected. Women over the age of 40 were predominantly involved, and the commonest reaction was an affective illness.

There appears also to be an association between bereavement and mortality. Rees and Lutkins (1967) in a semi-rural area of Wales found that 4·76 per cent. of bereaved close relatives (spouse, child, parent or sibling) died within one year of bereavement, compared with 0·68 per cent. in a control group: i.e. there was a sevenfold increase in the risk of mortality amongst the bereaved. The increase in risk was particularly great for widowed people. Parkes and Benjamin (1967) have reported that the increased mortality rate amongst London widowers is largely attributable to deaths from coronary thrombosis and arteriosclerotic heart disease.

The associations between bereavement and physical and mental illness have not yet been fully explored, far less explained. What has certainly been identified is a group of people who are at risk of becoming ill, and who will benefit from closer medical attention and support from their family doctors.

Unemployment and Loneliness. Unemployment, as well as unsuitable work, has been shown to lead to neurotic illness. There is a biological need for activity, the frustration of which will produce inner disturbance, certain boredom, sometimes apathy and sometimes mental illness. In addition, work has other values by giving the worker prestige within a community, without which he becomes uneasy. It has to be remembered too that unemployment often means a disintegration of the patterns of life which the individual has woven for himself. This may have a catastrophic effect on some individuals, or a more gradual undermining effect on the peace of mind of others. Those who lose much, in social status, financially or otherwise, particularly if the blow has been sudden, are more likely to break down than those who have always been used to little.

Few things are more striking than the number of lonely people among those who attend psychiatric out-patient clinics. Some of them are constitutionally inclined to solitariness, but others have it forced on them, with consequent limitation of interest, and dissatisfaction from frustration of natural needs. The parental deprivation, which we have discussed above, is one form of social isolation. Man is a social animal, and loss of contact with or rejection by the herd renders him both vulnerable and unhappy. Feelings of loneliness, the response to some loss of love or springing from feelings of being unwanted or useless, are prominent motives in many suicidal acts, at all ages. Those individuals, particularly in later life, who are not integrated in the activities of the community (for example, those who are living alone or in lodging-houses) are more prone to nervous breakdown, and particularly to depressive reactions. Our present social organization, especially that part of it which is comprised in suburban life, does not cater adequately for these social needs. Some new housing schemes have community centres but many more areas of suburbia are without them; and there is a great dearth of social clubs which might offset the isolation which so many feel in our great cities.

The Epidemiological Approach. Epidemiological studies complement investigations of individual patients, and data from such mass or population surveys may throw light on the aetiology of mental diseases as well as providing the kind of social information which is necessary for the logical planning of public health services, both for preventive measures and in the provision of treatment facilities. So far epidemiological or ecological studies in psychiatry have produced few new facts of importance. The difficulties surrounding such investigations have of course been considerable: in particular, the complicated and often multiple aetiology of nervous and mental illnesses; the notorious unreliability of psychiatric diagnosis; the relative naivety of sociology as a scientific discipline; and the lack of well-trained field workers—all these factors have inhibited research. The techniques of such research and its potentialities have been discussed by Reid (1960) and by an Expert Committee on Mental Health of the World Health

Organization (1960). The latter Committee considered that 'epidemiological methods can be appropriately applied to three aspects of the aetiology and pathogenesis of mental disorder: the genetic basis, the physical and psychological experiences during development which may favour the onset of clinical disease, and the social or other precipitating environmental circumstances'.

Epidemiological studies in psychiatry require the collaboration of psychiatrists and sociologists, and both must proceed with a lively sense of their limitations. Statistics is a necessary tool. From the psychiatric standpoint, where the subject of research is a biological entity, which can be both defined and readily ascertained, progress can be made, as it has been in the study of suicide. The psychoses and states of subnormality (mental defect) can be studied fairly well by epidemiological methods. It is in the field of the neuroses, character anomalies and psychopathic states that the great difficulties arise. What is socially accepted as being illness depends on the sophistication and tolerance of the society and of the various groups within each society, on the generally accepted ideas of right and wrong and of what constitutes delinquent or criminal behaviour, on how aberrant an individual's conduct can be without causing social concern or rejection, and on the readiness with which both the lay members of the society and the medical profession itself will refer problems to psychiatrists. The sociologist for his part will look at the community which it is proposed to study, to see if its social characteristics have been recently and competently defined and recorded: and if these data are not already available from census or other investigations, to see whether he has the resources in trained manpower and the access to the community's homes which will make possible a new survey of a representative sample of the population. The sociologist will also be aware that at best he will be using rather unrefined concepts and classifications in his investigations: the estimation of social class, for example, as usually recorded in this country is graded simply according to the occupation of the individual or her spouse, and satisfactory differentiation is certainly not achieved at the lower end of this, the Registrar General's, social scale of five classes.

The Prevalence of Treated Mental Illness. For several reasons, which include the lack of adequate clinical data in past years and rapidly changing facilities for diagnosis and investigation, incidence trends in the neuroses and other so-called minor psychiatric disorders cannot be computed. The psychoses which are treated in mental hospitals offer a more promising area for study. A careful and critical investigation has been made by Goldhamer and Marshall (1949) in Massachusetts, where for long mental hospital facilities and records had been at a relatively high level. These workers, using records going back as far as 1840, compared the nineteenth century and contemporary age-specific first admission rates for psychoses. Their main findings were as follows. Age-specific first admission rates for ages under 50 were revealed to be just as high during the last half of the nineteenth century as they are now. There had been, however, a very marked increase in the age-specific admission rates in the older age-groups—an increase which appeared to be due for the greater part to an increased tendency to hospitalize people suffering from the mental illnesses of the senium. In the nineteenth century there was relatively a much higher concentration of admissions in the age group 20–50; and now a relatively high concentration in ages over 50 and more particularly over 60. They concluded: 'there has been no long-term increase during the last century in the incidence of the psychoses of early life and middle life', and 'social trends probably have little influence on the incidence of psychosis'. The latter finding accords with what we know of the importance of physical factors in the aetiology of the psychoses.

Shepherd (1957) studied the admissions to an English county mental hospital during the years 1931–33 and 1945–47. He found that a large increase in the number of patients admitted took place in the latter period, but there was a quicker turnover of patients (a shorter period being spent in hospital) and there was no expansion of the hospital accommodation. The latter-day hospital population was older and included a higher proportion of female, married, voluntary and readmitted patients. The functional psychoses, particularly the affective psychoses, constituted more than one-half of all the patients admitted and were principally responsible for the changes found in the admission pattern to this hospital.

It has for long been believed that urban rates for mental illness are higher than rural rates, but this is still uncertain. Urban and rural areas differ widely in their access to treatment facilities and in their tolerance of deviant behaviour, so that comparisons are hazardous.

Influence of Neighbourhood on Mental Illness. Faris and Dunham (1939) pioneered these studies in Chicago. They plotted the residence of 20,000 patients admitted for the first time to mental hospitals and computed the rates for hospitalization in various areas or subcommunities of the city. Race differences they did not find an important factor in the incidence of breakdown, except that schizophrenia and general paralysis were reported to be commoner in whites and negroes where they were locally in a racial minority. Social conditions on the other hand were found apparently to be highly significant, mental hospital admission rates corresponding closely to the city's socio-economic structure. The highest incidence of mental illness was found in the central, densely populated slum areas: and here cases of schizophrenia (most notably), senile psychosis, alcoholism and general paralysis were concentrated. The incidence of treated mental illness in the periphery of the city was low. Cases of manic-depressive psychosis and epilepsy were randomly distributed. The central, lodging-house areas were characterized socially by high residential mobility, poverty and ethnic heterogeneity.

Other American investigators have reported similar results, and in particular the concentration of cases of schizophrenia in and around the central business districts of large cities. Two hypotheses have been advanced in explanation of these facts: the first, that the social *milieu* of these areas of social disorganization predisposes to the development of schizophrenia; and the second, the 'drift' hypothesis, that these areas are the termini for those who, due to their illnesses, have deteriorated in their social adjustments. Faris and Dunham favoured the first explanation: Gerard and Houston (1953) in Massachusetts supported the second, having compared the distribution of schizophrenia in those living alone with the incidence in those living with their families, and finding that the excess of schizophrenia in the central areas 'is principally due to the fact that schizoid individuals seek to protect themselves from close personal relations by moving away from their families to the lodging-house areas, and, in addition, by frequently moving from one lodging to another'. Hare (1956) working in Bristol, England, confirmed Gerard and Houston's main findings and stated that in a quarter of his cases separation from the family appeared to have been a factor of importance in the development of schizophrenic illness.

That the social environment in which schizophrenics in cities are most typically found is more a result than a cause of their illness, was confirmed by a later finding; that in England and Wales where schizophrenics preponderate among the unskilled young men of social class V, the fathers of schizophrenics are ordinarily distributed among the social classes, and that after leaving school schizophrenics have been non-starters in their parental class (Morris, 1959).

Social Class and Mental Illness. The most thorough research to date on the relationship between social stratification and mental illness has been carried out by Hollingshead and Redlich (1958) in their study, in New Haven, Connecticut, of an American urban community of 240,000 people. Their investigation was concerned only with individuals under psychiatric care or treatment at the time of the investigation (1950), but they believe that they found nearly all the cases of psychosis in the community. The patient's social status was recorded in terms of Hollingshead's Index of Social Position, which, using not only the individual's occupation but also his educational record, and the ecological area of his residence, breaks the population down into five social classes not dissimilar to the Registrar General's five social classes in this country. A 5 per cent. sample census of the general population was made as a control.

Hollingshead and Redlich found, first, that the prevalence of mental illness in New Haven was related to social class. This relationship was an inverse one, the lower the social class the greater the proportion of patients in the population: and the greatest difference lay between social classes IV and V, the latter contributing many more patients than its proportion of the population.

Second, they found that the types of psychiatric disorder were related to social class: directly in the case of the neuroses, which were commonest in the higher social classes, and inversely in the case of the psychoses, which were most prevalent in the lower social classes. For the psychoses, the lower the class the higher the rate: and this inverse relationship was found in affective, schizophrenic, senile, organic and alcoholic reaction-types. Also, they found a relationship between social class and types of neurotic reaction: phobic anxiety reactions and character neuroses were most prevalent in social classes I and II, while hysteria was found predominantly in classes IV and V.

Third, these investigators reported that social class position played a part in determining the type of psychiatric treatment given, the cost of treatment, where it was given and for how long. Furthermore, social class position tended to influence the decision as to whether or not a person should be treated by a psychiatrist at all for his disturbed or delinquent behaviour: those in social classes I and II tended to be treated in much 'more gentle and insightful ways' than those at the other end of the social scale.

Similarly detailed investigations are required in this country, but it is unlikely that under the National Health Service such disparities will be found between the social classes in the availability and effectiveness of psychiatric care and treatment. The direct relationship found between class status and the rate of treated neurosis may well reflect not only the incidence of neurosis but also the greater sophistication in medical matters and the greater financial affluence of the higher social classes in Connecticut.

Hollingshead and Redlich's data on the social class distribution of schizophrenia are reported in the chapter on Schizophrenic Reaction-Types.

Suicide and Attempted Suicide. Suicidal acts are a social phenomenon of great importance and concern not only to psychiatrists but to society as a whole. In the economically vital group of young adults aged 25–34 years, suicide is the cause of 1 in 10 deaths. The problem can be met only by a broad programme of mental hygiene, resocialization and medical treatment, in which the psychiatric services have a key rôle since it is generally accepted that the large majority of those who attempt or commit suicide are mentally ill or suffer from serious personality disorders. Such a mental hygiene programme must be based on a clear understanding of the factors, both social and individual, which predispose to suicidal acts.

According to figures quoted by the World Health Organization in 1961, West Berlin had the highest suicide rate in the world—37 per 100,000 of the population. Amongst European countries Hungary ranked first with 25·4 per 100,000 and Austria second with 21·9 per 100,000. The suicide rate in this country is only about half as high (11·3 in England and Wales, 7·9 in Scotland), but the problem is still a considerable one.

Prior to the Second World War, apart from a period of diminished incidence associated with the First World War, the suicide rate in Britain had been rising for many years. Again the rate fell during the Second World War, but since then it has been rising, in women more quickly than in men. In an ageing population suicide is becoming increasingly a disorder of elderly people, and about 20 per cent. of suicides now occur in people over the age of 60. Men more often commit suicide than women, and more often use violent methods: but since the Second World War there has, by both sexes in this country, been an increasing use of sedative drugs or gas in suicidal acts. The suicide rates are highest in social classes I and II: medical and dental practitioners, lawyers and retired Army officers are amongst the occupational groups with the highest rates. The high suicide risk amongst doctors has been reported also from the U.S.A., Denmark and Italy. More than 1 in 50 doctors in this country takes his own life, usually by an overdose of drugs: most are under the age of 50, and many had previously become addicted to drugs or alcohol. Seasonal graphs for suicide show peaks of incidence in late spring and in autumn.

F

Undoubtedly social factors are operative in the differential incidence of suicide, and important researches have been directed towards identifying these factors. In 1897 Emile Durkheim (1951), the French sociologist, divided suicides into three aetiological types, the egoistic, the anomic and the altruistic. Durkheim claimed that there is a direct relationship between suicide and the degree of integration of social groups. Egoistic or individualistic suicides he regarded as due to a slackening of family, religious and other social ties, so that the individual was left socially isolated or unsupported. Anomic or lawless suicides occur, he believed, when the individual's needs are no longer in harmony with his means and he ceases to be regulated by the collective conscience of his society: when he is thrown on his own resources, for example, at times of economic crises, by unexpected wealth or poverty, by widowhood or divorce. Altruistic suicides, on the other hand, are due to the over-integration of the individual in his group, to his domination by what he feels the group expects of him, so that he sacrifices himself on the altar of duty.

In support of his thesis that those who are not integrated in the life of the family and the community are more likely to commit suicide, Durkheim could point to well-established facts: the higher incidence in single than in married people; the higher incidence in childless women than in those with children; the higher incidence in Protestants than in Roman Catholics (the latter seem to be more closely knit socially in their Church and less prone to religious individualism); and in time of war the fall in the suicide rate which is probably associated with the heightened sense of social purpose and the greater social integration which war brings to a threatened community. Altruistic suicide is always rare, and in our peace-time society is exemplified by the captain who refuses to leave his ship when it sinks.

Durkheim's sociological approach has been developed particularly by Halbwachs (1930) and Sainsbury (1955). The latter tested the hypothesis that differences in the suicide rates of the London boroughs would reveal their social differences. Using mainly data from the Registrar General's publications and Smith's *New Survey of London Life and Labour* (1930–35), Sainsbury correlated the suicides notified in each borough with indices of that borough's social characteristics: he also examined the case records of all suicides reported to the North London coroner during the years 1936–38. Sainsbury found that the London boroughs showed significant differences in their suicide rates, and that the suicide rates correlated with the following social characteristics; with social isolation (measured as people living alone and in boarding houses), with social mobility (expressed in the daily turnover of population and the number .of immigrants), and with two indices of social disorganization, divorce and illegitimacy. Unemployment and overcrowding rates showed no correlation with suicide rates, which tended to increase in the middle class and to decrease with poverty: the unemployed, however, were found to have a significantly higher suicide rate than the corresponding employed population. 'Suicide rates were highest in the West End and North-West London where both class and spatial mobility are highest, small flat and boarding-house accommodation preponderates, shared mores are absent, and relationships impersonal. Suicide rates were low in the peripheral southern boroughs where family life and stability prevail, and in many of the working-class districts whose residents are locally born and where life is more neighbourly.'

Sainsbury concludes: 'These findings support the view that a lonely mode of life is an important adverse factor accounting for differential rates of suicide in the (London) boroughs and their subdistricts. Social isolation also provides a consistent explanation of the high incidence of suicide found in a wide variety of social groups: the aged, unemployed, divorced and among immigrants.' These important conclusions from a careful ecological study complement findings reported in cases of attempted suicide: for example, in a study of attempted suicide in old age Batchelor and Napier (1953a) reported that feelings of loneliness were the commonest psychological precursors of suicidal attempts in this age group.

Almost any mental disorder may eventuate in suicide. A depressive psychosis is the most common reaction; chronic alcoholism probably next commonest. Suicide may be a symptom of any psychosis, functional or organic, in which there is marked depression of mood. The young schizophrenic may kill himself: so, to take another example, may the elderly cerebro-arteriosclerotic patient who, realizing his increasing limitations, decides that it would be intolerable to be a mental or physical cripple. Psychopathic personalities not infrequently kill themselves. More rarely suicide occurs in the setting of a neurotic reaction. It may be a panic response to some sudden grave stress, such as bereavement or financial ruin or a police charge. The motives are many and complex: despair of course, feelings of loneliness and of being unwanted, anxieties and fears of many kinds, identification with a dead person (in younger people, most often with the mother—in older people, with the spouse), hatred, guilt and the need for self-punishment, experimentation and defiance. Attempted suicide is much commoner than suicide in Western communities: how much commoner we do not know accurately. Investigating the incidence of attempted suicide in Sheffield, Parkin and Stengel (1965) found the ratio between suicide attempts and suicide was 9·7:1, and thought that this was an underestimate. Stengel (1958) has investigated the relationship between suicide and attempted suicide and some of the social aspects of suicidal attempts. He suggests that those who attempt and those who commit suicide constitute two different populations, pointing out that the majority of those who commit suicide are males while the majority of those who attempt it are females; that the average age of those who commit suicide is higher; and that a minority of those who commit suicide have previously attempted it, while only a small proportion of those who attempt it later commit suicide. Nevertheless, the two populations overlap, and it would not accord with the facts, but lead in practice to an underestimation of the risks to life inherent in suicidal attempts, to draw any sharp distinctions between attempted suicide and suicide itself. In old age those who attempt and those who commit suicide seem to come from very closely allied, if not identical, clinical groups (Batchelor, 1957).

Ettlinger (1964), following up 227 patients who had attempted suicide (children under 16 years were excluded), found that 13·2 per cent. had committed suicide during an observation period of approximately 12 years—an incidence of suicide considerably higher than that in the general population of Stockholm. The statistically most significant difference between the attempted suicide patients who subsequently committed suicide and the other attempted suicide patients, was the more frequent occurrence of suicidal attempts in the suicide group: 53 per cent. of the suicide group had made more than 3 suicidal attempts, whereas in the remainder there were only 15 per cent. who did so. Here, in those who make repeated suicidal attempts, one can identify clearly a group of individuals who are especially at risk and who require particular medical attention. Those who had had psychotic symptoms in adult life, and those who had abused alcohol, were also as one would expect commoner in the suicide group. Dorpat and Ripley (1967) have reviewed 24 published studies bearing on the relationship between attempted and committed suicide, and report that both the incidence of completed suicide among attempters and the incidence of prior suicide attempts amongst those who completed suicide was many times that of the general population.

In the past decade there has been a notable increase in Britain of cases of self-poisoning, particularly with barbiturates and more recently with tranquillizing and other psychotropic drugs. In 1965 in England and Wales there were 3774 suicidal deaths by poisoning, and a further 289 deaths in Scotland. Recently these cases of self-poisoning have constituted 4–7 per cent. of the admissions to the medical wards of our general hospitals. The majority of these acts are impulsive: they are often the response to a quarrel or other frustration of a temperamentally unstable or psychopathic individual, whose already defective self-control may have been further weakened by the influence of alcohol or drugs. Kessel (1965) stated that 'for four-fifths of (these) patients the concept of attempted suicide is wide of the mark . . . what they were attempting was not suicide.' Certainly that there has been an attempt to seek attention and to manipulate the environment is often obvious: but Kessel goes too far in recommending that 'we should discard the specious concept of attempted suicide'.

In the individual case it is often difficult to be sure about the seriousness and dangerousness of a patient's intentions. No firm line can be drawn between suicidal gestures and suicidal attempts: and the circumstances of some genuine suicidal attempts indicate clearly that consciously or unconsciously there has been a wish to manipulate the environment. Stengel has drawn attention to what he believes is a marked social element in most suicidal attempts—an appeal, usually unconscious, to society for help. He calls attempted suicide Janus-faced, orientated both to self-destruction and to a revision of human relationships. Stengel believes that the majority of genuine suicidal attempts are carried out in such a way that the intervention of others is possible or even probable. This is doubtful; but Stengel's emphasis on the appeal function of suicidal attempts and on the participation of the patient's group very properly draws attention to social aspects of individual suicidal acts which must be regarded if these acts are to be prevented, and adequately treated. Suicidal talk and threats must not be minimized, since they are often both calls for help and danger-signals; and 'an understanding of the individual significance of the appeal inherent in the suicidal attempt would enable those who want to help to do so rationally and effectively and thus prevent repetition'. Hostility towards others is commonly a component in the psychopathology of suicidal acts, and this in part explains why society's response to these acts is still often itself aggressive and punitive.

RACE AND CULTURE

Our clinical psychiatry has been developed on the basis of findings made almost exclusively in Western civilization. Where the mental illness is dependent largely on organic pathology, this limitation will seldom be important. The psychoses and subnormality are probably very similar in different parts of the world; the basic symptoms at least are probably the same, though they may be variously expressed and elaborated, according to the customs and beliefs of the country. In the case of reactions more psychogenically determined we would expect the social and cultural setting to be much more important, affecting the incidence, the types of reaction favoured, tolerated or repressed, and the methods of care and treatment. The recent development of the sciences of social psychology and anthropology is enabling us to take a more balanced view of nervous and mental illness, by placing it more definitely in its social setting. Every individual is moulded by the culture in which he has been educated and by the culture in which he lives. In the culture he has a place (status) and a part to play (rôle), usually more than one, and he is subject to the stresses and conflicts peculiar to that culture. There is at least a suggestion that some of the psychological ill health in Western communities to-day is due to the indeterminacy and rapid changing of social rôles. We know that certain types of individual are happiest if their environment is stable and their obligations defined (*e.g.* obsessionals), whereas others because of their temperamental instability cannot adjust themselves to any social *milieu* (*e.g.* psychopaths). The more subtle interactions of personality and culture are now a promising field of research, and important work has been done by Benedict, Mead, Linton and others.

We cannot distinguish clearly the effects of race from those of culture. We meet the old difficulty of separating effects of nature from those of nurture.

We know comparatively little about the distribution, prevalence and incidence of nervous and mental illness in Britain and in the U.S.A. We know less of conditions in most other countries, and very little indeed about any country outside Western civilization. The two main obstacles to making comparisons of mental disorder in different races are that there has been no classification of mental disorders common to different countries, and that everywhere the development of psychiatric services has lagged behind those devoted to physical disease. Our knowledge of the influence of race or nationality on nervous and mental illness is therefore very slight and insecure, and much of it has been derived from observation of foreign-born immigrants into the U.S.A. Here the situation is particularly complicated: the immigrant may not have been a stable member of the society he has left, and he has all the strains of immigration and resettlement in a foreign country to contend with. There is evidence also that migration or other rapid and extensive social changes (for example, those due to the introduction of Western civilization to a primitive society) may be associated with an increased rate of mental breakdown.

Certain reaction-types are commonly mentioned as being more or less specific to certain racial or cultural groups. For example, latah and amok have been described particularly in Malays: the former is a trance-like state with automatic obedience and coprolalia, precipitated by fright and most often found in women past their prime (Yap, 1952); the latter is an acute, clouded excitement with homicidal violence. Amongst certain North American Indians a Wihtigo psychosis has been reported, in which the individual believes that he has been possessed and transformed into a mythological beast, a Wihtigo, and may become cannibalistic (Hallowel, 1934).

The resemblances between nations and cultures as regards mental illness are, however, on the whole more impressive than their differences, which seem to be mainly of quantity and degree. Williams (1950), working in the Indian theatre of war during the Second World War, found that Indian and British soldiers broke down in rather different ways and in response to different stresses. Fifty-two per cent. of the British psychiatric casualties developed anxiety states, but only 8 per cent. of the Indian casualties: whereas amongst the Indians hysterical reactions, often of a florid type, were much more common, comprising 31 per cent. of the breakdowns. Williams linked these variations of clinical reaction with the fact that loss of face was the basic stress factor to Indians. The maintenance of face was of paramount importance in their close-knit patriarchal society and in the maintenance of personal morale, and shame rather than guilt occurred in the event of their personal failure. Coming from martial races, they had also little guilt about killing in combat. To exhibit anxiety meant great loss of face to them, whereas hysterical symptoms such as fits were face-saving. Seligman noted among the Japanese that delusions of a religious nature with a sense of guilt were practically absent in Japan, where religion is cheerful and assumes primitive virtue rather than original sin.

In Scotland we seem to see a larger number of cases of melancholia than is the case elsewhere, and there is some evidence that the incidence is highest in the more northern parts of the country. In an earlier section we have noted also the higher incidence of alcoholism in Scotland than in England and Wales.

The culture is a shoe which pinches certain members of each society, and societies vary very much in the number and nature of their misfits. Malinowski, for example, believed that the neuroses are very rare among the Trobrianders in comparison with the inhabitants of neighbouring islands, on account of the sexual freedom of the former and the family organization, which is characterized by the virtual absence of anyone in the rôle of the father. On the other hand, many writers are prepared to link the prevalence of neuroses in Western civilization with the impact of the industrial revolution and the culture's encouragement of competitive, acquisitive strivings.

While the culture may elicit symptoms in certain individuals who come into conflict with it, the majority it supports. Hebb has drawn attention to this aspect, describing the culture as a protective cocoon. 'The well-adjusted adult therefore is not intrinsically less subject to emotional disturbance: he is well-adjusted, relatively unemotional, as long as he is in his cocoon.' The culture buffers the individual from emotional provocations and disturbing experiences of many kinds, tending as it does to eliminate sources of acute fear, disgust and anger, and to ensure that each member of society will not in general upset others emotionally by aberrant conduct.

The question of culture is important in assessing the import of a delusion. A delusional belief that would be ominous in a Londoner might mean little that was abnormal in a Sandwich Islander, on account of the special superstitions and folk-lore of the latter. This consideration holds, but to a lesser extent, for different cultural strata in the same population.

AGE

The part played by age in causation is in general indirect, a function of the changes in experience, in mental outlook and in the tissues which accompany the passage of the years. Of tissue changes, those affecting the endocrine glands and the brain are of greatest importance. Certain psychoses occur typically in certain age periods: hebephrenic schizophrenia between 15 and 25 years of age; chronic alcoholism, general paralysis and paranoid states in the fourth and fifth decades; melancholia in the involution; Alzheimer's and Pick's disease in the sixth decade; and, in old age, senile and arteriosclerotic dementia.

Generally speaking, the maximum incidence of mental disorder in males lies between the ages of 30 and 40, and in females between 25 and 35. After these periods there is a fall, followed by an increase at the involutional period and in the senium. The increasing age of the population has been associated with an increase in the depressive reactions and organic, degenerative mental disorders of later life.

In this country suicide is becoming increasingly a disorder of elderly people, and the highest suicide rate is found in men over 65 years. Most types of crime decrease with advancing age. The age group with most offenders is 13 years, and about one-half of all crime is committed by people under 21. Nearly half of those, however, who are found guilty of indictable sexual offences are aged 30 or over.

SEX

Sex has a complicated bearing on the incidence of nervous and mental disorders, and the types of stress differ considerably in the two sexes. In the male the effects of alcoholism and syphilis are seen to a far greater extent than in women, and on them also the stress of economic competition falls more heavily. Women, on the other hand, have to face the physical and psychological stresses of pregnancy, the puerperium and the menopause. Affective psychoses and Alzheimer's and Pick's pre-senile psychoses are commoner in women. Two-thirds of the patients aged 65 or over in the mental hospitals of England and Wales are women; no doubt mainly because women live longer than men. Crime and delinquency, head injuries and most of the 'psychosomatic' disorders are commoner in men. More women than men attempt suicide, more men commit it. These sex differences in the incidence of maladjustment and disease are extremely interesting, and their full elucidation would throw much light on aetiology. Despite particular differences, however, the total incidence of mental disorder is probably about equal in the two sexes.

ENDOCRINE FACTORS

Mental diseases being as yet very imperfectly understood and their causation frequently a matter of surmise, it is not surprising that the endocrines should have been implicated in their genesis much more often than the clinical facts justified. Premature attempts to correlate endocrine and temperamental make-up, and the over-enthusiastic, though usually unavailing, therapeutic use of endocrine preparations by some clinicians have also led to rather widespread scepticism about the value of this approach to aetiology and treatment. However, the functions and dysfunctions of the endocrine system must have considerable importance in the psychiatric field. It is probable that the endocrines are among the primary factors determining personality, and that they influence considerably the individual's constitution, his physical and mental growth, and his behaviour. We know that epochs which are of particular significance in the emotional life of the individual and at which there is a tendency to mental breakdown—e.g. puberty, the puerperium, the menopause, are times when profound changes are taking place in the endocrine system. We cannot yet define the mode of action of the various parts of the endocrine system in producing many of these great biological effects: but endocrinology is a young subject in which rapid advances are being made and, as techniques of investigation and assay become more accurate and subtle and as knowledge of the composition and actions of the hormones increase, we can expect more data to become available which will be relevant to the understanding of nervous and mental illness. The borderlands between endocrinology and psychiatry have been very incompletely explored.

It is important to recognize the complexity of the relationships which are involved. The endocrines are under neural control, and their hormones reciprocally affect the functions of the central nervous system. The hypothalamus acts not only as a central co-ordinating station for the endocrine system, but also as a mediator between the environment, the higher nervous centres, and that system. For convenience, we speak of the disorders of certain endocrine glands, but this is in most cases a simplification. The endocrine system functions as a whole, and is apt to be disturbed as a whole.

When one comes to link physical with mental events, the intricacy of the interactions becomes even more apparent. Endocrine disorder may be either a cause or a consequence of mental disorder, and it may be very difficult to identify the primary factor, so closely do the two interact. Psychological disturbance may upset the endocrine balance: for example, when emotional stress

induces amenorrhoea or precipitates thyrotoxicosis. Gibson (1962) in a review
of the literature of the effects of the emotions on thyroid activity, found only
anectodal evidence for the opinion that a single episode of severe stress can cause
thyrotoxicosis in a previously euthyroid individual: but there is a good deal of
evidence that long continued or repeated emotional stress may precipitate thyrotoxicosis in a genetically predisposed subject. Equally, endocrine disturbance
may act as an internal stress, and precipitate mental breakdown.

With the possible exception of cretinism, there is no endocrine disease which
presents an unvarying psychiatric picture: and none of the mental symptoms
occurring in endocrine diseases are peculiar to them. One cannot diagnose an
endocrine disorder from the mental symptoms which may be present, but must
depend upon the physical symptoms and signs and the results of laboratory and
other specialized investigations. Nevertheless, in certain endocrine syndromes
the mental symptoms are more or less characteristic: for example, the anxiety
and emotional lability of hyperthyroidism; the retardation and paranoid reactions of myxoedema; the neurasthenia of Addison's disease. Patients treated with
cortisone or corticotrophin not infrequently develop hypomanic reactions. In
general, and it is what we would expect, the clinical picture is conditioned both
by the endocrine disturbance and by the constitutional mental make-up of the
individual. Both functional and organic psychiatric syndromes may occur, the
former more commonly: as examples of the latter, one may instance the delirium
which may develop in severe cases of hyperthyroidism, and the confusion which
may be associated with the tetany of hypoparathyroidism.

The depression of spirits which may be evident in certain cases of endocrine
disease is often a very understandable reaction to the physical changes. Anyone
who has seen a full-blown case of Cushing's syndrome or acromegaly or Sim-
monds' disease will appreciate the tremendous psychic wound which such a
transformation may cause.

The endocrines influence profoundly the sexual life of the individual. Particularly is this noticeable in the case of women, who so commonly experience
emotional disturbances in association with menstruation and the menopause.
In the week before menstruation about a quarter of all women experience a
marked degree of emotional irritability, depression and tension, with headache
and sensations of swelling in the breasts and abdomen (Rees, 1953; Kessel and
Coppen, 1963). This state of 'pre-menstrual tension' has been thought to be due
largely to retention of water in the soft tissues of the body: but Bruce and Russell
(1962) in water and sodium balance studies of 10 patients found no evidence to
support this view. The hormonal changes of the menopause also produce both
physical and emotional upset in perhaps 50 per cent. of women. It is doubtful if there is a true male climacteric: but adult castrates are known to be apt
to manifest neurasthenic and anxiety symptoms, while pre-pubertal castrates
are said to show schizoid trends. The endocrines may play some rôle in the
genesis of certain cases of homosexuality, but the situation here is obscure: it
may be said, however, that the endocrine treatment of homosexuality, as also of
impotence and frigidity, usually fails. Hyperfunction of the adrenal cortices may

give rise to a number of rare and dramatic syndromes of sexual abnormality—virilism, feminism, pubertas praecox, which merit fuller psychiatric investigation than has yet been made of them.

A diversity of endocrine anomalies has been reported in schizophrenics: but no endocrine anomaly occurs consistently amongst them. Kretschmer described under the heading 'dysplastic' various physical types (hypoplastic, eunuchoid, masculinism) which he found commonly amongst schizophrenics, and which he thought might be the expression of endocrine disturbances. It is a common finding that schizophrenics are abnormally insensitive to certain glandular extracts, *e.g.* thyroid and insulin. Perhaps the most significant discovery has been Gjessing's: investigating cases of periodic catatonia, he found that in some a phasic alteration of nitrogen balance was associated with the mental symptoms, and that the mental symptoms could be relieved by the giving of thyroxine [see p. 268].

There are few psychiatric syndromes which respond to endocrine treatment. Indications for prescribing endocrine preparations should be based on the presence of physical signs and laboratory evidence of endocrine disorder. Thus, in the management of menopausal disturbances, oestrogens may be prescribed if there are vasomotor symptoms such as hot flushes and sweats: in the absence of these physical symptoms, such treatment is likely to be ineffective. Depressions occurring at or after the menopause do not themselves call for endocrine treatment.

Very much more work requires to be done before any general understanding of the rôle of endocrine dysfunction in mental illness can be reached. In the majority of cases of endocrine disease there are no psychiatric symptoms of note, and in most cases of nervous and mental illness no clear evidence of endocrine disorder. Despite this, the study of endocrine factors should not be neglected.

PHYSIQUE AND PERSONALITY

The study of the association between temperamental traits and body build goes back at least as far as the Greek physician Hippocrates. The layman too has for centuries held pragmatic opinions on this subject. When Shakespeare's Caesar exclaims, 'Yond' Cassius has a lean and hungry look; he thinks too much: such men are dangerous', he expresses not only his private apprehensions but the venerable popular belief that fat men who sleep well are more likely to be good-natured and reliable.

Ernst Kretschmer (1925) pioneered careful psychiatric studies of the problem, studying the physiques particularly of schizophrenics and manic-depressives. He isolated four main types of physique—pyknic, athletic, asthenic and dysplastic. The pyknic is the John Bull, short, thick-set with a round belly and small extremities; the athletic is muscular; the asthenic is long and weedy; the dysplastic approximates to the effects of various kinds of endocrine dysfunction, for example, the near eunuchoid or infantile. Kretschmer found that pyknic physiques were more than normally common amongst manic-depressives, while asthenic, athletic and dysplastic physiques were usual amongst schizophrenics.

From the study of psychotics Kretschmer proceeded to family studies and the investigation of healthy people, and distinguished two clearly recognizable types of personality, the cycloid and schizoid. The cycloid, open, extraverted and affectionate, prone to swings of mood, is associated with the pyknic physique, and, if there is mental breakdown, tends to develop a manic-depressive psychosis. The schizoid, inhibited, introverted and cold, is associated with the asthenic type of physique and with schizophrenia. These two types were by Kretschmer vividly contrasted: 'when we come out of the psychic milieu of the schizophrene family into that of the circulars (manic-depressives), it is like stepping out of a cool shut-in vault into the open sunshine'. He emphasized rightly that cycloid and schizoid personalities 'have no foundation in disease, but indicate certain biological tendencies of which only a small proportion comes to pathological culmination'.

The finding of links between personality, physique and psychosis is in accord with genetic expectations, since they may all be expressions of the same genotype: the existence of clear-cut, discrete physical and personality types amongst the normal population is not. In nature, mixed types are far commoner than pure examples. Kretschmer's work may be criticized on the grounds that his brilliant characterizations are perhaps in their contrasts too sharply drawn, the correlations he found between physique and temperament too close, and the methods of physical measurement he used comparatively crude: but his remains a major contribution.

Sheldon (1940, 1942) carried research on this subject further. He adopted the procedure of photographing the individual in a standardized posture from three positions, and then made detailed anthropometric measurements on the films. Examining in this way 4000 normal young men he found evidence not of discrete types, but of 'dimensions of variation' of physique. The presence of three primary components of structural variation seemed to be revealed and appeared to depend upon the relative development of tissues derived from each of the three embryonic layers. These three primary components Sheldon named endomorphy, mesomorphy and ectomorphy. Endomorphy, reflecting the predominance in development of the entoderm, is characterized by massive digestive viscera and weak development of the somatic structures; there is 'softness and sphericity'. The hallmark of mesomorphy is 'uprightness and sturdiness': somatic structures derived from the mesodermal layer—that is, bone, muscle and connective tissue, are in the ascendancy. In ectomorphy there is relatively slight development of the visceral and somatic structures, and the ectodermal predominance is expressed in 'fragility, linearity, flatness of the chest and delicacy throughout the body'.

Sheldon rated the strength of each of the primary components of physique on a 7-point scale, and his concept of the somatotype can best be illustrated by direct quotation. 'The somatotype is a series of three numerals, each expressing the approximate strength of one of the primary components in a physique. The first numeral always refers to endomorphy, the second to mesomorphy and the third to ectomorphy. Thus, when a 7-point scale is used, a 7–1–1 is the most extreme endomorph; a 1–7–1 is the most extreme mesomorph, and a 1–1–7 the most extreme ectomorph. The 4–4–4 falls at the midpoint (of the scale, not of the frequency distribution) with respect to all three components.'

Sheldon's books should be consulted for further details. He emphasized that when the somatotype has been determined, analysis of the physique has only begun. There are many important secondary variables; for example, dysplasia, and the secondary sex characters.

In studying personality, Sheldon used a variation of the technique of factor analysis applied to quantitative ratings on a group of traits, and claimed to have standardized the description of 'sixty-traits—twenty in each of three correlated clusters—which collectively make up a scale for measuring what appear to be the three primary components of temperament'. The first component, viscerotonia, is characterized by general relaxation, sociability and love of comfort and affection. The second, somatotonia, is expressed predominantly in muscular activity and assertiveness. In the third, cerebrotonia, behaviour is dominated by shyness and inhibition. Sheldon further claimed that these three components of temperament correlate closely with the three components of physique already described—viscerotonia with endomorphy, somatotonia with mesomorphy, and cerebrotonia with ectomorphy. Studying 200 young men he reported correlations of the order of $+0.80$ between the two levels of personality, the morphological and the temperamental.

This work has provided a valuable stimulus to research. Genetical factors governing bodily build are probably distributed normally in a community, and Sheldon's delineation of 'dimensions of variation' is therefore more likely to be accurate than a classification into types. It will be noted, however, that his three categories of physique do bear a clear resemblance to Kretschmer's pyknic, athletic and asthenic types. Sheldon's anthropomorphic measurements improve on those employed in earlier studies. His work on temperamental traits, on the other hand, is less convincing and seems over-simplified.

Eysenck (1947) examined neurotic soldiers, deriving an index of body build on the basis of a factorial analysis of physical anthropometric measurements. He too reported no evidence for the existence of discrete bodily and personality types. In this investigation neurotics as a whole were found to be more leptomorph (cf. Sheldon's ectomorph) than normals; and hysterics had a higher preponderance of lateral growth, as compared with dysthymics (those showing anxiety, depression, irritability), who had a higher preponderance of linear growth. The results of this carefully planned study seem considerably at variance with the reports of work already quoted, and these discrepancies point to the need for further investigation.

REFERENCES

Alcoholics: Report to Scottish Home and Health Department (1965), London, H.M.S.O.

Allen, G. (1965) in *Progress in Medical Genetics*, Vol. IV, New York.

Anderson, E. W . (1961) Proceedings of the Third World Congress of Psychiatry; forensic, 1169.

Andry, R. G. (1957) *Brit. J. Delinq.*, **8**, 34.

Baird, D. (1965) *Brit. med. J.*, **2**, 1141.

Bartlett, F. C. (1943) *Proc. roy. Soc. B*, **131**, 247.

Batchelor, I. R. C. (1957) in *Clues to Suicide*, New York.

Batchelor, I. R. C., and Napier, M. B. (1953a) *Brit. med. J.*, **2**, 1186.

Batchelor, I. R. C., and Napier, M. B. (1953b) *Brit. J. Delinq.*, **4**, 99.

Bowlby, J. (1944) *Int. J. Psycho-Anal.*, **25**, 19.

Bowlby, J. (1951) *Maternal Care and Mental Health*, Geneva, W.H.O.

Bowlby, J. (1958) *Brit. J. med. Psychol.*, **31**, 247.

Bowlby, J. (1961) *Int. J. Psycho-Anal.*, **42**, 317.

Brooke, E. M. (1967) *A Census of Patients in Psychiatric Beds*, London, H.M.S.O.

Bruce, J. T., and Russell, G. M. F. (1962) *Lancet*, ii, 267.

Davis, R. (1946) *J. Neurol. Psychiat.*, **9**, 23, 119.

Dennehy, C. M. (1966) *Brit. J. Psychiat.*, **112**, 1049.

Dorpat, T. L., and Ripley, H. S. (1967) *Comprehens. Psychiat.*, **8**, 74.

Durkheim, E. (1951) *Suicide*, Glencoe, Ill.

Ekblad, M. (1955) *Acta psychiat. scand.*, Suppl. No. 99.

Ettlinger, R. W. (1964) *Acta psychiat. scand.*, **40**, 363.

Eysenck, H. J. (1947) *Dimensions of Personality*, London.

Faris, R. E. L., and Dunham, H. W. (1939) *Mental Disorders in Urban Areas*, Chicago.

Fraser, R. (1947) *The Incidence of Neurosis among Factory Workers*, London H.M.S.O.

Gerard, D. L., and Houston, L. G. (1953) *Psychiat. Quart.*, **27**, 90.

Gibson, J. G. (1962) *J. psychosom. Res.*, **6**, 93.

Goldfarb, W. (1955) in *Psychopathology of Childhood*, ed. Hoch, P. H., and Zubin, J., New York.

Goldhamer, H., and Marshall, A. W. (1949) *Psychosis and Civilization*, Glencoe, Ill.

Greer, S., Gunn, J. C., and Koller, K. M. (1966) *Brit. med. J.*, **2**, 1351.

Halbwachs, M. (1930) *Les Causes du Suicide*, Paris.

Hallowel, A. I. (1934) *J. abnorm. soc. Psychol.*, **29**, 1.

Hare, E. H. (1956) *J. ment. Sci.*, **102**, 349, 753.

Hollingshead, A. B., and Redlich, F. C. (1958) *Social Class and Mental Illness*, London.

Höök, K. (1963) *Acta psychiat. scand.*, Suppl. No. 168.

Jansson, B. (1965) *Acta psychiat. scand.*, **41**, 87.

Jellinek, E. M. (1960) *J. Canad. med. Ass.*, **83**, 1341.

Keller, M. (1962) in *Society, Culture and Drinking Patterns*, ed. Pittman, D. J., and Snyder, C. R., New York.

Kessel, N. (1965) *Brit. med. J.*, **2**, 1265, 1336.

Kessel, N., and Coppen, A. (1963) *Lancet*, ii, 61.

Kretschmer, E. (1925) *Physique and Character*, London.

Lemert, E. M. (1951) *Social Pathology*, New York.

Lewis, H. (1954) *Deprived Children*, London.

Lindemann, E. (1944) *Amer. J. Psychiat.*, **101**, 141.

Miller, H. (1961) *Brit. med. J.*, **1**, 919.

Morris, J. N. (1959) *Lancet*, i, 303.

Munro, A. (1965) *Brit. J. prev. soc. Med.*, **19**, 69.

Parkes, C. M. (1964) *Brit. J. Psychiat.*, **110**, 198.

Parkes, C. M. (1965) *Brit. J. med. Psychol.*, **38**, 1.

Parkes, C. M., and Benjamin, B. (1967) *Brit. med. J.*, **3**, 232.

Parkin, D., and Stengel, E. (1965) *Brit. med. J.*, **2**, 133.

Penrose, L. S. (1950) *Congrès International de Psychiatrie*, Paris, **6**, 44.

Rees, L. (1953) *J. ment. Sci.*, **99**, 62.

Rees, W. D., and Lutkins, S. G. (1967) *Brit. med. J.*, **4**, 13.

Reid, D. D. (1960) *Wld Hlth Org. Publ. Hlth Pap.*, No. 2, Geneva.
Roberts, J. A. F. (1967) *An Introduction to Medical Genetics*, 4th ed., London.
Sainsbury, P. (1955) *Suicide in London*, London.
Sargant, W., and Slater, E. (1940) *Lancet*, ii, 1.
Sheldon, W. H., and Stevens, S. S. (1942) *The Varieties of Temperament*, London.
Sheldon, W. H., Stevens, S. S., and Tucker, W. B. (1940) *The Varieties of Human Physique*, London.
Shepherd, M. (1957) *A Study of the Major Psychoses in an English County*, London.
Shepherd, M., Cooper, B., Brown, A. C., and Kalton, G. W. (1966) *Psychiatric Illness in General Practice*, London.
Smith, H. L. (1930–35) *New Survey of London Life and Labour*, London.
Stengel, E., Cook, N. G., and Kreeger, I. S. (1958) *Attempted Suicide*, London.
Thomson, G., *et al.* (1947) *The Trend of National Intelligence*, London.
Walton, H. J. (1958) *J. ment. Sci.*, **104**, 884.
Watts, C. A. H., Cawte, E. C., and Kuenssberg, E. V. (1964) *Brit. med. J.*, **2**, 1351.
Williams, A. H. (1950) *Brit. J. med. Psychol.*, **23**, 130.
World Health Organization (1960) *Wld Hlth Org. techn. Rep. Ser.*, No. 185, Geneva.
Yap, P. M. (1952) *J. ment. Sci.*, **98**, 515.
Yarrow, L. J. (1964) in *Review of Child Development Research*, Vol. II, ed. Hoffman, M. L., and Hoffman, L. W., New York.

5

METHOD OF EXAMINATION

In the practice of psychological medicine a not infrequent obstacle enters which is not found, or found very little, in other branches of medical practice, namely a relative or total unwillingness on the part of the patient to co-operate. Co-operation may be slight or altogether lacking in many instances, for example in schizophrenia from absorption in an inner world of phantasy, in paranoid psychoses from suspicion, and in manic excitement from sheer inability to sustain attention; while in other syndromes there may be apparent willingness to co-operate, but inability to do so, for example in profound depression of spirits where thinking is so retarded that the patient may repeatedly open his mouth as if to speak and be unable to utter any more than a syllable.

It is to cases of the psychotic sort that a greater part of the following description of the manner of examination refers. It includes the method of approach to individual patients who are more or less incapable of co-operation in one or other of these ways.

In those instances of psychological ill health which are in the great majority, where the patient presents himself for examination and treatment, where he is morbidly anxious or excessively worried and depressed without being robbed of his volition, or still more frequently where he complains of headache, dyspepsia, palpitation or some other discomfort for which no sufficient and relevant physical cause can be found, the procedure may be summed up as that of taking a detailed *history* along certain lines.

After obtaining a statement of the symptoms in the order in which the patient complains of them, and noting associated qualities such as time, incidence, relation to what the patient does and so on, it is necessary to trace the chronology of their development. When did the symptoms first appear, and in what circumstances? It will sometimes be found that the first statement on this point is inadvertently erroneous, and further exploration may show that in fact symptoms of a similar sort existed at some previous date. The history of the development of the symptoms is, however, of importance, principally in relation to the patient's personal history. What were his circumstances at the time the symptoms first appeared or at the time of any recurrence or exacerbation? The task, in fact, resolves itself into taking a life-history of the patient as an individual in relation to his home, the people in it, his friends, his married life, his work, his career and so forth. One looks, first of all, for evidence of external stress existing at or near the onset of symptoms, such as frank anxieties, disappointment in a career, other personal frustrations, conflicts with wife or husband or work associates, jealousies and rivalries, from the nursery upwards; in fact, whatever human beings do and suffer has to be explored by the psychiatrist in relation to the occurrence of symptoms which are presumed to be signs of mental uneasiness or distress.

Where nothing of this sort appears in the history, or nothing that seems to account for the symptoms, either in the external circumstances or, what is much more difficult to ascertain, in the patient's inner attitude to his life and his fellows, then the investigation must be extended, as indeed in some degree in most cases it must be extended, for the sake of a proper understanding, into his early life, his relationship to his parents, his brothers and sisters and so forth. An attempt should also be made, primarily on the basis of the life-history, to make an estimate of the patient's temperament and character. Here the examination may follow the same lines as is discussed under 'Personality' later in this chapter.

In this way it will be possible to arrive at a provisional formulation which exhibits the symptoms as a reaction to contemporary circumstances, or shows the condition as one of much earlier origin connected with miscarriages of psychological development, starting at an early age and tending to produce feelings of insecurity and inferiority, or faulty attitudes of a more subtle kind; and on the other hand producing faults of character, such as vanity, tendencies to dodge important issues, or to bear grudges. More subtly still, emotional attitudes may be formed around certain individuals in the family and round certain episodes in the past which preclude a normal attitude to various aspects of life subsequently until these earlier attitudes have been uncovered and modified. For example, over-dependence on one or other parent may produce an apparently causeless anxiety at the prospect of marriage. More detailed exposition of topics of that kind will be found in Chapter 8.

It will be seen that what is wanted where the patient is co-operative, and especially where there is no question of mental alienation and of the existence of a radically different general attitude to the world from that of the ordinary man, is a history of the patient as a person, his character and temperament and his modes of reaction to the emotional stresses of life.

Where, however, the degree of co-operation is less than this, and where, even if co-operation is superficially good, the patient's attitude and ideas are such as to suggest that he has been developing a psychotic form of illness, then the following scheme should be closely followed, because an accurate, systematic form of examination is indispensable, and should be of material aid in the progress of psychiatry. It has seemed to us that physicians in general practice are reluctant to deal with psychiatric or 'mental' cases, largely because they do not know how to approach and examine them in an orderly way. No one expects a general practitioner to be fully conversant with every speciality, nor does one expect from him a detailed argument in regard to diagnosis and prognosis, but the general practitioner should be familiar with methods of examination, so as to be able to elicit the facts and present them systematically, even although he may not be able to interpret them correctly. This is fundamental. The interpretation of symptoms will only come on the basis of wide experience.

It has been unfortunate that in psychiatric case-taking there has not been a more settled, uniform policy, and too often the person studying psychiatry has either worked out methods of examination to suit himself, or has blindly followed the ways of his teachers and colleagues, even although those ways were recognized to be far from satisfactory. Hence psychiatric records have often left much to be desired, and it has not been possible to correlate accurately the clinical picture with the pathological findings, nor has it been possible to compare cases occurring in one psychiatric unit with those in another. From this there results confusion and incongruity, where it is essential to have clearness and uniformity. One hears various excuses made for this. A common one is that the patient is so disordered mentally as to be quite unco-operative, and on that account a complete examination is impossible. How seldom is this really the case! It is true that it may not be possible to make an absolutely complete examination until after a number of attempts have been made, and certain points may not at once be elicited, but sufficient should always be obtained (whether there is complete co-operation or not) upon which to base an independent opinion. Where it is not possible to elicit all the facts, the case-record should contain an explanation of why this is so.

Although a good descriptive record of the behaviour and symptoms of the patient is of importance, it will not be of any great value unless information is collected elsewhere regarding the setting in which the symptoms have occurred, and the causes which have been instrumental in producing them. The causes are so often of a family or environmental nature that a study of the social conditions and of the family life is essential. The plan of examination, therefore, consists of two parts—the history or 'anamnesis' obtained from the relatives or friends, and the examination of the patient. The one is no less important than the other.

There are several general points which should be kept in mind in making this examination. An effort should be made to record the case in simple, non-technical language, rather than by using hackneyed terms. Further, the physician should not be satisfied with an account from any one source, but should interview several of the intimate relatives or friends of the patient.

In examining the patient a great deal depends on the method of approach. The physician should realize clearly that he is dealing with a person of disordered mentality, who cannot be treated in the same way as a patient in a general hospital, and he should therefore be more than usually tactful, very patient, understanding and sympathetic. Many medical men in examining their mental patients repeatedly fail to get hold of the essential points of the case, either because of an undue sense of delicacy, or because their manner and method do not inspire confidence in the patient. The patient should be made to feel at once that the examiner has his best interests at heart, that he is willing to do everything that he possibly can to help him, and the doctor should be quite frank in stating his position. If the patient asks who was responsible for his coming, why he was brought and so on, these questions should be answered fully at the time. The patient should be informed that all the facts will be carefully investigated. It not infrequently happens that patients are more talkative and more willing to explain their illness at the first interview than they are later on, and this time should be seized to take as complete a record as possible. Sometimes the physician feels that he may upset the patient by going thoroughly into the case initially, but this

G

is incorrect. It is much better to make a comprehensive note at once of the patient's condition, and, at the same time, to give him any explanations which he asks for. The complete systematic examination should be conducted as early as possible. If this is not done, a change may very soon occur in the patient's attitude, and often a most valuable part of the record is lost. Until the physician has gained considerable experience in history-taking, we consider that it is advisable that the plan suggested below should be followed closely. Later, after experience has been gained, it can be changed to suit the individual case. Under these circumstances, and using this plan of examination, we believe that the different mental fields (*e.g.* behaviour, affect, intellect, personality and insight) can be examined just as thoroughly, as completely, and as systematically as any bodily organ.

The plan suggested was first formulated by Dr. Adolf Meyer when he was Director of the Psychiatric Institute, New York. In 1921 Dr. George Kirby edited for the New York State Hospital Commission a series of guides for history-taking and clinical examination, which were largely based on Meyer's original plan. We have followed these closely, but have modified them here and there, and have eliminated parts which might be considered redundant.

The form of examination which we suggest may be considered under the following headings:

1. Family history.
2. Personal history.
3. History of the present illness.
4. Examination of the patient, including the (*a*) mental and (*b*) physical condition.

FAMILY HISTORY

It is notoriously difficult to get a reliable statement of the family history. The relatives often feel sensitive about their position; they are apt to think that the patient may resent information being given, and the maternal side is apt to blame the paternal side, and vice versa. Even where evidence of definite nervous or mental disturbance is obtained, the positive statements are often glossed over, and any description of the state is usually qualified by some such phrase as 'Of course he was not insane, Doctor.'

We have already emphasized the value of the accurate study of the facts of heredity in relation to mental illness, and at this point we would merely reiterate the necessity of having as complete and as detailed information as possible, dating back for three generations. It is not always easy to get this, for various reasons, but, where the information is defective, a statement to that effect should be made in the case-record. On the other hand, where a positive history of abnormality in the forebears is obtained, then the age of onset, the duration of the illness and a description of it should be recorded. A one-word diagnosis is not satisfactory, because it is necessary to have the facts so that anyone could come to an independent opinion. This is why it is so important to avoid such vague terms as 'nervousness', 'shock', 'nervous debility,' and 'worry'. In addition to having information regarding the direct line, the collateral lines should also be closely inquired into. We not only want to have information about the occurrence of the more gross types of mental disorder, but we should also have as much information as possible in reference to subnormality in any degree, epilepsy, alcoholism, and eccentricities and peculiarities of any kind. Apart altogether from the purely nervous and mental aspects, we should attempt to obtain information about the general physique of the family, and the bodily, as well as the mental, morbidity.

PERSONAL HISTORY

This may have to be obtained from several different sources, from the brothers and sisters, or from other intimate relatives and friends. The personal history should cover the *development of the patient* from the time of conception up to the alleged onset of the illness. We want to know as much as we can about the life, habits and social circumstances of the parents at the time of conception, the condition of the mother during gestation, the character of the labour—whether it was unduly prolonged, complicated, or aided by instruments. The development and career of the individual should be followed, and such points inquired for as: whether he was strong and healthy, or sickly; the susceptibility to childish ailments; whether there were convulsions, tantrums or sleeplessness; the time of teething, of learning to walk and speak, the control of sphincters (bed-wetting) and the response to darkness, tunnels, thunder and lightning and other childish bogies.

Following this, the stage of *intellectual and social adaptation* must be inquired into, and our inquiries should concern school reports, the degree of intellectual attainment; what the patient's attitude was towards his fellows, whether he was a leader or led; how interested in, and proficient at, games; whether a spontaneous, keen, straightforward person, or cunning, a truant, untruthful. In short, we should have as much evidence as possible in regard to the individual's interests and hobbies, including such things as fondness for animals, or cruelty towards them; and interest in religion—whether it was merely formal, or had a deeper side. Special inquiry should be directed towards *sex development*, the establishment of puberty, whether much interest was taken in it, whether there was worry about masturbation or a tendency to associate freely with the other sex; and the possibility of venereal disease. In females, one should have an accurate history of the development of menstruation, of any irregularities, of pregnancies, abortions and the response to the menopause. In this connection one should also inquire into the psychosexual interests—love attachments, perversions, and attraction or antagonism to the parents, or to various members of the family.

Inquiry must also be made regarding *general diseases or injuries*, the possibility of infection from whatever source, and the state of the endocrine and vegetative nervous system (as suggested by abnormal desire for sweets or fluids; frequency of micturition, etc.). Addiction to alcohol and drugs and the presence of other toxic factors must be inquired for.

Previous attacks of mental disorder should be carefully investigated.

The object of the examination, therefore, is to get a description of what the individual was at his or her best, what the response was to social, business and domestic life, and what were his ambitions, dreams and hobbies. All this should be recorded in narrative form.

HISTORY OF PRESENT ILLNESS

Before attempting to take a detailed history of the symptoms, it is of even greater importance to inquire carefully about possible aetiological factors and precipitating causes. It may be that the cause is neither physical nor mental nor endocrine, but that it is a combination of all these factors, acting on a soil predisposed by hereditary and environmental influences acting over a long period of time. It is well to recognize this, because the relatives often feel that one factor is very much more important than another, whereas it is often the one which has seemed of least importance to the family that has been chiefly responsible for the break-down.

The date of the first deviation from the normal should be stated as accurately as possible, and then the development of the symptoms should be followed step by step. Such a description helps considerably in understanding whether the onset has been insidious and gradual, or sudden. It cannot be too strongly emphasized that general statements are of no value; we must get an exact description of what the patient's conduct has been, and how he has reacted to his difficulties. We must, therefore, endeavour to find what the attitude has been towards his intimate relatives and friends, whether there has been a change in mood, and whether peculiar ideas, delusions, suspicions or unusual interests have been spoken about and cultivated. It is not enough simply to have the statement, 'He is delusional', or 'hallucinated', but what is of value is to get an exact description of the delusions and hallucinations, and how the patient has reacted to them.

The memory and general intellectual faculties should also be closely inquired into. Where a variation of symptoms has occurred, it is important to give dates for the development of the various stages. In addition, one should always be quite clear whether there have been suicidal or homicidal tendencies, and whether there has been an impairment of physical health, as shown by sleeplessness, disordered appetite, a loss of weight, and constipation or diarrhoea.

EXAMINATION OF THE PATIENT
(See also Chapter 6)

Personality

In 1923, Amsden published an article dealing with the 'Practical Value of the Study of the Personality in Mental Disorders', and in this he described the study of personality under four main headings:

1. The intellectual faculties.
2. 'Somatic demands' (physical activities).

3. The individual's self-criticism and self-estimate.

4. The urgency or imperative to adaptation.

It stands to reason that such a scheme must have a definite value in helping one to come to an understanding of the individual case; for is not the colouring of the psychosis largely dependent upon the original make-up, constitution or personality of the individual? Furthermore, the prognosis of any case, no matter how serious it may seem on the surface, depends essentially on the 'stuff' of the individual, the inherent character. A person well-endowed intellectually, who has met his difficulties in his social, business and sexual relationships in a healthy, straightforward way, and who has had interests outside himself, who has been 'exteriorized' in his everyday relationships, has always much more chance of making a good readjustment than his introverted, 'shut-in' neighbour. With an exact, detailed description of the patient's likes and dislikes, hopes and fears, or of as much of them as it is possible to elicit, we are better able to guide the patient along the paths which are in harmony with his disposition, and which he can most easily accept. A study of the personality is therefore not only of importance after the development of the psychosis, but it seems to us to be particularly important in connection with prophylactic work, and in connection with the training of children. If we have clearer ideas about what the difficulties of make-up are likely to lead to, then we may be able to prevent the development of serious break-downs. The scheme which Amsden formulated is difficult to improve upon, and we would summarize it as follows:

1. In a description of *intellectual activity*, the points which we specially desire information about are: (a) the readiness with which knowledge is acquired; (b) the power of retention; (c) the ability to be guided by past experience. These points can be elicited by having a detailed account not only of the patient's schooldays, but also of his business and family life. We want to determine whether the well-endowed type is able to co-ordinate his activity in a healthy-minded, constructive way, whether he is in touch with things as they are, or whether he is apt to be diffuse, absent-minded, lacking in purpose and easily side-tracked. The questions to elicit these various points must be left to the individual examiner.

2. The *somatic demands* concern themselves especially with motor activities and the demands of sex. Motor, or, better, psychomotor, activity involves the questions whether the patient was lively or sluggish, *i.e.* whether there was push and energy as evidenced by talkativeness and enthusiasm, or whether he was inert and lacked initiative; whether there has been much interest in sports, games, hobbies, or whether there has been idleness and lassitude. Regarding sex, it is important to know how much the topic has interested the patient, whether the reactions to it have been hygienic or unhygienic, whether there have been unhealthy habits, persistent masturbation, prudishness or its opposite. Some importance has been attached to vaguer matters, such as nail-biting, and response to mucous-membrane stimulation—eating, drinking, smoking.

3. *Self-estimate and self-criticism* depend largely on comparing ourselves with others. Such comparison may bring with it a feeling of satisfaction, or a feeling

of failure, according to whether the comparison is favourable or unfavourable. If the comparison is favourable, the reactions are likely to be capable and adequate, but if unfavourable, a variety of responses may be elicited. Either the individual may realize his deficiencies, and attempt to correct his shortcomings in a healthy way, or else the individual may shrink, become sensitive, self-effacing and dependent. Again, evasions and compensations may be called into being. A sidelight on these various aspects may be obtained by the knowledge of whether the person is greatly influenced by the opinion of others, whether he is proud, fussy and makes much of discomforts. Other important sidelights are the individual's ability to make friends, the degree of easiness or uneasiness in the presence of strangers and the tendency to jealousy. The questions of over-conscientiousness, and the ability to take advice, also come in.

4. *The urgency or imperative to adaptation* centres on the question why we need to adapt ourselves at all. This, as Amsden said, is the crux of the whole study, because it is just these tendencies which favour or impede adaptation which are so important. A constructive assertion of it is seen in ambition, courageousness and vigorousness generally. Where we find a diminution of such tendencies we must attempt to get some explanation for it.

Mental Examination

We will attempt in the chapter on 'Symptomatology' to describe the great variety of mental symptoms which commonly occur, so that the plan of examination as here laid down will be put as briefly as possible. It will concern itself mainly with the order to be followed, and the method of eliciting the required information. Where a technical term appears of which the meaning is not evident from the context, an explanation of it will be found in the chapter on 'Symptomatology'.

General Behaviour

The general behaviour of the patient is usually the first indication to the relatives that all is not well. The facial expression, the dress, the attitude, often tell at a glance the underlying state of the patient, and we note at once whether there is depression, or elation and talkativeness, apathy and listlessness, co-operation or resistance, stupor or undue suggestibility. We must note whether the activity is free or constrained, changeable or stereotyped, whether there is anxiety and agitation, with scratching and picking at the skin, and whether there is any reaction to imaginary sense-perceptions. A good deal can be learned from the way the patient adapts to a new environment, as, *e.g.*, on admission to hospital, and it is always wise to get a description from the nurse of how the patient accepted the formalities of admission, *e.g.* having clothes taken and marked, bathing, and the association with other patients. The description should be made as vivid and telling as possible, but it should be couched as far as possible in non-technical language, and it is perhaps best written at the end rather than at the beginning of the examination, because facts will be observed during the examination which were not at first apparent.

The Stream of Mental Activity

This is easily and quickly determined by a number of simple questions, *e.g.*
'What is your name in full?' 'Are you married or single?' 'How old are you?'
'What is your occupation?' 'What do you complain of?' 'Do you know why you
are here?' The response to such questions will demonstrate at once whether there
is any formal disorder—that is to say, whether there is over-talkativeness or
mutism, whether questions have to be repeated, whether the answers tend to go
into too much detail, with flight of ideas and distractibility, whether there is a
considerable pause before a reply is given (retardation), or whether there is an
element of suspicion, *e.g.* 'Why do you ask me such questions?' Again, questions
may be answered promptly and to the point, or there may be irrelevance with
incoherence, verbigeration, perseveration, echolalia, neologisms, stereotypies.
On the other hand, the response to questions may indicate a total lack of understanding, and point towards some organic change. It is a most excellent plan to
take, if possible, a verbatim report of the patient's spontaneous talk.

Emotional Reaction (Affect)

The superficial manifestation of the patient's affect (facial expression, etc.)
will have been noted already under general behaviour, but we want to analyse
more deeply not only the affect, but also the situation producing it, whether it is
dependent on domestic, social or business difficulties. We have to depend a great
deal upon what the patient himself tells us regarding his feelings. We note at once
what his general attitude is, and we point our more specific questions in accordance therewith. It is a false move, and an insult, to ask a patient obviously
depressed whether he is happy; in consequence, it is always best to ask some such
general question as 'How do you feel?' and then, according to the reply, this can
be followed up with such questions as, 'Are you happy?' and then, 'Why?';
or, 'Are you sad or depressed, or out of sorts, or worried?' and, again, 'Why?'
Where possible, the mood should be described in the patient's own words. After
these more or less formal questions, the patient should be asked to tell his story
from the beginning, and should be kept to the topic with a minimum of questioning, until the condition has been thoroughly detailed. If the patient is allowed to
tell his story in this way, it usually means that a satisfactory basis of co-operation
is established, which permits of not only completing the examination expedi-
tiously, but also gives a foundation for future work. Furthermore, the patient at
once recognizes that a real effort is being made to understand him. This produces
gratitude, and establishes confidence. Our questions must largely be dictated by
our common sense, and must simply suffice to keep the patient to the topic in
hand, without unduly suggesting things. The points which have particularly to
be kept in mind are the intensity of the affect, whether it varies, the response to
reassurance, and the question whether it is in harmony with the ideas expressed.
The affective state can be approximately gauged even when the patient is unresponsive and mute, by noting such things as pallor, flushing, perspiration, the
respiration rate and the pulse.

Mental Trend: Content of Thought

It often happens that when a patient is describing his 'feelings' he will express ideas pointing to a disordered content of thought, and at this point he should be encouraged to detail the development of his ideas. This may be done quite spontaneously, and without much urging, but, on the other hand, there may be evasion and hedging, and more direct questions may have to be asked. The narrative, however, does not read so tellingly when questions are interposed, and it is usually best to omit them, and to continue the story as it is given. In case of necessity, however, we must ask such questions as, 'Do you believe that you have been watched, laughed at, or spoken about?' 'Have people been behaving strangely towards you?' 'Do they seem to take undue notice of you?' 'Have attempts actually been made to persecute and injure you?', and 'With what motive?' 'Does it seem as if your mind or your body is being influenced by electricity, wireless, drugs?' 'Do your thoughts seem to be read?' 'Have you been influenced by hypnotism?' 'Do you feel as if you had a mission?' It must be determined whether the patient is convinced that all this is being done for some special purpose, and whether these ideas occur in a setting of complete intellectual clearness. When it is evident that hallucinations play a prominent part, one should not hesitate to put direct questions, as 'Will you describe your imaginations to me?' 'Do you hear voices or noises?' 'Are they imaginary?' 'Do they occur in one ear or in both?' 'Do you see things?' 'Have you ever had visions?' 'Is this condition worse at night-time?' 'Have you noticed whether your sense of taste or smell is affected?' One should determine whether these experiences appear real (lack of insight), or whether they are regarded as being something strange and peculiar, and the result of imagination. When a positive history either of illusions or hallucinations is elicited, a detailed account should be obtained of how, why and when such disturbances appear. With regard to the condition described as 'compulsive' thought or action, or obsession, inquiry should be made whether thoughts come with insistent force into the patient's mind, and dominate completely. Have actions to be repeated? Is there 'a ritual' in regard to any of the daily tasks?

Orientation

This can be determined by the following simple questions: 'What day is it?' 'What time of day is it?' 'What month is it? 'What year is it?' 'Do you know the date?' 'What place is this?' 'What kind of place?' 'Who am I?' 'What is my occupation?'

Memory

The most convenient way to test the memory for remote events is to ask the patient to give a chronological account of his life from the date of birth. The patient should be asked for the date and place of birth, the age on going to and leaving school and what standard was reached. After leaving school what was the further development in occupation or training, the first place of employment and the subsequent career? If the patient is married, one should ask when the marriage took place; and the names and ages of the children. Where is the patient presently employed; what has been the longest time in one job; was he ever previously ill? It is wise to get as exact dates as possible of the various important events of the patient's life, in order to determine whether or not they are properly correlated.

The memory for recent events can be tested by such questions as 'When did you come here?' 'Where from?' 'What were you doing yesterday?' 'Who came with you?' 'How many meals have you had since you were admitted?'

Retention (Immediate Memory)

In order to test the power of retention, the patient is given verbally and asked to remember a street address, a person's name, a colour and some object such as a cabbage, a table, a house, and then, after a period of one to five minutes, or an hour, or several days, is requested to repeat what he was asked to remember. More specialized tests can be given, such as the memory for digits or letters or words. Franz, in his book on Examination Methods, gave these various tests in detail. We would particularly mention the test by word-pairs. The patient is asked to repeat five or ten word-pairs, and after this has been done, the stimulus word is given again, and the patient has to supply the second word, *e.g.*:

Head	—	hair	Window	—	door
Room	—	hall	Book	—	pencil
Chair	—	table	Lake	—	river
Grass	—	tree	Apple	—	pear
White	—	red	Pipe	—	tobacco

Further attempts to give more precision in tests for failure of memory and of intellectual capacity in general are described on pages 95–6.

Apperception (ability to assimilate and comprehend impressions)

Franz's second useful test was to give the patient a short story or paragraph to read, and then ask him to give the gist of what he had read. The cowboy story is a good test for this purpose:

A cowboy from Arizona went to San Francisco with his dog, which he left at a friend's while he purchased a new suit of clothes. Dressed finely, he went back to the dog, whistled to him, called him by name and patted him. But the dog would have nothing to do with him in his new hat and coat, but gave a mournful howl. Coaxing was of no effect, so the cowboy went away and donned his old garments, whereon the dog immediately showed his wild joy on seeing his master as he thought he ought to be.'

The following two stories are taken from Bleuler's *Textbook of Psychiatry*:

THE DONKEY LOADED WITH SALT

'A donkey, loaded with salt, had to wade a stream. He fell down, and for a few minutes lay comfortably in the cool water. When he got up he felt relieved of a great part of his burden, because the salt had melted in the water. Longears noted this advantage, and at once applied it the following day, when, loaded with sponges, he again went through the same stream.

'This time he fell purposely, but was grossly deceived. The sponges had soaked up the water, and were considerably heavier than before. The burden was so great that he succumbed.

'The same remedy does not apply to all cases.'

NEPTUNE AND THE LABOURER

'A day labourer worked along a stream. By accident his axe fell in, and as the stream was so deep that he could not get it out, he sat on the bank and bemoaned his fate to the river god.

'Neptune took pity on the man's poverty, dived down and brought up a golden axe. "Is this yours?" he asked the labourer. The latter honestly answered "No". Suddenly Neptune dived down again and appeared before the wood-cutter with a silver axe. To this one, too, the labourer made no claim. For the third time the god dived and brought up the right iron axe with the wooden handle. "Yes, that is it. That is the right one. That is the one I lost", the labourer exclaimed joyfully. "I only wanted to test you", replied Neptune; "I am glad that you are as honest as you are poor. There, take all three axes; I present them to you."

'The honest man told this story to several acquaintances. One of these wanted to misuse Neptune's goodness, and for this reason he purposely threw his axe into the stream. Hardly had he begun to bemoan his fate to the river god when the latter appeared with a golden axe. He asked, "Is this the one that fell into the stream?" He quickly exclaimed, "Yes, that is it", and grabbed for it. But Neptune denounced him as a shameless liar because he wanted to deceive even a god, and turned his back on him. With him disappeared the golden axe, and the labourer had to go home without even his own axe.

'Honesty is the best policy.'

The *thinking capacity and the power of attention* are important topics. In order to test these a series of digits or letters are read aloud to the patient, who is required to tap each time a certain digit or letter recurs. Or the lists may be given to the patient with the instruction to cross out the designated digits or letters.

Other tests to illuminate the same topics are the Heilbronner test, where familiar objects are drawn with varying degrees of completeness and the patient asked to indicate their defects; and the Ebbinghaus test, which tests the patient's ability to fill in blanks in a short story:

'Once upon a time —— heard a —— chirruping in the ——. "Ah," he said to himself, "if I could —— like that, how —— I should be." So he bowed low to the ——, and said, "Kind friend, what —— do you eat to make your —— so sweet?" "I drink the evening dew", replied the ——. The foolish —— tried to live on the same ——, and died of ——.'

School and General Knowledge

It is necessary in testing school and other knowledge to keep in mind the nationality, the educational level and the general experiences of the individual. School and general knowledge can be tested by giving simple questions in arithmetic, in history and geography, as follows:

7 times 9?   3 times 17?   63 divided by 7?

Subtract 7 from 100 consecutively and aloud (*i.e.* 93, 86, 79, etc.).

If the patient is able to accomplish these satisfactorily, then such questions as the interest on £200 at 4 per cent. for a year and a half can be asked, or such simple problems as—If 6 times X equals 18, how much is X?

In regard to history, one can ask questions in reference to the two World Wars. Who fought at Waterloo? Who was Napoleon? Wellington? Caesar? Name the oceans. Where are Brussels, Rome, Vienna, Berlin, Melbourne? What is the capital of France? of U.S.A.? Name the chief rivers in England. What is the highest mountain in the world? the largest lake?

Approximately correct replies to such questions in some instances would of course stand, and a number of failures must be allowed for.

General Intelligence

This can be gauged by the general character of the responses, or in special cases by tests for intelligence described on pages 466-7.

Sometimes it may be useful to ask more abstract questions, or to read a fable to the patient, and ask what is implied by it. One can put such questions, for instance, as the difference between a lie and a mistake, idleness and laziness, character and reputation.

Insight and Judgement

The questions here relate to the amount of realization the patient has of his own condition; does he realize that he is ill, that he is mentally ill, that he is in need of treatment in a mental hospital? Does he acknowledge that his ideas have been due to his disordered imagination? Does he show poor judgement regarding the question of discharge, plans for the future, family responsibilities, and ethical standards?

The foregoing outline applies more particularly to patients suffering from a psychosis. For modifications in cases of subnormality, and of neuroses, see the corresponding chapters, as well as the first part of this chapter.

Tests of Mental Deterioration

Various psychological tests have been devised which can be of much assistance in confirming and refining clinical observations in brain-damaged patients.

Wechsler (1958) pointed out that the measurement of mental deterioration involves three separate problems: '1. the reliable measurement of the individual's actual or present functioning ability; 2. the evaluation of his previous functioning level; 3. the expression of the difference between the two in meaningful quantitative terms.' He developed a differential-test-score method of measuring mental deterioration, which uses the fact that some abilities decline relatively little during adult life and others to a considerable degree: abilities tapped by performance tests, for example, decline more rapidly with age than those involved in verbal tests; general information and comprehension are maintained better than the memory span for digits. Tests are allocated to two groups, those which 'hold up' with age and those which do not. Tests which hold up with age are: 'information, comprehension, object assembly, picture completion and vocabulary'. Tests which do not hold up with age are: 'Digit span, arithmetic, digit symbol, block design and similarities'. To obtain a measure of deterioration, one compares the sum weighted scores of the two groups of tests. Pathological deterioration is defined by Wechsler as follows: 'An individual may be said to show signs of possible deterioration if he shows a greater than a 10 per cent. loss, and of definite deterioration if a loss greater than 20 per cent. than that allowed for by the normal decline with age.'

The observation that the formation of new associations is hindered has also been utilized in a small group of tests adapted by Zangwill (1943). In the first test the total memory span with a series of digits, such as 3.1.7.2.9.4., is contrasted with the time taken to learn to repeat gradually a series which is one digit longer than it is possible for the patient to reproduce immediately without error after one reading by the examiner. Thus a patient with a basal digit span of six digits may be unable to learn a sequence of seven digits even after ten consecutive trials.

The second test is adapted from Babcock's scale and consists in counting the trials necessary for the patient to learn a sentence of rather unusual syntax: 'One thing a nation must have to become rich and great is a large secure supply of wood.' The sentence is repeated alternately by the examiner and the patient until the latter gives two consecutive word-perfect versions. While an intelligence test may show no appearance of intellectual defect yet the deteriorated patient may not be able to learn to repeat the sentence perfectly even after ten trials. Even this test, however, may show nothing when the patient has been originally of superior intelligence.

The assessment of minor degrees of organic impairment should depend on a combination of total clinical impressions and the results of specific tests. Taken together these give a more accurate picture than either in isolation.

Physical Examination

A thorough physical examination is absolutely essential in every psychiatric case. This follows the ordinary lines.

REFERENCES

Amsden, G. S. (1923) *Amer. J. Psychiat.*, **11**, 501.
Wechsler, D. (1958) *The Measurement and Appraisal of Adult Intelligence*, 4th ed., Baltimore.
Zangwill, O. (1943) *Proc. roy. Soc. Med.*, **36**, 576.

6

SYMPTOMATOLOGY

An attempt will be made to define the terms used in clinical psychiatry, and this in the order in which they occur in the scheme of mental examination. Their discussion in the categories of the usual type of normal psychology, which has not proved fruitful in psychopathological practice, is thus avoided. Although the observation of individual symptoms is very important, it is only in connection with the whole life-history and the general clinical setting that they have their full meaning.

In the great majority of psychological illnesses there is little or no outward change; but in others there are alterations in demeanour, especially in the psychotic reactions, where the changes in social attitude and behaviour are sometimes both conspicuous and persistent. In most instances, however, we meet mainly or entirely subjective discomforts which may, however, be as great a handicap as the disability of physical disease, which indeed they often resemble, in the form of pains, 'indigestion', palpitation, headache and the like, without discoverable physical basis. The commonest type of subjective complaint is fear of something, whether it be of crowds, of open places, of being alone, of anything resembling dirt, of certain thoughts or of disease.

BEHAVIOUR

Behaviour will be used here in the general sense of the conduct and deportment of the patient as seen by the physician, and as related to him by the patient's friends. A change in behaviour can be one of the earliest and most striking indications of mental disorder. A man of hitherto ordinary normal habits becomes different from what he was previously. The change may be evidenced predominantly either in his emotional (affective) manifestations, in his activity, or in his intellectual performance. If previously cheerful and capable, he may become dull, morose and lacking in initiative; or, on the other hand, he may become unduly optimistic and enterprising, undertaking much more than he is fit to do. Another type of individual, with different characteristics, becomes an idler, unable to concentrate, dreamy and sensitive. Often with these changes goes lack of care of the person—slovenliness in dress and in habits of personal cleanliness. A good indication of the general condition is obtained from the facial expression and the general bodily posture, both of which may help to portray the prevailing affective state.

Intellectual disorder, e.g. of memory, may profoundly influence conduct by the resulting failure to carry out the ordinary everyday tasks, and, further, by the depression, restlessness or irritability which may result from the patient's realization of his inefficiency.

A definite delusional or hallucinatory condition is apt to reveal itself in a bizarre type of conduct, entirely out of keeping with the person's known habits.

The degree of *co-operation* which the patient displays towards those who wish to help him is of considerable importance. An attitude of suspicion, or even actual antagonism, will show itself either in speech or in gesture.

In general, these are indications of the kind of information that can be obtained from observation at first meeting the patient. Disorders of behaviour will be considered in greater detail in the general and special sections.

Motor behaviour comprises: 1. bodily movement; and 2. stream of talk.

1. Bodily movement may be abnormal either in degree or quality. *General over-activity* may consist in a rapid succession of purposive acts, with few of them carried to a conclusion, and not directed to a continued objective ('psychomotor excitement', 'push' and 'pressure' of activity). The over-activity is said to be playful when accompanied by a tendency to mischievousness, the whole having an 'infectious' character. On the other hand, over-activity may consist of a repetition of movements, with little or no diversity, *e.g.* wringing of hands, pacing up and down. Such an oft-repeated movement is known as a *stereotypy*.

Stereotypy shows in several types of motor behaviour. It includes stereotypy of attitude, of movement and of speech. An action, or group of actions, or words monotonously repeated, or a posture maintained long after fatigue would ordinarily have caused relaxation, is a stereotypy. Such monotonous activity may begin as an expression of emotional perturbation, or may have at first a special complex-determined significance; but in either case it gradually becomes a habit, from which meaning has partly or wholly departed.

Perseveration, or the repetition of a recent movement in spite of the patient's effort to produce a new movement, is to be distinguished from stereotypy. It is in its particular instances transient, requires a stimulus and is associated particularly with cases showing changes in the brain substance.

Stereotypy of attitude is excellently exemplified in the 'Egyptian mummy' position maintained sometimes for years—the patient sitting with head bowed, palms downwards on the thighs. Stereotypy of speech consists in such phrases as this, which was a question asked by a patient day after day for years: 'Is the door open yet?'

A *mannerism* differs from a stereotypy in that it is not so monotonously repeated, and is more in keeping with the personality.

Partial over-activity may take the form of isolated movements such as the tics or habit spasms, which are to be differentiated by the relatively simple nature of the movements involved, by the general setting in which they occur and by the fact that the subject is acutely aware of them, and complains of them.

General reduction in activity shows all gradations up to complete immobility. It may be associated with diminution in initiative, or with actual resistance to movement (negativism, *vide infra*). Slowness of initiative and slowness of execution ('psychomotor retardation', initial and executive) usually accompany each other, but may be found apart.

Negativism, like stereotypy, shows itself in various spheres of activity. In general, it consists in responses exactly opposite to those normally elicited by a given stimulus. In the muscular field, it may show itself either as an actively opposite performance to that asked for—*e.g.* shutting the mouth when told to open it—and as a resistance to passive movement. In speech it forms a variety of mutism. Negativism is seen also in the retention of saliva, urine and faeces, and in lack of general co-operation.

Contrasting with negativism is the so-called *automatic obedience*, showing itself in echopraxia (repetition of actions seen), echolalia (repetition of words heard), and flexibilitas cerea (the maintenance of imposed postures).

Automatic movements or automatisms occur in a pathological sense, without the subject's being aware of their meaning, and even without his being aware of their happening at all. They have not the full co-operation of the personality; they may, in fact, when generalized, occur in the complete abeyance of the normal personality. Automatism may be local, *e.g.* automatic writing, or general, as in the fugues and somnambulisms. Stengel restricts the term fugue to describe a state of alteration of consciousness combined with an impulse to wander. He has drawn attention to the relationship between vagrancy in childhood and episodic wandering in adult life, the common factor being a broken or disturbed home life. Very frequently a fugue occurs in a state of depression, and indeed the going away or wandering is often symbolic of suicide. An epileptic disposition is also often associated.

The significance of *impulses* varies with the clinical setting in which they occur. The term impulse has usually been applied to sudden outbursts of activity which are supposed to occur with little or no deliberation. Our experience is that the great majority of impulses, although apparently sudden, are the outcome of a long preceding period of mental unrest. Hence it is impossible to make clear differentiation between impulses and compulsions. The latter have been supposed to arise against the subject's wishes, and to make him uneasy until they are carried into effect. The term compulsive is also used in a similar sense which will be dealt with under obsessional neurosis.

Posture may be defined as static motor activity. It is often a telling expression of the general condition, physical and mental, and especially of the emotional (herein called 'affective') state. The bent head, furrowed brow and drooping shoulders of sadness are well known. The over-erect attitude of the vain and proud man is sometimes seen in an exaggerated form in mental disorders, associated with phantasies of self-importance. Strained and unnatural positions may be maintained ('fixed positions') over long periods of time. These may be produced by the observer by virtue of the 'flexibilitas cerea' already mentioned. The absence of apparent fatigue in such cases is remarkable. 'Catalepsy' is a term sometimes used for any form of sustained immobility.

2. In the stream of talk a distinction has to be made between content and form—the content meaning what the patient says, and the form, how he says it. Form only will be discussed here. Content is more appropriately dealt with under 'thinking'. Talk may be more copious than normal ('pressure' or 'push' of

talk), but still perfectly coherent and logical. This is mere *volubility*, and is spontaneous, irrespective of the asking of questions. In *circumstantiality* there is much unnecessary detail and great spontaneity, but the object in view at the beginning is ultimately reached. Mrs. Nickleby is the classical example. In *flight of ideas* the stream is continuous but fragmentary, the connections being determined by chance associations between the fragments. The connections can be followed— there is a certain coherence—but the direction is frequently changed, often by chance stimuli from the environment (*distractibility*), and the original objective is quickly lost sight of. *Punning* and *rhyming* (sound or 'clang' associations) are not infrequent in a flight of ideas.

Slowing of the stream of talk shows itself, like slowing of activity, in initial and executive retardation. In certain states of emotional exaltation the utterances may be slow and stately; but this is a deliberate slowing—an affectation. There may be no utterance at all, even in response to repeated questioning—*mutism*. This may be associated with one of several conditions—as an accompaniment of extreme depression, an expression of complete indifference to the environment, a form of negativism, the result of a hallucinatory command, of a complex-determined belief, or of an extreme degree of difficulty in thinking. When mutism is an expression of negativism, it may be only partial, occurring in response to questions, while spontaneous utterance takes place.

Blocking is a sudden stoppage of the stream of talk, occurring usually apart from any environmental influences, and without the patient's being able to account for the stoppage.

Deprivation of thought is an extreme degree of blocking, when the stream is arrested for a time, and there is no longer any apparent content whatsoever.

Relevance of the patient's answers is an important point. In the types of disorder of the stream of talk so far mentioned, the answers, when given, are relevant; but there are many other types where the disorder of thought shows itself by an answer not in harmony with the question, or even conveying no meaning at all. This irrelevant type of answer is closely related to *disconnection*.

Disconnection may be of all degrees up to complete *incoherence*. The minor degrees of incoherence are known as 'scattering' and 'dilapidation'. The most complete disconnection has been called verbigeration—simply a flow of unconnected words, some of them often repeated. A 'word-salad' is a string of substantives poured out in a similar manner.

To be contrasted with these disorders of the stream of talk which result from disorders of thought are the paraphasic disorders depending on a focal organic lesion. These, too, consist of a jargon, and on this basis Stransky applied the term 'intrapsychic ataxia' to the incoherent types of talk found in certain purely psychogenic disorders. *Perseveration* is often associated with a true paraphasic disorder, and consists of the persistent repetition of one word or group of words, in spite of the patient's attempt to change the topic, and the observer's attempt to introduce other stimuli (in contrast with stereotypy).

Neologisms are words of the patient's own making, often portmanteau condensations of several other words, and having originally had a special meaning for the patient.

EMOTIONAL REACTION

'Affect' and 'mood' are both used to denote the emotional condition. 'Affect' is the term of preference, for it has none of the popular connotations of 'mood'. Affect is difficult to define. The language of emotion is in any case very inadequate. Affect can, perhaps, be called the subject's inner feeling at a given moment, but this is not a definition. The automatic (*i.e.* self-regulating) nature of affect is well known. The commoner normal affects are those of sadness, elation, fear and their variants—joy, happiness, gladness, sorrow, anxiety, etc. Pathological states show exaggeration or mixtures of normal moods, or apparent complete absence of affect (apathy). The chief criteria of abnormality are depth, duration and setting—*i.e.* how great the affect is, and under what psychological and material conditions it occurs. *Incongruity or disharmony* of affect—inappropriateness of affect to thought-content—is very important, and should always be looked for and noted.

Elation is a joyful affect, and is used for sheer happiness. It is pathological when out of accord with the patient's actual circumstances. *Exaltation* means something in addition to elation—an element of grandeur and pomposity is usually implied. In pure elation and in exaltation, everything that could not harmonize with the general emotional condition is shut out. Pure elation is generally 'infectious', the observer having a sympathetic sense of the patient's happiness. *Ecstasy* is a less robust happiness, usually with a mystical colouring. *Euphoria* is a generalized feeling of well-being, not amounting to a definite affect of gladness.

Affective depression or sadness is pathological when not warranted by the patient's condition or surroundings. The patient may say that he feels 'down-hearted' or 'sad'; but often no statement of affect can be elicited, and a conclusion has to be reached from posture, facies and other sources.

Anxiety as a technical term is a fear of danger usually from within, *e.g.* impending physical illness. It may occur either as a continued state of fear, or in episodic attacks. The episodes have the well-marked physical manifestations usually associated with fear. It is said that a typical acute anxiety attack has nothing but somatic symptoms: there is usually, however, a conscious fear, generally of illness, sometimes undefined.

Apprehension is usefully confined to the fear of external danger.

Apathy is an absence of affect, and can only be inferred from the patient's statement, or, failing that, from his failure to respond to stimuli which would otherwise call forth an affect of some kind. It carries no subjective sensation with it, and should thus be differentiated from sadness. Apathy may exist in a setting of depression—the patient complains that he cannot respond with any feeling to incidents which should arouse emotion of some kind. 'Indifference' and 'dullness' are used almost synonymously, and are descriptive of the lack of objective response, while apathy refers specifically to a lack of feeling.

H

Irritability, as a description of affect, is used in the ordinary sense of response elicited with undue readiness. It is usually associated with some other prevalent affect, and is a symptom of lack of harmony of the subject with his environment, and especially with a feeling of 'subjective insufficiency'—*i.e.* inability to perform ordinary tasks with the usual facility.

Morbid anger is an unprovoked angry outburst. It occurs in children, and in states of subnormality, and is then designated as 'tantrums'. The striking features are the lack of provocation, the violence, and the transient nature of the outburst.

It is disputed whether *suspicion* is an affect. Bleuler considered it more an intellectual than an affective condition. It is best included among the affects for practical purposes.

Emotional instability or *lability* is characterized by fluctuations in the affective condition without external cause. It occurs especially in gross organic lesions.

Emotional deterioration is a progressive failure to show the normal emotional responses, and is usually characterized by a childish, easily suggestible (facile) state.

THINKING

The general characteristics of thinking are altered in mental disorders. Phantasy assumes large proportions—*i.e.* there is less correction by reality than in the normal; and thinking passes but little into action. These are the two chief characteristics of 'autistic' thinking (Bleuler, 1950).

It follows that the content and course of thought are much more at the mercy of the affects and wishes of the mentally ill than in the case of healthy persons. Disorders of thought have to be inferred from the patient's utterance, including his own statements about his thinking, and from his conduct. Disorders of the form of thought have, for the most part, been discussed in disorders of the stream of talk. In certain conditions the patient makes complaint of *difficulty in thinking*. This may.be due either to difficulty in concentration on one topic from preoccupation with another, or to actual slowing of the thought processes.

In *preoccupation*, the patient continually reflects on one topic or group of topics, to the exclusion of environmental interests, and to the detriment of useful activity.

Obsessive thoughts (or obsessions) persist with full realization on the part of the subject that they are abnormal, and in spite of his endeavours to rid himself of them. In these two respects they differ from simple preoccupation.

Autochthonous ideas are 'thoughts coming to the patient in some unaccountable way, strange but not dependent on hallucination' (Meyer). In other cases the patient believes that someone reads his thoughts. This condition is an example of 'passivity' (*v. infra*).

The *idea of reference* consists in the subject's being acutely aware that something in the environment is intended to have a meaning for him, when, as a matter of fact, no such personal reference is intended. The idea of reference is thus partly based on some external circumstance, and is open to argument, whereas a fully developed delusion more often arises with apparent spontaneity. Moreover, the idea of reference is usually transitory, and is an example of a general tendency. It is based on personal sensitiveness, and is easily understood as an exaggeration of the normal; the abnormality lies rather in the source and acuteness of the sensitiveness—the source being affective in origin, and depending, for example, on feelings of exaltation or of guilt.

Ambivalence is a term coined by Bleuler to denote the co-existence of two contradictory ideas or feelings in consciousness, both of which cannot be true, but which are allowed to co-exist without rejection by the patient of either one. *Double orientation* is a case in point—the patient, for example, stating almost in the same breath that he is in Glasgow and in London. But ambivalence is also used by the Freudian school in a somewhat different sense to denote the entertaining of two opposite feelings towards the same person, *e.g.* both love and hate of a parent by the child.

The term *katathymic* has been used to characterize thinking along the lines determined by some complex.

DISORDERS OF THE CONTENT OF THOUGHT

A *delusion* is a belief which: 1. is not true to fact; 2. cannot be corrected by an appeal to the reason of the person entertaining it; and 3. is out of harmony with the individual's education and surroundings. As Mercier pointed out: 'The delusion is not an isolated disorder. . . . It is merely the superficial indication of a deep-seated and widespread disorder. . . . As a small island is but the summit of an immense mountain rising from the floor of the sea, so a delusion is merely the component part of a mental disease, extending, it may be, to the very foundations of the mind.'

The type of individual most likely to have delusions is one who normally shows a suspicious, argumentative attitude.

The nature of the delusion is important—to what extent it displays judgement or lack of it. There are degrees of reasonableness even in delusional beliefs, and their unreasonableness varies directly as the degree of impairment of judgement and as the depth of the affect which supports them.

Insight in the form of the patient's own criticism of the fact of his holding delusional beliefs is a related problem of even more significance. A person who entertains a false belief, but at the same time admits that it may be unjustified, and who may spontaneously talk of it as a delusion, is, as a rule, more amenable to treatment than one whose beliefs admit of no criticism.

Systematization denotes that the delusions are well knit, and that they form a fairly coherent system, logical within itself, if the premises once be granted. In other instances, the delusions are not correlated with each other; they are more or less isolated, and little or no attempt is made at logical correction.

Delusions have frequently been classified, but this is a matter of convenience only. A delusion has its full meaning only in the setting of the whole mental state of the individual possessing it. There are, however, certain uniformities which enable us to mention certain general types.

Delusions of grandeur and *delusions of persecution* are very common varieties, which are frequently found together. They result from the projection of instinctual trends. They are sometimes obviously compensatory for failure in some direction. For example, a girl deformed from poliomyelitis believed that she was descended from Royalty, was married and had a family. In other instances their foundations are not so clear, and for the persecutory type psychoanalysts have postulated a repressed homosexuality.

Another general type is formed by delusions of *sin*, delusions of *poverty* and *nihilistic* delusions. In the nihilistic variety, the patient declares that he does not exist, that there is no world, etc.

Hypochondria consists in a settled conviction of physical disease in the absence of any evidence thereof. As a symptom it occurs in many forms of mental illness. It is most common in depressions, especially in the depressions of the involutional period. It also occurs as part of a schizophrenic syndrome, when the hypochondriacal ideas are of the most grotesque kind. Sometimes hypochondria is hysterical in origin, and not infrequently what appears on superficial examination to be hypochondriasis is actually a chronic anxiety state. But a hypochondriacal conviction and preoccupation is sometimes found in which it is impossible to demonstrate that it is part of one of the larger syndromes. This occurs sometimes, for example, in elderly men, whose whole life centres round their supposed ailments—a withdrawal of interest, perhaps never strong, having occurred from the outer world, with a corresponding intense concentration on their bodily functions. Hypochondriacal delusions are closely connected with disordered bodily feelings. For example, delusions that the bowels are obstructed, and the stomach cancerous, are associated with dyspepsia and constipation.

Ideas of unreality are probably sometimes psychologically related to nihilistic delusions, but they are not usually delusional, the patient recognizing their abnormality, and complaining of the distress which they occasion. Everything is expressed as seeming different—the streets and houses look unusual, the patient wonders whether his friends are the same people as they were, or whether indeed they exist at all ('derealization'); he feels differently in himself, and may wonder whether he himself exists ('depersonalization'). Such ideas, and the feeling associated with them, are not at all uncommon in older children, especially the more intelligent, and as neurotic or depressive symptoms in adults. But even strong, healthy, normal people may experience such disturbing sensations. Sir Walter Scott in his *Journal* under date 17th February 1828 at Abbotsford wrote as follows: 'Yesterday at dinner time I was strangely haunted by what I would call the sense of pre-existence—videlicet, a confused idea that nothing that passed was said for the first time, that the same topics had been discussed, and the same persons had stated the same opinions on the same subjects. It is true there might have been some ground for recollections, considering that three at least of the company were old friends, and kept much company together; that is Justice-Clerk (The Right Hon. David Boyle), (Lord) Abercromby, and I. But the sensation was so strong as to resemble what is called a *mirage* in the desert or a calenture on board ship, when lakes are seen in the desert, and silvan landscapes in the sea. It was very distressing yesterday, and brought to my mind the fancies of Bishop Berkeley about an ideal world. There was a vile sense of want of reality in all I did and said. It made me gloomy and out of spirits, though I flatter myself it was not observed. The bodily feeling which most resembles this unpleasing hallucination is the giddy state which follows profuse bleeding when one feels as if walking on feather-beds and could not find a secure footing. I think the stomach has something to do with it. I drank several glasses of wine but these only augmented the disorder. I did not find the *in vino veritas* of the philosophers. Something of this insane feeling remains to-day, but a trifle only.'

Hallucinations are mental impressions of sensory vividness occurring without external stimulus. They are distinguished from *illusions*, which are similar impressions, depending, however, on a misinterpretation of an external stimulus.

The psychopathological basis of hallucinations is usually stated as follows: a wish is disowned by the ego and is repressed and so becomes unconscious, when it assumes independent activity, and forces its way back into the consciousness by the only method permitted to it—in disguise. The disowning by the ego makes it necessary that the disguised wish should appear to come from outside; it is accordingly projected, assuming an external sensory appearance when presented to consciousness.

Hallucinations may of course be physiogenic and not psychogenic in origin. Hallucinations occur in toxic states as the result of physiological disturbances, and brain lesions are responsible for hallucinations of a special type. Mechanical irritation of the uncus may cause hallucinations of taste and smell; and the same cause in the occipital lobe may produce flashes of light apparently before the eyes. The content of the hallucination is to some extent determined by individual psychological experience. In the case of at least one toxic substance, however, namely mescaline, the hallucinatory content is often entirely novel, and may even, in an apparently normal person, have characteristics that resemble schizophrenic experience.

Hallucinations occur even in normal people on rare occasions. William James gave several interesting instances in his *Principles of Psychology*.

The evidence for the presence of hallucinations is various—the patient may state frankly that he hears voices, but he more usually does so only after some time and trouble have been spent in obtaining his confidence. He may be seen in a listening attitude, or he may talk aloud as if answering someone, or his lips may be seen to move. The subject's response to hallucinations may be that of a passive listener, or he may reply to them. More active responses may be made to hallucinatory commands, which are often obeyed. Hallucinatory insults may lead to attacks on bystanders. In any case, hallucinations entail a certain amount of preoccupation.

The general setting in which hallucinations occur is of great significance, especially in relation to the question whether the setting is one of mental clearness, or of disorientation (*v. infra*).

Hallucinations may occur in any of the sensory fields. Auditory hallucinations are the most common. The simplest form is 'buzzing' or ringing in the ears.

More usually hallucinations are of the nature of voices, the spoken words being distinguished as a rule. They may occur in one or both ears, and sometimes appear, like hallucinations in general, to be determined in their incidence by local disease or irritation (*e.g.* chronic otitis media). It is their *content* that is of special interest—and it has to be remembered that their content is just as much a part of the patient's mental life as his ordinary thought, however foreign in origin they appear to be. Illustrating their affective basis and their dependence on factors similar to those producing delusions is their similar colouring—grandiose, persecutory or accusatory as the case may be. Thus the voices may be those of exalted personages, conversing with the patient, who derives therefrom much satisfaction; or they may call him unpleasant names, or accuse him of vile practices. Occasionally the voices seem to the patient to come from inside his body.

Visual hallucinations occur in their simplest form as flashes of light and colour. More complex visual hallucinations commonly occur in a setting of general disorientation, but they also appear in states of ecstasy. Organic disease of the optic connections in the central nervous system is a cause of hallucinations either of the simple or of the complex type.

Toxic factors such as alcohol and morphine produce complex hallucinations often of a terrifying kind, sometimes associated with withdrawal of the drug; and they may or may not be accompanied by disorientation. When of purely psychological origin, the hallucinations are usually in accord with the prevailing affective tendencies, *e.g.* the religious ecstatic sees angels in his visions.

Hallucinations of smell may (rarely) be the result of irritation of the uncus from organic disease. When they occur in a psychosis, they are usually unpleasant odours, *e.g.* a patient stated that there was a skunk in bed with him. Odours may be interpreted by the patient as gas being pumped into the room to annoy him. There is evidently a frequent relation between hallucinations of unpleasant odours and a sense of guilt with reference especially to sexual topics.

Hallucinations of taste are often associated with those of smell, and, like them, may rarely be the result of organic disease. They occur infrequently in psychoses. Illusions of taste are more common, and are related to affective conditions (usually suspicion)—the food tastes queerly, and is inferred to be poisoned.

Hallucinations of touch (haptic hallucinations) and other skin sensations are common—for example, in the form of creeping sensations under the skin (*formication*—the 'cocaine bug'). Sensations 'like electricity' are related to sex-feelings, unrecognized as such by the patient. All kinds of paraesthesia—numbness, tingling, pains, etc.—occur, and are sometimes used as part of a delusional scheme, the persecuted patient inferring that some injury to him is being attempted. Sensations in the genital or anal regions help to substantiate delusions of assault.

In *pseudo-hallucinations* the patient has the vivid sensory experience, but realizes that it has no external foundation.

Reflex hallucinations occur in one sensory sphere as the result of irritation in another. An auditory sensation may in this way arise from irritation in the region of the inferior alveolar nerve (due to a carious tooth).

In *Lilliputian* or *microptic hallucinations*, the objects seen appear much reduced in scale. They are usually of very pleasant content and bright in colour. The patient is amused at seeing diminutive women and children in bright clothing. They have been observed in cases of scarlet and typhoid fever and in intoxications by alcohol, chloroform and ether.

Hypnagogic hallucinations occur in the state between sleeping and waking. They can be recognized from the conditions under which they occur, including the accompanying sensation of drowsiness, and from their dream-like nature, as well as from the fact that the subject who experiences them usually realizes their hallucinatory nature.

Impressions that part of one's body is being moved are sometimes described as *psychomotor hallucinations*. These are better understood under ideas of passivity.

Ideas and feelings of passivity or influence include such diverse ideas of the patient as that his thoughts are being read, his limbs moved without his control or consent and without visible agency, or even that he is entirely under the control of someone in the environment. Such ideas, or less well-defined feelings, may be associated with motor phenomena—flexibilitas cerea, and the maintenance of fixed attitudes. They are then expressions of a general attitude of passivity, and are sometimes the reflection of a wish, not consciously formulated, to be under another's control. From the psychoanalytic point of view, such ideas and signs have been interpreted in certain conditions as part of the attitude of the passive homosexual. In some conditions, especially where the phenomena are less generalized, the ideas of influence are more probably the interpretation of certain automatic motor acts—automatic because occurring without the co-operation of the personality, and dependent, it is supposed, on the activity of certain dissociated tendencies. The idea that one's thoughts are being read may in some instances rest on an affective basis of guilt.

ORIENTATION

Orientation is the appreciation of one's temporal, spatial and personal relations at the present moment. It may be deranged on either a psychogenic or a physiogenic basis. It is important to know whether the disorientation is complete or partial. Simple inattention, from distractibility or from general lack of interest, may cause partial disorientation. Strong affects may also do so, causing a patient to give for the actual date an erroneous one in which he is particularly interested. The answer in these cases must be judged from the general setting of memory, orientation in other respects and general clearness. Inattention and lack of interest may also cause random answers to be given, when closer questioning may elicit the correct information.

It is in organic conditions that orientation is most frequently lost, wholly or partially. In cases of this kind, a false orientation is often given, and this statement of orientation itself changes rapidly.

MEMORY

Disorders of memory are commonly divided into *amnesias, paramnesias* and *hypermnesias*.

Amnesia, or absence of memory, may be complete or partial, continuous, periodic or circumscribed. Complete amnesia, *i.e.* for the entire previous existence, is rare. Amnesia, confined to recent events and progressive (*anterograde*), is characteristic of senile cerebral degeneration. In the gradually extending amnesia of advancing degeneration, rote memory tends to be retained better than other kinds. *Retrograde amnesia* involves only past events, and is not progressive.

Circumscribed amnesia involves some isolated event, or group of events, which usually have had a strong affective meaning; but in many cases of brain trauma there is a localized amnesia which persists for events immediately before and immediately after the accident.

Paramnesia denotes false recollection—the patient relates with conviction and circumstantiality events which never took place, or gives a false colouring to those that did happen. *Confabulation* is the term applied to the fabrication of memories in this way, and *retrospective falsification* to the adding of false details and meanings to a true memory. *Pseudo-reminiscence* covers both these meanings. An outstanding example of fabrication of memory occurs in *pseudologia phantastica* (*pathological lying*).

Hypermnesia or excessive retention of memories, especially of detail, is found in certain prodigies, and in certain mental disorders, especially paranoid psychoses and hypomania. In the former of these two conditions it is related to the general affective tendencies, and any detail is remembered which might possibly have a bearing on the delusional topics.

A variety of paramnesia, known as the *déjà vu* phenomenon, refers to the not uncommon experience of seeing something (or hearing it) with the feeling that one has seen it before, but does not know when or where. Such an experience occurs sometimes in epilepsy, as well as in normal persons. The basis may lie in some real experience, which has been forgotten; something which one has read and does not clearly recollect; or in some previous phantasy, conscious or unconscious, of waking- or dream-life. Where the feeling of *déjà vu* is continuous, as in an epileptic recorded by Kinnier Wilson, the term 'reduplicative paramnesia' has been applied. Zangwill (1941) has made a careful study of a case of paramnesia from a volume of English memoirs entitled *Our Old Home*, by Nathaniel Hawthorne. Zangwill points out that theories regarding *déjà vu* fall into two broad groups. On the one hand the phenomenon is explained in terms of transient inability to distinguish old from new and past from present. This difference is not considered to be dependent on the external setting, the condition being regarded as endogenous and due to a momentary disorder of mental synthesis. It has been thought that there may be an associated organic predisposing condition, such as fatigue or constitutional inadequacy. On the other hand, the phenomenon is regarded as reactive or determined by some specific peculiarity of the setting or environment in which it occurs. This theory suggests the possibility of a psychological linkage between the constitution in *déjà vu* and some previous experience or disposition in the history of the individual. The matter is one which may be determined by unconscious trends and, in consequence, this theory stresses the psychogenic factors. On the basis of the study of the particular case of Hawthorne, Zangwill concluded that Hawthorne's experience of *déjà vu* was a reactive state co-determined by an early (and probably unconscious) phantasy and an accident of circumstance.

ATTENTION

This is sometimes loosely called 'mental tension', or regarded as a manifestation of that ill-defined entity; it may be increased or diminished. Decreased attention to the environment may be the outcome of lack of interest, or of a more deliberate shutting-out (in its extreme form a manifestation of negativism). A patient's attention varies inversely with his preoccupation with his own problems. Hence any affective disturbance may cause a diminution in useful attention.

Inability to attend, in spite of the wish to do so, is seen in organic diseases (toxins and in structural cerebral lesions). 'Fluctuation of attention', in which the attention varies to a much greater extent than in the normal, is a fairly characteristic disorder in these conditions, in which also perseveration of previous impressions is sometimes an interfering factor in attention, new impressions being hindered by the persistence of old ones. It has been pointed out by Bleuler that active attention is often good in organic cases, while passive attention is poor; and that in 'functional' disorders (*e.g.* schizophrenia) the reverse is true. *Blunting of attention* is an extreme form of inattention, and occurs in stuporous states, when even nocuous stimuli, *e.g.* pin-pricks, fail to elicit a response.

Increase of attention (*hyperprosexia*) is less common, and is sometimes associated with a sensory hyperaesthesia, *e.g.* auditory hyperaesthesia, and with certain excitements (hypomania). But increased attention is usually affectively and selectively determined. *Distractibility* is a disorder of the attention in which the patient gives attention to every passing stimulus; consequently his attention passes very rapidly from one object to another.

Comprehension (or *apperception*) is impaired by organic (cerebral) disorder, whether from toxins or from grosser lesions. Comprehension may be modified in certain directions by affects—misunderstandings occur in line with them, or comprehension may suffer from the inattention that comes from apathy.

JUDGEMENT

Judgement depends on the ability to bring together two contrasting propositions, and to discriminate that one which is in closer accord with the general body of the subject's knowledge. Anything which interferes with associative processes will therefore impair judgement; hence toxins, organic lesions and congenitally defective cerebral organization lead to defective judgement. But it is now also generally admitted that judgement is much more dependent on affect than was formerly believed. A delusion is the result of a judgement in which affect has had excessive weight. It is not, however, difficult as a rule to distinguish the affectively perverted judgement from a judgement defective from the other causes mentioned; the latter will be displayed in a wide variety of general topics of indifferent interest.

SUGGESTIBILITY

This becomes abnormal when the patient habitually conforms with unusual readiness to suggestions made to him. It is common in neurotics, and Babinski attempted to make suggestibility the fundamental factor in hysteria, on which all the wide variety of symptoms depends. Suggestibility is very much influenced by the relation of the patient to the person making the suggestion. A suggestion is much more likely to be effective if coming from someone whom the patient likes and trusts. Crude examples of suggestibility, not seen in neurotics, are the forms of automatic obedience—echopraxia, echolalia and flexibilitas cerea, already described.

Negative suggestibility, in which the subject habitually does the opposite to what is suggested to him, is seen in spoiled children, even in early infancy—the infant refusing the bottle offered by the over-solicitous mother, but taking food readily if the mother's fussiness is corrected. It is seen in more obvious and more direct form in certain mental disorders as the so-called negativism, already described.

Suggestibility plays a part, among other factors, in the genesis of *folie à deux* or 'communicated insanity', which is the term applied when two persons closely associated with one another suffer a psychosis simultaneously, and when one member of the pair appears to have influenced the other. The condition is not of course necessarily confined to two persons, and may involve three or even more (*folie à trois*, etc.). It is commonest in persons living secluded lives. Husband and wife, brother and sister, or parent and child, or friends of the same sex living closely together are the usual subjects of the condition. It is usually either a paranoid or manic-depressive state. Craike and Slater (1945) drew attention to a case of *folie à deux* in uniovular twins reared apart. The twins were separated at nine months, were brought up in different families in different parts of the country, met for the first time at the age of 24, never lived together or had any close contact with one another, but each in due course developed a paranoid psychosis, each involving the other in her own system of delusional ideas.

CONSCIOUSNESS

Under disturbances of consciousness are usually included sleep, various psychogenic disturbances (*i.e.* produced and removable by psychic means, and occurring without demonstrable physical basis), such as the multiple personalities, transformations and depersonalizations, somnambulisms, twilight states, trances, hysterical deliria and stupors; and the physically determined disorders such as deliria, stupors and comas.

SLEEP

All kinds of disturbances are possible. Sleep may be diminished, abolished or increased in quantity (hyposomnia, insomnia and hypersomnia), or the sleep rhythm may be inverted, so that the patient sleeps by day and is awake by night. Diminution in sleep may be due to delay in falling asleep (from preoccupation, anxiety, habit or physical disease), to early waking (from depression), or from interruption, *e.g.* by terrifying dreams.

The most nearly complete deprivation of sleep occurs in certain psychotic patients (manic-depressives). Experimental deprivation of sleep in man for three days has failed to show any change in metabolism. The subjective symptoms produced by artificial insomnia are quickly abolished by permitting sleep. Many normal people, including intellectuals, require comparatively little sleep. William Hunter habitually slept only four hours per night.

Apart from mental disorder arising from demonstrable physical disease, of the brain or of the body generally, there are few mental disorders accompanied by increase in the amount of sleep. Of physical disorders, increased intracranial pressure from whatever cause, tumours and inflammatory disease of the base of the brain, and general toxaemia are the commonest causes of increase in the amount of sleep. The drowsiness that appeared in some cases was the reason for the term 'lethargic' applied to what is now known as epidemic encephalitis. In epidemic encephalitis inversion of the sleep rhythm was not infrequent.

A *somnambulism* is a general automatism occurring in the course of, and interrupting, normal sleep. In this condition the patient rises from sleep, disregards the ordinary significance of his environment and those in it, and behaves as if he were living in an environment conjured up by himself. If spoken to, not brusquely, he may reply in terms of the phantasy which he is enacting. If roughly stimulated, he may regain full consciousness, or pass into a trance state of immobility, muscular flaccidity and lack of response of any kind. Patients in somnambulic states have sometimes met with unfortunate accidents, *e.g.* scalding, or even death from drowning.

STUPOR

In stupor the subject's activity is reduced to a minimum. There is no response to any stimulus, external or internal. In the deepest variety, not only is there no muscular activity even with regard to nutrition and evacuation, except (in some cases) that involved in the maintenance of posture, but there is no response to external stimuli, whether these be supplied by questions or actual pain. Stupor may be either of psychogenic or organic origin, or both. The maintenance of postures with resistiveness occurs more characteristically in cases of psychogenic origin, but it may occur, *e.g.*, in uraemic stupor.

In the lesser degrees of stupor, the patient may sometimes be partially roused for a moment or two to pay some attention to, or even to answer, simple questions. A very striking feature of the stupor (so-called 'lethargy') of epidemic encephalitis was the ability of the patient to answer questions to the point when roused for a time. In psychogenic stupor, the suddenness with which the patient may pass from stupor to considerable activity is in contrast with the gradual recovery from the stupor of physical disease.

Coma is but the profoundest degree of stupor; all consciousness is lost; there is no voluntary activity of any kind.

DELIRIUM

Delirium is a symptom-complex consisting essentially in disorientation and hallucination, and very commonly having an accompanying affective disturbance, especially of fear. It is in its typical form the result of a toxic process, but psychogenic deliria are not unknown. These are apt to be characterized by a certain grotesqueness, or by the appearance of a certain preponderant affect (other than fear) running through them.

TYPE OF PERSONALITY IN PSYCHOSES

Personality, as used in clinical psychiatry, is the integrated activity of all the reaction-tendencies of the daily life of the individual. It is, in other words, the person as he is known to his friends. This is the simple clinical connotation of the word. It has lately been the custom to use the term also in a much wider sense, regarding personality as the total integrated expression of the various 'levels' of which the individual is constructed—the lowest, or vegetative level (endocrine-autonomic), the sensorimotor level (central nervous system) and the psychic level.

Certain personalities in this sense are less adapted to meet environmental influences adequately than others. This may be the result of inherited handicap or of faulty training and habit. The result is a malintegration, in the sense of biological inefficiency. It has been found that personalities of this kind are specially prone to develop mental illness (which is, by our definition, a phenomenon of maladaptation). Thus a 'psychopathic personality' is recognized in individuals who habitually display excess or defect of emotional reactions, together with impaired judgement and inadequate or antisocial behaviour, and in whom there commonly occur transient or persistent mental disturbances, which are merely exaggerations of their normal condition. In other instances mental illness appears to be not simply an exaggerated development of the personality, but implies also a qualitative change in it. In schizophrenia it is found that in a strikingly large percentage the personality that existed before the disease occurred or was recognized was of the so-called 'shut-in' type (see Chapter 11, 'Schizophrenic Reaction -Types', p. 257). This is similar to an extreme degree of introversion (Jung) and to the 'schizoid' personality type of Kretschmer. The type of personality that is prone to manic-depressive illness is the so-called syntonic (Bleuler) or cycloid (Kretschmer) or cyclothymic personality. This type represents a marked degree of extroversion, and is characterized by its affective lability and responsiveness. In epileptics, long before convulsions develop, it is sometimes possible to observe an overwhelming egoism, with moodiness, irritability, and sometimes a shallow hypocritical religiosity. Preceding the onset of paranoid psychoses, there is often a long-standing history of sensitiveness, tendency to suspicion, and inability to take criticism. These are the principal types of personality related to the development of mental illness which have so far been recognized. The importance of further work in this direction is obvious, not only from the point of view of prevention, but also for the prognosis of mental disorder—it is probable that the outlook in many psychoses depends as much (or more) on the type of pre-existing personality as on the type of psychosis.

MULTIPLE PERSONALITY

'Double' and 'multiple' personality are the terms applied when the same individual at different times appears to be in possession of entirely different mental content, disposition and character, and when one of the different phases shows complete ignorance of the other, an ignorance which may be reciprocal. Each 'sub-personality' (for the personality in these conditions at least is compounded of a series of sub- or partial personalities) is said to be 'dissociated' from the total personality, and from the other sub-personalities, on each occasion when its activities are fully conscious and control the motor apparatus of the individual. (See further under 'Hysteria', p. 153).

PERSONALITY IN MENTAL SYNDROMES

The phrase 'preservation of the personality' is used in clinical work to denote that, in spite of some disease process, the previous traits of personality are clearly recognizable, and especially in a narrower sense when the patient preserves his ordinary social decorum and keeps his clothes, etc., neat and tidy. Thus, general paralysis, which is a sweeping disorder, and involves complete and rapid disintegration of the personality, contrasts with arteriosclerotic brain disease, where in the early stages at least the patient has complete insight for his illness, feels it keenly and endeavours to preserve his previous social appearance.

Depersonalization

Depersonalization or a feeling of unreality is a subjective state which may occur in any morbid psychological reaction, but it is especially common in depressive states either in young people or in those at the involutional period of life. For convenience, this state of depersonalization can be described as occurring in the allo-, somato- and auto-psychic fields, e.g. the flowers do not look real; my legs are not legs at all; I am not I, I cannot die. Mapother suggested that in those cases in which the environment is implicated the term derealization is preferable to depersonalization; the two conditions, however, frequently occur together. For instance, a young lady talked as follows: 'Life is so funny, I look at things and I cannot realize them; I am not real, I am nothing, nothing at all,

I go about in a dream, I feel I do not know who my husband is or who my baby is; I feel that I am not a person at all; the wool I knit with seems strange, and as for reading I don't know that I can read.' A somewhat similar case has been quoted by H. K. Johnson: 'I have not a moment of comfort and no human sensations, surrounded by all that can render life happy and agreeable, still to me the faculty of enjoyment and of feeling is wanting—both have become physical impossibilities. In everything, even in the most tender caresses of my children, I find only bitterness. I cover them with kisses, but there is something between their life and mine, and this horrid something is between me and all the enjoyment of life.'

It should be emphasized that such cases often show a marked fluctuation in mood. Even when describing the most extraordinary sensations and feelings they may themselves be amused by their own descriptions and may talk with considerable animation and vehemence. It is this paradoxical situation, this apparent incongruity between mood and thought which has led some observers to relate such states to a schizophrenic process. That, however, is more apparent than real, because in Shorvon's (1946) review of a group of 66 cases he remarked on the frequency of an acute onset, and the close relationship to migraine and obsessional states. Irrespective of the time factor, the course of the disorder is towards spontaneous recovery.

Transformation of the Personality

This is a phrase sometimes used to designate the not uncommon condition when the patient has a delusional belief that he is some other person, and to some extent acts upon that belief—for example, an epileptic patient periodically believed himself to be Christ, allowed his beard to grow and wrote letters to the newspapers protesting against his detention, and signing himself 'Yours truly, Jesus Christ'. Another type of periodic personality transformation, but not of this bizarre type, is that furnished by the multiple personalities already referred to. More lasting and more bizarre transformations are seen in the schizophrenics, who believe themselves to be a king or some other dignitary. In schizophrenics these transformations are often fairly sudden, and the rôle is very poorly sustained—a 'princess of the blood royal' will scrub the floor without protest. A gradual transformation of the personality, where the behaviour shows more consonance with the delusional beliefs, is characteristic of paranoid psychosis.

A certain vagueness and diffuseness of the concept and feeling of personality is common in schizophrenia. There is a 'suspension of the clear distinction between the ego and the environment, in which, for the ego, the clear presence of the external world vanishes' (Jaspers).

The most extensive, and at the same time most profound, of all personality changes is the 'splitting of the personality' that occurs in advanced schizophrenia. This consists not simply in a disintegration of the personality, so that the latest acquired reactions crumble away and leave only the primitive functions, but there is rather a fragmentation or splitting-up of the entire personality, with apparent independent activity of the individual split-off functions, with the result that all kinds of incongruities of thought and action are possible. Hence the schizophrenic's conduct lacks coherence and purpose, and often appears utterly bizarre, and he may appear happy when his thought content is tragic, or apathetic when he believes himself the recipient of untold wealth. He may perform actions which he does not want to perform, or feel that his thoughts belong to someone else. Some of the split-off reactions are projected and appear as hallucinations, or as delusions.

REFERENCES

Bleuler, E. (1950) *Dementia Praecox*, New York.
Craike, W. H., and Slater, E. (1945) *Brain*, **68**, 213.
Shorvon, H. J. (1946) *Proc. roy. Soc. Med.*, **39**, 779.
Zangwill, O. L. (1941) *Character and Pers.*, **13**, 246.

7

GENERAL PSYCHOPATHOLOGY

Mental development occurs in response to the needs of adaptation. The mind grows in complexity as the necessary adaptations multiply. The adult mind is far more complex than that of the child; the European's more complex than that of the unsophisticated native of Borneo. Adaptation implies originally conflict, the conflict in human beings between certain forces inborn in them and the environmental circumstances. It will be convenient, therefore, to consider mental development under three heads: 1. the nature and working of the inborn forces; 2. the nature of the environmental influences; and 3. the methods and means of mental adjustments between them. The discussion of the genesis of symptoms (maladjustments) will then be possible.

INSTINCTUAL DEVELOPMENT

The inborn forces are commonly called *instincts*. They are primary data, being given in the innate equipment of the organism. A common confusion occurs in failing to distinguish between instincts in this sense, and the innate paths or patterns which they utilize for their expression, and which are probably fewer in man than in any other animal. The prevailing instinctive forces, however, are the same in man and animals. There are probably only two, *self-preservation* and *sex*. Some add a third—the so-called *herd* instinct. At birth in man the instincts have but few patterns of expression, but these multiply (under environmental influences) as the age of the individual increases, so that there are two varieties of pattern of instinctive expression—inherited and acquired. It is in the number and complexity of his acquired patterns that man surpasses the lower animals. Some of the patterns which are actually inherited do not mature till after birth— the myelinization of the brain is not complete. The patterns of expression of the self-preservative instinct are adequate from an early age (although they continually multiply), while those for sex are much less developed, and do not begin to approach completion till puberty is reached. The process of unhindered satisfaction of an instinct—*i.e.* where the reaction-patterns are in full play—is accompanied by a conscious feeling of pleasure, and frustration of the process by unpleasure—a kind of pain. In early life all the activities of the organism are concerned with the immediate increase of pleasurable, and the reduction of painful, stimuli (the so-called *pleasure-principle*). Later, the increasing demands of reality make necessary a postponement of pleasurable attainment until certain mediate conditions have been fulfilled—this has been described as obedience to the *reality-principle*. Instincts are in themselves not conscious, but the feelings that accompany their processes of satisfaction or frustration are conscious. The self-preservative instinct attains satisfaction fairly readily from birth onwards, although not without repeated and increasing effort on the part of the organism. The sexual instinct is much more persistently frustrated. The conscious expression of an instinct seeking satisfaction is a *wish* or desire. This wish or desire by virtue of the representative-imaginative function of consciousness can have a definite conscious *object*, through which the general *aim* of the instinct can be fulfilled. The sexual instinct has a development peculiarly its own, in that its object normally changes at various stages of life although its general aim remains the same (Freud). First of all it attains satisfaction in the body of the individual himself—the *auto-erotic* stage. In this auto-erotic stage, satisfaction giving a pleasurable feeling akin to sexual pleasure is attainable by stimulation of almost any part of the body surface, but especially of certain *erotogenic* zones (mouth, anus, etc.). Thus, for example, stimulation of the mouth area is associated with pleasurable sensuous feeling—an association which persists in adult life. Similarly stimulation of the zone of the anus is, at least in some individuals, associated with pleasurable feeling, and this persists in adult life in a few of them as 'anal erotism'. In the later stages of development of the sexual instinct, these regions usually lose most or all of their pleasure-giving possibilities, which are now largely confined to the zone of the genitals. In the second or *homosexual* stage, the object of the sexual instinct becomes another individual, but of the same sex, and in the third or *heterosexual* stage, of the opposite sex. This is probably the normal development in which the stages overlap. But it may be arrested ('fixated' is the technical term) at any stage—one of the erotogenic zones may continue to afford sensual pleasure to as great an extent, or greater, than the genital zone; or the development with reference to the object may not go beyond the auto-erotic or homosexual stage. Further, 'bi-sexuality' has to be taken into account. The individual's sexual instinct is capable of expression and satisfaction in two opposite ways—with the individual as active or the individual as passive. In either case the process of satisfaction gives pleasure, but in the passive rôle the general feeling-tone involves a certain amount of pain; while in the active rôle evidently a certain amount of the pleasurable feeling may be derived from the inflicting of pain on the sexual object. These are called respectively the 'sadistic' or active and 'masochistic' or passive part-expressions of the sexual instinct.

A later psychoanalytic theory came to regard these tendencies as expressions not of the sexual instinct but of an aggressive or destructive instinct. According to this view there are two broad groups of instincts; the life instincts or 'eros', using a collective term, and the death instincts. Most instinctive manifestations are held to be the results of the fusion of these two broad groups. Hence the appearance of sadistic and masochistic elements in sexual relationships. This distinction cuts across the distinction formerly made between self-preservative and sexual instincts. Instead we have a life instinct which directs itself either to the aims and objects of self or those of sex, and on the other hand an aggressive instinct or group of instincts which find their object more usually in the external world but sometimes turn back from that on to the ego itself, producing, according to Freud, such phenomena as automatic

I

self punishment, *e.g.* in patients with whom everything seems to go wrong all their lives.

Affect

'Affect' or emotion arises in consciousness when an instinct is prevented from attaining easy complete satisfaction. Emotion and feeling-tone (pleasure and unpleasure) are not the same. Pleasure occurs during the process of satisfying an instinct; emotion probably only if there is some obstruction to the process of satisfaction. All emotions can be divided into two classes—those with a pleasant and those with an unpleasant, feeling-tone, the latter occurring when obstruction is for the moment complete.

Consciousness

Consciousness (sensations, feelings, emotions, wishes or desires and ideas) arises when instincts, themselves unconscious, are in action, requiring certain complicated adaptations to the environment for the satisfaction of the instinct. Consciousness is not an otiose creation. It has a function, the representative-imaginative function, especially when satisfaction has to be delayed in accordance with the so-called 'reality principle', in facilitating the satisfaction of instinctive needs. The instinct is represented in consciousness by a wish, and its object by an image. The wish and the image are in some way associated by a tension furnished by the instinct, and this tension brings about the motor adjustment necessary for the fulfilment of the wish (satisfaction of the instinct).

In the course of the individual's experience, certain mental events have a peculiar intimacy; such events become welded together to form the ego or self. Another group of mental events is attributed to the environment—'projection' is the attributing of subjective impressions to external causes. But their conscious representations form part of the experience of the self. Mental events are retained (memory), but do not persist in consciousness unless they continue to minister to an immediate need. They are said to become *unconscious*. Thus one's knowledge of French, say, remains unconscious while one is talking English. Although the content of consciousness is small at any moment of time, previous conscious events, being retained (memory), can be revived (recollection or recall). Many of these revivable unconscious events have had the peculiar intimacy mentioned and have been incorporated in the ego; hence the ego or self is composed of certain conscious facts of the moment together with a great many revivable mental events. The latter are, at any moment of time, for the most part unconscious, *i.e.* not conscious. 'Preconscious' is the term often used for this easily accessible type of unconscious fact.

But there is another type of unconscious fact—one which has proved distasteful to the ego and has been disowned by it. The forgetting of such facts occurs in an automatic way, and this process is known as repression. The percipient ego may or may not be aware of the occurrence, the repression itself being done largely by a part of the ego which is jointly the product of the ego's conception of the environmental demands and, on the other hand, of the instinctive urges. The joint product is the super-ego which Freud believed to be composed fundamentally of the introjected images of persons, especially the parents and those on whose conduct the child has modelled himself.

The super-ego is therefore the result of a process of identification with the parents and of wanting to be like them. The nature of the super-ego, it should be noted, is held to be coloured very much by the component it contains from the aggressive instinct. The aggressive component is derived in this way: the child projects his own aggression on to one or other of the parents, picturing the rival parent as having the same aggressive impulses as himself. Therefore when the parental image is introjected the aggressive aspect is introjected along with it. Thus the super-ego is felt to be severe as well as kind. This aspect of severity is supposed to be responsible for the feeling of guilt so commonly encountered. It is recognized that the super-ego is to a large extent an unconscious formation and consequently the repression carried out by it occurs unconsciously and therefore automatically.

Yet another type of unconscious content has never reached consciousness. Such are many feelings and tendencies closely connected with the instincts. This unconscious reservoir of instincts and feelings and attitudes connected with them has been subsumed by Freud under the term 'Id'. Many of the items of the conscious content, and of the repressed unconscious content, were by Freud regarded as originally derivatives of this primal reservoir.

Strictly speaking, 'unconscious' feelings, emotions, wishes and ideas are a contradiction in terms. But particular aspects of the instincts of which feelings, etc., are the conscious representations can persist in an 'unconscious' form. The term 'unconscious' is itself a bad one, since it defines something in terms of what it is not.

That part of the individual's unconscious which is inherited, including the 'instinctive' part, has been called the racial unconscious (Jung).

The inherited and the acquired possibilities of reaction—the instinctive re-action-patterns—have something associated with them (something designated above, instinctive forces), which converts them from mere possibilities of reaction to actual functioning elements, and the reactions they subserve must occur if life is to be sustained at all. The something which forces these patterns into action it is usual to regard as analogous to the 'energy' of physics. This psychical 'energy', if we may call it so for brevity, is commonly labelled 'libido'. The libido is regarded as being at the disposal of any reaction which subserves an instinct. In Jung's original sense of the term, the energy designated 'libido' was of a general kind, and applied to any instinctive force; but in Freud's usage libido was always associated with the sexual instinct. It is to a certain extent transferable from one reaction to another. When it is transferred from the service of a reaction which fulfils the ordinary instinctive aim more or less closely to one which fulfils that aim in a less direct way, the libido is said to take part in a reaction of 'sublimation' of the instinct. Freud had a special theory of the libido, of which the barest outline follows. In early life, as we have seen, instinctive satisfaction is largely obtained from the individual's own body. The libido at the service of the instincts is then pictured as directed inwards—the auto-erotic direction of the libido. As development proceeds, instinctive satisfaction is obtained increasingly from without; and the libido is directed to external objects. The libido is then said to expend itself partly in keeping the mental representation of these objects in consciousness: it is 'attached' to these mental representations and is spoken of as 'object-libido'. By this time self is not only a succession of experiences with a common feeling of intimacy: it is a developed concept. Sometimes it happens that very little of the total libido is attached to object-representations, and most to the concept of the self. That part of the libido which is attached to the concept of the self is called 'narcissistic libido'. 'Regression' is the return to an earlier stage of development of the individual personality, and, in the language of the libido-theory, consists in a withdrawal of libido from its present object to objects characteristic of an earlier stage of psychosexual development.

A distinction is made in Freudian theory between the *aim* and the *object* of the libido, the aim being the mode of satisfaction and the object the person with whom satisfaction is desired. The aim may change with reference to the same object according to the developmental stage.

The aim is believed to be concerned first with the satisfaction of oral cravings and then with anal. Each of these stages is divided into two; satisfaction is obtained first by sucking and later by biting in the oral stage; and in the anal stage of libidinal organization first by expelling or annihilating and then by retaining, possessing or holding fast. These aims are sought with reference to an object in the environment, usually one of the parents or a parent substitute. It will be seen that in the second and third phases the aggressive aspect predominates and this aspect is directed towards an object otherwise loved, *i.e.* an example of ambivalence. In this way the foundations of guilt feelings are supposed to be laid in the pre-genital stages of libidinal organization. In the next stage, the so-called phallic stage, satisfaction is concerned with the genital zone, still with incomplete investment of the object with libido. The final stage is said to occur when the female genitals receive for the first time the recognition that the male genitals have previously obtained, and complete object-love is now said to be possible.

Phantasy

We have seen that an important mental function is the conscious representation of an object or end with which a desire is associated. The occurrence of this conscious representation creates a state of tension (furnished by the instincts whose end is the conscious representation) which issues in bodily activities adequate to attain the desired end. Sometimes, however, these activities are not permitted to take place, and satisfaction of the instinct does not then occur. But in such an event the representation sometimes continues to be held in consciousness, and even to be elaborated, the energy which should have actuated the necessary bodily movements dissipating itself instead in the elaborative process. This is the development of phantasy and the achievement of phantastic wish-fulfilment at the expense of application of energy and activity to reality—at the cost, in other words, of adaptation to reality. The state of conscious pre-occupation with phantasy is called *introversion*, to distinguish it from the normal adaptation, which is the direction of the energy or libido outwards to reality (*extroversion*).

Phantasy is an important part of normal mental life, and it can serve a useful purpose if kept in sufficiently close conformity with reality to form the basis of a scheme of future action. Ambition, for example, is a phantasy, and is patho-logical only if real striving is abandoned for indulgence in the phantasy alone. The child's formulations of reality are phantastic in nature. His father is a great man, his mother the personification of goodness. He may identify himself very closely with these *imagines* (embellished concepts not in strict conformity with reality), and when these illusions which lapse more or less into unconsciousness are encroached upon in later life by contact with reality, he will feel the encroach-ment keenly, although unconscious of the source of this feeling, since the source has lapsed long ago into the unconscious. The resulting emotional perturbation leads to much thinking—an obsessive preoccupation, which is really an attempt to reconcile the real with the unconscious ideal. Since the motivation of this continued thinking is unconscious, the thinking appears in consciousness as a 'symptom' and forms one type of the obsessional neuroses (see Chapter 8).

ENVIRONMENTAL INFLUENCES

In early infantile life the child remains in the closest association with the mother. The child being still in a primary undifferentiated phase of conscious-ness, the associations of the earliest days are entirely subjective, *i.e.* there is at this stage no objectivation, no differentiation of the mother from himself; and his interest follows the direction of his mother's interest—namely, his own body. At this stage and later, his slightest gestures are followed by satis-faction of his instinctive nutritional needs—the stage of omnipotence (of 'magic' gesture and 'magic' words—Ferenczi). Soon, however, this primary subjective phase begins to pass, reality makes increasing demands on his con-sideration and he has to conform increasingly to it if he would compass the satisfaction of his instincts. His consciousness increases in extent, and a distinc-tion arises mentally between self and objective reality—his conscious experience is divided into self-consciousness and object consciousness. Both are experiences of the self, but the source of the second is projected. Object consciousness is at first a vague affair, the details of which are poorly differentiated among them-selves. For example, objects are assumed to have a kind of organic connection with the persons to whom they belong—a connection which in later life is recognized not to exist. This stage of object-consciousness corresponds to one which primitive man never completely passes—the stage of sympathetic magic or participation. The most prominent objective facts for the child at this early stage are his parents, and so they become the objects towards which his interest is chiefly directed. But here a complication occurs, in that one parent becomes more important for the child than the other. Furthermore, each parent has a place in the interests of the other, as well as having a place for the child; and so the latter meets what is probably his first great environmental obstacle of a personal kind—his first rival—and the germs of hate may grow in association and contact with the group of emotions and feelings comprising the conscious expression designated love. Thus love and hate are said to begin that association which persists throughout life. Prohibitions and punishments also can produce a feeling of antagonism and play a part in the genesis of hateful emotion. The attachment of the child to his parent of the opposite sex is conventionally called the Oedipus situation or complex. The early identification with the parents has a formulation partly conscious, partly unconscious, in the creation of an ideal to be like the parents. The ideal is the *imago* already mentioned. The parents thus serve as an example to the child, and so unknowingly train him in the formation of habits. Deliberate training begins with example and later proceeds with precept, in earlier days from the parents, and later from school influences and the influence of companions. Morbid reactions, as well as healthy ones, may be impressed in this way, and not only specific reactions but general attitudes with emotional components—*e.g.* morbid gloom or anxiety. Training also makes use not only of rewards but of punishment and threats of punishment. Punishment implies either the frustration of some conscious wish and the production of unpleasant emotion, or the infliction of actual pain of physical origin. There is no doubt that the inflicting of pain in one of the erotogenic zones may be accompanied by a certain amount of pleasurable feeling, and frequent arousal of pleasure in this way may cause a desire for it to become fixed. This desire may appear as a sexual perversion in later life, just as any other premature fixation of the sexual libido may appear as a perversion. When the primary parental stage of the environment begins to be less important, and the child's mental environment widens and his contacts with it increase in number and complexity, a group of tendencies come into play which have been included under the term 'herd instinct'. The use of this term connotes that certain reactions necessary for adaptation to society in general are inborn. It seems doubtful whether it is necessary to make this hypothesis, rather than to attribute the more primitive less differentiated reactions to the social *milieu* as reactions derived from personal contact with it. In any case, it is in connection with adaptation to the requirements of the herd that the ego-ideal is further built up, and that the most powerful repression is exercised.

THE MENTAL RELATIONS OF INSTINCTIVE MANIFESTATIONS AND ENVIRONMENTAL INFLUENCES

The infant, receiving its first sensory impressions, treats them in the beginning as part of itself—'introjects' them—they have a purely subjective reference. But from his motor activity and the different quality of sensations arising in his own body from those not so arising, he learns to differentiate those of the external world and to attribute them to influences external to himself and less within his control—*i.e.* to 'project' them. Not only does he do this with his sensations, but he projects also his emotions. The emotions he experiences in certain situations, *e.g.* in beholding anything large and new to him, he attributes to the thing itself, so that what fills him with awe has an awesome quality attributed to itself. Furthermore, all his projections are of the personal type; he endows external objects with all his own conscious properties. This is comparable to the stage of animism in primitive man.

Imitation

Imitation of example, especially of parental example, is a training method which is used early. It is one of the modes by which suggestion operates. *Suggestion* seems to depend on a particular relation of operator (suggestor) and subject, analogous to but not identical with the active-passive relation in the play of the sexual instinct. Suggestion operates only in an affective relationship.

Intelligence

Intelligence is phylogenetically the last-developed of all the adaptive functions. It appears in rudimentary form in the highest apes, at least. Intelligence is said to grow in the individual till the age of sixteen. After that its apparent growth is mostly a matter of experience and consequently improved judgement. In the growth of intellectual processes which deal eventually with the adaptation of means to ends, not merely the end is consciously represented, but the means to it, and so *symbolization* plays an important part.

Symbolization

This consists in the conscious representation of experiences derived from the environment by something mental which *stands for* that experience. Language is made possible by symbolization. For example, a certain sensory experience of roundness and depth and colour and consistency becomes represented by the vocalization 'ball'. The word 'symbolization' has unfortunately attained many meanings. In ordinary life it has come to be specially used where some simple object has become endowed with great affective meaning, *e.g.* a country's flag as a symbol for patriotic feeling. A very similar use is now made of the term in psychopathology; but the object acting as a symbol is invested with a very strong personal affective meaning instead of a general one, as in the case of the flag. Symptoms are often symbolizations in this sense when the meaning is unconscious (repressed).

The association of one idea with another, or of an emotion or feeling with an idea, is an important adaptive function subserving both practical (real) and phantastic thinking. It works in a way analogous to the conditioning of reflexes in physiology, in that once a certain feeling has become associated with a certain idea the revival of the idea (or, unlike the conditioned reflex, of some similar idea) may revive the feeling. For example, if an article of food has accidentally been associated with a feeling of nausea, the same or a similar article may on a later occasion revive nausea simply by virtue of the previous accidental association.

Adaptation

Adaptation is not at all a matter of pure reason. It is eventually and at all times a matter of modifications of instinctive trends, which have a very much closer association with emotional than with intellectual processes. But wherever an adaptation is consciously made or results in conscious experience of some kind, an intellectual formation tends to occur, which by virtue of its conscious nature, contrasting with that of the instinctive reaction which is wholly unconscious or only indirectly conscious, is apt to masquerade as the reason for the particular adaptation. This substitution of an intellectual conscious 'reason' for the actual instinct-derived (unconscious) basis of a reaction, is known as *rationalization*. It is usually a formulation more closely in accord with herd or ego-ideal requirements than was the primary instinctive trend.

The gradual building-up of an ego or self has been stated to arise from a continuous synthesis of certain experiences having a peculiar intimacy, while at the same time a 'not-self' or external world has been mentally constructed (represented). There is here a contrast, which results, among other things, in the formation within the experiences of the ego of an idealized representation of the self, or ideal ego, of which the unconscious part is called by Freud the super-ego (*v. supra*). It is a very gradual growth, and consequently not at all fully conscious at any time. It gives rise to an important subservient reaction, in that where the attributes of the self are conceived as lacking in some of the qualities of the ideal self, the self makes an attempt to *compensate* in one direction what is lacking in another. These deficiencies which it is attempted to compensate may be of either physical or intellectual attributes.

The more intimate part of the environment constituted by the body has important relations to the mind. In the first place, the mental representations of bodily activities are regarded as part of the self. Secondly, mental events (ideas) are followed by bodily (physical) events in so regular and invariable a way that a relationship of cause and effect is universally assumed to exist, and the relationship is called a process of 'will'. Thirdly, mental events which have an emotional accompaniment have a bodily reverberation also, not in the form of directly adaptive movement as in the case of 'willed' sequences, but in the form of disturbances of function of a special kind, especially visceral disturbances, but involving also movement of the limbs of an apparently useless sort, *e.g.* tremors. Fourthly, most visceral functions go on without any conscious accompaniment, and the intervention of conscious accompaniment usually betokens malfunction. Conversely, in the absence of spontaneous malfunction, conscious attention to the working of the viscera tends to derange the latter. Attention alone would not do so, but such attention is usually accompanied by emotion (usually anxiety), which has visceral reverberations. Attention of this sort arises only when the normal direction of interest towards the environment is frustrated and turns towards the self. Frustration of any instinct causes emotion of some kind, emotion produces palpitation, etc.; palpitation draws the attention, already failing to find an environmental object, and a vicious circle is set up, since attention makes the palpitation, etc., loom larger, and so the emotion increases.

For the individual the combined result of the innate endowment, of the environmental impressions, and of the reactive-tendencies arising out of the conflict between them, is what is customarily called the *personality*. This is a more or less completely synthesized group of reactive tendencies, including not only all those that the ego acknowledges as its own, but some of which it is unaware, *i.e.* unconscious but not repressed tendencies. Certain mannerisms are a simple example of this latter class of components of the personality. No two individuals ever have exactly the same history, from the zygote stage onwards, and so no two personalities are exactly alike. But there are certain general types, representing different types of adaptation. Some of these are more successful than others, reality being more adequately dealt with. Those personalities that are less successful are *ipso facto* apt to develop substitutive reactions (Meyer) for healthy ones, *i.e.* to have symptoms of mental illness.

THE PRODUCTION OF SYMPTOMS

The very important part played by unconscious factors in normal conscious mental life has already been emphasized. Normally the unconscious factors co-operate harmoniously in facilitating conscious reactions. But in some cases the unconscious factors break through indirectly (symbolically in the second sense given above) into consciousness in a manner out of harmony with the conscious mental life of the individual; in other cases, the unconscious factors usurp the whole realm of consciousness (dreams and dual personalities, for example). In either instance, symptoms of mental disorder become apparent. It is obvious that to do this the unconscious factors must have an activity that is independent of consciousness; they are said to be *dissociated* from the rest of the mental content, and the field of consciousness to be 'restricted' with regard to them. This lack of connection between conscious and unconscious may result either from a simple failure on the part of the conscious ego to recognize a connection, or it may be due to a refusal of the ego to do so ('repression').

The first case (of simple failure of recognition) is not at all uncommon. A patient may have a great deal of emotional perturbation which is associated with visceral disturbance. The latter attracts his attention, and as its subjective accompaniments (symptoms) are the same as those of some organic disease, and as he fails to recognize their connection with emotion, he concludes that he has that disease. Then because affects are easily displaceable from one idea to another the emotional perturbation which originally arose from other factors becomes attached to the idea of disease—and in this way an anxiety state is set up.

In the second instance, where the dissociation depends on repression (the result of conflict of the repressed material with the ego ideal), the dissociated material has had originally a strong affective accompaniment. The formation of a symptom denotes a partial or complete failure of the ego to repress the affectively accompanied material ('complex'), the degree of failure being proportional to the directness of expression of the latter. The symptom may take a bodily (physical) form: in the motor field, a muscular movement (tremor, tic) or a paralysis; in the sensory field, an anaesthesia or amblyopia, or some other sensory disturbance. The particular form is a matter of minor determinants. In other instances the symptom may have a psychic form—a fear or an idea, either being apparently meaningless for consciousness. The commonest conscious emotional symptom is 'fear' in the special form of distressful expectation usually designated 'anxiety'. Conflict of any kind, whether self-preservative or sexual, may lead to anxiety. The anxiety tends to attach itself to an idea, since affects can hardly remain unrelated in consciousness. This idea to which the anxiety attaches is apt to be one consciously very far removed from ideas associated with originally repressed material—this is the so-called *displacement of affect*. Whatever the idea to which the affect (of anxiety) attaches, an attempt may be made to ward off the anxiety in a way reminiscent of the magic acts of infancy. Thus a schoolboy had to touch everything twice in case he should not pass a forthcoming examination. This is the genesis of some compulsive acts—a wish, a fear and a magic act to overcome the fear. A similar mechanism accounts for certain obsessive ideas (magic words).

Another fashion in which the ego may deal with an imperfectly repressed complex (of idea plus emotion) is by *projection*. The complex material is permitted to appear in consciousness but projected as external reality, so forming a delusion (*e.g.* a belief that other people are watching the patient wherever he goes), or as a hallucination (*e.g.* a voice accusing him of vile practices). The method of projection is more seriously pathological than the preceding modes, since it involves a distortion of reality.

The projected complexes are often considerably elaborated, being originally the phantasy-formations already mentioned. Phantasies may, however, appear directly as part of the conscious ego, instead of being projected, in one of two ways: 1. either the phantasy is not one involving the emotions of guilt or other emotions such as would cause the ego to disown it; for example, a delusion of grandeur may involve simply a turning to phantasy from disappointment with reality, as in an individual with inflated self-regard; or 2. the ego-ideal is so disintegrated that repression is not exercised at all, and any complex which involves material, no matter how distasteful originally to the ego, is admitted into consciousness. This occurs only in the most serious forms of illness, *e.g.* in schizophrenia.

Frank conscious indulgence in wish-fulfilling phantasies when disintegration of the ego is not too profound, is accompanied by the appropriate affect, viz. elation. In many patients in whom elation occurs there is, however, little conscious evidence of a wish-fulfilment; and it appears that elation may also colour the consciousness while the wish-fulfilment associated with it remains unconscious but active (dissociated).

The emotional state which we are accustomed to consider as the psychological contrast to elation, namely depression, reaches pathological intensity in several ways. When a wish is not fulfilled—when frustration occurs—depression results. Depression is more likely to occur when the aim of the frustrated tendency is abandoned: anxiety when there is frustration with continued striving. This is a normal occurrence, but the depression attains pathological significance, magnitude and duration when the frustration occurs in relation to some conscious but very much overvalued end, the depth of depression being proportional to the degree of overvaluation. Overvaluation of the end is common in 'neurotics', especially as this overvaluation is derived from an exaggerated ego-ideal. Hence the continual striving of neurotics (Adler's 'masculine protest'). Depression is also pathological when the frustration is in relation to some unconscious object. In the latter instance the depression appears pathological, because there is nothing in consciousness to account for it. Depression may also be the conscious accompaniment of a feeling of guilt or remorse, which itself may be derived from an unconscious trend imperfectly repressed. A conscious rationalization of the feeling of guilt may be produced in the form of self-accusatory ideas, which may reach delusional intensity. Guilt is particularly apt to be felt in connection with sexual trends, on account of social prohibitions.

The methods of symptom-formation which have just been described are used in response to contemporary environmental influences, and may or may not imply any developmental defect hindering adaptation. In some individuals the development of the libido's object-direction may be arrested at an intermediate stage (*e.g.* the auto-erotic or the homosexual). This hinders adaptation to adult reality, which is heterosexual in organization, and brings the individual into contact with social prohibitions, *e.g.* in fixation at the homosexual stage. If he accepts his homosexuality in a matter-of-fact way, no mental disorder results, but if he represses his tendencies from consciousness because of the socially induced feeling of guilt, and if the repression fails, depression or anxiety or projected wish-fulfilment occurs as a symptom.

Failure of adaptation at any level of development implies dissatisfaction. The individual may revert in phantasy to a previous level of development, *e.g.* the infantile stage of helplessness, and obtain a phantastic satisfaction which may be dramatized, *i.e.* the patient lies helplessly in bed, uttering baby talk, and having to be fed. 'Regression' is not an unimpeachable description of this state, since there is no recapitulation, and the reinstatement of the previous terms of existence is never an identical one.

All these reactions can be described as substitutions for healthy adaptations. Their general tendency is to lead the patient away from reality. Some are more pernicious in this respect than others; the further away from reality, the more symptomatically pronounced the mental disorder, and (on the whole) the worse the prognosis for recovery.

SLEEP AND DREAMS

It is not known why we sleep and need to sleep for about one-third of our lives, but there have been notable recent additions to our knowledge of how we do so, by Kleitman (1963), Dement, Jouvet, Oswald (1962), and other research workers.

Individuals vary widely in the number of hours of sleep which they seem to require to function at full efficiency. As people become older, the tendency is to sleep less at night and to waken earlier, before 5 a.m. (McGhie and Russell, 1962). This is an important finding in relation to the symptom of early-morning wakening in manic-depressive psychosis: in the case of the older man or woman it is not waking early, but a recent change to waking early and distress about it, which is a significant symptom of depression.

There are two kinds or phases of sleep, which differ in their psychological accompaniments and which alternate during the night. This cyclical sleeping pattern changes every 1½ hours or so.

The 'orthodox' phase is characterized by deep sleep, with, in the electro-encephalogram large, slow delta waves and brief bursts of faster waves which are called 'sleep spindles'.

The 'paradoxical' phase is characterized by lighter sleep, by a rather flat E.E.G. record with low-voltage waves, and by rapid jerky conjugate eye movements (Dement and Kleitman, 1957). This phase makes up 20–25 per cent. (decreasing with age) of the whole sleep period. Dreaming occurs typically and abounds during this phase, though it is not limited to it.

Probably everyone dreams during the eye-movement phases of sleep: for a period totalling about two hours nightly. These dreams, although extended in time, are usually rapidly forgotten—hence many deny that they dream at all. If subjects are wakened repeatedly at the onset of these eye-movement phases of sleep and are thus deprived of dreaming for a number of nights, they dream more than normally in subsequent undisturbed nights and have longer periods of the 'paradoxical' phase of sleep. This finding has stimulated the conjecture that dreaming is needed, that dreams have an essential function in resolving the tensions, frustrations and conflicts built up during everyday life: but it is not more than a possibility, since dreaming is only one, and not necessarily the most important, aspect of the 'paradoxical' phase.

Oswald and Priest (1965), in experiments on volunteers taking sodium amylo-barbitone or a non-barbiturate hypnotic, demonstrated that hypnotic drugs disturb the brain processes underlying normal sleep. The drugs caused a reduction in the percentage of 'paradoxical' sleep: and after stopping the drugs there was a rebound to abnormally high proportions of 'paradoxical' sleep, with night-mares. After only 18 nights of the administration of sedatives, some neuro-physiological functions took over five weeks to return to normal. These important findings help to explain why patients find it so difficult to relinquish an hypnotic, once they have become accustomed to it.

During sleep external stimuli, auditory or tactile, may be incorporated into the content of dreaming, but play only a very small part in it. The content of dreams reflects the interests and events of the individual's waking life, and in their phantasy his deeper drives and emotions.

Dreams are the representations, in the disturbed state of consciousness called sleep, of unconscious mental states, based on experience of both the lapsed and repressed kinds. It is customary to call the dream-content as remembered by the dreamer the 'manifest' content, and the unconscious processes which give rise to the latter the 'latent' content. This distinction is of considerable importance when applied to psychopathology, for it is held in Freudian theory that the manifest content is produced from the latent content in the same way that symptoms ('manifest') are produced from unconscious ('latent') factors. The latter are said, on the basis of the theory of repression, to be made palatable to the ego by various methods of transformation by which the manifest content is finally manufactured. It would perhaps be more generally correct to say that in a state of lowered consciousness such as occurs in sleep, more primitive mental processes occupy the field. Visual imagery, for example, which was shown by Galton to be much more used by children and the uneducated than by educated adults, plays a large part in dreams. Nevertheless, it also can subserve repressive ends, on account of the distortion involved in clothing everything in visual images.

The methods of transformation which unconscious material undergoes before constituting the 'manifest content' are chiefly condensation, displacement, secondary elaboration and symbolization. By *condensation* is meant that the manifest dream is a kind of abridged edition of the latent content, this result being obtained especially by the blending into one whole of several latent elements with some characteristic in common, *e.g.* one person in a dream may represent several people actually known to the dreamer. *Displacement* consists in the transfer of the emotional setting of one idea to some other apparently insignificant idea, as has already been explained for symptoms. *Secondary elaboration* consists in welding the dream-content transformed in the other ways described into something like a coherent whole. By *symbolization* is meant that certain objects which occur often in the manifest content of dreams have a fairly constant symbolic value—they stand regularly for the same unconscious content or latent dream thought. In Freudian theory the standard symbols have usually a sexual significance. Symbolizations of a more general type occur, *e.g.* a man recovering from a neurotic illness, anxious to get well and finding the way hard, dreamt that he was crossing a bridge, that it progressively narrowed, so that he had to clamber along the parapet, but that finally it widened and he could proceed safely and easily.

Dreams in general, like the one just related, are considered to be fulfilments of wishes, conscious or unconscious, and often of the repressed type.

Jung emphasized a purposive aspect in dreaming and also in the neuroses—an attempt to solve an immediate problem.

REFERENCES

Davis, D. R. (1966) *An Introduction to Psychopathology*, 2nd ed., London.
Dement, W., and Kleitman, N. (1957) *Electroenceph. clin. Neurophysiol.*, **9**, 673.
Deutsch, H. (1946) *The Psychology of Women*, London.
Freud, A. (1936) *The Ego and Mechanisms of Defence*, London.
Freud, S. (1953) *The Standard Edition of the Complete Psychological Works*, London.
Hart, B. (1957) *The Psychology of Insanity*, 5th ed., London.
Jones, E. (1948) *Papers on Psycho-analysis*, 5th ed., London.
Jung, C. G. (1923) *Psychological Types*, London.
Kleitman, N. (1963) *Sleep and Wakefulness*, London.

Maher, B. A. (1966) *The Principles of Psychopathology*, New York.

McGhie, A., and Russell, S. M. (1962) *J. ment. Sci.*, **108**, 642.

Mowbray, R. M., and Rodger, T. F. (1967) *Psychology in Relation to Medicine*, 2nd ed., Edinburgh.

Oswald, I. (1962) *Sleeping and Waking*, Amsterdam.

Oswald, I., and Priest, R. G. (1965) *Brit. med. J.*, **2**, 1093.

8

NEUROTIC REACTION-TYPES

Neurotic forms of reaction are the commonest kinds of manifestation of psychological ill health. The specialist in psychological medicine encounters conditions of this kind much more often in that part of his work which lies outside mental hospitals, while for the general practitioner they constitute no small proportion of his practice.

Meaning of the Term 'Neurosis'

The term neurosis has, from the standpoint of classification, two connotations. In the first and historical connotation its meaning is purely *descriptive*. It is a term referring to conditions characterized by certain mental and physical symptoms and signs, occurring in various combinations. The most usual of these combinations or syndromes have been distinguished as sub-types of neurosis called respectively anxiety neurosis, hysteria and obsessional neurosis. None of these is dependent on the existence of any discoverable physical disease. They are not mutually exclusive categories so far as individual symptoms are concerned, but they signify certain recurrent patterns of symptoms commonly occurring together.

'Neurosis' has, however, another connotation, more fundamental, since it is an aetiological one. This is to the effect that the existence of a neurotic reaction is an indication of mental conflict. Neurotic reactions are the commonest modes of faulty response to the stresses of life, and especially to those inner tensions that come about from confused and unsatisfactory relationships with other people, whether they are a legacy from the past or from early childhood onwards, which remain to hinder future adaptations; or arise in the present in relation to hopes, ambitions, jealousies and so forth. The constitutional factor, where it does operate, seems to facilitate the development of inner tensions, but this factor is less conspicuous than it is in the psychotic forms of illness, such as manic-depressive and schizophrenic conditions. The pathology of neurotic reactions, in other words, is essentially a pathology of personal relationships.

On this view the existence of mental conflict is the commonest reason for the existence of neurotic symptoms, but because the individual is unconscious either of the conflict within him, or at least of its connection with his symptoms, the neurotic symptoms appear in the ordinary sense to be irrational. Although they may consist for the most part of ideas, no rational explanation exists for them in terms of the rest of the patient's thoughts so far as he is able to give an account of them; or if the mental conflict expresses itself as physical disturbances, such as blindness or paralysis or tremor, no physical disease can be found that can be regarded as causal. A neurotic patient may be disconcerted by a morbid fear of travelling in a train or a bus, or he may be unable to go more than a few yards from his own door, but he does not have the faintest notion why; yet this fear may be so impelling that the attempt to walk a few yards in the open may prove utterly beyond him.

The irrationality is confined, however, to the account that he is able to give of his symptoms. If enough of his thoughts and feelings are known, what has seemed mysterious becomes logical and coherent with the rest of the contents of his mind. It has been demonstrated many times that there are undercurrents of feeling and thought, and connections between thoughts and feeling, of which the individual himself may be quite unaware until the connection is exhibited to him.

A complication must be considered here, in that neurotic reactions resulting from mental disturbances in earlier life may be perpetuated as habits of behaviour and attitude and so become part of the personality. Even simple stresses, such as fatigue, may allow these characteristics to appear in such exaggerated form as to constitute an inadequacy of adaptation in the symptomatic form of a neurosis.

Disturbances of constitutional origin, especially depression, may have a similar effect, and this probably accounts for some of the instances where symptoms of neurotic form cover an underlying depression.

Prevalence

Accurate figures of morbidity are difficult to obtain because diagnosis is often not precise in this field: neurotic reactions border on the one hand states of tension and unhappiness which can be considered to be within the range of the normal, and on the other hand 'psychosomatic' syndromes of still uncertain aetiology. There is no doubt also that many illnesses are diagnosed as neurotic by general practitioners which are in fact affective psychoses. In England and Wales a joint survey by the General Register Office and the College of General Practitioners (1958), based on the returns of 171 general practitioners, reported the patient-consulting rate (the number of patients suffering from an illness, regardless of the number of consultations) for various illnesses in general practice. Whereas the number of patients consulting for malignant disease was found to be 5·2 per thousand, the patient-consulting rate for neurotic and allied disorders was 45·7 per thousand: that is, about one in twenty of the population apparently came under the care of their doctors in one year for minor psychiatric disorders.

Kessel and Shepherd (1962) surveyed the information about the distribution of neurotic illness which can be derived from records of patients treated in Britain as in-patients and out-patients at hospitals and by their family doctors; and pointed out cogently the limitations of the available data. About half the total of psychiatric out-patients appear to suffer from neuroses: so also do many of those who attend surgical and medical clinics at general hospitals (Shepherd *et al.*, 1960). The percentage of cases in general practice which are clearly 'psychiatric' appears to be about 10–12 per cent.: if psychosomatic disorders are included, the total may rise by another 5–10 per cent. Shepherd and his colleagues (1964) reported from general practices in the Greater London area that 'minor psychiatric disorders' were diagnosed in 14 per cent. of the population at risk. Neurotic illness, most prevalent among middle-aged females, was diagnosed in 8·8 per cent., and psychosomatic disorders in 3 per cent.

It is uncertain whether there has been a real or only an apparent increase in these neurotic forms of illness in recent years. They are certainly now much more widely recognized, whereas they passed formerly for other things. Mythical diseases, such as 'mucous colitis', 'dropped kidney' or 'spinal neurasthenia' have been debunked: they were the labels formerly attached to the patients' complaints, *faute de mieux*, by doctors of generations who had not been taught that physical disease is often simulated by mental disturbance. The public themselves are now also much more knowledgeable about nervous and mental illness, and of the out-patient and other facilities available for early treatment.

That there has been a real increase has been difficult to prove, but figures obtained by Halliday (1948) from statistics of the Department of Health for Scotland have tended to show that an increase had in fact occurred between the world wars. If this is so, then the increase has probably been related to one or more of the general factors favouring neurotic forms of illness, namely insecurity in one of its many forms, whether due to social isolation, changing social mores, financial stress or an absence of mental values of the sort that transcend purely material issues.

General Clinical Features and Groupings

Clinically, a neurosis implies either a bodily disturbance without structural lesion and dependent in a way unknown to the patient on mental causes; or a mental disturbance, not the result of bodily disease, in the form of morbid fears of many different kinds, or episodic disturbed mental states such as losses of memory and trances, or persistent troublesome thoughts, or acts which the patient feels compelled to do—all of which the patient realizes to be abnormal but the meaning of which he is at a loss to understand. The bodily disturbances may be sensory and subjective, or motor and therefore directly observable, or visceral. The sensory disturbances may occur in any of the physiological systems of the body; disturbances which are emphatically real, not 'imaginary'. A hysterical pain is a real pain, and causes genuine distress. The motor and visceral symptoms are also multiform.

Whytt of Edinburgh, as long ago as 1765, distinguished three types of neurotic reaction—neurasthenia, hysteria and hypochondria. About 1880 Charcot's use of hypnotism focused attention on the symptoms of hysteria, in particular on those cases where the patient's neurotic reaction was expressed in physical disabilities of a rather bizarre kind. About the same time Beard popularized the diagnosis of neurasthenia, drawing attention to a syndrome of which the nucleus was complaints of mental and physical fatigue. Janet recognized two groups, hysteria and psychasthenia; in the latter group placing obsessions and compulsions, fears of all kinds and feelings of fatigue. Later Freud divided states of morbid anxiety into two varieties, anxiety neurosis and anxiety hysteria. In anxiety neurosis there was supposed to be a primary physical disturbance expressed in the form, for example, of tremor or palpitations, with a mental content

K

of discomfort or vague fear. In anxiety hysteria there was a fear of some definite external object or disease, and the physical disturbance was said to be less important. This differentiation proved to be unhelpful: the first variety did not appear to exist in a pure form, while the second, which was common, seemed to have been given a designation which was both confusing and incorrect: these patients showed usually no evidence of hysteria clinically, and psychodynamically no unusual 'capacity for conversion of psychic excitation into bodily innervation'.

The most acceptable clinical grouping of neurotic reactions now seems to us the simple one of describing them under the heads of anxiety neurosis, hysteria and obsessional neurosis. The criteria for the diagnosis of hysteria are given on page 146: the term should not be used just in the sense that the patient is overemotional or acting-out his or her emotions. When there is much mental perturbation in the form of fear, and when any bodily symptoms seem to be the outcome of this, the best term probably is anxiety neurosis (anxiety state). The term obsessional neurosis includes obsessive-ruminative and obsessive-compulsive states, and the central feature here is a feeling of subjective compulsion, so that the patient has fears or preoccupations or carries out motor acts of an apparently trifling or meaningless kind, against his better judgement. We will give our reasons later for doubting whether there is now any point in considering neurasthenia a clinical entity, among the neurotic reactions.

We make no distinction between the terms psychoneurosis and neurosis: they reflect psychodynamic theories which have been abandoned, and the shorter term seems preferable.

Differentiation from Psychosis

There are few clearly defined boundaries in nature, and there is many a case of mental illness which it is difficult to assign definitely to the neurotic or psychotic group. But between a well-developed psychosis on the one hand and a full-fledged neurosis on the other there is a world of difference, from the descriptive as well as from the therapeutic aspect. Transitions also occur; so that a patient who reacts neurotically at one time may react psychotically at another. We have, for example, seen a patient who began with neurotic anxiety symptoms subsequently develop obsessive compulsive ones and finally enter a paranoid psychosis, as if these were successive stages of mental disintegration. But such transitions are the exception and not the rule. The neurotic who has among his other topics of anxiety the fear of insanity can usually be reassured with statistical certainty that he will not 'go out of his mind'.

The distinctions between neuroses and psychoses are symptomatic, psychopathological and therapeutic. The symptoms of the neuroses will be enumerated later, when the divergences from the clinical pictures presented by the psychoses will be evident. Considered biologically, that is, regarded as types of reaction to environment, the neuroses are distinctive in several ways. A psychosis involves a change in the whole personality of the subject in whom it appears, while in the neuroses it is only a part of the personality that is affected. With the development of a neurosis there is often no outward change of personality of any kind. As Meyer put it, a neurosis is a part-reaction, while a psychosis is a total one. Furthermore, in a psychosis reality is changed qualitatively and comes to be regarded in a way very different from the normal, and the patient behaves accordingly; in a neurosis reality remains unchanged qualitatively, although its value may be quantitatively altered. But the neurotic acts always as if reality had the same kind of meaning for him as for the rest of the community. Psychopathologically the psychotic change in reality-values is partly expressed as projection, which consists in attributing an experience in origin entirely subjective to some external personal agency, *e.g.* an externally unfounded belief that one is being continually watched often depends on a sense of guilt, subjective but unconscious. Projection of this sort does not occur in the neuroses.

Language is the symbolizing function and the latest developed function for social adaptation. In the neuroses, language as such is never disturbed, whereas in the psychoses it often undergoes distortion. From the psychoanalytic viewpoint, the unconscious comes to direct verbal expression in the psychoses; whereas in the neuroses it never attains more than symbolic expression in some physical or localized mental disturbance. The reactions in the psychoses are of a much more primitive type on the whole than in the neuroses: there is often a regression to an infantile level of activity in the psychotic. For example, wetting and soiling without shame are not found in neurotics in the presence of clear consciousness.

AETIOLOGY—GENERAL ASPECTS

We have stated already that neurotic reactions develop most commonly as faulty responses to the personal problems of everyday life. Stressful situations of a great many different kinds, instead of eliciting an out-going and constructive response, may precipitate a state of continuing anxiety and mental conflict, with the development of neurotic symptoms. There are two variables: the stress, and the strength of the human material tested. The stresses which precipitate breakdown vary greatly from case to case in their nature, quality, intensity and duration: they may be either psychological or physical (or both combined), but the former are usually of first importance and predominate. Physical illness or injury or fatigue may reduce an individual's resistance to psychological stress. If the environmental stress is severe enough almost anyone may break down with anxious or depressive symptoms, as has been demonstrated repeatedly in war-time; in the sequelae, for example, of long-continued trench warfare or combat flying. The stresses of civil life which are most commonly important arise from personal relationships and social and sexual difficulties. These stresses are as various as the personalities which encounter them: if they elicit emotions of fear, guilt and hate which have to be repressed, they are particularly likely to produce mental conflict and neurotic responses. For facing these stresses the individual may be weakened or wholly disabled by his inherited constitution and the incidents of his personal biography: the personality traits which he has developed out of the interaction of his inherited constitution and early environment may, in other words, have predisposed him to neurotic breakdown. Hence the aetiology of neurosis is a multiple aetiology, of great individual variety and complexity. We are still far from understanding it fully.

During the Second World War it became particularly important to select for specially arduous combat duties men who would not be likely to suffer neurotic breakdown under very severe stress. Attempts were made therefore to identify at examination and to eliminate those liable to breakdown. Four groups of characteristics were found (Gillespie, 1944) to indicate neurotic predisposition and to correlate with neurotic breakdown: 1. pronounced morbid fears; 2. traits pointing to timidity and lack of aggressiveness; 3. 'nervousness'; and 4. 'physiological instability'. 'Nervousness' was defined to include proneness to instability of mood, obsessional characteristics, inferiority feelings and solitary habits. 'Physiological instability' was thought to be shown by habitual restless sleep and sleepwalking, stammering, nail biting, bedwetting, and fainting at the sight of blood. A concentration of five or more 'neurotic' traits in one individual was considered to be significant of predisposition. Selection along these lines proved effective: those thought to be resistant to stress proved to be so—for example, less than 5 per cent. of bomber aircrew in the Royal Air Force became neurotic casualties, though the casualty rate for killed and missing rose to 48 per cent.

As we shall see later when discussing the different neurotic reaction-types in more detail, psychodynamic formulations deriving from Freud have proved of much value in understanding how a great variety of mental and physical symptoms may arise from the anxiety and tension which are fundamental in neurotic illness. There is also another kind of aetiological explanation which has few points of contact with psychoanalytic hypotheses, and is based on Pavlov's concepts of the conditioned reflex. An emotional reaction first aroused by a certain mental event tends afterwards to be aroused by any other mental event which has become associated with the first one. This secondary mental event may be without emotional significance in itself, but by virtue of its association it becomes capable of arousing the emotional reaction without the presence of the primary event in consciousness, or (perhaps and more often) in the absence of any conscious connection between the primary and secondary events, which may both nevertheless be fully conscious. The signs of emotional disturbance, physical or mental, aroused in this way, without adequate conscious reason, are reflected upon by the subject and mistaken for signs of disease. Thus the necessary conditions for the formation of neurotic symptoms are reproduced—the presence of localized bodily or mental disturbances without adequate conscious explanation of their occurrence. A simple example of this type of conditioned response was that of soldiers returned from battle areas who jumped at the slightest sound—not because the sound brought back memories of warfare into full consciousness, but simply because sudden sounds had become associated with reactions of fear.

Pavlov's work has been the starting-point for the contemporary development of 'learning theory', of which Eysenck (1960a) has been one of the leading exponents in the psychiatric field. Eysenck considers all neurotic symptoms to be either surplus or deficient conditioned reactions.

Constitutional Factors

Brown (1942), from a study of the relatives of neurotic patients, produced evidence that neurotic syndromes of the anxiety, hysterical and obsessional types have in some instances at least a constitutional basis, that the inherited constitution may be specific in each group, but that there is also some common factor which shows itself in an anxious personality.

Brown found that 21·4 per cent. of the parents of patients with anxiety states had a similar disorder, while 17·5 per cent. had either an anxious, depressive or obsessional personality. The anxious personality was described as timid, apprehensive, given to excessive worry or to mild phobias. Five per cent. of the parents of patients with anxiety neuroses had had depressions. In a control group the proportions of relatives affected were significantly less. It appears likely therefore that there are inherited constitutional factors in anxiety neuroses, and that these factors may in some instances be related to the depressive constitution.

In this sample also 19 per cent. of the parents of hysterical patients had themselves had hysterical reactions, while 14 per cent. of them exhibited an anxious personality. 7·5 per cent. of the parents of obsessional patients had suffered from obsessional syndromes, and the same percentage had had depressions: 19·6 per cent. of the parents had anxious personalities.

The same tendencies were confirmed by a study of the sibs and first and second degree relatives of patients with neuroses, the differences from controls being in all groups significant.

Slater (1943) investigating the relationships between personality traits and subsequent neuroses, found significant correlations between pre-existing traits and types of neuroses developed: the neurotic symptoms appeared as exaggerations of the personality traits. In the obsessional group in particular the correlation was high. A positive correlation was also found between hysterical traits of personality and hysterical symptoms; between anxious characteristics and subsequent symptoms of anxiety; and between depressive traits, such as mood swings, and subsequent depressive illness—in that diminishing order of relationship. If one assumes that these personality traits are inherited rather than acquired, this is additional evidence of a constitutional predisposition to neurotic types of reaction. The correlations were not high enough to indicate that constitutional predisposition is an essential factor in all cases. Slater (1944) proceeded to develop 'a heuristic theory of neurosis': that the neurotically predisposed individual represents one of the extremes of normal human variation, having more than average susceptibility to environmental stresses, and that this constitution is preponderantly determined by a very large number of genes of small effect. 'The effects of these genes, at least in so far as they are qualitatively similar, may be additive; and they become manifest by producing a reduced resistance to some form of environmental stress, and so facilitate the appearance of a neurosis. In so far as the effects of the genes are qualitatively dissimilar, the type of stress effective in producing breakdown, and the neurotic symptoms produced, will tend to differ.'

What is further required is a collaboration between the psychopathologist, the student of personality traits and the statistician in an attempt to establish what the fundamental and presumably inherited characteristics may be, and how they may produce in the course of psychological development in secondary fashion the traits which we recognize as predisposing to the development of certain types of symptom. In the obsessional type of character, for example, does the inherited factor essentially consist in an excessive degree of aggressiveness, which by happy accident and happy upbringing may result in a dominant and forceful personality in the one case; or which, on the other hand, as a result of a miscarriage of psychological development, may produce reaction formations, such as extreme scrupulousness devised to keep the aggressiveness in constant check, leading in the long run to the development of inner tension and ultimately of symptoms; or does the obsessional possibly inherit a nervous system which is distinctively organized? How far is the habit of anxiety, which appears to favour the development of anxiety symptoms, based on inherited emotionality; how far a mere infection, as it were, from an anxious parent; and how far an inner conflict, never properly resolved? Some of these are questions to which there can be no general answer. Studies of inheritance and constitution must be blended with studies of the life history of the individual and if possible with that of his parents. Probably only in this way can a true understanding be obtained, and at the same time scientific methods of prevention and treatment be gradually devised.

In the meantime it can be said that the individual constitution alone may be enough in some instances to determine the onset of an obsessive-compulsive state; while in the case of the hysterical, anxious and depressive syndromes much more depends upon accidents of experience and upbringing. It appears, in effect, that if an experience is severe enough these latter forms of reaction may appear in anyone, whereas it would be difficult to develop obsessional symptoms without a relevant constitutional predisposition.

Intelligence plays a part in determining the occurrence of neurotic reactions as a whole, which are relatively commoner among people of superior, than among those of inferior, intelligence. Intelligence also has an effect in determining the form of reaction, hysterical symptoms being commoner amongst dull individuals.

Environmental Factors

The environmental situations which may elicit neurotic reactions are multiform and may occur at any time throughout the individual's life. Each person has his own peculiar vicissitudes as he develops and ages: and at certain periods, in infancy, at puberty and in adolescence, in middle and old age, he is subject to stresses which he shares with all his coevals.

The earliest adverse environmental situation is a disturbed relationship with, or separation from, the mother. The infant's mind is dominated by the need to retain the mother, the primary source of love and food and protection, and in a state of nature vital of course to the offspring's survival. At the age of 83 Thomas Carlyle wrote, 'It was the earliest terror of my childhood that I might lose my mother and it has gone with me all my days.' Later the infant develops emotional bonds with his father and siblings, and, as he grows, with people outside the family circle, so that he becomes dependent on others not only for his material existence but for love and satisfaction in its many forms. The seeds of neurosis are sown often in these early relationships, when they are disturbed or distorted. How this may occur is described in Chapter 20, where problems arising from the child's emotional development are considered in greater detail.

Some of the social factors which may influence the incidence of neurosis, and the relationships between neurosis and social class, have already been discussed in Chapter 4, in the section on 'Social Factors and Aspects'. Here we wish in addition to draw attention to aspects of the life of the suburban areas of our large cities, which might be inimical to mental health and productive of neurosis.

Taylor (1938) described 'the suburban neurosis' of young women with anxiety states. He thought that these neurotic reactions developed because the environment had failed to interest, sustain or inspire these young married women, and they seemed to have little to live for. He thought the immediate causes were: 1. boredom occasioned by lack of friends, not enough to do and not enough to think about; 2. anxiety about money, the house and having another baby; and 3. a false set of values, due to the decline of religious faith and its replacement by the values of the advertisers and fetish-worship of the home. This paper of Taylor's was impressionistic. Martin and his colleagues (1957) studied the incidence of neurosis in a new housing estate in Hertfordshire and found a relatively high incidence of psychological disorder: their findings in fact suggested that the prevalence of neuroses in this environment might be as high as 77 per cent. in excess of the national rate. Tentatively they suggested that two adverse social factors might be operating: the effects of rehousing in producing family and social dislocation, and the loneliness of life on the estate, where each family tended to 'keep itself to itself'. An epidemiological study by Hare and Shaw (1965) has not confirmed these earlier findings. A comparison was made of the mental health of people in a new housing estate in Croydon with that of the inhabitants of an older area of the same town. No important difference in the prevalence of mental ill health in these two sample populations was detected. In each population, persons with poor mental health tended also to have poor physical health and to be dissatisfied with their neighbourhood.

Finally, we must take note that few persons are more suggestible than those who are anxious from any cause. Physical illness in other members of a family, or in near relatives may suggest symptoms to neurotic patients and focus their fears. Their suggestibility also makes the handling of neurotic patients or those potentially neurotic a delicate matter. We doctors, by mistakes in diagnosis and the injudicious handling of neurotic complaints, ourselves foster and fix neurotic reactions. Over the years there have been very many iatrogenic disorders, whose prevention has been wholly in our hands.

THE CLINICAL SYNDROMES

The main neurotic reaction-types have no hard and fast boundaries, and the classification we employ here—anxiety neuroses, hysteria and obsessional neuroses—is essentially a clinical one. Certain symptoms are held in common by each group—anxiety, for example. A given case may sometimes change so much that now it falls within one group, now in another: and cases showing admixtures of neurotic symptoms are commoner than those which exhibit the classical features of only one of the sub-types. Phobias can be classified either with the anxiety neuroses or with the obsessions: we have described them with the latter. There is also a considerable number of cases which may be difficult to classify definitively either as neuroses or affective psychoses: these are the so-called 'neurotic depressions', in which reactive emotional features are prominent and the symptoms are often clearly the response of an unstable personality to a situational problem. Some of these reactions are hysterical—it has indeed been suggested that this is the most typical contemporary form of hysteria: others, the majority we believe, are to be considered as belonging to the manic-depressive psychoses, the distinction between reactive and endogenous depressions being an arbitrary one.

Neurotic reactions may occur at any age, but are commonest in adolescence and in early adult life: women are more prone to them than men.

ANXIETY NEUROSES

These are the commonest of the neuroses, and fortunately the most responsive to treatment. Anxiety may occur as a symptom in almost any psychiatric syndrome: here it is the leading and predominant feature. It goes beyond any normal reaction of fear and worry: it is more intense, more persistent and more disabling. It is, however, always precipitated by some environmental situation or problem. A very similar syndrome may appear with no discoverable psychological cause, and subside spontaneously: in these cases anxiety has probably masked an underlying depression.

Clinical Features

Symptoms of morbid anxiety commonly develop in people of *anxious personality*—tense, timid, self-doubting, worrying people, who tend to expect the worst to happen and 'to cross their bridges before they come to them'. They often set high standards, there is a gap between their expectations for themselves and what they can in fact achieve, and this leads to feelings of insecurity and inferiority.

The symptoms of an anxiety neurosis are both mental and physical.

The mental symptoms take the form usually of a state of persistent anxiety, tension, apprehension and worry. The patient describes himself or herself as 'strung up', 'on edge', constantly expecting trouble or calamity: there is restlessness, impaired concentration, 'absentmindedness' and forgetfulness in day-to-day affairs, jumpiness, irritability and intermittently depression of spirits. The patient's tension makes him feel fatigued and he has difficulty in falling off to sleep at night because worries and forebodings crowd his mind. His sleep may be broken by unpleasant dreams or nightmares, of pursuit perhaps or attack or falling or failure.

The patient's anxiety may be unfocused, 'free-floating' it has been called, a nameless dread, or attaching itself to obvious trifles: or it may become specific, channelled into fears of many kinds, especially of insanity and cancer and other bodily illness. The locus of fears of bodily illness is often suggested by the bodily symptoms of the neurosis itself: palpitations and praecordial pains will be interpreted as evidence of heart disease, for example (a situation often given the unnecessary label of 'cardiac neurosis').

In some cases the apprehension recurrently rises quickly to a crisis in the form of acute attacks of anxiety or panic, which may last for a few minutes to half an hour or longer. The patient may describe these panics in physical terms, calling them feelings of dizziness or faintness; or may even not mention them, out of a fear of mental illness or of being thought a weakling. The attacks begin often with unpleasant sensations in the epigastrium, feelings of unease or tension or nausea which may resemble the aura of an epileptic fit. Then the symptoms mount towards the throat and head. The patient may feel his chest so constricted that he cannot get a full breath, and he pants for air. Palpitations, choking sensations, sweating, tingling of the limbs, feelings of lightheadedness, are accompanied by a fear of collapsing, fainting or dying: a terror, often, quite plainly of impending death. Then gradually the fear recedes, leaving the patient shaken and limp and afraid of being left alone. These panic attacks may occur both during the day and at night, in bed, and the patient may understandably feel afraid to leave his house because of them. The German poet Rilke, in his autobiographical *Notebooks of Malte Laurids Brigge*, described his own attacks: 'Why should I pretend that these nights had never been, when in fear of death I sat up, clinging to the fact that the mere act of sitting was at any rate a part of life: that the dead did not sit. . . . One wakes up panting. . . . Higher it mounts, here it passes out over you, rising higher than your breath, to which you flee as to your last stand. . . . Your heart drives you out of yourself, your heart pursues you, and you are almost frantic. . . . Your slight surface hardness and adaptability go for nothing.' And Rilke, a grown man, would call for his mother, remembering how she had come to him as a child when he had had a night terror, saying 'It is I, do not be afraid'—and his fear had gone.

The somatic symptoms of an anxiety state may involve any one or all of the bodily systems: most cases complain of a number of physical symptoms with the emphasis usually on one or other bodily system. Rapid heart beats, breathlessness, lack of appetite, a lump in the throat, flatulence, fullness in the stomach, water-brash, constipation, diarrhoea, frequency of micturition, twitching of muscles, weakness of limbs, tremors, pains and other paraesthesiae, blurring of vision, tinnitus, general fatigability—all these are common symptoms. There is evidence both of sympathetic and parasympathetic over-action: the former displayed, for example, in dilated pupils and rapid pulse, the latter in diarrhoea and frequency of micturition. Pains derived from muscle tension are very common and are often miscalled rheumatism: they may occur anywhere in the patient's back or at the back of his neck (so that he 'can't get his neck comfortable'), in his scalp muscles, his face and jaws, the left side of his chest and his limbs. Praecordial jabbing pains, due to spasm of intercostal muscles, draw the patient's attention to the state of his heart.

The patient suffering from an anxiety neurosis may exhibit no abnormality on physical examination; or he or she may show some of the somatic signs of anxiety, as described above—dilated pupils, tremors, cold and clammy hands, a raised systolic blood pressure, and very brisk tendon reflexes. There may be some loss of weight.

Aetiology and Psychopathology

In the genesis of an anxiety neurosis there are to be found some or all of the following factors. There is commonly an inherited predisposition. Frequently also, there is what in its effects may be mistaken for heredity, namely, a morbid family environment such as may be produced by maternal anxiety or much parental quarrelling or some other form of 'broken home' situation. These are the predisposing factors. The immediate factors include any source of dissatisfaction, whether in personal relationships, domestic, sexual or social, or in connection with employment or financial stress, or elsewhere. Exposure to some overwhelming, and usually sudden, external stress, for example a terrifying experience involving threat to life, can produce an anxiety syndrome in the absence of mental conflict, especially in people of timid temperament.

Anxiety neuroses may originate from any type of collision between individual needs and reality. These needs may be sexual, but are not necessarily so: and childhood conflicts which had been incompletely resolved (for example, an Oedipus complex) may or may not be reactivated, so that consciousness is threatened with the return of repressed material. Freud maintained that excessive anxiety, even when attributed to obviously reasonable objects of concern such as business difficulties, would not arise in the absence of faulty organization of the libido; and that in these cases the libido had remained partially attached to an infantile and incestuous object-choice. The result was that in face of a situation producing conflict, libidinal regression would occur in an infantile and still forbidden direction, with the production of anxiety. This hypothesis, that the basis of an anxiety neurosis is always in the sexual life, while valid for some cases is too narrow to be generally applicable, even if 'sexual' is interpreted in a very wide sense. One encounters sometimes a more straightforward connection between the sexual life and morbid anxiety, in the cases of women whose failure to obtain satisfaction in sexual intercourse (as a result, for example, of coitus interruptus) is expressed directly in heightened physical and emotional tension, in vague aches and pains and ill-defined fears.

When anxiety arises from any situation which arouses intense feelings either of fear or hate or guilt and which is not squarely faced, it diffuses itself generally throughout the mind, and in the course of its diffusion tends to become concentrated again (in a manner determined by the individual mental history) around some special topic in itself apparently of more indifferent emotional value. Fears, vague or 'free-floating' at first, may thus become attached to some particular idea or situation, remote from the original source of the anxiety: that is, displacement of affect occurs. This displacement has the result of enabling the patient to escape from the painful contemplation of a personal difficulty. It should be noted that displacement of affect does not necessarily involve repression into the unconscious: the original difficulties may remain in consciousness, on the fringe as it were, while preoccupation is focused elsewhere. The individual usually rationalizes this preoccupation, thus making the displacement of affect more effective. Displacement and rationalization are the two main mental mechanisms employed.

The symptomatic form of an anxiety neurosis, in its somatic aspects, is determined by the influence of emotional perturbation on the functioning of various bodily organs. Emotional disturbance produces bodily symptoms: these bodily symptoms may then attract the affect displaced from other problems, and become the patient's chief complaints and apparent source of worry. Alternatively, displacement of the anxiety may take place in the mental sphere without bodily reference.

That general problems—for example, of business or other material circumstances—may be an adequate cause of an anxiety neurosis by displacement or diffusion of affect is well shown by the following case history.

CASE NO. 1
A married man of 47, who complained especially of attacks of diarrhoea in trains, of sweating of feet and hands, of dizziness, tremblings, irritability, insomnia and poor memory. He was a conscientious, hard-working man of artisan stock who had worked his way up to a position of responsibility in a large business. Most of his symptoms had begun three months before, when he was transferred by his employers from an indoor to an outdoor job, another employee being discharged to make room for him. The latter had been in the business for thirty years, and the patient felt very 'heavy and miserable' at usurping this man's position. The new post involved much travelling by train, and the patient began to suffer from diarrhoea from the very start of his train-journeying. He became so weak that after ten days he had to stay at home, where he remained till he entered hospital, after 'convalescence' at the seaside had failed.

Investigations showed that some of the symptoms—insomnia and irritability—had existed for some time before the diarrhoea began, that he had attributed them to overwork and had actually resigned from his previous (indoor) post. His resignation had not been accepted, but he was hurt nevertheless at the small amount of attention that was paid to him. Further, he divulged that he had been afraid of supersession by his employer's son. His fear was to some extent justified, for his removal to an outdoor traveller's position, although ostensibly for his health, was carried out to allow of his former post being taken by his young rival. He was a quiet, unaggressive man, who disliked a traveller's work intensely and embarked on it with great reluctance. It seemed likely that much of his regret for the dismissal of the other employee was a reflection of his feeling about his own supersession. The connection between his mental perturbation and his symptoms was pointed out. He accepted the explanation willingly and his symptoms ceased with dramatic rapidity, and did not recur. He said that he now felt confident, and that he never had understood his symptoms previously, having thought he had some physical disease.

The foregoing patient illustrates several points. The diffusion of affect from his own plight to that of his fellow-employee, showing itself as an unusual degree of regret, is an example of 'displacement'. The bodily symptoms were all those that are associated with fear; and he had a fear of his new job, plus a reluctance to leave his old one. He was also jealous—although he would not permit himself to feel it—of his employer's son, and he had a grievance towards his employers for their apparent lack of commiseration. His symptoms could be viewed as: 1. the result of his fear; 2. a protest against leaving his former post; and 3. retaliation against his employers, since he, as a matter of fact, proved their most efficient traveller, in spite of his handicaps, and his incapacity through illness penalized them financially. This threefold origin is a good example of 'overdetermination' as Freud has called it. The kind of process seen in this patient is one that is not uncommon in everyday life, perhaps especially in children and young persons. There is a grievance: the child is sorry for himself, he finds an ache or a pain easily enough, and he complains about it, either for sympathy or as an excuse from duty or for both. The process is not far removed from full consciousness. In the above case it was so near full consciousness that the patient quickly saw the explanations that were put to him, and laughingly, but a little shamefacedly, admitted their truth.

Differential Diagnosis

An anxiety neurosis must be differentiated from other abnormal mental reactions, and from physical disease. The commonest mistake is to call an agitated depression an anxiety neurosis. It is a serious mistake since the former is accompanied by a suicidal risk which may thus be ignored and the proper treatment of the two conditions is very different. A man or woman who develops symptoms of morbid anxiety for the first time in middle or later life should be suspected of suffering from a depression rather than a neurosis. The depressive symptoms associated with an anxiety neurosis are not so persistent, nor does the neurotic patient complain of early morning wakening nor of being at his worst in the first half of the day. One's clinical sensitivity is called fully into play in deciding whether the patient is more anxious than depressed, and how deep may be his depression: and the differential diagnosis may be really difficult, since particularly in the involutional melancholia type of depressive reaction anxiety is often in the forefront of the clinical picture and there is no retardation. Before the diagnosis of neurosis can be established, one must be able to demonstrate an adequate cause of the neurotic reaction. But psychoses may be reactive too, and it is all too easy to find a spurious psychogenesis.

Discrimination between the symptoms and signs of anxiety, and physical disease, also calls for good clinical judgement. The autonomic upsets of anxiety may suggest disease in any of the bodily systems, and the neurotic patient is often referred initially to the medical departments of a hospital, suspected of suffering from heart disease or peptic ulcer, rheumatism or endocrinopathy; or to the ophthalmologist to have his eyes examined or to the orthopaedic surgeon for relief of the pains in his back. Perhaps the most difficult differential diagnosis on the physical side lies sometimes between an anxiety neurosis and primary hyper-thyroidism. The anxious neurotic patient may have a rapid (waking) pulse, a raised systolic blood pressure, slightly enlarged thyroid gland and some upper-lid lag. Radio-iodine estimations may be necessary to establish the correct diagnosis in these borderline cases.

HYSTERIA

Hysteria has been known since antiquity. In Hippocratic times it was supposed to occur only in women and to result from 'wandering of the womb' into another part of the body. Later, the more dramatic aspects of hysteria—the convulsions, for example, were for a long time attributed to demoniacal possession. Many of the dramatic cures by exorcism and other preternatural methods recorded in popular and religious history occurred in hysterical patients. The study of neurotic symptoms was on the whole haphazard until Charcot, who was pri-marily a neurologist, began a systematic study of them, confining himself to the hysterical type of manifestation. Applying the methods of clinical observation which he had used for organic nervous diseases, he succeeded in formulating a group of clinical pictures, of paralyses, contractures and convulsions which con-stituted a graded series of increasing complexity, and all of which together he called 'hysteria'. The one causative factor which he found uniformly in his patients was a morbid inheritance, and he considered hysteria a malady of degeneration. A relatively minor observation of Charcot's had far-reaching effects in the hands of certain of his pupils. He reproduced paralysis in his patients by means of hypnotism, proving that hysterical paralysis could be the result of specific ideas existing in the patient's mind. But Charcot believed that such paralyses could be hypnotically reproduced only in hysterics and in *grande hystérie* at that. It remained for his successors to develop and modify his views. These modifications were on very divergent lines, and the principal varieties of theory and practice were associated with the names of Bernheim, Dubois, Dejerine, Janet and Freud.

Bernheim gradually came to the opinion that all the phenomena which Charcot had described as hysterical were capable of being produced by suggestion. He declared that not merely hysterical patients were hypnotizable, but that prac-tically everyone could be hypnotized. 'Suggestion', said Bernheim, 'consists of the influence exercised by an idea that has been suggested, and has been accepted by the brain.' Hysterical symptoms were therefore in Bernheim's opinion the result of suggestion. Babinski went further and stated that nothing is hysterical which cannot be produced by suggestion and removed by persuasion. The views of Dejerine, Janet and Freud will be discussed later, when we deal more fully with the psychopathological aspects.

Not only have there been many changes in the theories elaborated to explain hysteria, the clinical features also of the reaction have changed over the years. Patients displaying the features of Charcot's *grande hystérie*, women resting on their shoulders with their bodies and legs in the air, or in opisthotonos, are no longer seen. Cases of multiple personality have become very rare since Morton Prince was interested in them. Gross physical symptoms, in the nature of paralyses or bizarre gaits, have also become very uncommon in civilian practice. Perhaps the most frequent hysterical complaints are now 'blackouts' and bodily pains of one sort or another, which present more subtle problems in differential diagnosis. Both the public and their doctors have become more sophisticated.

Definition of the Reaction-type

Hysteria is more than a symptom or collection of symptoms: it is a special type of reaction to difficulties displayed in a number of syndromes which are distinctive both clinically and psychopathologically. It has a relationship with anxiety states in that an anxiety state may in certain circumstances replace hysteria in a given patient, and a case may begin as an anxiety neurosis and end as a hysteria. But these are not usual transitions. On the whole, in any one patient the type of reaction tends to remain fairly pure. It is important to distinguish between anxiety in the sense of mental conflict and its accompanying distress, which is a normal reaction, and an anxiety neurosis which is a clinical syndrome, is abnormal and has already been defined. In the former sense hysteria always begins with anxiety.

If the symptom or sign produced in hysteria is a physical manifestation such as a paralysis or anaesthesia the result is called *conversion hysteria*, the psychic energy derived from the repressed drives, emotions and ideas being said to be 'converted' into a physical symptom or sign.

Clinical Features

Commonly, though by no means invariably, the previous personality is an unusual one. An aggregation of traits is found which comprises what has been called the '*hysterical or histrionic personality*'. Such people tend to be highly egocentric and immature, both in talk and appearance, and to be conspicuous for the demands they make on people around them. There is a lifelong theatricality of behaviour and a desire to impress and gain sympathy, a contrast between actual shallowness of the feelings and the intensity of the expression of them and between external shyness and intense erotic interest, a lack of persistence of emotion and of effort, and much compensatory day-dreaming. Most often they are women, though adult still to a great extent dependent on one or other parent, sexually frigid, prone to react with sudden spites and piques and to try to dominate others with their tempers, whims or suicidal threats. They seem to have carried with them into adult life the infantile need for exclusive love and attention. There is an excellent description of such a personality in Lord David Cecil's biography *The Young Melbourne*, where the author reconstructs the character of Lady Caroline Lamb.

All neurotics are suggestible, and it has for long been held that hysterics are the most suggestible of all and show in fact an exaggerated suggestibility. Eysenck (1947) formulated the view that there are different types of suggestibility and distinguished a primary suggestibility of an ideomotor kind. 'The main feature of the tests which go to define this trait is the execution of a motor movement by the subject consequent upon the repeated suggestion by the experimenter that such a movement will take place, without conscious participation in the movement on the subject's part.' The test most commonly used to demonstrate this primary suggestibility is Hull's Body-Sway Test, in which the subject stands still and relaxed, with eyes closed, while the experimenter suggests to him that he is falling forward: the amount of sway is measured and a suggestibility score can be constructed. Using this and a number of other tests Eysenck found that primary suggestibility is closely related to hypnosis; that suggestibility is strongly correlated with neuroticism—'both when comparing neurotics with normals and when comparing the more seriously ill with the less seriously ill it was found that degree of neuroticism was reflected in the suggestibility test scores'; and that hysterics are not more suggestible than other types of neurotics.

According to Rivers and MacCurdy environmental factors in the way of training and education are of importance in determining the hysterical form of a neurosis. A training in implicit obedience, such as occurs in soldiers, is said to heighten suggestibility to an extent that makes hysterical symptoms more easily produced; while lack of education makes possible gross signs, such as a paraplegia, the arbitrary appearance of which an educated mind would not tolerate.

Hysterical symptoms may be found as secondary features in both 'functional' and organic psychoses. One may, for example, find stuttering or an hysterical weakness of the legs in a psychotic depression, or aphonia in the course of a schizophrenic illness. A brain tumour or other organic nervous system disease may release hysterical symptoms.

Symptoms and Signs

Both mental and physical symptoms are developed, but usually one or other type of symptom predominates in the individual case. These symptoms may mimic closely those of other diseases and the greater the patient's medical knowledge the closer will be the resemblance: it is advisable therefore always to ask the patient what he thinks or fears his illness is. The particular symptom chosen depends on a number of factors which vary from case to case: it may clearly have symbolic meaning (hysterical vomiting, for example, may symbolize rejection of an unwanted pregnancy); or it may be based on the residuals of some earlier injury or disease; or it may be suggested to the patient by previous medical examinations or the recent illness of a friend or relative.

Hysterical signs and symptoms have certain general characteristics. Taking those with a physical reference first, it may be said almost universally that there are no physical signs or symptoms in hysteria that could not be produced in the beginning either by volition or by emotion, although they could be so sustained only for a short time. Long-standing contractures, for example, which may persist during sleep and anaesthesia, require some additional explanation to account for their continuance. It can also be said that the physical aspects of hysteria correspond strikingly with the usual concepts of disease entertained by the lay mind. Thus a paralysis is always of an entire limb or of a movement, and never of an individual muscle; a tic is always a co-ordinated movement of synergic muscles, never a chaotic movement of muscles not functionally associated; and an anaesthesia does not follow a segmental or peripheral nerve-distribution, but is of the 'glove' or 'stocking' variety. Hysterical symptoms in general are readily produced and removed by suggestion in the waking state or in hypnosis.

Hurst showed that if a group of normal medical students in the pre-clinical years were asked to suppose that they had suffered from some bodily injury, the signs and symptoms they developed upon suggestive questioning had the characteristics of hysterical symptoms above described.

Physical Symptoms. These may be conveniently considered as motor, sensory, visceral and trophic.

The *motor symptoms* which are in the nature of some incapacity, partial or complete, involving the voluntary musculature, include pareses with or without contracture, mutism, aphonia, tremors and tics. The incapacity is often sudden in onset, variable, and only superficially like that of neurological disease. If paresis exists, it may affect the proximal muscles of a limb more than the distal ones, which is the reverse of what commonly happens in organic paralysis; and the muscles may be used in some movements and not in others. When asked to make the movement that is paralysed, the patient only succeeds in producing a spasm of the antagonistic muscles. Thus an artisan of 63 when asked to walk faster (his right leg had a hysterical paresis) threw his body into such strenuous jerkings that he was very breathless in two minutes and perspired freely. There is no reaction of degeneration in hysterically paralysed muscles. The reflexes are not grossly disturbed; but they may be much increased in amplitude. Not infrequently one notices a certain amount of what seems like voluntary exaggeration —the patient either jerks his limb before it is struck, or he jerks it again immediately after the true tendon-jerk has occurred. In hysterical flaccid paralysis the tendon reflexes may be very much diminished, but they are not lost. The plantar reflex is always flexor. If atrophy occurs, it is usually secondary to long disuse. Hysterical hemiplegia may involve the face on the same side, and may involve speech as well, even when left-sided.

Mutism and *aphonia* are distinguished from similar conditions resulting from organic disease: 1. by their completeness—every phonated word and sound is lost; 2. the absence of any intellectual disorder; 3. the preservation of the ability to communicate by writing or by signs; 4. the absence of paralysis of the lips and tongue; and 5. the vocal cords can be seen to be fully adducted in inspiration. The mute individual may be able to cough normally. These features are not always all present.

Hysterical *tremor* is usually coarse and often involves the whole limb. It may occur at rest, but commonly only when attention is drawn to it, or when the patient makes a voluntary movement.

Motor *tics* involve a co-ordinated group of muscles. They range from an occasional jerking of a limb to choreiform movements. Hysterical movements are apt to be more co-ordinated than those of true chorea and to be less varied, involving the repetition of a comparatively few movements. Rapid jerking move-

ments of the head occur, and may be indistinguishable from spasmodic torticollis: the latter, however, is probably in the majority of cases due to organic
disease of the extrapyramidal nervous system. A respiratory tic, for example,
hiccough, may be hysterical; but it has frequently been difficult to distinguish the
respiratory disorders of epidemic encephalitis from those of hysteria. The encephalitic or post-encephalitic tics have often had some of the marks of an hysterical
disorder. For example, post-encephalitic tics may be influenced by emotional
factors and may come on at precisely the same hour each night. It does not
of course follow that hysterical and encephalitic tics are identical.

Curious gaits of all kinds may occur. The patient may attribute them to pains
in the back or to loss of power in the lower limbs.

It is understandable that in pilots and other members of aircrews manifestations of hysteria should affect the eyes rather than the limbs, for what his legs
are to an infantryman, his eyes are to a pilot (Ironside and Batchelor, 1945).
Many hysterical signs were reported—coarse tremor of the eyelids, blepharo-
spasm, nystagmoid jerkings, all degrees of heterophoria, convergence weakness
and dissociation between convergence of the visual axis and contraction of the
pupils. Variable convergence spasm and spasm of accommodation were also
recorded.

Sensory Symptoms. Anaesthesias, paraesthesias and hyperaesthesias are common. It has been said that they are produced by suggestion from the physician,
but this is certainly not true of all. They are commonly distinguished by their
distribution, which is not that of an organic disturbance; by their variability at
successive examinations; and by their susceptibility to suggestion. In the case of
anaesthesias also, the lack of sensation is much more sweeping than in organic
lesions, all kinds of sensation being abolished in a given area; it is also deeper,
pain not being felt at all; and its margin is much more sharply defined—there is
no gradual transition to a normal area as in neurological lesions.

The susceptibility to suggestion can be shown very easily in certain patients
with a hemi-anaesthesia. This can be transferred to the other side of the body by
suggestion in the waking state. In a chronic hysterical patient in whom this
was done, the anaesthesia could be very readily transferred from the left to the
right side of the body, so that she would tolerate the passing of safety-pins
through her skin; but it had invariably returned to the left side the following
morning.

Hyperaesthesias most commonly are localized in the head or the abdomen,
and may be described as pains of any type or in bizarre terms, as constant (even
during sleep) and as unassuageable.

The special senses can be affected also. A concentric diminution of the visual
field is not uncommon. If the perimetric examination is continued through 360
degrees a spiral field may be obtained. Amaurosis and amblyopia also occur.
There may be a bizarre contradiction in the symptoms—the patient may be able
to read a paper and yet may be unable to see to get about. Hysterical blindness is
often sudden. The bilaterally blind hysteric commonly avoids obstacles placed
in his path. Hysterical unilateral blindness can be detected in various ways. For

L

example, pressure on one eye may produce double vision. Specially coloured spectacles to read correspondingly coloured types can also be used for its detection, the patient reading type of a colour which can only be seen by the 'blind' eye. Subjective disturbances of vision are usually associated with intact pupillary reflexes and intact extra-ocular movements, but the light reflex may actually be lost, to return when the blindness is cured.

Visceral Symptoms. Anorexia, bulimia (excessive appetite), vomiting, air-swallowing, hiccough, fullness or pain in the abdomen, flatulence and regurgitation may occur as hysterical symptoms. Since gastric functions are so readily affected by emotions, it is easy to see why they should so often be disorganized in hysteria and why they should so readily have a symbolic significance: vomiting, for example, may signify a repressed disgust. Hysterical vomiting is rapid and easy, often occurring just after a meal and usually without nausea.

Anorexia nervosa, an uncommon, interesting and puzzling condition, is commonly classified with the hysterical reactions but it is not certain that it is correct so to describe it; it is a syndrome which is not fully understood, either from the psychological or the physical aspects, and whose boundaries have not yet been clearly delimited. Valuable studies have been made by Nemiah (1950), Kay (1953), and Crisp (1965), amongst others.

Anorexia nervosa occurs typically in girls in their later teens and in young unmarried women: it is doubtful if the same syndrome is found in men. The typical triad of symptoms is anorexia, amenorrhoea and loss of weight. The illness has an emotional basis and begins often with a voluntary restriction of the diet. One young woman said afterwards, 'It was a silly idea to get into my head' (to starve herself), 'but I thought I was too fat, and then I couldn't get rid of the idea. I just wouldn't eat.' The girl may have been teased by her friends about putting on weight or have become unduly sensitive about the development of her breasts. Crisp has pointed out that these girls tend to come from families with a history of nutritional disturbances, obesity and anorexia; and themselves to have experienced an early puberty and to have been of above average weight at this time. They develop a phobia of the physical and particularly the sexual developments of adolescence, which are epitomized by the normal adolescent gain of weight. There is refusal to take an adequate diet. Appetite may be lost and is replaced by a repugnance for food. Or there may be phases of compulsive overeating countered by vomiting or excessive purgation. A state of carbohydrate starvation results (Russell, 1967). Amenorrhoea may precede, be contemporaneous with or follow the refusal of food. The patient becomes markedly constipated and as a result of not eating loses weight, commonly to between 5 and 6½ stones; the resulting emaciation may prove fatal. A remarkable feature that these patients sometimes display is tireless activity in spite of their emaciation. The B.M.R. is low, hypothermia, hypotension and a poor peripheral circulation are also typical, and the patient may show a fine downy (lanugo) hair on her back.

It is usually the mother who brings the patient to the doctor. The patient herself may declare that she is perfectly all right and that she does not know why people are fussy and worrying over her. In this she may exhibit the *belle indiffér-*

ence of the hysteric, but this is by no means always the mental state. Depression of spirits may be prominent, with feelings of guilt and isolation and suicidal thoughts. Nor is the previous personality by any means always hysterical, though it is usually immature, with evidence of neurotic predisposition. Several other personality types are encountered, the obsessional, the anxious, the hypochondriacal—and of these the obsessional is probably the commonest. There may be a history of previous food fads and alimentary preoccupations. Insight is minimal and co-operation in treatment often poor, the patient covertly disposing in various ways of the food given her.

The psychogenesis of these cases is complex. There may be a severely disturbed mother-daughter relationship, the patient at one and the same time being unduly dependent and rebelling against maternal domination: or a preoccupation with phantasies of pregnancy and birth. From some of these immature girls one elicits fears of oral impregnation, and they appear to have identified growing fat with being pregnant.

Some of these patients recover mentally and physically, marry and have children: many do badly. The syndrome may persist for many years, or there may be a change to compulsive overeating and overweight; a few become psychotic, usually if so developing schizophrenia. Kay (1953), who doubted whether anorexia nervosa is a specific clinical entity, came to the following conclusions from a follow-up study of 37 patients: 1. these patients tend to have a poor prognosis; 2. when clear-cut psychotic features are not present from the outset, there is little tendency to develop a psychosis; 3. only 10–20 per cent. recover to the stage of good adjustment. Up to about 15 per cent. may die, and the commonest causes of death are inanition and suicide. Dally and Sargant (1966) have reported a better prognosis: by the end of 3 years about two-thirds of their 57 patients had made a satisfactory recovery. The prognosis for those who had been ill for more than 5 years was, however, poor. Most authorities agree that the return of regular menstruation is prognostically a good sign.

Trophic Symptoms. The *vasomotor* disturbances of hysterically paralysed limbs are well known. The limb is often blue and cold. This is partly the result of disuse and of posture (the dependent position of a paralysed arm, for example), but there is possibly another element, since the vasomotor changes may be rapid and considerable.

The spontaneous appearance of *skin lesions*, blisters, erythemas, etc., has usually been considered an artifact (dermatitis artifacta): but it has been known for more than 50 years that skin blisters, localized urticaria and oedema could be produced hypnotically at specified points on the body surface. Moody (1946) reported a striking case of bodily changes during the abreaction in a somnambulist of an incident when many years previously his hands had been tied behind his back during sleep to restrain him from violence. During abreaction this man developed on both forearms deeply indented weals like rope marks. However, many such lesions are undoubtedly more properly regarded as simulation than as hysterical. Some cases respond fairly readily to suggestion.

Mental Symptoms. The symptoms of hysteria which are obviously from the first of a mental kind are chiefly amnesias, somnambulisms, fugues, trances, hallucinations, dreamlike states and fits. They are all of dissociative type; that is, they are all to be regarded as the result of detachment and independent functioning of a part of the mental content. *La belle indifférence*, the typical mental attitude, is by no means always found. It tends to be a late feature, developing when disabling symptoms have become established. The lack of insight may then be striking. The patient denies any worries and insists that his symptoms are purely physical.

Amnesia is commonly of a circumscribed series of events in the patient's memory. It is as if a part of his life had dropped out, although the hysteric may not be aware of the gap in his recollection till it is pointed out to him. This amnesia usually hides some incident about which the patient has felt guilty, and he has forgotten what it would be painful for him to remember. Henderson recorded that amnesia sometimes served as a defence for desertion in war-time.

In some cases the amnesia is for the entire life up to a certain recent point. The patient may forget his own identity, the names and faces of his friends, even his wife and children. The amnesia is always for something with which a strong emotion has become associated. For example:

CASE NO. 2
A young flying officer who complained of insomnia and a terrifying dream of an aeroplane crash, with which he always awoke, could remember nothing of the events of a period of three days which began while he was at his flying depot, but ended with his finding himself in a hotel in London in mufti. In response to persuasive insistence, he reconstructed the period little by little. Asked to begin with the events preceding the first day of the amnesia, he gradually gave a consecutive account, although with many pauses and transient inability to recall, which were overcome by encouragement. It appeared that he had been for some time under stress, as he disliked and feared flying, and was at the same time engaged to be married. If he stopped flying, it meant breaking the engagement, for financial reasons. Finally his fear became so intense that he deserted. The amnesia was for the episodes connected with his desertion, including the exchange of some letters with his fiancée, announcing the step he had taken. The recovery of the lost memory was followed by disappearance of the insomnia and anxious dreams.

Fugues and Somnambulisms. In a hysterical fugue the patient suddenly leaves his previous activity and goes on a journey which has no apparent relation to what he has just been doing, and for which he has more or less complete amnesia afterwards. The lost memories may be recalled under hypnosis.

Somnambulisms are dissociated states identical with the above except that they begin during sleep. They are common in childhood, when their motivation often appears on the surface. For example, a boy much attached to his mother and antagonistic to his father, who treated him badly, in his somnambulisms would make for his parents' bedroom and endeavour to get in at the side of the bed on which his mother slept. Janet described 'monoideic' and 'polyideic' somnambulisms according to the poverty or wealth of mental content of the dissociated state. He pointed to the regularity of the development of each attack, the same features repeating themselves each time or (more rarely) each attack beginning as far as mental content is concerned where the other left off. Janet distinguished fugues from somnambulisms chiefly on the ground that the former last longer, and consequently require for their continuance more rapport with the surroundings. During the somnambulism the patient commonly lives through a vivid experience, little or not at all related to his surroundings, and therefore hallucinatory in character. By talking to him, not insistently, but in a persuasive attempt to enter into his experience, the patient may be got to describe the nature of the experience while he is still in the somnambulistic state. Although such patients appear to be 'walking in their sleep', they are not really asleep. Their perceptions are often acute. A somnambulist schoolboy had his eyes apparently closed, but when one door was shut he turned away without hesitation and chose another which allowed him to pass from the hospital ward into a corridor.

Fugues occur in conditions other than hysteria: in epilepsy, for example, as post-ictal automatisms or as ictal phenomena in psychomotor seizures; and in depressions, when they may be suicidal equivalents.

Stengel (1941, 1943) has made interesting contributions to the understanding of fugues. Of the 25 cases reported in his earlier paper 10 were related in some way to epilepsy, 1 was a schizophrenic and the remainder were typical manic-depressives, hysterics and psychopaths. There appear to be, Stengel stated, 'three essential conditions without which fugue states do not develop: the tendency to indulge in periodic changes of mood, a disturbance of home conditions in childhood, and a tendency towards the production of twilight states, the last factor being most prominent in epileptics'. He drew attention to the similarity between fugues and wandering states in children with disturbed home circumstances. Stengel's second paper reported 11 further cases in detail. In all these a tendency to depressive reactions of the constitutional type was noted, and in a number the transformation of a suicidal impulse into the impulse to wander was demonstrated.

Berrington and his colleagues (1956) reported findings in 37 cases. The following were the diagnostic categories: psychopathic states 24, hysteria 6, reactive depression 4, involutional depression 2, schizophrenia 1. They stressed the common factor of a depressive mood, and the rôle of head injury: severe head injury was found in 16 cases and doubtful head injury in 3 cases, as against 3 in controls. Ten of the patients were also alcoholic. Hysterical mechanisms were found to be fairly common and compulsive features rare. With regard to the rôle of head injury these authors concluded: 'We are not of the opinion that the organic trauma produced the fugue directly, but rather that it produced impairment which facilitated the occurrence of a psychogenic fugue, or that the concussion and subsequent amnesia formed the basis for the suggestion of a psychogenic amnesia at a later date. We incline to the latter viewpoint.'

A fugue should therefore not too hastily be diagnosed as hysterical. Detailed psychiatric and neurological assessment is required.

In *double* or *multiple personalities* there is a further elaboration of the process occurring in fugues and somnambulisms. The groups of dissociated functions are now so extensive that any of the dissociated groups is capable, when fully conscious and in charge of the motor functions, of appearing superficially as a complete personality. Stevenson's *Dr. Jekyll and Mr. Hyde* is a fictitious instance of this kind. William James recorded a case which has become famous:

CASE No. 3

A clergyman, the Rev. Ansell Bourne, disappeared from a town in Rhode Island. Eight weeks later a man calling himself A. J. Brown, who had rented a small shop six weeks previously in a town in Pennsylvania and had stocked it with confectionery, etc., woke up in a fright and asked who he was. He said he was a clergyman, that his name was Bourne, and that he knew nothing of the shop or of Brown. He was subsequently identified as the Rev. Ansell Bourne by his relatives, and remained terrified by the incident and unable to explain it.

In Morton Prince's patient, Sally Beauchamp, there were not two but several distinct personalities, which alternately occupied the field of consciousness.

Hysterical Fits. Hysterical fits can usually be distinguished from epileptic seizures, although there is an intermediary group very hard to assign definitely to one or other class. A true epileptic seizure can be provoked by emotional factors; and an epileptic may have hysterical fits.

The typical hysterical fit usually occurs only in the presence of others, and in the daytime, does not involve any but very minor injuries, is often provoked by an emotional situation, has a very variable duration and does not show the tonic-clonic succession, but consists of irregular movements, which have been supposed to have sometimes a symbolic significance, representing some emotional episode which the patient is re-living. Attempts to restrain the patient usually result in increased struggling. Tongue biting, incontinence and reflex changes do not occur: nor is the hysterical seizure followed by confusion, headache or nausea.

There are numerous anomalies in hysterical fits. Thus an elderly woman bent her head on her chest, screwed up her eyes (especially on an attempt to examine her pupils, which reacted normally during the fit), extended her right arm and rotated her forearm to and fro. She resisted both passive flexion and extension of the arm. The 'aura' was of a peculiar, visual hallucinatory kind in which she saw her mother's grave.

Hysterical *trances* and *stupors*, '*twilight states*' of altered consciousness, states of ecstasy, and hallucinations, are rarely encountered; and these types of reaction are much more often psychotic than hysterical. Much more common are dramatic scenes, in which the patient becomes acutely excited (usually following some frustration), 'acts out' and may threaten or attempt suicide.

Hysterical Pseudo-dementia. In situations in which a lack of mental responsibility, if recognized by the authorities, would bring some advantage, gross hysterical mental symptoms of a clearly purposeful nature may be developed. In prisoners awaiting trial, for example, and in persons still at large who have committed some illegal act, a state *non compos mentis* may excuse, or be conceived to excuse, the misdoer from the immediate legal consequences of his acts.

The patient may be unable to answer very simple questions: for example, he cannot tell the date. He cannot give a coherent account of himself and behaves in a simple, childish way. As Bleuler pointed out: 'What is characteristic is the disappearance of the memory for elementary knowledge and experience, which remains intact in the organic disturbances.'

The *Ganser syndrome*, or 'syndrome of approximate answers', was described first in prisoners. The patient gives bizarre replies to questions; for example, asked how many tails a sheep has, he will reply 'two', or if asked how many legs a horse has, he may say 'five'. Similarly asked to multiply 5 by 6, he will say (perhaps) 32. If requested to perform some simple action, the patient goes about it clumsily. Thus given a key and asked to lock a door, he will fumble and use the wrong end of the key. Dates will be given only approximately. We have seen the Ganser condition also in an acute hallucinatory paranoid state in one patient, and among the residuals of such a condition (probably alcoholic in origin) in another.

In some instances a much more elaborate attempt is made at dramatization, and in these the voluntary (simulated) element is much more clear.

CASE No. 4
A banker from one of the Southern American States furnished a good example of an elaborate reaction which was very probably simulated. His bank had failed at a time when he had utilized, for investments in companies in which he was interested, money from the funds of the bank in excess of the 10 per cent. permitted by the laws of the State. When admitted to hospital he was mute, shook his head in answer to questions and refused food. An hour later he took supper, and answered some questions relevantly and coherently. Then he became mute again, and the same evening he got out of bed, lay on his back on the floor and propelled himself towards the wall with his feet. He next proceeded to make a show of 'climbing the walls'. He mildly but firmly resented being put to bed, smiled, showed his teeth and moved his lower jaw rapidly up and down. When being carried to another ward he held himself rigidly, so that he could almost have been supported horizontally by his head and heels. For the following two weeks he alternately was mute and talkative. When he did talk it was in a disconnected fashion with sometimes a peculiar verbigeration, as 'Mother—Mary—Mary—Mother —All Marys—All Mothers'. After two weeks he recovered suddenly. He denied that any legal trouble was pursuing him, but some weeks after he left hospital, completely well, a telegram was received from his lawyers asking for a certificate that he had been in a mental hospital, as the patient had been arrested for irregular dealing with the moneys of his bank.

There is a *hysterical puerilism* which is related to this 'pseudo-dementia'. In this there is a return to the behaviour of early childhood. McDougall (1926) cited a good instance, which he regarded as an example of regression to an ontogenetically earlier mode of behaviour.

CASE No. 5
An Australian private, aged 22, after a series of experiences, including a bombardment and an air raid, 'reverted to the mode of life, bodily and mentally, which is normal to a child of some months of age'. With certain exceptions he showed no trace of comprehension of spoken or written language, and had little or no apparent understanding of the use of ordinary objects or utensils. He walked jerkily with feet wide apart, and, when allowed to do so, crawled on his buttocks. He had to be spoon-fed, and would take only milk and slops; if he took anything else, he complained of belly-ache and

curled up in bed. A doll was his chief toy. Fears of animals, sudden noises, etc., were prominent. However, there were some aspects of his behaviour which were of a more adult kind—he smoked a cigarette when offered it, showed some knowledge of finger speech and swam well. From time to time he showed progress in learning, especially in handwork, and the use of gesture-language, but he repeatedly relapsed after small frights. Once he wrote his own nickname spontaneously, and he sometimes tried to kiss his nurse. He recovered gradually 'to an approximately normal condition'.

Hysteria and Simulation. The differentiation of these uncommon pseudo-dementias from simulated mental disorders is often difficult. To distinguish sharply between hysteria and simulation is in fact arbitrary. Simulation is the voluntary production of symptoms by an individual who has full knowledge of their voluntary origin. In hysteria there is typically no such knowledge, and the production of symptoms is the result of processes that are not fully conscious. Kretschmer rightly pointed out, however, that the criteria 'conscious or unconscious?' will not serve to distinguish simulation from hysteria, for not all the motives of a healthy mind are conscious, and not all hysterical ones are unconscious. There are all graduations between hysteria and simulation.

We would emphasize the importance of contradictions in the patient's story, discrepancies between his subjective account (of pain, for example) and his behaviour (whether he knows himself to be observed at the time or not), the presence of marked hysteriform symptoms with great profession of concern about them and clumsy unwillingness to be cured, *e.g.* complete forgetfulness for what has been told him at previous interviews. All these strongly suggest simulation.

Estimation of the aim of the illness, and of discrepancies between the loss occasioned by it and the apparent gain, is often not easy. The patient conceals the gain—if he is a hysteric, he conceals it from himself as well as from others—and there may be objects other than avoiding justice or gaining pecuniary advantages from disability, of which the value for the patient is difficult to assess.

Aetiology and Psychopathology

Despite intensive research over the past century by psychiatrists, neurologists and psychologists of great ability, hysteria remains in many of its aspects mysterious. Neither its aetiology nor its psychopathology has yet been fully worked out. The relationships between suggestibility, hypnosis and hysterical symptoms are complex. Hypnosis is a state of heightened suggestibility. Hypnosis can remove hysterical symptoms and induce phenomena akin to hysterical symptoms: but the hypnotic state, which can be induced in many normal individuals, is not an illness.

According to Dejerine (1911), hysteria resulted from emotional disturbance, but only in subjects with a peculiar emotional constitution. The emotional constitution of the hysteric was, he believed, shown in his or her tendency to react much more intensely than the normal to an emotional stimulus, and to react in a specific region, that is, in a particular organ or group of organs: the psychic representation of the function had a distinctive tendency to become dissociated from the seat of consciousness, and there was a peculiar passivity in the patient's attitude to the dissociated function. Dejerine performed a considerable service in stressing the part played by emotions and preoccupation with their bodily results, but his explanations of hysterical reactions lacked the precision and detail which were to be supplied by Freud.

'Hysteria', said Janet (1911), 'is a malady of the synthesis of the personality.' It is a form of mental depression characterized by restriction of the field of personal consciousness and a tendency to dissociation (that is, independent functioning) and emancipation of the systems of ideas and functions that constitute personality. There are two kinds of psychological functions, according to Janet—easy ones, requiring the co-operation of only a few elements; and difficult operations, which require the systematization of an infinite number of elements, involving a very new and intricate synthesis in each operation. When the 'nervous tension' or 'psychological force' is lowered by puberty, disease, fatigue or emotion (the last named involving great expenditure of nervous strength and therefore approaching fatigue) there is a general lowering of the level of psychological performance. Hence only the simple acts can be performed. In hysteria the lowering of psychological tension is localized in one particular function, which disappears in consequence from consciousness; it is 'dissociated' from the rest of the conscious personality. This dissociation is mainly of a function which has been weak or disturbed, especially if the function has been in activity at the moment of a great emotion. The function that disappears is commonly one that is very complicated and difficult for the subject: in this way, for example, professional and social paralyses are developed.

The objection to Janet's views is that they are a matter not so much of explanation as of description in terms of doubtful physical analogies. Except that the hysterical dissociation is said to occur at moments of great emotion, his hypotheses offer no explanation of what brings about the dissociation.

Freud, also a pupil of Charcot, began where the latter left off. Following up a discovery made by his colleague Breuer, that a hysterical patient became apparently well after a forgotten event of a personal and emotional nature was recalled under hypnosis, and after establishing further in some cases that the forgotten event had been of a sexual kind, Freud formulated the generalization that hysterical symptoms are memory-traces of sexual traumata—'the hysteric suffers from reminiscences'. Soon he modified this view to include among memories of aetiological importance not only those of actual traumata, but those of sexual experiences which had existed only in the patient's childish phantasies. He developed the concept that this sexual trauma (real or imagined) was the Oedipus complex, that it was repressed in early childhood, that this repression failed in later life only if some contemporary event reactivated by association the early repressed memories, and that a repressed Oedipus complex was in fact the necessary condition for the development of hysteria in later life. Sexual frustration in adult life led to an infantile type of (forbidden) love-object being again sought out. The hysterical symptoms are the result of a conflict between the super-ego and wishes not palatable to the super-ego which seek expression. Repression is only partially successful: the forbidden wishes succeed in gaining a disguised expression by 'conversion' into the symptom, which is therefore in a sense a symbol. The localization of the physical sign or symptom is determined by various factors—especially the appropriateness of the particular sign or symptom to symbolize the repressed wish, but also by accidental factors such as a previous physical disability.

The Freudian explanation can hardly be accepted as having universal validity; it is probably true only for a proportion of hysterics. It is impossible, for example, to see anything sexual in the aetiology of hysteria occurring in the soldier on the field of battle, or in peace-time as the result of injury involving questions of compensation. The purposive aspect of hysterical dissociations is particularly evident in the hysterias of war-time, the hysterical disability making further service in the danger zone impossible. The reaction is to observers obviously purposive and self-protective, but the hysterical individual is not himself consciously aware of his evasion. Therefore he is not malingering.

A case history will serve to bring out the more frequent complexity of the situations in which hysterical symptoms are developed, the emotions involved, the influence of both heredity and environment, the part played by patterns of reaction acquired in childhood, the unconscious determination of the locus of the symptoms, the purpose of the individual symptoms and the aim of the illness, and its unsatisfactory nature as a solution of the problem.

CASE No. 6

The patient, a married man of 40, complained of exhaustion, tremor of right side of body, giddiness, pain in right side, photophobia (right eye) and jerking of body and limbs.

A maternal uncle had had a brief episode of elation followed by depression. A maternal aunt died in a mental hospital of 'religious mania' at 45 years. The maternal grandfather died from jumping out of a window. The patient had no children, his wife being 'delicate'.

Personal History—He was always 'very nervous' of his father, who was very severe in his punishments. In his boyhood the patient was thrashed every day for a week, put on dry bread and water and deprived of his clothes. While at school (from 5 to 15 years) the father made his son work in the garden before school hours from 4.30 a.m. The father was a very large man physically, and the patient was terrorized. His ambition was to be an engineer, but his father frustrated him, and he took up clerical work. He remained at this and has been fairly successful.

After the war he returned to his previous business, not from a strong desire to do so, but ostensibly from a sense of obligation because his employers had treated him very well during his absence.

He was a very ambitious man, fond of decorations and of social distinction, and was somewhat ashamed of the fact that he did not occupy an executive position in the office. His general attitude was one of some superiority, but this was not marked, and tinged with a good deal of uncertainty about himself and his position. His financial position was an unusually good one, largely from his own efforts.

Present Illness—In October the patient was transferred to work of a type which displeased him in several ways. He was told that excess of work had been deliberately added to his predecessor, 'in order to make or break him'. His predecessor had succeeded in doing it, although he had had a 'nervous breakdown' previously. Further, the work was much less congenial than the patient's previous work, and involved much more writing. It also savoured of degradation in rank. His immediate superior was domineering, and the patient disliked him, and, on account of his position, feared him. The superior had the reputation of being unable to keep assistants. The patient decided to make the best of it and to give the new work a three months' trial. Soon he found the work very difficult to overtake, and on most days he was exhausted even in the mornings. He began to sleep badly and obtained sick leave in the following May. In the previous November his father had had a stroke, and the patient for three months thereafter made a special journey every day to shave him. He 'couldn't stand being at work all day and then doing this'. While on leave he received a letter asking him to resign. This 'hurt' him very much, and he 'got such terrific pains', especially on his right side, that tears ran out of his eyes. He felt he was very badly treated. The pains in his right side were so bad that he could not lie on it for a time. Right-sided tremor began also at this time. His doctor reproved his superior for sending such a letter, and the patient returned to work. Four days before his return, however, his right hand swelled, with shooting pains in it. He thought, 'Am I getting some creeping paralysis?' He subsequently remembered that many years previously at business he had noticed his hand numb after much writing, and still earlier after writing impositions at school. His hand had been swollen for some time in France (frost-bite?). This painful swelling of the hand incapacitated him for anything except the type of work he had done before his transfer in October. On his return to work he was in consequence placed on an easy but menial task, which hurt his dignity still more. His condition did not in any way improve, and when his chief ultimately told him he was slacking, he felt this was the last straw, and practically did not sleep at all afterwards till he finally abandoned work two weeks later.

He was slightly depressed, and displayed considerable subdued resentment towards his business superiors, mingled with a fear of them and of their opinion, although he had no reason to fear the financial consequences of losing his job. He recovered rapidly with psychotherapy.

One of the most striking aspects of this patient's make-up was his ambition for the outward signs of success. Another was his timid, schoolboyish attitude to his superiors. Both these characteristics were marks of an underlying feeling of inferiority; and the manifestations of both of them entered largely into the foundations of his illness. His ambitious vanity produced an intense emotional revulsion from the new conditions of his work (which was a preponderating interest despite his financial independence), while his juvenile attitude helped to prevent his taking any action. Even verbal expression of his resentment he found difficult. If it is attempted to trace the origin of his feeling of inferiority with its special manifestation of timidity towards his superiors, it is difficult not to suppose that his remarkable early experiences at the hands of his father were responsible for it. Furthermore, his father's denial of an education to him while it was given to his younger brother added to his inferiority in another direction.

This patient exemplifies also the transition from a condition of conflict with anxiety into hysteria with 'conversion' symptoms (paralysis of arm, pains, right-sided tremor). The hysterical solution, however, was an unusually poor and incomplete one. The patient remained uncomfortable in mind for the greater part of the time. He was much too ambitious to be pleased with such an unsatisfactory compromise. The unsympathetic attitude of his immediate superior, while it helped to produce the illness, also seemed to shorten it, since the symptoms were not permitted to achieve their object—resignation was suggested and not reinstatement. The case is interesting also in that it shows with unusual directness the symbolic nature of certain bodily pains—the receipt of a letter whose contents were painful to his self-respect was followed at once by 'great pain' in his right side. The relation of the paresis of his right arm to his reluctance to do his new work has to be inferred, but with considerable certainty, from the connections of the facts recorded.

Hysteria seems to occur chiefly or entirely in persons particularly predisposed, either by inheritance or the effects of their early environment, to mental dissociation. The actual occurrence of this dissociation depends on the problems which the individual encounters on his or her way through life. The symptom developed is symbolic in the sense that it has a meaning for the patient. This meaning is eventually purposive, the symptom being a solution, however unsatisfactory, of some problem of everyday adaptation. The patient is unaware of the real meaning. If he thinks about it at all, he believes the symptoms mean simply an illness in the ordinary sense. From these two facts—that the symptom is a solution of a problem, and that it is misinterpreted by the patient's consciousness—arises the patient's *belle indifférence*. The onset of the symptom may not always involve repression, but only a mental conflict without repression. The conflict leads to emotion and its physical manifestations. These are misinterpreted as the outcome of physical disease, and physical disease suggests disability of the part affected. Suggestion operates powerfully where there is mental conflict, and as the suggestion of disease is in harmony with one side of the conflict—the desire to escape—the suggestion is accepted and the symptom results. There is a gain of mental composure, since the conflict is solved, but at the expense of part of the personality, since suggestion operates primarily at the mental level, and can isolate a function only at that level. The actual problem may remain in the patient's mind; but it is no longer acute, since the symptom has provided a solution of an indirect kind. But the connection between the problem and the symptom is not seen by the patient. The connection cannot so much be said to be repressed as to be neglected. Only in some such way as this can it be explained that in many a psychological analysis of hysteria nothing that was not conscious before—although it may not have been clearly defined, or alluded to—may be brought out, and yet the symptoms disappear as their causations and connections are exhibited.

Where repression does occur, the same processes will serve to explain the occurrence of symptoms. For the production of symptoms at all means a partial failure of repression: if repression has partly failed, conflict conscious or unconscious exists, and conflict is the condition that led to the formation of symptoms in the way already set forth. These theories hold for the physical symptoms of hysteria.

With the mental symptoms of hysteria a similar process occurs. In hysterical amnesia, for example, there has been a period of conflict; then emotional preoccupation prevents the subject's noticing events in the ordinary way, consequently the memory of them, when the conflict has died down (they are registered marginally), is vague; vagueness of memory suggests complete failure of it, the patient does not wish to remember in any case—again the emotional symptom coincides with the wish—we accept what we wish to believe, and so does the hysterical patient—and an amnesia results.

An exactly similar process will account for fugues—the patient starts out on his fugue simply with a consciousness whose clearness is disturbed by emotional conflict, and ends with an amnesia. In a fugue there need not be repression at the beginning—the amnesia is an end-product. Where a fugue-habit has once been established, however, dissociation appears to occur at the beginning of each fugue.

Differential Diagnosis

In every case a careful physical examination is essential either to exclude physical disease or injury, or to define it if it is also present. There may of course be no physical disease and this is the usual situation: but on the other hand there may be hysterical aggravation of an existing injury (for example, a hysterical paralysis of an arm with a flesh wound), or organic nervous system disease may have released hysterical symptoms. Hysteria is often mistaken for physical disease, and physical disease is often called hysteria. Central nervous system disease is not infrequently miscalled hysteria in its earlier stages: cases of brain tumour, encephalitis and disseminated sclerosis may be thus misdiagnosed. Myasthenia gravis may be thought to be hysterical weakness. It is helpful to remember that the hysteric does not usually look physically ill (anorexia nervosa is, of course, an exception), and that hysterical symptoms in young people are often of dramatically sudden onset—which is unlike physical disease at that age. Hysterical-seeming symptoms occurring for the first time in middle age or later should always be suspected of being organically determined.

Hysterical fits may be difficult to distinguish from epileptic fits. A careful description of the attacks is essential. A full examination will include electroencephalography.

To establish the diagnosis of a neurotic reaction, it is essential not only to exclude physical disease but to demonstrate that the illness is psychogenic. There must be positive as well as negative grounds for diagnosing hysteria. One must be able to link the hysterical symptoms understandably with a life-situation which has presented difficulties to the patient. His or her previous personality must, of course, be taken closely into account in assessing these environmental factors.

If the reaction is clearly neurotic, then the doctor must assess the importance of the hysterical features and determine whether they are primary or secondary. Hysterical symptoms may, for example, be developed by a patient with an anxiety neurosis, or anxiety appear in a reaction which is predominantly hysterical. Too much should not be made of these distinctions, but they may have some bearing on treatment.

Hysterical reactions rarely appear like psychoses. Fugues and stupors here present the chief problems in differential diagnosis. The personality of the individual, and the development and whole setting of the symptoms, must be taken into account. A stupor in a young person is more often schizophrenic than hysterical.

In reviewing cases diagnosed as hysteria at the Bethlem-Maudsley and National Hospitals, Slater (1965) found it easy to show that misdiagnosis is common. Patients formerly diagnosed as suffering from hysteria were found on follow-up to have various kinds of organic nervous system disease, epilepsy, schizophrenia, manic-depressive psychosis and so forth. Some of the diagnoses made by specialists were glaringly inept: *e.g.* a man aged 43 with a history of three attacks of right-sided weakness accompanied by vomiting and disturbed speech, with impairment of recent memory and variable right-sided signs, was held to be suffering from hysteria. Slater's dispirited and illogical conclusion from this demonstration of medical error, was that the diagnosis of hysteria 'is in fact not only a delusion but also a snare'. Those who think that cases of hysteria are hard to find might consider how far the impulsive self-poisoning has replaced the hysterical fit.

OBSESSIONAL NEUROSES

Definition of the Reaction-type

In common usage the terms obsession, obsessed and obsessional signify that an individual is in some way preoccupied or harassed or haunted. In delimiting an obsessional neurosis the term obsession must be used with more precise meaning. Schneider proposed the following definition of obsessions—'contents of consciousness, which, when they occur, are accompanied by the experience of subjective compulsion, and which cannot be got rid of, though on quiet reflection they are recognized as senseless'. This was later modified by Aubrey Lewis, to give a definition which is now widely accepted—'Whenever a patient complains of some mental experience which is accompanied by a feeling of subjective compulsion, so that he does not willingly entertain it, but, on the contrary, does his utmost to get rid of it, that is an obsession.' The three essential elements are the feeling of subjective compulsion, the resistance to it and the retention of insight.

Obsessional symptoms may occur in many different kinds of nervous and mental illness, neurotic and psychotic, 'functional' and organic. In an obsessional neurosis they form the kernel of the illness and its presenting and predominant symptoms. The patient's peace of mind is seriously disturbed by these symptoms and his daily life is to a lesser or greater extent hindered and disrupted by them.

The term obsessional neurosis includes both obsessive-ruminative and obsessive-compulsive states.

Clinical Features

Obsessional neuroses are the most constitutionally determined and the least common of the neurotic reaction-types, comprising less than 5 per cent. of the total of cases.

The majority of those who develop an obsessional neurosis have shown previously personality traits which are conventionally described as constituting the *obsessional personality.* These traits are an unusual conscientiousness and adherence to method, order and cleanliness. Their possessors are described as fastidious, meticulous, fussy and tidy, punctual, persistent, painstaking and hardworking, prone to recheck rigorously what they do, liking to have everything 'just so' and 'cut and dried', rigid and often pedantic. Samuel Pepys said of himself—'My delight is in the neatness of everything, and so cannot be pleased with anything unless it be very neat, which is a strange folly.' Though these characteristics are commonly called obsessional, it is obvious that very many normal people who never become nervously ill exhibit these traits. Also, if the possessor of these traits is subjected to stress and breaks down, he is more liable to develop a depression or a 'psychosomatic' syndrome than an obsessional neurosis. Furthermore, some of those who develop an obsessional neurosis have not had obsessional personality traits: Pollitt (1960) in a review of 115 cases found that 34 per cent. had had no obsessional traits before breakdown. It may be said therefore that the grouping of these particular traits together and the giving to them of the title 'obsessional' does not have a faultless theoretical basis.

Lewis (1935) described, in the nuclear group of chronic severe obsessionals, two types of previous personality—'the one obstinate, morose, irritable, the other vacillating, uncertain of himself, submissive'.

Psychoanalysts, notably Freud, Abraham and Ernest Jones, have called these obsessional traits 'anal' or 'anal-erotic' (constituting the '*anal-erotic character*'), believing that these traits preponderate in persons whose instinctual life has been anally orientated, and that these traits are partly reaction-formations against anal-erotic activities and partly sublimations of them. The main anal-erotic traits are held by psychoanalysts to be orderliness, frugality and obstinacy. Frugality is considered to be a continuation of the anal habit of retention, orderliness an elaboration of obedience to the environment's requirements about excretion, and obstinacy a continuing rebellion against these same requirements. The instinctual conflicts are commonly fought out around problems of money and time—'no compulsion neurotic can handle time and money rationally'—he is stingy or prodigal or both alternately. Psychoanalytic explorations of these anal-erotic traits have been carried out in fascinating detail and many acute observations have been made (they are summarized by Fenichel, 1946). Attention has been drawn to the irritability and frequent bad temper of the obsessional, the evidence of aggression and sadism he often reveals and his reaction-formations against these trends. Ernest Jones (1948), in a classic exposition of anal-erotic character traits, demonstrated the complexity of the interrelations of the different anal-erotic components with one another and with other constituents of the whole character.

Like the other neurotic reactions, obsessional neuroses develop usually in early adult life. In Pollitt's (1960) series of cases the mean age of onset of the main illness was 28 years, but about half the patients had previously suffered from obsessional symptoms, either very transiently or in attacks which had cleared up after some months: many had had their first obsessional symptoms between the ages of 11 and 15 years. An obsessional neurosis may be a single illness, lasting only months, or it may take a phasic or cyclic course; but there is a marked tendency for it to become insidiously established and to develop in severity over a period of many years.

Symptoms and Signs

Obsessional symptoms may take several forms—phobias; intrusive ideas or images or rumination; impulses and compulsive acts.

A *phobia* is a recurrent intense, unreasonable fear associated with some situation or object or idea. The external focus of the fear varies according to the individual sufferer's history. The patient realizes that his fear is irrational, but he is dominated by it. If he enters the fear-producing situation, anxiety, acute tension or panic assail him. Various Greek and Latin names have been assigned to these phobias—agoraphobia—fear of open spaces, claustrophobia —fear of closed spaces and so on. The phobia may be a fear of a recurrence of an attack of anxiety with pronounced somatic symptoms which has once previously occurred, for example, in a crowd (agoraphobia) or in a railway compartment or in Church (claustrophobia). Or the phobia may be of dirt, or disease, or animals, or sharp instruments—or many other things. The relationship with anxiety states is close, but the fear has the typical obsessional quality.

Obsessional ideas and *images* are disturbing and often very distressing: they may be frightening, blasphemous, disgusting or obscene. Their intrusive nature is characteristic. One patient described it as—'it is like being chained, my mind is gripped by the thought, it is torture to me': another said, 'If I try to divert my attention from the thoughts, the more I seem to get back to them. If I keep trying to tell my mind to forget about them, I seem to remember them all the more.'

A few examples may be given. A man aged 39 complained that his mind seemed to follow the same pattern all the time, certain words ('vivid thoughts') went persistently through his mind—'cancer, heart attack, mouth'. Sometimes these words were grouped into a phrase, 'I won't have a heart attack worrying about cancer in the mouth.' Then he had the thought that if he worried about this, he 'wouldn't go wrong in the mind'. Another young man had recurrent frightening thoughts about violence, about how he would react in an emergency if he were attacked, thoughts of fighting and being killed, of being buried alive or drawn into machinery. A single woman aged 38 was tortured by blasphemous thoughts: 'God is ——', the thought would come into her mind, some obscene epithet being used. Then she tried to fight this thought by doing or saying something before the obscene thought was complete: she would repeat to herself, 'Nobody's a ——', or in order to prove that she did not mean it she would perform certain movements, lifting her arm sideways or forwards.

The characteristic feature of *obsessional rumination* is the continuous preoccupation with some topic or group of topics, to the exclusion of most other interests and to the distress of the patient. The relationship of some obsessive-ruminative conditions to anxiety states is close. Nevertheless there is a clear clinical difference between an anxious preoccupation and a true obsessive one: in the former it is the anxiety that is objected to by the patient, in the latter the thought-content itself is seen by the patient to be morbid. The topic of the rumination is commonly religious, philosophical or metaphysical, something that permits interminable, inconclusive thought, the origin of the universe or the destiny of man. The subject of one young man's rumination was—'we are all like that, the animals of the forest are like that, creedless and without thought and we were like that once'. Dan Leno proposed an ideal subject: 'Ah, what is man? Wherefore does he why? Whence did he whence? Whither is he withering?' It may take the form of an internal debate or catechizing, the pros and cons stated again and again and argued without cease, or be like, as one patient described it, a trial in a Court of Law. 'I must analyse my thoughts and must repeat them but I'm always aware they are my own thoughts. Its like a prosecuting counsel. He gets up to say something and the defence counsel makes an objection. It may be shouted down but he has planted a thought in the jury's mind. The prosecuting counsel makes the suggestion to me and I'm the jury.'

On the borderland of obsessional rumination are those states of obsessive thinking where the ideas themselves are not meaningless nor of indifferent interest or irrelevant—they are on the contrary legitimate subjects for reflection: but 1. their persistent obtrusiveness is inexplicable; and 2. the patient does not regard them as pathological intruders. In such cases the subject with which the individual is preoccupied has a clear relation to the rest of the content of consciousness and an obvious affective relationship. The following case was an example of this type:

CASE No. 7

A tall, very thin young man of 20, who had recently been unable to follow his occupation because his mind was totally occupied by speculations about religion. To his friends he had seemed to think and talk of nothing else. He explained that for two years he had been very much troubled by the divisions he saw existing in the Church, and said, 'I can't get them out of my mind. I can't assimilate the attitude of religious meetings.' At one of these where a woman evangelist had spoken, the patient was 'very much upset'. 'She laid down the law. It made me feel very uncomfortable. There always seems to be some sort of mystery about the Church. . . . What is Christianity?—that is the point. Why are some people so religious?—There is something funny about their appearance. . . . The different religions—that's what bothers me.' Hymns in church disturbed him: 'They seem so ruthless, sweeping everyone aside.' He spoke of the awed feeling with which he looked on a king as similar to his feeling towards religion generally. He had also a feeling of 'suspicion' regarding his choice of profession, as he felt he had been pushed into it. But it was significant that he designated his attitude to the world generally as 'suspicious'. It transpired that his feeling of being upset at a religious meeting was closely paralleled by an emotional experience which he had when 12 years of age, when he had listened to a difference of opinion between his parents and had sided with his father. The patient came to define his attitude to religious matters and to the world as one of fear, which made him physically sick and his mind a blank. This attitude was closely similar to the attitude he had held towards older boys when he first went to school. 'It goes very far back—those young boys at school.' In other words, it appeared that in facing the problems connected with emancipation from home he was reproducing in part and more intensely the affective attitudes belonging to an earlier age, and further that the obsessive preoccupation with religious matters depended on a discrepancy between religion as he found it in the world and his preoccupations regarding it. The discrepancy reanimated the fearful type of affect which had characterized his childish attitudes, and the fear supplied the motive power for the obsessive thinking.

M

In the case of this young man there was an obvious conflict between his childish concepts and reality, and an inability to modify the former in the light of real experience: the rôle of the unconscious concepts was not realized by the patient. He ceased to be preoccupied after three months' psychotherapy.

Another form of obsessional thinking is *persistent doubting*—'*folie du doute*': the individual is never sure that he has completed a certain action, and may have to go back repeatedly to assure himself that he has done so. He may have to look several times to see if he has turned off the gas downstairs, or check repeatedly his addition of sums or measurement of lengths of material, or he may feel unsure whether or not he has behaved wrongly. A woman, who had impulses to strike children in prams, would when a pram had passed her wonder if she had in fact hit or killed the child. She would then become intensely and painfully preoccupied with trying to reconstruct in her mind exactly what had happened, becoming in the process more and more certain that she had killed the child, requiring repeated reassurance that she had not, but never quite reaching certainty either way, always doubting. The obsessional may be continually vacillating, like Mr. T. S. Eliot's J. Alfred Prufrock, who found that 'In a minute there is time for decisions and revisions which a minute will reverse.'

Some obsessional patients become preoccupied with numbers and have, for example, to count letters in words or do or avoid doing certain things a certain number of times. A patient under our care was obsessed with the number two. He delayed his admission to hospital because he had noticed that it had been arranged for the second day of the second week of the fourth month. He refused his night sedative because it consisted of two capsules, and would not make a rug in the occupational therapy department because he was given two colours and a pattern which he saw in multiples of two. He carried this avoidance of the number two into every sphere of his life, even in tying his shoelaces.

Obsessional Impulses and *Compulsive Acts*. The impulses of the obsessional are often aggressive—to attack, injure or kill. They may be directed against other people, for example, a puerperal woman may have impulses to strike or kill her baby; or the patient may have a recurrent and strong urge to kill himself, by throwing himself from a height, it may be, or under a moving vehicle. A young unmarried woman, to give another example, had recurrent impulses to kick, beat or otherwise interfere with children and other defenceless people: this caused her to keep her hands in her pockets when she was outside or to carry a shopping bag to keep her hands engaged. An impulse to injure is commonly associated with a phobia of weapons or potential weapons, razors, knives, scissors, etc. The impulse can be on the other hand to commit some social aggression—to laugh or swear aloud in church, for instance. The obsessional aggressive impulse nearly always remains an impulse; it is not carried out. The exception to this generalization is that the individual with obsessional impulses to self-injury may, if he or she becomes depressed, commit suicide. The obsessional's illness does not drive him to crime.

Compulsive acts are stereotyped, usually innocuous behaviour, which the patient feels compelled to carry out. The urge to carry out these acts is pressing, even imperative, and if the patient resists this urge he becomes tense and anxious. Many of these compulsive acts resemble the superstitious observances of every-day life, but the latter are much more easily resisted; they can often be under-stood as prohibitions or penances. One of the classic examples is compulsive handwashing, which is accompanied often by a phobia of dirt or contamination, and which may readily be interpreted as a symbolic cleansing of impulses and memories of which the patient feels guilty. Lady Macbeth is an examplar.

A few further examples may be given. A man aged 41 had had for eleven years a compulsion, when he passed any scrap of paper in the street, to return and pick it up: he felt that if he did not do this, his parents would die. This caused him to be seen in many ridiculous situations as well as to be constantly late for work, appointments and his meals. Another man, 31 years of age, always an extremely neat and tidy person, could not bear to see things unfinished or in disorder, and had to straighten out creases and wrinkles wherever he observed them. He had also the compulsion to touch things with his right thumb. He would pass a telegraph pole and try to avoid touching it, and then have to turn back to touch it ('*folie du toucher*'), feeling that if he did not touch it something would befall himself or the people he loved. He also felt compelled to cross the road at a certain point so that he could step over a manhole, and he was often unable to resist the urge to stand for a certain period of time on the manhole cover. A man in his twenties developed a phobia of infection and connected this with a cousin whom he resented. He felt compelled to wash money because this had been in contact with his clothes which in turn may have been in contact with a door handle via his hands or with furniture in his mother's house, and this furniture had been touched by his cousin or his cousin's father. This chain reaction became almost unending, so that there was scarcely a thing in his house or on his person that he could not have reason for washing and which he had not in fact at some time washed.

In all his symptoms the obsessional shows a great tendency to perseveration and repetition, to rituals and protective devices, to self-doubt and self-torment: and he is prone to become more and more involved in a tangle of fears, impulses and compulsive acts. He cannot argue himself out of his preoccupations, nor banish his phobias by trying to drive himself through the situations in which they occur. He is usually tense and anxious, and very often becomes intermittently depressed in spirits. His insight is maintained, except at times of crisis when it may temporarily be swamped in his emotional upset. Usually he manages, though with great difficulty sometimes, to carry on with his daily job: rarely does he become quite disabled or even immobilized by phobias and rituals.

Aetiology and Psychopathology

The main aetiological factor in obsessional neurosis appears to be heredity. Obsessional traits and obsessional illness are found in significant concentration in the families of obsessionals—in about one-third of the parents and one-fifth of the sibs. Lewis (1935), in a review of 50 cases of obsessional neurosis, found that 37 of the parents showed pronounced obsessional traits, and in a number of instances both parents were obsessional: 43 of 206 siblings showed mild or severe obsessional traits.

Perhaps one should say, at a time when our knowledge is still very incomplete, that the main causal factor appears to be the individual's constitution, since the effects of heredity and early environment are so difficult to separate and we do not have findings from any large group of twins to guide us. The obsessional child or adult may either have inherited these trends from an obsessional parent or parents, or been drilled into obsessional modes of behaviour by them. Certainly one frequently obtains the history of an unusually strict or puritanical upbringing, with much insistence on rectitude and cleanliness.

The obsessional personality may shade into the illness, by the insidious aggravation of the pre-existing trends. In many cases, but not in all, some emotional stress, some situation producing major worries or conflict, may be seen to have precipitated the illness.

Physical factors may also be of aetiological importance. An obsessional neurosis may be precipitated by physical illness or prolonged fatigue. Encephalitis lethargica may produce obsessional symptoms, with or without forced movements, in an individual who has not been obsessional before.

The mental mechanisms most prominent in the development of obsessional symptoms are repression, displacement and substitution. Repressed earlier drives and memories gain symbolic representation in the symptoms. The writings of Freud and his school should be consulted for a full exposition of the complicated psychoanalytic theories of the illness's genesis. If one may paraphrase very briefly and superficially the analytic viewpoint, it can be stated somewhat as follows. There is in the obsessional neuroses regression to the anal-sadistic stage of libido development, at which there has been a developmental fixation. Memories of early traumata and difficulties at that stage, either spontaneously or because they are revived associatively by some contemporary experience, tend to return to consciousness. The ideas and emotions, often aggressive, are of a kind intolerable to the patient's super-ego and in relation to this the affect is usually one of reproach. The ego has to defend itself and tries to keep the intolerable ideas out of consciousness by substituting other ideas, indifferent in themselves. In the compulsive variety of the illness, not ideas but acts are substituted. What maintains the substituted ideas or acts in consciousness is the affect of reproach, which the patient does not succeed in getting rid of when he treats the intolerable ideas in this way: the reproach attaches itself to the substituted ideas or acts.

In the case of phobias there is a displacement of the fear from its real source to some associated object. For example, a girl had such a persistent phobia of bichloride of mercury tablets that she remained confined to her room for two years. Such tablets were associated in her mind with an illicit pregnancy, which had been both desired and feared. Aggressive impulses may be displaced into a phobia of knives, forbidden sexual drives into a venereophobia. The phobia serves as a defence against realization of the real problem.

A simple type of obsessive thinking is initiated by a desire to keep some unpleasant thought out of one's mind by thinking continually of something else.

The obsessive idea continues as long as the necessity for repression of the unpleasant thought lasts, and sometimes to all appearances longer, as a habit. Freud recounts the case of a woman who was continuously brooding over such questions as, 'Why must I breathe?' She had been afraid of becoming insane, and to reassure herself she had begun to catechize herself on serious problems. This quieted her at first, but soon her fear was completely replaced by the habit of speculation, which lasted for years.

A very frequent basis of an obsessive rumination is an opposition between a desire and a fear. There is a desire, more or less unconscious, for something which the ego itself cannot permit, and a conscious dread as a reaction to the desire. This conflict may be fairly simply expressed. Greenacre quoted the case of a clergyman, who had distressing impulses to sing 'Dim-dam-dimmity, dammity' to the tune of some hymn. Even here, however, the matter was not simple, for there was a certain amount of symbolization. The obsession to use profane language symbolized his desire to be rid of the burdensome restrictions of his calling. An extension of this principle of the basis of obsessive preoccupation in the conflict between a wish and a fear enables us to understand the following case, in which there was an obvious wish followed by fears of homicide.

CASE No. 8

A Russian Jewish tailor, aged 35, married, and with three children. He complained that for six months he had been obsessed, to his immense distress, by a desire to kill his wife and children and to commit suicide. If he saw a river he wanted to jump in; a window would tempt him to jump out. He had had to leave work, and suffered from insomnia, his obsessive thoughts being worst during the night. It transpired that six months before the development of obsessive symptoms business had become very bad, and he was worried and mildly depressed. One evening he read in the newspaper that the Home Secretary advocated the deportation of aliens. This angered him and he 'wished he were the Lord that he might dismiss the Home Secretary'. Then it occurred to him that such thoughts portended madness. At this he felt 'hot all over', left his room and went out of doors, where he felt he wanted to assault a bystander, just as he would have liked to assault the Home Secretary. This alarmed him still more, and he became afraid that he would assault his wife and children in the same way.

The transition from an obsessive-ruminative condition to an obsessive-compulsive state is easily understood. The compulsion is a method of mastering the fear. The act chosen as a defence against the desire is usually mentally connected with the latter in some way—as a simple association, or as a symbol. The origin of certain compulsive acts is well seen in children, where they are motivated by a fear of some impending disaster. This is exemplified in the next case, where the fear was that of scholastic failure.

CASE No. 9

A boy of 13 was brought by his mother because he 'had to touch everything twice'. He would often go back to a door which he knew to be closed, reopen it and close it again. He frequently was seen to smell his cap. All these symptoms had existed for six months. He had had a scholastic examination three months after the symptoms began, which, however, he had successfully passed. With considerable reluctance and some tears, the boy, who was a fresh-complexioned well-built youngster, related how he had been dreading the examination, that he wanted very much to pass, but was afraid he would not do so, and that he had begun to touch articles twice and go through the other ceremonials mentioned because he feared he might be 'unlucky' if he omitted them. The compulsive acts had persisted as habits after the occasion for them had passed, and his fear of bad luck became generalized. With this confession, which he had refused to his mother, and some simple reassurances, he quickly improved.

In the obsessive-compulsive states of adult life the mechanisms may be similar, but they are not usually so superficially clear as in the case just quoted.

Differential Diagnosis

We have already pointed out that many normal people show obsessional traits in their personalities, and under the influence of fatigue or physical ill health these traits may become more prominent: the individual may indulge temporarily, for example, in an unusual amount of obsessional re-checking (going back to see if the light has been switched off, the back door shut and so on). But these minor things do not amount to a neurosis.

Many children, too, have ritualistic activities, and apparent obsessive-compulsive traits, but these are not usually to be taken very seriously unless they are unduly marked or persistent: some of these repetitive activities the child obviously enjoys, which is quite unlike obsessional neurosis. It is recorded of the poet W. B. Yeats that when he was a boy, before he had any knowledge of Latin, he loved to repeat the phrase 'Magna est veritas et praevalebit', and that he went about for days repeating a phrase which he had heard from a village boy, 'I saw thee and the little brothers and the maids at church.'

Occasionally the severe obsessional's rituals seem so bizarre and his trains of thought so far-fetched, that he is diagnosed to be schizophrenic. Much more often, the differential diagnosis lies between an obsessional neurosis and a depressive psychosis with secondary obsessional symptoms (a common conjunction of symptoms). The differentiation may be very difficult. Some obsessional neuroses, in their lack of external precipitants, in their recurrent attacks or cyclic course, closely resemble manic-depressive depressions, and some of these apparently obsessional illnesses may in fact be masked depressions. But not all these cases, where the illness is of more acute onset and the course limited, are depressed. It is only by close scrutiny of the history and of the patient's whole behaviour and symptomatology that one can determine whether the illness is fundamentally affective or obsessional.

Transitions to Psychosis. Rarely an obsessional neurosis passes into a psychosis.

Case No. 10

A man, aged 50, complained at first that he could not stop worrying about such apparently senseless topics as where he had thrown a match, and could not sleep for wondering whether the house door was closed. He was also much preoccupied with his anal zone. He remembered that he had had much itching there, and that he had scratched himself to the effusion of blood. Although no interpretations were given him of any kind he contemplated with horror the possibility that he might have scratched himself for pleasure. Soon also the fear occurred to him that he was thinking of his anus and his masseur in conjunction. These fears and homosexual thoughts took the place of his earlier obsessive preoccupation with indifferent topics, and drove him to avoid completely the company of men. He used such phrases as 'It's *not* a wish; it's a fear that the dread will turn into a wish.' Then he began to believe that he had been homosexually assaulted. There had been a gradual clearly evident transition from obsessive preoccupation with indifferent topics to obsessive sexual ideas, and finally to delusions of assault, with the development of a paranoid psychosis.

Gordon (1926) described 6 cases in which an obsessive-compulsive state had been followed by a psychosis: in 4 of the 6 patients the development was to a paranoid psychosis. It may be noted that both obsessional and paranoid states show a marked tendency to systematization and chronicity, and that the previous personality is characteristically rigid. Stengel (1945) found no report in the literature where the psychotic reaction occurring in an obsessional neurotic was of the hebephrenic or catatonic variety, and commented that schizophrenic reactions occurring in obsessionals show a tendency to remission and that if deterioration does set in it develops slowly over many years. Stengel's paper, in which 14 cases are presented, gives a comprehensive review of the relationships between obsessional neuroses and psychotic reactions. He draws attention to the prevalence of aggressive-destructive obsessional ideas and compulsions during depressive states occurring in obsessional patients, and to the suicidal risk in this type of case: and expresses the opinion that the obsessional personality structure, by exercising a strong integrating influence, is capable of subduing and aborting schizophrenic reactions.

OTHER NEUROTIC AND ALLIED REACTIONS

Neuroses following Trauma

The terms 'traumatic neurosis' and 'traumatic psychoneurosis' should be abandoned. The neuroses which follow trauma differ in no essential way from the neuroses which have other precipitants.

The trauma may be psychological or physical: and when it has been of primary importance in the aetiology, it has usually been sudden and intense. In the cases where physical trauma has occurred, the effects of physical injury may complicate the emotional reaction, and after head injury in particular it may be difficult to separate physical from emotional sequelae. Post-concussional syndromes are discussed on page 368. In all these cases questions of compensation may arise.

A psychologically traumatic, terrifying experience may produce an immediate response of extreme anxiety or wild panic: or there may be apparent calm with development of symptoms after a latent period. The symptoms that follow the fright are usually insomnia with terrifying dreams from which the patient wakes time and again—these dreams representing the accident in more or less distorted form. Anxiety symptoms occur during the day, especially lack of concentration and uneasiness of mind, and the bodily discomforts of anxiety, such as tremor or palpitation. Such symptoms may appear even in the most stable individual if the experience is severe enough; but they usually diminish and ultimately disappear, although it seems likely that they are readily revived by subsequent analogous experience.

The following is an example of a neurosis consisting in acute anxiety at the time, subsequent anxiety symptoms and prolonged associative or conditioned revival of the symptoms amounting to panic when the situation encountered reproduced, after nearly twenty years, more closely than ever before, the circumstances of the original experience.

CASE No. 11

An air gunner, aged 33, who had previously flown without symptoms, occupying the rear turret of a bomber for the first time was seized with acute panic on a practice flight. When he was released from the turret his breathing was observed to be deep and noisy. It was remarked by his medical officer that on the ground he had shown no symptoms at all. His history revealed that at the age of 14 he had a particularly disturbing experience when he found himself one Saturday afternoon shut in the vaults of the office in which he worked; moreover, soon after he found the exit closed against him, the lights went out and the watchman went off for the week-end. He became increasingly uneasy, and the intensity of his anxiety can be gauged from the fact that it was only after many hours that he noticed in the darkness a little red bulb which had the word 'Pull' printed on it. This set off the burglar alarm throughout the building, which after nearly 24 hours' incarceration brought people to his rescue. The air had become increasingly hot and dry, or so it seemed to him, and his prevailing fear during his imprisonment was that of being suffocated. The door was opened and he ran out in a state of extreme tension. He was off work and in bed for the two days following. For nearly two years afterwards he had nightmares in which usually he was in a tunnel which caved in on him. He remarked, apropos of the episode in the rear turret, that his breathing when he left the turret was very much the same as he recollected it when he got out of the vault. His pilot remarked that he 'sounded like a steam engine'. He was a man of stable character and temperament, and in the intervening years he was apparently well; but closer investigation showed that he had had mild claustrophobic symptoms all the time since the original trauma. When he drove a car it was always with the windows open, and he chose to drive a tourer rather than a saloon. On the first occasion in which he travelled in a tube train he had the thought that it was a risky business, but he was reassured by the lights and the open platform. For some time after his original experience he refused to take the elevator to his place of work, which was on the fourth floor—he walked up the stairs. This phobia he ultimately surmounted.

The period which normally elapses between an acute emotional trauma and the onset of neurotic symptoms is of considerable interest, both from the point of view of differential diagnosis from organic conditions as well as psychologically. Evidently the latent period is filled with ruminations, but the memory of these is usually difficult to recover—they were probably ill-defined in the first instance and underwent repression with the development of the symptoms.

It is reported that after a Vesuvian eruption all the survivors were at first emotionally upset; after three months only a few—and those obviously predisposed—showed neuroses; and after six months no one showed any ill-effects. There was no question of compensation in this instance, and the short duration of the neurotic phenomena, even in those predisposed, is an interesting contrast to what very frequently occurs in cases where monetary compensation is concerned—in workmen after accidents in their work, in railway passengers after a rail smash, and the like, when the symptoms tend to remain till compensation is settled. In some cases following trauma a sense of grievance, and even a desire for revenge, help to sustain the symptoms until compensation or some other satisfaction is obtained. This will obviously be more common where an employee is dissatisfied with the general conditions of his employment, or where the employer does not make satisfactory arrangements for rehabilitation. It is claimed that in large organizations where the disabled workman is given some kind of job as soon as he is fit to do any at all, and is gradually restored to as near his previous status as possible, compensation neuroses virtually do not exist. Sometimes an accident impinges upon an individual who is in the throes of a mental conflict on some personal issue and the symptoms may then be exploited unconsciously as an escape, however temporary, from an apparently insoluble problem.

Neurasthenia

This syndrome classically comprised the following symptoms—complaints of mental and physical fatigue, associated with sensations of pressure in the head, poor memory, inability to concentrate, irritability of temper, poor sleep and various aches and pains. It was first described by Beard in 1880 and quickly became so popular a diagnosis that by 1894 Muller was able to furnish a bibliography of fourteen pages. Now it is rarely recorded by clinicians, though the individual symptoms of the syndrome are of course still commonly complained of by both neurotic and psychotic patients. Being suggestible, neurotic patients mirror medical preoccupations. Neurasthenic symptoms were common while physicians were interested in fatigue syndromes, expected them frequently and sought them diligently: and they became much less common when medical interest in them waned.

Overwork being obviously related to fatigue, it was assumed by many that neurasthenic symptoms were identical with fatigue and must have an identical cause. On this assumption was based Weir Mitchell's treatment by absolute rest, in which the patients were not allowed even to feed themselves, lest they incurred unnecessary expenditure of energy. Overwork is an aetiological theory sometimes offered by neurotic patients because overwork is a creditable thing, but a closer investigation of the history does not often reveal that the hours worked have been excessive. It is emotional disturbances which produce fatigue, much more often than physical fatigue initiates illness.

Fatigue and allied complaints may, in our experience, be the expression of one of several types of emotional perturbation. They may be the simple result of conscious mental conflicts. If the conflicts persist, the symptoms also persist, and the latter may come to be autonomous, the patient observing them and dwelling upon them and shifting this preoccupation from the original problem to his physical health. Or fatigue may be the expression of some less conscious difficulties: it is then often a conversion phenomenon and really a hysterical symptom. Again, affective depression is commonly accompanied by fatigue; not uncommonly it is the fatigue rather than the depression of which the patient complains; or fatigue may wholly replace depression and is then a symptomatic equivalent of the latter. Finally, fatigue symptoms may arise in the course of any psychosis, 'functional' or organic.

Unreality States

Feelings of unreality may take two forms—the patient himself feels unreal (depersonalization) or the world around him seems unreal (derealization). The affected individual may complain of both types of change, but derealization is very uncommon without depersonalization.

Reactions in which unreality is a leading symptom do not comprise a distinct clinical entity. Mild feelings of unreality may be experienced by the normal individual in the setting of unusual fatigue. Feelings of unreality may also be symptoms of almost any neurotic or psychotic illness, occurring in anxiety and obsessional neuroses more often than in hysteria, in depressive psychoses and in schizophrenia, in cases of temporal lobe epilepsy (in close association with *déjà vu* phenomena) and in other organic reaction-types. The abnormal feelings may be very transient, or recurrent, or persist for months or years.

As presenting symptoms feelings of unreality are commonest in young adults of anxious or obsessional temperament: but many patients with unreality do not complain of it spontaneously, either because they find it hard to put their experience into words, or are not sufficiently introspective, or are afraid of being thought insane. The abnormal feelings are unpleasant and distressing.

The onset is often sudden, with sensations of faintness or dizziness, followed by a fear of impending collapse or insanity—the latter often persists. The patient complains of feeling unreal, emotionally dull or flat, mechanical and like an automaton; his voice or his face in the mirror may seem strange to him, and his experience of time may be altered, so that for example the recent past seems remote. If he experiences derealization too the outer world may seem far away, indistinct, misty, drained of colour. Sometimes the patient says that it is as if a shutter or glass screen had come down between him and the outer world, from which he has become shut off in some subtle but frightening way. The patient retains his insight, realizing that he is nervously unwell; he has no delusions that he or the world has altered fundamentally, it is 'as if' there had been a great change. Neither the psychological nor the possible physiological basis of these feelings is fully understood.

Shorvon (1946) gave a comprehensive and valuable review of 66 patients with depersonalization (46 females, 20 males), and suggested that these cases could be considered to form a distinct clinical entity, the depersonalization syndrome. He drew attention to a 'constellation of constitutional deviations', which included obsessional personality, migraine and mild non-specific cerebral dysrhythmia; and to the tendency of the syndrome to occur in more than averagely intelligent but emotionally immature individuals, with a history of unsatisfactory parent-child relationships. Thirty-eight per cent. of his cases suffered from migraine, and in 21 per cent. there was a family history of migraine: many ceased to have migraine attacks with the onset of depersonalization. Shorvon also noted that the onset is often related to relaxation following intense or prolonged stimulation or stress, and that a few cases are helped by stimulation by ether abreaction. This study increased our knowledge of depersonalization symptoms, but Shorvon did not make out a convincing case for accepting depersonalization as a separate syndrome: his patient material was selected, being drawn from out-patients and those seen at a neuropsychiatric unit, and excluded obviously psychotic patients.

Ackner (1954) reviewed the literature, and concluded that depersonalization should be used as a generic term for a number of different syndromes, often related only by a loose similarity of complaint.

TREATMENT OF THE NEUROSES

Psychotherapy is the main form of treatment of neurotic reactions. It developed out of the 'moral treatment' of the nineteenth century, and there are now numerous methods of psychotherapy, superficial and deep, eclectic and specialized by the various schools (Freudian, Jungian, Adlerian and others). It may take the form of counselling, support, abreaction, analysis, conditioning, suggestion or hypnosis, or be a mixture of these techniques. It may be conducted individually, that is with a single patient, or in groups large or small.

The neurotic patient should usually have psychotherapy as an out-patient, individual treatment sessions lasting up to one hour and being spaced (daily, weekly and so on) according to the individual patient's needs. These needs range from good advice at one end of the scale to prolonged and detailed analysis of a complex illness at the other. Successful treatment takes usually a matter of months: it may be quicker, and if it is taking longer than six months or so the situation should be very carefully reviewed. The initial diagnosis and approach may have been mistaken, or the patient be so limited constitutionally that psychotherapy could be interminable and still unavailing.

The general practitioner should be competent himself to carry out the simpler forms of psychotherapy, and is best placed to treat neurotic symptoms quickly, before faulty habits of reaction have become entrenched. If his psychotherapy is not successful within a few months, he should refer the patient to a psychiatrist for more detailed assessment and investigation. It is better to refer to a specialist too soon than too late.

Much depends in psychotherapy on the quality of the attention which the doctor gives to these unhappy and bewildered people, and therefore on his own personality, insight and wisdom. He must be interested, sympathetic, patient and above all a good listener. If he is critical or censorious, these timid people will shy away from him: and unfortunately many doctors, despite the improvements which have taken place in both professional and lay education in the field of mental health, still feel irritation at the sight of personal failure and still too often tell the patient to 'pull himself together'. On the other hand, if the doctor is over-sympathetic and paternal, he may foster a dependence which will be as unhealthy for the patient as it is likely to be inconvenient and embarrassing to himself. It is probably true that the outcome of psychotherapy depends more on the personality of the therapist than on the particular technique employed. Truax and his colleagues (1966) have shown that three qualities of the therapist are particularly important—accurate emphatic understanding, genuineness and non-possessive warmth: neurotic patients treated by psychiatrists who have these characteristics show greater improvement than those treated by psychiatrists who are relatively lacking in them. Furthermore, the successful therapist is usually modest enough to allow that much depends on time and changing circumstances, and on the patient's native powers of readjustment and recovery. One's attitude should be melioristic rather than too ambitious, aiming at an improvement in happiness and efficiency rather than at dramatic cures.

Two preliminaries are essential to psychotherapy—the taking of a detailed chronological history and a careful physical examination.

It is advisable, before proceeding with any explanation or reassurance (and these are frequently asked for by the patient even before the end of the initial interview), to find out what the patient himself thinks is wrong with him. Usually he has his own views and theories about his symptoms defined to some extent, and the longer he has been ill the better defined and elaborated they will be. It is also useful to know what he has been taught by other doctors, so that one may not be unsuspectingly led into the position of contradicting another man's opinion. The other physician may be, at least in the patient's eyes, a greater authority than you are: in which case, unless you are forearmed, your dicta may not avail much if they should chance to be in opposition to his. Views that the patient has already formed of his illness are commonly of a physical aetiology, and acceptable to his ego-ideal. If these views are discovered by the doctor beforehand, they can be dealt with much more effectively.

The doctor, whether he be general practitioner or psychiatrist, should carry out the physical examination of the patient himself. It is nonsense to say, as some psychoanalysts have claimed, that to do this is to prejudice one's psychotherapeutic relationship with the patient. The opposite is true: not to carry out a full and painstaking physical examination is both bad medical practice and poor psychotherapeutic strategy. If physical disease is found, this should be fully investigated and dealt with at the outset: it may of course have played some part in causing the neurotic breakdown.

The next step is to inform the patient that his symptoms are not due to any physical disease. The doctor must be able to reassure his patient on this point, with confidence; any hedging or hesitation may be fatal to one's ability to help the patient. Occasionally this reassurance is curative: the anxious patient with fears of heart disease, loses them, or the patient of low intelligence with hysterical symptoms recovers when following an impressive physical examination he is informed authoritatively that recovery is imminent. In the vast majority reassurance is not enough. The disclosure to the patient that he is not, as he had thought or feared, physically ill, must be done very tactfully: it is a critical moment in handling the patient's problems. The patient is liable to react acutely, with the feeling 'He thinks there's nothing wrong with me, that I am imagining it all or putting it on.' The doctor must therefore go on immediately to say that the absence of physical disease is a matter for congratulation, and that it does not mean that the patient's symptoms are imaginary. He should say that he realizes that the patient's symptoms are real and distressing, and that all doctors recognize that the symptoms caused by nervous and emotional upset are as unpleasant and as painful and disabling often as those caused by physical disease. He must then explain how anxiety, worry, depression or other emotional upset can produce both nervous and physical symptoms: how anxieties tend to be repressed into a subconscious part of the mind, with the production of inner tension, and how this inner tension gains expression in symptoms. He may tell the patient how, for example, emotional tension is accompanied by muscle tension, and how tense muscles become painful and fatigued; how excitement makes the heart race and may cause frequency of micturition or looseness of the bowels; and how anxiety may be expressed alternatively in panic attacks or phobias or obsessions. In this way the patient is brought to an understanding that there have been good reasons for his symptoms, but reasons probably of a kind quite different from what he had believed.

The general nature of psychotherapy and its objects must now be explained to the patient: and here we must add that the patient's relatives should not be left out of the treatment situation—normally the nearest relative should be interviewed, not only for the purpose of obtaining a full history of the patient's illness, but also to be told in general terms what is wrong with the patient and by what method of treatment it is hoped to help him. The patient himself is told that, with the doctor's help, the influence of various events on his mind and feelings will be explored, that there may have been important events and connections which he has forgotten or of which he has not been fully aware, and that it will be an essential part of the treatment that he talks freely of his memories, feelings, motives, attitudes and so on. If the doctor fails to give this explanation of the treatment, the patient is liable soon to conclude that he is getting no treatment, that there is just talk; and he may well cease to attend for something so esoterically different from the kind of medicine he had expected. The patient may ask how long the treatment will take. The doctor should on no account commit himself in reply, but say only that they will both have to see how quickly progress can be made. The patient may be reassured, if he asks, that this kind of treatment is likely to be helpful, but he should not be promised a cure. It is very important from the beginning to make it clear that the treatment will be a co-operative effort, and that success will not depend on the doctor alone.

At this stage one goes back usually to the patient's history. A detailed account must be obtained, not only of the illness but of the patient's life generally: and usually a number of exploratory interviews are given over to this. It is a good rule to accept almost nothing that seems at once important in the history, at its face value. Reports of previous physical illnesses, especially if they have borne such equivocal labels as influenza, anaemia, rheumatism or debility, must be investigated closely. It is desirable to survey the patient as widely as possible, and to regard the symptoms as arising not usually as an isolated response to one factor but as part of a wide problem of adaptation. Any mental unrest forms a fertile soil for the development of neurotic reactions. There is often fairly easily traceable an immediate cause which has precipitated the symptoms: but behind this there is usually a predisposition, the nature and determinants of which are much less easily ascertained.

It is now the task of the physician in collaboration with his patient to collate the chronological development of the patient's symptoms with the events of his life, or more strictly with the mental events which have accompanied them, so that the reasons for his present behaviour and symptoms can be found. It is best to take the most prominent symptoms first, and to take the patient back over his mental history to their onset. Then he is asked to recall as far as possible all that happened at that time, and what his thoughts were about the events and about himself. If he cannot reconstruct sufficiently what was going on in response to ordinary questions, or preferably as a narrative in response to a vague general question, the method of free association may be tried: but this latter is a method that works well only with a minority of patients.

By this time the chronological relation of most of the symptoms, and the relation of their first onset and their recurrences to events in the patient's life and to his phantasies (ambitions, reflections upon events), will be fairly clear to the physician. They will also have begun to be clear to the patient. Often at first he will deny that anything occurred at the time of onset of a given symptom. He will assure his doctor that nothing whatever took place at that time. But often a little later he will remember and will communicate what he has recollected—fragmentarily at first, more fully later. This may occur without pressure, the original question having set a train of thoughts going. For example, a woman of 35 complained that she had suffered from abdominal symptoms (nausea and discomfort) since she was 19. She at first denied altogether that anything had happened at that time. Two days later, without further reference to the subject in the meantime, she volunteered that she had been disgusted at that age by an assault from a very ugly man. Another patient who had recurrent attacks of trembling (at first associated with being called up for military service) had an attack in November 1923, which had lasted till he came under observation, and had disabled him from work. He at first denied that anything whatever had occurred in November 1923; but finally, in response to a general question, and after much reflection, saying he knew of nothing important at that time, he said—'Why, I got married then!' He saw the point, and laughed. His tremors disappeared, and he returned to work.

This, the development of insight, is one of the most important elements in successful psychotherapy. The more the patient can be allowed gradually to see things for himself, and the less direct explanation given to him in consequence, the better and the quicker in the long run. The more the patient contributes to his own recovery, the more permanent that recovery is likely to be. There is a considerable difference between the demonstration by the doctor of a cause and the patient's acceptance of a causal explanation. There is often some reluctance ('resistance') on the patient's part to accepting it, which is not surprising since a neurosis is an intensely personal affair and is usually in some degree a defence against unpleasant truth.

During the exploration of the patient's mental history, the objective is to bring back into full consciousness, against more or less 'resistance' on the patient's part, the mental events and conflicts which have been associated with the development of symptoms. The recall of these events and the uncovering of forgotten memories may be emotionally very disturbing to the patient, especially if these events have been associated with strong and painful feelings (of guilt, for example). The patient should, however, be helped always to recover both the memories and the feelings associated with them, and to experience these feelings again intensely. The release of pent-up, repressed emotions is often a vital part of the therapeutic process: it is known as abreaction or catharsis. It may be necessary to take the patient back again and again to the memories of a period of great unhappiness: and to give barbiturate drugs, by mouth or intravenously (so-called 'narco-analysis'), to disinhibit the patient and make recall and emotional expression easier.

It must always be kept in mind that the exploration and revival of past mental events is designed to be part of a process of re-education. The repressed material which is recovered must be used constructively, to increase the patient's self-awareness and to help him to deal more adequately with his life's problems. Like surgery, psychotherapy must have a plan of action, and sewing up must follow opening up. Neither the patient nor his therapist should lose touch with the realities of the patient's everyday life. Successful psychotherapy should strengthen the patient's ego, as well as relieving his symptoms: it should make him by re-learning a more self-reliant human being.

Frank (1966) in a lucid and persuasive paper has stressed the importance of such an adaptational approach. He emphasizes the need for understanding the meaning and function of the patient's complaints in his current life situation. His symptoms can profitably be read as 'disguised or oblique attempts to gain a reassuring response of some sort from other persons as a means of allaying subjective distress'. They are meaningful communications which are miscarrying. The clues to their interpretation are to be found in the interactions between the patient and other people, and in the social rôle which the patient is playing and others have adopted in relation to him: other people, especially near relatives, by their responses to him may be perpetuating in a vicious circle reaction his maladaptive behaviour. The function of psychotherapy is to help to increase the patient's awareness of the meaning of his symptoms: understanding them, he may learn to communicate his needs more clearly and constructively.

When the symptoms are not found to be accounted for satisfactorily in terms of external situations, and when consequently they appear to be mainly constitutionally determined, the investigation has to be carried further back into the early formative influences of the patient's personality—his relation to parents, brothers and sisters and companions, his reactions to dangers real or imaginary, and to sexual experiences, his ideals, aims, religious attitudes and the like. Something of this kind is desirable in practically every case. How far to go in this deeper exploration depends upon the requirements of the particular patient. One aims to help the patient to unravel the tangle of childhood memories, phantasies and feelings, and at the same time to realize more comprehensively his personal assets and liabilities, to bring the former into use and to mitigate the latter by understanding how they have arisen and how they may be compensated for.

There are patients whose resistance to becoming well is considerable, who leave all effort to the physician and believe stultifyingly in his miracle-working powers; and it is necessary to discover why the patient wishes to be so dependent and to lead him to independence away from his or her childlike or actually erotic attitude to the physician. Other patients who are among the most difficult to help well are those with a general attitude of superiority. Their symptoms are even more with them than with others an emblem of their attempts to preserve their self-respect. To teach them a new attitude to life is the task of the physician. This new attitude may not be necessary for the disappearance of the symptoms: these patients may rush off to some spa or special nursing home where they are treated with ultra-violet rays, or radiant heat, or colonic lavage or what not, and these treatments, implying as they do a physical and therefore objective or even heroic aetiology of their trouble, may bring about symptomatic relief. But the illness is not cured in these physical ways, and the patient's liability to breakdown is as great as, perhaps greater than, before.

The deeper exploration of a patient's personality concerns itself much with unconscious factors, and is the province of the specialist. Special techniques are used, the discovery of which we owe almost entirely to Freud and to his development of psychoanalysis. The main psychoanalytic techniques, which will only be outlined here, have been free association, dream interpretation and analysis of the transference. They are now used to a greater or lesser extent, with numerous modifications, by most psychotherapists and not only by those who have been trained by other analysts.

The technique of 'free association' consists in asking the patient to relate without reserve whatever comes into his mind, no matter how irrelevant it may seem or how personally objectionable it may be. The doctor should intervene seldom, except to urge the patient when the flow of his talk becomes temporarily arrested. Where an arrest of this kind occurs, it is said to be due to 'resistance', which may be either a more or less conscious desire to withhold some unpalatable piece of information or may be due to influences that are wholly unconscious— those of the super-ego. At suitable junctures interpretations of the material offered by the patient are given by the therapist, who bases these interpretations on the general theory of psychoanalysis and makes use of such concepts as repression, displacement, sublimation, rationalization and other 'defence mechanisms'.

Similarly, to obtain an account of the patient's dreams is often useful, both for suggesting topics for investigation and especially for throwing light on unconscious factors: but interpretations have to be very carefully based upon the patient's associations and not the physician's, and the time for unveiling them has to be carefully chosen.

Between a doctor and his patient there is normally rapport, and a feeling on the patient's side of trust and confidence. This rapport becomes heightened during any prolonged psychotherapy, and the feeling which then springs up in a patient towards the doctor with whom he or she is closeted for so long a time has been called the 'transference'. It is usually a mixture of affection and dislike. There are two aspects of transference. In the first place, it is held that the psychotherapist is made to occupy in the patient's mind various rôles formerly played by the patient's parents, brothers, sisters and others, in early life. Secondly, in accordance with this, the patient feels with regard to the analyst the emotions of love, hate, fear and so forth, which he once experienced towards those other people in his infancy and childhood, some of which he sooner or later repressed. Undoubtedly something of this kind happens, particularly when psychotherapy is lengthy or pushed deeply: and the therapist must be sensitive to the complexity of the emotional situation. Later psychoanalytic theory and practice has gone further, and by many analysts the analysis and interpretation of the transference is now considered the essential therapeutic process. The task of the analyst is said to be to employ this transference of emotion to overcome the patient's 'resistances', and to take advantage of the revival of the old situations to have them dissected consciously, and the reason for their repression clearly exhibited. This process also gives the patient an opportunity to abreact the original feelings connected with these early situations.

Psychoanalysis as a Therapeutic Measure

Any well-founded psychotherapy will employ some at least of the principles so fruitfully emphasized, if not always first propounded, in psychoanalytic theory. As a theory, or congeries of theories, there is no doubt of the epoch-making importance of psychoanalysis not merely in the field of mental disorders but in normal psychology. It was of course founded by Freud on his observations of neurotics. But when it comes to assessing the value of classical psychoanalysis as a method of treatment of neurotics we are on much more uncertain ground. There can be no doubt that wrongly used psychoanalysis can be dangerous, and at best it is a therapeutic method of limited applicability.

'Psychoanalytic therapy was created through and for the treatment of patients permanently unfitted for life.' Freud himself mainly restricted his treatment to chronic neurotics, and we are of the opinion that this restriction is a very proper one. He considered that the conditions peculiarly favourable for psychoanalysis are hysteria and obsessional neuroses. But probably most analysts would now agree that whatever may be the theoretical justifications for treating obsessive-compulsive states analytically, they are peculiarly resistant to psychotherapy.

Freud also laid it down that the patient must be intelligent, and that he must have a certain amount of education, and a certain degree of 'ethical development —deep-rooted malformation of character, traits of a degenerative condition . . . can scarcely be overcome'. Further, the patient must not be too old: if his age is 'near or above the fifties . . . the mass of psychical material can no longer be thoroughly inspected, the time required for recovery is too long and the ability to undo psychic processes begins to grow weaker'. The patient must also be

N

co-operative and desire help in this way. Finally, as far as the patient is concerned, he must have considerable resources of time and (usually) money, since psycho-analysis is long, arduous and often expensive. The patient may have to devote an hour five days a week to the treatment, over a period of two or three or more years. The expense of the treatment is usually considered to furnish a valuable motive to benefit from it. It should be added that neuroses complicated by com-pensation issues are not suitable for psychoanalysis.

The limitations of psychoanalytic therapy appear, therefore, on Freud's own showing to be considerable and to narrow the field so as to exclude the great majority of those who attend our psychiatric clinics. We consider that there are further limitations which may arise in individual cases. It seems necessary to estimate beforehand the possible effects of submitting to a prolonged analysis even a patient who conforms to all the above requirements; whether, for example, persons of a sensitive, idealistic type who have met their difficulties by interest in social, philanthropic and religious works should be submitted to the profoundly disturbing influence of psychoanalysis rather than be treated by the simpler methods described earlier in this chapter. The physician must also have a clear view of the circumstances surrounding the onset of a neurosis: where immediate material circumstances, for example disappointment in a career, financial diffi-culties and the like, play a large part, it is superfluous and often harmful to enter upon a course of psychoanalysis.

For details of psychoanalytic treatment the reader is referred to the volumes of Freud's complete psychological works. He was a most lucid expositor of his own methods.

Jung was the most important analyst to diverge from Freud's theories and methods. Laying less emphasis on the sexual interpretation of symptoms, he regarded each neurotic illness as an attempt at solution of the general problems of the patient's life. Symptoms and symbols generally he interpreted in a more abstract way than Freud did, in terms of an unconscious which is not only indi-vidual but collective (an inheritance of the experience of earlier generations), and of archetypes, which are mythical ideas and images of particular importance and at the same time of esoteric significance. Jung found his technique of analytical psychology of most value with older patients.

Group Psychotherapy

In group psychotherapy the individual patient is the subject of treatment and the group itself is the main therapeutic agency. Psychotherapeutic groups consist usually of less than a dozen individuals, with a therapist who acts the rôle of 'participant observer'. Free, uninhibited discussion is encouraged amongst the group, and interpretations are offered by the therapist, usually along psycho-analytic lines with elucidation of interpersonal relationships and dynamics: but methods vary as much as do those of individual psychotherapy. In the group the patient shares a social experience with a substitute family. His social isolation may be overcome and his social readjustment effected. Group psychotherapy can certainly be justified on economic grounds, since psychotherapists are few and patients many: and it is claimed that it has beneficial effects of its own which cannot be obtained from individual psychotherapy. Foulkes and Anthony (1957) have given a comprehensive account of it.

Behaviour Therapy

The techniques of psychotherapy which have been developed recently under the general title of 'behaviour therapy' were given their initial impetus by Wolpe (1958) and Eysenck (1960a), and have been refined in method and theory particularly by Gelder and Marks in this country. They rest theoretically on the principles of conditioning discovered by Pavlov, and on the later contributions to theories of learning made by Hull, Skinner and other psychologists. For the purposes of these treatments the neuroses are looked upon as determined by actual stressful experiences, which have led to learned faulty habits of reaction: their symptoms are conditioned maladaptive patterns of behaviour which require to be unlearned. Treatment is directly symptomatic: unconscious conflicts are disregarded, and the gaining of insight is not promoted. There are two main types of techniques of treatment—desensitization and aversion.

Desensitization therapy was introduced by Wolpe who, from the result of laboratory experiments with animals, had realized the possibility of treating human neuroses along these lines. The anxious person, like the 'neurotic' animal, avoids fear-provoking situations and stimuli, with the result that his normal pattern of behaviour becomes disturbed: the treatment is a method of reducing his anxiety-loaded associations to these situations, so that he can re-enter them and resume his normal activities. The patient is gradually reintroduced to the situations or objects which evoke his anxiety, while his anxiety is itself neutralized by a response which inhibits anxiety: the method Wolpe chose to produce this inhibition was deep muscle relaxation. The patient does not, in the treatment, face the anxiety-evoking situations or objects in real life, but in his imagination. He and the therapist draw up a list (a hierarchy) of anxiety-evoking situations (adversive stimuli), graded by their severity: and in phantasy he is reintroduced to these repetitively and progressively while he is relaxed, until he can tolerate the most severe of them without relapsing into avoiding behaviour. Having then relearned normal behaviour in situations created by his imagination, he must make the transition to retraining in everyday life.

Wolpe's explanation of the undoubted success of this technique of treatment in certain cases was that it makes use of a mechanism of reciprocal inhibition: *i.e.* the morbid stimulus-anxiety bond (the neurotic symptom) is weakened by a response inhibiting (incompatible with) anxiety being elicited at the same time as the stimulus which had come habitually to provoke it. This is probably not an adequate explanation of how the therapy works: more likely there is a reduction in the level of arousal which promotes habituation and relearning, and no doubt, as in all other kinds of psychotherapy, suggestion plays a part.

Only a minority of neurotic symptoms can be understood at all adequately as uncomplicated learned patterns of behaviour, and of these simple phobias provide the best examples. It is such simple phobias, *e.g.* of snakes or thunder, or rather more complicated anxieties such as travel phobias, which respond best to desensitization therapy: and for them it is probably now the treatment of choice (Gelder, Marks and Wolff, 1967). It may be of benefit in milder cases of agoraphobia. But where there are many neurotic symptoms, where the anxiety is severe and particularly where the personality and personal relationships are deeply involved, the method is ineffective. It is not a treatment to be recommended for obsessional or hysterical neuroses.

In *aversion therapy* an unpleasant or painful stimulus is associated repeatedly with a symptom or mode of behaviour which it is desired to eliminate. The unpleasant stimuli may be chemical (emetics such as apomorphine or emetine) or electrical (mild faradic shocks delivered through electrodes strapped to the patient's arm). These stimuli must be given at carefully chosen times, and the electrical method, now usually preferred, permits more accurate timing, as well as being safer and less unpleasant for the patient. Alcoholism, drug addictions, and sexual deviations, including homosexuality, transvestism, fetishism and sadomasochism, have been treated by this method. The aversion treatment of alcoholism and its results are discussed on page 415: there have also been some promising reports of the results of treatment of sexual deviations (Marks and Gelder, 1967)—but longer experience of the treatment in such cases is required before firm conclusions can be drawn. Aversion techniques may arouse in patients suffering from sexual deviations strong feelings of anger and depression, which require skilled management.

There is also a technique known as *positive conditioning*, of which the chief example is the pad-and-buzzer treatment of nocturnal enuresis. When the patient wets his bed, electrical contact is made between two metal plates and a bell or buzzer is then rung loudly, awakening the patient. By this means bladder distension comes to be associated with arousal, and the patient wakes to empty his bladder instead of being incontinent.

These behaviour therapies constitute an important advance in treatment. They are still specialized methods, requiring special training or experience in the therapist. They hold out good promise of relief for certain types of neurotic symptoms and sexual deviation; and even more promise of advancing our understanding of the mechanisms which are involved in the genesis and cure of these symptoms. They can be used in conjunction with individual or group therapy of a dynamic kind: desensitization of phobias may, for example, take place more speedily after group therapy (Gelder and Marks, 1968). Both behaviour therapies and psychodynamic methods have their particular uses and limitations; and they have also a good deal in common, since behaviour therapy is not carried out in an emotional void—a patient-therapist relationship is inevitably created, which is a potent factor in the results achieved. It was expected that such a superficial-seeming removal of one neurotic symptom would be followed by its replacement by another: but symptom-substitution is reported not to have proved a major problem in behaviour therapy. It is nevertheless likely that these new techniques will be found to have considerable limitations, since they do not promote the increase of psychological awareness and maturity upon which the achievement of greater emotional stability seems so often to depend.

Physical Methods of Treatment

The neurotic patient's general health must be cared for, and if there has been a considerable loss of weight, admission to hospital for a short period and the giving of modified insulin treatment to bring about a gain in weight, may be very helpful.

Drugs should be used very sparingly in the treatment of neurotics: and it is better, if possible, to do without them. The neurotic patient easily becomes dependent on tension-easing drugs, and addicted to them. It is also bad therapeutic tactics to make the patient too comfortable, since the discomfort of his symptoms acts as a spur to drive him through their psychological treatment. If the patient's tension is relieved by drugs, all too often he feels that this is sufficient; and he goes on taking the drugs because when he ceases to do so his symptoms return in full force. He is like the patient in cardiac failure who manages fairly well while he is digitalized: but compensation is never properly achieved and the neurotic usually needs his drugs in increasing doses.

The drug most effective for the relief of neurotic tension is amylobarbitone sodium, in 60 to 120 mg. doses given twice or thrice a day. It is particularly effective in the relief of anticipatory tension and in the treatment of acute anxiety attacks. Other barbiturates may be prescribed instead, and it is often advisable to ring the changes on them, if sedation is necessary for a prolonged period. Three of the most useful, quickly acting sedatives for those who cannot get to sleep at nights because of their anxiety, are pentobarbitone sodium, 100 to 200 mg., quinalbarbitone sodium in the same dosage, and cyclobarbitone, 200 to 400 mg.

The newer tranquillizing drugs have not been of much assistance in the treatment of neurotics. Euphoriant drugs should be avoided, again because of the risk of addiction: so should alcohol.

Environmental Adjustments

Where adjustments can be made in the domestic circumstances, or in the conditions of work, and where such adjustments are justifiable, the circumstances and conditions being positively morbid or disadvantageous, the physician derives much indirect therapeutic aid from whatever changes in this direction he is able to effect. The services of a psychiatric social worker are often of great value in this respect. In the case of hysterical patients in particular, to take the patient out of the stressful environment—whether this be a school where he is unhappy, or a job which is disliked, or a situation of war-time danger—may be sufficient for complete relief of the symptoms. But this is the easy way out, and it must be kept in mind that to follow such a course of action may be demoralizing. The neurotic patient commonly himself or herself suggests changing the environment, often in a dramatic way—a different spouse is wanted, or a new house, or a move to a new country, and the physician has in most cases to say that this will not do, that difficulties must be faced and overcome, not burked.

Cases following trauma when a legal action for damages is pending, or compensation is involved in some form or another, are very refractory to treatment. Such cases should be assessed by a consultant. Too much may be hoped from the settlement of claims; it may not result in a rapid cure. There are some cases in which the persistence of symptoms depends on a dread of return to the particular class of work at which the accident occurred, and in these the remedy of transfer to other work is obvious.

Treatment of Hysterical Symptoms

Suggestion plays some part probably in all psychotherapy (see Frank, 1961): it may have to be used deliberately in the treatment of hysteria. Like other neurotic patients hysterics are suggestible, and their symptoms will often be influenced by therapeutic suggestions: but one of the dangers of treatment by suggestion alone is that the disappearance of one hysterical symptom is apt to be followed by the appearance of others. Treatment should therefore not be confined to suggestion and to a superficial, symptomatic level, but should include exploration and explanation along the lines already described in the general discussion of psychotherapeutic procedures. The cause of the symptoms must be found and dealt with. The peculiarly disabling nature of certain hysterical symptoms may however mean that they have to be treated before a deeper psychotherapy is possible: deafness, mutism and amnesia are obvious examples of this.

In the great majority of cases it is possible, by gaining the patient's confidence and by the exercise of firmness as well as tact, to persuade him that the lost function is recoverable, that he can move his hitherto rigid arm, or walk upon his seemingly powerless legs. For this kind of treatment, immediate complete success is necessary and the doctor must believe it can be achieved. Piecemeal improvement is tedious and often temporary. The doctor should choose a day when he can devote, if necessary, an hour or more to the patient. The patient must be informed that the doctor does not intend to leave him until the limb is moved. The doctor then shows (often against actual physical resistance) that the movements can be done passively, and this being done he orders the patient to walk or to use the arm as the case may be. In walking, support is given at first, but the patient is told that if he tends to fall the support will be insufficient. Complete function must be restored at one sitting by this method. Incomplete restoration means the perpetuation of an incomplete function for weeks or months. In a proportion of cases the symptom is a hysterical habit which has outlived its usefulness, and which the patient would gladly be rid of, if he knew how. Such patients are easily amenable to treatment. The difference between 'trying' to move a limb—which involves a fear or a belief that it will not—and belief that it will move must be explained to the patient. Baudouin put it crudely but cleverly when he said that for the removal of symptoms the power of the imagination is inversely as the square of the will.

Mutism can be dealt with at a sitting by a determined attempt at persuasion and re-education. The patient is told to place his mouth and lips in certain positions. He readily does so. He is then shown that by placing them in certain positions and making sudden movements of them he can whisper consonants. Soon he can whisper sentences. It should then be pointed out that he thought he could not whisper, whereas it is proved that he can. He has then to be told with assurance that he can put his voice into it. He usually responds by doing so. Aphonia is usually a more difficult symptom to treat, partly because it causes less inconvenience than mutism.

If simple persuasion and suggestion fail, recourse can be had to intravenous barbiturates (amylobarbitone sodium or thiopentone) or hypnosis. In patients who have already shown a decided tendency to dissociations (in amnesias, trance-states, fugues, etc.), hypnosis is usually easy and may be the simplest method of recovering the content of episodes for which there is amnesia. Barbiturate narcosis is perhaps to be preferred, since hypnosis tends to make the patient unduly dependent on the therapist. By neither method are memories likely to be recalled unless the patient is willing that they should be. Amnesias which involve the whole of the individual's past life, with loss of identity, clear up spontaneously.

Cases of anorexia nervosa should be admitted to the psychiatric unit of a general hospital. Special feeding with a high calorie, high carbohydrate diet and nursing, initially in bed, should begin at once. Meals, light and nutritious, should be supervised until everything is being eaten, and the patient must be given no opportunity to conceal food instead of consuming it or to vomit immediately after meals. Chlorpromazine in large doses, with or without soluble insulin in small appetizer doses, may be helpful; a few cases are helped by E.C.T. When the patient's physical state no longer causes anxiety, psychotherapy should commence. Even superficial exploration may reveal some of the originating ideas—they may be fully conscious, and such an approach will also serve to show the patient that at last there is some understanding, and so gain her confidence. Where the basis is a fear of fatness the patient should have it pointed out to her that she will not be expected to eat so as to become too fat, and that, since she has been able to make herself so thin this time, there is no fear of adiposity. Whether a deeper exploration of the psychodynamics of the illness is possible and advisable, depends on the features of the individual case.

Other gross hysterical symptoms, such as blindness or fugues, or the poor general physical health of the patient, may make admission to hospital necessary; but it should be avoided if possible. Hospital tends to become a refuge which the patient may be very reluctant to leave. Admission to hospital should be a part therefore of a constructive plan of treatment. Otherwise it is apt to lead to therapeutic stalemate and when the doctor in frustration decides to discharge the patient still not symptom-free, there may be emotional outbursts, recriminations and suicidal threats.

It is essential in all these cases that the patient's relatives should clearly understand the therapeutic situation. If they do not, the patient may manipulate it so that the relatives come to blame the doctor for any lack of progress. The relatives must be taught also how at home to handle the patient's problems so as to give him understanding and encouragement but not too much solicitude.

Treatment of Obsessional Symptoms

Many phobias respond reasonably well to psychotherapy. While an under-standing is being obtained of the determinants of the phobia, the patient should be advised to avoid phobia-eliciting situations. A vicious circle development is thus broken. When the patient has lost some of his apprehension and gained some confidence and understanding of his symptoms, he may be advised to re-enter the situations which had previously caused him distress, fortified by a sedative such as amylobarbitone sodium. He should be told he can leave again as soon as he feels uncomfortable, and that he is not being weak in doing so. Gradually he is likely to find that he can tolerate the difficult situations for longer, the sedative becomes a standby which he carries with him, and then if all goes well he can dispense with it altogether.

Where obsessive rumination depends on an inability to reconcile objective facts with desires, or facts with childish preconceptions, discussion and modifica-tion of the desires helps to bring relief. Also, where the motive power of the obsessional preoccupation is remorse—and much of the malignancy of obses-sional states may depend on their basis in feelings of guilt and remorse—discus-sion of the foundations of the remorse, when they are discoverable, and readjustment of the mental attitudes to them, may be of considerable assistance: but this deeper exploration has to be carried out with great care, and too much analytic probing may precipitate greater distress and a depression of spirits with a suicidal risk.

One cannot hope to rid the obsessional of his obsessional personality, but he can be taught how best to live with it by understanding both its strengths and its disadvantages. Obsessionals drive themselves very hard, and they may have to be guided about taking adequate rest and holidays, and advised against over-loading themselves with duties and too many responsibilities. Promotion is some-times better avoided by the obsessional. He is more than normally sensitive to major changes in his way of life and upset by them. Many obsessional patients are helped very much by the opportunity now and again of a talk with their doctor, when they can ventilate their problems and get his reactions and encouragement.

Environmental readjustments may be all that is required in the case of the child who has developed obsessional symptoms under stress at school, for example, or is being brought up too strictly at home.

The patient with obsessional impulses will want to know whether or not he should give in to them. Usually he is forced to do, because not to give in to them creates intolerable tension: the doctor therefore in his reply should accept the *fait accompli*. But he cannot advise the patient not to withstand his impulses, if these are to antisocial actions or so frequent that he cannot get on with the business of life.

Treatment of the classical obsessive-compulsive type of case is a matter often of great difficulty. In those cases which are particularly resistant to any form of psychotherapeutic treatment and where the person's life and conduct is entirely dominated by obsessive symptoms, the operation of leucotomy should be seriously considered—particularly if the illness has been for some years disabling. In our experience leucotomy has proved very effective in certain malignant cases, and has made life much more bearable.

PROGNOSIS

There are great individual variations in the outcome of these illnesses, which is easily understandable since the reactions themselves range from transient responses to stress to states of chronic invalidism. In general, the prognosis depends not so much on the specific symptoms developed, as on the adequacy of the personality for the demands made on it by the circumstances of daily life. The prognosis may therefore be seen to depend on at least four factors:

1. The type and duration of the neurotic reaction.
2. The previous personality of the patient.
3. The circumstances of his life.
4. The treatment given.

Usually, the shorter the duration of the illness the better the outlook, since some neurotic reactions have a tendency to become habitual and the longer they persist the more likely is it that the development of hysterical symptoms may complicate the issue. Anxiety states usually clear up satisfactorily over a period of months; hysterical reactions may be very superficial and short-lived, or longer lasting, and in a few cases become so ingrained that they may be said to be malignant; while obsessional neuroses (which are more endogenously determined than other neurotic reactions), except for those which run a cyclic course or present as phobic states, tend to be persistent. We must stress the individual variations, and how unwise it is to generalize dogmatically. Anorexia nervosa, for example, is a serious condition, often intractable, sometimes fatal: but a considerable number of cases respond well to treatment, menstruation becomes re-established, and they remain well. Again, while obsessionals have in general the poorest prognosis, the outlook here is also very variable and usually not unsatisfactory. Lewis (1935) reported that in an unselected sample of obsessional patients roughly one-half may be expected to do well. He followed up 50 cases ('a good sample of the obsessionals of London'), five years or more after they had been treated at The Maudsley Hospital. Sixteen were then quite well (free of symptoms), 7 were much improved, 5 had been well but had relapsed, 5 were a little improved and 17 were no better or worse. Lewis noted that many obsessionals show a late improvement, after years of illness. Pollitt (1960), reviewing the published reports of follow-up studies, found that 43 per cent. of obsessional patients have a good prognosis.

The more stable and mature the previous personality, the better the outlook; except for those cases where the obsessional personality shades over into the obsessional illness. The neuroses are illnesses of young adult life, and there appears to be a general tendency for people to grow out of them. The immature, hysterical personality, after many alarms and excursions, may mature late and become much better adjusted. On the other hand, if neurotic symptoms are essentially an expression of the persistent maladjustment of an inadequate psychopathic personality, the outlook is far poorer.

Obviously the circumstances of the patient's life play an important part in determining the prognosis. These illnesses are responses to environmental stresses, as well as to inner conflicts. If these external stresses are relieved, either spontaneously or by deliberate manipulation of the environment, psychological healing can take place and the patient tends naturally to recover. On the other hand, circumstances which have been the main cause of the illness, may be irremediable; for example, a woman unhappily married to a drunken husband may on account of her children be unable or unwilling to leave him: in such a case the neurotic reaction will tend to chronicity, and it can be seen often to be to some extent self-protective and adaptive, a way of diverting and dulling the distress of the domestic predicament.

So individual are these reactions and so various, with in many cases a spontaneous tendency to readjustment, that the effects of psychotherapy and other methods of treatment are difficult to gauge. There is a good deal of evidence that, whatever the form of treatment employed, about 70 per cent. of neurotic patients may be expected to recover or become much better within a year or two. Ross (1936) in a follow-up study of 1186 cases treated at the Cassel Hospital, found a year after discharge that 40 per cent. were well and 25 per cent. improved. The more or less corresponding and contemporary figures from the Berlin Psychoanalytic Institute were 40 and 18 per cent. The Berlin cases were treated by psychoanalysis in its strictest sense, for an average of 17 months: the Cassel Hospital cases were treated by hypnosis, explanation, persuasion and sometimes by a modified form of analysis, for an average of 4·1 months. The results of treatment in these two groups were remarkably alike, in spite of considerable differences in methods and duration of treatment. Similar results have been reported by other workers since then. Denker (1946), investigating 500 cases of neurosis treated by general practitioners with superficial psychotherapy, found that 72 per cent. had recovered in 2 years.

This suggests that there are biological factors present in neurotic illnesses which promote improvement, independently of therapeutic efforts. On the other hand, the experience of individual cases and of watching the relation of their progress to the steps in treatment carry to the clinician conviction of the efficacy of psychotherapeutic methods. Statistical surveys of the results of treatment in large groups involve the lumping together of individual differences where the differences themselves may be of great importance, and the very varying standards by which improvement is measured make comparisons of dubious worth.

Eysenck (1960b) reviewed the literature on the effects of psychotherapy and came to challenging conclusions. He stated that 'when untreated neurotic controls are compared with experimental groups of patients treated by means of psychotherapy, both groups recover to approximately the same extent'; and he went on to say, 'We have found that neurotic disorders tend to be self-limiting, that psychoanalysis is no more successful than any other method, and that in fact all methods of psychotherapy fail to improve on the recovery rate obtained through ordinary life experiences and non-specific treatment'. These conclusions should not be considered as final, but they point very clearly to the need for more research, and research carried out with control groups (however difficult this may be).

The often quoted figure of 70 per cent. improvement with psychotherapy masks the fact that some patients are helped to a more impressive extent. Truax and his colleagues (1966) found that the difference in the improvement rate for neurotic out-patients treated in brief psychotherapy by psychiatrists might be as much as 40 per cent.: in their study one group of patients showed 90 per cent. improvement, the other only 50 per cent. It is also too seldom remarked that psychotherapy makes some patients worse: and that this is a situation which equally calls for further investigation.

The quality of the recovery which the patient makes can only be fully gauged by his ability to withstand the strains of life over the subsequent years.

PSYCHOSOMATIC DISORDERS

The word psychosomatic has been used with two main meanings: first, to describe a method of clinical approach to all patients; and second, to delineate a group of physical diseases or syndromes.

In its first sense, the term has much the same connotations as Adolf Meyer's psychobiological. It expresses a holistic approach to clinical problems, an interest in the vicissitudes of the whole organism rather than in the activity of single organs, a belief that psychic and somatic are two complementary and equally necessary angles of observation, understanding and management. So far as it assists to promote such an approach, the term is unexceptionable. It calls attention to the close relationship of mind and body, and especially it impresses upon doctors in general that many of the symptoms that they have been accustomed to treat along physical lines are really of psychological origin. Psychogenic, especially neurotic, conditions as a whole probably present themselves more frequently in a somatic guise than a mental one. Patients come more often to the family doctor with a complaint of palpitation or headache than with irrational fear of crossing the road. But in the past it has commonly happened that symptoms referred to by the patient as indigestion were accepted as such by the doctor and labelled 'dyspepsia', which was then treated as a disease *sui generis*, although no physical lesion had been demonstrated. Similarly, vague pains were labelled 'rheumatism'; complaints of fatigue were attributed to a 'weak heart' or 'anaemia'; breathlessness was called 'asthma'; localized pain was often disposed of as 'neuralgia' or 'neuritis'; and complaints both general and vague without discoverable physical causes were labelled 'debility'. The attachment of the diagnostic label gave form and substance to the syndrome in the patient's mind, and in this way neurotic invalids who were always complaining, improving a little and relapsing, were created in considerable numbers. Such chronic conditions might well be called iatrogenic, fostered, if not produced, by the doctor's failure, arising from shortcomings in his medical education, to recognize or even to look for the emotional factors that were upsetting digestion or causing pains or fatigue or what not.

The term psychosomatic has also been used with a much more limited reference to describe a certain group of diseases or syndromes. These are physical illnesses, in which one physiological system is predominantly affected, autonomic disturbance is usually apparent, and emotional factors are believed to be of decisive importance. The following list includes many, though by no means all, of the syndromes commonly described under this heading: vasomotor rhinitis, asthma, essential hypertension, coronary artery disease, duodenal ulcer, ulcerative colitis, primary dysmenorrhoea, persistent enuresis, primary hyperthyroidism, diabetes mellitus, rheumatoid arthritis, migraine, and various forms of urticaria, pruritus and neuro-dermatitis. It will be readily appreciated that this list comprises many syndromes with no obvious similarities, but many psychiatrists and physicians have thought that its heterogeneity may be more apparent than real and that there is some justification for a tentative grouping of this kind.

The skin was one of the first organs to get detailed attention, and this century many investigators have claimed that skin blisters, localized oedema and petechial haemorrhages can be produced at particular points of the body surface by hypnotic suggestion or during abreaction. In 1943 Wolf and Wolff, examining an apparently otherwise normal man who had a gastric fistula, were able to observe a sequence of events beginning with emotional upset (*e.g.* resentment), accompanied by prolonged hyperaemia of the gastric mucous membrane, increased acid secretion, and increased motility of the stomach, leading to haemorrhages and erosion of the gastric mucosa, and culminating (in the absence of protecting mucus) in the development of gastric ulceration. Similar detailed investigations have been made of the colon (Grace *et al.*, 1951). Holmes and his colleagues (1950) showed that prolonged emotional tension may be associated with oedema of the nasal mucous membrane, diminished ciliary activity, and lymphatic stasis—a state which predisposes to infection. Though the mechanism of many of these events is still obscure, a great many other findings have been reported which lend more or less plausibility to the concept of psychogenic lesions.

Halliday (1948) pointed out that a striking feature of the public health of this country in the present century had been an apparently rising incidence of these psychosomatic affections. He linked this rising incidence with socio-environmental changes which he believed had led to an increasing proportion of the population developing physiological dysfunctions and obsessional modes of behaviour. These affections appeared to be commoner in urban than in rural areas, and in certain social classes and occupational groups. Kessel and Munro

(1964), in a review of the epidemiological investigations so far made of these disorders, thought that little evidence had been found which supported theories of their psychological aetiologies. They took exception to the 'blanket term psychosomatic illness' and thought it only useful to examine particular illnesses. All this demonstrates the need for further, more critically conducted epidemiological studies.

There have been many enumerations of the traits of character and temperament, or delineations of the personality profiles, associated with the various physical syndromes. No specific personality type has been found to be correlated with any particular syndrome. In different affections, however, the same type of personality has seemed to occur very frequently—people described as anxious, sensitive, over-conscientious and covertly aggressive, who tend to 'bottle-up' their feelings, and who are often labelled as 'obsessional'. These traits, easily recognized and perhaps also rather readily extracted from the patients' accounts of themselves, have not been shown to have any inevitable connection with the physical symptoms. Those of apparently similar personality may develop quite different somatic lesions or, even more significantly, remain physically fit. Complementary and prospective studies are certainly required of different groups of people selected according to their temperaments and followed up to find out to what physical disorders they may be prone.

Various theories have been advanced as to why one system of the body should be involved rather than another, if emotional trauma or continued emotional tension can in fact facilitate the appearance of certain organic diseases. Many psychopathological explanations have been proposed. Some workers have found symbolic meaning in the symptoms, others have delineated emotional constellations, conflicts or attitudes which seem to have pathological results: but none of these psychological explanations now carry much conviction. It is very possible that an already existing organic defect, due to previous injury, could determine the locus of symptoms: for example, the sufferer from dysentery might be left with bowels more sensitive to emotional stimuli. It may also be readily supposed that an individual can have a specific, systemic weakness or locus of lower constitutional resistance. It is in the individual's constitution that the explanation seems likely in most cases to be found. Most of the psychosomatic disorders show a familial incidence, and study of the genetic factors is very properly getting increasing attention. The sufferers from psychosomatic affections may inherit abnormally labile autonomic nervous systems, and their temperamental traits may also have an inherited foundation.

After a period during which the psychogenesis of these syndromes was overemphasized, it is becoming widely recognized that their aetiology is multiple, and that the weight to be given to the psychological factors varies from syndrome to syndrome and from individual to individual. In the case of coronary artery disease, for example, there is currently more emphasis on the importance of physical inactivity, smoking and diet, than on emotional stress, temperament and behaviour patterns; though the latter are still considered to be of some significance in the aetiology. This is further exemplified in the views about asthma which are based on recent research, notably by Rees (1964) and by Leigh and Marley (1967). Infective, psychological and allergic factors are all recognized to be of importance in individuals who are constitutionally vulnerable. The emotional factors are obvious in the majority of asthmatic children, whose attacks are so frequently precipitated by psychological stresses, who are more than averagely prone to psychological disturbances of other sorts, and who tend to have emotionally tense, particularly over-protective, mothers. But asthmatics, young and old, come also often from families who are subject both to psychosomatic and other nervous disorders. The genetic predisposition is of much importance, and the mode of inheritance is probably multifactorial. Leigh and Marley, in a study with controls, have shown in convincing detail how in the relatives of asthmatics there is a higher incidence not only of asthma but also of chronic respiratory disorders, neuroses, hay fever and eczema.

Attacks of the psychosomatic disorders are commonly precipitated by emotionally disturbing circumstances. These precipitating stresses are not specific but are very various, depending upon individual sensitivities, age and the vicissitudes of life. Studying these disorders in a wider biological context, Harold Wolff (1953) considered them as purposive, though inappropriate, protective responses to stress, *i.e.* to problems and challenges in day-to-day life; and he emphasized that biological protective devices, elicited by danger or threats of danger, are for short-term use, and that bodily disorder or disease may arise if the threatened individual sustains such patterns of response unduly long or as a way of life. This is a stimulating formulation and it may be brought into relation with the work of Selye who, studying particularly the complex interplay of nervous and hormonal mechanisms in the individual's adaptation to stress, also proposed the concept that when normal adaptation breaks down certain physical disorders ('diseases of adaptation') may result. Both the autonomic nervous system and the adrenal cortex are intimately concerned with the individual's response to stress. Further research is required into these mechanisms, into the constitutional factors which may be hereditarily determined (twin studies will be useful here), and into the detailed physiology of the emotions.

The psychosomatic concept in therapeutics implies that each patient must be treated with many-sided understanding, both as an individual and as a member of a community, in all the aspects of his sickness, suffering or maladjustment. Attention to these principles will ensure a broader, more humanitarian and effective handling of all medical problems, and will avoid the reproach voiced by the philosopher Amiel in his Journal (Aug. 22, 1873):

'Why do doctors so often make mistakes? Because they are not sufficiently individual in their diagnoses or their treatment. They class a sick man under some given department of their nosology, whereas every invalid is really a special case, a unique example. How is it possible that so coarse a method of sifting should produce judicious therapeutics? Every illness is a factor simple or complex which is multiplied by a second factor, invariably complex—the individual, that is to say, who is suffering from it, so that the result is a special problem, demanding a special solution. . . . The principal grievance which I have against the doctors is that they neglect the real problem, which is to seize the unity of the individual who claims their care.'

These therapeutic principles apply also of course to the limited group of so-called 'psychosomatic' syndromes with their multiple aetiology; but it is proper to add that at present the psychiatrist has a modest rôle to play in their management. Many of these conditions tend to run a chronic and relapsing course. The psychiatrist who claims too much in this field does his speciality no service. A fuller knowledge of aetiology is essential if we are to make progress.

REFERENCES

Ackner, B. (1954) *J. ment. Sci.*, **100**, 838.
Berrington, W. P., Liddell, D. W., and Foulds, G. A. (1956) *J. ment. Sci.*, **102**, 280.
Brown, F. W. (1942) *Proc. roy. Soc. Med.*, **35**, 785.
Crisp, A. H. (1965) *Proc. roy. Soc. Med.*, **58**, 814.
Dally, P., and Sargant, W. (1966) *Brit. med. J.*, **2**, 793.
Dejerine, J., and Gauckler, E. (1911) *Les Manifestations Fonctionnelles des Psychonévroses*, Paris.
Denker, P. G. (1946) *N.Y. St. J. Med.*, **46**, 2164.
Eysenck, H. J. (1947) *Dimensions of Personality*, London.
Eysenck, H. J., ed. (1960a) *Behaviour Therapy and the Neuroses*, London.
Eysenck, H. J., ed. (1960b) *Handbook of Abnormal Psychology*, Chapter 18, London.
Fenichel, O. (1946) *The Psychoanalytic Theory of Neurosis*, London.
Foulkes, S. H., and Anthony, E. J. (1957) *Group Psychotherapy*, London.
Frank, J. D. (1961) *Persuasion and Healing*, Baltimore.
Frank, J. D. (1966) *Amer. J. Psychother.*, **20**, 564.
Freud, S. (1955) *Complete Psychological Works*, London.
Gelder, M. G., and Marks, I. M. (1968) *Brit. J. Psychiat.*, **114**, 323.
Gelder, M. G., Marks, I. M., and Wolff, H. H. (1967) *Brit. J. Psychiat.*, **113**, 53.
Gillespie, R. D. (1944) *Psychological Effects of War on Citizen and Soldier*, London.
Gordon, A. (1926) *Amer. J. Psychiat.*, **5**, 647.
Grace, W. J., Wolf, S., and Wolff, H. G. (1951) *The Human Colon*, New York.
Halliday, J. L. (1948) *Psychosocial Medicine*, London.
Hare, E. H., and Shaw, G. K. (1965) *Mental Health on a New Housing Estate*, London.
Holmes, T. H., Goodell, H., Wolf, S., and Wolff, H. G. (1950) *The Nose*, Springfield, Ill.
Ironside, R. N., and Batchelor, I. R. C. (1945) *Brit. J. Ophthal.*, **29**, 88.
Janet, P. (1911) *The Mental State of Hystericals*, London.
Jones, E. (1948) *Papers on Psycho-analysis*, 5th ed., London.
Kay, D. W. K. (1953) *Proc. roy. Soc. Med.*, **46**, 669.
Kessel, N., and Munro, A. (1964) *J. psychosom. Res.*, **8**, 67.
Kessel, W. I. N., and Shepherd, M. (1962) *J. ment. Sci.*, **108**, 159.
Leigh, D., and Marley, E. (1967) *Bronchial Asthma: A Genetic, Population, and Psychiatric Study*, London.
Lewis, A. (1935) *Proc. roy. Soc. Med.*, **29**, 325.
McDougall, W. (1926) *Outline of Abnormal Psychology*, New York.
Marks, I. M., and Gelder, M. G. (1967) *Brit. J. Psychiat.*, **113**, 711.
Martin, F. M., Brotherston, J. H. F., and Chave, S. P. W. (1957) *Brit. J. prev. soc. Med.*, **11**, 196.
Moody, R. L. (1946) *Lancet*, ii, 934.
Nemiah, J. C. (1950) *Medicine (Baltimore)*, **29**, 225.
Pollitt, J. D. (1960) *J. ment. Sci.*, **106**, 93.
Rees, L. (1964) *J. psychosom. Res.*, **8**, 101.
Ross, T. A. (1936) *An Enquiry into Prognosis in the Neuroses*, London.
Russell, G. M. F. (1967) *J. psychosom. Res.*, **11**, 141.

Shepherd, M., Cooper, B., Brown, A. C., and Kalton, G. W. (1964) *Brit. med. J.*, **2**, 1359.
Shepherd, M., Davies, B. M., and Culpan, R. A. (1960) *Acta psychiat. scand.*, **35**, 4.
Shorvon, H. J. (1946) *Proc. roy. Soc. Med.*, **39**, 779.
Slater, E. (1943) *J. Neurol. Psychiat.*, **6**, 1.
Slater, E. (1965) *Brit. med. J.*, **1**, 1395.
Slater, E., and Slater, P. (1944) *J. Neurol. Neurosurg. Psychiat.*, **7**, 49.
Stengel, E. (1941) *J. ment. Sci.*, **87**, 572.
Stengel, E. (1943) *J. ment. Sci.*, **89**, 224.
Stengel, E. (1945) *J. ment. Sci.*, **91**, 166.
Taylor, S. (1938) *Lancet*, i, 759.
Truax, C. B., Wargo, D. G., Frank, J. D., Imber, S. D., Battle, C. C., Hoehn-Saric, R..
    Nash, E. H., and Stone, A. R. (1966) *J. cons. Psychol.*, **30**, 395.
Wolf, S., and Wolff, H. G. (1943) *Human Gastric Function*, New York.
Wolff, H. G. (1953) *Stress and Disease*, Springfield, Ill.
Wolpe, J. (1958) *Psychotherapy by Reciprocal Inhibition*, Stanford.

9

SEXUAL ANOMALIES

The social and medico-legal problems which arise in cases of sexual anomaly present many perplexities of an intricate nature involving both aetiology and treatment. But it is usually only after the social, ethical and legal codes have been transgressed that the advice of the physician or psychiatrist is sought. Otherwise the sexual deviate remains secretive, either because he does not wish to change his nature in the belief that it gives him a certain superiority over his fellow-men or, on the contrary, if guilt feelings predominate, he lives in the vain hope that some time or other he may reach an adequate solution for himself. A psychiatric opinion may only be requested when he has fallen foul of the law and been arrested for lewd and libidinous behaviour. Then it becomes essential to reach a decision as to whether the offence was committed during the course of some form of mental or nervous disorder, or whether it arose *sui generis*. In the former instance the sexual anomaly is regarded as one of the symptoms of an otherwise disordered mind which requires the care and treatment a hospital provides; in other cases of a neurotic nature with obsessive-compulsive symptoms the Court may sanction probation with the proviso that the individual co-operates in medical supervision and treatment.

In the absence of nervous or mental illness the position is more complex; if the psychiatrist can, with justice, emphasize any mitigating factors, which may have influenced the conduct of the individual, he should not hesitate to do so, but he must be most scrupulous in his ascertainment of all the relevant facts so that the Court may be given every assistance to come to a fair decision. The cordial relations which now exist between the medical and legal professions has led to a greater emphasis on treatment and rehabilitation rather than on an arbitrary prison sentence. The better understanding of the man himself is aimed at rather than the quality of his act. But even if the sexual offender is sentenced to a term of imprisonment, specialized medical facilities for treatment are now available.

Anomalies of sex conduct affect all ranks of society and all age groups. Our case records show that we have been consulted in relation to members of the aristocracy, lawyers, doctors, professors, clergymen, scoutmasters, business executives, and manual workers; the young, middle-aged, and elderly have all been implicated. Alcohol has been one of the most outstanding precipitating agents. Even a small amount, given the particular circumstances and opportunity, may be sufficient to trigger off impulsive and instinctive conduct which otherwise would have been controlled. That of course is by no means invariably so for there are many sex deviates who are total abstainers. The fact that the person may be deeply under the influence of alcohol at the time of the offence does not, necessarily, excuse his conduct.

In the great majority of cases which have been referred to us the accused has been found to be of sound mind and fit to plead to the charge against him; in a considerable number there were extenuating circumstances which the Court took into consideration in assessing punishment or treatment. Our examinations showed that the offence was rarely an isolated one, it had been repeated on many occasions, but surprisingly enough it had not interfered with the person's ability to pursue his duties, or to lead a happy life at home; his employer, and his wife and family, often, had no knowledge of his incongruous conduct. For the accused, arrest and Court appearance came, sometimes, as a blessed relief. There was no need for further duplicity, an opportunity had been provided whereby the secret life which had dominated his conduct and his conscience could now be fully disclosed, and a restart made to reach a higher and more mature level. The younger the person the greater the chance of readjustment. The older group, many of them married men with families, presented tragic situations jeopardizing their careers and their homes. Their history often showed that they had been hard-working capable persons occupying positions of responsibility, happy in their homes, kind to their children, but who for one reason or another, *e.g.* predisposition, drink, sexual deprivation, impotence, sought relief from their inner tensions by lewd conduct, irrespective of the inherent risks. Many admitted their guilt, expressed remorse, and did not know why they should have behaved in such a way, but others took refuge in specious excuses or pleaded amnesia.

In this sophisticated age when the sexes mix with so much freedom it is surprising that so many remain profoundly ignorant of the facts of life. Inborn constitutional factors influencing or retarding normal sexual development may be one element, but parental over-solicitude, prohibition, threats of punishment, *e.g.* castration, are even more likely to inhibit the onset of the natural instinctive biological urge. Sex becomes taboo, a sense of shame and guilt is generated, and a mature heterosexual level may never be reached. We meet such situations in civil cases, as apart from criminal, where non-consummation of marriage due to impotence, of a physical or psychogenic nature, may lead to nullity proceedings. E. B. Strauss (1950) in his impressive and detailed account of this topic writes as follows: 'No medical practitioner can afford to be ignorant of the aetiology and nature of this sexual disability, and should always be prepared to give a sympathetic hearing, and informal advice to his unfortunate patients'. We concur entirely with that point of view for its full acceptance might be the means of preventing many disastrous marriages. For instance, a general practitioner had advised a sensitive, prudish, middle-aged schoolmaster to marry in the hope that his impotence and sense of inferiority would thus be cured. The result was disastrous. Investigation showed that a strong Oedipus situation existed, and even despite all the willing help his wife gave him he was unable to consummate the marriage. In contrast the powerful sexual reactions he experienced when he gave a boy a thrashing caused him the most intense alarm. The deep-seated nature of the psychogenic factors, and his age precluded the possibility of successful psychotherapeutic treatment and led to nullity proceedings.

(For a detailed, factual study of sexual behaviour as it affects male and female we refer readers to the authoritative investigations of Dr. Alfred C. Kinsey and his associates, 1948, 1953.)

Masturbation

In infancy and early childhood it is more correctly regarded as an instinctive search for a pleasurable sensation rather than as an overt form of sexuality. Even the normal warmth and security of the mother, sucking, rhythmic movements, cuddling and accidental stimulation of the sexual zone, during bathing and cleansing, may produce it. It is only when puberty or adolescence is reached that the child becomes conscious of sexual feelings as such, and may experience alarm, horror, shame and fear. The investigations of Havelock Ellis, Kinsey and many others have shown that practically all persons of both sexes have practised masturbation during some period of their lives, and it can therefore be regarded as a normal stage in one's sexual development. It is something to be lived through, and to be replaced at a later stage by heterosexual interests. This, however, may not always occur. There are some unfortunate people who remain stuck at the narcissistic level, and who learn to accentuate their erotic feelings by phantasy thinking. Sooner or later anxiety, shame, guilt, rear their ugly heads, and the victim may believe that he has done himself irreparable harm, committed the unpardonable sin, and deserves to be punished. An attempt at self-mutilation may seem to be the answer to his problems. Such persons are of a shy, sensitive, introspective make-up, they shun company, are sure that people can tell by looking at them that they are guilty of sinful conduct, and believe that bodily, mentally and spiritually they are doomed to failure and defeat. Some attempt to sublimate their problems by burning the midnight oil, by having recourse to philosophy and religion, and it is only when they are near breaking point that they seek advice and assistance. Others of stronger fibre—and they are the majority—pass through this ordeal of development unscathed.

The habit may be continued into adult life but gradually becomes less insistent, and does not interfere with the prospect of marriage, or ability to carry out one's marital duties. It does not lead to insanity or moral deterioration, as was at one time supposed, but if it has been practised excessively (several times a day) over a period of years it may produce a state of lessened potency. It is, therefore, of importance in relation to one's biological development to put away childish ways and habits at as early a date as possible—and strive for more healthy and mature outlets.

Scoptophilia and Exhibitionism

Scoptophilia and exhibitionism have been described by Clifford Allen as the counterparts of one another. Scoptophilia is the state of sexual excitement and pleasure derived from viewing sexual scenes, or the genitalia of a member of the opposite sex. Exhibitionism or 'indecent exposure' is the habit of displaying the sexual organs to persons of the opposite sex; it accounts for from one-quarter to one-third of all sex offences.

The above tendencies or anomalies are part of the play-life of the normal child. Most of us have indulged in them in one way or another, and have gained physical and moral satisfaction by comparing ourselves with others; even in later life our sexual gratification and curiosity may be satisfied by pornographic literature, drawings and pictures of an erotic nature, tailor's 'dummies', statues, *e.g.* Pygmalionism, rock 'n roll dances, strip-tease acts, glamorous young women in the theatre or on television. All such actions are harmless enough, but when they become of such a compelling nature as to inhibit or prevent further biological development they can produce dangerous situations.

The so-called *voyeurs* or 'peeping Toms' are usually emotionally immature persons who, in their search for satisfaction, travel alone (sometimes in disguise), and constantly court recognition and disaster, by repeating their offence time and again. The risks they run are amazing because during the day as well as at night they are driven into behaviour which, in their inmost being, they may despise. It is in complete contrast to the mask of respectability they present to the public.

They frequent public parks, playgrounds, or other places where they are likely to observe loving couples; even seeing them walk hand in hand, or kissing may be sufficient to stir their erotic fancies by identifying them with the participant. They go on holidays by themselves, seek secluded spots where there may be better opportunities to observe. We have known some who have made a habit of lurking in hotel corridors, of listening at bedroom doors, of peeping through the key-hole; others emulate the exploits of the cat-burglar by climbing up to windows in the hope of seeing people undressing, in the nude, or indulging in sexual intercourse.

Such persons do not lead dissociated lives, there is no absolute split in their personality, they are fully conscious of their actions, and know they are unbecoming to their pride and prestige. The conflict of forces between their conduct on the one hand, and their inability to control their perverted desires on the other may give rise to intense psychosomatic symptoms which not infrequently show themselves as nausea, abdominal discomfort and vomiting, symbols of overwhelming disgust. When such is the case, and when it becomes accentuated by phantasy thinking, then business efficiency and power of concentration may be seriously interfered with; appropriate treatment, however, can solve many such problems.

Exhibitionists also demonstrate the frailty and ambivalence of human nature. They, too, may prefer the by-ways and secluded places where they may display themselves to women and children with less chance of detection by the police. Three-quarters of them, however, display themselves in public places, in the streets or parks. Daylight, however, on occasions, does not daunt them. For instance, a man who had been brought up by an over-solicitous, possessive mother obtained his revenge and a false sense of freedom by exhibiting himself from a window in his mother's house to a group of girls who were employed in a factory opposite. The Court accepted the suggestion that he should be placed on probation in the hope that he would benefit from psychotherapeutic treatment.

Usually the exhibitionist displays himself to strangers: practically always to females. He may or may not have an erection and masturbate, but he seeks no further relationship with those whose attention he craves. There is a compulsive quality often about the act, the perpetrator experiences an overwhelming urge to do it and commonly feels dejected and guilty after it. He appears also often to be uncertain what sort of reaction he had been seeking from his 'victim'. He may select a certain type of woman or child or age group, but just as often he appears to act on impulse, as an opportunity presents itself. The offence is commonly repeated: exhibitionism has the highest rate of recidivism among sexual offences.

Most exhibitionists are in their twenties: a further largish group are adolescent. Cases occurring in the middle-aged and the more elderly illustrate a compensatory phenomenon whereby their exhibitionistic endeavours become indicative of their dwindling potency; the regression to a more primitive instinctive level is not so strange as it might appear. In certain cases it may be an indication or symptom of a beginning organic deterioration of the central nervous system. As a case in point and as an unusual outcome of psychosurgery a man, 47 years old, who never previously had committed sexual offences was charged with exhibiting himself, and interfering with a child aged 5 years. He had undergone a leucotomy ten years previously on account of paranoid symptoms. He was the type of person who required to be under constant medical supervision.

It is far from easy to understand the mental mechanisms which can influence and dominate people so dangerously. The ordinary standards of social conduct are thrown aside, ugly facets of the personality seem to take on individual activity and precipitate situations which can be alarming and tragic. The psychoanalytic school postulates the view that all such conduct is determined at an unconscious level, and that its root is embedded in castration fears (the denial of castration). No doubt there is much truth in that opinion. Some of these youths and men can be seen to have had unsatisfactory relationships with their parents— to have suffered from over-protective mothers or authoritarian (or absent) fathers, with the result that their sexual development has been inhibited. Others have developed feelings of sexual inadequacy in marriage. Probably we can rarely think in terms of one underlying mental mechanism; there are extraneous, accidental, unpredictable factors which also play a part. It is our opinion that many emotionally distorted and inadequate persons continually strive for dominance and power by the use of over-compensatory mechanisms.

Transvestism

This condition, the wearing of clothes of the other sex for sexual gratification, like so many other sex anomalies, may start naturally and innocently as a state of make-believe, of play acting, of a 'lark' which has no apparent or obvious relationship to sexuality at all. The roots must be deep in our unconscious. Most of us have had fun in dressing-up, in pretending that we are different from what we really are, and of reverting to an earlier period of our development. Flag days for charity conducted by students provide many examples. It is only when the practice is continued into manhood and womanhood and becomes established as a mode of life to produce sexual gratification that a dangerous state of abnormality is reached. It can, however, have its romantic aspects as well: James Barry (James Miranda Steurt Barry) was a little woman, barely five feet high, who assumed male clothing and was successful, in 1812, in becoming a doctor of medicine of Edinburgh University. In 1813 she joined the Army Medical Service, and after 46 years achieved the rank of Inspector-General of Army Hospitals. Only at her death in 1865 was the secret of her sex revealed. She seems to have carried out her duties admirably and was such an accomplished surgeon that in 1815 when stationed at the Cape of Good Hope she performed a Caesarean section on a Mrs. Munnik and delivered her of a son who, appropriately enough, was christened James Barry Munnik. A daughter of James Barry Munnik married a Hertzog, and their son became the Prime Minister of South Africa—James Barry Munnik Hertzog.

Miss Russell (1943), to whom we are indebted for the story of James Barry, also records that in 1904 an article written by G. E. Marvel and published in the *Cape Times* throws some light on the unconscious motivation which may have determined James Barry's remarkable sex impersonation. She is supposed to have been an illegitimate daughter of the Prince Regent, and her real name was Joan Augusta Fitzroy. After learning the story of her birth and bringing up, and of her mother's seduction she rejected the name of Joan Fitzroy, and became James Barry—a dominating aggressive personality who was a law to herself, and in her mental attributes over-compensated for her small stature and physique.

The story of another lady who was well known to us has certain points in common. Before she was born her mother had anxiously anticipated the birth of a boy. In consequence she was brought up as a boy, became interested in boyish sports and games and despised her femininity. When 5 years old she was sexually assaulted by a man in the family's employment. Later in life, during her adolescent period, she identified herself closely with soldiers who were being trained for service overseas. When she read of the casualties the regiment had sustained she passed into a delirium during which she identified herself with them and believed that she also was serving in the trenches. When she resumed her ordinary life she became conscious that other women seemed to be attracted to her, wrote her passionate letters, expressed undying affection, and said they did not know how they could live without her. She was so pestered by these attentions that she contracted a marriage in the hope that she might escape from the fatal attraction which she appeared to exercise. If she had fully realized what marriage meant, she said, she would never have undertaken it.

In *The Diary of a Country Parson*, Parson Woodforde tells how on May 21, 1778, he walked up to the White Hart with Mr. Lewis and Bill to see 'a famous Woman in Men's Cloathes, by name Hannah Snell, who was 21 years as a common soldier in the Army, and not discovered by any one as a woman. Cousin Lewis has mounted guard with her abroad. She went in the Army by the name of John Gray. She has a pension from the Crown now of £18 : 5 : 0 per annum and the liberty of wearing Men's cloathes and also a cockade in her hat which she still wears. She has laid in a room with 70 soldiers, and not discovered by any of them. The forefinger of her right hand was cut by a sword at the taking of Pondicherry. She is now about 60 years of age and talks very sensible and well, and travels the country with a basket at her back, selling buttons, garters, laces &c. I took 4 pr. of 4d buttons and gave her 0 : 2 : 6.'

The reverse situation, whereby men may desire to reject their sex and become registered as women, is more common but by no means frequent. Such states may involve fathers of families who throw up successful careers, and commence a new life; their wives may never discover the motive of their actions. After finding a new home such persons dress as women, wear extravagant jewellery, and occupy themselves with feminine pursuits, *e.g.* knitting, embroidery and cooking. Often they may wish to adopt a woman's name, to undergo a surgical operation, if permitted, so as to transform their sex organs, and to become registered officially as women. After attaining even a part of their purpose it is astonishing how their states of restless tension are replaced by contentment.

There are, of course, many much less clearly defined cases of men who from an early age have identified themselves with girls rather than with persons of their own sex. Usually they are of sensitive, artistic, aesthetic dispositions, refrain from team games of a robust nature, and derive their main pleasure by employing themselves in tasks of an essentially feminine nature. They love to dress themselves in women's clothing, bedeck themselves with jewellery, use lip-stick, scent and powder, and try to imitate the graces of beautiful women. If they do form friendships with other men they prefer those with a similar effeminate nature to their own. Some have expressed a desire to become pregnant so that they might undergo the experience of giving birth to a baby. Usually, however, they are inclined to shun physical contact, and sexual gratification may only be obtained in their phantasy and dream life. There are many who realize that they are living dangerously, that they may involve themselves in unsavoury episodes and be arrested by the police. We have known others, however, who have been able to learn to conduct their lives at a more mature and responsible level.

Fetishism

In all such cases the normal sexual act may not reach attainment in the absence of some accustomed stimulus. A particular scent, hair, fur, silk underwear, slippers, high-heeled shoes, garters, handkerchiefs, may all be necessary accompaniments. It is only when the particular fetish becomes completely detached from the person, and is itself utilized as the sexual object that we regard the condition as pathological. A youth described his irresistible desire to purchase women's shoes or slippers (he had accumulated a considerable quantity) which he had to fondle and kiss before he attained complete sexual satisfaction. A man, 42 years old, described how when he was 4 years old he used to obtain pleasurable excitement from swinging on his mother's foot. In later life he had a compelling desire to touch the feet of women with whom he might be associated, *e.g.* the chambermaid in an hotel. Sexual satisfaction was only attained when a foot was visualized.

Bestiality

This unnatural sexual offence is usually perpetrated by farm workers of low intelligence, by psychopathic personalities, or those who are of unsound mind. It may be associated with aggressive sadistic tendencies. Fortunately it is not common.

Homosexuality

Homosexuality is a sexual propensity or attraction between members of the same sex, and does not necessarily lead to overt sexual conduct which is offensive to public decency. We all know 'the man's man' type, the person who is happier and more at ease with other male companions than in female company. Where the relationship is maintained on a purely platonic basis we should not read more into it than is warranted. All of us probably have a latent homosexual component in our make-up. We may, in our youth, have passed through a homosexual phase so that we must be discreet and sensible in our outlook, and not read meanings into friendships between members of the same sex unless we have substantial proof that the relationship is a prejudicial and injurious one. Those men and women who do not marry until late in life may have many reasons of a personal, family or economic nature which prevent them from doing so, but the factors may be more complex, and may be concerned with unresolved doubts in relation to potency, latent homosexuality and so on which make them play safe in a companionate marriage rather than in one involving heterosexual intercourse. The same mechanisms may determine the marriage of partners where the age difference is quite remarkable. These matters were clarified by Freud (1910); he explained how the narcissistic, auto-erotic phase of development is replaced by a homosexual one which in turn is supplanted by a heterosexual one. Some persons are unfortunate enough to remain fixed at an immature level, and may never develop any heterosexual instincts at all; indeed a person of the opposite sex may be viewed with such repugnance that no possibility exists of normal sexual relationship. On the other hand there are persons of a bisexual nature who are indiscriminate in their choice of a partner whether man or woman.

Homosexuality is no respecter of persons; it involves all manner of men and women drawn from all ranks of society. Many are sensitive, artistic, aesthetic types who seek an outlet in poetry, music, the theatre, dress designing, interior decorating, etc. Doctors, lawyers, professors, clergymen, youth leaders, business executives and manual workers are by no means exempt. The majority are capable efficient persons who in every other respect lead their lives at a responsible and highly successful level. In Great Britain we have no accurate statistics regarding the prevalence of homosexuality—no detailed investigation has ever been carried out—but we may be able to draw deductions from the investigations which were conducted in the United States by Kinsey (1948). He concluded that 4 per cent. of adult white males are exclusively homosexual throughout their lives after the onset of adolescence. He suggested that 10 per cent. of the white male population are more or less exclusively homosexual for at least three years between the ages of 16 and 65, and that 37 per cent. of the total male population have at least some overt homosexual experience to the point of orgasm between adolescence and old age. The above statistics are difficult to accept, they appear to be on the high side, but they give more than an indication of the prevalence of sexual anomaly and experience. Sweden's statistics are more modest. In that country it was found that 1 per cent. of all men were exclusively homosexual, and 4 per cent. were bisexual.

Many of the cases we have examined have been proud of their homosexuality; it has given them a sense of superiority so that they have rejected, with scorn, the suggestion that medical treatment might be made available. Schofield (1965) investigating homosexuals who were receiving psychiatric treatment, found that those who had consulted a psychiatrist specifically about their homosexuality were bisexual. The exclusively homosexual individual sought psychiatric help only after he had come into conflict with the law or had felt unable to cope with a hostile social environment. Some prefer a prison sentence for a defined period rather than the indeterminateness of psychotherapeutic treatment. That holds true even in cases of gross indecency involving sodomy with boys or adults and accompanied by sado-masochistic components: for example a man, 68 years old, who had held a distinguished position but had developed the unfortunate and dangerous habit of inviting boys to his own house, exclaimed: 'This is what you get for being kind to boys.'

In contrast to those who refuse medical help we have met others who seek, urgently, for all the assistance they can get. The poignant distress contained in the following letter requires no emphasis: 'Once upon a time I had a will to fight, there were times when I felt that religion, art, literature, music were all that mattered to me, that no other things, particularly wrong things, had any hold over me. Now I have no such moments, my whole life is becoming one horrible obsession. . . . I have no longer any will-power with which to fight; no diversions, no refuge in the arts . . . they are being killed by this one disease. . . . Do try to help me, please. . . . If it be true that with God all things are possible, then it is also true that men may rise over stepping-stones of their own dead selves to better things.'

Another became alarmed at the great change which seemed to be occurring in his disposition. The homosexual tendencies which had existed since he was 8 years old became, while he was in the Services, acutely intensified. He had proved to be a most capable officer, reached a position of responsibility, but was insecure in his personal relationships with his subordinates; he recognized that his tyrannical, impatient and inconsiderate behaviour was closely related to his underlying homosexual tendencies.

The above brief extracts illustrate the various reactions to which homosexual persons are prone, and demonstrate the conflicting, ambivalent feelings and compensatory mechanisms which influence the conduct of many men.

Much remains uncertain or unknown about the causation of homosexuality. Homosexuals are probably a heterogeneous group, aetiologically. In some, constitutional physical factors may be of paramount significance: in others, psychological influences operative in childhood or adolescence.

Genetic influences may be important. Kallmann (1953) in a series of 44 identical (monozygotic) twin pairs found concordance of homosexual conduct in all of them: a finding which should be subjected to further research. Slater (1962) reported that homosexuals show a late mean maternal age—differing in this widely from the general population; and that they tend to be born late in sibship order. However, no chromosomal abnormality has been found to account for homosexuality. Homosexuals have no distinctive physique, only a minority of them being of effeminate appearance and manner.

Probably the individual's upbringing, if biased in certain ways, may predispose him to homosexuality. No specific statement about this can yet be made. Many homosexuals have obviously been very closely attached emotionally to their mothers. The combination of a dominating, over-protective mother and a weak or absent father is almost certainly a situation which makes it particularly difficult for a boy to mature emotionally and to find his sexual identity. Puritanical attitudes in the home, provoking neurotic attitudes to sex and an idealization of women, may also be prejudicial to normal development. It is probably true to say that homosexuality, whether due to genetic or environmental influences, is inherently an immature type of reaction.

It must be recognized that homosexual behaviour is commonly indulged in by those who are basically heterosexual, if they are deprived for long of female company: for example, in boarding schools, prisons, on board ship or on military service abroad.

Under the Sexual Offences Act 1967 homosexual behaviour in private between consenting adults (*i.e.* men aged 21 or over) is no longer an offence: but the law continues to be brought into action against those who offend against public decency or victimize children. With regard to the latter situation, it should be added that the majority of practising homosexuals are not interested in prepubertal boys, and that there is much evidence that those who become sexually involved with children (paedophiliacs) are in general more closely allied to the group of exhibitionists than to the homosexuals.

Homosexuality is less common amongst women, is probably less often fulfilled physically and is less associated with promiscuity than is male homosexuality. It is not punishable in law.

TREATMENT

To give adequate help to the patients who consult us, and to aid the Court in dealing fairly with the sexual offender, we must have an understanding of the forces at work, instinctive or conditioned, which produce the disturbing, dangerous and sometimes tragic states which we have described. Only rarely can we be content to accept such matters at their face value, to differentiate black from white is not enough; there are always ever-changing shades and hues which must be inquired into; and by doing so we may find the key to an enigmatic situation. Freud taught us how to carry out such investigations. His imaginative concepts enabled us to get behind the scenes, to penetrate the depths of the unconscious and to relate our findings to the actual situation.

The sexual anomalies we have described have usually developed insidiously and innocently during childhood and if not overcome may persist as fixed habits which exercise a profound influence over the psychosexual life. The essence of successful treatment is to prevent or anticipate their occurrence, and to deal with them in their incipiency. This is not a matter for the doctor only; it may require the co-operation of parents, social workers and schoolmasters, all of whom must be able to produce in the child a sense of security. There is much that can be done. A complete physical and mental examination should be made, and while doing so the opportunity should be taken to inquire into the sexual life as naturally as one asks about other bodily functions. It can be done in a delicate and sensitive manner. To avoid it merely surrounds the topic with greater mystery and secretiveness and adds to the perpetuation of sexual habits which are better avoided. The explanation that the sexual function constitutes a fundamental biological need, that it is not wicked, obscene, taboo, brings comfort, trust, confidence and co-operation. It is tact and understanding which help to obtain satisfactory results; arbitrary prohibition, blows and threats lead to resentment, and a feeling of not being understood. An attempt should always be made to sublimate unhealthy sexual activities and interests by directing them into more constructive channels, and by avoiding those things which may, inadvertently, lead to greater sexual stimulation. For instance, over-solicitous mothers who constantly cuddle their children, allow them to sleep in their beds even when they are past puberty, are too possessive, disapprove of their children's friends, and Olympian fathers who create terror rather than friendship, can be advised to alter their ways because of the danger of provoking attitudes and fixations which can be devastating. It is the fretful, sensitive, rejected children, the artistic, aesthetic ones who indulge in phantasy thinking of a sexual nature, who require all the help we can give them. Emancipation, however, is a slow process, it should be allowed to develop gradually otherwise emotional crises may be precipitated which are better avoided. It is a matter of timing, of choosing the appropriate psychological moment rather than trying to force a person into a situation before he is fit to cope with it. At a later stage of development explanatory psycho-therapeutic interviews are indispensable. Forebodings and fears can be dispelled, reasons and arguments can be advanced to show that sexual anomalies are not unique experiences but are common to all mankind, and need not be regarded too moralistically. The assurance that they do not lead to insanity, that they can be cured—especially when the person is anxious to be cured—that they are the aftermath of childish habits, and that they need not interfere with a normal married life, constitutes a great comfort, and lessens the tension and fear which have been prominent.

The understanding and treatment of established sexual anomalies is a most complex matter, doctors and lawyers should co-ordinate their approach, but that will never be accomplished so long as angry judges thunder moralistic platitudes from the Bench, and indiscreet psychiatrists indulge in optimistic theorizing; there is much common ground between such extremes.

When public offences have been committed and Court proceedings have been instituted we must appreciate that, medically, we have a duty to protect society as well as to do the best we can for the offender. Sometimes it may be the offender's first appearance in Court, the first time he has been found out, but investigation often shows that the sexual offences which are charged against him have been committed over a period of months or years; his whole personality has to be inquired into before we can present a fair, unbiased report to the Court as to whether or not he is likely to benefit from medical treatment. We must try to ascertain all the facts on the basis of such questions as: Is this man willing to co-operate in treatment in the hope of being made better? or does he merely wish to escape a prison sentence? Has he sufficient intelligence to understand what psychotherapeutic investigation attempts to do? Is he of an age (under 40 years) when treatment is most likely to prove successful?

We must always be careful not to promise more than is likely to be accomplished. If, however, we can answer the above questions affirmatively then we are justified in asking the Court to consider the advisability of probation on the understanding that medical supervision and treatment would be instituted. The crowded conditions which prevail in most prisons militate against successful therapy there, but prison doctors with psychological insight can accomplish a great deal.

We suggest that much can be accomplished by a psychotherapeutic approach. The mere fact that someone is anxious to help is a tremendous relief from the secret, losing personal conflict which has been waged for so long. The method of therapy must be adjusted to the needs of the individual patient: the choice ranges from psychoanalysis on the one hand, to education, persuasion, injunction and encouragement on the other. The goals of treatment must also be clearly defined: in the case of homosexuality, for example, if the patient is a young man, basically bisexual and eager for help, cure can be aimed at; while if the individual is over the age of 30 and has never been conscious of other than homosexual interests and desires, his constitutional predisposition will have to be acknowledged and treatment will be concerned with helping him to understand and accept his deviation and with improving his social adjustment. Recent developments in behaviour therapy [see p. 184] seem to hold out some promise of success in carefully selected cases of sexual deviation. But whatever the method of treatment, a great deal depends of course on the quality of the patient's motivation and co-operation.

While we have stressed the psychogenic aspects of sexual anomalies, yet the possibility of physical impediments to a normal sexual life should not be forgotten.

REFERENCES

Allen, Clifford (1949) *The Sexual Perversions and Abnormalities*, 2nd ed., London.
Ellis, Havelock (1933) *Psychology of Sex*, London.

Freud, Sigmund (1910) *Three Contributions to the Sexual Theory*, New York.

Kallmann, F. J. (1953) *Heredity in Health and Mental Disorder*, London.

Kinsey, A. C., Pomeroy, W. B., and Martin, C. E. (1948) *Sexual Behavior in the Human Male*, Philadelphia.

Kinsey, A. C., Pomeroy, W. B., Martin, C. E., and Gebhard, P. H. (1953) *Sexual Behavior in the Human Female*, Philadelphia.

Mohr, J. W., Turner, R. E., and Jerry, M. B. (1964) *Pedophilia and Exhibitionism*, Toronto.

Rickles, N. K. (1950) *Exhibitionism*, Philadelphia.

Russell, M. P. (1943) *Edinb. med. J.*, **50**, 558.

Schofield, M. (1965) *Sociological Aspects of Homosexuality*, London.

Slater, E. (1962) *Brit. med. J.*, **1**, 69.

Strauss, E. B. (1950) *Brit. med. J.*, **1**, 697.

Wolfenden, Sir John (1957) Report on Homosexual Offences and Prostitution, London, H.M.S.O.

10

AFFECTIVE REACTION-TYPES

MANIC-DEPRESSIVE PSYCHOSIS

The term manic-depressive psychosis was introduced by Kraepelin to characterize disorders of affect consisting either of elation or depression—disorders which had previously been termed mania and melancholia in the belief that they were quite separate diseases.

The first attempt to formulate a clearer conception was made in 1854 by Falret senior and Baillarger, who independently described recurring attacks of mania and melancholia in the same patient. This was followed in 1879 by certain observations by Falret junior, who published a paper on what he termed *folie circulaire*. This he described as 'a hereditary affection generally found in a similar form both in ascendants and descendants'. His paper contains a detailed description of the typical alternation of mood from periods of excitement to periods of depression. In addition, he specifically mentioned the existence of 'mixed states', which he considered were transitory stages between attacks of mania and depression. In 1882, Kahlbaum spoke definitely of the phases mania and melancholia not as two separate types of mental disorder, but as two stages occurring in the same disease. He used the term cyclothymia to designate the milder, recoverable types, while the more grave, lasting types he called 'vesania typica circularis'. Hecker likewise used the term cyclothymia, and drew attention particularly to the non-dementing features. These observations preceded the observations of Kraepelin, who made a further advance when, in 1896, he formulated his conception of the manic-depressive psychosis. In this group he included the whole domain of periodic and circular insanity, simple mania, the greater part of the morbid states termed melancholia and also a considerable number of cases of confusion or delirium. He considered that all these conditions were representations of a single morbid process, and he showed that the different phases might succeed and replace one another in the same case—mania might lead to melancholia, with transition stages. His contribution was a stimulating and important one, because it not only conduced to a more careful analysis of symptoms in the individual case, but was of even greater importance from the point of view of prognosis; for Kraepelin declared that such attacks might occur throughout the life of the individual, and would never lead to profound dementia.

When manic-depressive attacks develop without any precipitant, as they often do, they have been termed constitutional or endogenous. But to refer to 'endogenous depression' as a clinical entity is misleading, since in many instances manic-depressive psychoses follow upon and have evidently been precipitated by some stress, psychological or physical; that is, they are also reactive. There is as one would expect an interaction between constitutional and environmental, between endogenous and exogenous, factors: the relative weights of these two elements vary from case to case, and may change in the individual case from time to time. Astrup and his colleagues (1959) reported that the first attacks of manic-depressive psychoses are often precipitated by external factors, but in later relapses it is usually difficult to establish such factors and the disease seems to take its own course.

Other depressive illnesses with obvious precipitants show an ability to react to intercurrent stimuli (such as the doctor's visits), combined often with bouts of weeping, with anxiety or hysterical symptoms, and a tendency to blame others rather than themselves. The difficulty in falling asleep is a product of the anxiety in these cases, there is little or no consistent diurnal variation in the intensity of the symptoms, and delusions and hallucinations do not occur. These Kraepelin called 'psychogenic depressions'. They are more properly classed with the neuroses—as neurotic depressive reactions, occurring most often in individuals of hysterical personality.

Clinically, the differentiation between a manic-depressive psychosis and a neurotic depressive reaction is often difficult to make. A manic-depressive psychosis may develop in an individual of hysterical personality. Some depressive illnesses in younger women, which run a rather long course with much apparently neurotic acting-out and attention seeking, are found by their good response to E.C.T. to belong to the psychotic end of the spectrum of depressive illness. Stenstedt (1966) has in several studies drawn attention to the difficulty in distinguishing between neurotic and 'endogenous' depression.

Kiloh and Garside (1963) in 92 cases made a factor analysis of 35 clinical features, and concluded from the results of this that 'the group of depressive states consists of two separate entities conforming with the conditions known so long as "endogenous" depression and "neurotic or reactive" depression.' In the neurotic depressive group they found a pattern of reactivity, inadequacy, hysterical or other neurotic features, initial insomnia, hypochondriasis and self-pity: in the 'endogenous' group a tendency to be over the age of 40 and to have had previous attacks, to be more deeply depressed, to be retarded, to wake early and to be worse in the morning, and to lose a lot of weight. These covariant patterns of symptoms, selected by factor analysis, correspond fairly well with clinical experience: but the differentiation of depressions into the two groups is over-sharply drawn.

It is uncertain if a syndrome called 'involutional melancholia' can be differentiated from manic-depressive psychosis: this is discussed on pages 233–4.

AETIOLOGY

Hereditary predisposition is the most important predisposing aetiological factor. Kraepelin and numerous others have stated that 60 to 80 per cent. are hereditarily predisposed. It is probable that manic-depressive psychosis is due to a single dominant gene, transmitted by an affected parent to half of the offspring, but with incomplete penetrance so that many who possess the gene do not develop the illness. Rosanoff, Handy and Plesset (1935) reported that of monozygotic twins both were affected in 69·6 per cent., and of dizygotic twins both were affected in 16·4 per cent.: Kallmann (1953) confirmed these findings in a study of 27 monozygotic and 58 dizygotic twin pairs. In this series he found that the expectancy of manic-depressive psychosis varied from 16·7 per cent. for the half-sibs to 22·7 and 25·5 per cent. for the sibs and dizygotic co-twins, respectively, and to 100 per cent. for the monozygotic twin partners. The corresponding rate for the parents of index cases was 23·4 per cent. The perfect concordance in the one-egg twin pairs was explained by Kallmann as probably due to the fact that only hospitalized manic-depressive patients were chosen as index cases. There is certainly no evidence that the usual degree of expressivity of the genotype is 100 per cent., or any figure near to that. In Kallmann's sample there was no twin pair with a schizophrenic psychosis in one partner and a manic-depressive psychosis in the other.

Kallmann stated that amongst Western peoples the average general frequency of manic-depressive psychosis does not exceed 0·4 per cent. in the population: if involutional cases are included the risk rises to about 1 per cent. Women are more liable to the disease than men; it is estimated that 70 per cent. of the patients are women. All social classes are about equally affected.

Kretschmer attempted to differentiate mankind on the basis of their body build. He termed the short, stocky people with thick necks his 'pyknic' type, in contrast with the thin, visceroptotic, 'asthenic' or leptosomatic type, and the long-limbed, muscular 'athletic' type. The pyknic or endomorphic (in Sheldon's classification) type tends to be associated with people showing a manic-depressive psychosis.

From the purely mental side, Meyer, Hoch, Kirby and Bleuler have pointed out that the mental make-up which frequently characterizes the individual in whom a manic-depressive psychosis occurs deserves close study. The previous personality, often described as cyclothymic, is typically one in which the affect swings from moods of elation to moods of depression in people who are generally recognized to have frank, open personalities. They may be bright, talkative, optimistic, aggressive people, who make light of the ordinary affairs of life, or else they take a gloomy outlook, bewail the past, make mountains out of mole-hills; or there is a combination of the above moods, rendering the person emotionally unstable and variable. This variability of affect may never go beyond normal limits. The mood of most people does swing to a certain extent: and such changes are transitory, interfering little with daily activities.

There is no well-attested evidence that parental deprivation in childhood, either by death or other causes, is of aetiological importance. This was the conclusion of Stenstedt (1952) and it has been confirmed by Hopkinson and Reed (1966) who, studying the incidence of childhood bereavement in 200 cases of manic-depressive psychosis, found that the loss of one or both parents before the patient reached the age of 15 was no commoner than in the general population. While not being an aetiological factor, emotional deprivation may however possibly influence the degree of severity of a depressive illness. Munro (1966), in a carefully controlled study, found that 'severe depressives' report a highly significant excess of disturbed relationships with both mother and father during childhood.

The possible precipitants are legion and individual. They may be psychological or physical: amongst the emotional stresses one might instance bereavement, a move of home, business failure and the strain of promotion; on the physical side virus infection, surgical operations, the puerperium—and many others. Often the illness develops 'out of the blue'.

PSYCHOPATHOLOGY

A number of suggestive indications of the psychopathology of these conditions will be derived from a study of the case-histories to be given below. The following account in psychoanalytic terms is largely derived from MacCurdy (1925).

Manic States

The elation that is so prominent a symptom of manic states is to be regarded as the mood appropriate to the fulfilment of a wish; its pathological intensity is a measure of the strength of the wish. What makes the elation pathological is not that there is nothing in the conscious content that would justify it if it were true —there often is, in the form of fleeting grandiose ideas, for example—but that there is nothing in the external circumstances that apparently justifies the elation. The reason for the elation lies outside of consciousness, although often very close to it, breaking through sometimes in the fragmentary utterances of the flight of ideas. What happens is that from some very strong wish that has been repressed into unconsciousness, the repression is at least partly removed, and the patient feels and behaves as if the wish had been fulfilled. Sometimes the wish is for some adult gratification, e.g. marriage, but more often the wish is one that has developed at the childish stage of mental development and has persisted into adult life, e.g. for the death of a disliked parent. Sometimes external circumstances contribute to the wish-fulfilment, and so precipitate a psychosis. For example, the hated relative dies—let us suppose it is the mother of an individual who has from childhood had an abnormally strong liking for her father, and so, as a child, wished her mother out of the way (the 'Electra complex'—the feminine counterpart of the 'Oedipus complex'). This wish was repressed at the time and ever since. Then if the mother dies the wish is fulfilled, and the now adult woman, with the childish fixation of her affection on her father, has the chief obstacle to her exclusive possession of his affection removed. She becomes elated, but the elation appears causeless, i.e. pathological, and the fulfilment is poorly formulated in consciousness, if it appears there at all—either because repression continues to operate to some degree, or because the conscious formulation of unconscious wishes is a difficult task. The degree to which conscious expression is attained varies very much. Often the releasing causes of a manic psychosis are entirely within the patient's own mind, consisting in phantasy.

P

Depressions

If, on the other hand, there has been a strong feeling of guilt associated with the wish, adult or infantile, its fulfilment, whether in fact or phantasy, is apt to lead to a depression, which again appears pathological, especially because here repression continues to operate much more decisively, since the ideas are altogether unpleasantly coloured, and must be kept completely out of consciousness.

In many depressions a precipitating cause is not recognizable. In others, the depression results from disappointment or deprivation. In a third group, the precipitant is the reanimation, often by some external event, of an unconscious trend ('wish') which, if allowed to reach consciousness, would ultimately destroy the personality. Hence a gigantic effort is made at repression (inhibition), and the inhibition becomes generalized, so that all thinking is interfered with. The trend may have a strong feeling of guilt attached to it, because something antisocial is the object of the trend, *e.g.* the death of a near relative. As in the manic, such trends may be either infantile or adult in origin. In any case, repression of the guilty trend having occurred, depression appears as the conscious correlate of the now unconscious guilt-feeling. The depressive ideas which appear in consciousness are largely rationalizations, but may have also some disguised relation to the repressed wish.

The psychoanalytic view of the psychopathology of the depressive phase is that the following factors are involved:

1. A constitutional factor in the form of inherited accentuation of oral erotism.
2. A special fixation of the libido at the oral level, that is the patient's erotic interests have lingered round the mouth zone when they should on the contrary have developed to the genital zone with complete object love. The fixation is considered to be at the second oral stage when ambivalence first becomes possible (biting is an aggressive act, not co-existent with suckling).
3. A severe injury to infantile narcissism brought about by early disappointments in love, especially love of the mother.
4. The occurrence of the first disappointment in love before the Oedipus wishes have been overcome.
5. The repetition of the primary disappointment in later life as the exciting cause of the depression.

Bowlby (1961) has stated that in the small child separation from the mother produces a psychological disturbance, a process of 'mourning', which has three phases: a period of protest with the urge to recover and scold is followed by a reaction of despair (the equivalent of adult mourning) and this in turn is replaced by a defensive detachment. There are analogies here with the phenomena of adult depressive illness; and Bowlby, developing the Freudian concept of depression which stressed the links with mourning and ambivalence towards the lost object (or person), has further suggested that the process of mourning in the child is apt to take a pathological course and that if it does so the individual will be more prone in later life to react badly to loss—and to develop a depression. This explanation might account for the increased vulnerability of certain people to depressive reactions: but against it must be ranged the facts that in the case of those who develop depressive psychoses in later life only a minority have been bereaved in childhood and no more than in the general population.

Muncie (1963) has propounded a psychopathology of depression which may be particularly applicable to Western middle-class cultures and to those of obsessional personality. He points out that the incentive to strive is part of the cultural air we breathe, that such striving is derived from childhood efforts to please parental figures whose approval is contingent upon it, and that, if the parents are particularly pathogenic or the child unduly sensitive, the individual may embark upon an 'interminable treadmill of earned worth'. Such a person, finding himself in adult life unable to produce the effort necessary to gain contingent approval, becomes bankrupt in self-esteem. A depressive illness may be precipitated by a material or personal loss or disappointment, or even a trivial hurt to his self-esteem, which brings home to him the futility of striving. Muncie finds that in many depressed patients the first and foremost complaint is of 'a loss of spontaneity and initiative and potential directed especially toward that aspect of the daily, habitual living, of greatest importance for the patient's sense of worth and well-being'. In the psychotherapy of depression he seeks therefore to rid the patient of the guilt associated with his inability to strive towards his habitual goals, and to bring him to accept the relativity of personal ideals and their achievement and that there are worthwhile satisfactions and illuminations which can be had without effort.

SYMPTOMATOLOGY

Manic Phase

We have become accustomed to describe four main varieties of mania, termed respectively: 1. hypomania; 2. acute mania; 3. delirious mania; and 4. chronic mania. The cases which we include in the group of chronic mania run a course so different from the cases in the other groups that it will be best to consider the chronic manias together under a separate heading. All of these varieties, however, are characterized by three main symptoms, which vary in duration and in intensity in each case. These three symptoms are (a) elated though unstable mood, (b) flight of ideas, (c) increased psychomotor activity. In some cases the elated mood may predominate clinically, whereas in other cases it may be the restlessness or the over-talkativeness. Other features may complicate the picture; irritability, cantankerousness, suspicion, and more rarely a clouding of consciousness, with delusions, hallucinations and disorientation, may all appear. Such symptoms as suspicion, hallucinations, etc., are usually transitory, occurring at the height of the illness, and are not of the same ominous significance as they would be if they occurred in a setting of clear consciousness. There is rarely any insight.

Another important general point which should always be kept clearly in mind is the fact that practically in all cases the attacks are acute in onset, the history dating back only for a few days or a few weeks.

While such conditions as hypomania, acute mania and delirious mania can readily be recognized, we wish to point out that the differentiation of these states is not by any means clear cut, and that many cases pass through such stages without any definite gradation; some may never pass beyond the hypomanic stage, while others may from the very beginning be either acutely excited or, very rarely, delirious. Manic reactions occur probably in less than 10 per cent. of cases of manic-depressive psychosis. They are commonly prefaced by a mild degree of depression or irritability which lasts for a week or so.

MANIC STATES

Hypomania

Hypomania is the mildest variety, and although it is characterized by the individual symptoms previously mentioned, *e.g.* elation, over-activity, flight of ideas, these are not greatly developed. The patient continues to have a keen realization of his position and environment, and does not exhibit such extreme disorder of conduct as to bring him into conflict with his fellows. For a time he is merely considered a 'live wire', witty, a man with ideas and aggressiveness, a social success; and it is only in the further course of the illness when he becomes interfering, irritable, domineering and has too many schemes on hand, that his friends suspect that something is wrong. He tends to monopolize conversation, expresses his views dogmatically, drifts from one topic to another and shows a flight of ideas. His schemes, though feasible, are never thoroughly worked out. He is inconsistent and changeable; yet he feels more fit than ever before. When reasoned with, he is intolerant of criticism, becomes sarcastic or rude, changes the subject, thinks that the person who does not see eye to eye with him is a fool and does not hesitate to say so. He is lacking in moral control, and may indulge to excess both sexually and in regard to drink. It is frequently on the basis of such disordered conduct that he comes under hospital treatment or is apprehended by the police and taken to prison; *e.g.* a man with a very distinguished record was apprehended for buying motor cars with worthless cheques, and it was not until he recovered that he became fully conscious of the significance and seriousness of his actions. Under hospital conditions such a patient is most difficult to manage. He resents restraint, wants to better the ward arrangements, is arrogant towards officials, staff and other patients, and constantly lodges complaints, writing long letters to the Board of Management of the hospital, the Home Secretary, Members of Parliament and others. In his conversation, all manner of trivial details are introduced, but the talk never develops into incoherence; whatever he says can be followed and understood, but the patient rarely completes any topic. His memory is excellently preserved. Although many incidents may be distorted, ready explanations are given. Perhaps the most striking symptom of all is the extreme restlessness; such a patient must be doing something all the time; he feels that he can do everything better than anyone else, is never still and yet does not seem to experience an ordinary sense of fatigue There is no clouding of consciousness; his orientation for time, for place and for person is correct; and there is no evidence of hallucinations or delusions. As a general rule, he does not realize that he is seriously ill, his judgement being impaired.

CASE NO. 12

An enterprising successful man almost continuously ill for the past sixteen years with alternating attacks of depression and elation; now in a state of hypomanic excitement; over-active, talking continually and writing numerous letters; both talk and writing showing obvious flight of ideas and play upon words (rhyming and punning); his mood elated, but changing rapidly to irritability when he is crossed; and the content of his utterances showing a strong erotic trend.

P. S., 50 years old; a professional man. He has been ill more or less continuously for 16 years, with alternating attacks of depression and excitement. One sister was stated to have been in a mental hospital, and another was described as a 'nervous wreck'.

The patient himself had been an extraordinarily capable man, who had taken a high place in examinations, and had reached a position of great distinction. He was always of an aggressive type, very much a leader, described by some as too independent, by others as an agitator and, by his son, as one who could not brook opposition.

He has been treated in various mental hospitals. In his first excited attack in 1919 he was so exalted that it was suspected he might be a case of general paralysis. At that time he said that he was very wealthy, that he was the deputy of Lord Kitchener. He was taken to prison because of insulting behaviour towards a Jew, whom he accused of being a German spy.

The state which he has shown since he has been under our care has been essentially a hypomania.

He had been admitted to a mental hospital but was transferred to a private home. His condition there was described as follows:

After arrival he stated that it seemed as if he had entered Paradise after escaping from Hell, but he immediately wished to alter the domestic arrangements to meet his own whims. He woke early, and passed the time whistling in opposition to the blackbirds and thrushes. When asked by the nurse not to disturb the others, he abused and cursed her. At breakfast he talked incessantly, and made offensive personal remarks. He pointed out that one of the Matrons did not look well—that no doubt she had 'spent the night on the tiles'. During the day he wandered about, acting in the most unconventional and irresponsible way. He called on the local lawyer, and wasted his time, telling him of all the actions he intended to bring. He troubled the doctor, who in consequence tried to avoid him, but this could not be done, as the patient stood beside his car until the doctor was forced to appear and listen to his rambling talk. He threatened to get the banker into serious trouble, so that the latter complained. He disturbed the postmistress, and abused her loudly before the public, so that she also was compelled to lodge a complaint. He called on strangers, who were relatives of the staff, and demanded tea. He hinted by innuendoes, by winks and gestures, that one of the Matrons drank, and that he was going to keep his eye on her. At table, in the presence of others, he was disrespectful to her. He suggested that gross immoralities were going on, and he thought this must be so because there were 'one male attendant and twelve beautiful nurses'. He himself would go to the kitchen quarters to talk to the maids and when reproved by the Matron, flew into a temper and went to bed. He made a formal proposal of marriage to one of the nurses, and decided to divorce his wife for desertion. He told all his intimate affairs to complete strangers, such as his coming marriage, his intended divorce and so on. At table his conversation was most objectionable, as he discoursed among the ladies about public conveniences. He asserted that he himself was a lady-killer, and provided details. He was in communication with many lawyers, requesting actions to be brought and demanding money. On one occasion he forged the name of the lady in whose house he was staying, and sent a telegram to his wife demanding £25, which was forwarded immediately.

A good example of his condition is obtained from the following letter, in which he makes his proposal of marriage:

'My dearest G.—Y'day, I fondly believe, was as happy a day as I ever spent in this weary world of Drink, Work, & Sin. All on A/c. of you "Matey".

'Do you not believe in love at first sight? I do most emphatically assert that *the moment I met you at N. station my fate was sealed.* I am not an old Turk, or even Mahommedan, but I believe in *FATE.* And if I have your "promise true" ("which ne'er forgot shall be" mind) then "*I* am yours, and *YOU* are mine"—(For ever and Beyond) as the grand old Hymn phrases it. "And *ye* sall walk in silk" (real—not celanese) "attire an' siller hae tae spare"—bonnie sang that, a' aboot *LOVE*?
      "And we shall all the beauties prove,
      Of Hills and Valleys, Seas and Towns, etc., etc., etc."

'When I give my promise I make good. With St. Paul it is a case of "What I have said, I *have* said" always.

'But perhaps you will rejoin: "You have a wife?" Yes, but after many years' treacherous thieving, lying, failure to do that which she vowed, viz.: "Love, *Honour* & Obey", instead of putting me into vicious Asylums, I am not risking her company again. So, as I *know* she won't (*and cannot even if she would*) resist my Divorce Action for her Desertion of me in 1921, you must wait until Autumn for Ct. of Session Judge's decision. The cost is small for undefended actions nowadays under the 1922 Act, which allows "desertion" as a reason for granting Divorce. (It used to be that Adultery must also be proved, but that was amended.)

'So you are not taking an adulterous *lunatic* (?) If you'll have me, of course I'll settle a big sum on you for your own use, and make over my insurance and estate by Will in your favour, less one or two legacies for Charitable Institutions.

'Meantime you are my nurse—I am your Guide, Philosopher, Humble Servitor, and Lover. I could not sleep after 5 A.M. for thinking of you—and my songs were all of thee, my ideal woman, for face and figure and grace, and gracious womanly sympathy for a man without friendly relations when he is in "these places", but whose relations were proud of him when his income was large. "Telle est la Vie", m'amie fidèle.

'"I fear no foe with thee at hand to bless", as Toplady wrote together, in his immortal Hymn, "Rock of Ages".

'Tout à vous.'

The above letter, with its underscored passages (here printed in italics), interpolations, brackets and flight of ideas, yet at the same time coherent, is completely characteristic of a hypomanic state.

Since his arrival under our care his condition has been very much as already outlined. He is diffuse and circumstantial in his conversation, his statements are apparently quite accurate, and dates in his career are given rapidly and without confusion, and are remembered in minute detail, even to the hour and the day when certain things happened. He talks so continuously that it is almost impossible to get in a question, but he usually answers correctly and to the point; a few seconds later, without any break in the continuity of his flow, he is talking about something totally different. Yet after a long digression he is capable of coming back to the main point at issue—usually, however, only to leave it again. His mood is one of constant elation. At times he is definitely euphoric, and his list of wrongs, which is very long, he recites in a whimsical, jovial way; but every now and again, especially when interfered with, or when his wishes are not immediately conceded, he becomes very irritable, often obscene, and always scurrilous and threatening. There has, however, not been any evidence of hallucinations, nor does there seem to be the slightest impairment of his intellectual faculties, except, of course, that he has no realization of his condition, and therein shows defective judgement.

He spends a great deal of his time writing letters to various members of the staff, to the Sheriff of the County, to other high officials and to his own relatives and friends.

A letter, addressed to the Matron, is typical:

'Matron B.—Do you want to get hung at the Yard Arm as Pirates used to get hung for Piracy on the High Seas?

'If not, better come to terms with P. before the Directors are apprised of *your* piratical ways at G.

'And that may be sooner than you dream.

'Do your duty first—attend to your own private down-town pleasures when off duty here. Otherwise the consequences may send you into retirement without a pension, and with only a bad character from your last place. P.'

So long as this patient's threats are not taken too seriously, he is quite pleasant to get on with, but he has to be handled with a considerable amount of rope. He is able, however, to conform to regulations to a wonderful extent; he has now had the privilege of parole for a good many months, and has not in any way misused it.

The case is a good example of the constitutional reaction-type—repeated attacks, with no sufficient precipitating causes to be found.

In the following case there is a clear indication in the content of the patient's utterances of the factors leading to his illness:

CASE NO. 13

A brief mild hypomanic excitement in a hitherto quiet, docile youth, following upon a transitory mild depression. The hypomanic elation showed the usual characteristics— over-activity (with erotic tendencies coming to the fore), an infectious and excessive gaiety, over-talkativeness with some punning and rhyming and lack of sustained attention. The flight of ideas and the general over-activity are not so marked as in the previous case and the whole condition was comparatively short-lived—features which are probably related to the essentially shy, quiet type of personality in whom the illness developed.

L. M., 24 years; male; single; farmer. The patient had been a very quiet, sensitive, docile youth, who was not fond of company, avoiding the society of girls especially. He had been clever at school, and had just missed obtaining a medal in his last year. Since leaving school he had worked on his father's farm. He had seemed to think that having done well at school he was too clever for farm work. Nevertheless, he worked hard on the farm, except when suffering from 'stomach' troubles—he had headaches, and had to go to bed sometimes after food. During the War he showed no anxiety to join the Army, but afterwards he expressed regret at not having done so. In the early months of the year he was mildly depressed, but nothing remarkable was observed till April, when he began to behave oddly and was removed to a nursing home. There he was mildly elated, talked diffusely and circumstantially, rhyming and playing on words, and was distractible. He was restless and sleepless, and in the latter part of May he had brief influenzal symptoms, his sputum being blood-stained and watery, and containing pneumococci and pneumobacilli, *Micrococcus catarrhalis* and diphtheroid bacilli. On admission to hospital in June from the nursing home he showed all the above mental symptoms to a mild degree. He walked about aimlessly, smiling and laughing. Anything presented to him distracted his attention. He was mischievous, and tried to caress the nurses.

The following is a sample of his speech in response to questions: (Do you want to do some work?) 'Yes, I want to get out and practise music for a while.' (Do you want to earn a living?) 'Yes, I got a gold disc with a lion in the centre, with a wild cat down below and a tree above, from the King.' (Why?) 'For bravery, service to my country—and writing letters to my friends.' (Have you always been happy at home?) 'No, at times I was very angry—had wanted a shift—had seen these things too long—got into arguments.' (When you were young what did you do?) 'Well, that was a long time ago. I may have felt queer—I hurt my chest climbing trees—my lungs grew, but my stomach was too small—I could have gone without food for a long time.' (Do you sleep well?) 'I don't care to sleep—I've so much energy.' (Do you dream?) 'I dreamt I was flying—and if that doesn't prove that your spirit roams at night when you're in bed—electricity in your backbone which attracts eyes.' (What else?) 'I'd like to be married—hadn't money—I was shy—there's a change in me—I was kind of entranced—lifted clean out of myself.'

In addition he mentioned that he felt that his stomach would have to be very different before he could get married, and that he had read many sentimental books, and 'thought it might be very nice sometimes—buying rings and then taking a tiff'.

His memory was good, except for events of the very recent past, which had not been attended to and therefore were not well retained. Orientation was slightly interfered with for the same reason. Insight was lacking for the nature of his illness—'I was supposed to be in consumption.'

Within ten days he became less restless, his elation gave place to uneasiness and his talk became more connected and relevant. Within two weeks of admission he had returned to his normal state, i.e. a docile, quiet and agreeable fellow, rather self-conscious in manner.

Several trends were obvious in the content—the compensatory phantasy of the award of a medal (which he had missed at school), which also served to compensate his lack of war service; the remark indicating dissatisfaction with his employment on the farm—'he wanted a shift'; his erotic preoccupations and overt tenderness (caressing nurses); and his references to his bodily ill health. The conditions which these trends indicate combined to produce a mild degree of depression, followed by an elation, in which his failings were compensated in phantasy, and in which his personality underwent a change of which he was conscious—'I was shy—now there's a change in me.'

Acute Mania

There is no sharp distinguishing line between hypomania and mania—the one grades into the other. There are cases in which a state of acute excitement develops at once without any previous hypomanic stage. Acute excitement may be preceded by a short period of sleeplessness and irritability. In this stage the elation, flight of ideas and over-activity are all more intense. The patient affirms he 'never felt better in his life'; he has an air of utter superiority, he orders everyone about, and his conversation and conduct are so disordered that residence in a mental hospital is imperative. The mood is merry, gay, infectious, but periods of irritability and anger are frequent. At such times his conversation becomes obscene, and his conduct unrestrained. Assaults may be made on the officials and nurses, or the furniture and bedclothing broken and torn, but just as suddenly there may be a return to a state of good humour, and apology may even be expressed for the previous conduct. The speech shows a typical flight of ideas, and this may proceed to incoherence. He is extremely distractible, and his attention can be held only momentarily, because whatever he sees or hears he comments on. Such a patient is 'on the go' night and day. He may not be quite clear in regard to time or environment; he tends to misidentify people, and to greet perfect strangers as old friends.

Hallucinations are occasionally present, but they are transitory. The delusions expressed are of a wish-fulfilling kind, and are in harmony with the patient's excited mood.

It is impossible to carry out an accurate examination of the memory and intellectual functions, but there is nothing to indicate that they are disordered *per se*. The insight and judgement are very poor, as a secondary result of the disorders of affect and attention.

The following case illustrates the more acute type of manic excitement, and shows the rapid transition which occurs from one stage to another:

CASE No. 14

Rapid onset of an acute manic excitement in a healthy young woman of energetic happy disposition; extreme restlessness; excessive talkativeness with continuous screaming at times; elation reaching at intervals a pitch of ecstasy; distractibility so great that comprehension was vastly impaired and the patient disoriented in consequence; shamelessly erotic behaviour along with a pronounced religious trend in her talk; gradual subsidence with occasional exacerbations of destructiveness; complete recovery with insight.

A. L. A young lady, 32 years old, single, a school-teacher, had been ill for four days previous to her admission to hospital. She had come from a healthy stock, and had developed quite normally. She was a bright, happy, cheerful girl, who at school took many prizes in English, arithmetic and French, and after leaving became a pupil teacher. She was fond of fancy sewing, played the piano, sang in a choir, liked dancing and company, mixed with boys as freely as with girls and was a general favourite. She may have been somewhat over-sensitive, and is stated sometimes to have imagined slights where none were intended. On the whole, however, her personality was that of a very steady, normal, efficient girl. For about one year previous to her breakdown she had been teaching a special class of physically defective children. A few days previous to the onset of her illness she was noticed to be more 'on the go'—at the pictures, at a dance, and attending a meeting in church. She showed an unstable emotional state, burst into tears without provocation and next moment would be laughing and saying that she was all right, 'just needing a rest', 'just tired'. Soon she became more talkative and restless; she took little food, she did not sleep, except under the influence of a drug; she tended to recall the past, and to talk about former imaginary slights. Subsequently, she expressed peculiar ideas, declaring that her mother was dead, and when reassured about this, that her friend upstairs was dead. She declared that she was acting under God's orders, that she had spoken to God, and a good deal of her conversation consisted in her repeating what she said God was telling her.

At the time of her admission she asked the doctor to kiss her, and because he refused she said she could not trust him. She talked incessantly, accused the doctor of having been drinking and then immediately began to talk about God, and about how God meant her to suffer. 'I have got a pain here', pointing over her heart. 'It is me that is going to have the baby; God has made me say it now that I am going to have a baby; it was my fault—his fault—he was selfish; it is that that has nearly driven me out of my mind.' She explained how God meant everybody to be happy—God had told her to have a baby, and, at the same time, she felt sure that she was going to die. This idea of death constantly recurred throughout her conversation. At times she refused any nourishment—she would not even take fluids. She screamed at the pitch of her voice, saying that the doctor was to 'die, die, die', shrieking it till her face was livid, the veins congested almost to bursting, and her pulse racing at about 160 per minute. On account of her great excitement she had to be tube-fed, and had to be given paraldehyde to help her to rest. The intense excitement was accompanied by great motor restlessness. She was distractible, commented on things around her, misidentified people and was disoriented both in regard to time and place. Her conduct at times suggested that she was seeing visions. Her condition approached a state of ecstasy, when she would sing, 'How blessed are the messengers that preach the Gospel of Peace', and then would continue the air in a kind of recitative, interspersed with questions and conversation. She maintained that she still heard God's voice talking to her, believed herself to be God's spokesman and frequently identified herself with God. In contrast, she was foolishly erotic in her behaviour, made attempts to embrace the medical officers, exposed herself and was quite shameless.

In the course of a few weeks improvement began to take place, but at intervals she had very excited periods, when she smashed the crockery, tore her bedclothes, smashed the glass panels in her room and flung the fragments at the other patients. These periods gradually became fewer and briefer, and finally she reached a stage where she was able to discuss her illness, and gained complete insight for the fact that she had been mentally ill.

Here, then, was the history of an acute illness of rapid onset, rapidly passing through the various stages of the manic reaction and terminating in an excellent recovery. The condition seemed to be partly explained by exogenous causes, *e.g.* the strain of teaching, and the fact that she was the main support of her home. Her psychosis exposed erotic trends, and the fulfilment of her wishes, at the expense of sane thinking.

Delirious Mania

This is the extreme stage. It may spring from a hypomania, and then pass through a stage of acute mania, or may develop at once without the other stages having preceded. It is not simply an acute mania complicated by a delirium precipitated by intercurrent infection or some other secondary factor: but a specific form of the manic-depressive reaction-type. It is now very rarely seen.

The individual is disoriented for time, place and person. Conversation is incoherent, and the patient is so excited that he can be restrained only by a powerful hypnotic. He is never at rest; he tosses and rolls about, is in a ferment of activity bodily and mentally, and unless this is controlled by means of drugs or otherwise he rapidly exhausts himself. Auditory and visual illusions and hallucinations, and suspicions and delusions, develop. Such patients behave in the most shameless way; they not only do not take any pride in their personal appearance, but they are careless in all their habits. They have no realization at all of the serious nature of their illness, and do not therefore co-operate in treatment.

Such cases were first described by Luther Bell in 1849 and were known as Bell's mania. From their acute nature and high death-rate they were also named typhomania, delirium grave, or collapse delirium. If recovery occurs, the condition, when arising *de novo*, does not usually recur, or at least there is a long interval between attacks. Kraines (1934) gave an excellent review, and suggested that they should continue to be known as Bell's mania.

DEPRESSION

Depression exhibits three main grades of severity, termed respectively simple or mild depression, acute depression and depressive stupor.

We again recognize a triad of symptoms which though not present in all cases is characteristic of all of the above grades, namely, difficulty in thinking, depression and psychomotor retardation. Many other symptoms may be super-added—delusions, hypochondriacal, self-accusatory or persecutory; hallucinations, irritability, etc. The mood change gives the impression of being the fundamental feature. The depression is not infrequently accompanied by anxiety. The other features are such as might be expected to go with a depressed mood: for example, difficulty in thinking and a small output of talk. Sometimes there is considerable talk with much reiteration, while instead of reduction in activity there may be agitation.

The most important feature of depression in general, from the point of view of care and treatment, is the danger of suicide. Of all mental illnesses, it is in the affective psychoses that the risk of suicide is greatest: it is present often throughout the illness and far into convalescence. The risk may be at its most serious early in the illness and if there is a relapse in convalescence: in the depth of the illness the mental and executive retardation may not infrequently act as a safeguard—but this cannot be relied upon.

The depressed patient should always be asked if he has had gloomy thoughts, if he has felt discouraged or despairing or hopeless. If questioned with sympathy and delicacy, he may with relief speak spontaneously about his suicidal ruminations or impulses. If he does not and yet admits to feelings of hopelessness, he should be asked gently if he has had at any time thoughts of harming himself. He should be given ample time to speak about his feelings and to unburden himself of preoccupations about which it is likely he has felt ashamed and guilty. He should be reassured that suicidal thoughts are not evidence of moral weakness or sinfulness, but symptoms of the depressive illness: and that they will pass. A person who is very depressed and sharply denies any thoughts of suicide, is particularly to be distrusted. On the other hand, hints or talk or threats of suicide are always to be taken very seriously in the setting of a depressive psychosis. The majority of those who kill themselves have given at least hints to others of their intentions. A family history of suicide, and a previous suicidal attempt, increase the risk of suicide.

It is depressions of the anxious, agitated type which carry the greatest suicidal risk—particularly those of middle and later life. Amongst the warning symptoms are intense self-blame, feelings of guilt and failure and of being a burden upon others, feelings of loneliness and of being unwanted, fears of having a fatal physical illness or venereal disease or of becoming insane, a terrifying feeling that something is going to snap in the head, fears of losing control and of harming others, actual attacks upon others, a fugue and intense concern about insomnia. The essential thing is never to ignore the risk but to assess it as carefully as possible, to gain the patient's trust and to take the relatives into one's confidence. Those patients who say that they do not have the courage to commit suicide should not be believed: nor should any confidence be placed in the assertion sometimes made by relatives that the patient is the sort of person who would never carry out such a desperate act.

Simple Depression

This type is characterized by depression of mood and by a general slowing, both mental and physical. The bearing of the man is altered. He has a sad, care-worn expression, his brow is wrinkled, his eye is dull, and he looks older than his years. He may describe himself as a failure, or hopeless, or a disgrace. Thinking is difficult and slow. The slowness may not be apparent, and the only evidence of retardation may be the complaint of difficulty in thinking. Everything is an effort and a burden. He is unable to take an interest in what goes on around him, is often forgetful, irritable, and indecisive. His answers tend to be monosyllabic: he speaks in a low voice, in typical cases with a delayed reaction-time. Sometimes questions have to be repeated before an answer is obtained. What he does say, however, is relevant. He blames himself for trivial misdemeanours in his past, makes mountains out of mole-hills. In the psychomotor field the retardation is also conspicuous. The patient may sit for long periods brooding, and when asked to do anything there is usually a delay, and then the action is carried out in a slow, deliberate way, as if his limbs were weighted. The patient understands everything that goes on in his environment. There is no clouding of consciousness, there is no disorientation, no defect of memory or intellect. The patient himself recognizes the need for specialized treatment.

In depressive psychoses of all degrees of severity, a diurnal variation in the intensity of the symptoms is a common though by no means invariable feature. The patient tends to feel at his worst in the mornings, and to improve in the second half of the day. If such a patient is examined in the afternoon, a false impression of the seriousness of the illness may be obtained.

Milder forms of depression occur, which often masquerade under some other guise. Patients will consult the doctor in general practice, or come as out-patients, complaining sometimes of mild depression, but more often of anything but depression. They have vague or emphatic complaints of headache or facial pain, often of an ill-defined and ill-localized type and very persistent, of dyspepsia of various kinds, including lack of appetite, feelings of weight in the abdomen, a bad taste in the mouth, constipation, blurring of vision, irritability—especially to noises, lassitude, general weakness and (what is very common) fatigue or actual exhaustion. When thoroughly examined physically, they present nothing that will satisfactorily account for their symptoms. They are probably continuing at their work, but finding it very difficult, and on closer inquiry it will be found that although their difficulty is at first attributed to the complaints just enumerated or to the exacting nature of their work, as a matter of fact they have lost confidence, cannot concentrate, and it is an effort for them to keep to the task in hand. Reading may be easy enough, but when it comes to writing, it is difficult for them to do it, words and phrases come with difficulty, and if the latter requires any invention it takes a very long time. Sleep is frequently, but not always, disturbed, with early wakening and it is always unrefreshing. It is especially difficult to get started in the mornings. It may be impossible to get a clear statement of mood disorder from these patients; they may even deny that they are sad or depressed in any way. But when a patient presents a number of the above symptoms and when no adequate physical lesion can be found, and especially if the condition has persisted more or less unchanged for some months, and if there has been a previous similar attack perhaps some years before, it is probable that one is dealing with what is primarily a mental disorder —in these cases a mild depression. If, further, it is found that the patient has been of an anxious, gloomy, foreboding disposition, or, on the other hand, of an habitually or even unusually cheerful turn of mind with perhaps very transient episodes of depression of spirits (the 'cyclothymic' temperament), the conclusion is strengthened. A family tendency to affective disorders is also of confirmatory value. Such patients as these do not usually enter a mental hospital. They can be treated outside, and are sometimes better so treated. After a time, usually months, they recover gradually or suddenly, and the particular method of treatment they were undergoing at the time gets the credit of their cure; but that is fallacious; they recover often in spite, rather than because, of the irrelevant physical treatment still often meted out to them. In a few instances there is not this happy result. We have known cases, almost monosymptomatic in character —perhaps only a persistent headache, without physical signs, but with a good deal of concern about it—who committed suicide.

CASE No. 15

A second attack of simple retarded depression of acute onset in a quiet, shy girl, with a suicidal attempt early in the illness. Inactive, hopeless, slow and brief in her replies, with ideas of unworthiness, but some insight. Recovery in two months with insight, probably hastened by stimulation of interest in simple occupations.

A. B., 18 years old, is a good example of a simple retarded depression. She had had a former attack one year previously, which had lasted only for about one week, and from which she made, apparently, a good recovery. The family history indicated suicidal tendencies, because a paternal grandmother had taken her life when she was 62 years old, and a maternal uncle had committed suicide at the age of 45. This family history seemed to have a definite bearing on the case.

She had always been a strong, healthy child. She was not nervous, but was quiet, shy, reserved and not inclined to make friends easily.

She did quite well at school, but was described as being more practical than intellectual, and was especially interested in housewifery tasks. It was while she was attending a course of instruction at a School of Domestic Science that she broke down. The illness developed acutely, and three days before her admission she suddenly told her parents that she had drunk a bottle of eye lotion that had been in the house. On the night following this she got out of bed, and attempted to leave the house. It is of interest that preceding the onset of her previous attack she had overheard talk about suicide. This reminded her of similar incidents in her own family, and she was depressed for about a week afterwards.

At the time of her admission she was in a dull, depressed state, feeling hopeless and that she had not been learning and concentrating as she should have done. She feared in consequence that she would become a burden on her friends. Suicide had therefore seemed the simplest solution of her difficulties. She was slow in answering questions, replied for the most part in monosyllables, readily admitted that she was melancholy and that her mind was not at peace, but was occupied with morbid feelings and thoughts. As a result she had not been sleeping well. She said, 'I seem just to have been slipping along, and not doing my duty. I feel as if I had got everybody into a mess. I thought I was not so efficient as others, and that I could not hold my own with them.' Her answers to questions were always quite coherent and relevant. She denied ever having suffered from ideas of reference, from hallucinations or delusions. Her memory, her grasp of school knowledge and her intellectual faculties generally were not impaired. She realized that she was ill and in need of treatment in a mental hospital. Her general physical state showed that she was in good condition, and there was no evidence of physical disease. She had an erosion of her lower lip, due to the eye lotion which she had swallowed.

After a short period in bed she was allowed up, an attempt was made to cultivate her interest in the occupational department and this she readily took to. She found that she was able to do certain simple pieces of work comparatively well, and in consequence her self-confidence rapidly returned, and in the course of two months she made a good recovery. She put on weight, her sleep improved, she realized more clearly than heretofore what her actual difficulties had been and was able to return home.

A case such as the above illustrates very clearly a simple, depressed, retarded state, occurring in a somewhat shy, sensitive girl. There is no reason to suppose that she will not be able to carry on satisfactorily in the future.

In some cases retardation is not to be detected, at least by the ordinary clinical methods; yet the depression may be profound. In others, instead of depression, there is a total loss of feeling—the patient complaining bitterly of the lack of any emotion whatsoever, including a loss of affective response to those whom he formerly loved. As our appreciation of reality depends so much on our ability to 'feel ourselves into' the activities of other people (or more technically to project our feelings as well as our perceptions), patients suffering from emotional deficit of this kind frequently complain that everything seems unreal to them. This *feeling of unreality* may be distressing in itself and may even be the chief complaint.

Acute Depression

In this stage the retardation is more marked. The patient may never make any spontaneous remark; he is asocial, sits apart, refuses to mix with his neighbours. The whole attitude is one of great misery and dejection. The patient may accuse himself of the most heinous wrongdoing, sexual lapses and of bringing misfortune on others. There is nothing for it, he says, except to go to prison to expiate all his misdeeds. Hypochondriacal ideas and delusions are frequently expressed, often centred on the abdomen and bowels and suggested by the constipation which is so common a symptom. The depressive delusions of these patients are usually concerned with conscience, as delusions of sin; with health, as delusions of disease; and with fortune, as delusions of poverty. The patient is thoroughly convinced that no one ever suffered as he does, that he is doomed, that it is hopeless to think of the possibility of getting well. Sometimes he feels that his whole personality is changed, that he is altogether different from what he was before. The environment seems unreal to him. Occasionally hallucinations (usually auditory) occur, and orientation may not be quite correct (from inattention), but the memory and the intellectual faculties are well preserved. The patient usually realizes that he is ill, and that he needs careful looking after.

Depressive Stupor

This condition may be defined as a state of intense psychic inhibition during which regression may occur to an infantile, if not more primitive level. The patient, usually, is confined to bed, is mute, inactive and unco-operative. His eyes are open and eye movements are preserved. His bodily needs require attention in every way; he has to be fed, washed and bathed. Precautions have to be taken to prevent the retention of faeces, urine and saliva. In some cases all attempts at movement are strongly resisted. In other cases the muscles are more flaccid, and the body and limbs can be moulded into any position. On the surface it may seem as if there was a total absence of feeling or emotion, but that is often more apparent than real, for, after recovery, many patients give a vivid account of the distress which they have experienced. The idea of death is believed by some to be almost universal in stupor reactions, and may be regarded as a form of expiation for the wickedness for which they hold themselves responsible. Some patients have a clear appreciation of their position and surroundings throughout the whole period of the stupor, but in the majority a considerable dulling of consciousness occurs; and in these latter cases there is on recovery a partial or complete amnesia for the period of the stupor.

On inspection at the bedside, depressive stupor cannot be distinguished from schizophrenic (catatonic) stupor. Joyston-Bechal (1966) followed up 100 cases of stupor which had been treated at the Bethlem Royal and Maudsley Hospitals. The diagnostic incidence in this series was depression 25 per cent., schizophrenia 31 per cent., neurotic reactions 10 per cent., organic cases 20 per cent., and uncertain 14 per cent. In only one case was depression reclassified on follow-up as schizophrenia, and the concept of 'benign' stupor in manic-depressive psychosis was therefore strongly vindicated. Twenty-two of these patients suffered multiple attacks of stupor, and the likelihood of recurrent attacks was similar in depression and schizophrenia—approximately one in three.

CASE No. 16

Depression with hypochondriacal ideas of a somewhat grotesque kind in a previously healthy but somewhat anxious man of 52, following influenza and business worries; extreme taciturnity, refusal of food, retention of urine and general resistiveness—in short, the manifestations of a type of negativism; clear orientation; fairly rapid improvement with general care and encouragement; interest in occupational pursuits followed ' recovery.

B. W. A severe grade of disturbance occurred in a married man, 52 years old, who for about one year previous to admission had been experiencing a good deal of business worry.

About six months before admission to hospital he had suffered from an attack of influenza, and was in bed for a period of about ten days. He gradually made some improvement, but two months prior to his admission he seemed to change completely. He expressed the idea that he might have cancer, then that he had syphilis; he did not wish his wife or children to come near him in case they should get infected. He feared to go to the lavatory lest it would become choked, and infection would spread all over the house. This condition was followed by a period during which he would talk only in monosyllables. It was difficult to get him to take his nourishment; he tended to retain his urine, and on account of the difficulties of management he was sent to the hospital. He would not speak or answer questions when spoken to. He became restless, moaned and cried, and said, 'I cannot, I cannot.' He refused to take his food, and resisted being touched; and it was with the greatest difficulty that a physical examination could be made.

This man had come from a healthy stock. He had developed normally, and was described as a 'wild youngster, with lots of go'. He did well at school, and after leaving became a successful business man. He had been married for ten years, had two children and had a happy married life. He was always even-tempered and good-natured. He took life seriously, was rather inclined to worry, but was generous to his friends, devoted to his family and considerate to everyone. He had many outside interests, including art, drawing and latterly photography. His principal hobby had been his garden.

At the time of his admission he was in a miserable physical state, greatly emaciated, with small abrasions over the back of the left scapula and over both shins. His bladder was distended, and he had to be catheterized immediately. There was no evidence of any gross organic disease. For the most part he lay in a dull, depressed state. He answered one or two questions in monosyllables, but usually he refused to reply to questions. There was no evidence of any hallucinatory or delusional formation. He was able to tell the month correctly, but refused to reply to questions as to the day or the year. He seemed to realize quite clearly that he was in a mental hospital. He had to be tube-fed, and had to be catheterized. His condition, in short, was one of stupor. Even five weeks after admission he was more or less unchanged, except that artificial feeding had improved his general health. Gradually improvement was effected, so that he began to show more initiative, shaved himself, went out walking, spoke a little more and started to take his food better. Gradually it was possible to interest him in the occupational division, where he soon began to do satisfactory work, and after a residence of several weeks at a convalescent home at the seaside he made a complete recovery, returned home and resumed his work.

Alternating States

Some patients alternate continuously for years between states of depression and states of elation, with little or no interval of normality.

MIXED STATES

Kraepelin described 'mixed states', which he formed by a combination of the cardinal symptoms of the manic and depressive states. He differentiated six principal types as follow:

1. Maniacal stupor.
2. Agitated depression.
3. Unproductive mania.
4. Depressive mania.
5. Depression, with flight of ideas.
6. Akinetic mania.

These conditions, according to Kraepelin, not only occur singly in the course either of an acute excitement or an acute depression, but as transition stages during the change from excitement to depression.

In our experience mixed states, other than agitated depression, are not uncommon and are often misdiagnosed as schizophrenia. They show an admixture of manic and depressive symptoms, rapid fluctuations of mood are commonly noted, and perplexity may be a prominent feature. Such mixed states tend to run a rather more prolonged course than the average case of manic-depressive psychosis. Briefer mixed states also occur as transition phases, and the condition known as maniacal stupor is usually a transition stage between a depressive stupor and a manic attack.

The following is an example:

CASE No. 17

A shy, timid Italian girl of 18 who became mute and incontinent, but retained certain simple responses to her environment; then passed into a typical manic attack; recovered incompletely and without insight; became seclusive, expressed some religious ideas and relapsed into her former condition of mutism, etc., from which again she passed into an infectious elation, but this time with curious inhibitions in her flow of talk; once more recovery, again without insight.

A young Italian girl, 18 years old, who had always been shy and timid, was admitted to the hospital in a state of mutism. There was no evidence of infective-exhaustive factors, or of hallucinations, so that the diagnosis seemed to lie between a katatonic and a manic-depressive condition. The expression of the patient was impassive, but not unobservant. She obeyed commands promptly and quickly, her movements were free and graceful, and when given a pad and pencil she would cover pages with scribbles. She was incontinent both as to bladder and bowels, and on several occasions she smeared herself with excreta. She reacted very slightly to pin pricks. There were no assumption of fixed attitudes, no stereotyped movements, no catalepsy; on the other hand, there was no evidence of depression. Retardation or blocking or negativism could be inferred from the mutism.

This girl had had a previous attack, which lasted for a period of eight months. Before her first attack she had complained of some headache, and one day while in church said that it was full of cats. On admission to hospital she presented features similar to those seen in the condition above described, but later she exhibited a playful mood, free, graceful movements, some distractibility, flight of ideas and sound associations—a typical manic state.

She recovered from this attack, but at the time of her discharge she had very little real insight into her condition, and was rather careless and indifferent.

For five months she was able to remain at home. At first she did a certain amount of housework, but gradually she lost interest, became seclusive, sat in a room by herself and could hardly be got to leave the house. On one occasion she expressed the wish to become a nun, complained of seeing devils at night-time and seemed afraid.

During her second attack the patient gradually developed a condition of elation, becoming talkative and restless. Her talkativeness was peculiar in that there was no steady flow of words, as is usual in the frank manic, but rather an abrupt, inhibited mode of speech, a short sample of which is as follows:

'You know I'd love—you know—let me have a pencil—you know, you know—you know sometimes when—we didn't have any—we didn't have any news—you know sometimes (hums a tune)—I love the Italian band. You know sometimes we——' The content of her remarks was not specially odd or peculiar. She was extremely alert, and was much more in touch with the situation than her conduct seemed to indicate. She laughed excessively, but her laughter was gay and infectious. She was distractible, and occasionally showed clang associations.

She made a good recovery from this attack, but again without any real insight.

Q

The essential part of the picture had been her elated mood, with restlessness, alertness and talkativeness. Apart from her make-up, there was little that could be considered ominous. At the beginning of the attack the association of mutism with a slightly happy, smiling mood and free movements constituted a fairly typical example of a mixed phase of the manic-depressive psychosis. A similar mixture was shown later by the association of inhibited talkativeness with bright, happy, alert behaviour and increased psychomotor activity.

PUERPERAL PSYCHOSES

In the large majority of cases puerperal psychoses are manic-depressive illnesses, and they are therefore described here. Neurotic, schizophrenic and organic (toxic) reactions also occur: the latter two much less commonly in this country than the affective psychoses.

Tod (1964) in a prospective study of the development of puerperal depression in over 700 consecutive pregnancies in an urban general practice, diagnosed depression in 2·9 per cent. of the series. In each case there were also symptoms of pathological anxiety during the pregnancy.

While an unhealthy reaction to motherhood, a disturbed relationship with the husband or the fact that the pregnancy was unwanted by wife or husband or both, and other psychological and social stresses, may increase the likelihood of breakdown in the puerperium, the main factors are almost certainly constitutional. But it must be added that this constitutional predisposition is by no means regularly expressed: the recurrence of a puerperal psychosis is not usual, far less invariable—the risk has been calculated to lie between one in three and one in seven. If recurrence occurs, however, the illness is very likely to be of the same type. Attacks of depression are much commoner than attacks of mania.

Puerperal depressions begin usually in the first 7–10 days of the puerperium, often quite acutely. Initially there may be a slight degree of mental clouding and a marked degree of perplexity is common. In her rôle as mother the patient feels inadequate and even panic stricken. She loses her normal feelings of affection for her husband and for the baby. Morbid fears of the baby being abnormal or fears of harming the baby or impulses to harm it may emerge: and as the depression deepens there is a considerable risk not only of suicide but also of infanticide.

The course of puerperal depressive reactions is very variable, though the prognosis is almost invariably good. Lactation has usually to be stopped. The milder cases may be treated at home with antidepressants: but the more severe require admission to a mental hospital and it may be many months before full recovery takes place, whether E.C.T. is given or not. It has not yet been demonstrated that the prognosis either for the mother's or the baby's subsequent mental health is enhanced by admitting mother and child together to a psychiatric unit.

PHYSICAL SYMPTOMS

The chief physical changes are disorder of sleep and loss of weight. These are more difficult to control in the manic than in the depressed case. A history of sleeplessness or loss of appetite, or both, is often said to have been the first indication of the patient's being out of sorts, but a careful analysis of the case history usually shows that these symptoms were dependent on some already existing mental change. Every case of acute depression suffers from sleeplessness and from a disorder of appetite. Whereas the manic patient is so restless, so distractible and so busy that he has no time either to sleep or to eat, the depressed patient may be so tormented by depressive ideas, and feel so unworthy, that he does not consider himself entitled to any food that is offered him, and either refuses it altogether or states that he has no appetite for it. In consequence the body weight diminishes, sometimes to an alarming degree. One of the first signs of beginning improvement is an increase in the bodily weight, usually with a relish for food, and improved sleep.

Particularly in depressed patients there is a sluggishness of the whole gastro-intestinal tract, and constipation is a very common complaint. Rarely the depressed patient gains weight due to the retention of body water.

The menstrual function tends to be disturbed or to disappear at the onset of any mental illness, and it frequently remains absent during its whole course. Return of the menstrual function is sometimes an early sign of improvement.

Recently there has been much research into the biochemistry of the affective psychoses, stimulated by the success of physical methods of treatment, and the undoubted importance of the hereditary factor in the aetiology. Amine and mineral metabolism and adrenocortical activity have been intensively studied.

A good deal of evidence has now been gathered which suggests an abnormality of indoleamine metabolism in depression; while reports of changes in the catecholamines have been conflicting. Reserpine, which depletes brain amine stores, is recognized to cause depressive illness in about 15 per cent. of cases. Ashcroft and his colleagues in Edinburgh (1966) have found in depressed patients a reduced concentration of 5-hydroxyindolic compounds in the C.S.F.: the metabolite of 5-hydroxytryptamine (5HT) mainly involved seemed to be 5-hydroxyindole acetic acid (5HIAA). The urinary excretion of tryptamine in depression is reported to be low (Coppen et al., 1965). On the other hand, the results of treatment with antidepressant drugs suggest that depression is relieved by increasing the level of monoamines in the brain: imipramine may act by increasing the proportion of unbound amine which is present, and the monoamine oxidase inhibitors by decreasing the rate of metabolism of brain monoamines. Also, in a recent preliminary communication, Coppen and his colleagues (1967) have reported that tryptophan (the precursor of 5HT) may be almost as effective as E.C.T. in treating a depressive illness, and that the results may be improved by giving a monoamine oxidase inhibitor concurrently. None of this evidence is, however, conclusive.

During attacks both of depression and of mania there are changes in electrolyte distribution, of still uncertain significance. During depression, 'residual' sodium (intracellular sodium and a small amount of exchangeable bone sodium) is increased by nearly 50 per cent., and returns to normal after clinical recovery (Coppen and Shaw, 1963). At the same time, cellular potassium is depleted

(Shaw and Coppen, 1966). During mania, the 'residual' sodium has been reported to show an average increase over normal of 200 per cent., and to return to normal after recovery (Coppen *et al.*, 1966). It is not known if these electrolyte shifts occur in the central nervous system, altering the excitability of the neurones. In patients recovering from depression, Coppen and Shaw (1967) found an increase in intracellular, extracellular and total body water; and have suggested that lithium salts may exert their therapeutic action by altering the mechanisms responsible for these changes in body water, and not (as was earlier thought) by altering sodium distribution.

It is still uncertain if adrenal cortical function is specifically affected by depressive illness, or by certain types of depressive illness. A considerable number of investigations have been made, mainly of cortisol and its metabolites, and these have tended to show a moderate increase in adrenocortical activity. Gibbons and McHugh (1962), for example, found an increase (within the normal range) in mean plasma cortisol levels during depression, the more depressed patients tending to have the highest levels, and a decline in these levels during recovery: but not all their depressed patients showed this even when severely ill. One would of course expect some increased adrenocortical activity due to the stress of the illness itself and of admission to hospital and other environmental changes: and cortisol, which shows a diurnal variation in its secretion with a peak in the early morning, is the adrenal cortical hormone most responsive to emotional stress. Sachar (1967) has in fact found in a small sample of depressed patients that the urinary 17-OHCS response to admission to hospital far exceeded the change which took place during recovery. There is a need for studies also of aldosterone metabolism, in view of the electrolyte abnormalities which are found in affective illnesses.

In summary, one may say that the biochemical changes reviewed above are rather slight, of uncertain significance, not clearly related to discrete symptoms and of no diagnostic value. It is not known how they may be interconnected. But they are of much interest, and the further study in affective psychoses of brain monoamine metabolism in particular may well be very rewarding. A critical review of the literature on the biochemistry of affective disorders has been made by Coppen (1967).

INVOLUTIONAL MELANCHOLIA

The involutional period is a physiological epoch common to men and women, bringing in its train certain mental and bodily changes. The mental faculties in general become less acute. There is a tendency to bewail the past, and to feel that the future has little in store. The mind is occupied with the 'might-have-beens', and in consequence doubt, indecision, fear and anxiety readily show themselves. It is impossible to state definitely when the involutional period begins and when it ends, but, roughly, it ranges from 40 to 60 years in women, and from 50 to 65 years in men.

When Kraepelin made his broad differentiation between the manic-depressive psychosis and schizophrenia, he kept cases of depression occurring at the involutional period apart, and termed them melancholia. Some years later Dreyfus reviewed the material on which Kraepelin had based his findings, and concluded that the great majority of 'melancholias' should be included in the manic-depressive group, that cases of involutional melancholia corresponded to mixed states of manic depression, and that there was no such entity as involutional melancholia. Kraepelin accepted and concurred with the conclusions of Dreyfus. Kirby, however, in commenting on the work of Dreyfus, stated: 'In a number of cases the manic-depressive symptoms were plainly in evidence, the cases having been improperly placed with the melancholias'.

Kallmann (1953) referred to 'involutional psychosis' as 'those common but clinically diversified psychoses in the involutional period characterized by agitated anxiety, and a combination of paranoid and depressive features'. He considered the aetiology to be multiple, and the illness to be precipitated typically in a schizoid individual when the strains of the involutional period had overcome his or her powers of adaptation. He reported an excess of involutional psychosis in the families of schizophrenics, and a higher incidence of schizophrenia in the relatives of involutional cases than in the general population. Kallmann further declared that there was no genetic connection with manic-depressive psychosis. It was on the basis of this work by Kallmann that it came to be commonly believed that the evidence supporting the identity of involutional melancholia as a distinct reaction-type was largely genetic. Kallmann seems, however, to have investigated a heterogeneous clinical material, his findings have not been confirmed and Stenstedt's [see below] appear to be more soundly based. The conclusion is that there are probably, so far as present knowledge goes, no genetic grounds for separating involutional from manic-depressive psychoses.

Sir David Henderson believed that, clinically, involutional melancholia is separable from the manic-depressive psychoses. He emphasized the features of depression without retardation, anxiety, a feeling of unreality and hypochondriacal or nihilistic delusions, the last being in the allo-, somato- and autopsychic fields. At the same time he qualified his description, calling it a tentative formulation and making the following reservations: 'there is no one of the above-mentioned symptoms which is peculiar to the involutional period, but their occurrence together is unusually common at that time of life. A very similar syndrome may occur at an earlier age.'

There is no doubt that in recent years in Scotland, where this syndrome used to be very common, it is now much less often recorded. This may be either because it has become less common or because customs in diagnosis have altered. The syndrome may have been in part at least culturally determined, and cultural changes may have affected its prevalence: or it may have become less obvious because depressive illnesses are now treated earlier in their course, before the grosser symptoms have developed. Or it may be disappearing, because of a well-based judgement by clinicians that there are no longer sufficient grounds for distinguishing it from manic-depressive psychosis.

We believe that the last is probably the correct view. There is no doubt that an attack of manic-depressive psychosis may present the clinical picture said to be characteristic of involutional melancholia. Involutional melancholia may well be a manic-depressive illness affected in its clinical expression by the patient's personality type and its development in later life. We let the syndrome stand meantime, since it serves to draw attention to the rather marked symptomatic differences between depressions associated with much anxiety and agitation and without retardation, and those associated with obvious psychological and physical retardation. These two and other types of depression merit more detailed scrutiny, in their psychological and physical aspects and their response to different kinds of treatment, before it can be concluded definitely that they are aspects only of a single syndrome.

AETIOLOGY

There is often a history of exciting factors, either psychic, physical or a combination of the two.

The underlying type of personality in many cases has certain characteristics. These people have a record of hard work behind them. They are sensitive, meticulous, over-conscientious, over-scrupulous, busy, active men and women who take a pride in their work and have a high sense of duty towards others. Titley described them as showing 'a narrow range of interests, poor facility for readjustment, asocial trends, inability to maintain friendships, intolerance and poor adult sexual adjustment, also a pronounced and rigid ethical code and a proclivity to reticence and sensitiveness'. It will be readily appreciated that such an obsessional or anankastic type of pre-psychotic disposition has little or no relationship to the cyclothymic constitution.

Naturally the theory has been advanced that in women, at least, such conditions are due to hormonal alterations associated with the menopause; but treatment with oestrogens, though it may relieve the troublesome vasomotor symptoms of which many menopausal women complain, will not cure an affective psychosis.

It is the genetic factors which are of the greatest importance in the aetiology. Here the work of Stenstedt (1959) has been outstanding. Investigating a series of 307 cases diagnosed as involutional melancholia, of whom 74 per cent. had had only one depression and the remainder had had two or more, he found that the syndrome was from the aetiological point of view heterogeneous: both genetic and environmental factors could be identified and he thought that psychogenic factors, the climacteric and the age of onset (55 or over) might all be significant. There was no increased risk of schizophrenia in the relatives of Stenstedt's cases: but the risk for manic-depressive psychoses was high (at least twice as high as that for the general population), though not as high as that for the relatives of manic-depressive cases. His conclusion was as follows: 'There is a significant difference between manic-depressive psychosis and involutional melancholia as regards predisposition to endogenous depression. For patients suffering from the latter state the risk of endogenous depression among parents and siblings is about 6 per cent., whereas with manic-depressive psychosis the risk is about 12 per cent., or twice as high.' Stenstedt added that aetiologically it is possible that we cannot distinguish clearly between manic-depressive psychosis, involutional melancholia and exogenous forms of depression, hereditary factors playing a greater or less part in all three forms of depressive illness.

SYMPTOMATOLOGY

The term involutional melancholia is a convenient label for a group of depressive illnesses occurring at the involutional period of life, because cases exhibiting the characteristics to be defined are particularly common at this epoch. It should be reserved for those cases who have never previously suffered from any form of mental illness. There is no known reason why a person should not suffer from manic-depressive symptoms during the earlier period of life, and then at the involutional period exhibit an agitated state. When such is the case, it is considered better to keep it in the manic-depressive group.

The most characteristic involutional qualities lie in the content of the psychosis, especially in the apprehension, hypochondriasis and nihilism, and these qualities are the result of the psychological changes associated with advancing years.

The outstanding feature is the anxious depression, without retardation. This has often been preceded by a stage during which the patient has complained of tiredness, of feelings of inadequacy, of being easily fatigued and of sleeplessness. The development tends to be insidious, over several months, and the illness in its earlier phases is often misdiagnosed as an anxiety neurosis. The appearance and attitude of such patients may become one of great misery and intense agitation: they feel frightened, are restless, wring their hands, moan or groan, and tend to rake over their past, the slightest faults becoming crimes. They feel that there is no future for them, that they have an incurable physical or mental disease, that they may be thrown out or taken to prison. In their misery, loaded with feelings of guilt, failure and unworthiness, they may refuse food or attempt to mutilate themselves. The danger of suicide is great. Besides blaming themselves, they may hold themselves responsible for the condition of others with whom they are associated. Paranoid features are not uncommon: food may be refused because of a suspicion that it is being poisoned. Usually the individual realizes that he is ill and may respond to some extent to reassurance: but this alleviation is transient, the patient's beliefs and apprehensions become delusional and dominate him. The delusions are frequently hypochondriacal or nihilistic. Depersonalization may be severe. Orientation is preserved and memory retained.

These patients may complain bitterly of physical symptoms, such as feelings of pressure upon or bursting sensations in the head, flushing, vertigo, loss of appetite, feelings of weight and pressure after meals, and constipation. There is often a considerable and sometimes rapid loss of weight, due in part to the intense agitation and in part to the loss of appetite or refusal of food.

CASE No. 18
Gradual onset of depressed, anxious, apprehensive state in a man of 65; ushered in by apprehension over financial losses, followed by depression, loss of interest, irritability,

insomnia and headache; stereotyped anxious queries and stereotyped expressions of distress; increasing automaticity of actions and emotional expression; noisy, gluttonous and careless of his appearance; but ultimate recovery in two years.

E. F., male, 65 years old, was admitted to the hospital in a very restless, depressed, excited state. He threw his arms and legs about, knocked his head against the wall, pulled at his hair and cheeks and frequently made strange noises. The condition had been of about six months' duration.

He had been a strong, healthy man, successful in business, and had been married for a period of about thirty-eight years. He had always been reserved and silent but kindly, and had very few interests outside his business. Three years before his admission he had been able to retire, but during the war years his investments began to depreciate, and he worried greatly about his financial state, and exaggerated his losses. He began to fear that his income would be insufficient, though his family asserted that he had no grounds whatsoever for such an assumption. His habitual reticence gradually gave place to a deepening depression; he brooded about himself, took no interest in the daily papers and continually accused his eldest son—on whose advice he had acted in regard to his investments—as the cause of his ruin. He was sleepless, suffered from headache and complained that his head felt as if it was in a vice. He was irritable over the smallest things, and was totally unable to rest. For a minute or two he would sit down but then would be up, jerking his legs, pulling at his hair or his face. A holiday at a farmhouse had been tried, but while there his excitement increased, and as he seemed to be getting rapidly worse he was brought to hospital.

The patient's condition was one of great depression and anxiety. He said that he had always been a nervous man, and that he could not seem to control his movements or what he wanted to do. He answered all questions on general topics without any hesitation or confusion, and his memory for remote and recent events was good. His knowledge of current events had been gained by hearsay, as he had not been able to sit down and read a newspaper for many months. He knew exactly where he was, and expressed deep regret at the worry that he was causing his wife and family.

Physically his condition was satisfactory. There was no evidence of any organic disease. His hair was rubbed bare in patches over the temples.

Following his admission, he slept very badly, and he frequently had to get medicine to help him. He was always in a state of panic about himself, was constantly demanding an explanation of his condition and wanted to know the prognosis. He was treated by prolonged baths and as much nourishment as possible, but his excitement and restlessness continued undiminished. Whenever spoken to he was quiet, but when left alone he would continue to pace up and down the ward, shouting out some stereotyped phrase such as 'Oh, my God', at constant intervals. He never could give any explanation of why he shouted—whether he was impelled to do it, or whether he derived any special relief from it. His stereotyped attitude was also seen by his daily queries. 'Do you think I will ever get better?' 'Is there anything wrong with my brain?' 'Am I insane?' 'If I could stop the shouting would I get home?' 'What is it that makes me shout?' 'Could I live as I am just now in a tenement?' These questions, or similar ones, were repeated day after day. Attempts were made to interest him in various kinds of work both in the garden and in the house, but he never could be made to apply himself to anything.

Five months after his admission, his excitement and his manifestations of grief became more and more automatic, and were often continued, though with diminished vehemence, even when conversing. At this time his weight was persistently falling. He never passed a night without more or less frequent outbursts of shouting. It sometimes happened that he did not sleep at all; he would then jump in and out of bed, and pace the floor of his room shouting, 'Oh, my God', or meaningless and inarticulate sounds.

He stopped before the mirror, where he examined his reflection, and increased the din by striking the chest of drawers with his fist or the back of his hair-brush. When in this highly excited condition he would pull at his nose, or pull his too closely cropped hair. During the daytime he was even more noisy, and attempts to keep him in check were unavailing. Later his appetite became capricious, and gluttony alternated with abstemiousness. His sons usually brought him cakes and other 'tit-bits'. These he would put away in a drawer in his room, and at odd times in the day he would bolt various articles of food either in the way of fruit, fancy cakes or confections. While he was still a patient he was left a certain amount of money, which completely made up for all the money which he had lost as a result of his investments, but in spite of this his state of anxiety and depression continued. He continued to express abhorrence of his own conduct, and constantly asked 'Why do I make this noise? Can I not help it? Will you not give me something to keep me quiet?' Gradually a certain amount of improvement was effected in his condition, and after a period of two years he was able to be discharged.

During the whole of his illness his intellectual faculties remained perfectly clear. A certain continuity of personality and subsequent psychosis is clear in this case. His financial losses were the precipitating cause, but were not in themselves by any means sufficient to account for such an illness; and their redemption led to no immediate improvement. The fact that his chief topic in his illness was his health suggests strongly that his financial losses merely served to bring to the surface the general concerns of advancing years. The stereotypy of his utterances ('Oh, my God', etc.) and his deterioration in personal habits, both of which would have seemed prognostically ominous, are interesting in view of the fact that he ultimately recovered.

CHRONIC MANIA

At one time chronic mania was regarded as the aftermath of an attack of acute mania which had persisted for a period of twelve months or longer. A time limit, however, did not prove a very reliable guide, as in the absence of the specific methods of treatment which have in recent years proved so successful in manic-depressive states, many cases did eventually make good recoveries even after several years. This led Schott, in 1904, and a number of later workers to consider whether chronic mania had a symptomatology which was peculiar to it, or any other features which differentiated it from the manic-depressive psychosis. The four cases which Schott reported exhibited a manic state which had persisted for thirty, twenty-five, twenty-one and seventeen years respectively. All of them had had previous manic attacks of a similar nature to the final persistent one. All of the psychiatrists who had treated these cases were impressed by the long duration of the final attack, by its intensity, and by the astonishing integrity of the intellectual functions even after a period of many years.

In our original investigations of such cases, published in 1927, we suggested that chronic mania was the counterpart of involutional melancholia, that it started comparatively late in life, and might be maintained for many years at a persistently high level. We further suggested that the diagnosis should be reserved for those cases in which the first manic attack had occurred after the age of 40 years. Under such circumstances the condition was likely to be intractable. The absence of emotional fluctuations or periodicity seemed to justify its separation from the much more familiar and recoverable manic-depressive psychosis. In 1929 Wertham's review of a group of 'prolonged manic excitements' which had persisted for periods of from five to eleven years was valuable. He reported seven cases, in three of whom, aged 58, 52 and 60 years respectively, there was no history of previous attacks. He was impressed by what he termed 'the psychobiological rigidity' of these patients in conjunction with a manic constitution.

In a few advanced cases of chronic mania which we have seen there has been little motor over-activity, irritability and paranoid features have been prominent, and they have been misdiagnosed as suffering from schizophrenic or paranoid psychoses.

We do not wish to over-elaborate the position, but as examples of the clinical states which were not uncommon previous to the introduction of electric convulsion therapy, we submit the following.

CASE No. 19

Chronic mania. An excited, noisy, elated state with over-talkativeness and distractibility. Frequent angry episodes. Paucity of ideation, but a caustic wit. Hallucinatory and delusional trends. Ten years' duration.

A single woman, 49 years old, was admitted to hospital in an excited, elated, hyperactive state. Her conversation was imperious, domineering and abusive. Her language was obscene. Her mood fluctuated so that she had phases of irritability which might give place to the expression of grandiose ideas, or else she lapsed into a happy, humorous, witty stage, in which she cracked *risqué* jokes, and laughed heartily at the ensuing consternation. She was destructive of her clothing, or dressed grotesquely in a red dressing-gown adorned with gaudy bows. An example of her pressure of speech is as follows: 'You are not able to write. Give me a clean page. You are not a doctor—if I had a son like you I would drown myself, but first I would shoot the man—I see a vision—very fine—you are insane—I never met anyone worse—these bloody men—I loathe men.'

Throughout her illness her memory and general intellectual faculties remained intact, and she showed that she had considerable insight into her disordered state.

CASE No. 20

Chronic mania. Sudden onset of an elated, over-active, talkative state in a widower, 44 years old. Condition continued unchanged for five years.

A farmer went to a neighbouring estate where he liberated all the horses from their stables. He rapidly became so excited and irrational that his admission to hospital became a matter of urgency. He addressed the doctor as King Edward, King George, the Pope or as plain Geordie Boyle. He said he had been to Windsor Castle and had let the horses out to grass.

In hospital he was restless, excitable and noisy. He was constantly 'on the go', never stopped talking and showed a typical flight of ideas with clang associations: *e.g.* 'They were all stolen from me—King of Spain, Queen of Spain, twins, Heavenly twins, Esau —he sold his soul for a mess of pottage. Shah, Shaw of Persia I suppose you are.' When he was asked to explain his behaviour he replied: 'Mad, sir. Mad as a mad dog sir.'

The intense pitch of his excitement continued unabated for five years. There was no evidence of hallucinations or delusions; his memory and intellectual faculties remained intact.

COURSE AND PROGNOSIS

Affective states run, usually, a comparatively short course with a good prognosis. That is true, particularly, when the attacks are of an isolated nature or of the intermittent type which occur so frequently in younger people. In Rennie's investigation and analysis of 200 cases 93 per cent. of the patients recovered from the first attack but, unfortunately, 79 per cent. had recurrences. If the manic or depressive episodes are of a mild or simple nature they may resolve quickly under home care, but if there are frequent repetitions the duration of the episodes is inclined to be more prolonged, the care and treatment of the patient becomes more hazardous, and it may be imperative to arrange for the patient's admission to a psychiatric unit. Irrespective of that fact, and often in virtue of it, ultimate recovery can be expected even although it may be impossible to foretell with accuracy the duration and course of the illness. It is, however, often a matter of urgency, for family, business, and economic reasons, to be able to give an approximate forecast. With the modern methods of treatment which are now in everyday use we can usually assure the patient and his relatives that recovery from the episode will probably occur in from one to three months. Naturally enough, depending on a variety of circumstances, some cases may tend to persist much longer. In those cases in which the aetiological factors precipitating the reaction are of an exogenous nature the prognosis is better, and there is less tendency to recurrence than in those cases of an endogenous or constitutional nature determined by an hereditary predisposition. The individual with well balanced, wide interests can usually be helped through his period of stress without too much difficulty.

When the psychotic episodes continue to recur, periodically, in persons who are over 40 years of age, or, even more significantly, if they appear for the first time after that age, then the prognosis must be more guarded owing to the possibility that the patient may be more vulnerable to incidental factors such as arteriosclerotic or other organic changes. We have already emphasized the persistence of attacks of excitement of the chronic manic type. In the few cases of affective disturbance which fail to recover there is an emotional deterioration characterized by a loss of interest, diminution of affect, and a state of chronicity which may persist indefinitely. It has been asserted that when hallucinations have complicated the clinical picture the prognosis has been rendered more unfavourable. That suggestion, however, has never been adequately substantiated. In our experience hallucinatory phenomena occurring in affective states are of a transitory nature determined by the acuteness of the psychotic process.

Previous to the introduction of electric convulsion therapy the depressive states associated with the involutional period of life constituted a great problem. The illness was usually of intense severity, caused great distress of mind and body, and might be prolonged over many years. Usually the intellectual faculties remained intact, and so long as the affect was maintained, and there was no organic cerebral involvement, we felt justified in maintaining an optimistic outlook. Now, we know, that with electric convulsion therapy at our command, we can usually give a good prognosis.

DIAGNOSIS

In the majority of cases the personality of the patient, the relatively acute onset and the unequivocal nature of the mood changes are typical of the affective reaction types.

There are, however, a number of cases in which the clinical picture may be complicated by symptoms such as hallucinations, or by conduct disorder which points to regression to a more primitive and instinctive level, *e.g.* exhibitionism, or incontinence of urine and faeces. Superficially it might seem as if such features were more indicative of a schizophrenic rather than an affective reaction but they serve to teach us not to divorce symptoms from the setting in which they occur. So long as the mood, thought and conduct of the individual are in harmony we can remain assured of the correctness of our diagnosis. It is true that affective states may show schizophrenic features and vice versa, but in diagnosis it is safer to pay more attention to the acuteness of the onset and the personality structure rather than be side-tracked by the symptoms which are subject to so much variation. The mood of the manic patient is a gay, happy, jolly, infectious one—you want to laugh with him because of the warmth of his personality. The excitement of the schizophrenic is a blind, confused, impulsive, episodic state, during which the conduct is bizarre and determined by the hallucinations and delusions which are so predominant.

The depressive stupor state may appear to be identical to the catatonic stupor of schizophrenia, and again it is safer to be guided, for differentiation purposes, by rapidity of onset of the illness and the personality type. On the whole, however, the depressive stupor is not so persistent as a catatonic one, and is not punctuated by episodes of wild excitement as the latter is.

Those cases of affective disturbance occurring at the involutional period may occasionally present a certain amount of difficulty in differentiation from paranoid states, but in the latter the heightening of affect is only related to certain specified paranoid ideas, and differs in quality and type from that of affective disorders; in the involutional states the affect dominates the entire clinical picture.

Differentiation from cases of arteriosclerotic brain disease may present certain problems. The fact that a marked degree of peripheral arteriosclerosis may accompany involutional states should not deceive us. That is exactly what might be expected, but provided there is no history of headache, dizziness, convulsive attacks, failure of memory and concentration, we can remain confident of our diagnosis.

TREATMENT

The affective psychoses are, for the most part, constitutionally determined, and may occur and resolve spontaneously. In other cases trivial or more serious precipitating exogenous factors may be required to trigger off the psychotic cycle which we must attempt to control. Our treatment is directed in a threefold direction: 1. to allay the acuteness of the symptoms; 2. to modify or alter the patient's environment; and 3. to assist the patient to a better understanding of his own personality so that he may learn to live amicably with his disability. No hard and fast rules can be laid down, each case differs in its psychological, physical and environmental components, and must be treated on its individual merits.

The rhythmic swings of mood so characteristic of the affective state may never over-step normal limits, and be very transitory. In consequence, domestic, social and business activities need not be seriously interfered with. Perhaps temporarily the patient may have to modify the pace of his life, to take things easier, to get more sleep, to maintain his physical strength. A few words of sympathetic encouragement plus a mild sedative to combat sleeplessness may be sufficient to enable the personality to resume a better balanced tempo. In other cases the mood swings may be of a higher and deeper intensity, are episodic, prolonged, alternating in nature, and occur with dramatic suddenness. Even so the tendency is always towards a spontaneous readjustment irrespective of the number of recurrences. To facilitate recovery and to allay the mental distress and excitement it is advisable, without delay, to utilize all the modern methods of treatment which are now at our command.

Before any programme of treatment is instituted, a decision as to where it most appropriately can be undertaken should be come to. The social, economic and business circumstances of the patient may be some of the important deciding factors, but the patient's ability to co-operate is paramount. If he has good insight into his condition, if his relatives are able to undertake the responsibility, or if a special nurse can be provided, his own home may be eminently suitable. Otherwise the advantages of a nursing home, the psychiatric department of a general hospital, or a mental hospital, have to be carefully considered. In milder cases treatment on an out-patient basis can be arranged. In-patient treatment, however, gives a greater sense of security both to patient and to doctor.

Acutely disturbed, non-co-operative patients are more suitable for mental hospital care, especially if the illness is likely to be prolonged. Such a hospital gives a greater sense of freedom, recreational and social activities are available, and the association with other patients can hasten the rehabilitation process. At the same time depressed patients obsessed with suicidal thoughts can be under constant observation, while manic patients have sufficient scope in which to dissipate their superabundant energy. In coping with the above issues a serious responsibility is involved but doctors and nurses must remain understanding, flexible, calm and tactful even under the most trying and aggravating circumstances. Too great rigidity, the inability to take a reasonable risk may lead to unfortunate consequences by creating antagonism between patient and doctor. Careful 'timing' of such decisions should be exercised. Supervision should always be carried out in as unobtrusive a way as possible. No one likes to feel 'policed'—it may create a sense of mistrust, irritation and frustration. In case of any untoward accident our conscience may remain at peace provided all reasonable care has been exercised.

On admission to hospital or nursing home these patients are often in need initially of bed treatment and careful nursing which should be continued until the patient has become rested mentally and bodily. Some prefer a single room, others a small dormitory where they may have companionship. These procedures ensure that the doctors and nurses in attendance become quickly familiar with the character, conduct and habits of the patient. The problems of insomnia, suicide, undernourishment and so on are kept under constant review. The human interest and attention given to the patient is not only a comfort, but also reassures relatives and friends that everything possible will be done to facilitate recovery.

The majority of depressed patients are dominated by guilt feelings, regard themselves as moral cowards rather than as estimable persons who are merely sick in mind and body. The only mistake they have made with their problem has been to struggle unaided, usually for far too long, and to have added bodily exhaustion to their other troublesome symptoms. They feel that they are lacking in will power, that their character has deteriorated, that they should make some superhuman effort to free themselves from all those tormenting thoughts which seem to control and bind them. Their suffering may be intensified by well-meaning, naïvely optimistic friends—and even family doctors—who prescribe cheering up methods, social activities, amusements, holidays or other experiments which the patient is unable to accept or enjoy.

The more sensible plan is to reduce life's activities to as simple a level as possible. The patient should be advised, as a general rule, to have a period of sick leave, to conserve his resources, and to avoid activities which might increase his sense of failure. Anything he undertakes should carry with it a reasonable chance of success. He should be reassured and informed that his illness is not an uncommon one, that it is as real as appendicitis or any other bodily involvement, that there is nothing to be ashamed of, that it is not a punishment for sin, and that the future can be anticipated with equanimity. It is by no means easy for the patient to accept such reassurances, but constant repetition eventually brings conviction.

Insomnia and the dangers of suicide, which are often closely linked, are the most troublesome symptoms to deal with. It is this combination which so often necessitates hospital treatment, and indeed may be a matter of extreme urgency. In the event of a suicidal attempt everything possible must be done to conserve the patient's life by administering first-aid for the injuries sustained and admission should then be arranged to a psychiatric unit. The security of a hospital atmosphere provides the best opportunity to discuss the many problems which it had seemed impossible to solve. Their revelation may constitute a blessed relief.

The Church and various lay organizations are helpful in their attitudes to the problem of suicidal acts. London's Anti-Suicide Bureau, the Save-a-Life League in the U.S.A., Vienna's Advisory Centre for those weary of life, Zürich's Anti-Suicide League, and Berlin's Suicide's Aid Society have all accomplished a great purpose. The Salvation Army, the Samaritans Association and the increasing development of psychiatric out-patient clinics are most essential prophylactic agencies.

Insomnia may also prove most difficult to deal with. The unconsciousness which characterizes sleep and death are closely akin, and it is often the fear of death, of sinking into unconsciousness which prevents sleep. Tolstoy expressed it in this way: 'One must not be afraid of falling asleep if one wishes to avoid sleeplessness.' That is the underlying reason why so many patients refuse sedatives, fight against an anaesthetic or waken up suddenly once they have gone off to sleep. It is because of such doubts and fears that it is so important to establish a good *rapport*. It is only then that hypnotics will operate to the best advantage. Chloral hydrate is a safe, quick acting and effective hypnotic: it is prescribed usually in doses of 1·3 to 2 G. at night. Many barbiturates can be most efficacious. We suggest pentobarbitone sodium, B.P. (*Nembutal*), 100 to 200 mg.; cyclobarbitone, B.P., 200 to 400 mg.; quinalbarbitone, B.P. (*Seconal Sodium*), 50 to 100 mg. The action of barbiturate hypnotics may be potentiated by giving in addition chlorpromazine, 25 to 50 mg. at bedtime. Most depressed patients require also some daytime sedation: amylobarbitone sodium, 60 to 120 mg., or chlorpromazine, 25 to 50 mg., or trifluoperazine, 1 to 2 mg., may be given 8-hourly with much relief of their tension and agitation.

Both electrical convulsion therapy (E.C.T.) and the tricyclic antidepressant drugs are effective in the treatment of depressions. E.C.T., given usually twice weekly in a course of 6 to 12 treatments [see p. 322], is the most potent therapeutic agent which we have at present: in the management of the depressive psychoses the more severe the illness, the greater the suicidal risk is estimated to be, the more definitely is E.C.T. indicated. The clinical trial conducted by the Medical Research Council (1965) showed that in the treatment of depressive psychoses over the age of 40, E.C.T. more than doubled the placebo rate of recovery in the first month. After the 8th week and up to the 24th week of the trial period the results of treatment with imipramine (which has a slower action) were as good as those with E.C.T. Half of the patients who failed to respond satisfactorily to one month's treatment with imipramine, were found then to respond to E.C.T.

Of the anti depressant drugs, we have found imipramine, prescribed in doses of 25 to 50 mg. thrice daily, the most valuable. Amitriptyline, given in similar dosage, is also a useful drug. In the treatment of depressive psychoses the amine oxidase inhibitors are ineffective: in the M.R.C. trial phenelzine was no better than a placebo in the treatment of male depressives and gave less favourable results than the placebo in women. (For further details of these antidepressant drugs see p. 336).

The results of these physical treatments of depressive psychoses must be considered in relation to the natural tendency to recovery. In the M.R.C. trial, for example, about a third of the patients wholly or almost wholly lost their symptoms of depression in the first 4 weeks without any specific treatment apart from general care in hospital. But there is no doubt that in about 80 per cent. of cases E.C.T. and the antidepressant drugs most usefully control and diminish the intensity of the symptoms. E.C.T. may possibly shorten the course of a depressive psychosis, but there is no evidence that the tricyclic drugs can do this—one has to find by trial and error when it is possible to withdraw them without causing relapse. Neither E.C.T. nor the antidepressant drugs prevent or diminish the number of recurrences of manic-depressive attacks. Recent claims that maintenance treatment with lithium carbonate may act as a prophylactic against further attacks (Baastrup and Schou, 1967) have not yet been confirmed.

In the treatment of manic states, which if acute always require admission to a mental hospital, control of the excitement, restlessness and insomnia is of prime importance. The most useful drugs are chlorpromazine and haloperidol. Chlorpromazine may be given initially intramuscularly, in doses of 50 to 75 mg.: by mouth 150 to 300 mg. daily or more may be needed in the more acute cases. The dose of haloperidol is 5 mg. parenterally or 3 to 12 mg. daily by mouth (divided into two doses). Both these drugs are apt in such large doses to cause extrapyramidal symptoms. If the patient will take drugs by mouth, lithium carbonate may also be effective as a tranquillizer (Schou, 1963; Maggs, 1963), in a dosage of about 500 to 600 mg. twice daily. Lithium can be a dangerously toxic drug, producing amongst other side-effects vomiting, diarrhoea, muscular weakness, vertigo and drowsiness. It should be used only if the level of lithium in the patient's serum can be carefully controlled. In all cases of mania the patients' nutritional state must be carefully looked after: and as the excitement settles, normal outlets must be given for their abundant energy.

We have every reason to hope that further psychopharmacological research into the treatment of distressing emotional disturbances will lead to even greater therapeutic accuracy.

It is the use of such drugs plus electric convulsion therapy which has almost transformed the treatment of affective states. As a result hydrotherapy in its various forms has been discarded, and tube feeding is very rarely necessary.

Occupational therapy is an indispensable adjunct. It can be utilized, in one form or another, throughout the whole course of the illness, and even after the patient has returned home. It should be prescribed in consultation with the occupational therapist, and should be varied according to the particular interest or 'bent' of the patient. The essential point is to create co-operation, a sense of accomplishment, an ability to concentrate, and to persist in whatever is undertaken. It is not merely a matter of learning a new skill or handicraft, but it may be that greater satisfaction will be derived from work in the garden, the kitchen, workshop, laundry or other department. Others with literary and artistic interests are also catered for not only through the Occupational Therapy Department but also by the generous voluntary assistance of the British Red Cross Society and other organizations, some of whose peace-time activities are directed to increasing the amenity of life in a mental hospital. They provide an excellent library service, and choose appropriate works of art with which to decorate the hospital wards. The recreational and social side of hospital life is also incorporated, to a large extent, in the Occupational Therapy Department. Remedial exercises, dances and other types of entertainment, *e.g.* tennis parties, hockey, cricket, do much to build up a sense of well-being and good bodily health and fitness. The ready co-operation of the medical and nursing staff in all the above interests and activities adds enormously to the development of a therapeutic community.

Our main task in treatment, however, is to attempt to give the patient a better understanding of his personality than he has ever had previously. As Dr. Samuel Johnson said: 'Stay [with me] till I am well, and then you shall tell me how to cure myself.' To cure his symptoms is one thing, but a much higher achievement is to increase the patient's subjective sense of strength, confidence and well-being so that he can look forward to the future in a spirit of greater optimism. Our psychotherapeutic interviews are therefore based on good history-taking and on an investigation of all the relevant data. It is never wise to minimize the periodicity of this type of illness or its seriousness, but at the same time ways and means can be suggested whereby stress, fatigue and other untoward precipitants can be avoided. Furthermore, the assurance can be given that the disturbance of mood is a temporary disability, that the intellectual faculties will remain intact, that recovery from the attack will occur though the length of time can not be predicted. In order to avoid undue suffering the patient should be encouraged to seek expert help at the first indication of oncoming symptoms.

The above suggestions regarding treatment apply equally to the affective disorders occurring at the involutional period, e.g. involutional melancholia and chronic mania. But these latter forms are not nearly so recurrent as the manic-depressive states, and chronic mania may remain intractable.

During the process of convalescence everything possible should be done by nutritious diet, holidays, etc., to build up a state of mental and physical fitness. It is only when the patient has returned home and has resumed his former occupation that his complete confidence becomes re-established. A return to work, therefore, should not be too long delayed. (For details regarding physical methods of treatment and occupational therapy, see Chapters 14 and 20.)

REFERENCES

Ashcroft, G. W., Crawford, T. B. B., Eccleston, D., Sharman, D. F., MacDougall, E. J., Stanton, J. B., and Binns, J. K. (1966) *Lancet*, ii, 1049.
Astrup, C., Fossum, A., and Holmboe, R. (1959) *Acta psychiat. scand.*, Suppl. 135.
Baastrup, P. C., and Schou, M. (1967) *Arch. gen. Psychiat.*, **16**, 162.
Bowlby, J. (1961) *Int. J. Psycho-Anal.*, **42**, 317.
Coppen, A. (1967) *Brit. J. Psychiat.*, **113**, 1237.
Coppen, A., and Shaw, D. M. (1963) *Brit. med. J.*, **2**, 1439.
Coppen, A., and Shaw, D. M. (1967) *Lancet*, ii, 805.
Coppen, A., Shaw, D. M., Herzberg, B., and Maggs, R. (1967) *Lancet*, ii, 1178.
Coppen, A., Shaw, D. M., Malleson, A., Eccleston, E., and Grundy, A. (1965) *Brit. J. Psychiat.*, **111**, 993.
Coppen, A., Shaw, D. M., Malleson, A., and Costain, R. (1966) *Brit. med. J.*, **1**, 71.
Gibbons, J .L., and McHugh, P. (1962) *J. psychiat. Res.*, **1**, 162.
Hopkinson, G., and Reed, G. F. (1966) *Brit. J. Psychiat.*, **112**, 459.
Joyston-Bechal, M. P. (1966) *Brit. J. Psychiat.*, **112**, 967.
Kallmann, F. J. (1953) *Heredity in Health and Mental Disorder*, New York.
Kiloh, L. G., and Garside, R. F. (1963) *Brit. J. Psychiat.*, **109**, 451.

R

Kraines, S. H. (1934) *Amer. J. Psychiat.*, **91**, 29.
MacCurdy, J. T. (1925) *Psychology of Emotion*, London.
Maggs, R. (1963) *Brit. J. Psychiat.*, **109**, 56.
Medical Research Council (1965) *Brit. med. J.*, **1**, 881.
Muncie, W. (1963) *J. Canad. Psychiat. Ass.*, **8**, 217.
Munro, A. (1966) *Brit. J. Psychiat.*, **112**, 443.
Rosanoff, A. J., Handy, L. M., and Plesset, I. R. (1935) *Amer. J. Psychiat.*, **91**, 725.
Sachar, E. J. (1967) *Arch. gen. Psychiat.*, **17**, 554.
Schou, M. (1963) *Brit. J. Psychiat.*, **109**, 803.
Shaw, D. M., and Coppen, A. (1966) *Brit. J. Psychiat.*, **112**, 269.
Stenstedt, A. (1952) *Acta psychiat. scand.*, Suppl. 79.
Stenstedt, A. (1959) *Acta psychiat. (Kbh.)*, Suppl. 127.
Stenstedt, A. (1966) *Acta psychiat. scand.*, **42**, 392.
Tod, E. D. M. (1964) *Brit. med. J.*, **2**, 1264.
Wertham, F. I. (1929) *Amer. J. Psychiat.*, **9**, 17.

11

SCHIZOPHRENIC REACTION-TYPES

Schizophrenia, in its most typical form, consists in a slow deterioration of the entire personality, which often manifests itself at the period of adolescence. It involves a great part of the mental life, and expresses itself in disorder of feeling, of conduct, and of thought, and in an increasing withdrawal of interest from the environment.

The term schizophrenia is more applicable than the term dementia praecox to the group of cases now to be described. In 1896 Kraepelin first made his differentiation between manic-depressive psychosis and 'dementia praecox'. The differentiation was of great importance, but the name given to the reaction-type was unfortunate. Many of these patients did not show a permanent dementia, and many became ill outside the adolescent period. The term dementia praecox furthermore implied usually a rather hopeless prognosis, and encouraged therapeutic nihilism.

In 1911 Bleuler introduced the term 'schizophrenia' for these dementia praecox cases and for others which he considered to be allied—paranoid states, hallucinoses and prison psychoses; and in doing so stressed the importance of splitting of the different psychic functions. Bleuler's was a wider conception than Kraepelin's: 'We designate a group of psychoses whose course is at times chronic, at times marked by intermittent attacks, and which can stop or retrograde at any stage, but does not permit a full restitutio ad integrum'. He used the term schizophrenia in the singular, but was in no doubt that he was dealing with a group of several diseases. The symptoms of schizophrenia he divided into two classes, the fundamental and the accessory or secondary. The fundamental symptoms Bleuler considered to be disturbances of association and affectivity, a predilection for phantasy as against reality, and a tendency to divorce from reality (autism). Hallucinations, delusions, illusions and catatonic symptoms he called secondary, while conceding that these were the symptoms which often made manifest the psychosis and caused the patient to be hospitalized.

There has been little advance in the classification of this reaction-type since Kraepelin and Bleuler, and their descriptive work has not been superseded. Both Kraepelin and Bleuler believed that schizophrenia was the outcome of a pathological, anatomical or chemical disturbance of the brain.

The point of view adopted by Adolf Meyer differed considerably from that held by the purely pathological and anatomical investigators. Meyer did not by any means disregard the latter, but rather sought to include, in a general biological formulation of schizophrenia, whatever is of established value in the field of physical pathology. The essence of his view was that schizophrenia is the outcome of progressive maladaptation of the individual to his environment. Schizophrenia is not a 'disease', but a congeries of individual types of reaction having certain general similarities. 'We must consider mental illness, not in terms of clean-cut groups, but of reaction types.' The individual may be loaded in various ways—by inheritance, by physical defects of an endocrine disorder or some grosser kind, by intellectual deficiency, or what not—but none of them is in itself a sufficient cause of schizophrenia. It is only when the subject, whether handicapped or not, has to face the usual concrete problems in his journey through life that reactions can appear which cumulatively lead to one of the numerous conditions which have been included under the designation of 'dementia praecox' or 'schizophrenia'. It was from a careful study of patients, and especially of their history before any breakdown was recognized by friends or relatives—a line of investigation commonly neglected—that Meyer concluded that 'schizophrenia' is the end result of an accumulation of faulty habits of reaction.

The healthy attitude to life's difficulties and problems is a direct, aggressive, matter-of-fact one, designed to overcome the difficulty once and for all, with the result that the individual feels satisfied, and can proceed confidently to his next problem. On the other hand, the individual may shrink from facing the situation directly, and may temporize in the hope that something will turn up, or that the matter will be decided for him. In other instances he may evade the necessity for definite action by indulging in some substitute, which is never satisfactory; for example, if unsuccessful in work, he may indulge in day-dreams of wealth; or if unable to face the responsibilities of marriage, he may take to sex ruminations or to auto-erotic habits. A sense of failure is no longer combated by renewed efforts, but by brooding over troubles and by blaming others. Such reactions, occurring only occasionally, are within normal limits; but if they become so frequent as to be habitual, they lead to inefficiency and social maladaptation, so that the individual exhibiting them comes to be regarded as abnormal. Certain kinds of faulty reaction are especially pernicious, such as hypochondriacal trends— blaming one's health for one's failures—ideas of suspicion or actual fault-finding, phantastic religious motives and persistent brooding and seclusiveness. Reactions which are not morbid when used sparingly and in certain circumstances may become diffused over the whole conduct, and are increasingly used because, being habitual, they are easier than anything else. Negativism, for example, is healthy enough as mere stubbornness in certain directions; but when it extends to every activity as an 'uncontrollable blocking factor' it becomes pathological, and constitutes what has hitherto been called a mental 'disease'.

Since the Second World War, particularly in the U.S.A., the concept of schizophrenia has been enlarged; in our opinion, without sufficient justification. Hoch and Polatin (1949), in an influential paper, introduced the term 'pseudo-neurotic' schizophrenia, describing a condition of persistent tension with multiple and changing neurotic symptoms, which is characterized further by a proneness to develop transient psychotic episodes and which may pass later into unequivocal schizophrenia. Other terms have been used for apparently the same kind of case: for example, 'borderline states', 'abortive' and 'latent' schizophrenia. Usually the presence of a thought disorder is considered to be a necessary criterion for the diagnosis: but the nature of this thought disorder is by some authors left vague and is variously described by many others. Egocentricity, coldness of feeling, inability to develop normal personal relationships, poor work record, and a failure to respond to psychotherapy, are frequently described: these features are said to be persistent, and a progressive and lasting deterioration unusual. This description suggests that many of these cases would be more correctly described as suffering from psychopathic states. Their close relationship to schizophrenia has not been established. It is of course common experience that many cases of schizophrenia, particularly those of insidious onset, begin with the development of neurotic symptoms: but these do not form a distinct group and need not be given a special label.

Langfeldt (1952), from the University Clinic of Oslo, has been prominent amongst those who have deplored any widening of the classical concept of schizophrenia. Langfeldt accepts the Kraepelinian sub-groups of schizophrenia; while noting that the paranoid cases seem to be of mixed aetiology, multiform symptomatology and very variable course. He proposes in addition that cases which seem to fall into the category of schizophrenia should initially be divided into two other sub-groups, according to whether they appear to be typical or atypical: one group he calls typical, genuine schizophrenias, the other schizo-phreniform psychoses. The former, nuclear group shows pre-illness personality deviation and the schizophrenia develops mainly endogenously with dominant feelings of depersonalization (feelings of influence and passivity) and derealiza-tion: these symptoms, with massive primary ideas of persecution and catatonic stuporous features, he calls 'process' symptoms. Such cases mostly carry a poor prognosis and are prone to dement early. The atypical, schizophreniform group, on the other hand, is said to be heterogeneous: the pre-illness personality is not schizoid, exogenous factors are often prominent, and the symptomatology is mixed, with clouding or strong affective features and without process symptoms. This group carries a better prognosis on the whole, though some cases in the group turn out to be dementing schizophrenics: others prove to be cases of affective psychosis or neurotic or organic reactions.

Langfeldt's call for greater discrimination in diagnosis is to be welcomed, and research would be more profitable if it were heeded: but it is doubtful if his clinical designation of a specific schizophreniform group brings any advantage. That many of his schizophreniform cases reveal themselves later as definitely schizophrenic, seems to demonstrate that his concept of the typical group is too narrow: while if the category were generally accepted, many cases would no doubt find their way into this schizophreniform group not so much because of their near resemblance to schizophrenia but because diagnostic acumen is often lacking. For example, there would be little to be said in favour of calling a case of mixed affective psychosis schizophreniform on the grounds that the individual is hallucinated, perplexed and his affect variable; except that to do so would be better than calling it schizophrenia.

The term 'schizo-affective psychosis' has probably created more diagnostic difficulties than it has resolved. Certainly in many cases of schizophrenia there are prominent affective symptoms: particularly depression, in the illnesses of more acute onset. A mixture of manic and schizophrenic symptoms is much rarer. In some of these cases of mixed symptomatology the patient appears to have developed at the same time a schizophrenic and an affective psychosis; in others, where the affective symptoms colour the clinical picture but are not so prominent, one can find a sufficient explanation for them in that they can be linked with the traits of the pre-morbid personality or understood as psychogenic reactions to other distressing or alarming symptoms of the disease. In a small number of cases a schizo-affective psychosis appears to be a clinical entity showing a familial distribution, is inherited as a Mendelian dominant and is probably distinct from schizophrenia (Leonhard, 1939). Much more often the term schizo-affective psychosis is a misnomer, applied to cases of mixed affective psychosis in which the admixture of depressive and manic symptoms has given rise to some apparent incongruity of affect; and the perplexity and difficulty of thinking have been wrongly diagnosed as evidence of schizophrenic thought disorder with blocking. These mixed affective psychoses are not rare, and are much more often misdiagnosed as schizophrenia than is schizophrenia mistaken for an affective psychosis.

Research into the many problems posed by schizophrenia has been frustrated by doubts and uncertainties about the heterogeneity of the clinical material being studied. Possibly the majority of observers now think that schizophrenia is not a clinical entity but a group of syndromes, of different aetiologies though with similarities in their clinical features: yet research has usually proceeded on the assumption that a biological entity was being investigated. The varieties of schizophrenia shortly to be described are clinical groupings of symptoms, they have no known pathological basis: but it might well now be more profitable to select for biochemical research these clinical subdivisions rather than schizophrenia as a whole, and particularly the most typical cases of hebephrenia and catatonia.

AETIOLOGY

Heredity

The evidence from genetic studies is clearly that hereditary factors are important in the majority of cases of schizophrenia. Some psychiatrists already hold it to be established that schizophrenia is an inherited biochemical disorder determined by a gene-specific type of enzyme deficiency. Major contributions to the genetic study of schizophrenia have been made by Luxenburger, Rosanoff, Essen-Möller, Kallmann and Slater.

Kallmann (1953) stated that his very large clinical material showed clearly that the chance of developing a schizophrenic psychosis increases in direct proportion to the degree of blood relationship to a schizophrenic individual. From an analysis of nearly one thousand twin index families he reported that the total expectancy of schizophrenia varies from 7·1 per cent. for half-sibs, through 14 per cent. for full sibs and two-egg co-twins, to 86·2 per cent. for one-egg twin partners. The expectancy rate for schizophrenia in the normal population is 0·85 per cent. For the children of one schizophrenic parent the expectancy is 16·4 per cent.; of two schizophrenic parents, 68·1 per cent.—that is, the children of two schizophrenic parents have the second highest expectancy of the disease, next to one-egg co-twins. These expectancy rates, which Kallmann recorded for the blood relatives of schizophrenics, could not, he believed, be explained in terms of increasing similarity of environment. 'About one-quarter of one-egg pairs have been found to develop schizophrenic psychoses in the absence of similar environments, while close to one-half of two-egg pairs remain discordant despite similar environments.'

With regard to the mode of hereditary transmission, Kallmann held to the hypothesis of recessive inheritance. He did so mainly on the grounds that the distribution of schizophrenia in affected families shows that schizophrenia is transmitted in the collateral rather than in the direct line of descent, and that there is an excess of consanguineous marriages among the parents of schizophrenics: he reported that in the U.S.A. approximately 5 per cent. of schizophrenics were the offspring of consanguineous marriages. Kallmann noted that the children of schizophrenics have a higher expectancy of schizophrenia than the sibs, and that this was not what one would expect if the disease was recessive. He suggested that this apparent discrepancy might be due to a selective process of 'negative mate selection—the unlikelihood of actual or potential schizophrenics having a normal chance to select their mates'.

Kallmann believed that in some homozygotes the genotype is completely inhibited, so that the individual is normal: some schizoid personalities are probably inhibited homozygotes also, while others may be heterozygotes. Kallmann also suggested that the apparently wide differences in the penetrance and expressivity of the schizophrenic genotype may be interpreted as being controlled by genetically non-specific constitutional defence mechanisms, which possibly are related to the effect of certain mesodermal tissue elements.

The hypothesis of simple recessive inheritance of schizophrenia has been criticized by a number of other authorities, mainly because if the condition is recessively inherited the frequency of schizophrenia should be greater among the sibs than among their children. But no other genetic theory, monogenic or polygenic, fits the facts better. That the mode of inheritance is not more obvious may be due to the fact that a heterogeneous clinical material has been investigated —the schizophrenias, that is, rather than schizophrenia.

Slater (1953) critically reviewed the literature of twin studies in schizophrenia and reported on a large series of twins personally investigated: of 297 pairs the propositus was schizophrenic in 158 cases. He found a concordance rate for schizophrenia of 76 per cent. in uniovular twins, and of 14 per cent. in binovular twins. While there were wide differences in the severity of the illness within concordant uniovular pairs, taking all pairs of affected relatives together there was a significant degree of resemblance in the course of their illness and the type of onset: but not in the outcome. The facts suggested, Slater commented, 'that genetical causes provide a potentiality for schizophrenia, perhaps an essential one, though environmental factors play a substantial rôle, which may be decisive in the individual case. Those environmental factors which affect personality and constitution appear to be the most important.'

The high concordance rates for schizophrenia in monozygotic twins reported by Luxenburger, Rosanoff, Kallmann and Slater, ranging from 67 to 86 per cent., have been subjected to various criticisms and there have been some contrary findings. The highest concordance rates, recorded by Kallmann, may have been inflated by too wide a clinical concept of schizophrenia, and possibly also by errors in sampling, in the establishment of zygosity and in the statistical techniques used in calculating morbidity risk. Much lower or nil concordance rates have been reported from Scandinavia by Tienari (1963) and Kringlen (1964). Of Tienari's 16 monozygotic twin pairs with a schizophrenic proband, all were discordant for schizophrenia: but 6 of the co-twins were diagnosed as neurotic. Of Kringlen's 8 male monozygotic twins, 6 were discordant for schizophrenia: but in 4 of these 6 cases the non-schizophrenic twin was notably unstable—one drank too much, another was described as schizothymic, a third as suspicious and unapproachable, and a fourth as sensitive and prone to depressive reactions.

Concordance for schizophrenia in monozygotic twins is, as one would expect, higher in the more severe cases: *i.e.* in those in whom the diagnosis is least likely to be in doubt. This is borne out by a recent study by Gottesman and Shields (1966) who investigated at the Maudsley-Bethlem Hospital 57 twin pairs of whom one twin at least had a diagnosis of schizophrenia. Seventy-nine per cent. of the monozygotic co-twins of schizophrenics were found to be abnormal psychiatrically to some degree: the rate for the dizygotic co-twins was 46 per cent. Defining severity as over two years in hospital, they diagnosed 77 per cent. of the monozygotic co-twins of 'severe' schizophrenics as themselves schizophrenic; contrasted with only 27 per cent. of the monozygotic co-twins of 'mild' schizophrenics. Corresponding figures for the small sample of dizygotic probands were 15 per cent. and 10 per cent. Gottesman and Shields summed up: 'From the fact that the identical twin of a schizophrenic is at least 42 times as likely to be schizophrenic as a person from the general population, and a fraternal twin of the same sex 9 times as likely, it would appear that genetic factors are largely responsible for the specific nature of most of the schizophrenias.'

While the mode of inheritance, whether monogenic or polygenic, is still uncertain, it seems to be established that genetic influences play a major rôle in the aetiology of schizophrenia.

Environmental Factors

The rate of concordance for schizophrenia in uniovular twins is not 100 per cent. The genetic studies quoted above indicate that inherited determinants are not all-important: and there is evidence that social factors, in the family and in the *milieu* of an urban civilization, may play some part in the aetiology.

The Family Environment. Psychotherapists who were treating schizophrenics analytically became interested naturally in the early relationships of their patients to their mothers: and by the late 1940's the concept of a 'schizophrenogenic mother' had gained wide currency in the United States. The typical mother of a schizophrenic was held to be severely rejecting, and the subsequent distortion of the mother-child relationship was believed to have much aetiological significance. Tietze (1949), for example, found the mothers of schizophrenics dominating, over-anxious and obsessive, covertly rejecting and often frigid. Much of this work was, however, based only on clinical impressions. At the same time maternal rejection was commonly believed to produce types of deviation other than schizophrenia.

This interest in the mothers of schizophrenics subsequently widened into several important researches into the nature of the total family environment in which schizophrenic breakdowns develop. The investigations by Lidz and his colleagues (1949, 1956, 1957) at Yale have been amongst the most careful of these studies. They reported initially on a group of 50 young schizophrenics. Only 5 of these patients were considered to have been raised in homes which seemed reasonably favourable and which contained two stable and compatible parents until the patient was 18 years of age. Broken homes, unstable parents and an unusual pattern of child rearing appeared to be almost the rule. Later, investigating more intensively in 16 middle-class families the intra-familiar environment in which schizophrenia had developed, Lidz and his colleagues reached the conclusion that 'serious pathology of the family environment is the most consistent finding pertaining to the aetiology of schizophrenia'. These researchers have found abnormalities wherever they have looked in the schizophrenic's family. The marital relationship of the parents is reported to be seriously disturbed, in one of two ways: either there is chronic disequilibrium, with derogation and undercutting of the marital partner and threats of separation ('marital discord'); or one spouse is dominant and imposes his or her psychopathology on the masochistic partner, who achieves some marital peace by submission ('marital skew'). The schizophrenic's father, they report, tends either to be a passive nonentity; or to sabotage his wife in her rôle as a mother, being himself motivated by jealousy of a son or by a wish to mould a daughter after his own arbitrary fashion.

These researches by Lidz and his colleagues cannot be said to be definitive. The work has lacked controls and suffers from the weaknesses inherent in all retrospective studies. It has stressed effects of environment in the explanation of facts which might be better explained in terms of inheritance. But it has been of considerable value in placing the schizophrenic in his home setting, in raising questions about the mental normality of the heterozygous parents, and in stressing the importance of the complex personal interactions which take place in the schizophrenic's family whether as causes or effects of his illness. It has drawn attention to an aspect which is too often neglected in the investigation and treatment of schizophrenic patients; namely their families, from whom we can always glean a great deal of relevant information, whose co-operation we must enlist if our plans for management are not to miscarry, and to whom, good or bad, stable or unstable, our patients will in most instances return. Brown (1967) has reviewed other studies of the family of the schizophrenic patient.

Heston (1966) in Oregon, U.S.A., has endeavoured specifically to separate the effects of an environment rendered 'schizophrenogenic' by a schizophrenic mother, from the genetic results for the child of having a schizophrenic mother. He studied adults who had been separated from their mothers in the first few days of life: 47 of them had had schizophrenic mothers, 50 (controls) had not. Schizophrenia was found only in the children of schizophrenic mothers. Five of those born to the 47 schizophrenic mothers became schizophrenic, while others were described as being schizoid psychopaths. The probability of this being a chance segregation of schizophrenia is less than 0·025; and the results of this investigation tend therefore to confirm the genetic aetiology of schizophrenia.

The Wider Social Environment. There is a disproportionate number of cases of schizophrenia amongst those of low socio-economic status both in Britain and in the U.S.A., but there is as yet no evidence pointing unequivocally to specific injurious social factors outside the family which may cause schizophrenia. Elements of the urban social environment and social stresses may contribute to schizophrenic breakdowns, may act as precipitants of such breakdowns in predisposed individuals, and may complicate the ascertainment, treatment of, and recovery from the illness; but our present evidence suggests that the rôle of such factors is usually of secondary importance in the aetiology.

In Chapter 4 attention has been drawn to the work of Faris and Dunham, Gerard and Houston, and Hare on the influence of neighbourhood on schizophrenic breakdowns. Here the important researches of Hollingshead and Redlich (1958) must get further mention. Schizophrenia was the most common mental illness in their New Haven, Connecticut, population, at all class levels: schizophrenics comprised 59 per cent. of the psychotic patients. The rate of schizophrenia per 100,000 of this urban population was for social classes I–II, 111; for class III, 168; for class IV, 300; and for social class V, 895. Hollingshead and Redlich state that their data support the conclusion that 'neither geographic transiency nor downward social mobility can account for the sharp differences in the distribution of schizophrenic patients from one class to another'. Ninety-one per cent. of their schizophrenic patients were in the same social class as their families: only 1·3 per cent. were in a lower class, 4·4 per cent. were in a higher class. Eighty-nine per cent. of the class V patients came from class V families: and they had lived in the slums all their lives. Neither was there any linkage between schizophrenia and international migration (immigration was the largest geographical movement in this population). Hollingshead and Redlich therefore support the conclusion of Faris and Dunham that schizophrenic patients committed to mental hospitals from slum areas have not drifted there as an effect of their illness.

In a detailed study of family and class dynamics in 50 cases which formed part of the New Haven research, Myers and Roberts (1959) produced some evidence that certain conditions of life in social class V may be conducive to the development of schizophrenia, by causing isolation and withdrawal. They did not suggest that social class position is a direct cause of schizophrenia, but only that life at a certain social level may expose the potential patient to certain potent stresses. They found that the developing individual in social class V is more exposed than people in other social classes both to adverse economic conditions and to social isolation from community institutions. They found also that he tends to be reared in a family environment where there is little affection, protection and stability: and they link this with the proneness of the adult in this social class to feel 'neglected, rejected, exploited and trapped by unfortunate circumstances'. Furthermore, they report that both intra-familial and community stresses bear more heavily on schizophrenic than on neurotic patients, both in class III and in class V. Myers and Roberts are cautious in their formulations, emphasizing the exploratory nature of their studies and suggesting that their results should be regarded as hypotheses for future research.

In the U.S.A. schizophrenia has been reported to be nearly ten times as frequent in social class V as in the upper two social classes. A similar great social class difference in the incidence of schizophrenia has been found in Britain, where schizophrenia preponderates amongst the unskilled young men of the lowest social class and is concentrated in two occupational groups, kitchen hands and labourers: Brooke (1959) reporting these facts, comments that in both these occupations we should expect to find a high proportion of casual labour and they might prove suitable temporary occupations for the unstable. The ratio of class V to class I rates for schizophrenia reported by Brooke were 4·2 for first admissions and 6·7 for other admissions. Goldberg and Morrison (1963) investigated further this relationship between schizophrenia and social class and their findings, which seem to be very soundly based, are different to those of Hollingshead and Redlich. In a survey of a national sample of male schizophrenics aged 25–34 on their first admission to a mental hospital in England and Wales they found the usual excess of patients in social class V. In contrast, the social class distribution of the fathers at the time of the patients' birth was similar to that of the general population. A complementary clinical study of young male schizophrenics confirmed the findings of a social drift downwards in this illness, of a decline in occupational status both from father to son and in the patient's own history. Goldberg and Morrison are therefore of the opinion— which seems inescapable—that gross socio-economic deprivation is unlikely to be of major aetiological importance in schizophrenia. Dunham and his colleagues in the U.S.A. (1966) have come to similar conclusions. A further interesting finding by Goldberg and Morrison was that social drift appeared to affect schizophrenics from the highest and lowest social classes most severely: so that there may be occupational factors, not yet defined, which exert some influence on the course of the illness.

Precipitating Factors

Exciting factors in the sense of immediate precipitants of the illness are often apparently absent; but a certain proportion of cases begin in association with such stresses as toxic-infectious illness, pregnancy and (more often) the puerperium, domestic unhappiness, love affairs and financial difficulties. During both World Wars, schizophrenic cases of acute onset were encountered which appeared to have been definitely precipitated by war stresses, and which were both of a simpler form and had a better prognosis than the average.

Model Psychoses

There have been various attempts to elucidate the obscure aetiology of this disease by inducing what have been called 'model psychoses' in normal subjects. Some of these experiments have produced psychological data of much importance, but they have thrown little direct light on the genesis of schizophrenia. So-called model psychoses have been produced in two ways: by administering hallucinogenic drugs, and by sensory deprivation.

The hallucinogenic (or psychotomimetic) drugs most often employed have been mescaline and lysergic acid (LSD 25). The effects of lysergic acid, an ergot derivative, have been particularly interesting because they are produced by minute quantities of the drug. These drugs, given to the normal subject, cause changes in attention and affect, as well as hallucinations. Typically, the individual's attention is abnormally arrested by his immediate environment; he becomes anxious, depressed or euphoric; and he has visual hallucinations, which may be coloured or monochrome, take mosaic or graticule forms or consist of human or landscape content. Synaesthesiae may be reported. These phenomena occur in a setting of clear or nearly clear consciousness: insight is retained and behaviour is usually not disturbed. Perhaps the individual under the influence of a hallucinogenic drug has some experience like a schizophrenic's: but the 'model psychosis' which is produced by this means belongs to the classical organic reaction-type, since, if the dose of the drug is increased, the subject becomes delirious.

Sensory deprivation may be produced experimentally by shutting the individual into a cubicle (Heron et al., 1953), where he lies on a couch with frosted goggles over his eyes, sponge-rubber pads over his ears, his arms splinted and his extremities swaddled; or by immersing him in a tank of water at body temperature (Lilly, 1956). These experiences proved more unpleasant than they sound and became intolerable after 24–72 hours. The subjects reported a craving for stimulation, became abnormally restless, and later developed visual hallucinations, alterations in body image and, occasionally, fleeting paranoid delusions. The resemblance to schizophrenia of the symptoms produced by sensory deprivation may be closer than the effects produced by drugs, though they are somewhat similar to the latter: but there is no real evidence that sensory deprivation phenomena are a paradigm of schizophrenia. These experiments seem in fact to have thrown some light on the mechanisms of schizophrenia in a direction opposite to what was originally intended, since Harris (1959) has found that a small group of schizophrenics were more tolerant than normal of sensory deprivation for short periods in a soundproof cubicle: it seemed to reduce the intensity of their hallucinations and to render these less troublesome.

The psychological aspects of phantasticants and the relationship between experimental and social isolation have been discussed by Mowbray (1958).

In summary of this section, we can say that the aetiology of schizophrenia challengingly remains to be fully elucidated. It appears to be a disease or group of diseases, mainly caused by unknown abnormal organic processes which are genetically determined. We are still wholly ignorant of the mode of action of the pathological gene or genes which we suppose are responsible for its diverse symptomatology and its often malignant course.

CLINICAL FEATURES

Schizophrenia affects particularly adolescents and young adults. It has been estimated that two-thirds of the cases occur between the 15th and 30th year, and the maximum incidence is reached about the 25th year. Few cases begin after the age of 40. The incidence in the general population in England and Wales is approximately 1·1 per cent. by the age of 55 (Slater). Schizophrenia is the diagnosis of about three-quarters of the long-term patients in mental hospitals in this country, and it appears to have a world-wide distribution. It constitutes one of the most serious disease problems of Western civilization.

Mode of Onset and Previous Personality

In a small number of cases, particularly those showing catatonic features, the onset of the illness may be comparatively acute. More usually, and in contrast to the affective psychoses, schizophrenia develops slowly and insidiously over a long period of months or years. In the vast majority of cases a close analysis of the history shows that the patient has exhibited peculiarities and oddities which perhaps did not seem to have any special significance until the grosser symptoms presented themselves. We believe, therefore, that close attention should be paid to obtaining very complete records of the development of the patient, and that the idiosyncrasies and perversities of childhood should be carefully scanned, because by so doing we may be able to determine traits which are likely to be followed by more serious symptoms. We would particularly emphasize the importance of noting such traits as day-dreaming, fears, solitariness, undue sensitivity, and bashfulness.

It is often difficult to fix a time of onset of the psychosis. It seems to develop more or less from the habits of reaction cultivated by the patient on his way through life. These habits make up in great part the 'personality' of the patient as it was before they were sufficiently developed to constitute a socially recognizable illness. Meyer and Hoch emphasized the frequency with which this psychosis develops in certain types of handicapped personality, especially in the 'shut-in', shy, seclusive type. The same general type of personality has been described by other authors by other names; for example, by Bleuler as 'schizoid', in contrast with the 'syntonic' or 'cycloid' personality in which, if mental illness develops, it tends to be of the manic-depressive kind. Farrar distinguished five main types of 'shut-in' personality: 1. the 'backward' type, lacking ambition, absent-minded, often playing truant; 2. the 'precocious' type, the bookish, serious, prudish, 'model' child; 3. the 'neurotic' variety, selfish and deceitful, with headaches and other minor ailments, and temper-tantrums; 4. the 'asocial'—seclusive and day-dreaming; and 5. the 'juvenile' type, which never seems to grow up.

Kringlen (1964), in his study of 6 monozygotic discordant twin pairs of whom one member of the pair had developed schizophrenia, found that in all cases but one the pre-schizophrenic twin had in childhood presented neurotic symptoms—phobias, stuttering, nocturnal enuresis and marked sensitivity; as well as being 'gentler' and more 'obedient'. These differences in temperament were also shown beyond puberty, the twin who was to become schizophrenic being more introvert, inhibited, sensitive and dependent.

In at least half the cases there is this special type of schizoid personality, probably partly inborn and partly acquired, out of which the psychosis develops. The morbidly sensitive individual may, for example, become worried about masturbation or a homosexual experience, and go on for years ruminating about it till his feelings of guilt, no longer bearable, come to be projected, first as ideas of reference and later as delusions and hallucinations. The guilty feeling may be treated in other ways—the patient goes into an ecstasy in which he feels himself forgiven, or (rarely) attempts expiation by castrating himself.

A clinical example will help to illustrate the gradual development of a schizophrenic illness as an accumulation of mental reactions.

CASE No. 21

Q. M., who was admitted to the Glasgow Royal Mental Hospital at the age of 26, was reported to have been always 'nervous'. He had stuttered at the age of 15, and as the consequence of a fright, when he had been left alone in a schoolroom, he was kept away from school for a year. He was easily led by companions, and very obedient to his parents. Once at school his teacher had drawn his face on the board and said it was 'like the moon'. He remembered this bitterly, and his personal appearance became an increasingly sensitive point. Partly as the result of this, he was shy, and felt 'like a kind of clown' in company. When he left school at 16, he was apprenticed as an engineer, but as he developed Raynaud's symptoms his over-solicitous parents considered the work unsuitable. Aged 18 he enlisted, and was discharged three years later, but he saw no active service, having spent most of his time in hospital on account of a supposed heart lesion. On his discharge he had an operation for cervical adenitis. He became increasingly preoccupied about his health, so that if he read a book in which a disease was mentioned he at once imagined that he had that disease. At 22 he courted a girl, but 'I felt if I kept it up I'd go wrong in my head'. He ceased seeing the girl, concentrated on his work and felt better for a time. This failure only increased his general sense of insufficiency. 'I never felt I was just a man. I wasn't taking my right place. I was going about things apologetic. I could never talk right clear. I could never take the place I should have taken according to my age. . . . I never let myself go—for fighting or anything like that or taking up with a girl.' After discharge from the Army he had worked for his father, but his anxious preoccupation about his health, his sensitiveness about his appearance and his general feeling of dissatisfaction with himself interfered so much with his concentration that his head 'buzzed', and he had done no work for ten months before admission to hospital. After leaving off work, his preoccupation increased, he became more and more depressed about himself, and more and more secretive, so that he did not wish to see any one, thought everyone was looking at him, and hinted at suicide. When admitted to hospital he was quiet and co-operative, but very jerky in speech and movements, hesitating in the middle of sentences as if his thoughts had been interrupted. Soon he began to express definite persecutory ideas. He was 'being made an example of', and to 'appear the biggest fool in the world'. Finally, there was 'a system being worked' against him. His conduct became impulsive —he escaped over the garden wall, and returned voluntarily, saying he thought 'a race might do him good'. Within four months of admission hallucinations appeared, and at times mutism, verbigeration and flexibilitas cerea. Physically, there was no evidence of organic disease.

This patient shows very well how faulty habits of reaction—shyness, sensitiveness, plastic obedience to others, extreme consciousness of inferiority (based on his physical appearance, his clumsiness of address and of speech and the remarks of others) and hypochondriacal preoccupation—can lead to invalidism and then to inactivity, depression and ideas of reference, and finally to delusions, hallucinations, impulsiveness, automatic obedience, mutism and verbigeration. These, in fact, are the 'symptoms' of the so-called 'catatonic' form of schizophrenia.

TYPES OF SCHIZOPHRENIA

Kraepelin first differentiated three principal types, which he termed hebephrenic, catatonic and paranoid; later he added a fourth, termed simplex. In the last edition of his textbook he added numerous other forms, *e.g.* simple depressive, delusional, circular and agitated. No useful purpose is served by a multiplication of such sub-groups. The main groups are reasonably distinctive, but even these are not clear cut, there are admixtures and transitions, and one could if one wished form almost as many groups as there are affected individuals.

Paranoid symptoms may be present in any type of schizophrenia, in the same way that they may be found as secondary features in many other reaction-types, in delirium for example, or in a depressive psychosis or in senile dementia. The term paranoid schizophrenia is no more required to designate such cases than the term paranoid delirium is required for a delirium in which the patient is suspicious. On the other hand, paranoid symptoms may dominate the clinical picture of an apparently schizophreniform psychosis. Where they do, the reaction is in most cases in our opinion much more closely allied to other paranoid psychotic reaction (paranoia, paraphrenia) and should be considered and classified with the latter. We therefore make a clear distinction between schizophrenic psychoses and paranoid psychoses, while recognizing that paranoid symptoms may occur in the former and that there may be cases which are difficult to classify neatly in one group or the other. Our reasons for making the above suggestion may be summarized as follows: paranoid psychoses—

1. develop later in life than schizophrenia, *e.g.* at 35 years, or over;
2. are symptomatically more homogeneous and do not show the same mutual transitions and admixtures as other types of schizophrenia do;
3. have a strong affective component, often of a transitory or cyclical nature, which may be responsive to treatment;
4. rarely exhibit the gross intellectual and emotional deterioration which is so characteristic of schizophrenia.

We suggest therefore that the sub-types of schizophrenia should be limited to the simple, hebephrenic and catatonic forms.

SYMPTOMATOLOGY

The detailed symptomatology is extraordinarily varied, but there are certain groups of symptoms which stand out more prominently than the others, and are common to all the varieties. A most prominent symptom is the failure of affect, or emotional blunting, showing itself in apathy and indifference. This description applies more definitely to cases of some duration. In the early stages the affect may be lively enough, and even in advanced cases there are sometimes more evidences pointing to affective activity than would, on the surface, be suspected. The emotional deterioration leads to a state of mental facility, in which the patient is, up to a point, easily suggestible, and his conduct is more easily affected by those in contact with him. On the surface one gets the impression of a certain mild depression and feeling of failure. The patient does not seem to appreciate joy or sorrow or fear, but his attitude is rather one of indifference to his condition, and 'I don't care' or 'I don't know' is a frequently repeated phrase. Associated with this is a certain dreaminess and a lack of contact with reality; the patient lives a life with which his relatives and his doctor cannot get in touch. The apathy and lack of interest are usually so marked that active attention to any specific problem is fleeting. On the other hand, passive attention is remarkably good, so that he may remember long afterwards events of which he had seemed to take no notice. Such patients may be induced to do some purely mechanical type of work, something which they can pursue without interfering unduly with their ruminations. Another impressive feature is the disharmony between the mood and the thought. It is this more than anything else that distinguishes schizophrenia from other types of mental disorder. Schizophrenic patients may express, without any show of emotion, ideas which in the ordinary person would produce remorse, or pity, or profound depression. Situations in which they find themselves, which would normally have a profound emotional value—as, for example, being placed in a mental hospital—are by them met with indifference. Frequently there are sudden, causeless outbursts of laughter, and a stereotyped, silly, smiling attitude, in which there is no real mirth or hilarity.

The disharmony revealed in these ways between mood and thought is not the only indication of a deep-seated psychic change. There is a general disintegration of all the mental functions, resulting in the appearance of queerness and oddity which is so striking to the ordinary observer. In part at least this disintegration resembles that seen in cases of cerebral disease—in temporal lobe epilepsy, for example, and in organic dementia. Chapman (1966) from a study of young schizophrenic patients adduced a good deal of clinical evidence which suggests a widespread organic impairment of mental functions, involving attention, perception, memory, motility and speech. Thought blocking (see below), for example, he interprets as 'transient disturbances in consciousness which develop in association with a failure to exclude irrelevant stimulation from internal and external sources'. Chapman reports that these various phenomena, which may be episodic and fleeting, are experienced subjectively by the patients before signs of established disease appear overtly. He considers them as basic features of the illness, which are commonly masked by neurotic symptoms in its earlier phases. Chapman's paper is detailed and closely argued, and is of considerable interest.

The result of the mental disintegration is a widespread change in the patient's personality, which vividly impresses itself on his friends. The patient loses his pride in his personal appearance, gradually becomes untidy and slovenly and needs constant attention.

Ideas of reference, illusions, hallucinations and delusions constitute another group of symptoms which are present at one time or another during the course of the illness. Ideas of reference are probably more common than the others. They arise from the patient's attitude, which is one of increased sensitiveness and suspiciousness, in consequence of which he believes that he is being spoken about, and that articles in the daily press have special reference to him and his affairs. He interprets the most commonplace occurrences as having some special reference to himself. Such a patient may feel that the whole world centres round him, and that he is marked out either for persecution or for some great honour. Hallucinations of hearing are particularly common. For a time they may not exercise much influence, but often they dominate the patient so that the halluci- natory suggestions may be acted upon. It is frequently in response to such commands that impulsive and violent acts are perpetrated. Visual hallucinations, hallucinations of smell and taste, are also frequent, but not so common as those of hearing. The striking feature about the delusional ideas is their changeable and transitory nature. Ideas of influence are very important. They take the form of a belief that the patient's thoughts are being read, or stolen from him, or that he is being influenced by wireless or by electrical machines. Not only the content but also the process of thinking may be disturbed, and 'blocking', a sudden stoppage of the stream of thought inexplicable by the patient, is a characteristic symptom.

The symptoms which have been described are all the more significant in that they occur in a setting of relative clearness, so that the patient recognizes clearly time and place and the people around him, i.e. there is usually no disorientation or clouding of consciousness. In addition, the patient has a good memory both for things of long ago and for more recent events. The general intellectual facul- ties are unimpaired, and the remembrance and grasp of school knowledge are not interfered with. Any apparent intellectual deterioration arises from lack of atten- tion and concentration.

The judgement of these patients is, however, greatly interfered with, and they have no proper appreciation of the serious nature of their illness. Gradually the thought-content becomes more and more involved, so that a formal disorder occurs, and incoherence of speech, which may go to the extent of becoming a 'word salad', is not uncommon.

S

Schizophrenic Thinking and General Behaviour

Some general account of the factors which contribute to the strangely dis-ordered appearance of the schizophrenic's mind is perhaps desirable. The peculiar qualities of schizophrenic thinking and behaviour generally seem dependent principally on four conditions: 1. the schizophrenic turns away from reality (introversion); 2. his thinking is dominated by his complexes (topics with a strong affective colouring) to an extent not seen in the normal; 3. he regresses to a childish or infantile or archaic (as it is variously called) mode of thought; and 4. his personality undergoes a progressive disintegration. These are not separate and distinct conditions, but different aspects of one and the same thing. Different writers lay different stress on the various aspects.

It has been pointed out elsewhere ['General Psychopathology', p. 121] that the individual's personality is the product of the interaction of his instinctive forces and his environment. His personality is not simply the sum of the qualities so produced. It is their combination into a new dynamic whole, in which some of the component forces are allowed direct or indirect expression and some are inhibited. Now if such a personality for some reason (*e.g.* persistent instinctual frustration) ceases to keep in contact with reality (introversion) the necessity for inhibition is removed. Modes of expression which are, from the social point of view, primitive and not permissible, can then come into action. In other words, regression can occur, and tendencies hitherto unconscious, because inhibited, receive conscious expression. But a personality in which such expression is per-mitted is *ipso facto* no longer the same personality; it is socially a deteriorated one. Moreover, since there is no longer the necessity for conforming to the real environment, which demands a consistent purposive adaptation, all the modes of instinctive fulfilment can be used in a go-as-you-please, haphazard way; now this and now that complex may receive some sort of conscious expression; and the personality not only deteriorates, but becomes disintegrated as well.

This concept of the schizophrenic's personality, with its introversion, domi-nance by numerous loosely connected complex-derived affects, and its regression to 'archaic' modes of expression, provides a key to a general understanding of the clinical manifestations of schizophrenia. It should, however, be understood that the disintegration seldom is complete. Fragments, so to speak, of the old personality remain with the corresponding conflicts and inhibitions.

The vagueness of the schizophrenic's thought may be attributed largely to his introversion. The schizophrenic patient no longer seeks to commune with his fellows, but lives instead in a world of his own. There is then no need for clear definition in thinking, and the very lack of clearness itself helps to make possible another of the conditions mentioned—that as much as possible in his introverted world may be as his wishes dictate. The lack of necessity for communication with others makes possible such 'telegrammatic' and metaphorical thinking as that described by Jung in the case of a dressmaker who fell ill in her thirty-ninth year. She said, for example, 'I am Socrates'. This delusional statement proved to be an ellipsis for the thought that, like Socrates, she had been extremely able and accomplished and had been falsely accused and placed in prison (the hospital) where she would have to die. That the vagueness and disconnection of thought which reaches its extreme development in the complete incoherence of some cases may be largely dependent on the factors of introversion and dominance by affects, and that it does not necessarily depend on organic cerebral changes, is well illustrated by an occurrence that is not very uncommon; namely, that a patient whose utterances have long been unintelligible may talk coherently and entirely naturally for a time if he is overtaken by some severe physical illness which brings him up against reality with a shock, so to speak. A woman of 60, admitted thirty years previously as suffering from 'dementia praecox' and who had remained in hospital ever since in an apparently demented condition, began during an attack of influenza to ask intelligently for the relatives and friends who had been dead to her those thirty years. Between the thought-processes in schizo-phrenics and the type of thinking found in primitive man there are certain similarities, but some writers on the subject have tended to go too far in their identification of primitive and schizophrenic thinking. Some schizophrenic utter-ances are superficially reminiscent of the 'sympathetic magic' of savages. For example, a male patient, 30 years of age, was observed to carry always dead leaves next to the left side of his chest. Closer inquiry revealed that his mother, to whom he had been specially attached, had died in the autumn some years before, and that at the funeral he had seen the withered leaves strewn on her coffin. He believed that his heart was weak, and that autumn leaves placed over it would have a curative effect, because they had been associated with his mother.

Ideas of death and rebirth, such as are common in primeval myths and in religious writings, are frequently found in schizophrenic patients, who tend, moreover, to act according to such ideas and to give dramatic representations of them. For instance, the stupor of some catatonics seems to be a dramatization of the idea of death, and some states of ecstasy have as their corresponding mental content the idea of being born again. Such conditions, however, are not peculiar to schizophrenia. Religious trends in schizophrenics are sometimes of a type that would perhaps have been permissible in persons still claiming to be normal in the Middle Ages, but now bear the stamp of grotesqueness. One young man, for example, hears a voice saying, 'Yea, we shall relish thee', while at prayer, sees a picture of the Last Supper scintillate and sparkle six times in one afternoon, finds that his room is illuminated with a bright unearthly light, and observes that a bottle of medicine momentarily assumes the shape of an angel. His personality being disintegrated, and working inco-ordinately, instead of as a harmonious whole, it has been said of the schizophrenic that he is at the mercy of his complexes.

Whereas in the manic, as in the depressive, there is one prevailing affect, in the schizophrenic numerous affects, associated with as many complexes, are at work and at war with one another in the disintegrated personality. This affective disorderliness probably contributes to producing the curiously chaotic appear-ance of the schizophrenic's mind. In the minds of normal people all things are

possible—a feeling of love, or its opposite, or apparent indifference, may be
entertained towards the same person; what determines the choice is external
circumstance and the individual mind as a whole—that feeling comes upper-
most which is most in harmony with the rest of the mental experience, conscious
and unconscious, of the individual concerned. But in the fully developed and
therefore mind-disintegrated schizophrenic this decisive solution is impossible.
He hesitates between one feeling and the other, so that he may waver between
strong like and dislike, between wanting and not wanting something—rejecting
and accepting almost at the same time. This is the so-called 'ambivalence'.
Hence, something rejected, which the schizophrenic still succeeds in inhibiting
from full conscious expression, does not remain totally inhibited, but, because
it is still keenly wished for, crops up in an indirect way as a projection, i.e.
as a delusion or a hallucination. Thus, a young married woman consulted a
physician, whose voice she soon afterwards began to hear following wherever
she went. She wrote letters to him and to the hospital authorities, protesting
vigorously against this persecution. Persuaded, however, to interview the physician again, she smiled a great deal, especially when reference was made to the
voice, and said that it 'spoke of love'. Further, at the same time as she complained
of the physician's persecution, she proclaimed her engagement to him. It is not
surprising that such an ambivalent affective attitude which follows from the
disintegration of the personality also contributes to it. Bleuler supposed that a
similar 'ambivalent' tendency is at the root of schizophrenic negativism, a
stimulus evoking with equal readiness the appropriate (normal) psychological
reaction and its opposite. But negativism is probably fundamentally an expression of the desire to shut out reality (introversion). In Bleuler's opinion,
ambivalence is simply one aspect of the not-yet-fully-understood disorder of
association which he supposed to be the fundamental defect in schizophrenic
thinking.

The combination of loss of contact with reality and domination of thinking
entirely by the emotions centred round certain complexes makes all kinds of
fantastic delusions possible. The patient in phantasy has anything he wants. For
example, a young medical student talked of his will-power, and said that he had
a motor-car, a house of his own, and that he was a doctor, having qualified at the
age of 21, and was going to marry the girl of his heart. This is a mild example.

Guilt complexes, e.g. remorse for masturbation, also lead to compensating
phantasies, at the same time as there exist delusions of reference (that everyone
can see his guilt, e.g. in his eyes). In such an instance the phantasy may be translated into acts of expiation. One young man, for example, mutilated himself by
sawing with a safety razor blade round his penis just behind the corona, in an
attempt at castration and 'purification'.

These are among the commoner instances of the very numerous types of
'autistic' (introverted) and 'catathymic'[1] thinking and consequent action found
in schizophrenics. Other examples will be found in the case-records included in
this chapter.

---

[1] Catathymic thinking = thinking along the lines determined by some complex.

PHYSICAL ASPECTS

The pathogenesis of schizophrenia is unknown, though many physical abnormalities have been reported. A few of those reported are now fairly widely accepted by critical opinion to be significant, but none of them, with the possible exception of the biochemical changes described by Gjessing, go near to providing a comprehensible physical explanation of the mental symptoms. From the genetic findings we might expect schizophrenia to have a specific physical pathology, but a great many research workers over the past fifty years have failed to find it; though several of them indeed have thought that they had succeeded. Some of what appear to be the most important findings will be described briefly here.

Central Nervous System

There is no unequivocal histological evidence that schizophrenia is a disease of the brain. There are no gross changes in the brain, and though many microscopical abnormalities have been reported, none of these is yet accepted by the majority of expert investigators to be both constant and significant.

The position here has in fact changed little since Dunlap, an American pathologist of great discrimination and technical ability, reported in 1924. Dunlap formulated certain conditions which should be fulfilled in studying *post mortem* the brains of schizophrenics. The clinical diagnosis must be so clearly established as to be acceptable to the most critical; the age of the patients should not be over 40 years; and death should be caused by some acute disease and not by a wasting condition such as tuberculosis. The post-mortem examination should be performed immediately after death.

Dunlap examined eight cases, contrasting his results with control material, and found very much the same nerve-cell changes present in the control brains as in the schizophrenic ones. He concluded that schizophrenia is a condition lacking in any fundamental or constant alteration of nerve cells, and that any nerve cell alterations which have been found in schizophrenia have probably been reactions to various other bodily conditions, post-mortem changes and the result of technical factors (that is, artifacts).

The various microscopical changes which have been reported by other workers include loss of nerve cells, mainly in the cortex, and cell changes of many kinds—amoeboid, shrinkage, sclerosis, vacuolization, lipoid infiltration, and the presence of inclusion bodies. Glial changes described have been microglial proliferation, macroglial hyperplasia, and swelling of oligodendroglia. It is a ragbag of a catalogue.

The Vogts and their co-workers (1948) directed attention to pathological changes in the thalamus in schizophrenia, particularly in the nucleus medialis dorsalis of young catatonic patients. They reported two special changes: 1. the presence of a large number of dwarf cells (schwundzellen), these being clusters of cells which show dissolution and disappearance of the cytoplasm with unaffected nuclei; and 2. alveolar degeneration, in which the cytoplasm has become vacuolized and the nucleus distorted. These investigations have been critically and painstakingly conducted; and they seem sufficiently promising to be worth pursuing in other laboratories.

It may be that insufficient attention has been paid in the past to the thalamus and hypothalamus in seeking the neuropathology of schizophrenia. New and more refined techniques are also being developed (Meyer, 1960), which may be used to discover abnormalities not revealed by earlier methods of examination. We would emphasize the importance of correlating good clinical records with the pathological investigations.

Hill (1957) reported on the encephalogram in schizophrenia. There is no specific pattern or constant type of abnormality. Some schizophrenics have abnormal E.E.G.s, particularly catatonics. 'Subcortical type discharges, similar to those found in some epileptics, occur particularly in young catatonic schizophrenics': but Hill did not think that these discharges were evidence for the organic-pathological process theory of the aetiology of schizophrenia.

Cardiovascular System

Lewis (1923) was the first to record hypoplasia of the circulatory system in the majority of schizophrenics. The abnormalities consisted in a small heart, weighing usually less than 300 g. and on the average 254 g.; an abnormally thin aorta; and a reduced lumen of other major vessels.

Olkon (1939) reported a reduction in capillary density, and abnormalities of capillary size, shape and blood flow, in the finger webs of schizophrenics.

Shattock (1950) made a detailed study of the vascular disturbances which schizophrenic patients, particularly catatonics, may exhibit and which are well known to all doctors working in mental hospitals. Peripheral vasoconstriction of the hands and feet may be severe, with cyanosis, oedema, atrophy and thickening of the skin and superficial ulceration. The nose and ears may also be cyanotic. The cyanosis is not always related to inactivity. Extreme constriction may be found of the brachial, radial and dorsalis pedis arteries; also of the retinal arteries: and vasoconstriction is relieved as the patient improves mentally. These vascular changes in schizophrenics resemble those seen in normal and cold-sensitive subjects exposed to cold, but they are elicited at room temperatures, and are unusually intense and lasting. Shattock was commendably cautious and critical in drawing conclusions: 'some of the abnormalities of behaviour observed in refractory patients may be related to a relatively inadequate cerebral circulation'.

It is unlikely that cardiovascular changes play more than an adjuvant part in the production of schizophrenic symptoms. The cerebral blood flow has been reported to be normal by Kety et al. (1948).

Physique

Kretschmer (1925) linked leptosomatic (asthenic), athletic and dysplastic physiques with schizophrenia [see p. 78]. By dysplastic physical types he denoted those approximating to the results of endocrine disease, and he found 34 patients of this kind of physical constitution among 175 schizophrenics, and none of this type in 85 manic-depressives. Bleuler (1948) reported an association found in Switzerland between schizophrenia and an acromegaloid physique.

Rees (1943) confirmed Kretschmer's theories in part. He found schizophrenics more leptosomatic than normal controls and manic-depressives: but there was also a considerable overlapping in the distribution of physical types between manic-depressive and schizophrenic groups of his subjects. He reported that the schizophrenic group gave statistically highly significant smaller measurements than the normals in stature, chest circumference and expansion, hip circumference and biacromial diameter.

Endocrine Aspects

Schizophrenia is not associated constantly with any known abnormalities in any endocrine gland. There have been numerous investigations, tending to link schizophrenia with disordered action of the endocrine system and in particular of the sex glands, since Mott in 1919 first reported a regressive atrophy of the cells of the testicular tubules in schizophrenia. Most of the reported findings have gone through a cycle of affirmation and denial similar to the fate of Mott's. Mott's work was most damagingly criticized by Morse, on grounds which included his failure to take into account the effects on the testes of physical disease and malnutrition. Blair and his colleagues (1952) could find nothing in the testes outside the limits of the normal. Apart from the paucity of securely established positive findings, the clinical features of schizophrenia give no hint that the clue to its aetiology will be found in the endocrine system.

Nitrogen Metabolism

In catatonics following a periodic course, who are said to form only 2 or 3 per cent. of schizophrenics, Gjessing (1938), as the result of painstaking intensive studies continued over many years, of the metabolic exchanges in patients of this type, described certain disturbances of nitrogen metabolism which appear to run parallel to the periodic clinical alterations. Such illnesses are described as occurring usually before the age of 20, the onset being sudden with a state of confusion and excitement or in other cases of stupor, which clears up after days, weeks or, rarely, months, and repeats itself at varying intervals of longer duration, and are characterized by apathy, lack of insight and gain in weight. Ultimately there is a permanent state of mental deterioration which made Kraepelin change his opinion and place the condition among the dementia praecox group instead of among the manic depressives.

Gjessing distinguished two types: 1. the 'syntonic' type, so called because the metabolic changes synchronize with the changes in mental phase and with one another; these patients enter the excited or stuporose phase suddenly and emerge into comparative clearness; and 2. the asynchronous group, in whom the change of phase is gradual and the intervals characterized by apathy and lack of initiative, and where the metabolic alterations are chaotic.

Gjessing's results are important because they were the first record of uniformly recurring metabolic changes running parallel with clinical alterations, the correction of which by chemical means is followed by disappearance of the episodic clinical disturbances.

The main methodological principle of the research was the simultaneous recording of many of the physical functions of the organism, over a considerable period of the illness, covering a number of phasic recurrences and intervals in the same patient. The patient served as his own control.

Gjessing described the changes in periodic catatonia, as follows. In type (1) the metabolic changes are the same whether the phase is one of excitement or of stupor, but the course of the changes shows two sub-types. In sub-type A at the beginning of the phase (of excitement or stupor as the case may be) there is evidence of generalized sympathetic stimulation. It is of special interest that, even in the stuporose phase although the patient is kept motionless, the O_2 consumption rises. The excretion of total N_2 is also increased whatever the kind of phase, compared with the more or less quiet intervals. In these intervals there is an N_2 retention and therefore a positive N balance, and N_2 goes on being accumulated until it reaches a threshold characteristic of the individual patient (between 15 and 28 g. N_2) and then at the point of maximum N_2 accumulation, stupor or excitement, as the case may be, sets in. It is not the excitement that causes the excessive excretion to begin, as the latter may begin a day or two beforehand. Similarly in the excited or stuporose phase retention begins again before the end of the phase.

What characterizes this group is that excitement or stupor sets in shortly after N_2 retention has reached its maximum. In the sub-type C stupor or excitement sets in just before the lowest level of N_2 accumulation. The stuporose or excited phase coincides with a phase of N_2 retention and the quiet intervals begin when the N_2 store has reached the maximum.

Gjessing early suggested that at the time of the change of phase in the N_2 balance, a toxic substance, derived through a disturbance of protein metabolism, might act through the blood stream on the diencephalon: later he thought that the diencephalic autonomic functions might be influenced by periodic alterations in thyroid activity. With the object of emptying the N_2 store he used thyroxine in large doses (as much as 44 mg. in 8 days—intramuscularly, 1 mg., increasing by 1 to 2 mg. each day) and later dried thyroid so that the N_2 consumption was stabilized at 10 to 15 per cent. above normal. In this way he found it possible to stop the periodic catatonic disturbance. He recommended immediate discontinuance of thyroid if the pulse becomes irregular, and continuing with it when the pulse has fallen to 80 or 90. In type A he recommended that thyroid should be given during the last 8 or 10 days before stupor or excitement begins, and in type C shortly before the patient becomes quiet and stupor free.

Gjessing's reports of nitrogen retention in periodic catatonia and the response to treatment with thyroid have been partially confirmed by other workers (Stokes, Danziger, Rowntree and Kay); but the causal relationships between the biochemical and mental changes, and questions of where and how the biochemical changes originate, have not been elucidated. Jenner (1967), exploring the biochemical aspects of periodic psychoses, reports that it is very difficult now to find cases analogous to Gjessing's—a statement with which we entirely agree. Furthermore, he states that Gjessing himself tended to see his studies as taking place 'on the border region between dementia praecox and the manic-depressive psychoses'.

Amine Metabolism

Osmond and Hoffer (1952–59) developed a hypothesis that schizophrenia may be caused by a defect in adrenaline metabolism, and reported evidence that adrenochrome and adrenolutin (adrenaline metabolites) may both occur in the human body and be psychotomimetic. Further, they found differences in adrenochrome metabolism between normals and schizophrenics. The theories of these Saskatchewan workers aroused a good deal of interest, though their findings were not confirmed.

Many other research workers are following up clues suggested by the psychotomimetic properties of the hallucinogens and resemblances between them and the cerebral amines: mescaline is, for example, a close relative chemically of noradrenaline. The hypothesis has been advanced that there is a disorder of amine metabolism in schizophrenia. The true hallucinogenic drugs are methylated derivatives of the cerebral monoamines: and it has been postulated that in schizophrenia there is a disturbance of the biochemical mechanism of transmethylation. Recent claims that dimethoxyphenylethylamine (D.M.P.E.—which is chemically close to mescaline) can be found in the urine of schizophrenics much more often than in controls, have not yet been substantiated: if they were, it would of course support the transmethylation hypothesis. Kety's critical review (1967) is valuable.

Again and again the schizophrenic is reported to show an unusual biological variability, but within normal limits: and no biochemical abnormality has yet been demonstrated which is specifically associated with schizophrenia. Further research is emphatically required. Psychiatrists and biochemists must work in the closest and mutually critical collaboration. Patients chosen as the subjects of study must be selected by skilled clinicians, they should be symptomatically similar examples of one of the sub-groups of schizophrenia, and variables such as physical condition, diet and drugs must be scrupulously controlled.

PSYCHOPATHOLOGY

Various psychopathological concepts have been employed above in describing the symptoms of schizophrenia and in trying to get a working grasp of their significance. Here we will refer more specifically but briefly to a few of the many detailed psychopathological theories which have been formulated in attempts to comprehend schizophrenia in psychodynamic terms. The pursuit of a unitary psychopathology of schizophrenia is probably as illusory and doomed to failure as is the search for a single physical pathology common to all cases: but whether or not the cause of schizophrenia is found ultimately to be physical, psychological interpretation of the clinical phenomena will remain a necessary aspect of our understanding of the total pathology of the disease.

Prior to 1907 Bleuler and Jung of the Zürich School of Psychiatry had become interested in Freud's psychoanalysis in relation to the psychoses. Developing Wundt's experiments in association by interpreting the findings in psychoanalytical terms, they made a bridge between experimental psychology and psychoanalysis. Freud (1914) acknowledged the importance of their work: '(Bleuler) showed that light could be thrown on a large number of purely psychiatric cases by adducing the same processes as have been recognized through psychoanalysis to obtain in dreams and neuroses; and Jung successfully applied the analytic method of interpretation to the most alien and obscure phenomena of dementia praecox (schizophrenia), so that their sources in the life-history and interests of the patient came clearly to light. . . . As early as in 1897 I had published the analysis of a case of schizophrenia, which however was of a paranoid character, so that the solution of it could not take away from the impression made by Jung's analyses. But to me the important point had been, not so much the possibility of interpreting the symptoms, as the psychical mechanism of the disease, and above all the agreement of this mechanism with that of hysteria, which had already been discovered. At that time no light had yet been thrown on the differences between the two mechanisms. For I was then aiming at a libido theory of the neuroses, which was to explain all neurotic and psychotic phenomena as proceeding from abnormal vicissitudes of the libido. . . .'

Jung wrote his *Psychology of Dementia Praecox* in 1907. The thought disorder in schizophrenia he considered to be due to the operation of unconscious complexes of ideas and feelings. The inner tension and conflicts produced by these complexes precipitate states of panic, and the complexes themselves become split off from the ego in autonomous activity: in the schizophrenic patient's conscious mind they come to replace the normal traffic with reality. These complexes also cause resistances, which are revealed by negativism. As a technique of investigation he made much use of word-association tests, in which a line of stimulus-words is read off to the subject and he is asked to respond to each word with the first idea that comes into his mind. Different types of response are noted, according to the length of time that elapses between the giving of the stimulus-word and the reply, and according to the nature of the reply itself. By this means Jung obtained clues to the unconscious mental content, especially to the complexes. The method is, however, not generally of much value clinically. Jung thought schizophrenia to be psychogenic in its origin, but suggested that there might develop secondarily a biochemical disorder with toxic effects. Later he came to interpret the mental content of the schizophrenic, much of which appeared to him to be archaic and archetypal, in terms of a phylogenetic collective unconscious common to all men, a deposit of primordial and primitive experience. Bleuler adopted many of Jung's earlier ideas. Jung's later esoteric preoccupation with religion and mythology has had little impact on clinical psychiatry. His papers on schizophrenia have been republished (1960).

In Freud's view (summarized by Fenichel (1946)) the central process in schizo-phrenia is a profound unconscious mental regression and turning inwards, with the withdrawal of libido from reality, its objects and relationships. This regres-sion may be precipitated by emotional traumata or conflicts of various kinds, and is particularly apt to occur at critical periods of biological development: it is facilitated by some earlier trauma in the development and organization of the ego, which has caused a fixation at a more immature level of auto-erotism or narcissism. Contacts with reality are progressively lost as the illness develops, and the ego, reinvested with its libido, becomes again egocentric and narcissistic. The abandonment of relations with reality and the withdrawal of libido from objects lead to the development of feelings of depersonalization and derealization, and to such delusions as those of the death of relatives or of world destruc-tion. The increased narcissism and inflation of the ego result in hypochondriacal preoccupation and delusions, and infantile feelings of omnipotence. Other symp-toms are interpreted along similar lines: regression is revealed in behaviour also, in oral and auto-erotic activities, in incontinence and smearing, in echolalia and echopraxia. In addition to these regressive symptoms, breaking with reality, Freud identified restitutional symptoms which indicate efforts on the part of the sick individual to regain reality. Delusional ideas of saving mankind are adduced as examples of this trend: hallucinations are interpreted as creating a substitute reality in place of the perceptions which have been lost, and certain catatonic symptoms, stereotypies and mannerisms, are seen as attempts to regain lost object relationships. Freud pointed to the particularly close resemblance between visual hallucinations and dreams, and stated that in the disordered language of the schizophrenic words are subject to the 'primary' process which produces dream images out of dream thoughts.

Federn (1952), whose views have been recently influential, interpreted schizo-phrenia in terms of an ego psychology which he personally elaborated and for which he provided a special terminology. The ego he described as having a fluc-tuating boundary, which delimits the self from the environment. The ego is driven (cathected) by libido. Ego feeling, conscious and unconscious, floods the area of the self and is sensitively involved with reality at its frontiers. In Federn's view schizophrenia is a disorder of the ego: the ego is weak, because its cathexis is weak. The ego boundary disintegrates, with the result that ego and environ-ment, thought and feeling and their objects, become confused, and reality is falsified. The production of delusions and hallucinations then leads to a with-drawal from reality, and the ego regresses to states of childhood functioning, with the appearance in consciousness of previously unconscious mental material.

Freeman, Cameron and McGhie (1958) follow Federn in regarding a dis-turbance of the development and maintenance of adequate ego boundaries be-tween the self and the not-self, and a deficiency in ego feeling, as the central features of the schizophrenic disease process. 'The illness of the ego results in an impairment of the functions usually associated with it, namely the loss of adap-tive capacities, perceptual disturbances, changes in the memory function, altera-tions in the relationship with reality, disorders of the motor apparatus, and varying degrees of loss of personal identity.' They emphasize that the ego is never completely lost even in the most demented patient. Their theoretical framework is used to develop a therapeutic programme which is, in its earlier stages, essentially non-verbal, and is dependent on the formation of durable nurse-patient relationships: treatment is orientated specifically towards the restoration of ego functions. These workers, like many others with a psychoanalytic orientation, are careful to state that their views do not have any fundamental aetiological implications: the causation of the dissolution of the ego is left an open question.

In the past decade psychologists have made increasingly important contributions to the understanding of schizophrenia. The researches of Norman Cameron, Weckowicz, Payne, Shakow, McGhie and their colleagues have been particularly notable. Kraepelin and Bleuler thought that there are no perceptual changes in schizophrenia; but Weckowicz and Blewett (1959) demonstrated that size and distance constancy is impaired, there being a tendency to underestimate the size of the distal parts of the body. McGhie and Chapman (1961) found that schizophrenic patients themselves became at an early stage of their illnesses aware of an impairment of their powers of attention and of their proneness to be easily distracted. These workers were able to demonstrate experimentally that schizophrenics are unable to attend to external stimuli in such a way as to allow only relevant information to be selected: schizophrenics cannot screen out irrelevant information in a normal way, and have particular difficulty with visual information, with the result that the processing and storage of information are impaired. There is evidence too that the perception of speech may be disordered in schizophrenia (Lawson, McGhie and Chapman, 1964). A lucid review of the present status of studies of these cognitive disorders has been made by McGhie (1967): it is an area of research which holds out much promise. Two further aspects of these investigations require mention. The disorders of attention and perception so far reported are most clearly to be identified in cases of hebephrenic schizophrenia; and they suggest that these 'nuclear' cases of schizophrenia have symptoms in common with the organic dementias. They tend also to support the distinction made on clinical grounds between schizophrenia and the paranoid psychoses. For example, whereas hebephrenics are highly distractible, patients suffering from paranoid psychoses have been found to be less distractible than normal control subjects.

Schizophrenia Simplex

In this type there is an absence of any definite trend. There is simply a general falling away of interest. Kraepelin described it as consisting of an 'impoverishment and devastation of the whole psychic life, which is accomplished quite imperceptibly'. The change in the personality may be so insidious that it is not recognized as being due to any definite type of mental disorder, but such individuals seem to lack ambition, and are content to lead idle, shiftless lives, constantly changing their employment, never being satisfied with what they have. People who suffer from this type of disorder fill the ranks of the unemployed, the vagrants and delinquents. They are able in mild cases to carry on a coherent conversation, and give an appearance of normality which is not borne out on further acquaintance.

Such conditions frequently have their beginning in early adolescence. At school the potential schizophrenic is content to slip along. Afterwards he never reaches a position of any special responsibility, because he is apt to be dreamy, to be lacking in attention and concentration, and is content usually with routine tasks. Such a person may do good work, but always in a subordinate capacity.

As time goes on, a certain change may occur in his temperament, so that he becomes irritable, moody, distinctly asocial, and rarely takes part in the pleasures of his comrades. Even from his own family he becomes estranged. Inability to sustain a conversation is noticed, and the thinking becomes disorganized, even to the extent of incoherence; but it is rare for such a patient to have ideas of reference, hallucinations or delusions. The memory is well retained, and the chief feature is the extreme apathy or emotional dulling. We are all familiar with this type of individual. These are people who at one time have looked as if they might develop into something much better. They are quiet, pleasant individuals who gradually sink more and more into themselves, and who never fulfil the promise of their earlier days.

CASE NO. 22

Simple schizophrenic deterioration. A quiet well-behaved patient with little initiative but performing simple routine tasks satisfactorily; shallow in his affective responses—a facile empty laugh, a lack of resentment at detention in hospital or of desire to leave it; absence of significant thought-content and complete want of insight.

A good example of this type is that of a single man (D. R.), 32 years old, who had served for a period during the war years.

He had a history of having been ill for about two years. At the time of his admission to hospital he was quiet, looked a little dull, but smiled pleasantly, and answered readily and agreeably. His memory was good, and there was no evidence of hallucinations or delusions.

Following his admission he has been employed at various jobs about the hospital, and has always led a contented and happy life, quite satisfied with his surroundings, and never asking to be allowed away. A good idea of his condition may be obtained from the following questions and answers:

He said that he had nothing special to complain of, that he was quite happy.

'Do you think it strange being here so long?' 'Yes, that's true.'

'How do you account for it?' 'I feel very well. I feel all right.'

'Is your head right?' 'My head feels quite clear.'

'No strange thoughts?' 'No.'

When these questions were asked, the patient often laughed or smiled, in a simple, foolish way. His laugh did not have the 'infectiousness' of manic cases. There was always an element of silliness in it. He stated that he felt just as well now as he had ever done, and denied hallucinations and strange ideas of any kind. His answers were given quickly and to the point. The impressive features were contentment and apathy; and yet he had been long resident under hospital conditions. He was able to tell the day, the month, the year quite correctly, and he was able to give a history of his life. He told when he was born, where he was born, mentioned the different members of his family, what he had done at school.

'Did you get on all right at school?' 'Oh, yes.'

'Were you clever?' Patient laughed, and said that he could always get through his lessons.

'Were you top boy in the class?' The patient laughed loudly, said that he was not, but that he had never been 'kept back'. He was able to do simple calculations correctly, and he had a good grasp on general information, but no appreciation of the serious nature of his disorder.

The picture, therefore, is a very good example of the so-called 'simplex' type. The patient had suffered from a general slumping of his interest, to reach a state of apathy and contentment, in which he calmly accepted his detention in a mental hospital. He is protected by the hospital, and has no fears; but neither has he any ambition of any kind, nor any great capacity for enjoyment. His war service had probably little or nothing to do with precipitating such a reaction.

Hebephrenia

This type may be difficult to differentiate, because often in it there are some symptoms pointing more to a catatonic reaction. Hebephrenia, however, seems to occur usually at an earlier age than the catatonic varieties, and it is especially characterized by great incoherence in the train of thought, marked emotional disturbance, periods of excitement alternating with periods of tearfulness and depression, and frequently by illusions and hallucinations.

The people who develop a hebephrenic disorder have in their earlier days shown an unstable emotional condition; they may give a history of tantrums, and have often been of the over-pious, ultra-conscientious type, apt to be too idealistic, and to brood on obscure topics. Their acquaintances generally have looked upon them as queer. In such people the emotional response is shallow, and they laugh and weep without very adequate cause, or have sudden violent outbursts of anger, explosive in character and rapidly passing away.

Hallucinations of sight and hearing are particularly common in hebephrenics, and are usually in the nature of symbolic interpretations. They come and go during the course of the disorder. It is the vivid hallucinations which especially dominate the picture. Kraepelin particularly remarked on the changeable, phantastic, bizarre nature of their delusions, and he gave certain examples: they 'have no brain any longer', their 'back is broken in two', their 'blood has been taken from them'.

The hebephrenic patient often suffers greatly from ideas of reference; he feels that he is being watched and made fun of. Feelings of influence are common.

The most prominent symptoms are the incongruity of effect, the incoherence in the train of thought, the strange, impulsive, senseless conduct and the vivid hallucinations.

The following is an illustrative case of the hebephrenic kind. The very rapid deterioration to a condition of silly, impulsive activity, with inadequate and inappropriate emotional manifestations, great incoherence of speech and thought, hallucinations and apparently absurd ideas, *e.g.* of influence—in other words, the 'molecular disintegration' of the personality—is very well shown.

CASE NO. 23

P. R., a girl, 20 years old, who had been employed as a nurse, was admitted in a restless, agitated state, but a few minutes later she was smiling and happy. These phases rapidly alternated, even in the course of a few minutes. It was difficult to get her to co-operate in a satisfactory examination; she spoke in a simple, childish way, said that she wished someone would do an operation on her head and make her better. She told how she had worked in various hospitals, but had not been able to continue steadily at her job, because she 'seemed always to be working in a maze'. Perhaps the question and answer method brings out certain points better than a mere description.

'You were at a fever hospital?' 'Yes, just a few weeks.'

'Why did you leave?' 'I am not sure.'

'Do you hear voices?' 'No—yes—very seldom. I seem to be going sort of dead.'

Later she admitted that she did hear voices, and that they terrified her dreadfully.

She was able to do simple calculations correctly, and answered some questions on general information correctly, but her diffuseness and inconsequent talk can be gathered from the following:

'Who discovered America?' 'Well, I think it was a Murray. I had an old Aunt Sally who died and an old brother went to Hudson Bay.'

She behaved in a disturbed, excitable way, and made such a noise that she had to be removed to a room by herself. While there she promptly smashed several panes of glass. Her impulsive, violent conduct continued at intervals. She refused food, so that for a time it was necessary to tube-feed her. Still later she deliberately poked her fingers into her eyes and caused conjunctival haemorrhage.

During her residence in the hospital she continued to be hallucinated, and talked freely about her experiences. She said that voices told her things had been done to her during the night. During the day also she hallucinated, and often sat gazing at the ceiling in an ecstatic way.

Gradually her impulsiveness subsided; she began to look after her appearance, to help the nurses in the ward, but often she would have outbursts of weeping without any apparent cause. She was asked about this time why it was that she frequently sat with her eyes tightly shut, and would only open them for a moment or two at a time. She explained that when her eyes were wide open the doctor, or the sister in charge of the ward, or the nurses, saw what she was seeing, and that they were therefore seeing through her eyes, and to prevent this she shut her eyes. She also explained that she had two voices; the one which was speaking she called her 'top voice', and what she said with the 'top voice' was true; but there was a second voice, an 'under-voice', which she apparently believed or felt was what her auditors at times heard, replacing the true 'top voice'. Consequently we were getting false ideas by believing this second voice. She also expressed the idea that the doctors and nurses used her as a 'medium' to affect others. She held up the three middle fingers of her hand to illustrate the idea clearly to us; pointed out the first outside finger as representing the number 'six', the finger in the middle was herself, and the other outside finger represented 'the others'.

Her condition became gradually worse. She wandered about in a restless, aimless way, and when the physician visited the ward she clutched him by the arm, and could only be detached with difficulty. Her thought-processes were blocked and her speech was incoherent, her sentences being composed of detached words and phrases which had no relationship to each other, except for an occasional superficial association. An example is as follows:

'Losh, I don't know what it is. You see—she says—I don't know, I'm sure. There's Cinderella. There is a much better play than that. "I don't know," I said. He is an awful idiot. O dear God, I'm so stupid. That's putting two and two together—saying I really don't know—saying Cathie, and so I observe and—flowers. An orange, and shoe laces. A gaberdine skirt. Pettigrew's and the jazz band, with cream cakes. She says no. They like my hair bobbed, but I'm so stupid. Contrary Mary. Statues at Copland and Lye's. "Oh," I said, "yes, yes, yes." I'd go off to sleep immediately afterwards. I said, "I know quite well." "Nothing," I said. I forget all that I saw next. The next thing was —eh? The poor man's mad. They'll be chopping off our heads next, and—calendars tied with blue ribbons. Oh, dear God. Contrary Mary again. What period—that's right. I don't like acting the goat at all. A cream-sponge sandwich. My memory is so slow, that all I'm sure. It was caramels then and fruit cakes. Well, well, I said, I can't help it— I don't want to help it, and well, I don't care. Contrary Mary again, and says—Nurse Grant—dogs barking. What's the matter with me anyway? I'm so terribly stupid. I'm fed up with this place—that's all. Sago pudding. She looks pale and tired often, but not —I know that. Sings "Take me over there, drop me anywhere, Manchester, Birmingham, Leeds, Well I don't care. I should like to see my best girl"—Mrs. Patrick, she says—"though 'tis time for parting, that's it, Jean, and my tears are starting". I've got the Kruschen feeling.—Blue belts and medals—three eggs for tea. No, that won't do. Oh, dear God, I'm so stupid. I won't see my way—white rabbits. "Back home in Tennessee"—that the way it's spelt. Oh, I don't know what I am going to do now. It's all wrong. Dear God, I'm so silly. It's killing, isn't it? Cream cakes, French cakes and meringues. Flies, fleas, butterflies,' and so on.

She had the idea that she was changed, and sometimes remarked, 'My face is changed.'

The course of her illness had already been of five years' duration, and she was steadily going downhill.

A sample of her letter-writing shows very well the incoherence and the tendency to repetition.

DEAR SIR,

I have just had dinner. I ate my dinner the monkey and I feel better. change I. Nurse is always making the tea. Betsy's nurse.

     Wearing for a cup of
  tea.
        Bathing patient.
        (Ogalvie).
           Your—
             I j g u.
          gins Druce,
           Yours
              sincerely,
                P. R.

DEAR DR. HIND,

I am just that watea ahe bring me som gin snap & I u—a lobster — — — 1 a. the water's hot what a monkey goes with.

        Y I am
        s incere.
        Nurse Bruce
          gave
             me two
             snaps.

Thursday.

Caristic.
  Soc.
        Sit up latest
Ruby was away with it—Shorthand. So that I don't get a bath.

Catatonia

The catatonic type of reaction is more easily differentiated than the other types of schizophrenia. This catatonic condition was first described by Hecker and by Kahlbaum as a variety of mental disturbance *sui generis*, with symptoms and a course peculiar to itself. Kraepelin, however, recognized that the great majority of cases of this sort ultimately ended in a state of considerable dementia, and therefore he included these catatonic cases in his dementia praecox group.

Catatonia is usually described as an alternating state characterized by a stage of depression, a stage of excitement and a stage of stupor. We would reserve the name catatonia, as Kraepelin did, for these cases in which one sees the conjunction of peculiar excitement with stupor.

There is no doubt that this type of schizophrenic reaction develops much more acutely than the other types. Kraepelin himself said that 41 per cent. of such cases tend to develop acutely, 31 per cent. insidiously and the others subacutely.

There is no group of symptoms which can be looked upon as in any way premonitory. The usual history is a more or less general statement that there has been a general falling off in interest, an apathy, a lack of concentration, a dreaminess and often episodes of an odd nature. Then a state of dull stupor develops, with mutism, refusal of food, and with such a diminution of all activities that the patient may sit idly in one position, with the hands stretched out on the knees, and the head bowed between the shoulders, the whole aspect being that of a mummy. The facial expression is vacant, and no apparent interest is taken in the environment or in the people around. The muscles of the mouth may become pursed up into the so-called 'schnauzkrampf'. Patients in this condition have to be dressed and undressed, and have to be moved in bed: they may have to be tube-fed. Urine and faeces are often retained, or there is incontinence. Mannerisms are common. Perseveration may reach an extreme degree; for example, a patient who took his meals in a singularly mechanical way, shovelling his food into his mouth with his fork and then with his knife, used to go through the same motions long after he had finished the food before him. The saliva may be retained, so that the cheeks become bulged out with it, or drooling occurs from the mouth. These patients are so insensitive that they may not react to painful stimuli, such as pin-pricks, nor even close their eyelids when told that a pin is going to be put into one of their eyes. They understand perfectly clearly everything that is going on around them, but their apathy is so great that they take no part in it. Not infrequently they are intensely negativistic, and an attempt to do anything for the patient is resisted with every ounce of his strength. On the other hand, he may obey everything automatically. There are also stereotypies of thought and action; the patients ask the same questions over and over again,

T

write words or letters in a stereotyped way, or walk in a peculiar fashion, perhaps always stopping for an instant after so many steps; or they assume strange attitudes, which are maintained unchanged for long periods of time. Flexibilitas cerea is common; they will allow their bodies and their limbs to be placed in awkward positions, which are maintained indefinitely. Other symptoms commonly present are echolalia and echopraxia.

Suddenly, without any warning, the picture may change at any time, so that the patient begins to speak, answer questions and often gives a detailed account of everything that has occurred. A state of extreme frenzy may alternate with the period of stupor, during which the patient behaves with extraordinary impulsiveness and assaults whoever comes into contact with him. During this stage he may not only be homicidal, but impulsively suicidal. Such episodes of excitement usually come from a clear sky, and there are no premonitory symptoms. For instance, one of our patients, who had been going about as usual, and had actually been in town with his mother, and had seemed rather better, suddenly got up early one morning and made a dive through a window two storeys high. The frames were of iron, so that he was not successful in precipitating himself, but the violence of the attack was so great that he broke his collar-bone and had numerous cuts about his face and arms. Following this attempt he tried to mutilate himself. Another patient used to prop herself against the wall, then stand on her head and attempt to screw her neck. She also repeatedly tried to smother herself in the bedclothes, and several times dived from her bed on to the floor. These episodes of violence are usually associated with hallucinations, but they are not necessarily so. Often at these times the patients express delusions; they feel that they are not only commanded to do such things, but that they are all-powerful, or that they are being persecuted. Sometimes they believe that it is the voice of God that they hear, and that it is God who has commanded them to destroy themselves. The duration of these paroxysms is usually short-lived, not lasting more than a few hours or days or weeks. It is in this type of schizophrenia that the vasomotor symptoms already mentioned are prominent.

The following is a typical catatonic state:

CASE NO. 24

Catatonic schizophrenia. Onset of a dull, listless state, with vague ideas of reference and feelings of influence. Later, auditory and visual hallucinations, unsystematized paranoid delusions, refusal of food and incontinence. Alternating periods of stupor and excitement, with progressive dementia. No response to treatment.

There was no family history of mental illness in the case of F. C. He had been an average scholar but introspective and solitary at school, with no liking for games and no hobbies. He became a mill-worker at the age of 15 and was 'more a boy for home, never keen on girls'. He served in the Army during the Second World War and had some sort of transient mental breakdown, of which no records are available. After demobilization he was idle for six months: he appeared depressed and mixed up, seemed to take no interest in things around him and did not even respond to questioning. Then he had a job for six months, but was dismissed and again hung around the house, making no attempt to seek further employment. Thereafter he became even more dull and apathetic, looked vacant and faraway, refused to get out of bed or take food. He declared that people were trying to take a rise out of him, that some unknown individual was 'making him think about things', and that he himself was a 'riddle of bones'. In the year following his demobilization from the Army he was admitted to a mental hospital, aged 23 years.

In hospital at first he lay in bed with an occasional vacant smile, and refused food. He was correctly orientated and could give his history with reasonable accuracy, but he had little insight, saying that he had been sent to hospital on account of fits of bad temper. He was both auditorily and visually hallucinated: he complained of hearing buzzing noises, sounds like someone squealing and voices which he could sometimes understand but whose messages he could not remember, and he described flashes of light and shadows in the middle of the room. He expressed the belief that the doctors and nurses could manipulate their shadows, and that there was another person in his bed. Later he complained of tasting soap in his mouth and of receiving poison from the post beside his bed. Often he could not be engaged in conversation, sat vacantly by the hour and had both to be taken to his meals and pressed to eat. At times he was incontinent, chewed the end of his tie and hoarded rubbish. For weeks on end he would be in a state of stupor or near to it, showing catalepsy and flexibilitas cerea. Then a period of excitement would intervene, when for days or weeks on end he would be hyperactive and talk a great deal in a disjointed and usually incoherent way. At these times he would strike out impulsively at the nursing staff. On occasion he clowned in a crude way and would walk on his hands.

Repeated courses of E.C.T., various tranquillizing drugs, and treatment in occupational and social groups, have had no effect, and he has become grossly demented.

DIAGNOSIS

Probably mistakes in the diagnosis of schizophrenia are made most often because undue attention has been paid to single symptoms and the clinician has failed to view these in perspective. Certain symptoms in a young person, feelings of influence and passivity, for example, and hypochondriacal complaints of a wholly unexpected, unjustified or bizarre kind, will quite strongly suggest the diagnosis of schizophrenia: but the diagnosis cannot safely be allowed to rest on isolated symptoms. Gillies (1958) in an illuminating account of the symptoms which are most characteristic of early schizophrenia, has drawn attention to the importance of recognizing the often subtle and transient evidence of disorders of thinking, affect and volition, and of autistic withdrawal, before the numerous secondary symptoms have become manifest: and he makes the observation that a social group setting, in hospital or elsewhere, tends to bring out a schizophrenic patient's anomalies. Disorders of thinking, including the replacement of abstract by concrete thinking and thought-blocking, may be elicited by asking the patient to interpret proverbs. Later, when the illness is obviously a psychotic one, the persistent presence of auditory and visual hallucinations occurring when there is no excitement, and when there is no toxic basis, are very much more in favour of schizophrenia than of anything else.

Much help is to be got from a detailed history. Schizophrenia is usually an illness of slow, insidious onset, developing over years; whereas a manic-depressive psychosis develops, if not very acutely, at any rate over a period of weeks or months. The patient's relatives may report strange, odd, inappropriate behaviour. One should find out always if there has been progressive deterioration in the level of performance, at work and socially: school reports, examination results at university or college, and the employment record will provide objective and usually reliable indices of intellectual performance, its maintenance or decline.

Adolescent turmoil of feeling and behaviour, and neurotic symptoms, usually of an anxious or hysterical kind, in a young adult may for long mask the true diagnosis. Usually external precipitants are suspiciously slight or hard to define, the response to psychotherapy is disappointing, there is a deficiency in rapport and the illness drags on. The clinical picture is often gradually recognized to be becoming more atypical. There tends to be a diffuseness and vagueness in thought and expression, one cannot follow the patient's thought processes without strain, his thoughts may become blocked, or an unexpected emotional reaction may jar the sympathetic observer into recognizing the patient's deeper disorder.

The young schizophrenic may become profoundly depressed, and he may come into medical care after a suicidal attempt. His schizophrenia may be revealed only after his depression has been treated, in residual symptoms. Whether or not the patient is acutely emotionally disturbed, schizophrenia in the adult has in fact most often to be differentiated from a manic-depressive psychosis. Superficially the apathy, listlessness and stupor which occur in schizophrenic cases are apt to be confounded with a state of depression. One or two questions may be sufficient to elicit the fact that the listless schizophrenic does not have any subjective feeling of sadness, but, on the other hand, often feels contented and prefers to be left alone. In the depressed phase of the manic-depressive psychosis, the individual not only looks sad, but feels miserable, and his thoughts are despondent. In general, the schizophrenic, as contrasted with the manic-depressive, is full of discrepancies between his mood and his thought, so that ideas of persecution or disaster leave him comparatively unmoved; and between his thoughts and his actions, so that he does little to fulfil his day-dreams or to stop his persecution. There are also discrepancies in his thought-content itself, clear contradictions going uncorrected.

The type of excitement which one sees particularly in catatonic cases is sometimes very difficult to distinguish from an episode of manic excitement, but here again there are certain points which help to differentiate the two states. The excitement of the schizophrenic is much more episodic; it may occur quite suddenly following a period of stupor, and it is usually characterized by a blind impulsiveness, during which the patient may be dangerous to others and himself. There is a poverty of ideas as compared with the free production of the manic: there may indeed be something in the nature of a flight of ideas, but it is stilted, and poorly sustained. On the other hand, the manic excitement runs a much more prolonged course, the mood is typically one of great happiness, flight of ideas and distractibility are prominent features and there is commonly a joy and an infectious hilarity about the patient which are very easily observed.

Close attention should be paid always to the nature of the previous personality and to the adequacy of the previous social adjustment: and one should ask oneself, under stress what kind of reaction would be expected from a personality so constituted or limited.

The difficulties of diagnosis are best illustrated by the report of two cases: the first, one in which the schizophrenic symptoms predominated, but which ended in complete recovery; the second, one in which for a time the manic-depressive features were preponderant, but which went on to considerable deterioration.

CASE NO. 25

A young unmarried woman, 28 years old, had shown mental symptoms for one month previous to her admission to the Glasgow Royal Mental Hospital. There had been an initial period of depression lasting for a few days, which was followed by the expression of strange ideas. She announced that she had cast a spell over the family, that neither she herself nor any member of the family had any sense of taste, that she had no blood in her body, that she could feel nothing. She tried to leave the house dressed only in her night clothes. Her language became obscene, a thing quite foreign to her. On admission to hospital she was in a state of stupor, which was punctuated by impulsive episodes. She would suddenly leap out of bed and destroy the ward furniture. On one occasion she struck her brother violently, tore her bedclothes with her teeth and in doing so broke one of her teeth. She constantly rubbed the top of her head, or picked her skin. She hung over the edge of her bed, spitting out large quantities of saliva, and she became very filthy in her personal habits, smearing herself with excreta. Thirteen months after admission she was still most difficult to manage, and her mood was one of angry resentment. The only explanation vouchsafed for her conduct was that she was 'in love with some other fellow', and that 'he was an actor'. When asked about her picking habits she explained, 'I have been shedding my life-blood for you.' Twenty months after admission she began to show signs of betterment, which went on rapidly to recovery. She co-operated in a review of her illness, and showed good insight. She stated that at the onset of her illness she had the idea that she might have become pregnant, and worried over the disgrace which this would mean both to herself and to her family. A study of her personality showed that she had been a bright, happy, jolly girl, and a great favourite at school, where she had done well.

CASE NO. 26

A young married woman, 24 years old, had shown mental symptoms for one year previous to admission. She exhibited a variable emotional state, having periods of excitement, talkativeness and restlessness, followed by periods when she was depressed, dull, 'lifeless' and lacking in interest. During her excited periods she talked of seeing lights and hearing bells, was erotic in her conduct, exposed herself and used filthy language. She gave the impression, however, of great happiness, showed a flight of ideas, was distractible and misidentified those around her. For a time her conversation was incoherent and obscene, but her mood was always one of elation. In the course of six months she had made a satisfactory adjustment, and was discharged. Fifteen months later she was readmitted. Her condition was now one of apathy and lack of interest. She grimaced, showed flexibilitas cerea, had periods of mirthless laughter, had to be spoon-fed and was careless in her personal habits. During the next four years her mental health showed a steady decline. There were times when she had periods of excitement, which superficially simulated a manic state, but these periods were poorly sustained, her conversation was incoherent and irrelevant, she hallucinated, was foolish in her conduct and utterly lacking in appreciation of her disordered mental state. An investigation of her personality showed that she had been vain, reserved, hypersensitive and had peculiar tastes.

In the first of these two cases the behaviour sank to a very low level. Yet the patient made an excellent readjustment, with considerable insight, and there seems no reason to suppose that she will have a further attack.

In the second case at the time of the first admission the picture resembled a manic excitement. In estimating the prognosis at that time, more weight should have been placed on the long prodromal period of one year previous to her admission, and on the vain, reserved type of personality.

PROGNOSIS

Over half the patients in our mental hospitals are suffering from a state of mental deterioration, which particularly involves the emotional sphere and habits, due to chronic schizophrenia; so schizophrenia continues to have in general a very serious prognosis. At the same time, an increasing number of these patients are readjusting themselves satisfactorily. There are more who make a social rather than a complete recovery; and many who though still disabled reach a quiescent stage so that they can be cared for at home. There is good evidence that the prognosis has improved over the past thirty years. Three groups of workers gave the following percentage of total remissions in cases followed up prior to the Second World War: Stalker (1939), 12 per cent., and Guttmann, Mayer-Gross and Slater (1939), 21·5 per cent., both in Britain; and Rennie (1939), 24·6 per cent. in the U.S.A. In contrast Wing (1966), in a follow-up study of early schizophrenic patients after 5 years, found that 38 per cent. of his cohort had no symptoms in the final 6 months: while about one-quarter were still severely ill and another quarter were handicapped by less severe symptoms. One can say, therefore, that nearly half of the first-admitted schizophrenic patients now have a fairly good prognosis, and will require little or no after-care in the following few years.

The specific symptoms developed are of very little help in estimating whether the outcome of the illness is likely to be favourable or unfavourable. One must look at the total clinical picture, its setting and evolution. A long history of insidiously developing withdrawal of interests and progressive inefficiency is very ominous. Cases of acute onset—in particular, the catatonic group—have generally a better prognosis than those developing insidiously, but although this holds true for the majority it is no absolute criterion. We have seen cases of very acute onset who, far from showing signs of improvement, exhibited a gradual deterioration. Those who have been ill for less than a year before admission to hospital have a better prognosis than those who have been ill for longer.

Emphasis should be placed on an attempt to estimate how the individual met his difficulties in the pre-psychotic period. If he handled them for the most part in a satisfactory way, and if his general interests have been well maintained, then he has a much better chance of readjusting himself than the shut-in, introverted individual. The preservation of more or less adequate affective responses and rapport during the illness is a hopeful sign.

Illnesses precipitated by obvious exogenous factors, physical and psychical, tend to be more favourable: but there is no hard-and-fast rule. In certain cases the exogenous factors seem even to release latent pernicious trends which can never again be thoroughly held in check. If the exogenous factors have been heavy, and are transient or reversible, the conditions for recovery are obviously made easier.

It has been claimed that cases which have a family history of affective psychoses, those which present with some clouding of consciousness and those which are in other ways atypical, have a better prognosis. This is hard to gauge. Undoubtedly some or many of these are cases of manic-depressive psychosis, not of schizophrenia. Langfelt has stated the situation succinctly in these terms: 'Schizoid character, leptosome body, insidious onset, lack of precipitating factors and initial symptoms such as massive influence and derealization phenomena as a rule indicate an unfavourable prognosis; cyclothymic temperament, pyknic body build, acute onset, demonstrable exogenic factors and a non-typical schizophreniform symptomatology on the other hand indicate a favourable prognosis.'

The prognosis depends also on how soon, how vigorously and how persistently the illness is treated. In treatment what matters most is perhaps the individual attention given to the patient; and even although the methods used are not in any way specific, the fact that doctors and nurses are constantly stimulating the patient along one or other line is helpful. After the patient's discharge from hospital much will depend on the understanding and support of relatives, on the tolerance of neighbours, on whether he takes the drugs prescribed and on whether or not the patient can be found suitable employment. There is nearly always a certain falling away from the pre-illness level of adjustment. Recoveries seldom occur with complete insight, and the patient who becomes re-employable is seldom able to return to his own job, something simpler being required.

TREATMENT

We have no specific and effective treatment for schizophrenia. Our attitude has to be melioristic: but much can and should be done which is helpful. In a considerable proportion of cases the treatment given determines the prognosis, at least in part. We can probably assist in arresting the disease process, we can certainly often limit the degree of deterioration, and we can sustain and develop the patient's undamaged assets.

Neither is there any sure way of preventing schizophrenia. Even if it were legally permissible, sterilization would not be a useful measure, since schizophrenia is inherited probably as a recessive and the parents are in most cases outwardly fairly normal individuals. We cannot for certain identify the carrier state, though we suppose that the schizoid individual may be heterozygous for the abnormal gene or genes. Fortunately, some biological circumstances tend to limit the spread of the disease. Schizophrenics have low marriage rates and low fertility rates, and few children are born to schizophrenics after the onset of their illnesses. If medical opinion is sought, one should usually advise a person who has had a schizophrenic breakdown not to marry: it is true that an understanding spouse might greatly help such a sensitive and predisposed individual, but child-bearing and child-rearing would be liable to bring stresses which would prove insupportable.

A more promising field for mental hygiene lies in the special care and under-standing which can be given to the child who is recognized to be shy and with-drawn and to have schizoid trends. We have as yet no proof that such special care of the schizoid individual at an early age can prevent the onset of schizo-phrenia, but it seems both humane and realistic to take deliberate precautions. We must encourage, stimulate, explain and try to 'exteriorize' those who tend to day-dream and to lead asocial seclusive lives. If there are difficulties in any part of the instinctual life, these difficulties must as far as possible be resolved; the shy and nervous and sensitive individuals who suffer from such difficulties must be encouraged to talk them over more freely, and must be urged to meet their problems face to face instead of dodging them. Consideration must be given to habit formation and character training, so that the child does not come to suffer from the kind of dangerous accumulation of faulty reactions to which Adolf Meyer drew particular attention. We may have to choose the sensitive child's school with care, and later by vocational guidance try to make sure that he enters the most suitable type of occupation or further training. These are tasks for parents, teachers, ministers of religion and family doctors: and, in the case of the more disturbed child, for the child guidance and specialized child psychiatric services. Every endeavour must be made to identify the child who is labouring with problems of adjustment, and to bring help at an early stage.

When the illness has been diagnosed or suspected, admission to hospital is in most cases advisable even if the patient's disturbed conduct does not make it imperative. The young schizophrenic patient is unpredictable and at home he imposes great strains on his family. The orderliness and discipline of a hospital regime, and the understanding attitudes of the staff, have a calming effect, the patient's mental condition can be more thoroughly assessed in hospital, and the effects of various methods of treatment can be more certainly ascertained. The co-operation of the patient's relatives must be secured from the outset by explain-ing to them something of the nature of the patient's illness, the objectives of treatment and the lines of management which are proposed; and the relatives should be encouraged to visit the patient regularly and frequently in hospital. The therapist should never imitate the patient in ignoring the claims of the world outside the hospital: and if the patient's home circumstances are reasonably good, the objective should be to return him home as soon as his more acute and disabling symptoms have been controlled. In considering discharge from hospital one has to weigh up both the patient's need for rehabilitation in a more normal environment and the ability of his relatives to sustain any residual mental dis-abilities which the patient may show. To discharge a patient prematurely is per-haps usually less of a mistake than to keep him in hospital too long, but it may lead to losing the ground gained therapeutically and may so antagonize relatives and the public that after re-admission to hospital the patient's next discharge may be very difficult to effect.

It has often been stated, erroneously, that the schizophrenic is incapable of rapport. In a state of stupor or acute turmoil he may be, and lack of rapport is a feature of advanced schizophrenic dementia. But most schizophrenic patients are accessible and capable of developing emotional bonds; and these bonds may be intense and ambivalent. The therapist first gains the patient's trust by himself taking his history in detail and listening attentively to his symptoms. Probing and interpretations of an analytic type are usually unwise, since they may easily result in the patient becoming more confused and disturbed. The therapist must not only seek to understand the symptoms of the illness, but also intimately the personality of the individual who has become ill, his defects and assets and the environmental pressures which have moulded him. He should orientate his treatment in much the same way as one does for a brain-injured individual, building upon what is uninjured or relatively intact in the personality, re-educating, encouraging, advising, praising, rewarding; directing the patient persistently towards normal ways of thinking and acting. This sort of supportive psychotherapy is relevant in every case. The therapist must be optimistic and not give up easily, since it is often a long haul until the patient can be discharged from hospital relieved. Analytic psychotherapy should be considered an experimental form of treatment in schizophrenia, to be undertaken usually only in hospital and only by most experienced psychotherapists. Modified analytic techniques for treating schizophrenics have been developed by Fromm-Reichmann, Federn, Powdermaker, Frank and other American workers (Brody and Redlich, 1952).

Individual interest in the patient is of prime importance. To be most effective, the doctor must leave his consulting room and the interview situation, to join the patient in the other business of hospital life. He must make contact with his patient at social functions, at games, dances and religious services, at the canteen and in the occupational therapy department. In short, the therapist must never limit himself to formal verbal exchanges with the patient. The nursing staff, more constantly with the patients and participating with them in many small activities and purposes, have commonly an even more important and potentially effective therapeutic rôle than the doctor. Nurses must be educated and encouraged to see that all their contacts with patients are potentially therapeutic, and not just those which have been conventionally described as nursing duties. All the time the patient must be brought sympathetically into contact with reality and helped to climb a ladder of social readjustment. Aggressiveness should be met with calm handling and explanation, as well as being diminished by the prescription of drugs. It is of the greatest importance to insist on good personal hygiene and posture, cleanliness, clean shaving, tidiness of dress, acceptable eating habits. The patient should be helped to take an interest in his clothes, to select new ones and to take an active pride in his appearance: anonymous clothing of the institutional type depresses morale. Exercises and games will help to restore the patient's physical tone and sense of well-being. All this gives the schizophrenic patient needed self-confidence. As well as being given individual attention, he should of course participate in group activities, and never be left to stand or lie about in lonely self-absorption. Group psychotherapy may be even more helpful to the long-term patient than individual psychotherapy.

The patient's general physical health must be cared for, his nutrition attended to and any concurrent physical illness actively treated. Though not in any way specific in their effects, other physical methods of treatment directed towards amelioration of the schizophrenic process itself play an important part in the total therapeutic programme. E.C.T. is often of value in alleviating depressive symptoms and in disrupting acute hallucinatory states. Tranquillizing drugs, in particular chlorpromazine and trifluoperazine, are useful in allaying turmoil and tension and in allowing the patient to become more accessible to other thera-peutic influences: and these drugs sometimes have a distinct effect in diminishing the strength and persistence of delusions and hallucinations. Chlorpromazine is prescribed usually in doses of 150 to 400 mg. daily by mouth, and as much as 800 mg. daily has been given; the dose of trifluoperazine is 5 to 25 mg. daily: both drugs produce Parkinsonian symptoms as their main neurological side-effects. A tranquillizing drug should probably be persisted in for 1 to 3 months, to give it a fair trial, and patients who respond to a particular drug may have to continue to take it regularly for many months or even years. Physical methods of treatment have also psychotherapeutic effects, and there is some evidence that the contacts of physical nursing may help the schizophrenic patient to recon-stitute the disturbed boundaries of his ego.

Occupational therapy assists the patient to regain his interests and to develop manual skills. When thus busy he is distracted from his delusional and hallucina-tory preoccupations; but distraction is only a step on the way to his rehabilitation. Occupational therapy must be followed by therapeutic occupation; first, in the grounds of the hospital or on a hospital farm, in an industrial therapy unit, or in one of the indoor departments of the hospital, the kitchen or joiner's shop or elsewhere. There every attempt should be made to train and fortify the patient to become fit to take a job outside hospital.

When the patient is discharged from hospital, he must not be allowed to fall into a social void. It is seldom of any use to return him to a lonely life in lodgings: if he has no home, boarding out with a suitable family should be considered. His return home must have been prepared by encouraging visits to him in hos-pital, by giving him increasing parole and later by allowing him home for short trial periods. The patient's relatives too must be prepared by an understanding of his illness, his needs and his limitations. A psychiatric social worker is often very helpful in smoothing the way for a patient's discharge by visiting the home and discussing with his relatives in that more intimate setting the problems and chal-lenge the patient's return home may bring. If the patient can be discharged to a job, so much the better: he must certainly not be allowed to return to a life of slippered indolence around the house. His relatives must often continue at home the work which has been done in hospital by nurses, and the patient's family doctor must attend to his medical needs, which include taking the drugs upon which his being able to live outside hospital may depend. Continuing visits by a health visitor or social worker may support both doctor and relatives in their efforts to keep the patient at a socially acceptable level in the community. Membership of a social club may draw the patient further out of his loneliness and diffidence.

The more enthusiasm and staying power we bring to the treatment of schizophrenia, the better are likely to be our results. All our treatments are empirical and limited in their effects: we are frustrated by our very slight knowledge of the aetiology of the illness. Schizophrenia still accounts for about two-thirds of those who require long-term care in our mental hospitals, and is thus one of the major unsolved problems in the whole field of medicine.

REFERENCES

Blair, J. H. (1952) *J. ment. Sci.*, **98**, 464.
Bleuler, M. (1948) *Arch. Psychiat. Nervenkr.*, **118**, 271.
Bleuler, E. (1950) *Dementia Praecox or The Group of Schizophrenias*, New York.
Brody, E. B., and Redlich, F. C. (1952) *Psychotherapy with Schizophrenics*, New York.
Brooke, E. M. (1959) *J. ment. Sci.*, **105**, 893.
Brown, G. W. (1967) in *Recent Developments in Schizophrenia*, Brit. J. Psychiat., Special Publication No. 1.
Chapman, J. (1966) *Brit. J. Psychiat.*, **112**, 225.
Dunham, H. W., Phillips, P., and Srinivasan, B. (1966) *Amer. sociol. Rev.*, **31**, 223.
Dunlap, C. B. (1924) *Amer. J. Psychiat.*, **3**, 403.
Federn, P. (1952) *Ego Psychology and the Psychoses*, New York.
Fenichel, O. (1946) *The Psychoanalytic Theory of Neurosis*, London.
Freeman, T., Cameron, J. L., and McGhie, A. (1958) *Chronic Schizophrenia*, London.
Freud, S. (1914) *The Standard Edition of the Complete Psychological Works* (1953), London.
Gillies, H. (1958) in *Topics in Psychiatry*, ed. Rodger, T. F., London.
Gjessing, R. (1938) *J. ment. Sci.*, **84**, 608.
Goldberg, E. M., and Morrison, S. L. (1963) *Brit. J. Psychiat.*, **109**, 785.
Gottesman, I. I., and Shields, J. (1966) *Brit. J. Psychiat.*, **112**, 809.
Harris, A. (1959) *J. ment. Sci.*, **105**, 235.
Heron, W., Bexton, W., H., and Hebb, D. O. (1953) *Amer. J. Psychol.*, **8**, 366.
Heston, L. L. (1966) *Brit. J. Psychiat.*, **112**, 819.
Hill, D. (1957) in *Schizophrenia, Somatic Aspects*, ed. Richter, D., London.
Hoch, D., and Polatin, P. (1949) *Psychiat. Quart.*, **23**, 248.
Hollingshead, A. B., and Redlich, F. C. (1958) *Social Class and Mental Illness*, New York.
Jenner, F. A. (1967) in *Amines and Schizophrenia*, ed. Himwich, H. E., Kety, S. S., and Smythies, J. R., Oxford.
Jung, C. G. (1960) *The Psychogenesis of Mental Disease*, London.
Kallmann, F. J. (1953) *Heredity in Health and Mental Disorder*, New York.
Kety, S. S. (1967) in *Amines and Schizophrenia*, Oxford.
Kety, S. S., Woodford, R. B., Harmel, M. H., Freyhan, S. A., Appel, K. E., and Schmidt, T. (1948) *Amer J. Psychiat.*, **104**, 765.
Kraepelin, E. (1913) *Lehrbuch der Psychiatrie*, 8th ed., Leipzig.
Kretschmer, E. (1925) *Physique and Character*, London.
Kringlen, E. (1964) *Acta psychiat. scand.*, Suppl. 178.
Langfeldt, G. (1952) *Proceedings of First World Congress of Psychiatry*, Vol. 2, 237 Paris.
Lawson, J. S., McGhie, A., and Chapman, J. (1964) *Brit. J. Psychiat.*, **110**, 375.
Leonhard, K. (1939) *Allg. Z. Psychiat.*, **112**, 391.
Lewis, N. D. C. (1923) *Nervous and Mental Diseases Monographs*, No. 35, Washington.
Lidz, R. W., and Lidz, T. (1949) *Amer. J. Psychiat.*, **106**, 332.
Lidz, T. (1956) *Amer. J. Psychiat.*, **113**, 126.
Lidz, T. (1957) *Amer. J. Psychiat.*, **114**, 241.
Lilly, J. C. (1956) *Psychiat. Res. Rep. Amer. psychiat. Ass.*, No. 5.

McGhie, A. (1967) in *Recent Developments in Schizophrenia, Brit. J. Psychiat.*, Special Publication No. 1.

McGhie, A., and Chapman, J. (1961) *Brit. J. med. Psychol.*, **34**, 103.

Meyer, A. (1951) *The Collected Papers*, Vol. 2, Baltimore.

Meyer, A. (1960) *J. ment. Sci.*, **106**, 1181.

Mowbray, R. M. (1958) in *Topics in Psychiatry*, ed. Rodger, T. F., Chap. 2, London.

Myers, J. K., and Roberts, B. H. (1959) *Family and Class Dynamics in Mental Illness*, London.

Olkon, D. M. Z. (1939) *Arch. Neurol. Psychiat. (Chic.)*, **42**, 652.

Osmond, H., and Hoffer, A. (1959) *J. ment. Sci.*, **105**, 653.

Rees, L. (1943) *Physical Constitution in Relation to Effort Syndrome, Neurotic and Psychotic Types*, M.D. Thesis, University of Wales.

Shattock, F. M. (1950) *J. ment. Sci.*, **96**, 32.

Slater, E. (1953) *Psychotic and Neurotic Illness in Twins*, London, H.M.S.O.

Tienari, P. (1963) *Acta psychiat. scand.*, Suppl. 171.

Tietze, T. (1949) *Psychiatry*, **12**, 55.

Vogt, C., and Vogt, O. (1948) in *Schizophrenia, Somatic Aspects*, ed. Richter, D., London.

Weckowicz, T. E., and Blewett, D. B. (1959) *J. ment. Sci.*, **105**, 909.

Wing, J. K. (1966) *Proc. roy. Soc. Med.*, **59**, 17.

12

PARANOID REACTION-TYPES

The history of paranoia and paranoid states as we know them to-day may be said to date from 1818 when Heinroth described them as disorders of the intellect under the term *Verrücktheit*. In 1845 Griesinger described similar conditions, but he regarded the intellectual disorder which was present as secondary to an affective disturbance either of a manic or depressive nature. The above contradictory opinions have never been completely resolved or co-ordinated.

Kahlbaum, in 1863, was the first to use the term paranoia. Krafft-Ebing defined it as 'a chronic mental disease, occurring exclusively in tainted individuals, frequently developing out of the constitutional neuroses, and having as its principal symptoms delusions'. These delusions were believed to arise independently of any disorder of affect. They were bound together systematically, and by reasoned judgement and inference were welded into a formal delusional system. This disease was slow in its course, was subject to a certain degree of remission, but showed neither a complete recovery nor complete mental deterioration. Particular attention was directed to a study of the personality prone to develop such a disorder, and it seemed remarkable how often shy, solitary and suspicious persons expressed persecutory delusions; the excitable and egotistic were grandiose; the over-conscientious and eccentric showed a predilection for religious topics.

Meantime, Magnan in France was making a determined effort to give an even more systematic account of this disease which he described under the general term of *délire chronique à évolution systématique*.

He described four main stages:
1. A hypochondriacal stage, or stage of subjective analysis.
2. A stage of persecution.
3. A transformation of the personality, characterized by the expression of delusions of grandeur.
4. Occasionally a stage of mental deterioration.

During the primary stage the patient becomes self-centred, believes that remarks he overhears, or things he sees, or items he reads in the newspapers have some special significance, and are directed to him personally. Naturally he resents such happenings, he worries about them, sees meanings in them which were never intended, becomes resentful, avoids his friends and colleagues and shows an inability to concentrate on his work as he had done formerly. In the second stage, the morbid introspection which has been described is replaced by the development of delusions of persecution which dominate his life and conduct. All his suspicions are transformed into beliefs so that he may seek the help of the police, or may employ all manner of devices to protect himself from his supposed persecutors. He may even change his home and his employment, but wherever

he goes he seems to be followed and feels that he is the victim of a huge organization which is determined to ruin him and to make his life unbearable. Occasionally he may turn on his persecutors and attempt to right his supposed wrongs by
criminal action. Such delusional states are not infrequently complicated by an
hallucinosis which may affect any of the special senses but is, predominantly,
auditory. In the third stage it appears almost as if a complete transformation of
the personality had occurred. The persecuted man becomes the grandiose man,
and he does so in his attempt to find an explanation or compensation for all the
trials to which he has been subjected. He appears to argue that because so many
people seem to be interested in him that therefore there must be something which
calls for special consideration and in consequence he may identify himself with
God, or at least with some very distinguished person. During the passage
of years a certain degree of mental deterioration may occur, but it is surprising that the memory and general intellectual faculties remain remarkably
intact.

Kraepelin (1919, 1921) in his effort to obtain a clearer clinical differentiation suggested a nosological grouping which he termed respectively paranoia,
paraphrenia and paranoid schizophrenia. Paraphrenia he described as a state
intermediate between paranoia and paranoid schizophrenia, and without the
characteristic dementia of the latter. The term paranoia he reserved for cases
showing a prolonged course, unfavourable prospects of recovery, and fixed
delusions. He laid particular stress on the insidious development of a permanent and unshakable delusional system, resulting from endogenous causes,
and accompanied by preservation of clear and orderly thinking, willing and
acting; there is no real or genuine hallucinosis. The underlying personality type
is usually consistent with the clinical state. They are apt to be violent, excitable
persons, self-willed, distrustful people with 'a chip on their shoulder'. Homosexual tendencies may play a significant part in their make-up. Kolle (1931),
who reviewed Kraepelin's amongst other cases of so-called paranoia, found
that the group resembled schizophrenia both symptomatically and genetically.
But he noted that many were of cyclothymic temperament and pyknic physique.

There are lesser states amongst the paranoid reactions which have been
described, notably by Gierlich and Friedmann (1908), as 'abortive forms and
formes frustes'. Their cases had recurrent tendencies which were precipitated by
certain situations or circumstances. 'These are patients who present the picture
of paranoia, who develop systematized, persecutory delusions, with great irasci-
bility, with happy or sad affective states which last for several weeks, without
sensory impairment, and who rather rapidly recover, with perfect insight into
their condition, with a tendency to a periodic recurrence.' In analysing their case
material both Gierlich and Friedmann had comments to make which are of
significance in helping us to understand the mechanism of such cases. For instance, Gierlich concluded that a compelling emotion, anxiety, expectancy, envy,
might lead to a delusional formation, provided it had sufficient strength and
duration. Friedmann's views were very similar. While he emphasized the sensitive, obstinate, egotistical nature of his patients, yet in addition many of them

had been struggling with complex emotional forces. It was usually a disturbing experience which had created uneasiness or mistrust and remained the sole topic of the abnormal trend of ideas. Such happenings give rise to shame and guilt feelings, to uncertainty in relation to others, and ultimately to delusions. Friedmann believed that the experience preceding the development of the disorder corresponded very closely to Wernicke's conception of 'overvalued' ideas, and that the entire condition rests upon congenital traits, particularly of character.

While the above descriptions give the basic features of paranoid psychoses, we must take notice also of the contributions which have been made by Bleuler, Adolf Meyer, Freud, and some contemporary writers.

Bleuler was critical of the symptomatological differentiations of Kraepelin, and was much more liberal in his interpretation of paranoia and paranoid states. Bleuler (1912) also took issue with Specht and sought to prove that paranoid states were not related to manic-depressive psychoses (as Specht had claimed) and that they were not dependent on the 'pathological affect of suspiciousness'. Bleuler maintained that suspiciousness was not an affect, that it was not a mixture of pleasure and displeasure, and that therefore paranoia could not be regarded as an 'affect psychosis'. On the contrary, Bleuler argued that suspicion and mistrust were the result of faulty perception and interpretation and were dependent on intellectual processes. 'Suspicion simply means that one cannot definitely foretell, and in consequence the affect may be either positive or negative, the former being what we term hope.' He analysed the position further when he pointed out that the manic-depressive state is the typical affect psychosis because of the variability of mood, whereas in paranoia the affect remains stable. Furthermore, in the affective psychoses any delusional formation which is present is secondary to the mood change, whereas in paranoia and paranoid states delusions are the predominant feature, and any change of affect is based thereon. If, for instance, the patient's attention is shifted from his delusions, his affect is similar to what it is in sane people. Furthermore, paranoia can actually exist without the feeling of suspicion, as it does, for instance, when the delusions of persecution are replaced by those of grandeur. Surprisingly enough Bleuler's experience led him to believe that many paranoid patients never become dangerous. Our experience is that the majority of male cases are, potentially, dangerous. And our view seems to gain support from Bleuler's formulation of the development of a 'catathymic state'. It appears to arise in consequence of a complex of ideas (usually of a delusional nature) associated with intense emotion which may show itself in some form of criminal conduct. It is of some significance to note that Bleuler found evidence of lack of sexual power almost invariably in his paranoid cases, and no doubt it was this failure which led so often to the expression of delusions of jealousy and infidelity. His general summing-up was as follows: 'The constitutional predisposition will explain why these people and not others suffer from paranoia (and paranoid states) and Freud's complexes will tell us why the critical events have brought out the paranoia and, eventually, why the developed paranoia immediately connects itself with the events.'

Meyer (1951) regarded all paranoid states as transformations of the personality, in which reason appears preserved, but side-tracked, and no longer fitting into the natural and real work of the world or of the individual, but still active along set lines. It is the type of personality which is continually ready to see a biased meaning in things, to be suspicious and asocial. They are always wondering what others think, and attribute deliberate intention to casual and indifferent actions. Such paranoid tendencies, for a time at least, may be compatible with formally correct conduct, but there is a certain inability to adapt the personal trend of thought and elaboration and attitude to the actual facts. He suggested that certain grades or stages might be recognized in the development of a paranoid reaction:

1. Uneasy, brooding, sensitive type, with an inability to correct notions and to make concessions;
2. Appearance of dominant notions, suspicions, or ill-balanced aims;
3. False interpretations with self-reference, and a tendency to systematization;
4. Retrospective or hallucinatory falsifications;
5. Megalomanic developments or deterioration, or intercurrent acute episodes;
6. At any period antisocial and dangerous reactions may result from lack of adaptability and excessive assertion of the aberrant personality.

Freud (1911) and his co-workers and pupils have, however, been much more bold in their formulation, and have not hesitated to propound an explanation for the origin and psychopathology of paranoid states which is most ingenious, and in certain instances seems to be borne out.

They state that paranoia and paranoid states are dependent upon homosexual fixation which is repressed, but when a failure of repression occurs the paranoid symptoms develop as projection phenomena. Freud's views stemmed from his analysis of the case of Dr. Schreber. He showed that in the genesis of delusions of persecution the persecutor is the one who, before the illness, had a great influence on the emotional life of the patient, or was an easily recognizable substitute for that person. The person who, on account of his supposed persecutory activities, is hated and feared, is the one who was formerly loved and revered. Schreber, for instance, had had at one time a great trust in and affection for his physician, Flechsig, but during his illness he called Flechsig a 'soul murderer', and also exhibited a feminine wish fantasy (passive homosexuality) which had taken Flechsig for its object. The person longed for had become the persecutor. Eventually Flechsig became replaced by God, and this seemed to afford a way of escape from the unbearable homosexual wish fantasy. Flechsig and God both probably symbolized the father. Freud then came to believe that all the recognized forms of paranoia could be represented as contradictions of the proposition 'I (a man) love him (a man).'

(a) *Delusions of persecution.*—The contradiction in this case is 'I do not love him, I hate him', but such a familiar principle cannot become conscious, the mechanism of projection comes into play and instead of saying 'I hate him' a transformation occurs into 'He hates me which justifies me in hating him.' Then the contradiction really becomes 'I do not love him, I hate him because he persecutes me.' The persecutor is always the former beloved one or a recognized substitute.

(b) *Erotomania.*—The contradiction is 'I do not love him, I love her.' Then the mechanism of projection causes the following change. 'I notice that she loves me. I do not love him. I love her because she loves me.'

(c) *Delusions of jealousy, e.g. alcoholic.*—A man disappointed in a woman may take to alcohol, which means that he may go to a public-house where he may meet other men. The contradiction then becomes, not 'I love a man', but 'She loves him', and in consequence he suspects the woman in relation to all the men whom he himself is tempted to love.

Analogous to this is the jealous paranoia of women: not 'I love the women.' 'He loves them.' The jealous woman therefore suspects the man towards all the women who please her.

(d) A fourth kind of contradiction is possible, 'I love nothing and no one', which is equivalent to saying 'I love only myself.' This is at the basis of delusions of grandeur, and may be regarded as a sexual overvaluation of the ego.

Kay and Roth (1961) described patients over the age of 60 whose presenting and chief symptoms were paranoid delusions, as suffering from 'late paraphrenia'. In their series of 99 patients females predominated over males in the ratio of about 7 : 1. In both sexes unmarried people were over-represented. Forty per cent. of the patients were deaf to some degree, and Kay and Roth attributed their frequent social isolation to three factors—their abnormalities of personality, deafness and the fact that they had few surviving relatives. There was no doubt that paranoid personality traits had predisposed most of these people to loneliness.

Kay and Roth agree with the great majority of other observers about the uniformity of the clinical picture; the conspicuous delusions and usually auditory hallucinations; the relatively good preservation of personality, intellect and memory; and the usually chronic course of the illness. They conclude that 'late paraphrenia' is the mode of manifestation of schizophrenia in old age: and in support of this contention they draw attention to certain clinical features of the illness and to its genetic background. They describe what they call 'schizophrenia-like' disorders of thought, mood and volition; and believe that there is an inherited predisposition to the illness, probably multifactorial and of lesser degree than in schizophrenia occurring early in life.

Post (1961), investigating a similar group of what he calls 'persistent persecutory states of the elderly', found at least three times as many first-degree relatives with affective as against schizophrenic disorders; and depressive admixtures were frequently seen in the patients themselves (53 out of 93 cases). Post agrees that these patients have only slightly more schizophrenic first-degree relatives than do healthy subjects. With regard to the symptomatology, he found that affective, volitional and psychomotor symptoms of schizophrenia tended to be 'vestigial'; and that in only about one-third of the patients did their symptoms shade over into those considered to be characteristic of paranoid schizophrenia—'and even they did not exhibit marked affective and personality

U

change of a schizophrenic kind '. Furthermore, the body build of these patients was not distinct from that of sufferers from affective psychoses. Despite these findings tending to distinguish the paranoid psychoses of late onset from schizophrenia, Post considers them to be partial or incomplete manifestations of schizophrenia. Post drew attention to two other clinical features of considerable importance: the episodic and recoverable nature of some of these illnesses, and the generally good response to treatment with phenothiazine drugs.

This review of some of the very extensive literature indicates that the peculiarities and differentiation of the paranoid psychoses are of considerable academic and clinical interest and worthy of much further study and investigation.

SYMPTOMATOLOGY

The onset of the illness is usually after the age of 35, women are more commonly affected than men, more patients are single than are married, and there does not seem to be the predominance of cases in social class V which is found in schizophrenia. The illness often develops insidiously out of the previous personality, and may in its earlier stages be difficult to detect, the claims of being unfairly dealt with or discriminated against having much plausibility. It is characterized by the development of delusions of a persecutory, grandiose or erotic nature, which become elaborated and systematized. Usually also there are hallucinations. The personality is well preserved, consciousness is clear, the memory intact and the emotions congruous.

It is only when paranoid symptoms are the presenting and main features of an illness that the diagnosis of a paranoid psychosis is justified. We include cases which have been diagnosed as paranoia, paraphrenia and paranoid schizophrenia, and see no merit in trying to distinguish subgroups. Cases of paranoia as defined by Kraepelin are very rare but probably do occur.

Paranoid symptoms occur as secondary features in many other psychoses, *e.g.* in schizophrenia, manic-depressive reactions and both acute and chronic organic psychoses.

The Previous Personality

The personality-type is one of the most potent predisposing factors. The sensitive, suspicious, jealous, ambitious person; the shy, prudish, dreamy and impractical; and the selfish and vain—these types all occur, particularly the first; but in some cases no suggestive personality traits are disclosed. The typical 'paranoid' personality is rigid, unwilling to compromise, humourless, sensitive to slights, a person who cannot be crossed or made fun of, often aggressive and resentful of discipline.

The rôle of inferiority feelings, on whatever ground, is considerable in the genesis of paranoid states. This sense of inferiority may be the result of disappointment in inflated ambition; or it may be associated with guilt feelings, auto-, hetero-, or homo-sexual in origin. There is frequently a 'complex' with a very strong affective component, often sexual in nature. The sexual desires being of a forbidden kind (heterosexual in women, and often homosexual in men) have been repressed. Or there may be a history, for example, of venereal infection accompanied by shame, guilt and self-consciousness. When a person is so involved the effect of some innocent and trifling incident may be profound, and memories and former associations are relighted; *e.g.* the routine visit of a policeman to a man who had long cherished in secret his shame of venereal disease. Conversely, in illnesses which seem to date from such an incident it is often possible to trace a particular predisposition, either of the total personality, or in the form of some more localized 'complex'.

Homosexual trends may, as Freud described, be repressed and projected on to individuals in the immediate environment: but homosexuality is not such a specific factor in the aetiology of paranoid psychoses as Freud believed. In women, heterosexual wishes are much more often projected: and many men who suffer from paranoid psychoses are preponderantly heterosexual, judged both by their ordinary lives and by the content of their delusions.

Anything which causes social difficulty, isolation or ostracism may be an important predisposing factor. Paranoid traits of personality in themselves of course tend to isolate the individual socially: he may be too prickly, proud and suspicious to marry or to make friends. When thwarted he tends to blame others, and his argumentativeness and aggression precipitate him into conflicts. Deafness may make an individual feel most painfully cut off from others and it potentiates any tendency to suspicion and misinterpretation. That paranoid reactions become commoner with advancing age is probably due in part at least to the social isolation and loneliness to which old people are so prone.

The Illness

These patients brood over grievances, and then project and rationalize their aggression, hatred or longing. Ideas of reference insidiously become delusions of persecution. Plots, they believe, are hatched against them: their thoughts, their persons and their property are interfered with. They are hypnotized, influenced by electricity or rays, machines are made to play upon them and control them, they are drugged or poisoned. Intruders enter their homes, spy upon them, remove things, cause disturbances at night, assault them sexually. Middle-aged women, especially spinsters, claim that they are pestered by men. Usually these delusions are accompanied by hallucinations, which in the large majority of cases are auditory: voices threaten, accuse or command them, and they receive fantastic messages. This persecution is greatly resented. The persecutors may not be clearly identified and are then referred to as 'they': when they are identified it is usually neighbours who are blamed, but it may be relatives, doctors, religious or political organizations, foreigners or some other group. If these patients think that they can identify their persecutors, they may attack them physically—there is a risk of serious assault or murder; molest their property; or go to law against them. Georgina Weldon, a Victorian campaigner against the Lunacy Laws and a paranoiac with an 'unexampled zest for litigation', issued a record fourteen writs within three weeks.

As they become gradually more deeply involved in their delusional beliefs these patients tend to scrutinize the past and to find evidence there too of persecution which they had not recognized before—a process described as retrospective falsification.

Delusions of persecution may characterize the illness throughout: or a sense of superiority, or at least a striving for it, may lead eventually to the development of grandiose delusions. Sometimes the development of the two delusional trends seems to be concurrent, but delusions of grandeur are not followed by delusions of persecution. The sources of secondary elaboration of the delusions, especially the development of grandiose trends concurrently with or after persecutory ones, are multiple—the affect of the original complex or complexes continues to operate; more or less logical influence is brought to bear on phenomena observed under the influence of the first factor; and the compensatory superiority feelings sometimes present in great force produce flattering rationalizations. The patients then come to believe that they have unique abilities or a divine mission, that they are of royal birth or married to someone of high estate, or that they are in some other way especially distinguished.

Such an illness usually develops over months and years, the delusions becoming progressively more fixed, unshakable and extensive. But illnesses which run a fluctuating course, abortive attacks, and formes frustes also occur. The most transitory of these should, however, probably not be grouped with the paranoid psychoses. For example, the brief paranoid reactions which may develop acutely after an operation or in the setting of a severe debilitating illness in the unfamiliar environment of a general hospital, are probably more accurately classed with the delirious reactions if there is mental clouding, and with the panic reactions if consciousness is clear [see also p. 444]. These reactions, in which the affect of fear or depression is prominent, usually subside almost as quickly as they arise.

The clinical picture of fully developed paranoid psychoses will be exemplified further in the following case histories.

CASE No. 27

In the timidity, shyness, sensitiveness and lack of application of his boyhood, he early exhibited a tendency to be out of touch with reality and with his fellows—a very common foundation for feelings of dissatisfaction and actual antagonism, and one which would readily be strengthened by the occurrence of such incidents as the homosexual adventures he met with. Homosexual incidents, being covertly focused upon, readily act as a basis for sensitiveness towards the 'herd', as the patient rather significantly called his fellows.

Lack of application to his work led to inefficient performance and failure, and a definite feeling of social inferiority from another direction. Masturbation seems also to have contributed to his many-sided sense of unworthiness. His attempt at compensating his inferiority, not unhealthy in itself, soon reached unhealthy dimensions. His compensating feeling of superiority went far beyond the bounds of reasonable possibility, and produced the grandiose ideas of his psychosis, of which the muddled, high-flown mystical trends were an example. His exhibitionist tendencies (Müller's exercises in full view of the public) were, of course, related to his other sexual trends. His overweening sense of general superiority and his exhibitionism are different aspects of what McDougall would have called his self-regarding sentiment, what the Freudians would call 'narcissism' and what others have called the paranoiac 'hypertrophy of the ego'.

The course of the symptoms is clear enough as far as the sexual trends are concerned— rumination over homosexual episodes, with the stirring up of homosexual desires; repudiation of them at first, and projection of them on the environment; but finally, increasing acknowledgement of their subjective origin.

The fact of transition from an attitude of inferiority to one of superiority is also sufficiently clear; but in this patient the ideas of superiority are certainly not a matter of logical deduction from delusional premises, but of something deeper—a craving for the satisfaction which life has denied him.

Symptomatically the clear thinking on other topics, the absence of hallucinations and the attacks of impulsive violence are all noteworthy.

The patient was described as a shy, sensitive, timid person, who did not interest himself in his school work, and was inclined to resent any criticism. His apparent backwardness at school was due much more to lack of application than to any intellectual defect. If teased or cuffed by any of his comrades he did not retaliate but went home and wept to his mother. He was unable to pass the university entrance examination, and went into an office in the city. He soon changed his occupation, and, after being in several positions, he set out on a voyage to South America, but, behaving in a strange, excitable way, he was put ashore at the Canary Islands, and eventually brought back to the British Isles. We have no description of what happened on board the ship. Prior to his voyage, however, it had been noted that his behaviour was strange, in that he had left his positions without adequate reason, but always on account of some imagined slight. Following this, he went to Canada, and stayed there for a period of seven months. On his return home he obtained a position in a laboratory, but after changing from one to another he decided that he was being persecuted. In consequence he entirely gave up his employment, and for twelve years previous to his admission he had not done any work. Gradually he began to express his ideas of persecution more constantly. Everything that went on around him seemed to have some special reference to himself, and everyone with whom he came into association seemed to be conspiring against him. The war preyed on his mind. He was much against it, gave the usual high-flown pseudo-philosophic reasons of war's insanity and uselessness and refused to do anything for his country. He began to state that the police were shouting in at his bedroom window at night-time, making insulting and obscene remarks, that people were pointing at him in the streets and that he was surrounded by a host of watchers. His suspicions became more and more diffuse, and every sound made, every action that was done, was interpreted by him as a sexual symbol. A night or two previous to his admission he rushed into the room where his sisters were and threatened either to rape them or kill them. At this time he was talking in a very grandiose way, stated that he had revolted from organized society, that he objected to vote as 'the herd' did and that law and government and social organizations were 'all nonsense'.

At the time of his admission the patient adapted himself pleasantly enough, but he resented having been brought to hospital, said that the whole procedure was quite illegal and that there was no necessity whatsoever to admit him on an emergency certificate. Without being urged, however, he began to tell the doctor how the police had been shouting in at his bedroom window. He spoke in an affectedly humble way of his knowledge of philosophy, and how few people understood it. He answered questions readily and correctly, but in his answers he was apt to become diffuse, and frequently dragged in some ideas connected with his delusions. He stated that he had known that sooner or later 'the herd' would 'get him down' and have him put in hospital, and he expressed the idea that the herd was always against those who had enough brains to think for themselves. He related an incident when he was 10 years old when a ticket-of-leave man from Perth prison had attempted improper practices with himself and a friend. No actual relation occurred, but the episode frightened him, and, looking back on it, he is certain that this man was a police spy. He could give no reason for this assumption save the light of his subsequent experiences. When he was about 14 years old, the same thing happened, he said, with a man who purported to be a night-watchman, but the patient then added, 'As he went home to bed at night, and did not appear to watch anything, I think I am justified in saying he was also a police spy'. At that time, and for some years following, he was greatly troubled with nocturnal emissions, and he now regards these as having been manifestations of some malign influence.

In reference to his beginning work in an office at 16, he said, 'I will not say I was persecuted, but I was just made to feel—as always—that I did not belong, that I was different and regarded with suspicion'. On this account he left the office and entered another one, but left for a similar reason and tried to enter the university. He is certain, however, that the Registrar was not sympathetic towards him, and told him that without his Leaving Certificate he could not enter. The Registrar seemed to be making much of two young men, and was saying to them, 'I see that you were at a public school. We are always very glad to get public school boys here', and while saying this he gave the patient a scornful glance, as much as to say, 'That is you washed out'.

The patient described how a system of spying and persecution had been going on for the past twenty years. Always his remarks were coloured by an artificially humble attitude about his own abilities. 'You can see, I expect, that perhaps I'm not just exactly below the average. I am not altogether shallow-minded.' He spoke a great deal about the interrelation of philosophy and science, how one could not have, or even think of, the one. without, or in terms of, the other, explaining that that was where Haeckel failed. 'A good sound man, unimaginative perhaps, but sound, and yet no-where, because he had no science. Now that is where I want to begin.' He related how when he had been working in a certain laboratory his urine had been examined, and that afterwards his teachers seemed to twit him rather unkindly about the presence of mucus and vaginal epithelial cells. He believes that this was part of the plot on the part of society to make him 'cave in'. Eventually he left there on account of 'petty attentions which I did not mind very much really'. He then told how he had fitted up a small laboratory at home, but when he mentioned this to a friend it seemed to be construed into an allusion to tender passages with some girl. It was about this time, he said, ten or twelve years previous to admission, that the police began to pay special attention to him. Insulting remarks were frequently shouted in to him through his open bedroom window while he was asleep. This was done by a policeman whom he knew quite well, who had no personal enmity to him, but was obeying orders. The police, he feels sure, were told to do this by the Chief Constable, because 'the herd' were outraged by the patient doing Müller's exercises before an open window, and had complained to the City Fathers. Having described this episode, he gave a diatribe on the theme, 'To the pure all things are pure'. He then related what he called his 'Blank Experiment'. It seemed to him that people might try to annoy him by jingling money in their pockets. He waited for a year, and never heard anyone doing it. This struck him as significant, and he wrote down, in a notebook he used for jottings, that people might, to annoy him, jingle money in their pockets. From that day onwards, more and more, he heard people jingle coins as they passed him. This proved that 'there must be a plot' against him, and also that his notes were being systematically perused by others. He related an endless number of such incidents—how beggars on the street made strange gestures as he passed, how people looked out of the window at him, how blinds were pulled half-way down on his approach, as a signal to those farther up the street, how bags were opened in the theatre as a special signal.

His memory, both for recent and remote events, was unimpaired; his grasp of general knowledge was excellent, and he had a clear realization of his position, but had no real insight into his condition.

Physically he was in excellent general health. He was a tall, well-built man.

Following his admission, he took up the position that he was misunderstood, that his detention was part of the plot of society against him, that it was quite unjustified, that it was a criminal proceeding, that the superintendent and all associated with him would be made to pay dearly for it. His attitude at all times was one of superiority and condescension; he always felt that he was on a higher intellectual plane than anyone else. For example, he stated that his coming here had interrupted a small job that he was on. He explained that he had been writing a piece of music on the subject of a chapter in *Travels with a Donkey*. When asked if this was for the piano, he said, 'No, for a small orchestra of about forty performers', adding, 'it was as easy as falling off a fence—to me at any rate'. The most insignificant, trivial happenings in the ward were interpreted as being done with the sole purpose of annoying him. He stated that he experienced pains in his abdomen, due to the movements of the mouth of the sister in charge, which he looked upon as a sex symbol. At night-time he did not sleep well, and he alleged that he was purposely prevented from sleeping. He constantly spoke about 'the herd', whom he described as 'haters of bravery and individuality', and then arrived (as he invariably did) at the sex aspect of the situation, and said, 'What they always do is to grab the unfortunate man by the genitals who dares to think for himself, and keep ragging at him until he gives in and lies down to it. It is just all part of the plot.'

A few days after his admission he rushed out of his bedroom at seven o'clock in the morning and attacked the attendant in charge. The assault was a violent one, and two other attendants had to come to the rescue before the patient could be controlled. He did not give any explanation for this assault, except to say that the attendant had annoyed him by walking up and down the ward, that there was no necessity for him to do such a thing and that it was done with the purpose of raising sex ideas. He said, 'It is the same old system of punishment for self-abuse. There can be no such thing as self-abuse; it is a contradiction in terms. I refuse to take orders from a man like you.' The explanation for this idea was obtained later, when he said that he supposed that one of the methods of treatment in an institution such as this was to nauseate him with the thing that was supposed to trouble him. A similar outburst occurred the following day. He rushed out of his room in the middle of the night and assaulted one of the attendants, who, he claimed, had been making a peculiar noise with his mouth with intent to annoy him. He declared that the attendant's conduct was 'equivalent to striking him in his privates'. He demanded to be set free at once, and used the most abusive language to all the members of the staff, accusing the superintendent particularly of instructing his nurses in such methods of persecution. On one occasion he admitted that when he was in the presence of other men he felt what he called a 'wild sexual urge', which seemed to dominate him. He also said that he had dreams, usually accompanied by nocturnal emissions. In the usual type of dream, which the patient said is 'quite free from any element of sex', and which is accompanied by a feeling of pleasure, he is plodding along a road, through a beautiful countryside. In this dream he is always alone. Once, however, he had a dream in which he saw himself walking outside his room along with one of the other patients. The other patient was striking him on the side of the neck with a newspaper at every step.

Six months after admission he was given parole of the grounds and was allowed occasionally to go into the city, accompanied by a male nurse. For a time he enjoyed these outings very much and appreciated the privileges, but he continued to suffer from impulsive outbursts. On one occasion he got into conflict with one of the other patients, and before they could be separated our patient had been put forcibly on the ground, and sustained a severe bruise on his left eye, a cut on the lip and a cut on the right ear. His attitude towards this was remarkable. He pretended to treat the matter very lightly, said that he had no recollection of what had happened, that he must have been in a phantasy and that it was the first time that he had ever been so affected.

Seven months after admission he again made a violent assault on one of the night attendants. He caught him by the throat, threatened to strike him and only after a severe struggle was he overpowered. When asked for an explanation he refused to furnish one, but demanded that he should be allowed into town to see his lawyer. Later in the morning he attempted to leave the ward without permission. He stated that he wished to be allowed out into the grounds to pass urine, because he was quite unable to perform the act in the lavatory. On this occasion, while the physician was talking to him, the latter happened to rattle some money in his pocket. This was immediately seized on by the patient as a form of annoyance, done with the object of inciting him to attack the physician. He made many wild accusations against the officials in the institution, saying that it was their object to 'down' him and to persecute him in every way.

In contrast to his delusional formation, and to his persecutory ideas, it was found that on ordinary topics he talked clearly and intelligently, showing no affective disturbance and behaving like an ordinary individual. If conversation with him was continued over any period of time, however, his persecutory ideas always came to the surface. He believed, for instance, that certain lady patients had been deliberately set to follow him by the medical superintendent, and that the object of this was to stimulate him sexually so that he would misbehave himself and therefore be subjected to some form of punishment.

His delusional system is unchanged. He refers frequently to his persecution by the police, who are under orders to annoy him by making 'disgusting sexual signs'. He continues to have a very high opinion of his scientific knowledge, and says, for example, that he has no difficulty in understanding Einstein's theory. On one occasion he resented being given lettuce to eat: 'Fancy giving a bachelor lettuce; that is an insult; lettuce contains vitamin E, the reproductive vitamin'.

Case No. 28

There was no evidence of inherent predisposition, either in the family history or in the personal make-up. A 'complex' of very long standing seemed to be the underlying cause—the memory of her husband's unfaithfulness, and the hurt he had done her many years before, had been accompanied (judging from the content of her psychosis) by a good deal of vengeful rumination, in which she had fancied herself unfaithful in her turn. Her illness began at a period of life when repressions are apt to fail, and the repressed material blossoms forth more or less indirectly as symptoms. Not all the paranoid developments occurring at this age are as completely elaborated as this one was.

Symptomatically, the case shows some common symbolizations of sex feelings— 'electricity' and feelings of influence of various kinds. The paranoid trends are to be considered largely as projections of illegitimate heterosexual fancies.

This patient was 52 years old. There was no history of nervous or mental disease in her family. The patient married when she was 18.

She was supposed to have been a very healthy child, and to have developed normally. She had five children. The second was still-born, the remaining four were alive and well.

Her husband stated that she had been a most capable woman. He always considered her 'a bit better than himself', and she was the leader of the household, though never domineering. Her interests were centred in her home and in her family. She was sociable, a good hostess, even-tempered and met her difficulties courageously. She was well read, and interested in affairs generally.

Her present illness was stated to have begun six years previous to her admission. At that time, while on holiday, a room in the house in which they were staying was kept locked. The patient complained that she thought there was someone in the room who came out when they had left the house and examined their property. At the same time she told her husband that she was certain that some man was following her. Her husband investigated this, and found that there was no foundation for her belief. She stated that she could not stay in the house any longer, and returned home after a fortnight, having intended to stay one month. On her arrival home she at once complained that the house was in a filthy condition. This was not true. She began to accuse her husband of allowing people to come into the house 'to show off the dirt', and so induce people to believe that she was not doing her duty. She also stated that she was certain that her husband had men in the attic of the house who influenced her by X-rays in order to prove her immoral. About the same time a young woman visited the house as a collector for a bazaar. When her husband returned home the same evening he was challenged with keeping company with this woman, whom he had never seen. She was told that her ideas were imaginary, that she was suffering from delusions, but in reply she stated that her husband was trying to make her out a lunatic, and that he would marry this girl. She refused to allow her husband to leave the house in the evenings; she accused him of making signs to his agents, the X-ray operators, to influence her. She changed in her disposition, became irritable and in fits of temper she struck several members of her family. A doctor was called in to see her, but he was informed that he was an agent employed by her husband to make her do things in order that her husband might get rid of her. She complained of the noise of the traffic, and said that the noise was made at her husband's desire, to annoy her.

At the time of her admission she denounced her husband for having brought her to such a place, saying that he would never be forgiven, and that there was no justification for it. Later she said that it had been a great shock to her, that her husband had exaggerated her illness in order to get rid of her and that he would live to regret it. She said that she had been annoyed and worried because electric sensations had been entering her body, and that she had seemed to see twinkling lights and shades in her own house, and also in the doctor's house, which was not far away. These phenomena were all produced by agents, unknown to her, but probably employed by her husband or by the church. The motive was to make her do and say things in order to make people believe that she had delusions, so that she could be put away by her husband. She stated that two years previous to her admission, she had had a quarrel with her husband, during which she had told him that he should give up his eldership in the church, as he was not good enough to hold it. He agreed to do this. Later on, in the same year, she had gone to stay with friends, and while there a gentleman in the house told her about a woman whom the patient identified with herself. This woman had had suspicions of her husband, and the description of her family and her household surroundings corresponded so closely with those of the patient that the patient became convinced that she was the woman referred to, and that this gentleman must have got all his information from her church people. She began to notice now that people in the street seemed to know about her domestic affairs and were talking about her; her husband, she thought, must be spreading tales broadcast. Later she was convinced that an agency was formed to influence her, in order to make her appear to be suffering from delusions, so that her husband could get a divorce and marry again; he exaggerated her illness to such an extent that there could be no other motive. She also became convinced that the family doctor was in her husband's employment. She spoke quite clearly and connectedly, and had an excellent appreciation of time and place and those around her. Her memory, both for recent and remote events, was excellent, and her power of retention, her grasp of general information and her memory for school events were all very well maintained.

Physically she was a stout woman, in good general health.

Following her admission, she requested an interview with the physician, and stated that she had neglected to tell him that when she was pregnant with her second child she suffered from venereal disease, for which she blamed her husband at the time. There was no evidence of hallucinosis at the time of her admission, and she denied that she had ever heard voices. She described her condition somewhat as follows: 'At times it seems as if words were being put into my head, as if I was being the mouthpiece of somebody else. I will tell you the sort of feelings I have had. I have had different experiences: I have had the feeling of being almost benumbed—like catching the handle of a galvanic battery—I have had other experiences of something that makes my pulse beat faster. Perhaps I would be in the middle of something, when suddenly there was something like a stop put into my head, and things forgotten would come back, songs perhaps, or even conveying some message to me.'

When asked if she had ever heard anything that sounded like a voice, she said, 'No, I have never heard a voice at all; but I gave utterance to things; in regard to the church —I have been the friend of the church, and I have been religiously inclined all my life, and yet I have spoken and said terrible things about the church while that particular thing was on me. I acted under influence. I have no tendency now to swear as I did before, a thing that used to make me shudder. Once or twice the electric forces worked on me since I came, but nothing like to the same extent.'

During her residence in the hospital her condition showed considerable progress. She was very well preserved in her general mentality, but she was now constantly dominated by auditory hallucinations. Often she could be heard talking and shouting in her room, in response to them. She would not go out into the grounds by herself because she felt that everybody was talking about her and making remarks about her, and she continued to believe that she was being persecuted by X-rays. In addition, she felt that she was being watched at all times, even when she was in her own room. She felt that it may be all on the basis of jealousy. She had been so tormented that on occasions she had refused to sleep in her room, and for a time refused to go to bed. She was certain that if she did so she would be interfered with when she was asleep. A sample of her talk is as follows:

'There is going to be no insane certificate for me. It is M——, N—— and Company who are doing this. I am only claiming my legal rights to leave the institution. My husband has been paying for me, but N—— puts it all in his pocket. It is thousands of pounds they are swindling. I would not have a medical man made a criminal to save me. I should have been home long ago. M—— and N—— have called me a forger, a prostitute, and I am a highly respectable lady. Please sign my letter of clearance from the institution. Would you believe what N—— had the audacity to say to me, "Would you, for a piece of money, allow M—— to commit adultery with you?" I would never sell my honour to anyone.'

Her condition showed no improvement.

CASE NO. 29

In this patient the paranoid development occurred late in life (at age 58). The significant points are the patient's personality—ambitious, sensitive and suspicious; and the origin of the condition in a very definite event—the failure of a cherished ambition. This case furnishes a very apt illustration of the psychogenesis of certain paranoid psychoses, as described by Bleuler.

G. H., a married woman, 58 years old.

Both her father and mother were stated to have been alcoholic. The patient had six brothers and sisters.

Her early life was a somewhat hard one, because her parents neglected her. She received a good schooling, however, and after leaving school worked as a dressmaker. She married comparatively late in life, when she was about 40 years old. There were no children. Her husband described her as being naturally ambitious, anxious to climb socially, of rather a suspicious cast of mind, 'apt to put two and two together very quickly', and to read meanings into things. She was sensitive, and apt to apply remarks to herself which were not intended for her.

She was stated to have been well until about six months previous to her admission. Two years before her admission she had suffered a serious disappointment, having failed to inherit from a millionaire relative a large sum of money which she had expected. Her brother, who was a trustee of the estate, told her quite definitely that nothing had been left to her. She felt that a gross injustice had been done her, and began to speak of taking legal action. A few months later she became definitely suspicious. She began to think that someone must have been slandering her reputation, so that she was kept out of the estate on the plea that she would be unable to manage it. She gradually elaborated this idea. First she became suspicious of her brother-in-law, then of her relatives in general and finally of her husband. She began to pour out her troubles to various friends, and even to the clergyman. She imagined that people would come in the night and take her away. She accused her husband of throwing dirty linen out of the house to expose her, so as to damage her reputation, and of spreading stories that she was addicted to drink. Her husband stated that she had not been in the habit of taking alcohol at all. Three weeks previous to her admission she began to believe that another millionaire had left her a large sum of money, and she called on various people to see what could be done about it.

At the time of her admission to hospital she was in excellent physical health, and there was no suspicion of any organic disease. She stated that she had been in a highly nervous state, that she was in need of a rest and had decided to come voluntarily. She spoke about her ideas quite freely, stating that she was certain that her husband and others had been working against her, that she had been left a large sum of money and an estate, that the money had actually been deposited in a certain bank, but that for some reason or other she was denied access to it. She declared that her husband was spreading tales about her to the effect that she was dissolute and immoral, that he was hand and glove with a man called Brown, a publican, and that these stories were spread with the idea of damaging her reputation, so that she would not be considered fit to receive the money left to her. When she was in Edinburgh, and walked in the Gardens there, she saw a woman talking to one of the gardeners. The woman lifted her elbow as the patient passed. The latter interpreted this act as an indication that the woman was signalling that she (the patient) drank.

After a month's residence she stated that she did not feel that she could stay any longer, and she was discharged.

Four months later she was readmitted under medical certificates. After she left the hospital, she stayed quietly at home for a fortnight; then she engaged a room in a hydropathic establishment, and remained there for a period of five weeks. She then went back to her own home, arriving late one night, and for some time after she behaved in a most extravagant way. She ran up bills with tradespeople and for motorcars, and began to express ideas of grandeur, saying that she was the laird of a vast estate, that her husband was bound to give her £5000 a year and that she would see that she got justice.

When she was brought to the hospital she was in an angry mood, saying that there was no reason why such an action should have been taken, that it was gross injustice and that she protested very strongly against it.

During this second admission her ideas of grandeur became even more marked, and were freely expressed. She maintained that she had estates, that she was a millionairess and that she was being kept out of her money and her estates by certain financial trusts. She claimed Mary Queen of Scots and King David of Scotland among her relatives.

A good idea of her condition may be obtained from one of her letters:

'I claim the privilege of a private citizen. After two years of annoyance, my house open to ladies and gentlemen, everything inspected by them, drawers opened, letters read, garments displayed, fun made of them, the most private relations of home life, I have been tracked both outside, and watched in my home, by land and sea. Men have been engaged to traduce my kith and kin, because of the inheritance which is the dowry belonging to the heirs of Queen Mary and King David, grandson of Robert the Bruce. Everything has been done to disgrace me. I was brought here by force, and am kept until the inheritance is divided.'

Her personality was well maintained. She was always most careful about her appearance. Her antagonism to her detention was undiminished, and her grandiose ideas went on increasing steadily. When she began to talk about them she became slightly incoherent, but her ordinary conversation did not show this.

AETIOLOGY

This is still largely unknown. Probably the causation of paranoid psychoses is due to a constellation of factors of a constitutional and environmental nature. Very similar symptoms, all with the general stamp of the paranoid reaction-type, are capable of arising on the basis of factors which differ considerably in their relative importance in individual instances. Heredity, the previous personality, unresolved unconscious complexes, the vicissitudes of life, real injustices and physical disabilities may all play their parts, together with the factors of age and sex.

DIFFERENTIAL DIAGNOSIS

It is still a matter of argument (which must be resolved by further research) whether or not the paranoid can be separated from the schizophrenic psychoses. In making the distinction we emphasize the sex incidence, the age of onset, the previous personality, the absence of many symptoms thought to be typical of schizophrenia (*e.g.* incoherence of thought, incongruity of affect, volitional disorders, catatonic symptoms), and the absence usually at least for many years of a state resembling that of schizophrenic dementia.

Many paranoid psychoses seem to be more closely allied to the affective than to the schizophrenic reactions. Paranoid symptoms occur both in depression and in mania. In rare cases of chronic mania irritability and paranoid delusions may be the presenting symptoms, and we have seen such cases diagnosed as paranoid schizophrenia. Much more commonly there are paranoid features in the depressive psychoses of middle and later life, particularly in women: and in some of these cases depressive can only be distinguished from paranoid psychoses by the longer-term development of the illness, or by the fact that paranoid symptoms remain after the affective symptoms have responded to antidepressive treatment.

Paranoid symptoms may also be prominent in the persistent epileptic psychoses which may occur in cases of temporal lobe epilepsy [see p. 428]. In differentiating these states from the paranoid psychoses, attention should be paid to the previous personality, the presence or absence of clouding of consciousness and more lucid intervals, the occurrence of bizarre behaviour and of course the history of fits and the E.E.G. findings.

Paranoid delusions and hallucinations may be the presenting symptoms of an amphetamine psychosis [see p. 397]. The patient is usually a young person, there may be little or no evidence clinically of intoxication, and a mistaken diagnosis of schizophrenia may easily and understandably be made. Testing of the patient's urine will reveal the presence of amphetamine: and the illness resolves fairly quickly after the drug has been withdrawn.

TREATMENT

As a preliminary it is essential to obtain from the patient a detailed and thorough account of his life history, since this may establish a basis of co-opera- tion and win the patient's confidence. The doctor must be extraordinarily patient, sensitive and impartial. He should not get drawn into argument or contradiction and he should decline to state prematurely any personal point of view. He can easily say that in a situation of such complexity and difficulty he must know much more about the facts and the feelings and attitudes of those involved, before he can come even to provisional conclusions. Adolf Meyer (1951) rightly stressed the importance of hearing fully the patient's point of view, of allowing him to unburden himself, and of not offending the patient before help can be given. 'Here the first rule is to accept the statements in an attitude in which neither the patient nor the physician need at any time be forced to recognize deception. I am as capable of listening calmly and politely to an account of a system of delusions as I am able to inquire into the religious and philo- sophical views of an oriental, and do not see why it should not be possible to do the two things with equal fairness and equal suspense of criticism and argument and to arrive at a working agreement without any need of deception or sheer humoring.' If rapport can be achieved in this way, the doctor should endeavour in what he says, advises and does, to act as the spokesman and agent of what might be 'the consensus and conclusion of thoroughly informed and fair- minded persons; and the ideal to be kept before the patient is that he or she gradually join the consensus and make unnecessary any subjection against his or her will'. The aim is to reach a relationship of co-operation, and in all his deal- ings with such patients the doctor must be unflurried and unequivocal.

A few of these patients appeal for help and are relieved to be taken into hospital to be protected and escape from their persecutors. But the great majority will not accept interference and control, and resent intensely any suggestion that they should be 'locked up'. They usually refuse to go to hospital informally, and to effect compulsory admission may not be easy. The desirability of arranging for admission to a mental hospital is determined often by the degree to which their delusional beliefs lead them into conduct producing discomfort and loss to themselves or into antisocial activities, whether these be in the nature of physical attacks upon others or simply of annoyances by accusations or petty ligitation.

For those patients in hospital a constructive programme of occupational therapy and work, either in a hospital department or an industrial unit, is of great importance. Phenothiazine drugs may be helpfully prescribed: and cases in which there is an affective component may be relieved by electric convulsion therapy. These patients can be allowed usually a good deal of freedom on parole, once the patient and the doctor have come to understand and trust each other and the possibility of employment outside the hospital as a step to discharge from hospital should always be kept in mind. A state of relative stability and self-control may be reached, despite the persistence of delusions: and many individuals suffering from paranoid psychoses are in fact accepted remarkably well by the community, despite their obvious eccentricities.

PROGNOSIS

The prognosis of well-established systematized paranoid delusional states is extremely serious. It is very seldom that such cases ever make an adequate, or satisfactory, adjustment irrespective of any form of treatment which may be employed. A person so affected believes that he is right, that he is justified in his beliefs, and that anyone who opposes his point of view is behaving maliciously or at least non-understandingly towards him. The illness in most cases runs a more or less autonomous course, with gradual worsening and increasing alienation from others.

There are, however, lesser states, conditions where the delusional ideas are not so firmly established, and where the affective element is powerful. A considerable number of such cases are transitory in nature, are developed often in reference to certain specific situations and subside when such situations are no longer present. These cases are of more acute onset, are more environmentally than constitutionally conditioned, and in consequence we expect a fair number of them to make a reasonable recovery. A number need never be admitted to a mental hospital because they will co-operate very well on an out-patient basis. It is impossible to lay down any hard-and-fast statement as to how long recovery may take; it depends on the insight and understanding of the patient, and on the skill of the therapist.

REFERENCES

Bleuler, E. (1912) *Affectivity, Suggestibility and Paranoia, State Hosp. Bull.*, New York.
Freud, S. (1911) *Collected Papers*, Vol. 3, 287, London.
Gierlich, N., and Friedmann, M. (1908) Studies in Paranoia, *Nervous and Mental Disease Monograph Series*, No. 2, New York.
Kay, D. W. K., and Roth, M. (1961) *J. ment. Sci.*, **107**, 649.
Kolle, K. (1931) *Die Primaere Verruecktheit*, Leipzig.
Kraepelin, E. (1919) *Dementia Praecox and Paraphrenia*, trans. Barclay, R. M., Edinburgh.
Kraepelin, E. (1921) *Manic Depressive Insanity and Paranoia*, trans. Barclay, R. M., Edinburgh.
Meyer, A. (1951) *The Collected Papers*, Vol. 2, 495, Baltimore.
Post, F. (1966) *Persistent Persecutory States of the Elderly*, Oxford.

13

PSYCHOPATHIC STATES

In Chapter 22 it will be noted that the Mental Health (England and Wales) Act, 1959, has differentiated four groups of mentally disordered persons. Psychopathic states form one of those groups. The official definition describes them as 'persistent disorders of mind (whether or not accompanied by subnormality of intelligence) which result in abnormally aggressive or seriously irresponsible conduct on the part of the patients, and require or are susceptible to medical treatment'. That definition may not prove acceptable to everyone, but it has the merit of providing a useful working basis whereby a large number of mentally abnormal persons can become more clearly delineated. Psychopathic disorder was not defined in the Mental Health (Scotland) Act, 1960.

We include under the above title persons who have been from childhood or early youth habitually abnormal in their emotional reactions and conduct, but who do not reach, except episodically, a degree of abnormality requiring compulsory detention; they show no intellectual defect, as measured by the usual intelligence tests, and therefore cannot legally be classified as subnormal (mentally defective); and they do not benefit under prison treatment. They are not sufficiently well-balanced mentally to be at large, nor yet are they sufficiently involved as to be suitable for mental hospital care. They have never seemed to be the particular province of anyone, and in consequence they have often been knocked about from pillar to post with no satisfaction to those looking after them and with no benefit to themselves. And yet they are desperately in need of help, of guidance, of encouragement, and the psychiatrist should be better qualified to assist them than anyone else. It is in their homes, in their schools, their factories and workshops that they should be studied and dealt with rather than under hospital conditions. To deal with them successfully requires the co-operation of all persons interested in the problem of human betterment.

Let us attempt a further description: They constitute a rebellious, individualistic group who fail to fit in to their social *milieu*, and whose emotional instability is largely determined by a state of psychological immaturity which prevents them from adapting to reality and profiting from experience. They may be adult in years, but emotionally they are so slow and backward and uncontrolled that they behave like dangerous children. They lack judgement, foresight and ordinary prudence. It is the sheer stupidity of their conduct which is so appalling. 'The judicial, deciding, selecting processes described as intelligence, and the energizing, emotivating, driving powers called character' do not work in harmony. They are the misfits of society, the despair of parents, doctors, ministers, lawyers and social workers. It is probably social workers more than any others who are impressed by the complexities of such cases, and by the difficulty in placing them in satisfactory employment. It is hoped, however, now that so much more attention has been directed to them that they will receive more skilful attention and understanding. They constitute a challenge to preventive medicine, and make us aware, not only of the necessity of ensuring that children will be born healthy but also of doing everything possible to improve the environmental conditions, so that the stability of family life can be ensured.

In 1835 J. C. Prichard, a Bristol physician, under the title of 'moral insanity' and 'moral imbecility' described a series of cases which included the prototypes of the psychopathic state as we know it to-day. The term 'moral imbecility' was incorporated and defined in the Mental Deficiency Act, 1913, but we consider it advisable to make a clear distinction between states of intellectual and so-called moral defect. Prichard made the position abundantly clear when he wrote: 'There are many people suffering from a form of mental derangement in whom the moral and active principles of the mind are strongly perverted or depraved; the power of self-government is lost or greatly impaired, and the individual is found incapable, not of talking or reasoning on any subject proposed to him, but of conducting himself with decency and propriety in the business of life.' While Prichard was the first person to give a systematic description of those so-called moral disorders, yet others before him, notably Pinel, Esquirol, Georget and Rush, had drawn attention to their existence, and had appreciated their significance. Then later came interesting contributions from Morel and Magnan in France; from Lombroso, Bianchi and Tanzi in Italy; and from Krafft-Ebing and Ziehen in Germany.

In 1888 Koch introduced the term psychopathic inferiority, and suggested that certain hysterical and obsessional states might be so regarded, or at least had a certain psychopathic component which might influence prognosis adversely. This conception was widened and elaborated by Kraepelin, who drew attention to the fact that a vast variety of syndromes occurred which could be described in terms of the most obvious presenting symptom, e.g. excitable, impulsive, eccentric, liars and swindlers, antisocial and quarrelsome. He further suggested that closer clinical analysis might show that the psychopathic element formed a constituent part of certain neurotic and psychotic states. During the present century the contributions of Healy, Kahn and Partridge in America, and of Birnbaum in Germany, each from their individual viewpoints, have been outstanding. While Healy and Kahn have attempted a more accurate clinical analysis and differentiation, Partridge and Birnbaum have drawn attention to the sociological implications of the group, and have suggested that the term sociopath might be more appropriate. This is not altogether a happy term, since society does not always suffer as a result of their instability; some, as will be seen, even benefit the society in which they live. For such a diverse group it is difficult to devise a satisfactory nomenclature. We feel that it is better to describe samples of the group under convenient but admittedly somewhat arbitrary headings, so as to give a foundation upon which experience may provisionally be based. It has never been easy to differentiate these cases from many of those who constitute the prison population. It may be suggested that the disordered conduct of the psychopath is determined at a subconscious or instinctive level, in contrast to the reason and intention and free-will which govern the conduct of the average criminal. This is a matter worthy of much more detailed consideration. In order to illustrate the general complexity of the group the following case may be submitted:

CASE No. 30

M. B., 24 years old, single, was a young lady of attractive appearance and address, who came from a neurotic stock. For a long number of years this patient had been creating a great deal of difficulty in the home, so that her brothers and sisters felt that their mother's life was not safe. It was stated: 'Her vindictiveness is so extreme that she is capable of anything, while, at the same time, she is so plausible and cunning that she is able to impress all strangers that she is a persecuted saint condemned to live in a family of criminals and savages.' A few instances of her conduct are sufficient to describe the case. She refused to sit by her father when he was dying, to prepare food for him or to relieve those who had been constantly with him night and day. On the contrary, she jeered at the constant 'morbid atmosphere' of the sick-room. The family tried to induce their mother to have a nurse in the house, but she refused to do this lest a stranger should talk outside about her daughter's conduct. She terrorized the home for years, and drove more than one of her sisters away from home by her threats and her violence. When her brother came home on leave she did not speak to him during the whole time he was in the house. She sat at meals with her face turned away from him, and when he left to return abroad he had to search her out to say good-bye, and his farewell did not meet with any response. Her mother had to sleep at night with her bedroom door locked for fear of her daughter's violence, and she also had to lock her door by day in order to guard against thefts. The patient for weeks on end would not speak to any member of the family, except to demand money or clothing. It was also stated that one of her brothers, who was an apprentice engineer, had to stand over the water which he had heated to have his wash, because if he relaxed his vigilance the patient would take the warm water and pour it down the sink. One day in mid-winter she threw a bucket of cold water and deluged his hens, which were his hobby, 'just to see what he would do'. Frequently she told her mother that she 'would make her suffer'. On one occasion she walked through the house and crumbled every gas mantle into dust. She lit all the gas jets of the gas stove, and put over them every pot, pan and kettle the stove would hold, and then slipped quietly out of the house. Her habit was to rise any time from 11.30 to 2 P.M. to cook a meal for herself, and then to leave the house without a word to anyone. 'What she does, where she goes, and who her friends are, none of us are quite sure.' Indian ornaments, sent home by a sister, disappeared, and some Greek metal-ware which was also in the house disappeared and was discovered hidden in the commode in the patient's bedroom, awaiting a chance to be smuggled out of the house. A brother came home unexpectedly, and found his sister arguing with a rag-woman for the sale of his boots—his second-best pair.

On account of the difficulties of management, she was admitted under compulsory powers to a mental hospital. During her stay there she was unreliable in every way. There were times when she was better controlled and better behaved, but sooner or later she got into difficulty again. When found fault with, or criticized, or restrained in any way, she had outbursts of great passion, during which it was almost impossible to control her. She was sullen, sulky, spiteful and destructive, making life difficult for the other patients, and even striking those who were most helpless. At other times she could be most attractive and charming, and seemed almost out of place as a patient in a mental hospital.

Schneider (1958) included in his concept of psychopathic personalities

X

'abnormal personalities who either suffer personally because of their own abnormality or make the community suffer because of it'. He did not differentiate psychopathic from neurotic reactions, which fall within the first half of his definition. This seems to us to be too wide a grouping, and one which fails to bring into sharp focus this major medical and social problem.

CAUSATION

There is no specific cause, no single traumatic event either of a psychological or physiological nature which need necessarily be present. On the other hand, in every case we require to think of a combination of hereditary and personality factors working in association with a great variety of environmental ones which may have affected the health or social circumstances of the individual. Some persons are much too prone to over-emphasize the predispositional or constitutional factors, while others pin their faith and their treatment on a modification of the obvious and difficult environmental situations. No such division is possible. The whole situation must be considered in the light of all the surrounding circumstances, and if this is done then conduct which has seemed meaningless, foolish, irrational, may be capable of being more fully understood. We know that conduct disorder may be in the nature of an over-compensatory reaction for those things which ordinary daily life has been unable to supply, e.g. for poverty, broken homes, illegitimacy, etc. We also know that physical mechanisms may be brought into play by organic disorders such as encephalitis, epilepsy, brain injury or leucotomy. In all of the above instances the conduct of the individual may be so affected as to render him unfit for ordinary society owing to the transformation of his personality. He becomes governed and dominated by thoughts and feelings which are uncontrollable. That is why it is always so imperative to insist on a comprehensive medical examination being carried out in those cases where the conduct is incomprehensible, and in complete contrast to the persons's real character. It should never be forgotten that intellect and emotion and character do not always go hand in hand; one may not develop any more than the other. In the case of the intellectually defective, the situation can be measured and assessed, but so far no yard-stick has been devised to allow us to estimate the emotional factors in a person's make-up. 'We thus have people in our midst, semi-insane or semi-responsible, if you like to use such terms, in every walk of life from the highest social and political offices to the ranks of the unemployed and the delinquent, who not only are unable to conform adequately in their own personal lives, but may even be responsible for some of the greatest social crimes in history.'

In a small number of male criminal psychopaths a chromosomal abnormality has been found, the individual having an extra Y chromosome [see p. 531].

Electroencephalographic studies have shown that 65 per cent. of aggressive psychopaths, and 32 per cent. of inadequate psychopaths, have abnormal E.E.G.s compared with 15 per cent. of normal controls (Hill and Watterson, 1942). Hill (1952) grouped the E.E.G. patterns into two classes, those found in normal children and sensitive to the age factor, and those not found in normal children, and not sensitive to age. He believed that the first class may be associated with maturation defects in the nervous system, and the second class with processes of homeostatic regulation. In cases of psychopathic behaviour no single type of E.E.G. has been found. Focal abnormality in the temporal lobes (especially the posterior slow wave type of defect) is often prominent in personality disorder with antisocial conduct.

In 75 criminal psychopaths, characterized either by aggressiveness or hostility, or by extreme selfishness, or by inferiority feelings and self-destructiveness, the great majority were found to have either an abnormal E.E.G. or an unsatisfactory early home life, or both (Silverman, 1943).

A social factor which stands out pre-eminently in a large number of psychopathic cases is a history of a broken home or illegitimacy. The influence of an adverse environment upon the development of the child's personality has been discussed at page 61, where the researches initiated by Bowlby are reviewed. In a personal study of 34 mothers of illegitimate children we found that 50 per cent. were psychopathic. Binder's analysis of 350 cases of illegitimate pregnancies showed that one-third of the mothers were normal, one-sixth subnormal (mentally defective) and 50 per cent. psychopathic. It was further noted that 113 of the women were under 20 years of age; the love factor had not entered into the pregnancy, and in many cases there was hatred towards the unwanted child. It is easy to see that any inheritance of psychopathy from the mother will be reinforced by a sense of insecurity in the child, with the possible consequence of antisocial behaviour.

CLINICAL GROUPS

The line to be drawn between psychopathic states as a medical problem and delinquency as a penal one is sometimes very narrow indeed, and a degree of overlapping is almost bound to take place. On some occasions, when face to face with such problems, it has been thought that the law should take its natural course, but on other occasions, when dealing with the same case, care and treatment under mental hospital conditions has been suggested. There are numerous delinquents who have psychopathic personalities but who are best treated and dealt with under prison conditions, and there are many psychopathic persons who may never come into conflict with the law at all. The term psychopathic state, therefore, is not to be applied indiscriminately to every type of delinquency; it should only be employed when it has acquired a degree of specificity which cannot be questioned, and it should never be advanced in a criminal court merely as a plea *ad misericordiam*.

There are a huge number of persons, unfortunately, who suffer from a psychopathic state or constitution which has often been present from their earliest days, and which has remained unaltered irrespective of all the medical and social measures which have been tried. They respond neither to kindness nor to a beating, they remain a law to themselves, show an absence of altruistic feeling and require very special consideration. The varying clinical states exhibited are almost as numerous as the persons involved, but to facilitate classification we suggest three broad groupings:

1. Predominantly aggressive.
2. Predominantly inadequate or passive.
3. Predominantly creative.

Predominantly Aggressive

Those who constitute this group exhibit disorder of conduct which may reach the highest degree of violence either directed towards themselves or others. The characteristic feature is that it is not sustained but occurs in the form of episodes of shorter or longer duration, and is followed by a period of relative calmness, often with considerable insight into the occurrence. The attack, whatever the nature of it, seems to clear the air just as an epileptic fit so frequently does. The principal clinical features of this group may be exhibited in the form of suicide, homicide, alcoholism and drug addiction, epilepsy, and sexual perversion. All of the above conditions may be part and parcel of an accompanying psychosis, but in the present instance we are considering them merely as features or symptoms of the underlying psychopathic state. A detailed investigation of the life-history will show that from an early age, and at intervals throughout their development, whether at home, school or place of employment, their conduct has given cause for alarm owing to its wayward, impulsive, violent and undependable nature. As has been explained already, this conduct may be determined on the basis of a multiplicity of factors, some of which may be entirely obvious, but its intensity and fierceness seem often to be related to feelings of hate and frustration which have their roots in the instinctive life of the individual. There is little or no pre-meditation, the action is almost in the nature of a reflex—a trigger-like reaction giving rise to the 'chance, affect and opportunity' criminals described by Asch-affenburg; there is usually a clouding of consciousness with a varying degree of amnesia. There is a coldness, a hardness, an insensibility to the feelings of others, and an absence of remorse which relates the condition to a primitive level, and exemplifies the catathymic crisis described by Hans Maier and Wertham.

While the above-described features are evident, especially in cases of suicide and homicide, yet it is the same type of impulsive, ill-adapted personality that may use alcohol or drugs, or show epileptic phenomena or sexual perversion. The drunken bout, the unconsciousness of the epileptic, or the retreat to sex-perversion, are sometimes methods of escape from situations which for the moment have proved intolerable. They are the immature ways in which the personality attempts to evade reality. The persons who constitute this group are, obviously, a very dangerous social class, and the problem is made even more difficult by the inadequate provision for caring for them, and the difference of opinion which exists in regard to them.

CASE No. 31

A young man, 18 years old, was charged with the murder of an elderly woman, 63 years old, who had befriended him. The facts of the case were as follows:

He was an only child, whose father died when he was very young; in consequence he was over-protected and spoiled by his mother, who subsequently married again. He was a big, sturdy, ungainly youth who suffered from a stutter on account of which he had been teased. He was educated at a good school, but a report from his headmaster described him as an unsatisfactory pupil who had no interest in school work, and was probably below normal mental capacity. He left school when 15 years old, obtained work in a factory but was dismissed on account of his lack of interest. When 16 years old he was charged with 'Serious assault, robbery and lewd practices'. At that time he was considered to be strange and lacking in control; he was treated in mental observation wards, was given a course of electro-convulsion therapy and was put on probation. His probation officer eventually reported that he was deceitful, cunning, untruthful and not suitable for probation. He was again put under mental observation, was considered unfit to plead to the charge against him and was certified as of unsound mind. After a period of nine months' treatment an appeal on his behalf for an independent medical examination was granted. Two experienced and distinguished psychiatrists testified to his controlled behaviour and sanity, and in consequence he was discharged. He obtained work on board ship and was away from home for several months. On the day after he returned he committed the crime with which he was charged.

The lady whom he murdered was a friend of one of his relatives and he had known her throughout his life. While in her home he battered in her skull with a poker or other blunt instrument. So far as could be determined there was no ostensible motive for this foolish, unprovoked crime. The prisoner had a clear memory of all the events preceding and following the offence. He denied being prompted by hallucinations or delusions, and yet he acted with great violence. He could offer no explanation of why he had behaved in so impulsive a manner.

During his examination the outstanding feature was his strange, smiling, callous, unconcerned manner, and his complete nonchalance in relation to the dangerous and serious position in which he was placed. On account of this mental attitude, his lack of insight, his disordered judgement and his emotional instability, he was considered to be of unsound mind and was ordered to be detained in a State Hospital.

The case illustrates very clearly the difficulties and dangers involved. Here was a youth with a poor school and work record who had been brought up under unsatisfactory home conditions, and who on account of his erratic conduct and unstable disposition had required care and treatment in a mental hospital. Under such conditions he had behaved well, and in the examination carried out by experienced psychiatrists he had so comported himself that he was considered fit to be discharged. His subsequent conduct showed how narrow his margin of control was, and how, without provocation, he again committed a dangerous assault which resulted in the death of the victim. Surely such a case teaches us the necessity of treating all such psychopathic states with the greatest possible care, with greater care than one would bestow on the psychotic patient who has recovered, or even on the so-called sane criminal. We would even go as far as to suggest that the psychopathic person who has committed serious offences of the type described should not be liberated except under the most stringent safeguards, and only after a prolonged period of stable conduct.

It is the occurrence of such cases which brings forward the advisability of introducing an indeterminate sentence into the criminal code.

Such partly affected, emotionally immature persons are far more dangerous than either the sane or insane criminal. The former may readjust, the latter may recover and never commit another crime, but the partially involved may never recover sufficiently to be considered as reasonably safe. Their margin of control is too narrow and delicate. Everyone knows how futile it is to sentence such persons to short terms of prison treatment. We appreciate likewise that the majority of such cases are not susceptible to psychological treatment, but at least they should be given an opportunity for readjustment.

Predominantly Inadequate or Passive

This again is an important and numerous group exhibiting symptoms which may not be so dramatic as those already described, but which may be more persistent and with less chance of readjustment. Roughly we see two main types: 1. the petty delinquent class with thieving, lying, swindling propensities; 2. those who develop types of invalidism closely allied to neurotic and psychotic states. The background in each is essentially the same. On the one hand we have placid, suggestible, rather charming persons who readily accommodate themselves to the domination of others, and always follow the path of least resistance; on the other hand we meet cold, frigid, apathetic persons who, irrespective of the fix in which they may find themselves, are utterly detached and individualistic. Under these circumstances and with such ill-balanced personalities it is not at all to be wondered at that a multiplicity of symptoms should on occasion present themselves as reactions to the various situations in which the persons become involved. For instance, we see the so-called kleptomanias and pyromanias, conditions which are more common in children than in adults, due to their greater state of emotional instability and their embryonic state of social development.

Pathological Liars. These are persons who lie habitually and without external need. The condition seems to involve two processes: 1. falsification of the memory of actual occurrences; and 2. entirely new creations of phantasy. The haziness which normally obscures the details of remembered events is filled in circumstantially, at first perhaps with a feeling of uncertainty, but later, when the true details and the false have become inextricably mixed up, with assurance.

The pathological liar never tires of phantasies, which are usually of the nature of wish-fulfilments (often compensatory for a felt inferiority), and which he recounts to others with apparent belief in their veracity. The condition is the continuance into adult life in an exaggerated form of a tendency not uncommon in children. One lie leads to another, since previous statements have to be substantiated. The usual topics of the phantasies are the possession of wealth and position. The phantasies do not develop, however, into actual delusions—the patient seems privately to realize that they are fabrications.

A patient of ours, for example, recounted how he could indulge in imaginations for hours at a time. 'I could go to a dealer's and buy a Rolls-Royce, pay for the car, drive it home, visit my friends and so on', and he could recount such events to any chance acquaintance. But he had full insight, and said he realized he must stop the practice. This attitude of reform and desire to do better is not by any means always present. Some deny that they ever made such statements, and assume the attitude of injured innocence. Emotionally they are usually light-hearted, and have very little sense of responsibility. The patient mentioned above gave up his post as ship's officer, and was entirely unconcerned that there was no prospect of any other occupation for him. This attitude of complacency is usually accompanied in such patients by confidence in their own powers. They make a good impression socially, being gay and talkative, and full of information, which is superficial and, of course, unreliable. Intellectually they are usually equal to the average, and sometimes above it.

The pathological liar develops readily into the *pathological swindler*. In him the phantasies are translated to some extent into reality. The swindler not only says he is the Earl of X., but acts as if he were so—putting up at expensive hotels, running up bills for motoring and clothes. Such cases are frequently reported in the newspapers. East described a good instance of this type:

CASE No. 32

The patient had an intellectual capacity considerably above the average for her station in life. There was no record in her family of mental illness, epilepsy or nervous disease of any kind. She was dismissed from her last school on account of pilfering. She was described as having had a good, but superficial, education, as being a singer and pianist of more than ordinary merit, with attractive conversational powers. At the age of 15 'Jane' became intimate with her mother's lodger, and subsequently married him when she was 17 years old, her baby being born shortly afterwards. Her married life was very unsatisfactory; she was recklessly extravagant, involved her husband in debt and they shifted about from place to place. She neglected her home and children, and led a gay life, on account of which her husband eventually left her. Before they actually parted she posed to a lady as an heiress having a guardian. After leaving her husband she obtained a situation in a hotel as a book-keeper, but was discharged on account of her unsuitability. It was then found that she had obtained goods from local trades-people, representing that she was the hotel proprietor's wife. She was arrested, and sentenced to a short term of imprisonment. After her discharge from prison she went to a home, from which place she wrote to Mrs. X., the lady to whom she posed previously, representing the home as the mansion of her guardian, Mr. Y., who, she stated, was asking her to marry him. She stated that as her fortune was tied up until she was 23 years of age she felt at his mercy, but was determined to resist his attentions, and she asked Mrs. X. to take her as a paying guest. This plan did not materialize, and J. was recommended to another home, where she made herself popular with the inmates on account of her social talents and engaging personality. She told them that she was about to be married to a young gentleman, who eventually arrived for the ceremony. As soon as he discovered that she was a married woman with children he left her abruptly. Later she stayed in a local hotel at a seaport town. Fire broke out a few days later in one of the bedrooms, and the place was gutted. The next day it was discovered that the cash-box and a sum of money were missing. J., who had left the town, was traced, pled guilty to the theft and received a short sentence of imprisonment. On her release she resided in a leading hotel, posed as a rich ward in Chancery and at this time had plenty of money. She took a situation, succeeded in introducing herself into the manager's home circle, and while there she met a gentleman, Mr. Z., who within a few days proposed marriage and was accepted. Ultimately she married Mr. Z., but her life soon became very unhappy. She involved him in debt with her reckless extravagance; at one time he was paying rent simultaneously for three different houses she had taken in his name. She alleged that she was ill-treated by Mr. Z. She was attended by various doctors, and to one she said that she was the illegitimate daughter of a lady, an admiral's wife, who had erred during the absence of her husband at sea, and that she was under guardianship. This doctor considered her to be morally insane, and informed Mr. Z. that she had already had children. On hearing this Mr. Z. separated from her. Soon after this J. wore her hair in public as a long plait reaching below her knees, but no explanation was given for this conduct. Later she obtained a situation, but was discharged for stealing. Next she was companion to a lady under treatment for inebriety, but J. continued to supply her with intoxicants, and the inebriate lady became so much worse that she had to go to an institution. She then set fire to this lady's bedroom, stole a large quantity of her clothing, saturated some of the other beds with water, lighted a large fire on the kitchen floor and so terrorized the other servants that they all left the house together. She was arrested, charged with theft and sentenced to imprisonment. Following this she carried out various impersonations. She called herself a nurse, and was engaged to take care of a lady who was dying of cancer. A night or two afterwards she was discovered bringing men into the house, and instead of attending the patient she was usually absent from her.

A form of psychopathic behaviour which occurs as a wartime phenomenon—masquerading in uniform—was described by Stalker (1945). He reported a group of seven cases in whom the underlying motive seemed to concern itself more with personal prestige than with any materialistic purpose. The cases in themselves were of great interest as showing the length to which people will go to attain their ends even although that end may be a source of discomfort and annoyance to themselves, their relatives and every one interested in them. In all Stalker's cases the constitutional element was prominent, but he draws particular attention to the over-compensation mechanisms which were at work, mechanisms which were determined by a state of physical or mental inferiority. One of the most amazing of these cases was that of a young man, the son of wealthy parents, who throughout the whole period of his supposed medical career led a life of make-believe. He eventually returned home saying that he had been the most distinguished student of his year—a story which was accepted by his parents, his family doctor and his friends. Later, when he was arrested for masquerading as a Naval Surgeon-Lieutenant, his life-story was exposed; he accepted the whole position in the most nonchalant manner, stated that he had always craved for adventure, and that he would like to join the R.A.F. as a pilot. Unfortunately their practice lags woefully behind their expectations and they do not succeed any better in the Armed Forces than in any other walk of life.

Pseudo-querulants. The pseudo-querulants are usually described as a separate type. It is really a matter of accentuating a trait that is not uncommon in the emotionally unstable. They are very irritable. Hence they readily come into collision with other people, and regard trifling differences as grave injustices. They are also arrogant, and this combination of irritability and arrogance leads them not only into quarrels but lawsuits. They seek satisfaction from higher and higher Courts, if permitted to do so. If frustrated in this direction, they try other methods—making charges of perjury against the witnesses, and indulging in other slanders. This quarrelsomeness never involves them in actual delusions. Their feelings would be legitimate in isolated cases; it is the aggregation and universality of their feelings of grievance, and the manner in which the latter lead them into falsifications and inventions, that mark them out as abnormal. They are further distinguished from the litigious paranoid type by the fact that in the pseudo-querulants the tendency exists from youth up.

Eccentrics. The group is one which does not usually come within the physician's purview. When it does, it is usually difficult to distinguish the symptoms from schizophrenic manifestations.

Numerous other types of constitutional psychopathic inferiority could be described. Thus Schneider (1958) mentions, among others, the 'insecure', characterized by feelings of insufficiency; the 'self-seeking', including the 'hysterical character', so called, which he rightly regards as a misnomer, holding as we do that the 'hysterical character' and 'hysteria' are not at all the same condition; the 'explosive', the 'weak-minded' and the 'asthenic', the latter including those whom we have elsewhere alluded to as the scanty group of 'congenital neurasthenics'.

There is considerable evidence to show that the inadequate, immature, dispositional background of the psychopath may exercise a considerable influence, prognostically, on cases which symptomatically might be classified as neurotic or psychotic.

Predominantly Creative

At first sight it may seem strange to associate creativeness developing to a condition of genius with the aggressive and inadequate groups already described. Popularly, genius and 'madness' have always been closely associated, but that is an over-statement, and just as the aggressive and inadequate groups do not include madmen (as that term is used generally), neither does the creative group. We find, however, intense individualistic people who carve out a way for themselves irrespective of the obstacles which bestrew their path. Genius in its truest and greatest sense is a multiple quality, it has many facets, and associated with it there must be sufficient energy to accomplish whatever has been conceived. Such persons are not many in number. It is understandable that the sensitive nervous system of the genius is one which might quite well show vagaries in many directions. It is something which crops up in the process of variation. When we study the lives of those who have been famous in many diverse fields we find with singular regularity dispositional traits which are in fairly close conformity to the psychosexual immaturity, and emotional instability, and individuality of others termed psychopathic. Joan of Arc, Napoleon, Lawrence of Arabia, may all be taken as examples of persons with great qualities of leadership and of vision, but yet associated with a certain unevenness in their make-up which differentiated them markedly from their more ordinary companions. There is an uncanniness and an inspiration about them which is far beyond what, ordinarily, may be expected. Their objective is gained by a feeling that their way is right rather than by thoughtful, methodical planning.

It is believed that the clinical groups delineated are of great psychiatric and social interest, and that while they may seem heterogeneous, yet they have a common background in their constitution and their psychobiological development.

PROGNOSIS

It is obvious that the prognosis of such a diversified number of clinical states cannot be discussed in a categorical manner. The prognosis is likely to be more favourable when the patient is young in years, referred early for expert advice, and proves co-operative in treatment. But when the hereditary loading is severe, and personality defects have been intensified by unfortunate environmental circumstances then we are faced with a set of factors which may prove difficult, if not impossible, to modify. In any case the course of the illness or mental disturbance is so prolonged that many months or even years may elapse before the patient's future stability can be regarded as reasonably secure. So many become dogged by a sense of failure and resentment that they feel that every man's hand is turned against them. In consequence, all too often they develop a cynical fatalism which seems to glorify their rebellious, individualistic, selfish conduct.

On the other hand it has been our experience that a much larger number of cases than might be thought have a genuine desire to obtain help, and are willing to co-operate to the best of their ability. They have their lapses and failures but if the physician continues to exercise individual care combined with great patience a *rapport* can be effected which breeds mutual trust and confidence, and leads to a sense of greater hopefulness. The importance of the ageing factor should never be lost sight of; a state of greater emotional maturity and stability may be delayed until the middle thirties. That fact by itself should encourage us to persevere in our therapeutic efforts. It may be that as our knowledge of personality structure and character formation increases, and more follow-up studies are made, we will be able to report a more favourable prognosis than heretofore.

TREATMENT

The successful treatment of psychopathic persons does not rest with the medical profession alone. It is a medico-social problem of great complexity which constitutes a challenge to society in relation to every aspect of social health and welfare. While we are unable to specify definite forms of treatment yet we can formulate some general principles which, in certain instances, may prove of value. We are never likely wholly to prevent the occurrence of psychopathic states, they will continue to appear during the natural process of variation of the species. Just as some persons, from birth or an early age, are handicapped physically and intellectually so there are others who, irrespective of their heritage and education, are lacking in mental stability, emotional maturity and social adaptability. In the former, precise methods of training can deal reasonably well with defects of intelligence and physical incapacity, but in the latter the problem presented is much more complex. For we are then called upon to deal with anomalies of character and personality which prevent the individual's adjustment to his social *milieu*. Every medical and social discipline may require to be called into action. Through our understanding of the psychobiological principles which govern reactive tendencies we should, medically, be able to give a lead as to how treatment might most profitably be directed. This entails the co-operation of parents, schoolmasters, social workers, probation officers and all others concerned with the health and welfare of young people. And this is also the reason why we so strongly support the development of organizations such as the Cubs, Brownies, Girl Guides, Scouts, Boys' Brigades, etc. It is during puberty and adolescence that everything possible requires to be done to inculcate high standards of decent conduct. It is at this preventive level when all deviations of conduct should be examined in their entirety that we are most likely to attain success. Undue delay may spell disaster, and may lead to Juvenile Court proceedings, referral to a Remand Home, and perhaps to indoor treatment in an Approved School or Borstal. We do not gainsay in any way the most valuable work which all the above-named organizations accomplish, but like tends to be attracted to like and the association of groups of psychopathic persons may constitute a dangerous complicating factor in their successful treatment. It is, however, by our intensive study of such case material that we are likely to acquire greater diagnostic skill whereby we can enlarge our concept of mental abnormality. There are shades and degrees of abnormality which do not amount to a psychosis but yet are accompanied by a diminution of responsibility which can lead to disastrous results. We want to avoid such catastrophes. If we are fortunate to deal with such conditions in their incipiency excellent results may be attained by an environmental adjustment. A modification in the school curriculum, a change of school or of occupation, a good foster-home, the skilled guidance of a child psychiatrist, an expert social worker or probation officer and above all, kindness, friendship and human understanding may work wonders.

Adult psychopathic persons frequently require indoor treatment over a prolonged period but how and where this can be best carried out has not as yet been definitely decided. Our experience, however, coincides with that of others who believe that the wards of an ordinary mental hospital are not suitable. The psychopath disrupts the lives of the more contented and amenable psychiatric patients. If the mental hospital is used for such patients then a separate department should be built detached from the main hospital. When special security measures are necessary a special department of a prison, where there is an adequate psychiatric service, could be utilized; or else a completely independent organization with its own highly skilled medical, nursing and social service personnel could be set up. A notable example of the latter organization was instituted in 1933 at Herstedvester, Copenhagen, Denmark, providing accommodation for 180 males and 20 females. Its object is twofold: 1. to effect satisfactory preventive detention; and 2. to treat patients according to their psychical needs so that they may return to a normal life. Detention is regarded as a security measure rather than a punishment. The majority of the patients at Herstedvester are relapsed criminals who have committed serious offences, *e.g.* murder, incendiarism, rape, indecency to boys and girls, and drug addicts. The same court which orders the detention of the patient decides, on the basis of a medical report, when he may with safety be released on parole. The Medical Director is the counsellor to the

Ministry of Justice, and the officers of any prison are encouraged to seek guidance from him in regard to the management of difficult cases. An atmosphere of great activity is present throughout the institution. There are workshops with modern machinery, where the detainees work an 8-hour day at a variety of vocational tasks, earning 10 kroner or more per week. A lively, social club life provides an agreeable opportunity for discussion; study circles and correspondence courses are available, and everything possible is done to promote a spirit of hope and encouragement. Stürup maintains that upwards of 50 per cent. are able to resume normal life in the community. Sexual offenders who have been repeatedly convicted are advised to submit, voluntarily, to castration. As an inducement to do so the hope is held out that there may be a remission of sentence and liberation on parole at an earlier date than normally expected. Castration, however, appears to us to be a dubious practice, and is in striking contrast to the other much more constructive methods which are employed.

Maxwell Jones (1952, 1959) at the Belmont Hospital, London, stressed the value of group therapy whereby the patients, in co-operation with the medical and nursing staff, worked out their life situations and specific problems. An imaginative, elastic technique was used backed up by infinite patience. Frequent staff conferences were held so that grievances—'real or imaginary'—could be talked out. Jones takes a conservative and modest therapeutic outlook and believes that we will require to know much more about personality structure before any fundamental changes can be effected. At present we have to be content with improving social attitudes.

In conclusion we would emphasize once again that the treatment of the psychopath is a many-sided affair. Our central aim, however, is to maintain a progressive, constructive outlook, to encourage and support the patient so that we can direct his interests and activities into healthy channels. By so doing we may be able to inculcate the art of living harmoniously.

REFERENCES

Craft, M. (1965) *Psychopathic Personality*, Bristol.
Hill, D. (1952) *Electroenceph. clin. Neurophysiol.* 4, 419.
Hill, D. and Watterson, D. (1942) *J. Neurol. Psychiat.*, 5, 47.
Jones, Maxwell (1952) *Social Psychiatry*, London.
Jones, Maxwell (1959) *Lancet*, ii, 1022.
Schneider, K. (1958) *Psychopathic Personalities*, London.
Silverman, D. (1943) *Arch. Neurol. Psychiat. (Chic.)*, 50, 18.
Stalker, H. (1945) *J. ment. Sci.*, 91, 383.
Stürup, G. K. (1948) *Danish Psychiatry*, Copenhagen.

14

SPECIAL METHODS OF PHYSICAL TREATMENT

In this chapter a few of the more important techniques will be described in some detail and reference will be made to others, but a comprehensive account of physical methods of treatment in psychiatry will not be attempted.

About 1935 a major advance in psychiatric treatment took place, with the introduction, on the Continent of Europe, of the so-called 'shock therapies'—insulin coma, convulsion therapy and leucotomy. These techniques were then used very widely in treatment of the 'functional' psychoses, and the results obtained were in very many cases remarkable: they constituted indeed a landmark in psychiatric progress. All these three treatments were, however, empirical, and they have remained so. Electric convulsion therapy has established itself as the most potent treatment for the affective psychoses. Leucotomy, on the other hand, holds now only a peripheral position, as a drastic form of treatment for cases of otherwise hopeless prognosis: while insulin coma, shown by Ackner, Harris and Oldham (1957) to be no more effective in the treatment of schizophrenia than barbiturate narcosis, has by most workers in mental hospitals been abandoned.

The latest major development in physical therapy has been pharmacological, the production of the tranquillizers (ataractics) and antidepressant or euphoriant drugs. These new chemical methods of treatment are also empirical. Some of the new drugs are undoubtedly effective, but we do not know how they work and their prescription is therefore very often of a hit-or-miss nature. Too many of them are being produced too quickly, and are being used without guidance from properly controlled trials of their efficacy. We are in fact repeating the mistakes made with the 'shock therapies' of the thirties, using these new therapeutic agents too enthusiastically, too indiscriminately and frequently naïvely. Far too often the latest drugs are prescribed before the patient's clinical state has been defined, and far too often he is rendered punch-drunk (as it were) by their cumulative effects. If they are used well, many mentally ill patients are benefited by drugs: and research into their modes of action, both in those cases where they succeed and in those where they are ineffective or harmful, may provide invaluable clues to the aetiology of the psychoses.

The methods which will be described are as follows:

1. Electric convulsion therapy.
2. Leucotomy.
3. Modified insulin therapy.
4. Continuous narcosis.
5. Various drug treatments: tranquillizers, antidepressants and narco-analysis.

CONVULSION THERAPY

The treatment of schizophrenic psychoses by induced convulsions was introduced by Dr. von Meduna of Budapest in 1934, on the basis of the dubious observation that epilepsy was rare in schizophrenics, and of the deduction that there might, therefore, exist a biological antagonism between schizophrenia and epilepsy. However that may be, he found that by producing fits in schizophrenics he could influence the recovery rate. The convulsant first used was camphor, injected in oil intramuscularly: later *Cardiazol* (pentamethylenetetrazol) was given intravenously, before Cerletti and Bini introduced in 1937 the present widely used method of inducing convulsions electrically (E.C.T.). It was not long before it was discovered that melancholic patients responded better than schizophrenics to this physical method of treatment.

The *modus operandi* of the treatment is still conjectural. Its effects are almost certainly due more to the bodily changes induced than to the psychological trauma it may be supposed to constitute. It has been suggested that it acts as a threat of death, and in some cases probably this is so, since we know that certain cases of depression get better rapidly after making a suicidal attempt and by atoning thus for the guilt which has overwhelmed them. A more important psychological effect is doubtless the disruption, by the fit and the subsequent period of amnesia, of recently acquired morbid patterns of behaviour and reaction. The physical changes caused by the treatment are often rapid and impressive: appetite and weight are regained, and normal sleep and menstruation re-established. These somatic changes suggest that the treatment affects diencephalic centres in a way beneficial to the whole bodily economy. From electroencephalographic studies also Roth (1952) produced evidence that the primary effects of E.C.T. may be on the diencephalon: his results suggested a cumulative influence of the treatment on some mid-line structure in the brain with access to all cortical areas, though with some special relationship to the frontal lobes.

Method

Since electric convulsion therapy (E.C.T. or electroplexy) has replaced the production of fits by drugs, this method will be described. Suitable patients can be treated successfully in general hospitals, nursing homes or out-patient departments, although we are not greatly in favour of the latter procedure. There are several convenient types of electro-convulsant apparatus on the market which are small, portable and designed both for A.C. and D.C. mains.

A careful physical examination must always precede treatment. X-rays of chest or spine, electrocardiographic and other specialized investigations may be indicated in cases where the physical state is impaired; and it is often advisable in such cases to obtain the advice of a medical or surgical consultant. Written permission for the treatment should be obtained from the patient or from the nearest relative, to whom the risks attendant upon the treatment should be explained. If the patient has been taking a long-acting sedative at nights, a shorter-acting hypnotic should be substituted—*e.g.* cyclobarbitone, B.P.C., or pentobarbitone sodium, B.P. (*Nembutal*).

Treatment is usually most conveniently given in the morning. If a muscle relaxant is to be used, food should be omitted that morning, since if food were taken there would be a risk of vomiting and regurgitation into the lungs. Half to one hour before treatment the patient is given a subcutaneous injection of atropine sulphate, 0·45 to 0·6 mg., to prevent salivation and vomiting: and the very anxious patient may at this time be given a small dose of amylobarbitone sodium. Immediately before treatment he should empty his bladder and bowels. His clothes must be loosened at neck and waist; dentures, hair-clips, jewellery, etc., are removed.

The patient lies on a padded table or firm couch, which most conveniently is of the same height as the ward trolley, so that heavy patients can be gently slid from one to the other after treatment.

The use of a muscle relaxant to modify the force of the electrically induced convulsion allows us practically to eliminate the risk of fractures and dislocations. A number of relaxants have been used; for example, curare, gallamine triethiodide (*Flaxedil*) and suxamethonium bromide (*Brevidil E*). The latter is very brief in its action, and is outstandingly suitable. Since the onset of paralysis is very frightening to the conscious patient, 0·2 to 0·25 G. thiopentone sodium, B.P., (*Intraval Sodium*) is first injected intravenously, to give light anaesthesia. The needle is left in the vein, and from another syringe suxamethonium bromide is injected in a dose of 30 to 50 mg. according to the patient's weight and muscular development. Its action is signified usually by fibrillation or twitching of the muscles: when these movements have ceased, or at some time between 30 and 60 seconds after the injection of the relaxant, the electrical current should be passed. Prior to the fit the patient is given a few breaths of oxygen through a mask.

In order to pass the electrical current the electrodes, covered by pads wet with saline or sodium bicarbonate, are placed firmly on the temples, and some workers consider it advisable to clean the temples beforehand with ether or cetrimide solution (*Cetavlon*). A mouth gag is inserted, and the current is then switched on by the operator. A typical setting of a McPhail-Strauss machine would be 120 volts for 0·3 second: if an Ectron machine is used, which delivers a fixed voltage of electricity, the current should be passed for at least one second and for not more than four seconds. The object is to produce a major fit.

Oxygenation should be continued after the seizure until breathing has restarted, which usually occurs within three to five minutes. Very occasionally, in individuals who as a hereditary defect have little or no serum cholinesterase, prolonged apnoea results, and aeration of the lungs with a pressure bag may have to be carried out for as long as 20 to 30 minutes. No one should undertake to modify E.C.T. with a muscle relaxant who cannot carry out the prolonged oxygenation of an unconscious patient, or who cannot pass an intratracheal tube in an emergency. We prefer therefore always to have an anaesthetist to assist us.

If muscular relaxation has been very complete, it may be difficult to be certain that a major seizure has occurred. Contraction of the frontalis or inversion of the feet and toes may be seen when there is little or no movement visible elsewhere. The passage of the current may in fact not produce a major fit, but only a 'stun' (simple or sub-shock). A 'stun', which is momentary with relaxation again almost immediately, is of no therapeutic value, and tends to cause headache and confusion: its production is therefore to be avoided, and no more than three 'stuns' should be allowed to occur at any treatment. If a major seizure is not produced by the first setting or timing of the machine, voltage or time or both should be increased and a further shock given.

After treatment the patient is returned to his bed, where he usually sleeps. On regaining consciousness he is often for a period suggestible, and may reveal previously hidden symptoms of his illness.

If for some reason it is not possible to employ a muscle relaxant, and E.C.T. has to be given 'straight', further and extra precautions have to be taken: and despite these, injury may be done to the patient. A small pillow is placed under the patient's back, extending the thoracic spine, and another under his head, and his movements must be controlled manually by a team of nurses. It is the initial jerk and jack-knife flexion of his spine in the fit which constitutes the chief danger to the patient. If only two nurses are available, one should hold the patient's shoulder girdles firmly to the couch by pressure on the clavicles and shoulders transmitted through her own extended arms, the other should similarly control the pelvic girdle by downwards pressure on the iliac crests. If four nurses are available, one should hold the patient's flexed arms to his sides and another keep his extended legs together at the ankles. The doctor giving the treatment should hold up the patient's lower jaw, thus keeping the mouth gag in position and preventing dislocation of the jaw by extreme opening of the mouth. When the gag is in position, the patient is instructed to bite on it and the current is then switched on by the operator. The patient's movements should be carefully controlled throughout the seizure, and at the end of the clonic phase he should be turned into the semi-prone position. If cyanosis is still marked or if breathing has not recommenced satisfactorily, he should be given oxygen from a cylinder through a face mask attached to a pressure bag: usually this is only required for a minute or so. The patient is then returned to bed. He may regain consciousness quickly, and be restless or emotional, or sleep for half an hour or longer.

Treatments are normally given twice a week but preferably they are spaced according to the needs of the individual patient. In those cases which respond satisfactorily, six to eight treatments are usually sufficient to promote recovery: and, in the great majority of instances, if a response to the treatment is going to occur at all, it becomes manifest in the period of the first four treatments. It is doubtful if more than twelve treatments should be given at a single course. Sometimes a patient who has improved during a course of treatment begins to relapse within a fortnight of its completion: in such a case, a further two or three treatments may be required.

Indications for and Results of Treatment

Imipramine (*Tofranil*) has been used with success in many cases of manic-depressive psychosis which would previously have been treated with E.C.T.: but imipramine has not replaced E.C.T., which appears usually to be more effective in the severer illnesses, to act more quickly and to shorten the illness.

The chief indication for convulsion therapy is the treatment of a depressive psychosis. Results are most dramatic in the involutional melancholia group: here about 80 per cent. of the cases respond, the illness is in most instances cut short, suffering is much reduced and management facilitated. Tube-feeding is now rarely necessary in these cases. The response of manic-depressive depressions is also often very satisfactory; the attack may be modified, though recurrences are not prevented. One has the impression, however, that in manic-depressive cases treatment is most effective if given when the nadir of the illness has been passed: it may then accelerate recovery, whereas if given very early in the illness a temporary improvement may be followed by a rapid relapse. E.C.T. is usually less effective in those less typical recurrent depressions which, before its introduction, tended to run courses longer than the average; in cases, that is, characterized by hypochondriasis, and in younger people by prominent feelings of unreality or anxiety. E.C.T. may in fact make such patients worse. In general, it is ineffective and not infrequently it is harmful where the depressive reaction is essentially a neurotic response to environmental difficulties.

We have not been impressed by the results in cases of mania; the patient may be quietened, but usually only very transiently so. Some workers have claimed more satisfactory results in mania from E.C.T., given intensively (*i.e.* 1 to 3 times per day initially), but we deprecate its use in this way. Where depression is a prominent affect in a schizophrenic or paranoid illness, E.C.T. may be helpful but its effects are seldom lasting.

Old age is not a bar to treatment with E.C.T. Patients in their seventies or even older may be treated successfully, provided that there is no organic deterioration of their mental faculties.

Physically, there are, since the introduction of muscle relaxants, few contra-indications to the treatment. Cerebral arteriosclerosis and recent coronary thrombosis debar the treatment; marked hypertension does not necessarily do so. In cases where there is evidence of myocardial damage the strain on the cardiovascular system incurred by prolonged agitation must be weighed against the strain imposed by a modified convulsive seizure. In cases of pulmonary tuberculosis also the risks must be weighed against the advantages, since it appears that E.C.T. might light up a tuberculous lesion. Orthopaedic disabilities frequently call for the use of muscle relaxants but rarely debar treatment.

Risks and Complications

Since E.C.T. evidently produces its effects by altering brain function, and indeed its effects clinically may resemble closely those which follow head injury, the question at once arises whether or not pathological lesions are produced in the brain and, if so, whether these structural changes are reversible. The results of animal experimentation have not given a clear answer: and pathological studies of human brains can rarely be made shortly after treatment. It may be

Y

said that there is no evidence that a previously normal brain suffers permanent damage of any consequence from a standard course of E.C.T. Organic sequelae may, however, follow the giving of too prolonged or too intensive treatment: memory gaps of weeks or months may then be produced and these must have a pathological basis. Corsellis and Meyer (1954) reported two cases in which irreversible histological changes in the brain may have been caused by unusually heavy electro-convulsive treatment. The changes, which were mild, consisted mainly of a proliferation of the marginal glia and of the glia of the white matter.

All patients have an amnesia for the fit and for a variable time afterwards extending over the period when they are drowsy or confused; a momentary retrograde amnesia is also usual, but may transiently be much more extensive. During the treatment course and for a week or two subsequently many patients complain of forgetfulness, particularly over dates, names and such details. This memory disturbance, after a normal course of treatment, may be expected to disappear within a month. With more intensive or prolonged treatment, however, memory disturbance may be more severe and permanent impairment may be caused. This complication points to the need for caution especially in the treatment of those whose livelihood depends on their memory and intellectual capabilities.

The main and commonest danger of convulsion therapy used to lie in the production of fractures and dislocations by the intense motor excitation of the fits. The commonest fracture was a compression of the vertebral bodies (more than one might be involved). When *Cardiazol* was used, this complication was recorded in as many as 40 per cent. of the patients treated (Polatin, 1939): with 'straight' E.C.T. an incidence of 23 per cent. has been reported (Lingley and Robbins, 1947). The incidence was highest in muscular men and in cases with osteoporosis. The injury varied from a slight crush in the extreme tip of the body of the vertebra, usually 4th, 5th or 6th thoracic, to a telescoping of the vertebral body. Fortunately many of these fractures were symptomless: in other cases there was complaint of pain in the back for a few weeks, but lasting disability has been exceptional. Dislocations of jaw and shoulder, and more rarely fractures of long bones, also occurred during treatment. With careful manual restraint of the fit the incidence of such physical injuries can be much reduced, and by the use of muscle relaxants they can practically be eliminated. If a fracture has occurred it may still be justifiable to continue the convulsive treatment, but a muscle relaxant must be employed.

We have had experience of manic-depressive patients who, as a result of treatment, have passed from a depressive into a manic phase. This is uncommon. In such instances the last state, at any rate so far as relatives are concerned, may be considered worse than the first. We once received a letter imploring: 'Please de-electrify my daughter'. More commonly, towards the end of a course of treatment, the patient may show for some days a euphoria which is probably organically determined.

If the patient has been carefully examined beforehand as to his physical fitness to stand the treatment and if the E.C.T. is properly carried out, the risk of death under treatment is negligible.

LEUCOTOMY

In 1935 Egas Moniz, a Portuguese surgeon, introduced this operation which divides the pathways between the frontal lobes and the thalamus. The original method consisted in the injection of small quantities of alcohol into the white matter of the prefrontal region, but this was superseded by the use of a steel leucotome to sever the white matter.

Rationale

The operation was devised on the basis of clinical and experimental observations. In 1848, in Vermont, U.S.A., a man named Phineas Gage had an iron crowbar driven through the frontal region of his skull, but lived for twelve years afterwards. Autopsy showed that only the prefrontal cortex was involved. After his injury Gage was described by Harlow in these terms: 'He is fitful, irreverent, indulging at times in the grossest profanity (which was not previously his custom), manifesting but little deference for his fellows, impatient of restraint or advice when it conflicts with his desires, at times pertinaciously obstinate, yet capricious and vacillating. . . .' Cases such as this showed that widespread and bilateral damage to the frontal lobes could produce a state of disinhibition and euphoria. Later, evidence from animal experiments led to the general conclusion that in monkeys, too, there was a change in temperament as a result of bilateral frontal lobe injury, J. F. Fulton remarking that the animal became like a 'good-natured drunk'. Chimpanzees which had developed an 'experimental neurosis' in that they became irritable over their mistakes in learning, lost all concern over them after leucotomy.

Ritchie Russell (1948) speculated that the beneficial effect of prefrontal leucotomy may be derived in one of three ways: 'Either the operation prevents the relay of the nervous activities engendered by mental conflict to the fronto-thalamic mechanism; or the fire of the mental conflict loses its fuel when no longer stimulated by the mechanism; or most likely the mechanism of mental conflict at a cortical level is highly complex and may be directly interfered with by this operation to such an extent that it can no longer develop the intensity required to stimulate the emotions'. Fulton (1951) suggested that its effects may be due to interference with a visceral afferent system—the so-called 'visceral brain', which is believed to include parts of the temporal lobe, the hippocampus, the amygdaloid nucleus, and nuclei of the thalamus and hypothalamus as well as the cingulate gyrus and posterior orbital cortex; and suggested that these two latter regions may be the optimum target for the operation. But it is impossible to do more than theorize until much more experimental work has been carried out.

Anatomical Considerations

The anatomical basis of leucotomy was discussed in detail by Meyer (1954) who emphasized the interdependence of the frontal region with the thalamus, hypothalamus and—indirectly—with rhinencephalic centres. The principal afferent connections with the frontal region arise in the thalamus: fibres run from the dorsomedial nucleus to areas of granular frontal cortex, and from the anterior nucleus to the cingular region. The thalamic nuclei which project to the medial orbital and cingular regions receive fibres from the hypothalamus. Efferent fibres from the granular frontal cortex run to the dorsomedial nucleus of the thalamus (particularly), and to the hypothalamus and pontine nuclei; while those from the agranular frontal cortex connect with the ventro-medial nucleus of the thalamus (particularly), the corpus striatum, corpus subthalamicum, substantia nigra, red nucleus and pons. The operation severs thalamo-frontal pathways. After it there is retrograde degeneration in the thalamus, most marked in the dorso-medial nucleus, and in the anterior nucleus following involvement of the anterior cingular region. The importance in the operation of damage to the diffuse thalamic projection system is still uncertain.

Indications for Operation

The general aim of the operation has been to modify the disordered behaviour of psychotic and neurotic patients whose illness has been of a prolonged type, and the tendency has been to select patients for treatment more on a symptomatic than on a nosological basis.

Strecker and his co-workers considered that a syndrome composed of fear, anxiety, actual mental suffering and aggressive violence was a better criterion for suitability than a diagnostic label. In involutional melancholias which had failed to respond to electric convulsive treatment, and which had lasted a very long time, leucotomy was justified by its results.

Our experience has been similar but we would exclude the aggressively violent. The best results have been obtained in severe involutional melancholic, obsessional and paranoid states, which have been characterized by great subjective suffering. The possibility of serious and permanent damage to the mental functions makes it necessary to reserve the method for cases where all other suitable methods of treatment have been tried and failed, where the illness offers no reasonable hope of spontaneous recovery, and where the patient is disabled more or less completely from useful occupation or from modest enjoyment of his life.

It is important to stress that, in giving symptomatic relief, the operation does not produce a cure. In depressives the apprehension and anxiety may be relieved or disappear, and obsessional thinking tends to die out perhaps because it is no longer sustained by its affective component. But hallucinations and delusions may remain, though the patient is no longer so disturbed by them; and recurrent illnesses may recur, *e.g.* manic-depressive psychoses. Apart from the relief of distress and tension, there is commonly a restoration of energy and interest, increased appetite, and a gain in weight.

These beneficial effects are won, unfortunately, at the price of some change in the personality, in the direction usually of coarsening and blunting. Symptoms of frontal lobe deficit appear, and may be disabling: euphoria, tactlessness, lack of initiative and foresight and laziness have been recorded in many cases. Intelligence tests show usually no measurable loss, but there is probably a tendency for thinking to become more concrete. These unfavourable personality changes are most marked if the cuts have been too extensive or placed too far posteriorly; or if there is involvement of the dorso-lateral white matter, and particularly the cortex of the lateral convexity (Meyer, 1954). Thus in every case the benefits of leucotomy must be weighed carefully against its disadvantages: while there may remain a certain bleaching of affect and a lack of the finer sensibilities, at the same time a peace of mind has often been attained which makes life bearable for the patient, and gives some pleasure to relatives who have often been intensely distressed.

The Surgical Operation

The mortality rate from the operation, the result usually of haemorrhage or infection, is about 2 per cent. Of after-results in the physical sphere incontinence is one of the commonest: it is usually temporary. Epilepsy occurs in 10 to 15 per cent. of cases, but can be satisfactorily controlled with anticonvulsants. A morbidly increased appetite may lead to obesity: and, if the cuts are too posterior, marasmus, restlessness, vasomotor and trophic disturbances, and uraemia, may lead to 'delayed death' (Meyer and McLardy, 1948).

There are evidently three main factors which govern the results obtained: the previous personality of the patient, his reaction-type and the extent and locus of the surgical cuts.

Much research has been directed towards finding out whether the benefits of leucotomy can be gained without causing adverse personality changes. and many attempts have been made to render the operations more precise. In a blind operation such as the original 'standard' Freeman-Watts leucotomy, it was difficult for the surgeon to know the exact location of the cuts made either in the anteroposterior or in the transverse planes. Meyer and McLardy, on the basis of 27 cases which had come to post-mortem, commented on the variability of the surgical lesions, and stated that only in a few cases was a bilateral lesion through the whole of the white matter actually effected. Though the clinical results of the 'standard' operation were on the whole fairly satisfactory, it should now be abandoned in favour of procedures more precisely localized and more limited in extent.

Other workers, in the pursuit of surgical selectivity and better clinical results, have performed open operations. Heath and Pool and their colleagues performed bilateral cortical ablations (topectomy) of Brodmann areas 9, 10, 11; Whitty and Cairns ablation of Brodmann area 24 (cingulectomy); and Greenblatt and Solomon (1953) a bimedial lobotomy.

Scoville (1949) introduced undercutting of the orbital area. Personality changes are said to be slight after this operation, and patients suffering from chronic neurotic tension states, with anxiety and depression, which have been unresponsive to psychotherapy, are said to benefit. Sykes and Tredgold (1964) reported favourably on a modification of Scoville's method introduced by Knight—restricted orbital undercutting, in the treatment of anxiety, depressive and obsessional states. Nearly all of their 350 patients had ceased before operation to respond to other forms of treatment. In their opinion about half had clearly benefited considerably from the operation: only just over 3 per cent. showed no improvement.

Of the various developments of leucotomy, orbital undercutting and the bi-medial lobotomy introduced by Greenblatt and Solomon have seemed the most satisfactory. The results obtained correspond also with the deductions which Meyer (1954) made from the pathological study of 102 cases mostly treated by a 'standard' leucotomy. Meyer stressed that this material showed that quantitative adequacy of the cut is a most important factor in the degree of improvement obtained, and that full social recovery may be obtained without involvement of medial orbital and cingular segments. But he concluded: 'While the quantitative factor thus retains its importance, a few facts have emerged which point to some regional localization. The dorsal and, in particular, the dorso-lateral sectors of white matter do not appear to be as significant for improvement as the mid-central, orbital and cingulate sectors.'

Present Position. Much relief of human suffering and important advances in our understanding of frontal lobe anatomy and function were brought about by the operation of leucotomy: but its value has never been definitely assessed in properly controlled trials. The indications for its use have been greatly reduced with the introduction of new drug therapies. Leucotomy is now rarely carried out in cases of schizophrenia, having been replaced by tranquillizing and allied drugs in the treatment of those whose behaviour is grossly disordered. Some cases of involutional melancholia, resistant to E.C.T., which would previously have been considered suitable for leucotomy, are found to respond to imipramine. Probably the main indication for leucotomy now is for the relief of cases of chronic depression and obsessional neurosis, where there have been many years of suffering and relief cannot be brought in any other way.

Stereotaxic techniques in brain surgery, which enable small and very carefully placed lesions to be made, have opened up new possibilities both of bringing about symptomatic improvement in cases previously thought suitable for leucotomy and for understanding the mechanisms by which this may be achieved. These new, more precise operations may also widen the clinical range of patients who could benefit from 'psychosurgery'.

MODIFIED INSULIN THERAPY[1]

This method derives from Weir Mitchell's treatment of neuroses after the American Civil War, when he prescribed with abounding success removal from stress, rest and feeding up. During the Second World War it was developed for the treatment of psychiatric casualties in the Services. Sargant and Craske (1941) selected cases of good personality, who after subjection to prolonged stress had

---

[1] This, the usual descriptive label of the treatment, is somewhat misleading: the insulin is not modified.

lost a good deal of weight and had developed neurotic or reactive depressive symptoms; and they found the method valuable. In civilian practice also it is sometimes useful as part of the treatment of both neurotic and depressive ill-nesses, where there has been exhaustion and considerable loss of weight: in the case of depressions it may be given either during or after treatment with E.C.T. Satisfactory results are also reported in the management of some cases of anorexia nervosa, and in alleviating the unpleasant symptoms of drug withdrawal in cases of addiction. There is much individual variation in response to the treatment.

The treatment promotes a gain in weight. In some cases it has also a noticeable calming effect. There is, too, an element of suggestion; and some patients accept a psychotherapeutic approach to their problems more easily if it is combined with more active, 'medical' treatment.

Technique of the Treatment. The treatment is given daily. The patient fasts overnight. At about 7 a.m. he is given subcutaneously an injection of soluble insulin: on the first day 10 Units, rising by daily increases of 5 to 10 Units, to a maximum of 40 to 50 Units each morning. He is then screened, the environment is kept quiet, and he is encouraged to relax and drowse. During this time he must be kept under constant nursing observation and details of his condition must be recorded half-hourly. The danger is that he may, while hypoglycaemic, drift into coma.

The symptoms of hypoglycaemia are feelings of weakness, emptiness, shaki-ness, faintness and hunger: the signs are alterations in the pulse rate, sweating and tremor. Instead of becoming drowsy the patient may become restless and disinhibited, laughing or crying. If there is muscular twitching or the patient becomes not easily rousable the treatment must be interrupted at once by giving glucose by mouth or intravenously, or 0·5 ml. of 1:1000 solution of adrenaline subcutaneously. If the treatment has to be interrupted in this way, the morning dose of insulin should subsequently be reduced by at least 10 Units.

At 10 a.m. (if a premature interruption has not been necessary) the patient is roused and given a breakfast of about 1000 calories, containing 20 to 25 g. protein. This breakfast must be appetizing, and the patient should be encouraged to eat all of it: it should be varied as far as possible from day to day. If on account of drowsiness the patient cannot get ahead with solid food, he should be given 2 oz. glucose in a tumblerful of fruit juice and water before he starts the meal. After breakfast the patient may be allowed up and about, and it should be seen that he takes his other meals properly. In the afternoon he may again become slightly hypoglycaemic, and he should be warned of this: the symptoms can be neutralized then by eating sweets or taking a drink of sweetened tea or fruit juice.

The patient's weight should be recorded at the beginning and end of the course of treatment, and weekly during it. The treatment should be continued usually for a few weeks, until normal weight has been attained.

CONTINUOUS NARCOSIS

Woolf originated this form of treatment in 1901 and it was extensively used by Kläsi (1922), with whose name it is usually connected. It was entirely empirical and it is now rarely employed. It is mentioned here because it has not yet been clearly shown to be of no value, and because drugs which have been introduced in recent years could make this a safer form of treatment than hitherto.

The essence of treatment by prolonged sleep is the spaced administration of hypnotics at such intervals as will keep the patient asleep for 18 to 20 hours out of the 24. If thoroughly carried out, the treatment is fraught with some danger—death rates as high as 5 per cent. have been recorded: and as is the case with all treatments which demand a very high degree of skill in the personnel administering them, the risk to the patient is proportionate to the experience of the therapists.

It has been said that continuous narcosis is of value mainly in curtailing the duration of psychotic conditions which would sooner or later recover spontaneously or by other methods of treatment. One can see now no indication for its use in the affective psychoses: and in the management of acute schizophrenic excitements of the agitated fearful type, for which it was advocated, it has been replaced by the tranquillizers. Claims have also been made, more substantial perhaps, for its effectiveness in the treatment of the reactive anxiety states seen in war casualties.

The rationale of the method is that deep and prolonged sleep allows natural processes of mental healing and reintegration to take place more quickly.

Technique of the Treatment. The patient is put to bed in a quiet and darkened room. The hypnotics used most often have been *Somnifaine* (each ml. containing 0·1 G. of diethylbarbituric acid and 0·1 G. of allylisopropylbarbituric acid), amylobarbitone sodium, other longer-acting barbiturates, and paraldehyde. The average amount of *Somnifaine* required was 6 ml. in 24 hours, given intramuscularly in 2 ml. doses: amylobarbitone sodium was given in 180–360 mg. doses, up to a total of 2 G. in the 24 hours. Chlorpromazine was not available when the treatment was most used, and a combination of chlorpromazine with short-acting barbiturates would be a good deal safer than *Somnifaine* (abscesses and damage to the sciatic nerve from the injections were well-recognized risks) and the longer-acting barbiturates. Up to 1200 mg. of chlorpromazine daily have been prescribed.

Continuous, highly skilled nursing care is essential, with frequent recording of the pulse, temperature and blood pressure; charting of fluid intake and output; and repeated examination of the urine for acetone. The patient must get three full meals each day and a large fluid intake is vitally important. The bladder and bowels, too, require close attention. The treatment is continued for a week to fourteen days. Then barbiturates must be withdrawn slowly, if confusion and fits are not to be precipitated.

While under this treatment the patient is on the verge of a drug-induced toxic delirium: he may also pass into coma, become seriously dehydrated, suffer cardiovascular collapse or develop pneumonia.

The risks are evidently very considerable, the rewards slight and inconstant, and it is perhaps time that the treatment was relegated to the histories of psychiatry.

VARIOUS DRUG TREATMENTS

Tranquillizers

This term has been introduced to describe a group of drugs which, unlike the usual sedatives and hypnotics, produce a calming effect without at the same time causing mental fogging or drowsiness. Some of these drugs appear to do more than tranquillize, and to have a distinct effect in reducing the force of psychotic delusions and hallucinations. The scope and details of their efficacy have as yet not been more than provisionally worked out. Much further research is required, in properly controlled trials, to elucidate their actions in various reaction-types and in the treatment of specific symptoms. Meantime they should be prescribed with as much discrimination as possible, and usually not in combination. Tranquillizers have usually to be given for a period of one to three months, before their effectiveness can be properly assessed.

The tranquillizing drugs can at this stage be separated into three main groups: 1. the phenothiazine derivatives; 2. a group which includes meprobamate (*Equanil*) and chlordiazepoxide (*Librium*); and 3. the butyrophenones.

1. The phenothiazine derivatives include, in the dimethyl subgroup, chlorpromazine, promazine hydrochloride and prochlorperazine (*Stemetil*): in the piperazine subgroup, perphenazine (*Fentazin*) and trifluoperazine (*Stelazine*): and in those with a piperidine side-chain, thioridazine (*Melleril*).

Of the phenothiazines, chlorpromazine is both the most generally useful and the most toxic. It was introduced by Delay and Deniker in 1952 for the treatment of schizophrenia: and it has proved of great value in controlling turbulent schizophrenic behaviour, with the result that mental hospitals have in recent years become much less disturbed by the outbursts of noisy and aggressive patients, and many chronic schizophrenics have been enabled to leave hospital and live in the community. It is also useful in controlling the agitation of depression, the excitement of mania and delirium, and the restlessness of senile patients. It potentiates the action of barbiturates.

The drug is given orally usually, in doses of 25 to 150 mg. three times a day. Larger doses have been given to schizophrenics: and the drug may also be given intramuscularly (chlorpromazine injection, B.P., in 25 to 50 mg. doses). The side-effects are many and may be serious: they include obstructive jaundice, agranulocytosis, oculo-cutaneous lesions, dryness of the mouth, constipation, hypotension, convulsions and extrapyramidal symptoms [see also below]. Of the more serious toxic effects, jaundice (1 to 2 per cent. cases) is the commonest, and occurs most often in the first two months of treatment: this, and agranulocytosis, call for immediate stoppage of the drug. General guidance cannot be given about the duration of treatment advisable in schizophrenia: it has usually to be extended over months, and one must find out by trial and error if the drug can be withdrawn without precipitating relapse.

The piperazine subgroup of the phenothiazines have been thought to have a more marked effect on the delusions of schizophrenics: they also produce extrapyramidal symptoms earlier and more severely, and in some cases severe anxiety and restlessness. Trifluoperazine is perhaps the most potent of this group of drugs. It has appeared to be of particular value in the treatment of chronic, withdrawn schizophrenics. Favourable effects become evident usually within ten days. Patients who respond to the drug become less impulsive and more co-operative in their behaviour, are less troubled by delusions and hallucinations (these may even be abolished), and show a renewal of interest in the world around them. The average maintenance dose required is 15 to 25 mg. daily, and the drug is administered by mouth. Treatment should commence usually with a small dose, e.g. 10 mg. daily, and this can be increased to 15 mg. after a week. For rapid, initial administration a preparation is available for deep intra-muscular injection: the dose by this route should be small, 1 to 3 mg. daily. Treatment may have to be extended over months.

The piperidine subgroup are generally both less toxic and less potent.

The main side-effects of the phenothiazine drugs are neurological. The symp-toms are extrapyramidal and may be florid: motor restlessness, jitteriness and agitation ('akathisia') are common; so are classical Parkinsonian signs, mask-like facies, salivation, tremor, rigidity and shuffling gait; more rarely there are dystonic phenomena, spasms of the muscles of the limbs, head and neck par-ticularly, even torticollis and oculogyric crises. The dyskinetic symptoms appear usually early in treatment and sometimes acutely; an expression, it is supposed, of individual sensitivity. The Parkinsonian symptoms are more closely related to the nature, amount and duration of the drug treatment. These extrapyramidal side-effects often disappear if the drug dosage is reduced; and they may be suppressed with appropriate drugs (for example, benztropine methanesul-phonate, 2 to 6 mg. daily), without impairing the efficacy of the phenothiazine treatment.

Studying 4000 patients treated with phenothiazines Ayd (1961) found that 21 per cent. had akathisia, 15 per cent. Parkinsonism, and over 2 per cent. dystonic movements.

Unfortunately, C.N.S. side-effects of treatment with phenothiazines are not always benign, but may continue even after the drug is withdrawn. As Sigwald and his colleagues in France first described, irreversible dyskinesia may result, based presumably on lesions in the basal ganglia. This persistent oral dyskinesis has been well delineated by Hunter and his colleagues (1964), who found 13 of these cases (5 per cent.) in a group of 250 patients who had been treated in a mental hospital for more than 18 months with phenothiazines. All were women over the age of 55 and demented due to brain damage from other causes—following leucotomy or E.C.T., or as a result of senile or arteriosclerotic brain disease. The dyskinesia had developed insidiously and usually secondarily to drug-induced Parkinsonism. There was continual and distressing grimacing and contortion of the face, with writhing, chewing, sucking and gaping movements of the mouth, tongue and jaws. Rapid protrusion and withdrawal of the tongue may interfere with eating and drinking, speech may become hoarse and even unintelligible, and sudden closure of the glottis may precipitate respiratory distress. These abnormal movements of the face region are frequently accompanied by akathisia and minor choreiform movements of the limbs. They are not relieved by anti-Parkinsonian drugs and persist after the phenothiazines are withdrawn (as they should be, always, in these cases). Hunter and his colleagues commented that the syndrome resembles the hyperkinetic viral encephalitic syndromes seen in the 1920's: it should also be noted that many old, demented women, not treated with phenothiazine drugs, show abnormal movements of the face and mouth.

Apart from the acute photosensitivity in summer, with redness and oedema of the exposed skin, which a few patients show, more significant oculo-cutaneous lesions may develop in patients treated with phenothiazines, particularly chlorpromazine, in high dosage over a long period. Greiner and Berry (1964) in Canada first drew attention to this complication. Eye changes usually precede skin pigmentation. Lesions of the lens have been recorded in a quarter to one-third of patient samples, and in at least a quarter of these affected individuals there have been corneal lesions also. In the lens a central stellate or disc-shaped cataract may be produced, and in the cornea a diffuse haziness, due to fine white granular opacities: pigmentation may also be seen in the conjunctiva. Fortunately these changes, though persistent, are seldom disabling, visual acuity apparently only rarely being impaired. The skin pigmentation appears gradually, aggravated in the summer, on the face, neck and backs of the hands. It is largely irreversible, slate or bluish-grey or lilac in colour, and due to melanosis around the small blood vessels of the dermis: probably breakdown products of the drug are involved too in the pigmentation.

The viscera also may become pigmented during treatment with phenothiazines, and it is possible that in some cases cardiac damage results from the deposition of a phenothiazine metabolite: certainly a few patients have died suddenly and unexpectedly when under treatment with these drugs, and there has often been little or no evident cause for this at post-mortem examination. Recently Richardson and his colleagues (1966), using histochemical techniques, have reported in 12 such cases which they autopsied, subendocardial lesions in the right and left atrioventricular conduction bundle and papillary muscles, consisting of an acid mucopolysaccharide deposited in and around altered arterioles and degenerating myocardial muscle.

The extrapyramidal signs and oculo-cutaneous lesions caused by phenothiazine drugs do not necessarily call for the cessation of treatment with phenothiazines when they have arisen, since the degree of disturbance of the patient's behaviour may justify continuation of the drug treatment. But they do call for caution, and continuing vigilance. The lowest possible effective dose of the drug should be used, the patient's condition should be reviewed at least every six months, and when medication is prolonged serial slit-lamp examination of the eyes will often be required, since this is the only way of detecting the eye changes at an early stage.

2. The second group of tranquillizing drugs is heterogeneous, and includes meprobamate, diazepam and chlordiazepoxide. These drugs are not effective in the psychoses, but they have been advocated in treatment of neurotic reactions.

There is, however, as yet no definite evidence that in the control of neurotic symptoms they are more potent than amylobarbitone sodium, and that they should be preferred to the barbiturates. Chlordiazepoxide is probably the most effective and has the fewest side-effects (little more than sleepiness usually) of this group. All are liable to lead to drug dependency.

3. The butyrophenones, haloperidol (*Serenace*) and triperidol, are useful in the control of psychotic excitement, particularly manic. They have extrapyramidal side-effects but are less hypotensive than chlorpromazine. The prescription of haloperidol is for 3 to 12 mg. daily, in two doses; or 5 mg. parenterally.

Antidepressant Drugs

Of the antidepressant drugs, the imipramine (tricyclic) group and a group of hydrazine derivatives, which are amine-oxidase inhibitors, are the most important. The former has constituted an important advance in treatment. These drugs are, however, in general less potent than E.C.T., and in cases of acute, severe depression E.C.T. is usually to be preferred. They appear to lessen the severity of the illness, often markedly so, but usually not to cut short its duration: and they have therefore to be prescribed normally for a period which approximates probably to the natural course of the depressive illness.

Kuhn in Switzerland introduced imipramine hydrochloride (*Tofranil*) in 1957 as a drug for the treatment of depression. It is an aminodibenzyl derivative, chemically closely related to chlorpromazine but with different properties. Its mode of action is unknown. It is undoubtedly effective in the treatment of depressive psychoses: some milder cases can be treated throughout satisfactorily in this way, so also cases which are unsuitable for E.C.T. on account of physical disease or injury, and some chronic depressions which have not responded to E.C.T.

Imipramine is prescribed in a dose usually of 25 to 75 mg. three times a day. The following is a typical full dosage schedule: 25 mg. three times a day on the first day, 25 mg. four times a day on the second and third days, and 50 mg. three times a day on the fourth and subsequent days for a month. If the drug is going to produce improvement, this is seen usually in the first 10 days of treatment: but in some cases the drug appears to be very slow in producing its effects, and continuance of it for a month at least, at full dosage, is often advised. As the patient improves, the dose can be gradually reduced. Imipramine's side-effects include parasympathetic symptoms—dryness of the mouth, difficulty with visual accommodation, constipation, sweating, skin eruptions, retention of urine, and falls in old people: increased agitation is common, a hypomanic reaction may be induced, and conversely suicide may be precipitated by reducing a depressed patient's retardation. Hallucinatory episodes have also been described.

Amylobarbitone sodium or trifluoperazine may be helpful in reducing the agitation which may be a very uncomfortable side-effect and cause a patient to give up treatment.

Of the other drugs in the imipramine group, amitriptyline (*Tryptizol*) is probably the drug of second choice, less powerful as an antidepressant, more sedative and sometimes to be preferred for depressed patients who are anxious and agitated. Desipramine and nortriptyline are less potent.

The monoamine-oxidase inhibitor drugs include the hydrazine derivatives—iproniazid (*Marsilid*), phenelzine (*Nardil*), and isocarboxazid (*Marplan*); and tranylcypromine (*Parnate*). The sphere of their usefulness is still uncertain. They are ineffective in the treatment of affective psychoses. Their protagonists claim good results in the alleviation of atypical, neurotic or reactive depressions; particularly in cases whose symptoms include anxiety, irritability, fatigue and autonomic overactivity.

Iproniazid is the most effective but also the most toxic of these drugs: its usual dosage is 50 mg. three times a day. Phenelzine is given usually in 15 mg. doses three times a day, isocarboxazid in 10 mg. doses three times a day; and tranylcypromine in a dosage of 15 mg. given twice in the first half of the day (because of its stimulating effects). These drugs are toxic to the liver, and may cause jaundice and in some cases a fatal hepatitis. Postural hypotension is a troublesome side-effect. Good effects, if they are to appear, do so usually within two weeks, and the general management of the treatment is as for imipramine. The M.A.O. inhibitors should not be combined with the tricyclic antidepressants, and a tricyclic antidepressant should not be prescribed within three weeks of giving a M.A.O. inhibitor, otherwise dangerous reactions may be precipitated.

Apart from their directly toxic effects, monoamine-oxidase inhibitors may cause serious, even fatal, reactions by interaction with other substances—which include tyramine, dihydroxyphenylalanine ('dopa'), amphetamine, morphine and ephedrine. If a patient who is taking phenelzine, iproniazid, or (especially) tranylcypromine, takes amine-containing food, in particular cheese which contains considerable amounts of the pressor substance tyramine, he may within an hour or two develop a hypertensive crisis, with very severe throbbing headache, nausea, flushing, sweating and raised blood pressure: in a few cases death has resulted from cerebral haemorrhage or cardiac failure. Cheddar cheese is particularly liable to precipitate hypertensive reactions: so may broad beans, yeast extracts, game and chianti. Hypertensive reactions had been reported in 4–20 per cent. of patients treated with tranylcypromine, before there was widespread realization of these serious side-effects of the monoamine-oxidase inhibitors. A good review has been made by Blackwell and his colleagues (1967).

Consumer Reactions. Though the psychotropic drugs at present available only alleviate or suppress symptoms and do not cure, it is obviously important that the patients for whom they are advised should take them when and as prescribed. Unfortunately, but not surprisingly, this is often not the case. Even in a mental hospital patient population, it will be found that many patients are for one reason or another not receiving the drugs which their doctors suppose that they are getting, while others are taking drugs which have not been prescribed within the hospital. Amongst out-patients, the situation is of course much worse: Willcox, Gillan and Hare (1965), examining 125 psychiatric out-patients to ascertain whether they were taking the chlorpromazine or imipramine which had been prescribed, found that the failure rate was 48 per cent. The causes of this are complex: though the failure rate varies with the patient's diagnosis and the nature of the drug, there are other factors which are still obscure—indicating the need for further investigation of a phenomenon of great practical importance.

NARCO-ANALYSIS

This inelegant term, coined by Horsley (1943), has been used to describe the method in which the intravenous injection of a sedative drug is employed to produce a disinhibited state of mind, so that the patient becomes more communicative and has less emotional control—in fact a temporary state of veritable intoxication, similar to that produced by alcohol. The drugs most used have been *Evipan*, thiopentone and amylobarbitone sodium.

The chief usefulness of the method is in the treatment of hysterical conversion symptoms, and the rapid recovery of memory in cases of psychogenic amnesia. It is more certain to work than hypnosis and gives, therefore, more confidence to the doctor; but with sufficient patience and time, the same and probably better results can nearly always be obtained with persuasion, without either hypnosis or drugs. The method gives the patient something tangible that he understands more easily than the purely psychological method of approach, and it has, in consequence, considerable value as a vehicle of suggestion. It also provides some individuals with a welcome and apparently honourable excuse for divulging what they profess to have forgotten. It is doubtful whether it ever leads the patient to disclose what he still means to conceal. On the other hand, the productions are not necessarily factual—some patients produce phantasies in this state: it is not a 'truth drug'.

The method is also of value in promoting 'abreaction' in neurotic cases, the patient giving his story and recalling memories with more emotion than he is able to do in the ordinary therapeutic setting. It may help to clarify the diagnosis or content of a psychosis, by eliciting symptoms from a stuporous or negativistic patient. It may also be useful occasionally to get over difficult situations where the patient's tension or shame make it impossible for him to co-operate in discussion of his problems.

Technique of the Treatment. It is essential that treatment should be entered on in an atmosphere of optimism and faith in the method. It is extremely likely that usually what is really effective in the situation is the doctor's confidence in the treatment.

If amylobarbitone sodium is used, 0·5 G. of the drug dissolved in 5 ml. of distilled water are injected intravenously, slowly, usually at the rate of about 1 ml. of the solution per minute; the patient counting backwards meanwhile until drowsiness and disinhibition are produced, without however seriously disturbing articulation. It has been said that if the narcosis is pushed beyond this, rapport is lost and is not fully restored in the state of emergence from narcosis; but this has not been our experience.

If the method is used for abreaction, a number of treatments may be required. **Excitatory abreaction,** by the use of intravenous methedrine or ether on a mask, was introduced by Sargant and Shorvon. Emotions of anger and fear particularly are aroused. A crescendo of excitement is induced, reaches a climax and is followed by collapse. Persistent neurotic reactions following traumatic incidents, in men of stable personality, may be helped in this way (see Sargant and Slater, 1964).

REFERENCES

Ackner, B., Harris, A., and Oldham, A. J. (1957) *Lancet*, i, 607.
Ayd, F. (1961) *J. Amer. med. Ass.*, **175**, 1054.
Blackwell, B., Marley, E., Price, J., and Taylor, D. (1967) *Brit. J. Psychiat.*, **113**, 349.
Corsellis, J. A. N., and Meyer, A. (1954) *J. ment. Sci.*, **100**, 375.
Fulton, J. F. (1951) *Frontal Lobotomy and Affective Behavior*, New York.
Greenblatt, M., and Solomon, H. C. (1953) *Frontal Lobes and Schizophrenia*, New York.
Greiner, A. C., and Berry, K. (1964) *Canad. med. Ass.J.*, **90**, 663.
Horsley, J. S. (1943) *Narco-analysis*, London.
Hunter, R., Earl, C. J., and Thornicroft, S. (1964) *Proc. roy. Soc. Med.*, **57**, 758.
Kläsi, J. (1922) *Z. ges. Neurol. Psychiat.*, **74**, 557.
Lingley, J. R., and Robbins, L. L. (1947) *Radiology*, **48**, 124.
Meyer, A., and Beck, E. (1954) *Prefrontal Leucotomy and Related Operations*, Edinburgh.
Meyer, A., and McLardy, T. (1948) *J. ment. Sci.*, **94**, 555.
Polatin, P. (1939) *J. Amer. med. Ass.*, **112**, 1684.
Richardson, H. L., Graupner, K. I., and Richardson, M. E. (1966) *J. Amer. med. Ass.*, **195**, 254.
Roth, M. (1952) *J. ment. Sci.*, **98**, 44.
Russell, W. R. (1948) *Lancet*, i 356.
Sargant, W., and Craske, N. (1941) *Lancet*, ii. 212.
Sargant, W., and Slater, E. (1964) *Physical Methods of Treatment in Psychiatry*, 4th. ed., Edinburgh.
Scoville, W. B. (1949) *J. Neurosurg.*, **6**, 65.
Sykes, M. K., and Tredgold, R. F. (1964) *Brit. J. Psychiat.*, **110**, 609.
Willcox, D. R. C., Gillan, R., and Hare, E. H. (1965) *Brit. med. J.*, **2**, 790.

15

THE ORGANIC REACTION-TYPES

Two organic reaction-types can be differentiated, the acute (delirium) and the chronic (dementia). There are also transitions between them.

The pathological difference lies in the fact that the acute organic reaction is usually the result of a temporary toxic, biochemical process affecting the function of the brain, *e.g.* the delirium of acute fevers or alcoholism; while the chronic organic reaction is the expression of a more severe tissue change, usually a progressive degeneration, as in syphilitic general paralysis and senile dementia.

The organic reaction-type as a whole comprises the following changes:

1. In the intellectual sphere there is impairment of comprehension, interference with the elaboration of impressions, defects in orientation, memory disturbance and marked fluctuation of the level of attention.
2. Affective disorder in the form of emotional instability, the patient laughing or weeping without sufficient cause, and often in an uncontrolled way.
3. Character-change in the form of conduct foreign to the patient's natural disposition, *e.g.* indecent behaviour in a hitherto self-respecting individual.

All these disorders must be taken together as constituting the organic syndrome, although in a given case one set of symptoms may be preponderant and the clinical picture of the acute reaction differs from that of the chronic.

THE ACUTE REACTION—DELIRIUM

Delirium is commoner in the young and in the old, than at other ages. Some individuals are apparently more prone than others to react in this way, and the reasons for these differences in susceptibility to the effects of intoxication are not known. The precipitants are very various: perhaps most commonly febrile illnesses, cardiac failure, and intoxication with alcohol or drugs. The basic disorder has its seat usually outside the brain.

Prior to the development of a frank delirium there may be a prodromal period of several days during which the individual feels exhausted, restless, irritable and sleepless: he may complain of headaches and dizziness, and of feeling muddled.

Confusion follows, with clouding of consciousness, at its worst usually at night; disorientation for time and also commonly for place; impairment of memory, recent memory being chiefly involved; illusions and hallucinations; and an affective change, usually to fear. 'Lucid intervals' of brief duration, variations in the level of consciousness in the direction of clearness, may occur in the course of a delirium. The mental grasp is always impaired, the individual cannot focus his attention more than fleetingly, cannot co-operate properly in an examination of his condition, is suggestible and may misidentify people in his environment. Illusions are common and so are hallucinations of all kinds, especially visual. Though fear is the usual affect and it may be extreme, some cases are euphoric. The mental clouding and its associated symptoms lead to feelings of great insecurity, and paranoid misinterpretations and delusions are common developments. Suicidal attempts or attacks on others may be made. Occasionally there is wild excitement, resembling acute mania. If the patient's condition further deteriorates speech may become incoherent, low and mumbling: and he may pass from drowsiness into coma.

Usually restlessness and insomnia are very prominent symptoms, rendering management difficult and causing prostration. The patient's physical condition is apt to deteriorate rapidly. He is tremulous, sweating, with tachycardia and often a rise of temperature. Epileptic seizures are not uncommon.

A delirium may usher in the terminal phase of a fatal illness; but usually it lasts for a few days and the patient then clears again mentally, with a patchy amnesia for the duration of his delirium. Rarely, instead of his mental state clearing, the patient passes into a Korsakoff's psychosis (e.g. after delirium tremens). Usually he takes some time to recover fully from what has been a serious illness, and symptoms and signs of debility may be present for some weeks. In this period there is commonly disinclination for exertion and easy fatigability, mental and physical; complaints of forgetfulness, often some depression of spirits, and irritability or apathy.

The so-called 'infection-exhaustion psychoses' are delirious or subdelirious reactions (and their sequelae), accompanying infective illness, haemorrhage, poisoning or other severe physical stress. Such a stress may also precipitate a 'functional' reaction, neurotic or psychotic, in a predisposed individual. After influenza and other virus infections, for example, depression is especially common.

DEMENTIA

The chronic organic reaction—dementia—is usually of more insidious onset, and often progresses to a profound change in the personality not seen in the acute reactions. It is typically progressive, but it is not necessarily so. Neither does the diagnosis of dementia mean that the condition is irrecoverable, though this is certainly implied in most cases: the dementia of general paralysis, for example, if the syphilitic infection is treated thoroughly and early enough, may not only be halted but reversed.

In states of dementia, the mental symptoms occur in a setting of relatively clear consciousness. There are changes in the intellectual and affective spheres, and in behaviour; all in the direction of deterioration and disintegration and based on tissue damage to the brain itself. Intelligence is progressively impaired, the intellectual horizon becomes ever narrower, the ability to learn new material diminishes, and the individual tends to react at a simple, factual, unreflective level, which Goldstein has described as the loss of the abstract attitude and a turning to concrete behaviour. Impairment of memory is a symptom of central importance: recent memory suffers more than remote memory, but it is seldom

Z

involved alone. Disorientation is progressive, involving time first and ultimately affecting all spheres. Speech may be impaired; most commonly there develops a nominal aphasia or paraphasia. The most characteristic affective changes are emotional lability and loss of emotional control ('emotional incontinence'). Behaviour becomes inefficient, inappropriate, slovenly; the patient tends to neglect his personal hygiene; he may react violently, indecently or otherwise out of character. Sooner or later there is incontinence of bladder and bowels. Perseveration in speech and other activities is another typical symptom (Allison, 1966).

The development of these various signs and symptoms of mental disorganization leads inevitably to a profound change, a coarsening, then bleaching of the individual's whole previous personality. Facets of it may remain relatively undamaged even to a late stage; and sometimes they become exaggerated, so that the previously sensitive and suspicious individual becomes paranoid, the introspective hypochondriacal and the irascible prone to temper tantrums.

Dementia is often described too exclusively in terms of deterioration in intelligence and memory. Certainly these are features of great importance: but they comprise only part of the clinical picture. Degradation of behaviour, affective changes and the defects of insight and judgement often secondary to them, are of equal significance. The deterioration, as it develops, tends to be a global one, all the individual's abilities suffer. If one mental aspect is particularly and disproportionately affected, speech for example or memory or orientation, a focal lesion is likely to be present.

An individual who is demented may become delirious—an acute organic reaction being then superimposed on a chronic one. A demented person may also develop any sort of 'functional' reaction, such as anxiety, depression or paranoid delusions.

THE KORSAKOFF (AMNESIC) SYNDROME

This is a type of dementia which is relatively well demarcated. Often it becomes a chronic reaction, but it may be brief and recoverable. Most typically it develops from a delirium tremens which does not clear up, and the major factor in these cases is thiamine deficiency: but it may have other causes, e.g. head injury, brain tumour, cerebral arteriosclerosis. It is distinguished from delirium by the clarity of the individual's consciousness and his unimpaired powers of perception; and from more global types of dementia by the relatively good preservation of intellectual capacity. The causal lesions lie in the diencephalon, and may be more or less confined to the mamillary bodies.

The cardinal features of Korsakoff's psychosis are a gross memory defect for recent and current events, the patients being unable to retain new sensory material for more than a minute or two; nearly always (but not necessarily) confabulation, to cover the memory gaps; disorientation; and a retrograde amnesia, which may cover a period of a year or more before the illness. The affected individual is usually lacking in initiative, euphoric, facile and without insight into the fact that he is ill and that his memory is so grossly impaired. Judgement also is severely damaged.

Zangwill (1966) and Brierley (1966) have provided critical reviews.

GENERAL PRINCIPLES OF EXAMINATION

In all cases suspected of being of the organic reaction-type and in all patients of the senile age-group, both a mental and physical examination must be made. The latter is essential: in the organic psychoses the symptoms are the result of a physical illness.

Attention should be paid to the way in which the patient tells his story. He may have some manifest, if slight, difficulty with names, dates and other details, may lose the thread of his account, be confused, or may if severely demented be quite unable to give a coherent account of himself. The patient's recent and remote memory must be meticulously tested: so must his orientation, for time, place and person. He should be required to perform simple arithmetical calculations and to write at least his name and address. His insight and judgement must be assessed. These are some of the essential elements in the full history-taking and mental examination which must be carried out. Abnormal symptoms and signs will indicate the need for more detailed observation and testing.

To assess intellectual deterioration at all accurately, one must know the level of the individual's capacity before he became ill. Apart from the results of intelligence tests which may sometimes be available (if, for example, the patient has recently been at school or in the Armed Forces), the patient's scholastic record and the nature of his subsequent employments will give useful clues to his previous intellectual status. Detailed psychological testing may reveal a discrepancy between the individual's achievement on tests of vocabulary and performance, indicative of organic deterioration, which tends to affect performance more than vocabulary.

A detailed and comprehensive physical examination is obligatory, with particular attention being paid to the nervous system. Laboratory and other specialized investigations are often required, including X-rays of skull and chest, and lumbar puncture. Every effort must be made to diagnose the basic physical illness and its site.

At least one relative or close friend must be interviewed; and detailed information should be sought also of course from the patient's family doctor. This is particularly necessary because many such organically ill people forget or are unaware of or deny their disabilities. The witness should be questioned about changes in the patient's personality, in his behaviour and in his family and social relationships. Inquiry should be made about his memory and judgement, his competence in money affairs, his handwriting, his ability to find his way about; and about any disturbances of consciousness, whether described as faints, fits or episodes of confusion. Inquiry should be made too about the patient's consumption of alcohol and drugs. Furthermore, it is a relative or friend who is most likely to be able to give a clear account of the evolution of the illness in time; its duration, speed of development and fluctuations.

TREATMENT

Whether the organic mental syndrome is acute or chronic, a delirium or a dementia, the underlying cause must be attacked if it is accessible to therapy. There is a host of possible causes—vitamin deficiency, infections, blood loss from haemorrhage, intoxication with alcohol or drugs, cerebral tumour, etc.: and it is this basic physical condition which is the main target for treatment; the disease process must be arrested, the deficiency made good. The remainder of the treatment and management is symptomatic.

In cases of delirium, the patient requires skilled nursing care in a calm and stable environment. Changes in nursing personnel should be kept to the minimum, the patient should not be moved about the ward or put behind screens or left unattended, and he should have a night light. If the home circumstances are favourable a delirious child or old person may well be best cared for there, where the familiarity of the environment is greatly reassuring. If he is in hospital, the relatives of a delirious patient should be permitted to sit by his bed. People and things which are known tend to counter the disorientation and to allay the fear and suspicion which are part and parcel of the confusional reaction. Restlessness is perhaps best controlled with chlorpromazine; paraldehyde and chloral hydrate are other useful drugs; only short-acting barbiturates should be used. Dehydration must be corrected and the patient's strength maintained by an adequate intake of nourishing food.

In states of dementia which cannot be arrested or reversed by specific treatment, the general aim of care and management is to keep the patient as contented, active and constructively occupied as his mental and physical condition will allow. He should remain in the community, at home and up and about for as long as possible. Sedative and tranquillizing drugs should be prescribed, not as an indication that the doctor is doing something, but only when they are really required and then in the minimum effective doses. Often the mental status of demented people is found to be considerably improved by stopping a harmful and unnecessary prescription of barbiturates; or by active treatment of a physical complication, e.g. cardiac failure or urinary infection, which had been overlooked.

Other aspects and details of the treatment of organic reactions will be given below, where the individual syndromes and diseases are discussed.

THE ORGANIC SYNDROMES

Only some of the numerous organic syndromes will now be delineated, which are of particular importance or interest. With individual variations, they exemplify the generalized description already given of the acute and chronic reaction-types. Further examples will be found in the following chapter, where the effects of dependence on drugs and alcohol are described. The following rough classification will indicate the field to be covered:

1. Psychoses of senescence and senility.

2. Metabolic disorders—portal systemic encephalopathy, porphyria.
3. Vitamin deficiency—Wernicke's encephalopathy, pellagra, vitamin B_{12} and folate deficiency.
4. Poisonings—lead, carbon monoxide.
5. Mental sequelae of head injury.
6. Brain tumour.
7. Infective diseases of the C.N.S.—syphilis, encephalitis lethargica.
8. Other diseases of the C.N.S.—Huntington's chorea, disseminated sclerosis.

PSYCHOSES OF SENESCENCE AND SENILITY

The care and treatment of the ageing members of the population who are no longer able to manage for themselves constitutes a national medico-social issue which can only properly be met by the co-operation of local authorities, government departments (health and national insurance) and charitable voluntary organizations, e.g. Nuffield Foundation, British Red Cross Society, Salvation Army, etc. As we advance in years we become more vulnerable to physical and mental incapacity, the machine slows down, it loses something of its resistance and elasticity, and there is no longer the spontaneous vigour and buoyancy of earlier times. There are, however, a favoured few whose physical and intellectual powers remain intact almost to the end of their days, but a far greater number, of a different habit, become old in mind and body long before their appointed time. Why such a difference exists we do not know. Heredity, prolonged psychological and physical stress and strain, endocrine function, may all play their parts. But in addition there are many socio-economic reasons, e.g. poverty, loneliness, faulty nutrition, poor living conditions, and family disharmony, any or all of which may be of equal if not greater importance. The pride and responsibility of maintaining a family group spirit appears to be dwindling in favour of a somewhat selfish individualism.

The problem, therefore, of ageing with its accompanying incapacity is in urgent need of much greater sympathetic understanding and more intensive research than ever has been accorded to it. It is one of the most important aspects of preventive medicine which should be familiar to and within the scope of every well-trained doctor, nurse or social worker. It is a mistake to regard it as a specialist geriatric issue which requires expert personnel. Such over-emphasis narrows the concept instead of encouraging everyone to play his or her part in helping to remedy it. For instance, it is imperative, whenever possible, to decrease the admission rates to all hospitals, and to expend every effort in caring for and treating elderly patients in their own homes, or in residential units which have been made suitable for that purpose. To ensure the success of such schemes an accurate medical diagnosis should be made as rapidly as possible so that an appropriate assessment can be made of the probable course of the illness, and the extent of the help required.

Thompson, Lowe and McKeown (1951) in their valuable and notable survey in Birmingham estimated that approximately 12 persons in every thousand aged

65 years and over were in hospitals for the chronic sick. They suggested that in order to reduce the demand for expensive hospital beds for the aged three things are necessary: 1. the provision of better social services in the home (nursing, domestic help, laundry, beds and bedding, and meals); 2. housing designed for the elderly; 3. residential institutions (other than hospitals) which afford domestic services and simple nursing (washing, feeding and dressing). All such amelioristic measures have met with universal approval, and should confer a great benefit. Their necessity becomes even more apparent as we become aware that the number of persons over pensionable age continues to show a continuous increase. Nearly 1 in 8 of the population is now aged 65 or over. In 1963 5·6 millions of people in England and Wales were aged 65 or more; by 1972 6·6 millions will be, and by 1982 7·4 millions. As a result mainly of this ageing of the general population, patients aged 65 or over comprise 39 per cent. of the patients in psychiatric units and hospitals, compared with 30 per cent. nine years previously (Brooke, 1967). In 1965 nearly 21,000 patients were admitted to mental hospitals in Scotland and of these nearly 21 per cent. were over the age of 65.

In addition, the prevalence of both neuroses and psychoses amongst old people in the community is known to be high. Kay, Beamish and Roth (1964) in Newcastle studied the prevalence of psychiatric disorder in old people who were living at home. Ten per cent. were considered to be suffering from organic brain syndromes—mainly senile and arteriosclerotic psychoses, which totalled 8·1 per cent.: brain syndromes due to other causes were found in 1·9 per cent. 'Functional' psychiatric disorder, predominantly affective disorders and neuroses, were found in 31 per cent. Only a small fraction of these, often very mentally disabled old people, are being cared for in hospitals and Homes: and Kay and his colleagues rightly pointed to the urgent need to extend to them better facilities for medical care.

Both in hospitals and in the community the facts about the mental illness of old people are grave, and call for urgent consideration, research and action.

Changes in the Senium. Many of our most famous essayists, poets and novelists have portrayed the characteristics, the vagaries of conduct, and the foibles of the elderly. For the most part they have done so in a sophisticated, kindly, understanding manner so that ample allowance can be made for the ultra-conservatism, arbitrariness and obstinacy which constitute so much of the clinical picture. Senescence is a slow progressive process. At first the changes may be very slight, and may not consist of more than a mere modification or caricature of the normal personality which can be maintained for a considerable time. A complete transformation or distortion of the personality only occurs coincidentally with a severe involvement of the brain tissue. It is only then that the disorganization of the intellectual faculties and the physical changes give cause for alarm.

One of the most prominent—and even irritating—features of the senescent state is inflexibility, a resistance to change, an inability to adapt to what are regarded as 'new fangled' ideas, or other ways of living. It is this lack of insight, this inability to recognize one's short-comings and limitations that may have led government departments, local authorities, universities, big business organizations, and the services to ordain compulsory retirement at the 60–65 age level. Sometimes such arbitrariness may seem a little unfair, and may even be a means of accelerating the senescent process rather than of retarding it. Judges, ministers of religion, Members of Parliament, and some business executives remain exempt from the above limitations—it is difficult to understand why—and it must be assumed that they have inherited the wisdom of the ages!

But when all aspects are taken into consideration it is probably an excellent plan to fix a compulsory retiral age. It provides the younger person with the opportunity and incentive for promotion, for the infusion of new blood, or the elimination of dead wood, whichever process seems to be the more appropriate. Elderly persons whose mental powers are showing a noticeable failure, and yet who persist in maintaining a senior position, often provide a sad spectacle. It is, of course, natural enough to want to maintain prestige, and to be proud of past achievements, but it is wearisome in the extreme to listen repeatedly to the same old story no matter how richly it is embellished in the re-telling. The refrain is always the same—how much better the old days and ways were, children respected their elders then, the world is going to the dogs, the wisdom and experience of age are being neglected.

In other words senescence creates a one-track mind so that any departure from the daily routine becomes anathema. To live in the past, to indulge in reminiscences, anecdotes, clichés and platitudes may be taken as indicative of inability to cope with present-day affairs. Lack of attention and concentration results in the repetition of questions the answers to which are easily forgotten. Such states of absentmindedness and forgetfulness may cause books, business papers, dentures, spectacles, etc., to be mislaid.

There is loss of weight, the body becomes stooped and bent, the features are fine-drawn, the hair is white and sparse, and the skin is wrinkled, dry and often discoloured by purpuric patches and petechial haemorrhages on the backs of the hands or other parts of the body. There may be tremor of the head and hands, and shaky hand-writing; the gait becomes stiff. Subjective complaints of headache, dizziness, and fatigue are common.

We may now direct attention to the various clinical senescent states which demand a more detailed description. They will be considered under three headings: 1. the pre-senile psychoses; 2. cerebral arteriosclerosis; 3. senile dementia. In this age group neurotic reactions, and affective and paranoid psychoses, are also of much importance: but they do not differ essentially from similar reactions occurring at an earlier age.

THE PRE-SENILE PSYCHOSES

Three main types are differentiated:
1. Alzheimer's disease.
2. Pick's disease.
3. Jakob-Creutzfeldt's disease.

Alzheimer's Disease

This condition is an organic brain disease with focal manifestations, due to a primary parenchymatous change, occurring in persons between the ages of 40 and 60 years; certain persons may be affected in youth or early manhood. For instance Malamud and Lowenberg reported the case of a child who when 7 years old had contracted scarlet fever and subsequently showed a lack of physical and mental development. After his death at the age of 15 years the histopathological investigation of his brain revealed the miliary plaques and nerve cell changes which are regarded as characteristic of Alzheimer's disease. And Biggart quotes Hallevorden as reporting that in 10 cases of post-encephalitic Parkinsonism, whose ages ranged from 10 to 50 years, he had been able to observe the presence of typical Alzheimer 'tangles' in the substantia nigra and tegmentum of the pons. It is evident, then, that Alzheimer's disease has a wider spread than was thought and that a variety of aetiological factors may be implicated. We have not seen any cases under the age of 40 years, and believe, with Grunthal, that any such should be investigated with the most careful scrutiny. Women are more frequently affected than men.

Alzheimer's original observation, in 1907, concerned a woman, 51 years old, whose clinical state was marked by a severe failure of memory so that she was unable to find her way in her own house. She was perplexed and puzzled, disorientated for time and place, and experienced states of transitory confusion accompanied by hallucinosis. She exhibited a paraphasic state with perseveration, and had difficulty in understanding spoken speech. Her illness progressed over a period of four and a half years; at the time of her death she was greatly enfeebled, and her limbs were contracted. Alzheimer described the histopathological changes in the brain as follows: 'In an otherwise normal cell there appear at first one or more fibrils which on account of increased thickness and stainability stand out prominently. In the further course of the alteration many neighbouring fibrils are similarly affected. These then form thick bundles which gradually come to the surface of the cell. Finally the nucleus and cell disintegrate and only a tangled bundle of fibrils remains to indicate the site of a former ganglion cell.' In addition to the so-called 'tangles' or 'baskets of fibrils' which were so characteristic, many miliary plaques were demonstrated throughout the brain cortex. It had been known that such plaques were usually present in the brain of elderly persons, and in cases of senile dementia their number was always considerably increased.

Clinical Symptoms and Morbid Anatomy. The clinical symptoms are so insidious in onset that it is only at a later date that their significance is fully realized. A previously capable and intelligent person may appear to lack concentration, to be absent-minded, to make mistakes in doing the simplest tasks. There is emotional instability which varies from facility to depression and irritability. Such symptoms are apt to be made light of, and a rest, a change of air, a tonic may seem to be all that is required. Gradually, however, it becomes recognized that the above symptoms are much more persistent and serious than was originally thought. The difficulties in attention, concentration and comprehension seriously interfere with the person's ability to perform ordinary daily tasks, and the tendency is to blame others for the growing incapacity; ideas of reference, suspicion and even transitory, unsystematized delusions of persecution may be expressed. As the illness pursues its slow and ominous course, the power of sustained attention becomes less and less and forgetfulness, both for recent and remote events, an ever more notable feature. Ultimately there is disorientation for time, place and person, and the patient becomes unable to name or recognize his most intimate relatives. There is coincidental bodily enfeeblement with inco-ordination of movements and emaciation. The patient becomes bedridden and helpless.

In addition to this gradually worsening dementia, nominal aphasia, para-phasia and apraxia usually develop, and there may be occasional epileptic fits.

Sim, Turner and Smith (1966) investigated 35 patients in whom the diagnosis had been confirmed by cerebral biopsy: 21 were female, 14 male. In 23 of these cases the age of onset was between 50 and 59 years: in 3 below the age of 50. Early memory impairment was a conspicuous feature in all these patients. The earliest neurological sign detected was a constructional apraxia, which could readily be demonstrated by the use of Koh's blocks. Personality and social behaviour tended to be preserved longer than might be expected. Disorientation and dysphasia with perseveration became more marked as deterioration proceeded, with the development of neurological signs: the latter were striatal features with rigidity and tremor and pyramidal signs, particularly in the lower limbs. Where epileptic fits occurred, they followed usually the onset of gross dementia. Only one patient had a sibling affected by a similar condition.

E.E.G. changes are early and generalized. Though characteristic of this disease, they are not pathognomonic. Letemendia and Pampiglione (1958), reporting on 17 histologically verified cases of Alzheimer's disease, recorded the common E.E.G. findings as follows: 'Absent or scanty alpha rhythms; generalized 2 to 7 c./sec. activity poorly affected by sensory stimuli, slightly increased by overbreathing but clearly diminished during drowsiness; well-preserved responses to photic stimulation; and poor fast activity response to barbiturates. Sleep spindles were recognizable though often of low amplitude; K-complexes were only infrequently evoked by sensory stimuli. The E.E.G. abnormalities were fairly uniform in all cases without constant relationship to the duration and severity of the clinical picture, the presence or absence of fits, or the patient's age.'

The neuropathological changes are a generalized cortical atrophy, similar to that seen in senile dementia, with enlargement of the ventricles. Histopathologically the nerve cells are replaced by neurofibrillary tangles arranged in the form of whirls or baskets. Senile argentophil plaques with a dense core of amyloid material are also typical. There is proliferation of neuroglia.

Pick's Disease

In 1892 Arnold Pick of Prague described a circumscribed atrophy of the frontal and temporal lobes which contrasted with the diffuse involvement of the

Alzheimer group. The persons affected are between 40 and 60 years old, and the illness may persist from fifteen to twenty years. The aetiology is obscure but in some cases there is a familial history of heredo-degenerative traits. Grunthal, for instance, reported its occurrence in two brothers, and in two generations of another family.

Clinical Symptoms. The clinical picture bears a close resemblance, especially in its early stages, to Alzheimer's disease. The onset is usually most insidious, and in general the symptoms correspond to those which are characteristic of organic brain disease, *e.g.* intellectual disorganization with a change in character and affect. The earliest indication of the disorder may be a failure of attention and concentration leading to forgetfulness, and apparent lack of interest. The previously capable, efficient person seems to be unduly casual, is perplexed and confused, and a constant source of worry and anxiety to relatives and friends. The true significance of the illness does not usually become appreciated until even more gross symptoms develop. These usually consist of a complete loss of spontaneousness and initiative so that the ordinary everyday acts such as dressing, eating, attention to bodily habits, and the simplest tasks cannot be accomplished without much assistance. There is a regression to a childhood level with lability of mood and stereotypy of speech and conduct. Disorientation becomes complete, memory for recent and remote events disappears, and life is continued at a purely automatic level. Aphasic, alexic, agraphic and dyspraxic phenomena occur depending upon the localized area of brain tissue involved. Epileptiform attacks occur occasionally but are not a special feature.

The terminal stage is one of mental and bodily enfeeblement so that the patient becomes bedridden.

Morbid Anatomy. The brain shows a circumscribed atrophy particularly affecting the frontal and temporal lobes; there may also be a shrinkage of the corpus callosum. The left hemisphere of the brain is the one more usually affected. The motor cortex and cerebellum usually remain intact.

Microscopically, the nerve cells in the third layer of the cortex disappear first and are replaced by neuroglial proliferation. The cells in the three first cortical layers are more intensely involved than the others. Many of them become swollen, 'ballooned', and show deep argentophilic staining. The chromatin substance of the cells disappears, the nucleus is displaced to the periphery of the cell, is pale in colour and vacuolated. Occasionally senile plaques and Alzheimer's cells may be present but they are not a conspicuous feature of the disease. The white matter may also atrophy.

Differential Diagnosis. Clinically it is extremely difficult—and sometimes impossible—to differentiate Pick's disease from Alzheimer's. They occur at the same age period, run a more or less identical course, and exhibit similar phenomena. Sjögren, Sjögren and Lindgren (1952) compared and analysed the symptoms in a group of 18 cases of each disease. The average age of onset in each group was 54 years. Amnesia and progressive dementia were especially prominent in Pick's disease, while the Alzheimer group showed an increase in muscle tone, unsteady gait and space disorientation.

In each group 3 of the 36 parents had suffered from senile or pre-senile dementia, and one sibling in each group was likewise involved. The risk of parental involvement was estimated as 10 ± 4 per cent. for Alzheimer's disease as compared with 19 ± 5 for Pick's; the risks for brothers and sisters was $3 \cdot 8 \pm 2 \cdot 1$ per cent. and $6 \cdot 8 \pm 2 \cdot 9$ per cent. Sjögren suggested that a dominant gene of incomplete penetrance was the important factor in Pick's disease, and that a multifactorial inheritance was responsible for Alzheimer's disease. A familial tendency appears therefore to be a feature of both diseases. It is only *post mortem* that an accurate distinction can be made. In Pick's disease the lesions are circumscribed, and the basal ganglia are rarely affected; in Alzheimer's disease there is a diffuse atrophy of the cerebral cortex, and changes are usual in the basal ganglia.

Jakob-Creutzfeldt's Disease

This syndrome differs from the other pre-senile states in the predominance of pyramidal and extrapyramidal involvement. At various times the syndrome has been described as a 'spastic pseudo-sclerosis'; 'encephalo-myelopathy with disseminated lesions'; 'cortical pallidospinal degeneration'.

It is a disease of middle life, but in some instances cases have been reported with autopsy findings in which the patients were not 30 years old. The aetiology is not known. Anxiety and depression are prominent clinical features, but the emotional picture varies considerably and sometimes a state of euphoria and incurable optimism is in marked contrast to the obvious physical and mental disabilities. A progressive deterioration of the intellectual faculties involving memory, judgement and insight occurs, and is sometimes accompanied by confabulation of the Korsakoff type. The terminal stage is one of complete dementia.

Physical Symptoms. A sense of tiredness and of weakness in the legs is an early sign. There is difficulty in raising the legs, so that the patient will walk round rather than step over any obstacles. Later considerable ataxia develops so that walking is a matter of great difficulty. The tendon reflexes are markedly exaggerated, ankle clonus can be elicited, and the plantar responses are extensor. The muscles of the arms and legs may show the atrophy and fibrillations which are so commonly associated with amyotrophic lateral sclerosis. Extrapyramidal signs take the form of spontaneous movements, tremor, athetosis, disturbance of muscle tone. Parkinsonian symptoms may be present, and dysarthria is almost invariably present. Death occurs usually in a period of two to five years.

The pathological change consists of a symmetrical frontal lobe atrophy which sometimes extends back to the parietal and temporal lobes. The histopathology shows a diffuse diminution of the cortical ganglion cells with moderate neuroglial proliferation. Similar destructive changes occur in the basal ganglia, ventromedial nucleus of the thalamus, bulbar motor nuclei, and anterior horn cells. The myelin sheaths and axis cylinders of the pyramidal and extrapyramidal tracts are seriously affected.

Other Pre-senile Dementias

A small group of pre-senile dementias do not fit neatly into any of the three syndromes already discussed. Amongst them is the very rare condition described by Newmann and Cohn (1967) as primary subcortical gliosis, in which the cortical changes are less marked than in Pick's disease and the subscortical more prominent. Clinically, its features can hardly be distinguished from those of Alzheimer's and Pick's diseases.

CEREBRAL ARTERIOSCLEROSIS

Arteriosclerotic brain disease occurs, for the most part, in persons over the age of 50 years. In those families, however, in which there is a distinct tendency to early arterial degeneration the members of the 30 to 40 age group may not escape. The onset is most often in the middle sixties: and the average expectation of life, which is very variable, is then 3–4 years. The outlook is worse for those suffering additionally from hypertension. Death results from a cerebrovascular accident or cardiac failure.

Mental symptoms may be ushered in with the dramatic suddenness of an apoplectic seizure. It may be of a minor nature—an arterial spasm—causing a state of mental confusion, a clouding of consciousness with word amnesia and paraphasia which may persist only for an hour or two. It should be taken as a warning, as an indication that, for a time at least, the strain and stress of life should be curtailed. No further untoward symptoms may develop and the patient may be able to lead a happy and efficient life. If, however, the apoplectic seizure should be of a major type accompanied by unconsciousness and followed by paralytic symptoms the situation is much more ominous. It is true that the patient may make a good recovery, that all residual symptoms may disappear, and that the patient's personality may continue to be well preserved; he is still the man he used to be. Sometimes, however, and this is more usual than not, his confidence in himself has been disturbed, he fears another 'stroke', is inclined to be introspective and obsessive so that there is a noticeable loss of efficiency. Such patients are very loath to give in, they struggle against their disabilities, and if frustrated in their efforts, bouts of anger and irritability occur which may precipitate another cerebral incident. Emotional instability in a middle-aged man who has never previously suffered from temperamental difficulties is most likely to be organically determined. In such states laughter and tears are never far apart— the one succeeds the other in an almost explosive way. Suspicion, jealousy, delusions of persecution, leading to violent outbursts which may have dangerous consequences, occur especially during periods of clouding of consciousness and disorientation. After these episodes have passed the patient may have a complete amnesia for their occurrence. In his more lucid moments he expresses great regret and sorrow to those who have been caring for him for causing so much trouble. His condition, however, may vary from day to day, or from week to week, and there is a gradual weakening of his personality structure, and an inability to contend with the tasks of everyday life. Accompanying his emotional lability and personality change, forgetfulness, lack of concentration, and memory failure particularly for recent events, become conspicuous features. This may be so much the case that it may become imperative to appoint an attorney or curator to look after his business affairs so that the interests of the family are properly protected. In contrast to his forgetfulness for recent events, his memory for the events of his childhood and early life may be retained to the end of his days. In those cases suffering from a repetition of 'strokes' the mental and physical disorganization may be much more rapidly completed.

Physical Symptoms. Headache, dizziness, tinnitus and nose bleeding are among the earliest symptoms. The pupils are small and sluggish in their reaction in about 25 per cent. of cases. The hands are tremulous, the gait is unsteady and tottering, and paraesthesiae of the lower extremities are a fairly constant occurrence. The tendon reflexes are usually exaggerated, and in those cases with a residual paralysis there is an extensor plantar response, and ankle clonus. In addition to the production of monoplegias, hemiplegias and a bilateral spastic state, all varieties of aphasia and apraxia may be in evidence. Epileptic seizures are common. There may be Parkinsonism. A pseudobulbar paralysis may occur due to a bilateral involvement of the pyramidal tracts above the medulla.

An ophthalmoscopic examination will often reveal a sclerosis of the vessels of the fundi, even when there is no indication of a peripheral arteriosclerosis. An increase of blood pressure is a usual, but not invariable, concomitant. The C.S.F. is usually normal, except for a week or two after infarction, when the protein may be slightly or moderately increased and there may be a pleocytosis.

Disease of the Extracerebral Arteries, Angiography has demonstrated that many of the cerebral lesions previously thought to be due to intracranial vascular disease, are caused by extracranial obstruction of the carotid or vertebral vessels. Probably atherosclerosis of these arteries in the neck is responsible for at least half of all cases of cerebral ischaemia. Typically, when the carotid arteries are stenosed or occluded, the cerebral hemispheres suffer: when the vertebral arteries become stenosed, there is brain-stem ischaemia. Often both systems are diseased simultaneously. Infarction of the brain may result either from reduction of its blood supply or from emboli derived from mural thrombi which have formed on atheromatous plaques in the vessels in the neck. Infarction may be preceded by transient ischaemic attacks.

The proximal 2 cm. of the internal carotid artery seems to be especially vulnerable: and the stenosis is commonly bilateral. It is the ipsilateral frontal and parietal lobes which are usually affected. Recurrent ischaemic attacks producing transient paresis or paraesthesiae of a limb or of one side of the face, with or without dysphasia, may preface a major disabling or fatal stroke.

In the syndrome called vertebrobasilar insufficiency, there are atheromatous changes in and stenosis of one or both vertebral arteries. Embarrassment of the vertebral blood supply may also be associated with cervical spondylosis. Ischaemia of the brain stem, cerebellum and occipital lobe results. The symptoms are in the early stages notably transient, and often related to movements of the neck or to standing upright abruptly. Vertigo is the most frequent of them: also characteristic are transient visual disturbances—blurring, visual field defects and even loss of vision; paraesthesiae of the face and distal parts of the limbs; and drop attacks, in which the patients falls without losing consciousness. There may also be brief losses of consciousness, ataxia and dysarthria. Infarction of the brain stem, major strokes and intellectual impairment are later, and not inevitable, developments.

It may be difficult clinically to differentiate internal carotid from vertebrobasilar occlusion. Symptoms of vertebrobasilar insufficiency may also result from occlusion of the first part of the subclavian artery, causing a reversal of blood flow in the vertebral artery ('subclavian steal') to supply the arm on that side.

It is of importance to diagnose these extracerebral vascular lesions at an early stage and if possible to forestall their disabling effects. If the stenosis is partial and accessible, reconstructive vascular surgery may be possible. Anticoagulant therapy may in some cases reduce the incidence of transient attacks. Hypertension should be controlled with methyldopa or other drugs. But once dementia has developed operation is contra-indicated and it is too late for effective treatment.

The Vascular and Neuropathology. Atherosclerosis affects the carotid and vertebral arteries and their larger intracerebral branches. It is distinguished by its 'signet ring' appearance—the whole circumference of the vessel is not uniformly affected. There is fatty degeneration and fibrous thickening of the intima, splitting of the internal elastic lamina and replacement of the medial muscle with fibrous tissue. Vascular occlusion may result from progressive narrowing, from thrombus formation on the inner surface of the atheromatous plaques or from emboli derived from these plaques. Ischaemic necrosis or infarction of cerebral tissue results, involving usually a considerable area of both white and grey matter. Later there is neuroglial scarring or cyst formation as the necrotic tissue is removed.

Cerebral arteriolosclerosis is manifest in a uniform fibrous thickening, and progressive narrowing of the lumen, of the small intracerebral arterioles. Commonly there is splitting of the media, and there may be hyalinization of the arteriolar walls. This process, which is associated with hypertension, produces multiple small foci of ischaemic damage in the white or grey matter, resulting in cell atrophy and glial scars.

The majority of strokes are due to infarction. Atherosclerosis gives rise typically to the gross and fatal cerebral lesions: while arteriolosclerosis tends to cause transient focal symptoms, confusional episodes and a progressive dementia.

Intracerebral is commoner than subarachnoid haemorrhage. Haemorrhage may result from the rupture of a fusiform arteriosclerotic aneurysm: or, especially in the case of hypertensive individuals, from the rupture of micro-aneurysms of the terminal branches of the lenticulostriate vessels in the basal ganglia.

SENILE DEMENTIA

There is no clear dividing line between the more or less normal mental changes of the senium, and the onset of a senile dementia. Its development is insidious.

The failure of memory for names, dates and recent events becomes more marked. Orientation begins to fail, at first for time. Concentration and thinking processes are increasingly impaired. The average age of onset of this progressive deterioration is about 75 years of age, and its duration usually about 5 years.

A diffuse involvement of memory both for recent and remote events marks the progress of mental deterioration. A charming, elderly gentleman who was well over 80 years old used always to say that he was only one day old. Obviously he lived in a 'day-tight' compartment so that neither the past nor the future disturbed his blissful equanimity. Disorientation for time, place and person becomes complete. Night and day cannot be greatly distinguished, the days, weeks, months and years pass unnoticed: he cannot recognize his own home; he fails to recognize intimate relatives with whom he has been on the most affectionate terms. The above symptoms can prove most troublesome and even dangerous especially at night-time. On awakening from a restless, disturbed sleep he may be in a confused bewildered state. In attempting to determine his whereabouts he may fall from his bed and sustain a fracture of his femur or pelvis, or he may wander aimlessly about the house or set it on fire, or leave it altogether. Such episodes are most alarming. Personal habits become faulty, he is unable to dress himself properly, stuffs his pockets with rubbish, and becomes uncleanly in his bodily care. The emotional disorganization is punctuated by bouts of explosive anger. Inevitably the intellectual and emotional life is reduced to a state of childish fatuity, a prattling mindlessness, and a purely vegetative existence. The patient becomes bedridden and requires every nursing care.

Some writers have been inclined to emphasize the melancholic, maniacal and paranoid states which may show themselves during the progress of the senile illness. We see no reason or purpose in doing so because the above states differ in no way from similar states occurring at any other period of life. They merely reflect the underlying constitutional make-up which has been exposed or laid bare by the profound organic disturbance.

Senile Delirium. Symptomatically senile delirium resembles the delirium of earlier years: there is hallucinosis, fear, disorientation and exhaustion. It has many possible causes: acute infections, respiratory and urinary most commonly; vitamin deficiency; cardiac failure; head injury; and it is common as a postoperative phenomenon, *e.g.* following prostatectomy or excision of a cataract. Insomnia may be extreme, and great care should always be exercised in choosing an appropriate hypnotic; injudicious medication may aggravate the condition we hope to cure. Delirious states may also occur more or less spontaneously as a result of the ageing process. For instance, a gentleman, 86 years old, who had experienced a birth phantasy, requested that his congratulations should be conveyed to one of his male nurses. He stated that during the night he had given birth to twins, and that the male nurse in attendance had assisted their delivery in the most skilful way imaginable. Another, when found lying under his bed, explained that he was fishing for pearls in a private loch, the property of a person in whom he had been intensely interested.

Neuropathology. The brain is small, and its weight may be diminished by as much as 200 g. The cortex and convolutions of the brain are shrunken, the sulci are widened and the ventricles dilated. The small blood vessels may exhibit a degree of degenerative change but not sufficient to cause areas of softening.

Microscopically, there is a loss of nerve cells and a disturbance of cortical layering. The neuroglia is proliferated but it may also undergo atrophy. Plaques occur normally in every senile brain but in dementia their number is considerably increased: they consist of a mixture of neural and glial elements and form a conglomerate mass. Basket-like formations of fibrils of the Alzheimer type are also characteristic. Marked nerve cell loss in the hippocampal areas may be related to the deterioration of memory.

Having carried out meticulous plaque counts, Blessed, Tomlinson, and Roth (1968) report that there is a relationship between the severity of dementia and the extent of senile plaque formation.

Aetiology. Hereditary factors undoubtedly play a part in the aetiology of senile dementia, but the mode of inheritance is uncertain. For senile psychoses (organic psychoses of the senium) Kallmann reported (1953) that the expectancy is significantly increased in senile twin sibships; varying from 6·5–8 per cent. for dizygotic twins and sibs, to 42·8 per cent. for monozygotic twins. Larsson, Sjögren and Jacobson (1963), in a review of 377 patients suffering from senile dementia, found in their relatives an incidence of senile dementia 4·3 times that in the general population, and have suggested that the genetic component in its causation is a major gene inherited as a Mendelian dominant. Kallman thought it to be polygenically determined. In the Stockholm study no cases of Alzheimer's disease were found in the relatives, and it was concluded therefore that senile dementia and Alzheimer's disease are different disease entities.

Larsson and his colleagues believe that environmental factors of a socio-economic nature play little part in the onset of senile dementia. In general we agree with this and with the conclusion reached by Kay and his colleagues (1964): namely, that advanced age is the main aetiological factor, while physical disease elsewhere in the body, sensory defects, inadequate diet and social isolation may on occasion contribute to the deterioration.

Differential Diagnosis. This is between senile and arteriosclerotic dementia and various other states.

It is a serious error to think that any emotional disturbance in the senium must be due to degeneration of brain tissue or cerebrovascular disease. Neurotic reactions in this age group are very common. Probably the majority of those who react in this way have shown neurotic traits when younger. The insecurity of old age promotes reactions of anxiety, and the wearing out of the bodily machine provides a basis for hypochondriasis. Self-concern tends to take the place of outside interests, and physical complaints compel the attention of other people—attention which the old person might otherwise not get. Depressive psychoses are also common, constituting the cause of about one third of mental hospital admissions after the age of 60.

Neither are organic mental illnesses in this age group necessarily either cases of cerebral arteriosclerosis or senile dementia. Cerebral tumour is not uncommon, and may cause as its most prominent symptoms intellectual deterioration and personality change: headache, vomiting and papilloedema may be late developments. A relatively rapidly developing dementia, with progressive focal signs and symptoms, should arouse suspicion of a tumour. Subdural haematoma is often difficult to diagnose in the old, and particularly so since there is often no history of trauma: severe headache and a fluctuating level of consciousness are very significant features of the clinical picture. A late developing syphilitic general paralysis or pre-senile dementia or vitamin deficiency or uraemia, are amongst the other diagnostic possibilities. The apathy of a depressive psychosis is sometimes mistaken for dementia, but usually only if the observation and mental examination of the patient have been inadequate.

Beyond the age of 75–80 it is difficult, if not impossible, to differentiate cerebral arteriosclerosis from senile dementia: parenchymatous and vascular changes so often at this advanced age co-exist. Between the ages of 60 and 75 discrimination is usually possible. On the average, cerebral arteriosclerosis begins about 10 years earlier. The onset is often acute, it runs a stormy course with fluctuations in intensity, punctuated by the development of strokes and focal neurological symptoms and signs. The general personality and insight tend to be retained for longer than in senile dementia, and emotional lability is a prominent feature. In senile dementia the typical development is much more insidious and progressively downhill. Its earliest symptoms are essentially mental, whereas in the case of cerebral arteriosclerosis they are often physical.

Prognosis

We must accept the fact that, once degenerative changes have occurred in the brain tissue and in the cerebral blood vessels giving rise to objective clinical symptoms, the prognosis must be viewed with grave concern. The probability is that the degenerative process will be progressive in nature and will lead to a state of mental and physical enfeeblement. While this, eventually, is the final outcome yet we are impressed by the frequency with which temporary betterment can be effected. This is particularly the case in cerebral arteriosclerotic states. For example, a man of 62 years had an apoplectiform seizure followed by inability to speak, and a right-sided hemiplegia. He became so difficult to manage that treatment in a mental hospital was imperative. Under skilled medical and nursing care a great improvement was effected, and in three months he was able to be discharged. He had regained his ability to converse, his paralytic symptoms disappeared, and he acquired good insight into his illness. His memory and general efficiency were only slightly impaired.

Apart from post-apoplectic states we have been gratified to see how frequently, as a result of improvement in nutrition and general management, irritable, suspicious, aggressive delusional states become so greatly modified that the patients may be able to live comfortably in their own homes.

These transitory improvements occur much more frequently than is generally recognized.

2 A

Treatment

The medico-social preventive aspects of the treatment of the elderly have been stressed by all who have studied the problem. It is of paramount importance and constitutes a challenge to our skill and humanitarianism. Elderly, lonely people with slender material and economic resources are often in a sorry plight and are in urgent need of all the assistance friends, relatives, voluntary organizations, and the Welfare State can provide. Such assistance must have been visualized when the National Assistance Act (1948) made it incumbent on the local authority to provide 'residential accommodation for persons who by reason of age, infirmity or other circumstances are in need of care and attention not otherwise available to them'. That Act has not yet been implemented nearly far enough, but certain local authorities have recognized that it is particularly applicable to the case of many elderly persons. There is, however, so much to do that governmental and local authority departments would make little impression on it unless they had the enthusiastic support of all the magnificent personnel engaged in voluntary and charitable work. These bodies recognize that if their efforts are to meet with the reward they deserve they must not be squandered in a haphazard way. The actual individual situation requires to be carefully defined, and an accurate diagnosis established so as to determine the best procedure. The family doctor may be able to do this, or if necessary he may refer his patient to a specialist for a domiciliary consultation, or to an out-patient clinic. We believe that in the first place if it is practicable every effort should be made to provide home care; to remove an elderly person from his accustomed surroundings may constitute an additional hazard. The help of relatives, friends, neighbours may require to be enlisted, and, for special services, home helps, social workers, district nurses and 'meals on wheels' can prove invaluable. Some elderly persons are very independent, they prefer to have their freedom and not be beholden to anyone. So long as they do not constitute too much of a danger to themselves or to their neighbours it is a good plan to reduce interference to a minimum. The family doctor, a social worker, a relative or friend, should be encouraged to maintain contact, not so much for a specific purpose as for security reasons.

If home-care is considered inadvisable it is possible to arrange for the patient's admission for observation pending the next step. Special units for elderly persons who do not require specialized nursing care have won the support of many private individuals, religious organizations and charitable agencies, e.g. British Red Cross Society, National Old People's Welfare Council and the King Edward's Hospital Fund for London. Such special units have much to be said for them. The patients lead a community life, have their own room, or may be in a small dormitory with others, are well nourished and maintained, and in many instances are able to go in and out with freedom and safety. In other cases, depending on the condition of the patient, it may be considered advisable to recommend admission to a mental hospital. It can be arranged informally and the patient can be assured of receiving skilled attention, kindness and understanding to an extent which the public do not sufficiently realize. Here the patient will find all that modern science can do to make life easier and more pleasant. Attention is paid to nutrition, sleep, hygienic habits, there is plenty of indoor and outdoor space to move about in, there is companionship, occupational therapy, radio and television, church services and social parties, so that life can be at a much fuller but yet more protected level than under home conditions.

Contractures of the limbs, deformity of the feet, the immobility of the paralysed, and the maintenance of the natural functions, are all matters for attention. Physiotherapy and chiropody are often most valuable. The great advantage of hospital treatment of the elderly is the constant supervision both night and day. Private nursing home organizations and small specialized residential units are apt to be much more expensive, and defective in nursing and night supervision. In hospital there is much less chance of serious accidents, and if they should occur an efficient medical and nursing service is at hand to deal with them.

General nursing measures which materially add to the comfort and contentment of the patient are warm clothing, a comfortable bed, a well-heated room, easily masticated food, a warm drink at night-time. Wet beds, bed-sores, faecal impaction, incontinence of urine, and the possibility of becoming bed-ridden should be avoided. Bed exercises, simple occupations, getting the patient up each day, and not tucking in too tightly at night-time may all help enormously.

Chlorpromazine is probably the best drug for controlling restlessness and sleeplessness in the aged. It may be given in a dose of 25 mg. twice or thrice daily; and at night in a dose of 25–50 mg. Chloral hydrate, 1–2 G., is another useful hypnotic. If barbiturates are given, they should be short-acting ones: too many old people are rendered confused and ataxic with barbiturates. For those who have been accustomed to alcohol a glass of whisky at bed-time may promote relaxation and sleep. It is wiser to induce sleep than to allow sleeplessness to become a habit.

METABOLIC DISORDERS

PORTAL SYSTEMIC ENCEPHALOPATHY

An association between liver disease and mental symptoms has been recognized since antiquity, being first described by Hippocrates: but it is only in the last decade that the neuropsychiatric syndromes have been clearly delineated and progress been made in understanding their aetiology and treatment.

Both acute and chronic organic syndromes occur, and have been included under the broader descriptive term portal systemic encephalopathy. In these patients, either as a result of the liver disease itself and the development of collateral venous channels or following surgical portacaval anastomoses, a circulatory pathway is formed by which portal blood enters the systemic system and reaches the brain without having been metabolized in the liver. From this bypassing of the liver, cerebral intoxication may result. The intoxicants are probably produced by the action of intestinal bacteria on nitrogenous matter (especially protein) in the gut. Ammonium is an important but not the only substance involved. Both deficiency and intoxication may be factors, and individual sensitivity may also play some part in the production of symptoms.

In the more acute cases drowsiness precedes delirium and coma. The clinical features have been described by Sherlock and her colleagues (1954). There is nothing pathognomonic about them. There is clouding of consciousness with impaired comprehension, disorientation, emotional lability and apathy or disinhibited behaviour. A 'flapping' tremor is commonly seen, due to rapid flexion-extension movements at the metacarpophalangeal and wrist joints: it is best demonstrated when the arms are outstretched and the fingers spread. A similar clinical picture may develop, for example, in cases of congestive cardiac failure and uraemia. Jaundice, ascites and foetor hepaticus may point to the seat of the disease, and the plasma ammonia level is usually elevated. Progressive slowing occurs in the E.E.G., until in the stage of pre-coma the rhythmic activity is less than 4 c./sec. There are characteristic pathological changes in the brain, the protoplasmic astrocytes showing a diffuse enlargement and proliferation while the nerve cells are relatively little altered.

Treatment is by protein deprivation and the administration orally of a broad-spectrum antibiotic (usually neomycin) to diminish bacterial action in the intestine: gastro-intestinal bleeding and electrolyte imbalance must also be corrected urgently. The mental symptoms are often reversible. The prognosis depends on the degree and duration of the impairment of liver function. In cases of acute hepatitis, if recovery occurs it is usually complete. In the more chronic cases of cirrhosis the course of the illness may be fluctuating, with recurrent periods of stupor or coma. It should be noted that sedatives or hypnotics may precipitate coma.

Survivors of hepatic coma occasionally manifest residual damage of a distinctive kind. This has been named acquired hepatocerebral degeneration, and a full description of it has been given by Victor, Adams and Cole (1965). It is a syndrome which is associated with gross liver disease and/or surgically created portal-systemic anastomoses, and it may become established even before episodes of hepatic coma have occurred. In areas where liver cirrhosis is common, this acquired type of hepatocerebral degeneration is likely to be much more common than the hereditary kind (Wilson's disease). A clinical differentiation from Wilson's disease is usually possible: Kayser–Fleischer corneal rings are not found, and there is no familial incidence. The neuropathological changes in the two conditions are however similar, and in neither is the mechanism of the production of the damage fully understood.

In these chronic cases the patient suffers from a generalized dementia of varying severity, with cerebellar symptoms and usually also choreo-athetosis. The cerebellar symptoms include dysarthria, ataxia and intention tremor: the choreo-athetosis may involve head, trunk, and limbs. There may also be mild pyramidal tract signs, coarse rhythmical tremor at rest resembling that of Parkinson's disease, and diffuse muscular rigidity. Diffuse hypertrophy and hyperplasia of the protoplasmic astrocytes is a dominant feature of the histopathology, with degeneration of nerve cells and medullated fibres in the cerebral cortex (particularly in the deeper layers), cerebellum and lenticular nuclei.

This syndrome is largely irreversible. The disease process can be fatal in a few months, but patients may live for ten years or more after the onset of the neurological symptoms.

Since the cirrhotic patient may give a history of alcoholism, this state of dementia with ataxia must be distinguished from a Korsakoff's psychosis. Here memory is not disproportionately impaired, and dysarthria and choreo-athetosis may be prominent features. The distinction must also be made from Huntington's chorea, another condition in which dementia is associated with choreo-athetosis. In cases of acquired hepatocerebral degeneration the absence of any family history of chorea, the presence of liver disease and the early development of cerebellar signs facilitates the differential diagnosis.

Several other neuropsychiatric syndromes (Read *et al.*, 1967) have been described in cases of chronic liver disease, including 'paranoid schizophrenia' and a hypomanic reaction. In these latter instances portacaval anastomosis and depression of hepatic function seem to have acted as precipitants of reactions which have no necessary connection with portal systemic encephalopathy.

PORPHYRIA

The porphyrias are not rare in this country, and constitute major health problems in Turkey and in South Africa. The commonest of these diseases is acute intermittent porphyria, where the seat of the abnormality of porphyrin metabolism is in the liver. It is inherited as a Mendelian dominant. In the acute attacks of illness and often also in remission excess amounts of porphobilinogen and delta-aminolaevulic acid are excreted in the urine. The urine may not be port-wine in colour. The most widely used test for urinary porphobilinogen (a porphyrin precursor) is the Watson–Schwartz test: Ehrlich's aldehyde reagent is added to an equal volume of urine, and if the test is positive, a reddish compound appears which is insoluble in chloroform. The results of this screening test should be confirmed by quantitative estimates of porphobilinogen and δ-aminolaevulic acid in the urine. If there are skin lesions, the faecal porphyrins must also be estimated.

The peak incidence of the disease is in the third decade, and women are more often affected than men. The affected individual comes under medical observation for abdominal, neurological or psychiatric symptoms, often acute and characteristically intermittent. Attacks of abdominal colic may mimic acute obstruction and the patient not uncommonly bears the scars of laparotomies. Various neuropathies may occur, with paraesthesiae and muscle weakness: most often pareses of the limbs of lower motor neurone type with loss of pin-prick sensation, and paralysis of the respiratory muscles, which may be fatal. Any of the cranial nerves may be affected. A minority of patients have epileptic fits.

The mental symptoms are not at all specific. There is emotional instability, irritability and apparent hypochondriasis. The patient's complaints of weakness or unsteadiness or inability to walk may be thought to be hysterical. Depression of spirits is common. There may be periods of confusion with disorientation.

A crisis may be precipitated in a susceptible individual by an acute infection, pregnancy or childbirth, by alcoholic excess or by drugs—notably the barbiturates, sulphonamides, oestrogens and griseofulvin. The barbiturates are particularly often the cause of serious deterioration in the patient's clinical condition and may bring on paralysis. Ackner and his colleagues (1962) found no evidence for a psychogenic factor in the aetiology of the disorder.

It is highly important to make the diagnosis in the patient's case as soon as possible: a history of recurrent attacks of emotional instability and colic should suggest it, and the urine should then be screened. Barbiturates must absolutely not be prescribed. The safest drug to use is chlorpromazine. Goldberg (1965) in his review of the disorders of porphyrin metabolism, stresses the importance of tachycardia as a sign of the disease and as a measure of its activity. Blood relatives should be tested, to detect latent porphyria if it is present and to advise them about how attacks may be precipitated and avoided.

VITAMIN DEFICIENCY

Vitamin deficiency is usually associated with malnutrition in other respects, and deficiencies in the intake or absorption both of vitamins and other dietary items are most often multiple. It is deficiency of the B group of vitamins which may lead to the development of mental symptoms. In cases of gastro-intestinal disease, following partial gastrectomy, in severely depressed patients, in confused old people and in alcoholics, deficiency of B group vitamins may be an important factor in the illness and the physical signs of vitamin deficiency should always be sought.

Vitamin B_1 (aneurine, thiamine) deficiency is probably usually a factor in the aetiology of delirium tremens, and it is the major causal factor in Wernicke's encephalopathy. Deficiency of an element of the vitamin B_2 complex, nicotinamide, causes the mental and physical symptoms of pellagra. Deficiency of vitamin B_{12} (cyanocobalamin) causes pernicious anaemia, subacute combined degeneration of the cord, and mental symptoms also. Deficiency of folic acid may be of some psychiatric importance. These syndromes will now be described. They are encountered not uncommonly in clinical practice in this country, while in many of the economically poorer countries they are of major importance.

WERNICKE'S ENCEPHALOPATHY

In 1881 Wernicke described a series of cases of acute superior haemorrhagic polio-encephalitis which were regarded as dependent on chronic alcoholism. Since then Neuburger and Campbell and Biggart have pointed out that the same condition may occur as a complication of other conditions in non-alcoholics. The pathological lesions consist of foci of vascular stasis and parenchymatous degeneration occurring symmetrically in the corpora mammilaria, and in other parts of the hypothalamus, the fornix, the juxtaventricular zone of the thalamus, the peri-aqueductal grey matter of the midbrain, the posterior colliculi and the floor of the fourth ventricle. Lesions may also be found in the corpus striatum, the substantia nigra, the anterior colliculi, the optic nerves and, rarely, in the cerebral cortex.

Campbell and Ritchie Russell (1941), in an analysis of 21 cases, pointed out that Wernicke's encephalopathy was not an uncommon condition, that it occurred as a complication of a wide range of other diseases, and that it could be diagnosed clinically. Eight of the cases were associated with alcoholism, but following Neuburger's suggestion regarding its occurrence in cases of gastric carcinoma and chronic gastritis, Campbell and Russell carefully investigated a series of cases of fatal gastro-intestinal disease associated particularly with a history of disturbance of memory or consciousness before death. In addition to alcoholism their case material comprised cases of gastric carcinoma, pyloric stenosis, chronic dyspepsia, macrocytic anaemia, chronic septic peritonitis, hyperemesis gravidarum, pernicious anaemia, pregnancy with vomiting, bronchiectasis, chronic pyosalpinx, meningovascular syphilis and a child of $3\frac{1}{2}$ years dying from (?) whooping cough.

The clinical symptoms were described as falling into two groups: 1. disturbances of consciousness and of higher cerebral functions; 2. focal neurological signs and symptoms. The first group of symptoms was a constant feature. The picture was of drowsiness, delirium and Korsakoff features, e.g. disorientation, amnesia, hallucinations and confabulation. Epileptiform convulsions are an occasional accompaniment.

Oculomotor disturbances were present in 10 cases and constituted the most frequent and most important group of focal neurological signs and symptoms. Unequal and irregular pupils, the Argyll Robertson phenomenon, paralysis of conjugate eye movement, diplopia, strabismus and nystagmus were all noted. There may be respiratory paralysis of central origin and pyramidal tract involvement, while polyneuritis was present in 9 cases.

Campbell and Russell, and others, stress the important aetiological factor as a deficient intake of some part or parts of the vitamin B complex; most probably of thiamine. Previously usually fatal, recovery may take place in these cases if large doses of vitamin B complex are given parenterally. At least 50 mg. of thiamine hydrochloride, B.P., must be given parenterally, daily.

PELLAGRA

Pellagra was described in the eighteenth century as occurring in Spain and in Italy, and in the nineteenth century cases were recognized in France, Rumania, Egypt, the United States and in the British Isles. In 1866 Howden of Montrose described the first case in the British Isles, but no further mention was made in the British literature until in 1909 Brown and Cranston Low described a second case. Since that time numerous cases have been described by other observers in many countries. Since from 4 to 10 per cent. of all pellagrins show mental symptoms, its psychiatric importance is considerable in countries where poverty and malnutrition are common. It may also result from malabsorption secondary to some lesion of the alimentary tract; and it occurs, though uncommonly, in cases of mental illness, where the diet has been defective. We have seen it complicating cases of senile dementia, alcoholism, involutional melancholia and schizophrenia.

Aetiology. At one time it was thought that this disease was caused by the excessive use of corn, or by corn that was diseased. But it affects persons who have never eaten corn or corn products, and, moreover, pellagra is occasionally absent from districts where corn preponderates in the diet. In 1915 the experimental work carried out by Goldberger, Waring and others of the U.S. Public Health Service proved that pellagra is due neither to diseased maize nor to an infective agent, but to a defective diet. Goldberger's conclusion that the disease was dependent on some fault in the diet has been amply confirmed by later work, which has demonstrated that pellagra can be promptly cured by administration of the appropriate vitamin, nicotinic acid, the pellagra-preventing (P.-P.) factor of the vitamin B complex.

Symptomatology. Pellagra is characterized by a combination of cutaneous, digestive, nervous and mental symptoms, which may show remissions and recurrences over a long period of years. Occasionally the disease may run an acute course and proceed quickly to a fatal termination.

The skin lesions consist of an erythema, followed by a dermatitis, and discoloration of the skin, resembling a severe sunburn. This condition involves the backs of the hands, extending as a band round the wrists, and in some cases involving the palms of the hands. The face, the neck, the elbows, the knees, the scrotum or vulva may show a similar condition.

The mucous membranes of the mouth and tongue become inflamed, so that the mouth is painful, and the tongue has a glossy, red, raw appearance. Associated with this condition there may be gastric symptoms, and a history of alternating diarrhoea and constipation.

The nervous symptoms are of a general nature, and consist mainly of paraesthesiae occurring throughout the body, tremor, increased or diminished reflexes, and occasionally convulsions.

The mental symptoms associated with pellagra are usually either in the nature of a depressive state, a dementia, or a delirium. The last is the most frequent. The depression is probably based on the fact that the patient realizes he is suffering from a severe physical illness, while the delirium shows no peculiar features.

Morbid Anatomy. The principal histopathological finding in cases of pellagra is an axonal reaction affecting especially the Betz cells of the motor cortex. This type of axonal reaction was described by Adolf Meyer and termed by him 'central neuritis'. The probability is that his cases of central neuritis were really cases of pellagra. The axonal reaction consists of a swelling of the cell body as a whole, while the centre of the cell exhibits a pale, more or less homogeneous appearance of the protoplasm, with a loss of stainable substance, which might or might not be well preserved at the periphery of the cell, and displacement of the nucleus towards the border of the cell body.

Treatment. We have already stated that pellagra is due to faulty nutrition, and the best way to prevent its occurrence is to take an abundance of fresh milk, eggs, fresh lean meat, peas and beans. For treatment, a suitable dose of nicotinic acid is 500 mg. per day orally or 40 mg. intramuscularly thrice daily: it should be accompanied by a well-balanced diet, supplemented with dried yeast, since other vitamin deficiencies are commonly associated with deficiency of nicotinic acid. In more severe cases massive doses of nicotinic acid are required: Sydenstricker advised 100 mg. hourly for 10 hours during the first two days. Most patients begin to improve within 48 hours after beginning the treatment.

VITAMIN B_{12} AND FOLATE DEFICIENCY

Pernicious (Addisonian) anaemia is in psychiatric practice the commonest cause of vitamin B_{12} deficiency: but there is an increasing number of cases which are the sequelae of gastro-intestinal surgery, and in some instances B_{12} deficiency is due to the inadequacy of the diet taken by an individual who is already mentally ill. In all of these states low serum vitamin B_{12} levels are found.

It has long been recognized that those with pernicious anaemia may develop mental symptoms. Depressive reactions, confusion and dementia all occur: the latter rarely, determined by cerebral lesions similar to the spinal lesions found in cases of subacute combined degeneration of the cord. Shulman (1967) pointed out that the association between pernicious anaemia and any of the so-called functional psychoses (in particular, manic-depressive reactions) has not been clearly established. That organic mental symptoms, either of confusion or dementia, can be produced by this deficiency state is however both understandable and well documented. There is nothing specific about these mental symptoms and cases of psychiatric disorder due to vitamin B_{12} deficiency can thus easily go undiagnosed. The mental symptoms usually respond to treatment with adequate doses of vitamin B_{12} (cyanocobalamin).

It is of particular importance to recognize that mental abnormality due to avitaminosis B_{12} may occur in the absence of anaemia, megaloblastic erythropoiesis or clinical evidence of subacute combined degeneration of the cord. Further difficulty arises from the fact that the condition may rarely occur in a young adult, that the pre-anaemic phase may extend over months or even years, that the mental symptoms may apparently remit and that E.E.G. changes are inconstant.

In an unselected population of 1012 psychiatric patients, Henderson and his colleagues (1966) found avitaminosis B_{12} in 0·88 per cent. There are, therefore, good reasons for instituting screening tests for vitamin B_{12} deficiency. In the pre-anaemic phase, the diagnosis can usually if not always be made by careful examination of peripheral blood films for evidence of morphological changes in the red blood cells: Shulman therefore recommends the haematological screening of patients suffering from confusional states and senile and pre-senile dementias of unknown origin. Henderson *et al.* (1967) report that the occult Addisonian state can be reliably detected by the antigastric parietal-cell antibody (A.G.A.)

test, though this test is inadequate for other causes of vitamin B_{12} deficiency: and they advocate the following procedure as the safest and least expensive screening for this avitaminosis: 1. a serum A.G.A. test in all patients; and 2. vitamin B_{12} assay in all patients over 60 years of age, or with any history suggesting the possibility of non-Addisonian vitamin B_{12} deficiency (*e.g.* dietary inadequacy, partial gastrectomy or other abdominal operation, or gastro-intestinal symptoms).

There are close metabolic relationships between vitamin B_{12} and folic acid: and there is some evidence that folate deficiency may cause mental symptoms similar to those which result from B_{12} deficiency. This condition should be looked for particularly amongst the epileptic patients in mental and mental deficiency hospitals, who may be especially at risk from prolonged drug-induced folate deficiency. Investigating 45 treated epileptics Reynolds and his colleagues (1966) found a megaloblastic haemopoiesis in 38 per cent. Examination of the bone marrow was essential: the patients were not anaemic and only a small minority showed a macrocytosis in the peripheral blood. Serum folate concentrations were subnormal in the majority, and the condition responded to treatment with folic acid. Apparently each of the major anticonvulsant drugs—phenobarbitone, phenytoin and primidone, may cause this deficiency: and the risk of it may be greater for those receiving combinations of these drugs.

POISONING

LEAD POISONING

Poisoning with lead occurs uncommonly in children and adults. The former may gnaw and swallow lead paint from toys or furniture, or eat old plasterwork: the latter may be exposed to lead in dusts and fumes, and in Britain about 50 cases of lead poisoning as an industrial disease are notified yearly.

It is most important to make an early diagnosis: irreversible cerebral damage or death may ensue, if the child is not treated. Pica in young children should alert the doctor to the possibility of lead poisoning. In Britain, the children of immigrants living in physically deteriorating Victorian property, may be particularly at risk. The development of otherwise unexplained abdominal pain, vomiting, anaemia or encephalopathy should prompt immediate further investigations, including the estimation of the blood-lead level (Moncrieff *et al.*, 1964). The administration of calcium edetate may be lifesaving.

The symptoms and signs of this poisoning in adults have been described by Dagg and his colleagues (1965). Both gastro-intestinal and nervous symptoms are prominent. Abdominal pain with nausea and anorexia usually occurs, often there is constipation and vomiting, sometimes diarrhoea. There may be abdominal tenderness, guarding or rigidity. The neurological signs are bilateral paralyses or pareses of limb muscles of lower motor neurone type. Pains, numbness and tingling in the legs and hands, and aching elsewhere, are frequent, fatigue is commonly complained of and asthenia may be profound. The patient may be depressed in his spirits, and if the organic nature of his symptoms is not recognized may be described as 'hysterical'. (Peripheral nerve involvement is very uncommon in children.) The poisoning is rarely severe enough to cause lead encephalopathy, with fits, delirium, coma and irreversible cerebral damage or death.

Dagg and his colleagues point to the striking clinical similarity between the symptoms and signs of lead poisoning and those of acute intermittent porphyria. Abdominal pain, constipation and vomiting is the commonest symptom complex of both conditions. Abdominal emergencies may be mimicked by both. The mental symptoms are similar, though they tend apparently to be more prominent in porphyria. The principal distinguishing features clinically are the occurrence of anaemia and the blue line on the gum-tooth margin (rarely seen in children) in cases of lead poisoning. In both conditions there is an abnormality in the metabolism of porphyrin or its precursors, and similar pathological changes occur in the peripheral nerves and central nervous system.

CARBON MONOXIDE POISONING

Carbon monoxide poisoning is of psychiatric importance, not only because inhalation of coal-gas and of car-exhaust gases are common modes of attempted suicide, but more particularly because the mental after-effects of this poisoning may be so severe that the patient comes under psychiatric care.

In the blood, carbon monoxide combines readily with haemoglobin to form carboxyhaemoglobin, the blood's capacity to take up oxygen is thus reduced and anoxaemia results. Symptoms do not usually develop until the blood is more than 10 per cent. saturated. Headache, weakness, nausea and vomiting precede the collapse which may be fatal. In the cases of more severe poisoning which are not fatal, the patient is usually first seen in a state of delirium or coma, with a cherry-red complexion and often pulmonary oedema. This acute confusional state may clear in a few days and the patient go on to make a satisfactory recovery, or dementia may ensue if there has been severe brain damage.

There is a third possible development, as Kraepelin first pointed out, which is typical of carbon monoxide poisoning. The patient may make an apparently good initial recovery: though this recovery, if a careful mental examination has been made, will usually be seen not to have been complete, some persisting defect at least in mental grasp and concentration usually being found. The patient may be discharged home from hospital. One to three weeks later relapse occurs, and this may be acute, severe and even fatal. The patient may then pass into a state of akinetic mutism, of dementia with parietal lobe symptoms, or (and this is usually a somewhat later development) may develop Parkinsonism. Garland and Pearce (1967) have given a detailed description of the clinical features of 4 severe cases, and draw attention again to the diffuse cortical damage and parietal-lobe disturbances which may occur. Two of their patients, discharged apparently recovered after the first 5 days, relapsed acutely within 48 hours. The prognosis of these later-developing mental and physical sequelae is very variable and on the whole bad: dementia and Parkinsonism may persist, the akinetic mute state may be transient.

Pathologically, the main damage is seen in the cerebral cortex and in the basal ganglia. The two main factors producing the cerebral lesions are believed to be anoxaemia and vascular damage. Most typical is a bilateral and symmetrical necrosis of the globus pallidus (Meyer, 1960). More rarely lesions elsewhere in the extrapyramidal system have been reported—in the putamen and substantia nigra. The cortical softening may be widespread.

The emergency treatment of coal-gas poisoning is to take the patient into the open air and apply artificial respiration. Then oxygen and carbon dioxide should be administered by mask, and shock actively combated.

MENTAL SEQUELAE OF HEAD INJURY

Mental symptoms may be precipitated by injury to any other part of the body as well as to the head, and in that event we are concerned with the psychological effects of the traumatic experience in precipitating either a neurosis or a psychosis according to the nature of the pre-existing personality or to the special circumstances. The symptoms are not different from those of neurotic and psychotic forms of reaction in general.

Head injury may precipitate or cause mental symptoms in one or both of two ways: either it acts as a non-specific psychological stress-like injury elsewhere in the body (though associated perhaps with greater fear of the consequences) and precipitates a 'functional' reaction, a neurosis or a psychosis; or it causes organic mental symptoms as a result of damage to the brain. To put it in other words: an abnormal mental state following a head injury may be due to the physical effects of the injury of the brain, or to the psychological effects of the experience on the personality, or to a combination of the two.

It is only the organic sequelae of head injury that are in any way specific, and with which we are mainly concerned here. A convenient subdivision of the mental after-effects is as follows:

1. Post-concussional and post-contusional syndromes; including deliria and transient dysmnesic states.
2. Post-traumatic dementia; including personality changes and Korsakoff's psychosis.
3. Other neurological sequelae; including epilepsy, aphasia and subdural haematoma.

After a minor head injury with concussion, the mental symptoms are transient, disappearing usually in a few days. In addition to complaining of headache, the patient may be dazed, irritable, restless and for some time confused. The effects of cerebral contusion, which implies a more significant degree of organic damage to the brain, are more severe and tend to be much more persistent. The patient may proceed through the phases of stupor, delirium and confusion as he slowly emerges from coma following a major trauma. He may then recover completely, or show residual disabilities of lesser or greater severity.

Post-contusional Syndrome. After cerebral contusion, the patient is apt on recovering full consciousness to complain for some time of a group of symptoms which has been called the post-contusional syndrome. These symptoms include headache, which is usually throbbing and aggravated by stooping and physical or mental stress; dizziness or giddiness; increased fatigability; impaired concentration; slowing of thinking processes, and forgetfulness; irritability and oversensitivity to noise; and a decreased tolerance of alcohol. Headache is not always present. The patient realizes that he is ill and is often anxious and depressed. Typically he prefers to keep away from all forms of amusement as well as from work, since the one is nearly as great an effort as the other: this distinguishes him from the malingerer.

The post-contusional syndrome is often accompanied by anxiety, and this complication is responsible for difficulty in diagnosis and prognosis, as well as for some of the confusion in terminology which has existed. When the majority of the above symptoms are complained of, there is no difficulty in concluding that true cerebral damage has been sustained and persists; but when the patient complains only of lack of concentration and difficulty in memory, and of headache not influenced by posture or by some movement, as well as of dizziness of an ill-defined type, and when he is obviously anxious, the diagnosis is much more difficult. The apparent mildness of the original injury is not conclusive: there may be little or no evidence of loss of consciousness after cerebral injury.

The previous personality is of importance. Symptoms are more likely to be due to persistent brain damage if they occur in a person of previous stable personality. It is essential to find out if the patient has domestic or other such worries, which may be complicating the situation. Questions of compensation favour neurotic developments. It is interesting that neurotic syndromes appear to be rare after head injuries sustained in the hunting field.

Many have emphasized that head injury is particularly apt to be followed by anxiety, since the individual attaches special importance to his head and brain; moreover, in those who have to earn their living by intellectual work, damage to the head is mentally disturbing. Another source of anxiety may be the feeling of insecurity produced by repeated experiences of dizziness.

The pathological physical effects of brain injury are both focal and diffuse, immediate and delayed. The focal lesions consist at first of capillary haemorrhages and oedema; and later in the occurrence of secondary degeneration, demyelination and the formation of scar tissue. Diffuse effects of the same kind are also produced. The circulation of the cerebrospinal fluid is usually disturbed, the pressure being either raised or lowered.

The prognosis is determined by a number of factors. The time taken for convalescence to be completed varies more or less directly with the length of the post-traumatic amnesia (measured from time of injury to time when continuous awareness is re-established). Where the P.T.A. has been less than 2 hours the patients are usually back at work within 3 months. Where it has been less than 48 hours they are usually back inside 4 months, but if it has been over 48 hours the time taken to return to work varies from 3 to 6 months, and in some cases longer, depending largely on personality and circumstances.

The prognosis depends also importantly on the adequacy of the previous personality. It has been said that what is often spoken of as the prognosis of head injuries in the post-contusional group is more accurately the prognosis of willingness to return to work in spite of the persistence of such symptoms as headache. Ritchie Russell (1934) recorded that of 120 patients whose symptoms persisted longer than 2 months, 66 per cent. still had symptoms after 18 months, but in many cases work, even heavy manual labour, was not interfered with. Some patients are driven back to work too soon by economic and other pressures.

Anxiety about compensation hinders recovery. Ritchie Russell reported that after 18 months 35 per cent. of his compensation cases had not reported fit for work, while in the non-compensation group only 9 per cent. had failed to do so.

The prognosis is also influenced by age, those over 40 being less successful in getting back to work quickly.

Details of the treatment of head injuries will not be discussed here: they can be read in textbooks of neurosurgery. Rest in bed is imperative at the beginning, but how far it should be prolonged is a matter for judgement. If his headache has gone the patient may usually be allowed up, by gradual stages, soon afterwards. Explanation of the symptoms and encouragement in what is often a long convalescence, are needed. Occupational therapy and graduated physical exercise prepare the way for a return to other normal activities and to work.

Post-traumatic Dementia. Gross and permanent dementia following head injury is rare: and one should not conclude that damage is permanent until at least 18 months after injury. The slighter degrees of residual disability are more frequently seen but are still uncommon. The brain-damaged individual may develop a post-traumatic personality change, in that he becomes more labile emotionally and mentally slower and forgetful, shows a diminished sense of moral responsibility, neglects his personal hygiene and may have outbursts of episodic violence. Frontal lobe damage is particularly apt to be associated with this sort of deterioration in the personality which is revealed in loss of the finer feelings, in childishness and in emotional decay. A less common sequel is a persistent dysmnesic syndrome or Korsakoff's psychosis, with euphoria, gross memory retention defect, disorientation and confabulation, which may last for weeks or months following the injury or become permanent. This, and other severe types of damage, may so incapacitate the patient that long-term mental hospital care becomes necessary.

Other Neurological Sequelae. Fits occur in the first week in 5 per cent. of patients with blunt head injuries and herald late epilepsy, which has the same incidence (Jennett, 1961). Nearly one-third of patients who suffer intracranial haematomas develop fits, and the incidence rises if the post-traumatic amnesia is long or the dura is penetrated. There may be an interval of years before fits commence, due to scar formation.

Lesions involving cortical areas associated with speech interfere more or less with the mental abilities also, since the individual is so dependent on speech and allied functions, both receptive and expressive, for his contact with the environment, and on verbal symbols for his thinking. Aphasic syndromes resulting from such lesions may on superficial examination be mistaken for a diffuse dementia.

The signs and symptoms of subdural haematoma may not develop until some weeks or months have passed, and the head injury itself may have appeared so slight as to have caused little concern at the time: the latter perhaps most often happens in the cases of old people and alcoholics. Intense headache, with the development of a state of fluctuating consciousness, is typical. Neurological signs are often slight, inconstant and misleading in localizing the site of the haematoma. If the haematoma is bilateral, a fairly rapidly progressive dementia results. It is of great importance to make the correct diagnosis and to make it as soon as possible. The response to surgical drainage through burr-holes is usually excellent.

BRAIN TUMOUR

Tumours of the brain are amongst the commonest of tumours and in the majority of cases are primary, originating in the brain itself or in its coverings. In less than a quarter of the cases the tumour is a secondary deposit, and then often multiple: of these the primary focus is most often in the lung. It is important to note that the primary lung cancer may be more or less clinically silent, while the secondary deposits are giving rise to symptoms of confusion or dementia. Brain (1958) reported that bronchial carcinoma itself may give rise to fluctuating clouding of consciousness and dementia, apparently without metastasizing to the brain. The chest should therefore be X-rayed in all cases of suspected brain tumour.

Mental symptoms are usually stated to be present in upwards of 60 to 85 per cent. of all cases of brain tumour, and in 100 per cent. of patients with tumours of the corpus callosum. Mental symptoms may be the earliest and presenting symptoms, and it is unfortunate that usually they are of a general and indeterminate character, not specific to tumour and without localizing value, being those associated with any condition producing an increase of intracranial pressure. The very earliest symptoms are often very slight—undue fatigability, difficulty in concentration, indefinite malaise and anxiety: they may easily be thought neurotic or depressive. If an epileptic fit occurs in such a setting, or indeed for the first time in adult life, whether or not there are accompanying symptoms, brain tumour should always be considered in the differential diagnosis.

The less equivocal symptoms and signs which are developed as the tumour grows fall into two groups: those due to the widespread effects of increasing intracranial pressure, and those due to the local effects of the tumour itself. Raised intracranial pressure causes typically headache, throbbing or bursting, at its worst often on wakening and increased by stooping or coughing; vomiting, with or without nausea; and papilloedema. In old age, when the shrunken brain leaves more space within the skull, this triad of symptoms of increased cerebrospinal fluid pressure may be unusually late in developing. The mental symptoms are those of confusion or dementia. The patient becomes dulled, irritable and forgetful, later apathetic and somnolent: disorientation and incontinence usually precede the terminal lapse into coma.

The nature of the local symptoms depends of course on the location and mode of spread of the tumour. Metastatic tumours, which are commonly multiple and rapidly growing, tend to cause mental confusion.

If the tumour is in a frontal lobe, or involving by pressure one of the frontal lobes, the presenting clinical feature may be a personality change, a frontal lobe deficit syndrome. The patient may become mildly euphoric, with a tendency to pun or joke (the so-called 'witzelsucht'), facile, tactless, degenerate and unconcerned. His behaviour deteriorates as his dementia progresses and he remains without insight. A grasp reflex may be pathognomonic. The mental symptoms do not help to locate the side of the lesion.

Mental symptoms may also be the earliest symptoms of a temporal or temperoparietal lobe tumour. The clinical picture depends on whether or not the lesion is in the dominant hemisphere. If the lesion is anterior, in the non-dominant hemisphere, the symptoms may be similar to those described above as typical of frontal lobe lesions and may precede the development of neurological signs. A left-sided lesion in a right-handed individual is likely to cause aphasia. The most frequent other neurological signs are a homonymous visual field defect and slight hemiplegia (initially most often a lower facial weakness): hemianaesthesia is less common. The patient with a temporal lobe tumour is often notably moody, intermittently depressed and irritable. Psychomotor seizures are also characteristic signs of tumours in this area. They may last for minutes or much longer, even for days: the patient is clouded mentally, and experiences hallucinations of taste or smell and feelings of unreality or *déjà vu*. In this clouded state he may act bemusedly or violently, or go off in a fugue.

Tumours of the occipital lobe are much rarer. Visual field defects are characteristic, and if the patient has fits the seizures may be prefaced by a visual hallucinatory aura.

Corpus callosum tumours are also very uncommon. Mental disorganization is a prominent feature and memory disturbance may be particularly severe. There is usually also early damage to the pyramidal tracts.

For a full description of the symptoms and signs of tumours in the various cerebral areas, the reader is referred to a textbook of neurology, such as Lord Brain's (1962).

INFECTIVE DISEASES OF THE CENTRAL NERVOUS SYSTEM

SYPHILIS

Following a sharp decline after the Second World War the incidence of venereal diseases is rising in Britain, as in many other countries throughout the world. Infectious syphilis is becoming more frequent, especially in men in the major seaports and among male homosexuals. Venereal diseases have also increased in teenage groups, with increasing promiscuity. As a result it is possible that cases of late syphilis, after a steady decline in the past decade, will begin again to increase in number.

Congenital Syphilis

A certain number of cases of subnormality or psychosis in the offspring are the result of syphilis transmitted by the parent. Those in whom the mental disease is certainly syphilitic are the uncommon cases of juvenile general paralysis (found in about 1 per cent. of cases of congenital syphilis) ; and cases complicated by cerebral lesions from other gross syphilitic brain disease (gumma, meningitis, endarteritis). But there is a residuum of cases of congenital subnormality where the syphilitic origin of the defect may be in doubt.

Though congenital syphilis does not necessarily affect the nervous system and many congenitally syphilitic children grow up to be mentally normal, a number of infected children sustain cerebral damage with a possible outcome in subnormality. It has been stated that about one-half of syphilitic infants show a positive Wassermann reaction in the cerebrospinal fluid. Nabarro (1944) reported that of 640 congenitally syphilitic children at least one-quarter gave evidence of clinical or latent neurosyphilis. The proportion of all cases of congenital subnormality which are due to syphilis is not accurately known. Tredgold (1947) was of the opinion that the proportion of syphilitic aments was probably about 3 per cent.: Berg and Kirman (1959) reported an incidence of 0·6 per cent. at the Fountain Hospital, London; and the incidence is probably continuing to fall. Reports on the proportion affected tend to vary with the age of the population studied, since with or without treatment the child's Wassermann tends to become negative as he gets older, and this reaction may be the only clue to the infection.

It is important to stress that congenitally infected subnormal children may show congenital syphilitic stigmata while the Wassermann is negative, and may not show other signs of congenital syphilis while it is positive. The subnormality may be accompanied by other signs of neurological damage (*e.g.* paralyses, blindness, deaf-mutism) and if these signs are gross the degree of subnormality is usually also severe.

PSYCHOSES DUE TO SYPHILIS

In adults syphilitic diseases of the nervous system consist of two main types, mesoblastic or interstitial, and parenchymatous. Clinically, pathologically and serologically, it is often impossible to draw a hard and fast line between them.

General paralysis of the insane or dementia paralytica and cerebral syphilis are examples of the organic reaction-types, the former corresponding to the chronic type of organic reaction and the latter to the acute type. In addition we will describe, briefly, a subtype—locomotor ataxia or tabes with psychosis.

The knowledge that syphilis has been contracted constitutes also for sensitive individuals an intense psychological trauma. There are few illnesses which carry a greater social stigma and are attended with more fears. In these circumstances a state of morbid depression or other form of mental breakdown may be precipitated.

2 B

General Paralysis of the Insane (G.P.I.)

The successful treatment of organic affections of the central nervous system due to syphilitic infection has constituted one of the triumphs of twentieth-century medicine. It has been a hard won struggle, a long process which has necessitated the correlation of observations derived from a variety of sources. Psychiatrists, neuropathologists, neurologists, ophthalmologists, serologists, and other research workers have all played a significant rôle; each has contributed from his specialized knowledge. It was not until 1913 that we could talk with confidence regarding the aetiology of this condition. It was then that the brilliant Japanese research worker Noguchi, working in association with Moore in the Rockefeller Institute, New York, announced that he had been able, in fourteen out of seventy cases of dementia paralytica, to demonstrate the presence of *Treponema pallidum* in the brain cortex. Their results were soon confirmed by other investigators, and now, with improved staining methods, organisms can be demonstrated in almost all cases. The categorical statement 'no syphilitic infection no paralysis', had become true. Syphilitic infection, however, does not necessarily lead to an affection of the central nervous system; only 1–2 per cent. are so involved. Why some people's nervous systems are more susceptible than those of others is still unknown. Is a special neurotropic strain of organism to blame, or are some nervous systems much more vulnerable than others? Evidence *pro et contra* is available.

Whatever the real explanation may be, it is necessary to discuss how a disease formerly so prevalent has become so much less of a scourge. Let us start with a definition: general paralysis is a diffuse organic parenchymatous disease of the brain cortex, resulting in mental, physical and serological changes which can be arrested, and in many cases successfully treated. This is a very different state of affairs from that which existed earlier. Up until 1917 the wards of every mental hospital were crowded with cases of syphilitic disease of the nervous system in various stages of mental and physical deterioration. The remedies we had were unable to stem the progress of a killing disease which achieved its purpose in five years or less. Death came as a happy release from a life of intense misery.

The situation was rendered even more poignant by the fact that such cases accounted for 5 to 15 per cent. of the admission rate to mental hospitals. The majority of those involved were in the prime of life, and there was the added danger that if the syphilitic infection was transmitted to their offspring, juvenile general paralysis might result. As a precautionary measure the blood serum and cerebrospinal fluid of all children of parents suffering from general paralysis of the insane should be examined.

It was in 1798 that John Haslam, the apothecary at Bethlem Hospital, published the clinical report of a case characterized by a state of mental euphoria or well-being which was completely out of keeping with the paralytic symptoms and bodily enfeeblement from which the patient suffered. In the early years of the nineteenth century a number of French investigators—Esquirol, Georget, Bayle, Calmeil—made relevant observations which helped us to come to a clearer idea of the definition and progress of this disorder. In 1805 Esquirol noted 'that paralysis was a common complication in cases of mental disorder and added considerably to the gravity of the prognosis'. Georget agreed with Esquirol's observations and suggested that it might more suitably be described as 'chronic muscular paralysis'. In 1822 Antoine Bayle, in his thesis for the Doctorate of Medicine of the Faculty of Paris, established a correlation between the clinical and neuropathological findings from which he concluded that general and incomplete paralysis accompanied by mental disorder was due to a chronic meningitis. It was that correlation which led to a series of further discoveries. In 1826 Calmeil confirmed Bayle's findings but demonstrated that it was not merely the meninges but the brain substance itself which was seriously affected by a chronic encephalitis.

These discoveries acted as a spur. While the clinical symptoms were becoming more clearly delineated, Charcot, Babinski, and many other neurologists were accumulating information of changes affecting the reflex arc. The Edinburgh ophthalmologist, Argyll Robertson, found that in a high percentage of cases of organic brain disease the pupils did not react to light but reacted on accommodation—a phenomenon known as the Argyll Robertson pupil. The neuropathological investigations of Nissl and Alzheimer, and the serological examinations culminating in the Wassermann reaction constituted a series of brilliant advances which led to the final elucidation of this disorder—the demonstration of *Treponema pallidum* in the brain cortex.

Time of Onset. This is often difficult to determine owing to the fact that the patient may never know of his syphilitic infection, and there may have been no residual signs of primary or secondary syphilitic lesions. From the available evidence it is reckoned that a period of five to twenty years elapses after infection before the symptoms of general paralysis show themselves. Some cases are of shorter duration than others but the usual period is from ten to fifteen years.

Symptomatology. The disease is usually insidious in its development and is characterized by episodes of strange behaviour which are at variance with the previous good character of the individual. A man who had attained a position of great trust and had been of irreproachable character disgraced himself by trying to steal golf balls from a club-house in which he was a guest. Another who had been an indulgent husband and father became irritable and cantankerous, drank to excess, was unfaithful to his wife, and ill-used his children.

Changes in character and mood may be the first signs of the disease. Even at the earliest period of the illness there may be a pronounced dulling of comprehension so that questions may require to be repeated, and even then the patient may quickly forget what he has been told or asked to do. Aesthetic feelings become dulled or lost, and the alterations in the patient's personality may be such that his relations and friends are puzzled and regard him as a changed man. This rapid deterioration of the personality in general paralysis is in striking contrast to its preservation in most other forms of organic brain disease.

A few patients, however, are aware of a change in themselves. They may appreciate that they are not so competent as formerly, that they cannot apply themselves to their work, are lacking in attention and concentration, are easily fatigued mentally and bodily, and are prone to make mistakes in dealing with the simplest tasks.

In another group the condition may be ushered in by physical symptoms, *e.g.* a transitory loss of speech, a hemiparesis, or a convulsive attack with unconsciousness.

During the progress of the disease one of the most significant features is the progressive loss of memory both for recent and more remote events. The main facts of the patient's life may be given correctly and relevantly but it is more usual for the patient to be unable to correlate important sequences in his life so that gaps can be demonstrated covering a number of years. The memory defect may be so great that knowledge acquired in school, including the ability to do simple calculations, becomes faulty, particularly when these calculations involve sustained concentration, as for instance in subtracting serial sevens from one hundred. There is disorientation particularly for time. An outstanding feature is the patient's usually complete lack of insight into his own deficiencies. He may resent attempts to correct him, or suggest a trivial explanation, or excuse. It is not long before he lapses into a state of facile, contented dementia.

In this setting of a progressive dementia grandiose delusions of a bizarre type may be conspicuous, but are not now nearly so common as used to be described. Depression is much more often present than euphoria or elation, and the patient may be thought initially to be suffering from an uncomplicated depressive psychosis. The delusional ideas in these depressive cases may be as fantastic and grotesque as those of the grandiose variety. But more often than either depression or elation the affective change is one of emotional blunting and facility.

A profound mental degeneration gradually occurs so that in the course of time the patient comes to lead a vegetative existence requiring to be cared for and nursed in every way.

This, of course, is a picture of the tragic mental and physical state which may develop if, for one reason or another, treatment is omitted or ineffective.

Physical Signs. It has been stated above that the first evidence of this disease may be the occurrence of a convulsive seizure. It is more usual, however, for the seizures to occur during the course of the illness. In some cases convulsive states may never develop at all, but when they do they are either epileptiform or apoplectiform in type. Following a fit, even after consciousness is regained muscular twitchings may continue for many hours or even days. In contrast the apoplectiform attacks are followed by focal symptoms such as hemiplegia, monoplegia, hemianopia and dysarthria which may persist for a few days or even longer. It is not necessary that a vascular lesion should be responsible for the above conditions as they may result from a more severe involvement of certain specialized areas of the brain tissue.

The facies is distinctive; the features become smoothed out so that the patient looks considerably younger than his years, and has a vacant or even mask-like expression. The cranial nerves are seldom involved, but pupillary changes should always be carefully noted. These consist of inequality of the pupils, irregularity of outline, and most striking of all, sluggishness or total absence of the light reflexes. The Argyll Robertson phenomenon, characterized by the absence of the light response and the preservation of the accommodation response, is present in from 50 to 60 per cent. of cases. In some cases the light response can be described merely as sluggish, and the amount of excursion as smaller than normal. When the accommodation response is absent as well as the light response (internal total ophthalmoplegia) then the disease process is usually associated with locomotor ataxia. Primary optic atrophy occasionally occurs but more especially in cases associated with locomotor ataxia.

The speech is characteristic. In the early stages the patient slurs his words, but as the disease progresses, the difficulties of pronunciation become so intense that words are distorted beyond recognition. An easy and rapid way of demonstrating speech difficulties is to ask the patient to repeat, consecutively, three times, certain test words such as 'hippopotamus', 'particular popularity', 'Methodist Episcopal', 'British Constitution'. Great effort is often required to articulate at all so that, finally, it may become impossible to understand what the patient is trying to say; the effort to enunciate is accompanied by gross facial tremors.

The writing is tremulous, syllables are missed out or transposed and the words become distorted. Generalized tremors affect the hands, tongue and facial muscles; the tremor of the tongue has been described as of the trombone type.

We recognize two main types of physical involvement—the cerebral and the tabetic. In the cerebral type the tendon reflexes are equally exaggerated on the two sides, but if focal symptoms are present the exaggeration is greater on the affected side. In the tabetic type the tendon reflexes are absent or diminished. It is only in cases with focal lesions that ankle clonus and an extensor plantar response can be elicited.

Loss of control of the organic reflexes may occur during the course of the disease so that particular attention should be paid to the possibility of retention of urine, or overflow from a full bladder, and incontinence of bladder or bowel. It is only by careful nursing and cleanliness that bed-sores and contractures can be prevented, especially after the patient has become bedridden.

Juvenile General Paralysis of the Insane. This condition, the result of congenital syphilis, was described in 1877 by Clouston. It usually becomes manifest at the end of the first decade but flagrant symptoms may not appear until adult life. The number who can be reasonably successful at school and even set up a good work record are more numerous than might be suspected. The disease does not differ essentially from the adult form.

Serology. Routine serological tests for syphilis should continue to be made in psychiatric units. In addition to the Wassermann reaction, specific serological tests have been introduced to increase the accuracy of diagnosis, notably the Reiter protein complement fixation test and the fluorescent treponemal antibody test.

In cases of G.P.I. the blood Wassermann is almost always positive: and the Wassermann reaction in the C.S.F. is positive in 95–100 per cent. of cases. In the C.S.F. pressure is often increased, usually there is a moderate pleocytosis of mononuclear cells, the total protein content is increased (up to about three times the normal in some cases) with a marked increase of globulin; and the Lange colloidal gold curve is of the paretic type, for example, 5 5 5 5 5 4 2 1 0 0 or 3 4 5 5 4 3 2 1 0 0.

The symptoms, signs and serological reactions of G.P.I. should be familiar to all clinicians. G.P.I., though much less frequent than formerly, has not died out: and the diagnosis is still too often made belatedly. The following is an illustrative case:

CASE No. 33

A married woman, 40 years old, four months previous to admission to hospital showed a character change as evidenced by her conduct and conversation. In hospital she was confused, forgetful, facile and expressed grandiose delusions. Treatment with penicillin resulted in a good recovery.

She was an average pupil at school. At the age of 15 years she had an illegitimate child before marrying another man when she was aged 17. Later she married again. Her work record as a waitress had been satisfactory. She denied any history of venereal infection.

Her relatives had noticed a marked change in her disposition and behaviour during the four months previous to her admission to hospital. She 'made silly remarks and did silly things', and told lies. Her gait was unsteady, her appetite voracious. At her brother's shop she had made a nuisance of herself, and on several occasions she had gone, unexpectedly, for long, solitary, motiveless walks; on one occasion the police brought her back from a railway line. In the month before admission she had twice been arrested for soliciting. Two days before admission to a mental hospital she had complained of acute abdominal pain, but examination in a general hospital proved negative. The pain subsided and she explained this by saying that she had had an appendectomy on the previous evening. She was mentally confused, gave a wrong home address, and stated that she had been working until the day before admission, when in fact she had not done outside work for several years.

In hospital she was in a foolish, happy, facile state. She was indifferent to her surroundings and answered questions at random. She announced that she was pregnant and expected a baby in two months; shortly afterwards she said she had had a menstrual period one month ago. Asked to name the capital cities of Europe she said that when in Rome she had gone, dressed in ermine and diamante, to dinner with Mussolini's son, and added, 'The Mussolinis did very well during the war'. Her memory was faulty, she lacked concentration and was disorientated.

Physically the pupils were unequal, the right was small, irregular and did not react to light. Her tongue was coarsely tremulous. The Wassermann reaction was positive both in blood and cerebrospinal fluid. The Lange curve was of the paretic type 5 5 5 5 5 3 2 2 1 0; there was no pleocytosis.

The patient was treated with procaine penicillin, 24 million Units.

At the time of her discharge she was mentally well, and no organic mental defect could be demonstrated. Her serological abnormalities persisted and arrangements were made so that her condition could be repeatedly reviewed.

Neuropathology. The brain membranes are thickened, and areas of pachymeningitis may be present. The pia-arachnoid is affected as well as the dura; the frontal tips are adherent, and the temporal tips may be tacked down to the under surface of the brain. When the pia-arachnoid is stripped it causes decortication of the brain substance. The Pacchionian granulations are increased. The brain looks smaller than usual, and its weight is diminished. The convolutions, particularly in the frontal and parietal areas, are atrophied, and in consequence there is widening of the sulci. A frosted-glass appearance due to granulations is visible on the ependyma of the lateral ventricles and fourth ventricle.

The histopathological changes affect the blood vessels of the cerebral cortex, as well as the nerve elements. In the former there is a proliferation of the endothelial cells with a tendency to the formation of new vessels through sprouting and vascularization of the proliferated intima. There is also a thickening both of the elastica and adventitia; the lymph spaces are widened and are infiltrated by plasma cells, lymphocytes and mast cells. In cases which have been of long duration regressive changes are present in the vessel walls.

In the brain cortex long or short rod-shaped cells are present; these are histiocytes with enlarged and elongated oval nuclei. The cell layering is disorganized, and the nerve cells show a great variety of degenerative forms; in some cases many of the nerve cells disappear altogether, while in others the Nissl granules are absent. The axis-cylinder processes are also degenerated. As a compensation phenomenon for the destruction and disappearance of nerve cells there is a marked proliferation of neuroglia. This may be so great that dense masses of glial fibres may be formed; the most marked increase is usually along the vessel sheaths. Another characteristic change is the large amount of free iron, which stains readily with Prussian blue, deposited in the cortex.

In addition areas of focal softening can be demonstrated, and *Treponema pallidum* are invariably present in the brain substance.

Diagnosis. The suggestion that a patient may be suffering from G.P.I. has so many serious implications that it is unwise to come to a final conclusion until the mental, physical and serological examinations have been completed, and found consistent with one another. When they are all positive the diagnosis can be made with certainty, and treatment started without delay.

Sometimes it may prove difficult to differentiate G.P.I. from other types of cerebrospinal syphilis but in the latter group we emphasize the acute inflammatory nature of the disorder, its onset within 5 years of primary infection, and the presence of headache, delirium, involvement of the cranial nerves, and the prominence of focal symptoms due usually to a syphilitic endarteritis.

In arteriosclerotic brain disease—non-syphilitic in origin—the onset is often ushered in by an apoplectiform seizure with ensuing emotional instability, but gross deterioration of the personality is not likely to occur until a late stage; the serological findings give negative results.

Cerebral Syphilis

This type of syphilis affects the interstitial and mesoblastic tissues and gives rise to acute organic mental symptoms. It occurs, usually, from 6 months to 6 years after primary infection.

Symptomatology. The mental symptoms are of an acute delirious nature characterized by hallucinations, sleeplessness, fear, disorientation and inability to concentrate. There may have been premonitory symptoms such as difficulty in thinking, a sense of uneasiness and emotional instability amounting to euphoria or depression. Once the condition becomes more fully established the memory may be found to be faulty especially for more recent events, but more diffusely as well. A confabulatory state of the Korsakoff type is not unusual.

In the more unusual cases of an endarteritis affecting the small vessels supplying the basal nuclei the clinical features may vary considerably, and may be difficult to recognize. In some instances they resemble a Parkinsonian state, and the patients suffer especially from a lack of sustained attention and concentration; there are none of the gross symptoms consistent with a meningitis, gumma, or large vascular lesion.

Subjective symptoms are often most distressing. There are complaints of severe headache, dizziness, a tendency to faint, a feeling of nausea, and sometimes vomiting unaccompanied by nausea. Such symptoms are indicative of increased intracranial pressure especially when accompanied by stupor and a slow pulse.

The physical signs are manifold, and particularly involve any of the cranial nerves. Eye symptoms of all kinds and degrees are among the earliest and most characteristic. A blurring and dimness of vision, diplopia, squint, ptosis may all be complained of. It is the coming and going of such symptoms, their transitoriness, which is so characteristic. The pupils are frequently irregular in outline, and unequal, but in contrast to cases of dementia paralytica the Argyll Robertson pupil is rarely present. Optic neuritis is common, and not infrequently precedes an optic atrophy; primary optic atrophy points to a more chronic process. The third cranial nerve is the one most frequently affected, but the fourth and sixth also suffer. Of the other cranial nerves the seventh and eighth are more commonly affected than the others.

Convulsive seizures occur especially in cases of endarteritis, but they are by no means infrequent in meningitic and gummatous cases as well. In the endarteritic group the residual focal symptoms may be of a permanent nature. When the small vessels of the basal nuclei are involved bilateral softenings may result in the production of cases of pseudobulbar paralysis with their characteristic spastic gait, slurring speech, and emotional instability.

Serology. The blood Wassermann reaction is positive in 60–70 per cent. of cases. The changes in the C.S.F. are similar to those in G.P.I., with the exception that the colloidal gold reaction may be less complete in the first six tubes as compared with the paretic curve, giving the so-called luetic curve—for example, 2 2 3 3 2 1 0 0 0 0.

Pathology. Three main types of cerebral syphilis can be differentiated—meningitis, endarteritis and gumma—but in any one case all these forms may co-exist. It may be difficult to make a histopathological differentiation of cerebral syphilis either from dementia paralytica or from arteriosclerotic brain disease. Cerebral syphilis and dementia paralytica can come so closely together as to be almost indistinguishable.

Diagnosis. The difficulty of differential diagnosis between this condition and dementia paralytica has already been referred to. We need only mention again that an acute onset accompanied by severe headache and cranial nerve palsies almost invariably means a syphilitic involvement of the meninges, rather than a parenchymatous change.

In relation to vascular involvement, arteriosclerotic brain disease is a disease of later life, usually after the age of 50 years, and the negative serological reactions would rule out the possibility of syphilitic endarteritis.

Tabes with Psychosis

There are certain patients, already suffering from tabes dorsalis, who at a later date develop G.P.I. Other instances occur, however, in which tabetic cases show mental symptoms which are not of a dementia paralytica nature. Kraepelin and Otto Meyer described such cases, and one of us reported a series of five cases in which there was no evidence of a paralytic process; in two cases the diagnosis was confirmed by autopsy. Two of the cases presented an hallucinatory state closely akin to the clinical picture described by others; two were accompanied by depression; one was characterized by hypochondria.

The clinical features which distinguish such cases from dementia paralytica are the absence of memory defect, and on the physical side the absence of tremors and of speech and writing defect.

TREATMENT AND PROGNOSIS

The credit for the introduction of the successful treatment of syphilitic diseases of the nervous system rests with Wagner Jauregg of Vienna who in 1917 recommended the use of malaria therapy. Initially he inoculated 9 cases of G.P.I. with malaria of whom 6 were greatly benefited; and 3, five years later, were maintaining themselves at work, and showed no signs of the disease. These were better results than ever previously had been recorded. Similar good results obtained by other workers from many different parts of the world confirmed Wagner Jauregg's findings.

The induction of one disease to cure another was a novel form of treatment. Its rationale depended on the observation that mentally ill patients who suffered from an intercurrent febrile illness seemed, for the time being, to become more normal and co-operative. They relapsed again, however, as soon as the fever had subsided. The temporary improvement, however, raised the hope that an artificially-produced pyrexia might be prolonged for a longer time and give correspondingly better results. Wagner Jauregg's courageous idea of using malaria infection was based on the belief—later disproved—that G.P.I. did not exist or at least was extremely rare in those countries in which malaria was endemic; the pyrexia was regarded as the potent agent: *Plasmodium vivax* (benign tertian) was the parasite used. Infection was induced either by allowing mosquitoes to bite the patient, or by the inoculation of blood from a malaria infected person.

Now malaria therapy is reserved for resistant cases, those which have failed to respond to treatment with penicillin. Penicillin is the treatment of choice both for cerebral syphilis and G.P.I., in doses of half a million Units twice a day for 10 to 28 days. If necessary, such a course of treatment may be repeated. The place of bismuth in treatment is at present uncertain.

Until the introduction of successful treatment by malarial inoculation and penicillin the course of the disease was rapid, the prognosis was poor, and death normally resulted in a period of from two to five years. Now we can hope to arrest the progress of the disease, to prolong life, and to effect a recovery whereby the patient can return home, and resume employment and domestic responsibilities. The earlier the case is recognized, and the more quickly treatment is instituted, the better the result. We can rarely speak in terms of a complete recovery, since nerve tissue once destroyed is not regenerated.

It is essential to follow up treated cases, and to re-examine them from time to time so as to ensure that no recurrence of symptoms takes place undetected. Further courses of treatment may be required. This, as indeed all other phases of the treatment, should be undertaken in collaboration with the specialist venereologists.

ENCEPHALITIS LETHARGICA

During and following the First World War an epidemic encephalitis, first described by von Economo in Austria in 1917 and called by him encephalitis lethargica, occupied an important place in psychological medicine. For example, 3350 fresh cases were notified in England and Wales between January 1919 and December 1922; and in 1924, when the epidemic was at its peak, there were 5036 new cases. In 1927 there were 644 men and women under care in psychiatric hospitals as a sequel of the infection.

Though the majority of cases of the disease showed mental symptoms of some degree, most of them however did not require admission to mental hospitals. Those that did require psychiatric care often presented difficult problems: in the case of adults the disability was prolonged, and in children the after-effects were of a type particularly difficult to manage. It was in order to facilitate the care of adolescents suffering from chronic epidemic encephalitis that the Mental Deficiency (England) Act of 1927 made it possible to certify a mentally defective person in whom the defect had arisen as late as 18 years of age.

The main incidence of the disease was between the ages of 15 and 50. It was almost certainly a virus infection: but the causal agent and its mode of transmission were not identified. Since that epidemic, which subsided in the late 1920's, many other neurotropic viruses responsible for virus encephalitis, epidemic and sporadic, have been identified. However, very few if any certain cases of epidemic encephalitis have been reported since the 1930's, and some authorities have stated that the disease had died out. This is not quite certain. Hunter and Jones (1966) reported in the south of England 6 cases of acute lethargica-type encephalitis, and they have suggested that such cases may be occurring more frequently than has recently been suspected. Their patients had a combination of cerebral, hypothalamic and midbrain involvement. The presenting symptoms were confusion, lethargy, visual disturbances and sleep disorder; the illness tended to run a fluctuating and relapsing course; and in three cases lethargy and confusion improved dramatically after lumbar puncture. Symptomatically, the illness resembled encephalitis lethargica: but it differed apparently in its more gradual development over months, and in the absence of a pleocytosis in the cerebro-spinal fluid. It is not yet known if this illness will be followed by post-encephalitic Parkinsonism.

Encephalitis lethargica is still therefore of some interest, and most mental hospitals care for a few of the chronic cases. Its clinical manifestations were protean, and their description will draw attention to the very various general and focal symptoms in the central nervous system which may be caused by neuro-tropic viruses.

Symptoms

Only the mental symptoms will be described here. They are best considered in two stages, the acute and the chronic; but the two varieties of symptoms merge into one another both in type and in time. The symptoms in both stages belong chiefly to the organic reaction-type, as might be expected, but there are some symptoms not ordinarily associated with the organic reaction-type which occur in some cases of epidemic encephalitis, and give it its striking and exceptional mental colouring.

Acute Stage. Delirium, stupor and psychomotor excitement have all been reported. It was from the frequency of stupor that the name 'lethargic encephal-itis' was derived. The stupor is of an unusual type, in that the patient can be roused for brief intervals, and can respond clearly to questions. An exceptional symptom in the acute febrile stage is 'pressure of talk'—the patient talking rapidly and incessantly, but with complete coherence and rapport with his environment, and without mood alteration. Neurotic symptoms have also been noted.

Sleep disturbances of all kinds are present, and insomnia is much commoner than the usual descriptions of 'lethargic' encephalitis would lead one to believe. It is not unusual for several nights of complete insomnia to precede the onset of lethargy. Complaints of headache are common. The mental symptoms of the acute stage may overshadow the neurological signs, and in a few cases have been the only symptoms detected during life. In rare instances, behaviour disorders (which are common in children in a setting of clear consciousness in the chronic stage) occurred in the early part of the illness.

The absence of mental symptoms in the early stages, or at least of a history of mental symptoms, does not make it impossible for them to appear in the chronic stage. The disease is so protean, even in its forms of onset, and the history given is often so vague, that the diagnosis of encephalitis had not infrequently to be made from the signs and symptoms of the later stages, both neurological and psychological.

Subacute forms have been described, with mood and character disturbances, polymorphous delusional ideas and psychomotor excitement, especially at night. These were succeeded by somnolence and stupor. Death in two to six months, or a chronic condition, ensued.

Chronic Stage. There are very considerable clinical differences between the symptoms seen in most adults and in most children affected by the disease. The symptoms common in adults will be described first.

The behaviour of adult post-encephalitic patients is usually in consonance with their affective condition. Thus the apathetic patient is usually inactive—a patient in whom consciousness is perfectly clear often lies motionless in bed or sits staring out of the window for hours on end, with only a casual type of mental content, *i.e.* the inactivity does not depend on preoccupation. In the Parkinsonian syndrome, however (and it is mostly, but not at all exclusively, in association with this syndrome that mental symptoms occur), there is a definite physical handicap to the patient's activity. His ordinary voluntary movements are slow ('brady-kinesis') although he can sometimes perform movements of rapid phase with apparent ease, *e.g.* he can play tennis with facility when it is laborious for him to walk. He has to devote a good deal of conscious attention to his movements, and this has a mental effect—it means a sense of unusual effort and a restriction of interest when movements normally automatic require much voluntary reinforcement. The restriction in interest can in itself be depressing, in addition to the discouraging effect of the knowledge of the presence of a chronic disabling disease. Corresponding to the physical slowing and lack of spontaneity, there is a psychic viscosity ('bradyphrenia'): a diminution of voluntary attention, of spontaneous interest, of initiative and of capacity for effort and work, together with objective and subjective fatigability and slight memory impairment. Extreme cases of this sort lead a vegetative existence.

Psychomotor excitement occurs sometimes. We have known 'pressure of talk' to persist for three years after the onset, accompanied by mild euphoria and lack of insight.

There is no affect which can be regarded as having a specific relation to this encephalitis, unless it be the remarkable apathy found in some cases. The apathy cannot be related directly to the Parkinsonian after-effects of encephalitis, since it occurs also in non-Parkinsonian cases, and Parkinsonian cases may not show it. Many other types of emotional reaction can occur. In a series of 23 cases we observed depression in 14 (with a suicidal attempt in 1 case), euphoria in 5, anxiety in 4 and emotional instability in 1. Depression is not to be regarded as specific. It is certainly in many cases a reaction to the physical disabilities, and can sometimes be removed by psychotherapy. Euphoria, in the face of physical disability, is more likely to be organically determined. Wimmer remarked that this type of emotional disorder is 'essentially different' from that in manic-depressive psychoses, and, with the reservation that we do not see why epidemic encephalitis should not sometimes unmask a latent manic-depressive predisposition, we are inclined to agree.

'The subjective (and objective) phenomena of the chronic stage seem sufficient, even after allowing for physical impediments, to indicate a profound mental change in the volitional sphere, with which emotional deterioration is closely connected.' This applied especially to adult patients with apathy, and to children in whom aggressive behaviour disorder was the prominent feature.

Disorientation, with or without hallucinations, memory defect and weakness of attention, are absent in the majority of chronic cases. They were present in 6 patients out of our series of 23. A Korsakoff syndrome may rarely occur (Wimmer). In adults lack of interest may give an impression of intellectual impoverishment.

All kinds of disturbances of sleep are possible—insomnia, hypersomnia, inverted rhythm, etc. Hypnotics are of very little use. We noticed that these patients do not seem to feel the lack of sleep to the extent that a normal person does.

Chronic Stage in Children. In children the chronic stage is noteworthy for the preponderance of behaviour disorders of a restless and aggressive kind. This is in obvious contrast to what is the rule (with some exceptions) in adults.

The characteristic change—it can be called characteristic since there is no other physical disease affecting children which leaves after-effects of this kind and degree and in such a large proportion of cases—is the appearance in a child, hitherto of normal decorum, of impulsive, unruly, shameless activity. Very rarely a reverse change has been noted. Grossman recorded the case of a very unruly child who became docile after epidemic encephalitis. The psychic disturbances in children are said by Wimmer to set in late and slowly, and are given by him as follows: restlessness, garrulity, meddlesomeness, excessive curiosity, erratic but active attention, foolish mirthfulness, irritability, temper-tantrums, scolding, mischievousness, destructiveness, abusive language, smearing with faeces and urine, micturition on surrounding persons, violence, attempts at murder and arson, cruelty to children and to animals, truancy, vagrancy, begging, dishonesty, pilfering and precocious erotism (sometimes with precocious puberty) with obscene language and conduct, including attempts on adults and small girls. These children seem to be very literally transformed into 'little devils'. Punishment has no effect. Asked why he does these things, the child will answer that he does not know, or that 'something in me makes me want to do it', as one expressed it. There is, in some cases, no evidence of shame or a sense of responsibility for their actions; others express apparently genuine regret.

Inverted sleep rhythm is very frequent, and the nocturnal wakefulness is accompanied by great psychomotor excitement. In some cases there is psycho-motor excitement in the daytime as well as at night.

Intellectually, there arises a secondary intellectual deficiency from lack of concentration and interest and fatigability, with consequent unreliable perception and imperfect retention, so that at school these children appear backward. There are, in addition, evidences of a temporary arrest of intellectual development, such as may result from any prolonged severe debilitating illness in children. This may sometimes prove permanent.

Tics, in the sense of habitual more or less complex co-ordinated movements occurring without reference to any apparent external need, are more common in children than in adults. Many of these encephalitic and post-encephalitic tics are more complex than those that have usually been considered 'functional'—i.e. not dependent on organic change. They include spitting, nose-picking, forced respiratory movements (sniffing, snorting, coughing), touching the shoe and putting the hand in the mouth, wetting the finger and rubbing the cheek and ear with it, shaking the hand, making the sign of the cross and stretching the arms laterally in rhythms of some multiple of three.

There is no evidence that behaviour disturbances are commoner in children of psychopathic inheritance or make-up than in children without this handicap. The prognosis of behaviour disorders in children is variable. Some go on to develop Parkinsonism, often with recession of the behaviour disturbance, others improve considerably but often with some form of instability remaining.

Neuropathology

The changes in the cerebrospinal fluid are never great. In the acute stages there have been reported lymphocytosis, increased globulin and precipitation in the 'luetic zone' in the colloidal gold test. In the chronic stages the changes are slight or absent.

The macroscopic post-mortem findings are frequently insignificant, but there may be congestion of the pial blood vessels, oedema of the brain and superficial haemorrhages. The most constant histopathological lesion is a perivascular infiltration, so that in sections the blood vessels in the affected region appear congested, with their walls packed with lymphocytes, plasma cells, adventitial cells, and in very acute stages polymorphs ('cuffing'). These infiltrations persist even in chronic cases. The parts chiefly affected are the basal ganglia and the region of the Sylvian aqueduct (especially the subthalamic region). Less frequently the grey and white matter of the cortex, and the medulla and spinal cord, are involved. Whether true parenchymatous infiltration occurs is not definitely decided; but extensive nerve cell degeneration does occur, and is very important.

Prognosis

The prognosis of the mental symptoms is intimately connected with that of the physical signs, but is not inseparably bound up with the latter. Death in the acute stages was estimated variously as occurring in 10 to 50 per cent. of the cases. The course of the mental symptoms is very changeable, so that in a single case there may be a sequence of *e.g.* delirium, stupor, exaltation and psychomotor excitement, with later hallucinations and delusions, a lethargic phase and finally recovery; or (in another case) initial psychomotor excitement followed by apathy and depression with retardation, inactivity and flexibilitas cerea. The delirium of the acute stage usually subsides after a few weeks: it may be followed by complete recovery, or by other mental symptoms.

The initial sleep disturbance may continue or disappear, or may show as heterogeneous a succession as the other mental symptoms, *e.g.* hypersomnia, followed by hyposomnia, or by inverted sleep rhythm with sometimes a return later to hypersomnia.

It is impossible to make a prognosis in an individual case, even in the acute stage, and very difficult in the chronic stage. We have known a patient recover symptomatically and return to his work, only to have Parkinsonian signs and affective changes appear nearly five years after the onset.

The adult patients coming under the notice of the psychiatrist in the chronic stage have usually a more or less extensive Parkinsonian syndrome. Parkinsonian cases are prognostically very unfavourable from the physical point of view, but when the affective symptoms are depressive or anxious, the mental prognosis is not necessarily bad. We have known anxiety and depression to disappear, and a return to work be possible. When euphoria accompanies the Parkinsonism, useful occupation is possible. The euphoria, like the other affective changes, may persist indefinitely. Apathy accompanying Parkinsonism, we have not known to disappear. In children, Wimmer recorded that of 25 acute cases, 11 died, 2 were untraced and 12 displayed psychic sequelae (chiefly behaviour disorders). We have not seen complete recovery occur from the behaviour disorder. The onset of Parkinsonism, however, is sometimes, but not invariably, associated with a cessation of impulsive conduct. Hohman recorded marked improvement or recovery in 6 out of 11 juvenile cases.

Differential Diagnosis

The apathy and lack of spontaneous movement in certain patients led to erroneous diagnoses of schizophrenia, and as such some of them were classified in mental hospitals. But closer investigation of such cases showed a normal grasp of the immediate environment without distortions, and no disorder of talk or of thought or other evidence of 'splitting' of the personality.

OTHER DISEASES OF THE CENTRAL NERVOUS SYSTEM

HUNTINGTON'S CHOREA

Huntington's chorea is a hereditary organic disease of the brain, characterized by choreiform movements and by gradually increasing dementia. It is due to a dominant gene. Every patient heterozygous for the disease has to expect an average of 50 per cent. of affected offspring. A small minority of cases are recorded without demonstrable inheritance, and these are due to new mutations.

It is a disease of world-wide distribution. The following are typical figures for its incidence per 100,000 population: Northamptonshire 5 (Pleydell, 1954); Minnesota 5·4 (Pearson, 1955); Essex, Herts, London 2·5 (Heathfield, 1967).

The onset is usually between the ages of 30 and 50, and the average length of life after the onset, about sixteen years. The physical and the mental symptoms are alike progressive. The mental changes may precede the physical signs by years. The early mental symptoms consist in deterioration of behaviour —slovenliness in dress, carelessness of social conventions, e.g. the use of obscene language, expectoration on the floor, great irritability issuing in altercation or in actual assault. Usually the patient is depressed, often suicidally so; a few are euphoric. There is poverty of thought, failure of memory, defective attention and judgement. Delusions, persecutory or religious or jealous, and often absurd in their content, are frequent.

Physically, there are continuous choreiform movements of the head, trunk and limbs—stretching, jerking and grasping, reminiscent sometimes of athetosis rather than of chorea. The movements begin usually in the lower limbs, and are often unilateral for a time. They cease during sleep, which is usually broken. The voluntary movements are irregular and incoordinate. Speech is hesitating and stumbling, and interrupted by clicking sounds, or so thick that it cannot be understood—a slurring, jerky dysarthria. Writing shows much irregularity. Swallowing may be impaired, and spasmodic jerking of the respiratory muscles may occur. Heathfield (1967) has drawn attention to the gait, which he describes as characteristic. The patients walk on their heels, with a wide base, and most show an exaggerated lumbar lordosis; in some, the attitude is one of flexion. Progression is irregular, lurching or zigzag, with increased choreiform movements of fingers and wrist, and arms held rigidly to the sides or abducted. Falls may lead to fractures. In Heathfield's series of 81 cases more than a quarter showed pyramidal tract signs, one-fifth extrapyramidal rigidity and one-seventh spasticity. The sphincters are intact.

The usual termination is dementia and physical helplessness, so that the patient is bedridden. The constant jerking movements continue to the last, and produce trauma to the skin, resulting in bed-sores.

Neuropathology. As a result of widespread neuronal degeneration, there is a gross generalized cerebral atrophy involving both the cortex and the basal ganglia, and both the white and the grey matter. The caudate nucleus and the putamen are usually particularly severely damaged, with a great reduction of their nerve cells. There is some compensatory ventricular dilatation.

Treatment. There is no way of detecting the gene and its carrier before the gene produces the disease. Nor is there as yet any treatment, pharmacological or neurosurgical, which can halt the course of this most distressing illness. The best that can be done is by the use of tranquillizing drugs such as trifluoperazine to ease the patient's unhappiness and bodily discomfort: these drugs have inconstant and usually slight effects on the abnormal movements (unless Parkinsonism is produced).

DISSEMINATED SCLEROSIS

Prominent emotional changes are common in this disease. Mild euphoria is characteristic, and has been said to be more frequent than any other single symptom, not excluding the physical ones—but this is doubtful. Coupled with the euphoria, and probably in part at least dependent on it, there is a lack of insight for the seriousness of the illness. In a smaller proportion of cases the affective change is towards more persistent depression and irritability: there may be dullness and apathy. As the disease advances the mood tends to vary too readily. Outbursts of laughing and crying, of an uncontrollable character and not necessarily accompanied by an appropriate change in mood, are not infrequent.

In a small minority of cases there is further evidence of dementia, in memory loss and impairment of judgement. This dementia may become profound. A

Korsakoff syndrome appears rarely. Persecutory and grandiose delusions, sometimes of a bizarre type, have also been recorded.

Some of the symptoms and signs of disseminated sclerosis—complaints of dizziness or paraesthesiae, pareses, the mood of euphoria mistaken for *belle indifférence*—may lead to a mistaken diagnosis of hysteria: but a neurological examination will nearly always reveal the true state of affairs. It must be added that a patient suffering from disseminated sclerosis may develop hysterical symptoms.

REFERENCES

Ackner, B., Cooper, J. E., Gray, C. H., and Kelly, M. (1962) *J. psychosom. Res.*, **6**, 1.
Allison, R. S. (1966) *Brit. med. J.*, **2**, 1027.
Berg, J. M., and Kirman, B. H. (1959) *Brit. med. J.*, **2**, 400.
Blessed, G., Tomlinson, B. E., and Roth, M. (1968) *Brit. J. Psychiat.*, **114**, 797.
Brain, W. R. (1958) *Lancet*, ii, 971.
Brain, Lord (1962) *Diseases of the Nervous System*, 6th ed., London.
Brierley, J. B. (1966) in *Amnesia*, ed. Whitty, C. W. M., and Zangwill, O. L., London.
Brooke, E. M. (1967) *A Census of Patients in Psychiatric Beds*, London, H.M.S.O.
Campbell, A. C. P., and Russell, W. R. (1941) *Quart. J. Med.*, **10**, 41.
Dagg, J. H., Goldberg, A., Lochhead, A., and Smith, J. A. (1965) *Quart. J. Med.*, **34**, 163.
Garland, H., and Pearce, J. (1967) *Quart. J. Med.*, N.S. **36**, 445.
Goldberg, A. (1965) in *Symposium: Disorders of the Blood*. Royal College of Physicians, Edinburgh.
Heathfield, K. W. G. (1967) *Brain*, **90**, 203.
Henderson, J. G., Strachan, R. W., Beck, J. S., Dawson, A. A., and Daniel, M. (1966) *Lancet*, ii, 809.
Henderson, J. G., Strachan, R. W., Beck, J. S., and Dawson, A. A. (1967) *Lancet*, i, 112.
Hunter, R., and Jones, M. (1966) *Lancet*, ii, 1023.
Jennett, W. B. (1961) *Ann. roy. Coll. Surg. Engl.*, **29**, 370.
Kallmann, F. J. (1953) *Heredity in Health and Mental Disorder*, New York.
Kay, D. W. K., Beamish, P., and Roth, M. (1964) *Brit. J. Psychiat.*, **110**, 146, 668.
Larsson, T., Sjögren, T., and Jacobson, G. (1963) *Acta psychiat. scand.*, **39**, Suppl. 167.
Letemendia, F., and Pampiglione, G. (1958) *J. Neurol. Neurosurg. Psychiat.*, **21**, 167.
Moncrieff, A. A., Konmides, O. P., Clayton, B. E., Patrick, A. D., Renwick, A. G. C., and Roberts, G. E. (1964) *Arch. Dis. Childh.*, **39**, 1.
Meyer, A. (1960) in *Neuropathology*, ed. Greenfield, J. G., London.
Nabarro, D. (1944) *Brit. J. vener. Dis.*, **20**, 65.
Newman, M. A., and Cohn, R. (1967) *Brain*, **90**, 405.
Read, A., Sherlock, S., Laidlaw, J., and Walker, J. (1967) *Quart. J. Med.*, **36**, 135.
Reynolds, E., Milner, G., Matthews, D., and Chanarin, I. (1966) *Quart. J. Med.*, **35**, 521.
Russell, W. R. (1934) *Edinb. med. J.*, **12**, 129.
Sherlock, S., Summerskill, W. H. J., White, L. P., and Phear, E. A. (1954) *Lancet*, ii, 453.
Shulman, R. (1967) *Brit. J. Psychiat.*, **113**, 252.
Sim, M., Turner, E., and Smith, W. T. (1966) *Brit. J. Psychiat.*, **112**, 119.
Sjögren, T., Sjögren, H., and Lindgren, A. G. H. (1952) Morbus Alzheimer and Morbus Pick, *Acta psychiat.* (*Kbh.*), Suppl. 82.
Thompson, A. P., Lowe, C. R., and McKeown, T. (1951) *The Care of the Ageing and Chronic Sick*, Edinburgh.
Victor, M., Adams, R. D., and Cole, M. (1965) *Medicine* (*Baltimore*), **44**, 345.
Zangwill, O. L. (1966) in *Amnesia*, ed. Whitty, C. W. M., and Zangwill, O. L., London.

16

DEPENDENCE ON DRUGS AND ALCOHOL

DRUG DEPENDENCE OR ADDICTION

The following definition of drug addiction was adopted by the World Health Organization in 1950: 'Drug addiction is a state of periodic or chronic intoxication detrimental to the individual and to society, produced by the repeated consumption of a drug (natural or synthetic). Its characteristics include: 1. an overpowering desire or need (compulsion) to continue taking the drug and to obtain it by any means; 2. a tendency to increase the dose; 3. a psychic (psychological) and sometimes a physical dependence on the effects of the drug.'

Where there is physical dependence on a drug, deprivation of it leads to specific symptoms and signs of withdrawal—the abstinence or withdrawal syndrome: as, for example, with heroin or barbiturates.

It is dependence upon the effects of a drug which is the basis of its abuse, whether that dependence is psychological or physical or both: and it has sometimes been uncertain whether or not a drug which is certainly habit-forming and harmful when taken habitually, should be called a drug of addiction. The W.H.O. Expert Committee on Addiction-producing Drugs (1964) recommended therefore that the term 'drug dependence' should be used to replace the terms 'drug addiction' and 'drug habituation'; and that drug dependence should be defined simply as a state arising from repeated administration of a drug, whether administration was periodical or continuous. The distinction between habituation and addiction is probably mainly one of degree: there may be habituation without tolerance, without the need for steadily increasing doses of the drug, and without a clear-cut withdrawal syndrome.

In the Second Report of the Interdepartmental Committee on Drug Addiction (1965) in Britain, the following definition of an addict was proposed: 'A person who, as the result of repeated administration, has become dependent upon a drug controlled under the Dangerous Drugs Act and has an overpowering desire for its continuance, but who does not require it for the relief of organic disease.'

Drug abuse is manifest either in injurious effects upon the individual or his society or upon both.

Dependence-producing Drugs

The chief drugs which may cause dependence may be listed as follows:

1. Opium and its derivatives, including morphine, laudanum (tincture of opium, B.P.), paregoric (camphorated tincture of opium, B.P.), *Dilaudid* (dihydromorphinone hydrochloride), heroin and codeine.
2. Synthetic opiates, including pethidine hydrochloride, B.P. (meperidine hydrochloride, U.S.P.) and methadone hydrochloride, B.P. (*Physeptone*, *Amidone*).

3. Cocaine.
4. Marijuana.
5. Sedatives and hypnotics, including the barbiturates, bromide, paraldehyde and chloral hydrate. Alcohol also comes into this group.
6. Stimulants, including amphetamine sulphate, B.P. (*Benzedrine*), dexamphetamine sulphate, B.P. (*Dexedrine*), phenmetrazine hydrochloride (*Preludin*), and ephedrine, B.P.

Probably the non-barbiturate sedatives and hypnotics, which include methylpentynol, meprobamate, glutethimide and chlordiazepoxide, should be added to this list. Chloroform and ether also are occasionally abused.

The Present Situation

Until recently Britain had few drug addicts and the distribution of drugs of addiction was tightly and effectively controlled. In 1961 the Interdepartmental Committee on Drug Addiction (Brain Committee) reported that the problem was a small one; the number of known addicts was 454, in a population of 52 millions. The highest occupational incidence was amongst those who had ready access to these drugs—doctors, dentists, nurses, pharmacists; and about a third of the male addicts were from the professions. Morphine, pethidine, diacetylmorphine and methadone were the drugs preferred by these addicts. There was also a relatively small number of people who, while being treated medically for a painful illness, had become dependent on narcotic drugs. These two addicted groups did not spread the drug habit to others.

Already at that time the drug addiction problem in the U.S.A., where control of the sources of the drugs is more difficult and less effective, was both absolutely and relatively much greater; and many young people between the ages of 14 and 25 were becoming involved. The problem was concentrated in the great cities, where ethnic and socially deprived minority groups, notably Negroes and Puerto Ricans, were chiefly implicated.

Since 1961 the pattern of drug addiction in this country has drawn closer to the American one (except in its ethnic aspects): the number of addicts has increased sharply and a greater proportion of young people have become affected. The Second Report of the Brain Committee (1965) documented the serious changes which were taking place. The number of known addicts to dangerous drugs had risen from 454 in 1959 to 753 in 1964, the number of heroin addicts from 68 to 342, and the number of cocaine addicts from 30 to 211 (nearly all of the cocaine addicts were taking heroin as well). There had been a striking change too in the ages at which people were becoming addicted. Whereas in 1959 11 per cent. were less than 35 years of age, in 1964 nearly 40 per cent. were, and the majority of these were taking heroin. Forty addicts were under the age of 20 years, 1 was aged 15: all were taking heroin. The male–female ratio is 2–3 to 1. The focus of these alarming changes was in London: Birmingham too showed a deteriorating situation. Since 1965 the figures have continued to mount: the number of heroin addicts in 1967 was 1299, the total number of narcotic addicts in 1967, 1729.

This new wave of addiction has not resulted primarily from medical treatment;

though the major source of supply of the drugs has been doctors who have prescribed in excess to established addicts, so that these addicts have been able to
supply other individuals and introduce them to drug taking. New recruits who
become 'hooked' on drugs of addiction may then themselves become patients of
these or other doctors. Thus dependence on 'hard' drugs is contagious and an
epidemic of drug addiction is initiated. It has now become a serious public health
problem.

Source of Supplies

Doctors prescribe the drugs which may cause addiction, and the profession,
being thus in a position of great social responsibility, must ensure that narcotics
are used for the relief of pain and distress only when this is necessary, and that
their use is abandoned (except of course in cases of hopeless prognosis) before
addiction can be developed. The Brain Committee (1965) concluded that the
major recent source of supply of dangerous drugs had been the activity of a few
doctors who had prescribed excessively for addicts, and that 'not more than six
doctors have prescribed these very large amounts of dangerous drugs for individual patients'. In this country at the present time there seems also to be much
laxity in the prescription of barbiturates and amphetamines to those who complain of neurotic or mild depressive symptoms.

Addicts ('junkies' or 'kicksters') get their supplies of drugs in many other and
often devious ways: by claiming that prescriptions and supplies already received
have been lost, by obtaining prescriptions from more than one doctor, by using
drugs prescribed for relatives, by giving false names, forging prescriptions and
committing theft. Drug 'pushers' are a further source of supply, the pushers in
their turn getting their supplies from over-prescribing, theft and smuggling.
'Pushers' are often themselves drug addicts, selling drugs to make money to buy
their own supplies: and they form one of the significant links between addiction
and crime. In Britain criminals are increasingly raiding chemists shops to get
supplies of drugs, chiefly amphetamines.

Vulnerable Personalities

Drug addiction is more a symptom than a primary cause of mental illness.
The addict has usually been a temperamentally unstable individual before he has
become addicted; but the contributory effects of a drug habit to this constitutional instability is always great. In the later stages toxic physical damage of
various kinds may occur, and the 'hard' drug addict frequently greatly shortens
his life. Though many alcoholics and drug addicts have similar psychological and
social problems, drug addiction does not lead to frank mental disorder to the
extent that alcohol does. The drug addict may, of course, become an alcoholic,
and vice versa. He tends to undergo a moral rather than an intellectual deterioration, and may be regarded by the community more as a degenerate to be despised
and perhaps punished, than as a person mentally ill and requiring treatment and
protection from himself.

There is no single deviant personality type which is exclusively or particularly prone to drug addiction: but it is those whose personalities are most unstable and most poorly adjusted to the requirements of their society who are in general the most susceptible, that is, the psychopathic group. The personality traits of these people render them not only very difficult to treat but also, on account of their importunate and threatening attitudes, much resented often by those who have to treat them.

These vulnerable personalities are to be found in all age groups. The problem of drug addiction is by no means confined to unstable, non-conforming adolescents, long-haired, bearded and unkempt.

The Natural History of Addiction

Little is known about the natural history of drug addiction, about what types of personality may be attracted to certain drugs, about which drugs predispose to the use of other even more addictive drugs, and what the cultural determinants may be. There is no doubt that many of those who have become addicted to heroin and cocaine have previously taken amphetamines or marijuana. Glatt (1967) states that while there may be a tendency for the more sophisticated 'intellectual and artistic' drug takers to prefer cannabis and L.S.D., and for the lower socio-economic groups to choose amphetamines, there is in Britain a large overlap between those drug users who take 'pep pills' and those who are attracted by hallucinogens and 'psychedelic', 'mind expanding' experiences. He reports that of 48 young addicts recently admitted to St. Bernard's Hospital, Middlesex, mainly heroin and cocaine users who had previously taken cannabis and amphetamines, 16 had also taken L.S.D. Glatt believes that the taker of cannabis is more likely to go on to experiment with L.S.D. than with heroin; cannabis being somewhat similar in its effects to L.S.D., though pharmacologically a different kind of drug.

Apart from heroin addiction the amount of adolescent drug taking in this country is an important problem, perhaps already a serious one. The size of the problem is difficult to gauge: only a few of those involved come before the Courts, still fewer are seen by psychiatrists. They are to be found in all social classes. Probably most of it is culturally determined behaviour, a currently fashionable type of experimentation and rebellion against adult, conservative mores; whether it be in university student groups or concentrated in certain coffee bars, clubs and cafes. It is not known how many of the adolescent experimenters who smoke 'reefers' or take amphetamine or amphetamine-barbiturate mixtures 'graduate' to 'hard' drugs or alcohol. The determinants may often be social, and the influence by contact with confirmed 'hard' drug takers crucial. On present evidence it seems likely that most of them do not become addicted to narcotic drugs.

The taking of L.S.D. appears to be at present a small problem in this country; but it might become more important and there is some evidence that here as in the U.S.A. its use is no longer confined to the higher socio-economic groups.

Social Attitudes

In the recent increase in drug addiction this country is facing a new medical and moral problem. So far relatively small numbers have been involved, but the contagion may spread. Society's attitudes are still uncertain. Amongst the general public the social taboos against narcotic addiction are still much stronger than those against alcoholism. At the same time there are minority groups, sophisticated and vocal, who want to 'liberalize' this society's attitudes to lay experimentation with drugs and in particular to get the sale of marijuana to the public legalized. They argue that marijuana (and other hallucinogens) can enhance one's perceptual appreciation of the external world and can lead to ecstatic and mystical experiences of great value. But being drug induced these mystical experiences are flawed and have usually no connection with the spiritual life. Marijuana has no medical uses, and there are no medical grounds for supporting a campaign to legalize its sale. It has not been conclusively demonstrated that marijuana itself is an innocuous drug: still less has it been proven that the taking of marijuana does not dispose the individual to take other drugs which are addictive or in some way dangerous. The widespread use of marijuana would be unlikely (to say the least) to enrich the quality of life in this country, by making its people more creative, more unselfish or productive: it would on the contrary tend to encourage detachment, passivity and self-indulgence. Though its effects might be less malignant than those due to alcoholism, the evidence so far available suggests that they would on balance be deleterious; and at a time when the excessive consumption of alcohol amongst the less stable members of the community is a cause of growing concern, it does not make sense to risk promoting another, possibly serious, social problem. Further consideration of a change in the legal control of marijuana should now await the results of a full scientific inquiry into the effects of this drug.

Legal Enactments

The manufacture, sale, possession and distribution of poisons and drugs of addiction in Great Britain have been rigidly controlled by legislative enactments —notably the Dangerous Drugs Act, 1965, which controls the opiates, pethidine, cocaine, marijuana; the Drugs (Prevention and Misuse) Act 1964, which controls amphetamines and L.S.D.; and the Pharmacy and Poisons Act 1933, which controls the barbiturates and many other substances.

The most recent of these laws to control drug addiction is the Dangerous Drugs Act 1967, which embodies the main recommendations of the Brain Report (1965), though it does not give new powers for the compulsory detention and treatment of addicts. Under this Act, medical practitioners are required to identify and notify addicts to a central authority; and are prohibited, except under licence, from prescribing for addicts certain specified drugs (initially, heroin and cocaine). To assist in the diagnosis of addiction, advisory panels have been set up to which a doctor can refer a patient if the doctor is in doubt about the patient being in fact an addict. Treatment of addicts will be concentrated in a limited number of special treatment centres, whose medical staff will be authorized to prescribe heroin and cocaine if and when required in the management of addiction.

In the present state of drug addiction in this country it seems entirely justified to transfer the responsibility for the medical treatment of addicts from the general practitioner to hospital-based specialized out-patient clinics and treatment centres, provided that the psychiatric services are given the extra facilities and staff which this transfer of responsibility entails.

Dependence upon or addiction to the following drugs will be described: morphine, heroin and pethidine; cocaine; amphetamines; barbiturates; marijuana; hallucinogens; and bromides. The characteristics of the dependence itself and the symptoms produced vary from one type of drug to another; and the dependence can be designated as morphine-type or amphetamine-type, for example. Morphine, heroin, pethidine and cocaine are often described as the 'hard' drugs.

MORPHINE, HEROIN AND PETHIDINE

Morphine, which has its most notable effect in the relief of pain, produces also sedation and a feeling of mental detachment. Tolerance is developed to these psychological effects and the dose may be raised gradually even to twenty times the original dose. Psychological and physical dependence become easily established. Diamorphine (heroin), which is less sedative, less prone to produce nausea and less prolonged in its action, is an even more addictive drug: it is used by addicts usually in conjunction with cocaine. Pethidine has effects similar to those of morphine and is equally addictive.

Addiction to heroin is now the main narcotic addiction in this country. It is usually self-administered (a 'fix') by intravenous ('main line') injection. When the addict has recently had a dose of the drug and is 'high', he feels dreamy and euphoric, looks preoccupied and detached and his pupils are small, reacting sluggishly to light. He resents disturbance and may become drowsy. As the time for the next dose draws near he becomes fidgety and irritable, unable to concentrate on other matters and more and more preoccupied with his need for the drug. The initial signs of withdrawal then begin to appear—yawning, running eyes, sneezing, sweating and a miserable feeling of malaise.

Most heroin addicts inject themselves at about 4-hourly intervals. The effects of deprivation of the drug are striking. Restlessness and apprehension mount in intensity over 12 hours or so, with tremor, yawning, lachrymation, rhinorrhoea and excessive sweating, and feelings of coldness. Cramps in the abdomen and elsewhere precede muscular spasms and twitching. Nausea, vomiting and diarrhoea may lead on to a state of severe physical collapse. Sudden withdrawal of the drug may also precipitate a delirium, occasionally of a quiet, dreamy type but more often characterized by restlessness and horrible hallucinations. These withdrawal symptoms last less than a week.

In all cases a character change, directly attributable to the use of the drug, sets in as soon as the habit is established for its own sake. The change consists in a gradual deterioration of the personality. There is a general falling off in efficiency, partly because the higher intellectual faculties become impaired, and partly because there is a lowering of aims, ambitions and energy. The whole life of the addict revolves round the procuring of an adequate supply. Ethical deterioration is a prominent feature; the sense of responsibility diminishes, and is lost; the addict becomes untrustworthy in all directions, and untruthful, especially regarding the drug habit itself. He neglects his appearance, is suspicious and furtive in his manner, perhaps on account of the social disapproval entailed by his addiction. His suspiciousness may develop into actual ideas of persecution. The mood is very variable, the degree of well-being varying inversely with the time that has elapsed since the last dose. Memory, attention and grasp of current events all deteriorate, partly as the result of progressive restriction of interest to the problem of obtaining and using the drug. When delirium (an excited hallucinatory episode with fear) occurs, it is very often because the patient has been taking some other drug as well, such as alcohol or cocaine.

The heroin addict deteriorates also markedly in his physical health. His appetite is poor, he becomes constipated and he loses weight until he may become emaciated. Muscular weakness and easy fatigability are usual: tremors, paraesthesiae and impotence are other developments. He becomes prone to both general and local infections. Injecting himself without sterile precautions he frequently produces local abscesses, hepatitis is another common sequel, and the often fatal complications of tetanus, septicaemia or bacterial endocarditis (especially, *Staphylococcus aureus* infections) may also occur. An overdose is the commonest cause of death.

COCAINE

Cocaine is not by itself so much indulged in as opium and its derivatives, but is chiefly used as an accompaniment or alternative to other drugs of addiction. Particularly it is used with heroin, to stimulate and to increase euphoria. It is taken hypodermically or as snuff.

The effects of a dose of cocaine are slight dizziness and headache, quickly followed by feelings of well-being and of enhanced mental activity. This increased activity is real, but does not endure. In this stage the addict is garrulous, witty, may write a great deal and has no sensations of hunger or fatigue. Vivid phantasies, illusions and hallucinations of a pleasant kind occur: these are generally in the nature of wish-fulfilments. After the acute effects wear off, there is general diminution of activity, with some motor incoordination, and the mood fluctuates from well-being to irritability, moroseness and suspicion. There is then a craving for a further dose of the drug. In addicts taking large doses delirious reactions with prominent paranoid symptoms may be induced; and tactile hallucinations, especially creeping sensations under the skin ('cocaine bug'), are said to be characteristic.

Cocaine potentiates the action of adrenaline. Dilated pupils, dryness of the mucous membranes, pallor, anorexia and emaciation are the common physical signs. When cocaine is taken as snuff, lesions of the nasal mucous membranes including perforation of the nasal septum may result.

Psychological but not physical dependence on the drug is developed. There being no physical dependence, there is no withdrawal syndrome and the drug can always safely be withheld from an addict.

It would be no loss if the prescription of cocaine was now prohibited.

AMPHETAMINES

Amphetamines are prescribed as appetite suppressants in the treatment of obesity or to relieve depression or fatigue; and annually in Britain millions of prescriptions for these drugs are written by doctors. Kiloh and Brandon (1962) in Newcastle found that probably over 500 out of a population of 270,000 were dependent on amphetamines. Yet, with the exception of narcolepsy, there is probably no physical illness for the treatment of which amphetamines are necessary; and there are no psychiatric indications for their use. Mild depression can be treated more effectively with the tricyclic derivatives: and though dependence on these newer drugs can occur, it presents a less serious medical and social problem.

By no means all, and perhaps only the minority, of those who become addicted to amphetamines do so as a result of medical treatment with them. Though unauthorized possession of these drugs is an offence under the Drugs (Prevention of Misuse) Act, 1964, they can be obtained illegally quite readily, from 'pushers' in pubs and clubs and elsewhere. Adolescents who take amphetamines probably do not often get their supplies from doctors.

In recent years adolescents have increasingly experimented with amphetamines, obtaining them easily in cafés and clubs and taking them for 'kicks', particularly at week-ends. Scott and Willcox (1965) have identified these as mainly youths with mild personality disorders, narcissistic, easily influenced by their fellows and rebellious against adult mores. Though they found that 16–18 per cent. of boys examined in London Remand Homes had amphetamine-like substances in their urine, they were unable to detect a definite relationship between the taking of these drugs and antisocial behaviour. Young psychopaths who go from amphetamines to narcotic addiction constitute probably a small minority of the adolescent group.

Any of the amphetamine group of drugs may cause addiction—amphetamine, dexamphetamine (*Dexedrine*), methylamphetamine (*Methedrine*) and phenmetrazine (*Preludin*). The one taken most often is *Drinamyl*, a mixture of amphetamine and amylobarbitone, known popularly as 'purple hearts'. These drugs have 'pep'-producing qualities, giving a stimulus and feeling of euphoria, which the temperamentally unstable or neurotic person may find irresistible. Brandon and Smith (1962) have suggested that as many as a fifth of those prescribed these drugs may become habituated or addicted to them. The dependence is psychological, not physical: there is no withdrawal syndrome. Multiple addictions, to alcohol, barbiturates and amphetamines are not uncommon: and the addict may go from one drug to another.

Doses which give mental stimulation may produce little or no evidence of sympathetic overaction. Psychotic symptoms may result from a single large dose, but are unusual unless the daily intake of the drug is more than 50 mg. The most prominent mental symptoms of intoxication are delusions of persecution, with auditory and visual hallucinations. There is often little or no clouding of consciousness, and the toxic reaction is commonly misdiagnosed as a paranoid psychosis or paranoid schizophrenia: it is, however, transient usually, responding in a few days to withdrawal of the drug. With higher doses a frank delirium may be produced. While acutely intoxicated, the patient may be violent towards others: and in the withdrawal phase there is a suicidal risk in cases where the amphetamine has been prescribed for an existing depression. The features of amphetamine intoxication are not peculiar to this intoxication, and an 'amphetamine psychosis' should not be described as a clinical entity. A full account of the condition has been given by Connell (1958).

The drug-addicted individual is likely to dissemble about his use of the drug and his urine must be tested. The methyl-orange test for amphetamine is unreliable and chromatography is required. This should be carried out in all acute paranoid reactions, to elucidate the differential diagnosis.

BARBITURATES

The barbiturates, the least often mentioned amongst the drugs which can cause dependence and intoxication, are probably the most often misused. The problem is to a considerable degree iatrogenic, these drugs being prescribed too readily and too lavishly for the relief of nervous tension by both general practitioners and psychiatrists. Women become more often dependent on barbiturates than men, and it is those who suffer from personality disorders, persistent neurotic tension and insomnia who are most vulnerable. The habitual taking of barbiturates is responsible for much minor disability in the home, by reducing efficiency and, through a vicious circle development, by perpetuating nervous instability. Where addiction occurs it is a classical addiction; the patient requires increasing doses of the drug and has distressing psychological and physical symptoms if deprived of it. Multiple addictions, to alcohol, barbiturates and amphetamines, are not uncommon.

The symptoms of chronic intoxication are difficulty in thinking, impaired recent memory, concentration and judgement, and emotional lability. Periods of euphoria, talkativeness and disinhibition are superimposed on the basic state of unhappiness, tension and irritability. It may be difficult to distinguish the symptoms due to neurosis from those due to drug intoxication or drug hunger. Speech is apt to be slow and may be slurred: there may be nystagmus and ataxia. With larger doses periods of confusion and obviously inappropriate behaviour may precede a state of stupor; and the borderland of suicidal acts is reached.

Particularly in cases where a number of different drugs are being taken concurrently, the clinical picture may be atypical and the diagnosis of drug intoxication may be missed. Endocrine disease, hypoglycaemia or thyroid dysfunction, may be suspected. An E.E.G. record, which reveals the excess of fast activity typical of barbiturate intake, may clarify the situation.

There is no doubt that both a psychological and a physical dependence on barbiturates may be developed, and in an individual so addicted, abrupt withdrawal of barbiturates may cause severe symptoms. Increased anxiety, tremulousness, insomnia and feelings of weakness are to be expected: but it is the onset within a few days of a delirium or of epileptic seizures which are the more serious developments. They are liable to occur after sudden withdrawal, if the intake has been more than 0·6 g. quinalbarbitone or pentobarbitone daily. Barbiturate withdrawal fits are not at all uncommon occurrences and the unexpected onset of fits in a patient who has been admitted recently to a psychiatric unit should suggest that drug withdrawal may be their origin. Withdrawal of barbiturates from a person habituated to taking them should therefore always be gradual.

MARIJUANA

Parts of the Indian hemp (*Cannabis indica*) plant have been used for centuries in many parts of the world to produce a pleasurable intoxication. Hashish is a form of the resin of the plant. Marijuana ('pot' or 'weed') consists of the dried leaves of the female plant, which in Europe and America are smoked as cigarettes ('reefers').

Intoxication produces usually a state of elation, with disinhibition and increased suggestibility, and distortions in time and space perception. Depersonalization and disturbances of body image may also occur. Appetite is typically increased, the breath has a characteristic odour, and the conjunctivae are reddened. Motor co-ordination is not seriously impaired. It is not specifically an aphrodisiac. Excitement is usually followed by 'delicious' lassitude and sleep. The effects of the drug are very variable, and instead of euphoria, anxiety, palpitations and nausea may be evoked; but it is of course for the way in which it stimulates and promotes a soothing withdrawal from life and its problems that its votaries smoke it.

No marked degree of tolerance of the drug is built up, its users do not develop a physical dependence such as is found with the opiates, and there is no withdrawal syndrome.

As with alcohol, the disinhibiting effects of marijuana may be antisocial. It does not seem to promote aggressive behaviour, but it may in some cases facilitate criminal activities, encourage sexual promiscuity and render the individual under its influence particularly dangerous when driving a car. It is known that many of those addicted to heroin and cocaine have previously indulged themselves with marijuana: but there is no evidence that this progression from a 'soft' to a 'hard' drug is pharmacologically determined, and no indication that the smoking of marijuana is in itself more dangerous than the drinking of alcohol. But both 'soft' and 'hard' drugs circulate in some of the same places and amongst some of the same sort of people, and it is as a channel of introduction to highly undesirable social contacts that marijuana may have its most dangerous influence. In this country possession of the drug is illegal: in 1967, there were 2419 convictions for possession of less than 30 g. of it. It has no medical uses.

HALLUCINOGENS—ESPECIALLY L.S.D.

Drugs capable of producing visionary states in normal people have been called the phantastica (Lewin, 1931): cocaine, cannabis, mescaline, lysergic acid diethylamide (L.S.D.) and psilocybin are included in this group. The effects of the first two of these drugs have already been described. Mescaline and L.S.D. produce similar mental symptoms: and since from the point of view of their abuse L.S.D. is much the more important drug, its actions will be set out here.

L.S.D., an ergot derivative, is a very potent drug and a minute dose of 30 μg. by mouth will elicit symptoms. It causes changes in attention and affect, as well as disturbances of sensory perception with illusions and hallucinations. Typically, the individual's attention is abnormally arrested by his immediate environment; he becomes anxious, depressed or euphoric; and he has visual hallucinations, which may be coloured or monochrome, take mosaic or graticule forms or consist of human or landscape content. Synaesthesiae may be reported, as well as distortions of time and space perception, body image disturbances and feelings of unreality. These phenomena occur in a setting of clear or mildly clouded consciousness: insight is retained and behaviour is usually not disturbed. There is considerable variation in individual sensitivity, and the personality of the subject has an influence on the symptoms elicited. The reaction-type is an organic one due to intoxication, and frank delirium will be manifest as it becomes more severe.

L.S.D. has been used medically in both psychiatric research and treatment. In research, it has been employed as a method of investigating the psychological phenomena which may occur in mental illness; and in particular it was hoped that by inducing a 'model psychosis' in normal subjects by the administration of this drug, light would be thrown on the genesis and symptoms of schizophrenia. Perhaps the individual under the influence of a hallucinogenic drug does have some experiences like a schizophrenic's: but the model psychosis induced belongs clearly to the organic reaction-type, and so far very little has been learnt about schizophrenia in this way.

In treatment, L.S.D. has been employed as an adjunct to the psychotherapy of neurotics, alcoholics and sexual perverts, to promote abreaction and the release of repressed psychic material and to foster insight: but there have been no controlled clinical trials which have demonstrated its value for these purposes.

Apart from the unpleasant short-term feelings of nausea, agitation, panic and depression which it may produce, L.S.D. may occasionally precipitate more severe and prolonged reactions. Hallucinosis may persist for 48 hours or longer; serious paranoid misinterpretations may be provoked; behaviour may become more sociopathic; and severe depressive and anxiety states may be precipitated (Cohen and Ditman, 1963). It is not clear whether these reactions are confined to people who are predisposed, who are pre-psychotic and would probaly have become mentally ill anyway: according to Cohen and Ditman it is those with already unstable temperaments, often hysterical or paranoid, who are particularly at risk. At any rate alarming and sometimes dangerous reactions have been reported by many psychiatrists, in cases particularly where there has been unsupervised and inexpert use of the drug. There has also been some recent evidence which suggests that L.S.D. may be a teratogen.

The vivid mental symptoms produced by L.S.D. have attracted some amateur experimenters and thrill-seekers, who have administered the drug to themselves illicitly, hoping to get from it ('psychedelic') experiences of a supposedly mind-expanding or life-enhancing kind. Professional, intellectual and artistic groups, including students, more so in the U.S.A. than in Britain, have been trying out its effects in this way. To serve these groups there has been illegal production of the drug and a 'black market' in its sale: it is both easy and cheap to produce, and its small bulk makes it easily concealed.

There is so far no evidence that L.S.D. itself is a drug of addiction. Its main dangers seem to lie in the psychotic reactions which it may precipitate, even in a single dose: and the possibility that its use may lead to further experiment with drugs of addiction. In Britain it is not available for general prescription and its supply is confined to a small number of psychiatrists, who wish to pursue trials of its possible uses in research and treatment.

BROMIDES

Bromide salts used to be prescribed so indiscriminately in nervous and mental disorders, and in epilepsy, that prior to the Second World War cases of bromide intoxication were common. They are now rare, because doctors have been so thoroughly warned of the toxic effects of bromides. Occasionally still one encounters an individual who has become addicted to a bromide and chloral mixture; or to one of the more than two dozen compounds containing bromide which are available, and the majority of which can be bought by the public without a doctor's prescription. Some individuals can tolerate a serum bromide level of 200 mg. per 100 ml. or over. Mental symptoms are unlikely unless the serum bromide is at least 150 mg. per 100 ml., but this toxic level may be lower if renal function is impaired (as it commonly is in old people).

The delirium produced by bromide does not differ from that caused by other toxic agents. The individual becomes in the earlier stages of the intoxication forgetful, irritable and generally sluggish. Later, as confusion increases, he shows a fear reaction in association with hallucinations and disorientation. In very severe intoxication, drowsiness may precede coma. He does not recover as quickly as a case of delirium tremens does, but more gradually over many days or even weeks, depending on the degree of intoxication and the rate of elimination of the drug.

Physically, the patient looks unwell and has commonly lost weight. Often he has a notably sallow complexion and he may (but does not always) have an acneiform rash on face and back. The breath may be fetid, the tongue is usually coated with a thick brown fur, and the bowels are constipated. Speech may be slurred, tremors and incoordination may be marked, and the pupils react sluggishly to light, so that in severe cases the clinical picture may resemble general paralysis.

The blood bromide should be estimated in all patients in whom the diagnosis is suspected. Treatment is by immediate stoppage of the drug and by giving plenty of fluid and sodium chloride.

TREATMENT AND PROGNOSIS

Prevention is infinitely the best approach to this serious medico-social problem. The strictest possible control over the distribution of dangerous and addictive drugs should be complemented by better education of the lay public, medical students and doctors about the causes, nature and often malignant effects of drug addiction. Doctors in their prescribing should keep constantly in mind the risk of inducing drug addiction. Society should see that no public encouragement is given to young people to experiment in this hazardous way, while it ensures that it provides for them every reasonable opportunity for ways of life which are more challenging and satisfying.

The main aspects of the treatment of the drug addict are psychiatric, and it is essential that specialized care be undertaken as soon as possible. Far too often the patient is referred to a psychiatrist only when the habit has become firmly established. He should be referred as soon as addiction is suspected.

In the case of the older person who has become addicted to a dangerous drug in the course of his professional life or following treatment of a serious physical illness, and whose addiction has not responded to withdrawal and the usual measures, it is sometimes best to accept the situation and to endeavour mainly to control the amount of the drug taken. A stabilized addict, who is prepared to co-operate in this kind of maintenance treatment, may be able to continue reasonably effectively to carry out even professional duties. But such patients are rare; and in the case of the young person the aim must always be to wean him from the drug upon which he has become dependent. Here the indications for with drawal are so strong as the stability of the individual's personality is (probably) weak. Here only too often one is dealing, not with a life that has become disorganized after a fairly good start, but with an individual who has never matured to an adult level of responsibility and self-control.

It is not possible to withdraw his drugs from an addict while he attends as an out-patient. But out-patient clinics have an important part to play in the treatment of addiction: not only as places where drugs will be supplied in a responsible and controlled way so that by the prescription of limited quantities the spread of addiction is contained; but as giving the opportunity to addicts to come into contact with a tolerant and understanding staff, and to form the rapport which is the necessary bridge to any effective treatment. If the addict can be brought to accept that he is a sick person and his co-operation can be gained, treatment may be successful: without co-operation, success is impossible.

When an addict attends at an out-patient clinic or doctor's surgery for the first time, one has too often only his word for what he has been taking. It is of great importance that the addict should not get more of the drug than is necessary more than he has already been taking. If possible, of course, reliance should not be placed on his own estimate of what he needs: and more accurate data may be obtained from his general practitioner or a pharmacist or from the Home Office, which obtains information about the abnormal prescription of dangerous drugs from the police scrutiny of retail pharmacists' records, from the medical profession and elsewhere. At out-patient clinics biochemical facilities must be available for the testing of urine and blood samples. There is also an urgent need for new laboratory methods to be developed for assessing drug levels in body fluids, which would enable an objective estimate to be made of the amount of the drug being taken.

A period of in-patient treatment, in a psychiatric unit or nursing home, where (theoretically at least) all access to drugs can be prevented, is essential for effective treatment. In most cases, the addict can only be persuaded to accept this. There is no legislation in this country which allows the compulsory detention of an addict purely on account of and for the treatment of an addiction. An addict can, however, be treated under legal constraint in the following circumstances: if he has become psychotic as a result of his drug taking he can be detained in the usual way as a compulsory patient; if he has been convicted by a Court of an offence punishable by imprisonment he can be detained in a mental hospital under Part V of the Mental Health Act (1959), Section 60; and after a criminal conviction also, a probation order can be made under the provisions of the Criminal Justice Act (1948), with the condition of residence in a mental hospital. There is no doubt too that in certain cases a period of compulsory detention in hospital can be in the best interest both of the patient and of society.

The first essential, when the patient is under in-patient care, is to withdraw the drugs which he has been taking. This should be done gradually over a period of 7–10 days: sudden deprivation is unnecessarily distressing, and may provoke severe symptoms of withdrawal. The unpleasantness of deprivation must be made more tolerable by giving the patient tranquillizing drugs, for example, chlorpromazine or diazepoxide. Drugs thus given in substitution should be prescribed only in sufficient quantity to provide relief, and should themselves be gradually withdrawn. The nature and amount of the medicines being administered should be concealed from the patient. During this period also the addict, his visitors and his other contacts, must be supervised very closely. Many addicts try to get in supplies surreptitiously and show very considerable initiative and cunning in their duplicity.

Methadone, which is itself a drug of addiction and used as such in this country by a small minority of 'hard' drug addicts, has been widely given to ease the withdrawal symptoms of morphine and heroin addicts. It is of course in its turn usually withdrawn after this short-term use. More recently it has been suggested by Dole and his colleagues in New York (1966) that in the case of the 'hard' drug addict who cannot be brought under control in any other way, maintenance replacement therapy with methadone should probably be accepted, and a single daily oral dose of this drug has been found sufficient. This cannot however in the case of the young addict be other than a measure of last resort.

As with alcoholics, it is often debated whether addicts should be treated in specialized units, separated from the general body of psychiatric patients. Shortage of beds and other facilities usually determines that they cannot be: but even were it possible to set up in each region wholly separate units, it is not at all certain that this would in practice be advisable though no doubt advantageous from the point of view of research. Experiment in this matter is necessary. All types of alcoholics cannot helpfully be grouped together for treatment, and the same probably applies to drug addicts. Difficulties arise both from the individual personalities of these people and their reactions to and with each other—their 'code', not to give each other away and to regard addiction as a sign of manliness or at least as some distinction; and their suggestibility, so that older addicts influence the others detrimentally, and the weaker take their cues from the disgruntled. This is of course not to say that group treatment may not be found as appropriate for selected cases of drug addiction as it is for certain cases of alcoholism.

After withdrawal of the drug, psychotherapy and active rehabilitation should be undertaken, or at least hopefully attempted. Psychotherapy is usually very difficult, the patient's will to co-operate may be feeble and insight lacking: and indeed psychotherapy is often not possible, owing to the resentful, reluctant or aggressively hostile attitude of these patients. But what is possible should be tried, with determination, on an individual or a group basis. Rehabilitation is always necessary. These patients should be employed about the hospital wards, in the occupational therapy department, in the hospital grounds or in any industrial unit which is at hand. It is as important for the addict as for the chronic schizophrenic that he should regain a habit of work and skills which will enable him to hold a job when he leaves hospital.

Even more essential than a constructive handling of the problem in hospital is the quality and persistence of follow-up after the patient has been discharged. If the addict is dropped abruptly into the outside world, he will sink. Very often he will need help in every direction, in bringing him into touch again with an estranged family, in finding somewhere suitable to live and somewhere suitable to work. To be accommodated for some weeks or months in a supervised hostel —which also has an occupation centre—would in many cases be the best solution: but such a hostel is hardly anywhere to be found. Persistent, patient follow-up, support and encouragement are necessary, over a period of years. Either his family doctor or a psychiatrist has to undertake this, with the help of a social worker or health visitor. A period of retraining in an Industrial Rehabilitation Unit may be valuable. So may introduction to a club where the patient will find new social contacts. His old haunts and friends are as dangerous and seductive as the drugs he has been taking, and he must break with all three if he is to be cured.

Such an outline is the required pattern of treatment, so far as we know it. Unhappily at every point one encounters frustration and failure in carrying it out. The prognosis for 'hard' drug takers is generally bad: worse even than the prognosis for chronic alcoholism. Many refuse to co-operate in treatment, many break it off prematurely, many relapse after apparent initial success. Rehabilitation and follow-up care are frequently neglected, both by the addicts themselves and by those who treat them. Bewley (1965), following up the 507 recorded heroin addicts in the United Kingdom between 1954 and 1964, found that over 82 per cent. of them had remained addicted or had died. The mean age of death of heroin addicts, who had acquired their addiction from other than medical sources, was 34 years. Clark (1962), at the Crichton Royal, Dumfries, followed up 50 drug addicts from the medical and nursing professions who had been treated there: though 28 per cent. of this group had overcome their addiction, only 14 per cent. of those addicted to drugs controlled by the Dangerous Drugs Acts had remained free. Retterstol and Sund (1965), in Oslo, reported that only 14 out of 62 addicted patients had stopped using drugs. Similarly poor results are recorded from the United States (Duvall *et al.*, 1963).

The darkness of the prognosis and the youthfulness of many of the victims of drug addiction point unequivocally to the need for further research into all the facets of drug addiction—into its physical, psychological and cultural aspects, its aetiology, prevention, control, and treatment. On none of these matters is our current knowledge sufficient.

DEPENDENCE ON ALCOHOL (ALCOHOL ADDICTION)

The influence of alcohol on the normal individual, the importance of alcohol as a factor in the aetiology of mental illness, crime and other antisocial behaviour, and the extent of the problem have been outlined in Chapter 4. Here we consider alcoholism more specifically as an illness. Alcoholism in this country is a far greater problem medically than drug addiction. A double dependence on drugs and alcohol occurs commonly, and the individual dependent on alcohol may change to drugs and vice versa. Dependence on alcohol has in fact much in common with dependence on drugs, in the underlying personality defects, the cultural influences, the social complications and the difficulties of treatment.

The following definition of alcoholism was proposed by the World Health Organization (1951). 'Alcoholics are those excessive drinkers whose dependence upon alcohol has attained such a degree that they show a noticeable mental disturbance or an interference with their bodily and mental health, their interpersonal relations, and their smooth social and economic functioning: or who show the prodromal signs of such developments. They therefore require treatment.'

The dependence upon alcohol, when it is established, may be both psychological and physical. Tolerance of the effects of alcohol usually increases (until in chronic alcoholism there is a reduction in tolerance): and the withdrawal of alcohol can undoubtedly precipitate an abstinence syndrome—a craving for more, with the development of anxiety and insomnia, tremors, sweating, nausea and in the more established cases of dependence, transient hallucinations, delirium and epileptic fits.

At some point in time, the excessive drinker is liable to become dependent on alcohol. He cannot then do without it, though its effects upon himself and others are clearly injurious. His alcoholism has become an illness and he is in need of understanding and treatment.

2 D

The Development of Dependence

Dependence on alcohol develops out of the interaction between social circumstances and a vulnerable personality: it is a psychopathological development, not a disease entity. Some of the determinants may be found in a disturbance of the individual's childhood environment, in parental alcoholism and quarrelling, and in the insecurity resulting from this or other disruption or deprivation of early child-parent relationships. Later there are the influences of the individual's employment, business habits, friends and peers, social attitudes to drinking, the impress of the culture he lives in and all the incidents and mishaps of his life-history.

The more social drinking there is, the more vulnerable people are placed at risk. Probably the previous personality is always faulty: it is sometimes grossly so. There is no single personality type which becomes dependent on alcohol. One finds amongst alcoholics inhibited, passive individuals, dominated by and over-attached to their mothers. Others have prominent feelings of tension and social inadequacy: in some cases there is a fear of being seen to have trembling hands, and the alcoholism is attributed by them to the need to control this physical tremulousness. Others again appear self-sufficient and self-confident, even omnipotent in their attitudes, having all the answers. Some have obvious difficulties in their sexual adustment. Some are self-indulgent, others guilt-ridden and self-punitive. Some are keeping at bay, as it were, in their restlessness, conviviality and drinking, complexes of which they are only dimly aware, if they are aware of them at all. A considerable number are inadequate psychopaths, shiftless, irritable and unable to form normal human attachments. Nor is this a full catalogue.

There is no evidence that alcoholism is due to a primary biochemical disorder, either inherited or acquired.

There are perhaps two main patterns of drinking to excess which lead to dependence and its sequelae. The one type, much the commoner in this country, is characterized by its compulsiveness or lack of control: the individual cannot drink moderately, he is frequently drunk, disorganized or incapable. Jellinek (1960) called this 'gamma' alcoholism. The other type is characterized by steady, heavy drinking, not impulsive and disorganized, and not till late leading to manifest drunkenness: but ending, as in the former type, in psychological and physical dependence. This was called by Jellinek 'delta' alcoholism.

The signs of developing dependence or addiction are as follows. The individual becomes preoccupied with his drinking, with the next drink, and begins to take alcohol earlier in the day. He begins to drink surreptitiously, and before social occasions. He drinks to relieve himself of tension and of the effects of abstinence, to be able to cope with his work and to face others. His efficiency at his job deteriorates and social problems accumulate. He often realizes that he is losing grip and has feelings of guilt. He may alternate between remorse and blaming others; become morbidly jealous and distrustful or frankly paranoid in his attitudes. Very significantly, he may begin to experience 'blackouts', which are not losses of consciousness but periods for which he has an amnesia.

When such signs of dependence have become apparent, there should be no further delay in attempting to arrest the process by initiating treatment. Otherwise, steady deterioration is likely with the development, sooner or later, of an alcoholic psychosis.

ALCOHOLIC PSYCHOSES

Symptoms of alcoholism may complicate many psychoses, *e.g.* manic-depressive psychosis, schizophrenia, syphilitic general paralysis. Alcoholism may be a symptom of an anxiety state; or much more commonly, a feature of a temperamentally unstable or psychopathic personality. It may be a complication of subnormality (mental defect). There are, however, various types of disturbance which are more or less peculiar to it.

The three main clinical types of alcoholic psychosis are delirium tremens, Korsakoff's psychosis and chronic alcoholism. Even this is not a sharply demarcated group of syndromes: Korsakoff's psychosis may have other causes, and alcoholic dementia, developing usually in the fifties or sixties, may be complicated by the onset of cerebral arteriosclerosis and senile changes. Dipsomania, a state of acute intoxication occurring at intervals, the intervening periods being free of any alcoholic indulgence, is probably usually symptomatic of recurring attacks of manic-depressive psychosis.

An alcoholic hallucinosis, an alcoholic paranoia and an alcoholic epilepsy have also been described. It is doubtful if alcoholic hallucinosis is a clinical entity —when transient, it may be an epileptic phenomenon, and when persistent a symptom of schizophrenia. Alcoholic paranoia is probably a misnomer, alcoholism being in these cases a symptom, not a cause, of an underlying schizophrenic or paranoid predisposition. It is well recognized that epileptic seizures occur commonly in the course of chronic alcoholism, but there is no reason why they should be placed in a separate group as alcoholic epilepsy. *Mania à potu* has been delineated as a state of pathological intoxication, consisting in extreme excitement, sometimes with homicidal attacks, and resulting from the ingestion of comparatively small amounts of alcohol by a susceptible individual.

Delirium Tremens

The condition is rare before 30 years of age. It usually arises after a prolonged debauch, when the individual has not only been persistently intoxicated but also been neglecting his food and vitamin intake: but it may follow withdrawal of alcohol, as an 'abstinence' delirium. Abstinence is probably the main factor in the delirium into which the alcoholic may unexpectedly pass after admission to a general hospital as a result of intercurrent disease or injury. Inquiry into some cases of 'abstinence' delirium will show, however, that the patient had left off drinking some days previously because of feelings of nausea; this suggests that an alcoholic illness was already developing, and that the distaste that led to abstinence was a premonitory symptom.

The chief prodromal symptoms are great restlessness, sleeplessness and fear— the patient starting at the least sound—and profuse perspiration. If he does sleep he has vivid nightmares, and wakes up repeatedly in terror. Unless one can induce sleep at this stage, it rapidly passes into a typical delirium, during which hallucinations, visual, haptic and auditory, make their appearance. The visual hallucinations are the most common. Illusions are prominent and can be easily suggested, *e.g.* spots on the counterpane which the patient mistakes for animals and attempts to catch. Given a blank piece of paper and asked to 'read' it, he may proceed to do so. Commonly visual hallucinations are of snakes and rats. Haptic hallucinations (probably based on paraesthesiae, and therefore more correctly called illusions) are usually of animals crawling over the skin. Sometimes the delirium is occupational in character—the busman drives his vehicle, and a station-master's wife constantly sees trains approaching, and crawls all over the bed to get away from them. In response to the hallucinations there may be impulsive conduct, the patient seeking to flee from his supposed persecutors, or attacking them, with the result that he may make suicidal or homicidal attempts. At the height of the delirium the patient is more or less completely disoriented, and the affect is nearly always one of great fear—of being taken away to be punished, for example, or of meeting some dreadful fate. Rarely the affective state is one of amusement or mild indifference to the hallucinations, or even euphoria. The talk may become incoherent and shows distractibility, usually in response to the hallucinatory experiences. The delirious patient is very suggestible, and can be readily made to confabulate. Kraepelin and Aschaffenburg pointed out that external stimuli play an important rôle in the character of the delirious content, and that the tendency to rhyme and to form sound associations is well marked. Misidentification of persons is striking, total strangers being recognized as intimate friends. Retention of immediate impressions is almost non-existent; the patient's attention can be obtained momentarily, but it is impossible to hold it.

Physically there is a generalized tremor, coarse in type, and affecting chiefly the fingers, facial muscles and tongue. The temperature is usually slightly raised, the pulse is quick and the patient perspires freely. The tongue is coated, the breath foul, there may be sordes on the lips and the patient has no appetite. Mild transitory albuminuria occurs in about 50 per cent. of cases. Epileptic fits may occur. The pupils are often widely dilated, and may be sluggish in their reaction. The tendon reflexes are in some cases diminished or absent.

Course and Prognosis. The usual duration is from three to six days. Improvement and recovery occur when sleep has been obtained. In uncomplicated cases death is rare (3 or 4 per cent.) but may occur from heart failure or pneumonia.

Morbid Anatomy. Besides the changes belonging to chronic alcoholism, punctiform haemorrhages in the brain substance and degeneration of nerve cells have been described.

Korsakoff's Psychosis

Probably the commonest cause is a deficiency of B-group vitamins. Clinically the psychosis is seen most often to develop in the course of chronic alcoholism, usually following an attack of delirium tremens. It is often associated with a polyneuritis, but not necessarily so.

The retention defect, and confabulation compensatory for it, is shown, for example, by a patient who assures the physician morning after morning that he has just returned from London that day; or by another who peruses the same book again and again. The retention defect can be clearly brought out by giving such patients short stories to read. Memory for remote events is usually good. Orientation for time is more completely affected than orientation for place or person. Korsakoff patients commonly are aware that they are in hospital, and they usually recognize doctors and nurses, although not by their names. They suffer from both visual and auditory hallucinations. There is a mixture of euphoria and irritability—they are affable at one time, and at another queruiously demand their release. Usually their conversation is clear and intelligent, and they are extraordinarily plausible in their confabulations. Insight is lacking, and after recovery, although they recognize they have been ill, it is extremely difficult to persuade them that their condition has been due to alcohol.

Physically, the signs are those usually of alcoholic polyneuritis, with diminution or abolition of the tendon reflexes, tenderness over the nerve trunks and, in pronounced cases, wrist- and foot-drop. Any of the peripheral nerves may be affected. Ocular palsies may occur, and nystagmus is very common. There is marked tremor of the outstretched fingers.

Course. These cases may run a prolonged course. Some begin to show improvement during the first six weeks. The neuritis may disappear entirely, and usually the physical health improves to a greater degree than the mental. The memory sometimes does not recover; and there may be some residual emotional deterioration evidenced by an easy suggestibility, emotional facility and lack of efficiency.

Morbid Anatomy. There are the usual polyneuritic changes in the peripheral nerves. In the brain, the lesions are bilateral and symmetrical. The mammillary bodies are nearly always involved, but usually not alone: lesions occur also in other hypothalamic nuclei, the thalamus and the fornix. All neural elements may be involved. The mammillary bodies are often shrunken, and show some loss of neurones with gliosis.

Chronic Alcoholism

By the chronic alcoholic we mean to designate the habitual drinker in whom there develops insidiously a change in intellect and character. He is often able to carry on his ordinary work sufficiently well to make a fair appearance to the casual observer; but he never reaches a high pitch of energy or efficiency, and his history is one of gradual deterioration, moral and intellectual. To his companions he is usually pleasant, sociable and sympathetic, entering boisterously into his alcoholic enjoyments, and shedding a ready tear in commiseration of others' misfortunes. At home, on the other hand, he is irritable and careless of his family's welfare. Sometimes the chronic alcoholic goes so far as to sell his home and furniture, thrash his children and assault his wife. It is at this more advanced stage that sexual crimes and indecent assaults are especially frequent.

The affect is often a very shallow and labile one, and is closely related to the disorders of conduct just described. The alcoholic is very frequently jealous of his wife. There is usually also a generalized persecuted attitude—the patient is never to blame, he is always the worst-used man in the world, constantly bewailing his fate and saying that every man's hand is against him. He is very untruthful, and is always making promises to reform which he never fulfils. He is cunning, evading arrangements made for his guardianship and twisting facts to suit his own ends. 'His heart is soft, and his head is full of deceit.' The memory tends to be faulty, but orientation is for a long time unimpaired. There is little or no insight.

Some alcoholics become depressed and attempt or commit suicide. It has been recognized from time immemorial that the drunkard drowns his sorrows. 'He dares not enter on a serious thought, or if he do so, it is such melancholy that it sends him to be drunk again', says Earl of the drunkard in his *Microcosmography*: and another seventeenth century writer, 'If you would know the reason why their Heaven is the Tavern . . . it is mostly that they may drive away time and Melancholy.' This association between depression and alcoholism is evident not only in the periodic drinking of the dipsomaniac, associated as it is usually with the cyclical return of depressive attacks, and in the dejection of the hangover; it lies frequently behind the alcoholic's mask of joviality. Alcoholism and suicide seem often to have similar or identical psychopathological bases. 'Alcoholism may be a fractional suicide, prepare the way for suicide, or provide a substitute' (Batchelor, 1954).

The risk of suicide in chronic alcoholics is in fact considerable. Kessel and Grossman (1961), following up two series of chronic alcoholics in London found that 8 per cent. and 7 per cent. respectively of the males killed themselves within a few years of their discharge as in-patients. This was 75 to 85 times the expected figures of suicide for males of their ages. Robins and his colleagues (1959) reviewed all the suicides which had occurred in one year in the city of St. Louis, Missouri. The great majority fell into two diagnostic groups: depressive psychoses 45 per cent., and chronic alcoholism 23 per cent. The danger of suicide was found to be greatest in the later stages of chronic alcoholism: but not all the cases were far advanced and 29 per cent. were under the age of 40. Robins and his colleagues emphasize that suicide is usually a premeditated act of which the alcoholic gives ample warning. Of the alcoholic suicides which they investigated, 77 per cent. had communicated their suicidal ideas to other people, 61 per cent. had specifically stated that they intended to kill themselves.

Course of the Illness. The course, if death does not result from suicide or physical disease, is slowly but progressively downhill. Permanent arrest of a well-established chronic alcoholic deterioration must be very rare outside of institutions. The moral and intellectual deterioration is gross in the terminal state.

The following is a typical example of the clinical picture:

CASE No. 34

R. P., a married man 50 years of age. He had always been of unusual temperament, having a difficulty in mixing with other people, so that even his own relatives did not visit him. He was always restless, never being able to enjoy a holiday because he wanted to get back to work. He owned a wine and spirit business, and had at one time a dozen retail shops of his own. Five years before his admission to hospital his disposition began to change. He commenced to grumble about everything at home, became irritable at trifles, swore volubly at his wife and children—a thing he had never done before. For some indefinite time he had been drinking secretly. Three years after this he fell into the hands of the police while drunk, and lost some of his licences in consequence. His ordinary daily programme at that time consisted in going out after breakfast, and returning drunk at midday, sleeping in the afternoon, going out again and returning drunk once more. He showed no care whatever for his family. His son, who was delicate, had sometimes to carry him home. While drunk he exposed himself to his family including his daughter. During their convalescence from influenza he turned his children out of the house. He would send his wife on errands and refuse to readmit her till she had obtained what he happened to want—usually more alcohol. He took no interest in anything, neglected his business and threatened suicide but made no real attempt at it. In hospital he was antagonistic and resentful, saying that he was unjustly detained, refusing food at times, doing his best to find fault with the ward arrangements. Occasionally, however, he was affable, making caustic jokes. He boasted of his athletic prowess (he was a puny unpleasant-looking little man). He showed no shame at his conduct, denied most of it and lied readily, often contradicting himself. A slight memory defect was revealed by the more difficult tests. He was persistently uncooperative and lacking in insight.

Morbid Anatomy. In the cerebrum there is nerve cell loss and astrocytosis: both the cortex and the basal ganglia, periaqueductal grey matter and corpora mammillaria are usually damaged.

The Physical Effects of Chronic Alcoholism. Apart from the effects on the peripheral and central nervous systems which have already been described, and the tremors, paraesthesiae and impotence which are commonly reported, chronic alcoholism and its often associated vitamin deficiencies have very damaging effects on other parts of the body. The following complications are well known— chronic gastritis, hepatic cirrhosis, hypoglycaemia, myopathy and cardiomyopathy. Nolan (1965), investigating 900 consecutive admissions to a general hospital in New Haven, Connecticut, found that in 13·8 per cent. of these alcoholism was a significant problem, contributing in three-quarters of the cases to the illness which had necessitated admission to hospital. Pneumonia, liver disease, gastritis, pancreatitis and neurological disorders were the commonest diagnoses. The mortality rate among the alcoholic males was 23 per cent., compared with 14 per cent. for the whole sample. No doubt many alcoholics are treated in general hospital wards for physical illnesses secondary to their alcoholism, without their alcoholism being recognized. Also, apart from suicide, alcoholics are more prone to deaths by violence and accidents than the general population: an important cause of this being of course that they drive cars when drunk.

Psychopathology. It is doubtful whether general statements can be made about the psychopathology of chronic alcoholism. It is commonly stated that chronic alcoholics as a class are essentially homosexual, either consciously or unconsciously. Alcoholic habits lead to a close association with others of the same sex, and at the same time offer a refuge from other situations which, on account of the homosexuality, are unsatisfactory. Marital jealously is explained on this basis, as a projection of the married alcoholic's unfaithful tendencies. It may equally be the psychological result of the impotence induced by the physical effects of alcohol. Support for the homosexual theory can be obtained from a study of the content of the delirium usually only with the aid of extravagant symbolic interpretation. The content of the auditory and haptic hallucinations in cases in which these are prominent, may lend some support, since it is sometimes clearly homosexual; genital paraesthesiae, for example, being interpreted by the patient as evidence of actual homosexual assault. But these cases are in a very small minority, and it has already been remarked that in them usually the alcoholism and the hallucinosis alike are symptoms, and do not stand in the relationship of cause and effect. In general, homosexuality is only one of many possible factors.

The psychological understanding of a chronic alcoholic is an individual affair, and each case must be tackled as a special problem on its merits. The factors which have helped to precipitate a chronic alcoholic habit and to sustain it do not differ in any kind from those which may produce other morbid mental reactions; and sufficient weight should be given to the influence of habit, to the influence of nagging friends and relatives in accentuating it and to the manner in which the alcoholism becomes a part of the ego-ideal, so that to keep on drinkng becomes a point of honour.

PREVENTION OF ALCOHOLISM

If it was possible to detect the alcoholism-prone individual before he became alcoholic, primary prevention might be feasible. But prediction is very difficult, so various are the personalities which may become involved, so complex are the predisposing and precipitating situations. Studying the possibly hereditary basis of alcoholism Amark (1951) in Sweden and Manfred Bleuler (1955) in Switzerland have shown that the incidence of alcoholism in the brothers and fathers of alcoholics is high, and that the relatives of alcoholics show a high frequency of psychopathy. Probably alcoholism as such is not inherited, but the individual who is brought up in contact with alcoholism is certainly at increased risk. Early influences in the home may be of major importance in warping personality development towards vulnerability. In elucidating these influences, longitudinal studies aimed at prediction are of the first importance.

A detailed prospective study has been carried out by the sociologists W. and J. McCord (1960). They traced to adulthood 225 urban, mainly lower-class American boys from Massachusetts, discovered that a minority of them became alcoholic, and found that certain traits 'set the alcoholics apart as a distinctive human type before the onset of their disorder'. Their most important finding was that in childhood the pre-alcoholic underwent a series of experiences in the home productive of what they call 'dependency conflict' and 'intensified dependency longings'. They report that the alcoholic is typically reared in a home riven by parental conflict and antagonism, where the mother, erratic and unstable, alternating between indulgence and rejection, induces in the son heightened dependency desires. The father typically has failed either to exemplify or enforce the male rôle. The child, emotionally confused, responds by aggression and asserting self-confidence: but behind this facade he 'continues to feel anxious, to suffer conflict and to be desirous of dependent relationships'. It is these repressed traits of dependency, inferiority and passivity that the McCords see as typical of the personality of the adult alcoholic. They have presented their data carefully and critically, and they make it clear that one cannot generalize from their study to all alcoholics. They point the way to further research.

Education undoubtedly has an important contribution to make to the reduction of alcoholism. Men and women must be educated to make good use of their increased means and leisure. And with regard to alcoholism in particular, the public must be educated to understand it as an illness, to recognize its early signs and symptoms, and to know where and what medical help can be obtained. Here the mass media of communication, local health authorities and Citizens' Advice Bureaux should be the main channels of information. Great or quick changes are not of course to be expected; men and women will not easily forego their pleasures or be warned in good time; and there is a rebellious element in most of us which wants and needs at times to revolt against the rules of society, its respectability and boredom, and to go to excess, to deny reality and to be impulsive and egotistical.

TREATMENT OF ALCOHOLISM

There is no specific cure for alcoholism, but in the earlier stages of the illness, before dementia has developed, much can be effected and the patient given a new start.

Delirium Tremens

The chief aims of treatment are to alleviate the excitement, to maintain the patient's strength, to promote the natural functions and to procure sleep.

A patient of this sort does much better with strangers and, particularly if he is to be treated satisfactorily in his own house, nurses experienced in the management of delirious patients should be provided. Alternatively and preferably, treatment may be carried out in a nursing home or in the psychiatric ward of a general hospital. Recovery is so likely to occur quickly that there is no justification for compulsory admission to a mental hospital. Compulsory powers should not be taken to detain a patient while he is under the influence of liquor. The delirious patient should be nursed in bed, constantly supervised, and reassured by changes and disturbances in his environment being reduced to the minimum.

There is general agreement that the amount of alcohol given must be carefully controlled, but disagreement about the advisability of an abrupt cessation of alcohol intake. In our view, it is illogical to continue to give a drug which, if it has not produced, has at least materially contributed to, a dangerous state of intoxication; and we have not seen ill effects from stopping the intake of alcohol as soon as the patient comes under treatment. Where the provision for nursing care is less adequate and the patient less confused, some compromise may have to be made until the patient comes under the control of sedatives: and some physicians make an exception of the elderly patient, giving small quantities of alcohol in the belief that a sudden cessation of the drug might precipitate collapse.

Sedatives to produce sleep are essential, and a large dose of whatever drug is chosen should be given initially. Cyclobarbitone, B.P., 400 mg. with a further 200 mg. in four hours if necessary, or pentobarbitone sodium, B.P. (*Nembutal*), 200 mg. with a further 200 mg., we have found satisfactory hypnotics in many cases. Paraldehyde, 10 ml. by mouth, is very useful; but in some cases it seems to increase the excitement, and there is also some risk of the alcoholic becoming addicted to it. Chlorpromazine (*Largactil*) either intramuscularly or by mouth is also effective in controlling excitement and restlessness, both by day and at night.

When there is much gastritis, it is well to begin by washing out the stomach. Food should be liquid or semi-solid, and in small quantities to obviate vomiting: it must have as high a caloric value as possible, with plenty of carbohydrates. Tube-feeding may occasionally be necessary. Since the patient suffering from delirium tremens sweats profusely, he becomes dehydrated. This lost fluid must be replaced and an intake of around 3 litres per day should be ensured. If the sweating is very profuse and particularly if it is accompanied by vomiting, an important deficiency of sodium chloride as well as of fluid results. This can be corrected by preparing beverages with 0·2 per cent. saline instead of plain water, or by giving sodium chloride, 2 G. in capsules 4-hourly. Constipation is usual, and should be treated.

It is probable that vitamin deficiency plays a significant rôle in the genesis of delirium tremens, and it is customary therefore to prescribe B group vitamins. At least 200 mg. thiamine should be given intramuscularly, and 500 mg. nicotinic acid parenterally or by mouth daily. In cases where the intake by mouth is unsatisfactory the vitamins should always be given parenterally.

Cardiac failure and pneumonia are two of the chief causes of death. Where there is evidence of commencing congestive failure, fluid intake must be carefully controlled and the patient should be rapidly digitalized. Any chest infection or infection elsewhere should be promptly treated with an antibiotic.

Korsakoff's Psychosis

Many patients suffering from this disorder have to be treated in mental hospitals, as the condition is prolonged, and difficult to manage at home. While acute symptoms of peripheral neuritis are present, the patient should be nursed in bed: massage, passive and active movements are advisable after the acute symptoms have subsided. The general physical state is usually considerably enfeebled and should be restored by giving a full diet, with Marmite. The prescription of additional specific B group vitamins is of doubtful value.

Chronic Alcoholism

The kind of treatment to be adopted, and the hope entertained for it, depends partly on the type of chronic alcoholic with whom one is dealing and partly on the stage at which he comes (or is brought) for treatment. Careful investigation from a physical and a psychiatric view-point is an essential preliminary. When alcoholism is found to be a symptom of some disease, mental or physical, such as a recurrent manic-depressive psychosis, the treatment is that of the underlying disease. When the alcoholic habit itself is in the forefront, the chief line of attack is a thorough investigation of the factors of the patient's life and personality. Usually the first step that should be insisted on is that the patient should place himself in a nursing home or in a hospital where he can be adequately supervised; but an arbitrarily fixed period of treatment, whether of one or three months, should not be prescribed. In-patient treatment, of course, is often what the patient refuses to accept, but with the exercise of tact and patience it is frequently possible in the early stages to get the patient's co-operation. In our experience, the psychological view-point is usually a revelation to the patient, and the physician who places it before him is at once at an advantage; for the patient has been taught by his friends that his condition is simply one of moral turpitude, and nearly always he has personally come to regard his alcoholism as mysterious and inevitable. The patient's goodwill having been gradually obtained in this way, it is usually possible to show him the factors, psychological and circumstantial, which have contributed to his illness; and to show him how they can be more satisfactorily dealt with. Abstinence should be the goal of treatment, and the patient has usually to be taught that it is not unmanly to be abstinent: fewer than 10 per cent. of alcoholics can return to 'normal' drinking (Davies, 1962). An avoidance of unnecessary opportunity for drinking is extremely important; for example, it is unwise to send him back to work as a bar-tender or an exciseman. The cultivation of hobbies and social recreation of a healthy kind, to replace the discarded alcoholism, is also important. When the immediate treatment is finished, and the patient returns to work, he should be encouraged to keep in touch with his medical adviser for a year or two. Follow-up is essential. With the more advanced chronic alcoholic, in whom definite and irreversible moral and intellectual deterioration has set in, the case is different; compulsory admission to a mental hospital is always necessary to prevent further deterioration. This in ordinary cases is very difficult, on account of the patient's plausibility and good superficial appearance.

Aversion therapy for alcoholism has a long history. In 1793 Benjamin Rush reported that he had tempted a Negro man 'who was habitually fond of ardent spirits', to drink some rum into which he had put a few grains of tartar emetic. This 'sickened and puked him to such degree that . . . he could not bear the sight, nor smell of spirits, for two years afterwards'. In this experiment by Rush the conditioned stimulus was the alcohol and the unconditioned stimulus which followed it, the emetic. Both emetine and apomorphine have frequently been used in the aversion therapy of alcoholism: the former drug is now usually preferred. Emetine hydrochloride is given by intramuscular injection to produce nausea and vomiting, and is usually combined with pilocarpine hydrochloride which produces intense sweating and with ephedrine sulphate which is supposed to provide cardiac support. As nausea develops, the patient is plied with alcoholic drinks, and encouraged to smell, taste and consume them despite vomiting. The procedure lasts about twenty minutes and is repeated on about five successive days.

Careful preliminary physical examination is necessary to judge the patient's fitness to undergo the rigours of the treatment. It is uncertain how strong a true conditioned aversion is created: probably suggestion has been an important factor in the results obtained. Details of the treatment are given by Lemere and Voegtlin (1942). Lemere and Voegtlin (1950), summarizing their results in over 4000 cases, reported '51 per cent. abstinent for 2 years or longer, 38 per cent. for 5 years or longer, and 23 per cent. for 10 years or longer after their first treatment'. This was not, however, an unselected sample of alcoholics.

Those who have specialized in aversion therapy state that many types of alcoholic are unsuitable for it. But this approach should be investigated further, for several reasons. Advances in psychological research should assist the refinement of conditioning procedures in practice: and stimuli other than the production of nausea, faradic shocks for example, may be used to produce aversion. Also, this method of treatment can be systematically and accurately described, applied and taught: and its results also critically evaluated. And very importantly, it may be applicable to the less intelligent patient, who may be inaccessible to dynamic psychotherapy. It has of course the obvious disadvantages that it cannot affect the deeper determinants of alcoholism and that insight is in no way fostered.

Tetraethylthiuram disulphide (*Antabuse*, disulfiram, I.N.N.) was introduced by Hald and Jacobsen (1948). This drug interferes with the normal oxidation of alcohol, and in doing so causes an increased liberation of acetaldehyde in the body. It is acetaldehyde poisoning that produces the symptoms upon whose discouraging effects the treatment depends. If an individual who is taking disulfiram takes alcohol within 24 hours of the last dose of disulfiram, he develops usually within 20 minutes a highly unpleasant reaction, which is characterized by intense flushing of the face, neck and upper chest, tachycardia and palpitations, headache, dyspnoea, nausea and vomiting, and in some cases cardiovascular collapse. In rare cases, acute right-sided heart failure has led to death. Other toxic symptoms have been reported, notably dizziness, diplopia, skin rashes, peripheral neuritis and delirium. At first it was thought that the disulfiram-alcohol reaction was the cause of these, but more recently it has been recognized that the drug itself, although relatively non-toxic, may produce side-effects. These are usually mild and include drowsiness, fatigue, headache and reduced libido. Disulfiram has, however, been very widely used now with relatively few serious ill effects and very few fatal ones, and though one must know the possible toxic effects of the drug their importance should not be overstressed. The individual who is given the drug must of course be in reasonably satisfactory physical condition: cardiac decompensation is an absolute bar to this treatment, as is any serious damage to the liver or kidneys. Disulfiram should never be given while the individual has alcohol in his body, and must never be given surreptitiously. A suitable commencing dose is 0·5 G. on the first day, then 1 G. daily for three days, followed by 0·25 to 0·5 G. daily as a maintenance dose which may have to be continued for many months. On the fourth or fifth day after the commencement of the treatment a test dose of 15–30 ml. of alcohol may be given, to indicate to both doctor and patient whether or not the treatment is effective: some workers now omit this as unnecessary and to some degree dangerous, and if it is carried out the patient should be in bed and equipment for his resuscitation must be at hand in case his reaction should be severe. Disulfiram is helpful in the treatment of intelligent and co-operative alcoholics, who come for treatment early in their illness and who feel that they require some extra safeguard in the early months of their abstinence, particularly on social occasions. The success of the method depends obviously on the degree of the patient's co-operation.

Unless and until a correctable metabolic disorder is found to be the cause of certain cases of alcoholism, the use of drugs in this field is likely to be a superficial method of treatment and of limited value. An approach through correction of the alcoholic's defective personal attitudes and relationships holds out more promise, and it is this which the group movement known as ALCOHOLICS ANONYMOUS (A.A.) has some success in effecting. Launched in 1934 in the U.S.A., A.A. now has groups in more than thirty countries and in most of the cities and large towns in Britain. In voluntary association the members meet regularly, discuss experiences and problems and the tenets of their movement, and work actively in the reclamation of other alcoholics. Against the 'defiant individuality and grandiosity' of many alcoholics, they set a belief that the alcoholic can overcome his trouble only by surrender and by accepting some power greater than himself. The essential element is therefore a form of religious conversion (Tiebout, 1944). Certain criticisms may be made of the movement; that it depends rather too much on emotion, and that its conversions are not always followed by a real maturing of the personality. But, in a field where the psychiatrist so often fails, its success may be outstanding.

Results of Treatment

Hill and Blane (1967) in a critical review of 49 studies, published in the United States and Canada between 1952 and 1963, which reported the results of psychotherapy with alcoholics, found that nearly all of them were descriptive and in method unsatisfactory: and they repeated the conclusion reached by Voegtlin and Lemere 25 years earlier, 'we are unable to form any conclusive opinion as to the value of psychotherapeutic methods in the treatment of alcoholism'. This commentary emphasizes strongly the need for far more critical investigation of our current techniques of therapy and their efficacy.

Davies, Shepherd and Myers (1956) reported the 2-year follow-up of 50 alcohol addicts (22 per cent. women) treated at the Maudsley Hospital. This was not treatment in a specialized alcoholism unit, but it was a selected group of addicts: the uncooperative and poorly motivated were excluded. Therapy was broadly based: there was individual but not group psychotherapy, and the management included the aid afforded by disulfiram and Alcoholics Anonymous. Thirty-six per cent. of these patients were found to be abstinent for the greater part of the time, and a further 42 per cent. were improved. These results compared favourably with those of many other previous follow-up studies. A good result from treatment was found to be correlated, as one would expect, with the quality and degree of stability of the previous personality, work record and social relationships; and with the strength of the motivation for treatment.

Glatt (1961), employing group therapy, A.A. and disulfiram (or citrated calcium carbimide, a similarly sensitizing drug) and emphasizing the after-care, found at a 2–3 year follow-up of 94 alcoholics who had been treated in a mental hospital that a third had 'recovered' and a third had improved. One-third of this sample were reported to be psychopaths and the prognosis for the psychopathic addict was found to be poor.

Two studies of the results of the treatment of alcohol addicts have been made recently in Scotland. In Edinburgh, Walton, Ritson and Kennedy (1966) reported the results in 83 patients (24 per cent. female), treated predominantly initially as in-patients of a specialized clinic with daily group psychotherapy, supplemented with individual psychotherapy and disulfiram; and given prolonged after-care either in weekly group-therapy sessions or in individual out-patient attendances. In this patient sample Social Classes I and II were over-represented, Classes III and V under-represented. The results after 6 and after 18 months were similar—the latter will be quoted: 51 per cent. were abstinent or abstinent with lapses, 17 per cent. were improved but drinking, 26 per cent. were not improved, 4 per cent. had died. It was noted that the number requiring out-patient support increased with the length of the follow-up period.

In Dundee, Freeman and Hopwood (1968) investigated the response to treatment of 100 unselected alcohol addicts (15 per cent. female) admitted to a mental hospital. In this sample too the main element in the treatment was psychotherapy, group and individual, patients were encouraged to participate in Alcoholics Anonymous, and follow-up was by social worker and out-patient clinic attendances. Social Classes IV and V were over-represented in the sample. Follow-up ranged from 3 to 18 months: 23 per cent. were abstinent or abstinent with some lapses, 73 per cent. were unchanged, 4 per cent. had died.

In these two investigations, the patient samples were different. In the Dundee study the sample was unselected, individuals from the lower two social classes predominated, 70 per cent. were unemployed, three-quarters were drinking cheap wines and sherry, the majority had police records, one-third were seriously physically ill, and co-operation in treatment was poor. This was the hard core of the alcoholism problem in an industrial city.

Both these patient groups received special and highly skilled psychotherapy: but only between a quarter and a half of the addicts were helped to make a good readjustment. In so far as the problem is a psychiatric one, we are therefore still far from reaching a satisfactory solution of the treatment problems of this addiction. Most cases come for treatment only after 10–20 years. Non-cooperation is only too common, relapse is often to be expected: but it is important for the doctor to remain optimistic, persistent and within reason tolerant. Help, at one time refused, may be accepted later. Far too often the patient is rejected after one or two failures to keep an appointment at a clinic or surgery, when a home visit by a social worker might re-establish contact and co-operation. Alcoholism should in principle be treated like any other relapsing disease; and it offers many opportunities for putting into practice the concepts of family psychiatry and family case-work.

REFERENCES

Amark, C. (1951) *Acta psychiat. scand.*, Suppl. 70.
Batchelor, I. R. C. (1954) *J. ment. Sci.*, **100**, 451.
Bewley, T. (1965) *Brit. med. J.*, **2**, 1284.
Bleuler, M. A. (1955) in *Etiology of Chronic Alcoholism*, ed. Diethelm, O., Springfield, Ill.
Brandon, S., and Smith, D. (1962) *J. Coll. gen. Practit.*, **5**, 603.
Clark, J. A. (1962) *J. ment. Sci.*, **108**, 411.
Cohen, S., and Ditman, K. S. (1963) *Arch. gen. Psychiat.*, **8**, 475.
Connell, P. H. (1958) *Amphetamine Psychosis*, London.
Davies, D. L. (1962) *Quart. J. Stud. Alcohol.*, **26**, 423.
Davies, D. L., Shepherd, M., and Myers, E. (1956) *Quart. J. Stud. Alcohol.*, **17**, 485.
Dole, V. P., Nyswander, M. E., and Kreek, M. J. (1966) *Arch. intern. Med.*, **118**, 304.
Drug Addiction: The First Report of the Interdepartmental Committee (1961), H.M.S.O.
Drug Addiction: The Second Report of the Interdepartmental Committee (1965), H.M.S.O.
Duvall, H. L., Locke, B. Z., and Brill, L. (1963) *Publ. Hlth Rep.* (*Wash.*), **78**, 185.
Freeman, T., and Hopwood, S. (1968) Personal Communication.
Glatt, M. M. (1961) *Acta psychiat. scand.*, **37**, 143.
Glatt, M. M. (1967) *Lancet*, ii, 1203.
Hald, J., and Jacobsen, E. (1948) *Lancet*, ii, 1001.
Hill, M. J., and Blane, H. T. (1967) *Quart. J. Stud. Alcohol.*, **28**, 76.
Jellinek, E. M. (1960) *The Disease Concept of Alcoholism*, New Haven.
Kessel, N., and Grossman, G. (1961) *Brit. med. J.*, **2**, 1671.
Kiloh, L. G., and Brandon, S. (1962) *Brit. med. J.*, **2**, 40.
Lemere, F., and Voegtlin, W. L. (1942) *Quart. J. Stud. Alcohol.*, **3**, 322.
Lemere, F., and Voegtlin, W. L. (1950) *Quart. J. Stud. Alcohol.*, **11**, 199.
Lewin, L. (1931) *Phantastica: Narcotic and Stimulating Drugs*, London.
McCord, W., and McCord, J. (1960) *Origins of Alcoholism*, London.
Nolan, J. P. (1965) *Amer. J. med. Sci.*, **249**, 135.
Retterstol, N., and Sund, A. (1965) *Acta psychiat. scand.*, **40**, Suppl., No. 179.
Robins, E., Murphy, G. E., Wilkinson, R. H., Gassner, S., and Kayes, J. (1959) *Amer. J. publ. Hlth*, **49**, 888.
Scott, P. D., and Willcox, D. R. C. (1965) *Brit. J. Psychiat.*, **111**, 865.
Tiebout, H. M. (1944) *Amer. J. Psychiat.*, **100**, 468.
Walton, H. J., Ritson, E. B., and Kennedy, R. I. (1966) *Brit. med. J.*, **2**, 1171.
W.H.O. Expert Committee on Addiction-producing drugs: Fifteenth Report (1964), *Wld Hlth Org. Techn. Rep. Ser.*, 273.

17

EPILEPSY

The term epilepsy has for long been used to designate a heterogeneous group of symptoms, of which the most prominent feature is the repeated occurrence of convulsive attacks. But it is now generally recognized that it is more accurate to speak of 'the epilepsies', or to consider epilepsy a symptom rather than a disease. The essential feature is not the convulsive seizure or the disturbance of consciousness, but the episodic sudden disturbance of function in the central nervous system. Hughlings Jackson from his clinical observations pointed to the nature of the neuronal process as an active discharge at some level of the central nervous system anywhere from the cortex to the diencephalon, with accompanying phenomena, such as automatisms following a major fit, conceived as release phenomena. That a neuronal discharge is the primary condition is supported by Penfield and Erickson's observation that an attack which seems to the patient and observer to be identical with the customary seizure can be provoked by electrical stimulation of the appropriate part of the brain. Both the physical and the mental phenomena can be conceived in the same way. For example, one of Penfield and Erickson's novel discoveries was that a visual memory of some old experience, which may have appeared also in a nightmare, as well as forming part of a seizure, could be elicited by electrical stimulation of a temporal lobe.

Epilepsy is an important condition in the psychiatric field for a number of reasons. Abnormal mental symptoms and disturbed behaviour may either accompany, or follow, epileptic seizures; and may be so severe or prolonged in some cases that the label epileptic psychosis is merited. Major and minor seizures must often also be distinguished from other disturbances of consciousness or motility due more purely to psychogenic causes. While in interparoxysmal periods the sufferer from epilepsy may show certain anomalies of personality or temperament which, apart from his overt fits, impair his social adaptation.

Recent research has increased the number of cases of epilepsy in which a causal lesion can be found by detailed physical examinations which include X-rays, air-encephalography, angiography and electroencephalographic recordings. However, the hope expressed by some that soon there will be no need for such a category as 'idiopathic' epilepsy, in which no physical basis for the attacks can be discovered, is probably illusory; and we are coming to appreciate better the importance of hereditary factors, which though they may be called physical are unlikely soon to be dissected.

AETIOLOGY

The aetiology of epileptic seizures is certainly a multiple aetiology, and much remains unknown, particularly about the so-called idiopathic group. We shall set out the causal factors under three main heads—constitutional, predisposing and precipitating. These are not to be understood as distinct or mutually exclusive categories, but as a means only of ordering the data. In cases where the constitutional factors appear to be of greatest importance, or the aetiology is unknown, the epilepsy is usually described as idiopathic, or genetic (Lennox): when predisposing factors predominate, it is called symptomatic or acquired. The precipitating or eliciting factors are common to both groups.

Constitutional Factors

Among constitutional factors we may include the rôle of heredity, the influence of the endocrine system, and age.

There is convincing evidence that *genetic* factors are important in the production of epilepsy. The incidence of epilepsy is higher amongst the near relatives of epileptics than it is in the general population. Lennox (1951), reviewing near relatives of 4231 epileptics, found that 3·2 per cent. had a history of one or more seizures; whereas the incidence of epilepsy amongst the young adult population of the U.S.A. (those of draft age) was about 0·5 per cent. Lennox found a positive family history of epilepsy in 1·8 per cent. of cases of symptomatic epilepsy, and in 3·6 per cent. of cases of idiopathic epilepsy. He also reported that the incidence of epilepsy amongst relatives declined progressively with increasing age of the patient at the time of the first seizure: thus in cases of idiopathic epilepsy which began in infancy, 6·4 per cent. of relatives were found to be affected, while amongst those cases with onset at age 30 years or over, the family incidence of epilepsy fell to 1·3 per cent.

Twin studies have been employed to elucidate the relative importance of hereditary and environmental causal factors. Lennox and Jolly (1954) studied 173 twin pairs subject to seizures. Concordance of epilepsy among 77 monozygotic pairs was 70·1 per cent., among 96 dizygotic pairs 12·5 per cent. If cases with acquired brain damage were excluded, the concordance among 51 monozygotic pairs rose to 88·2 per cent. Concordance for epilepsy among monozygotic pairs of around 60–70 per cent. has also been reported by Rosanoff (1934) from the U.S.A., and by Conrad (1935) from Germany. Figures for concordance among dizygotic pairs have a much wider scatter, from 3 to 24 per cent. Lennox and Jolly not only found a high concordance of epilepsy in monozygotic twins, both absolutely and in comparison with dizygotic twins, but reported that this high concordance extended to the type of seizure and particularly to the three per second wave-and-spike pattern of the E.E.G. The rôle of heredity appears to decrease progressively in the three groups, *petit mal, grand mal* and psychomotor seizures.

Though only a small percentage of the near relatives of epileptics have epileptic seizures, a considerable percentage have abnormal E.E.Gs. Lennox, Gibbs and Gibbs (1940) reported abnormal E.E.Gs. in 54 per cent. of the parents, sibs and children of epileptics, whereas only 6 per cent. of a control group unrelated to epileptics exhibited similar abnormalities. It has therefore been suggested that what is inherited is a cerebral dysrhythmia, a tendency or predisposition to abnormal cerebral discharge, which may show itself as fits or as anomalies of temperament, or may not manifest itself clinically at all.

2 E

The mode of inheritance of epilepsy has been much debated, and the action of single genes, recessive and dominant, as well as that of polygenes, has been postulated by various workers. Such discrepancies in the opinions expressed are not unexpected, since epilepsy is not a nosological entity and research has been much hampered by the great difficulty experienced in obtaining case samples for investigation which have not been in some way biased in their selection.

One may say in summary that hereditary factors appear to play a part in the genesis of both idiopathic and symptomatic epilepsy, but more particularly in the former, and especially in idiopathic cases with *petit mal* seizures; and that the mode of inheritance is not yet known.

The incidence of epilepsy is approximately equal in the two sexes. In women, there is an important relationship of fits with menstruation, seizures tending to occur in some cases shortly before or at the menstrual periods. Pregnancy may have no influence on the frequency of seizures: on the other hand, they may temporarily disappear during a pregnancy, or become more frequent.

Idiopathic epilepsy usually becomes manifest before adult life is reached. It is said that three-quarters of the cases have their onset in the first two decades, often about puberty. A history of infantile convulsions is obtained in about 20 per cent. of epileptics, compared with 4 per cent. in normal controls.

Predisposing Factors

Factors which predispose to epilepsy are those which cause directly tissue damage in the brain, or indirectly interfere with its normal functions. They are very numerous.

Amongst local cerebral causes may be mentioned tumour, arteriosclerosis, meningitis, cerebrovascular syphilis and general paralysis, cysticercosis and head injury. The latter may be inflicted at birth, by trauma or asphyxia; or in adult life, when epilepsy is most often a complication of penetrating injuries. The incidence of epilepsy after closed-head injury is 5 per cent. (Jennett, 1961), but may rise even to 45 per cent. if the dura has been penetrated (Ascroft, 1941). Epilepsy may also occur in cases of subnormality (*e.g.* in cerebral palsy, tuberous sclerosis); and in some cases of pre-senile dementia (*e.g.* Alzheimer's disease).

General causes include infections, intoxications and other illnesses leading to profound metabolic or circulatory changes. In infancy, epilepsy may be a symptom of an acute infection with high fever, or of tetany, for example; in adult life, of uraemia, eclampsia, delirium tremens, hypertensive encephalopathy, heart block.

Precipitating Factors

These may be primarily emotional or physical. Frustration may produce a fit in a susceptible individual; so may other strong emotions. Specific sensory stimuli are effective in certain rare cases—*e.g.* music, or visual flicker. Metabolic changes are especially important: hydration, hyperventilation leading to alkalosis, and hypoglycaemia are common precipitants. So also is sleep; and, less commonly general anaesthesia. Ketosis, on the contrary, tends to inhibit seizures.

Relationships with other Syndromes

Some writers have claimed an association between epilepsy and migraine, which others have denied. Migraine has been said to occur in the heredity of 60 per cent. of epileptics, compared with 17 per cent. in normals. A clearer relationship may be seen between epilepsy and aggressive psychopathic states, particularly the so-called 'epileptoid' group of the latter, whose intermittent outbursts of violent conduct often closely resemble clinically psychomotor seizures of temporal lobe origin: and in both conditions E.E.G. abnormalities may be found in recordings from the temporal lobes.

PHYSIOLOGY OF THE SEIZURES

The brain has a continuous spontaneous electrical activity and it is these changes in electrical potential which are recorded by the E.E.G. When sensory stimulation is reduced to a minimum the cortex shows a resting rhythm while the individual is conscious. The origin of the resting activity is not known: it has been suggested its pace-maker may be situated in the central grey matter, perhaps in the reticular system of the brain stem. This resting rhythm is markedly altered by incoming stimuli, and if the individual increases his mental alertness by concentration and attention or emotional excitement, or if he diminishes it by falling asleep.

In epileptic seizures the neurones discharge paroxysmally, and there is excessive electrical activity, which tends to be hypersynchronous. This epileptic discharge may be initiated either in the grey matter of the cerebral cortex or in the subcortical ganglia. The reasons for this abnormal activity are not clearly known. It is recognized that the metabolism of the neurones is very easily disturbed. They are particularly sensitive to changes in cerebral blood flow causing ischaemia or hypoxia, and this may be a common factor in causing epileptic discharges. The rôle of diminished H-ion concentration is uncertain.

Penfield and Jasper (1954) state that experiments indicate the following functional characteristics of epileptogenic nerve tissue:

1. Increased tendency to spontaneous activity and to self-sustained paroxysmal discharge.
2. Decreased synaptic resistance.
3. Increased and more prolonged discharge in response to afferent nerve impulses.
4. Hypersynchrony—greater number of cells firing together, though excessive discharge may also be relatively asynchronous.
5. More intense, higher frequency, discharge of impulses from each cell.
6. Spread of paroxysmal activity from a focus to adjacent tissue with progressive recruitment of larger masses of cells in synchronous discharge.
7. Projection and distant spread of paroxysmal activity over two-way neuronal conducting pathways between the cortex and subcortical structures, and over association pathways between distant cortical areas, and between the two hemispheres.

8. Non-synaptic spread of excitation by electrical field effects between adjacent areas of grey matter due to heightened facilitation and high-voltage discharge.

PATHOLOGY

In assessing the relevance of post-mortem findings in cases of epilepsy, it is necessary to remember that the changes found may be either the cause or the result of the epileptic process, whatever it is. There are no constant pathological findings.

Alzheimer discovered pathological changes in 'idiopathic' cases, notably sclerotic changes in the cornu ammonis (hippocampus) and superficial gliosis of the hemispheres. Many other workers have reported Ammon's horn sclerosis, laminar atrophy, particularly of the third cortical layer, and disseminated cerebellar sclerosis. These changes, which may be slight or severe, have usually been ascribed to anoxia.

More recent research has been focused on lesions of the temporal lobes. Penfield and Baldwin (1952) found that in case after case of temporal lobe epilepsy the cortex was tough in the anterior and deep portion of the first temporal convolution, extending into and growing more marked in the uncus and hippocampal gyrus. This condition was named 'incisural sclerosis', and Penfield and Jasper (1954) gave the following explanation of it: 'It seems likely that, at the time of the passage of the infant head through the birth canal, the mesial portion of one or both temporal lobes may be squeezed downward through the incisura of the tentorium. Thus, the margin of the lobe, including uncus and hippocampal gyrus, would be subjected to greater ischaemia than other portions of the brain. It also seems likely that the artery of supply, the choroidal artery, and even, at times, the posterior cerebral artery, might be compressed against the incisural margin.' Penfield and his colleagues believed that incisural sclerosis is the commonest cause of temporal lobe epilepsy.

This theory of transtentorial herniation of the brain, with consequent impairment of the arterial supply of the medial temporal areas, cannot account for damage of a similar kind found elsewhere in the brain: and Margerison and Corsellis (1966) have reported that hypoxic damage elsewhere is common. Investigating cases of temporal lobe epilepsy, they found hypoxic damage, often bilateral, in 80 per cent. The lesions were not confined to the temporal lobe: in 65 per cent. the hippocampal part of the temporal lobe was involved, in 45 per cent. the cerebellum and in 25 per cent. the thalamus. It is probable therefore, that hypoxic damage, which may be either a cause or an effect of epileptic seizures, in the majority of cases develops after and is secondary to seizures which have some other aetiology.

In 'symptomatic' cases various lesions are found, tumours, porencephalic cysts, angiomas and the scars of penetrating head injuries and infections.

SYMPTOMS

These can, for convenience, be divided into paroxysmal and interparoxysmal.

Paroxysmal

The clinical features depend on the site of origin and the spread of the cerebral disturbance.

Some epileptics become aware hours or even days before a seizure occurs, that one is impending; they may feel that they are 'working up' to it; they are usually depressed, restless and irritable, have sensations of tension or fullness in the head, or experience muscular twitchings. This is a true warning of a seizure. Gowers, from the examination of more than 2000 cases of epilepsy, concluded that 57 per cent. of the cases had some kind of warning. The 'aura', sensory, motor, visceral or psychic, the common immediate precursor of major seizures, is not a true warning but is in fact the first few seconds of the seizure itself. In some cases the epileptic discharge consists of a sensory aura alone (sensory fit). There are numerous varieties of aura, depending on the locus of discharge. Probably the most common is a sinking feeling in the epigastrium. Vertigo is also common. There may be headache, diffuse or one-sided, or feelings of heat or cold, or numbness or tingling of a limb. The special senses may be involved, the aura being a hallucination, *e.g.* of taste or smell (in temporal lobe seizures). Visual phenomena (occipital lobe discharge) may be specks or lights in front of the eyes; or they may be elaborate hallucinations, which may be grotesque and reach always a certain stage of development at which the loss of consciousness occurs. Hallucinations of sound (temporal lobe discharge) are usually simple, such as humming, but may be elaborate, as music; they are most often associated with dizziness. Motor auras may be sudden muscular twitches or complicated movements, such as running. A psychic aura may take the form of sudden disturbance in the use of words, or of obsessive thoughts, with irritability. It is of much importance in every case where there is an aura, to obtain from the patient a clear description of it, since this may assist the discovery of a focal lesion.

Grand Mal. The classic major epileptic attack, *grand mal*, consists of four stages. 1. The patient, falling to the ground with sudden and complete loss of consciousness, may injure himself. As he falls, there may be a cry. This is followed immediately by 2. the stage of tonic spasm, involving the entire body-musculature. In this stage, which lasts usually from ten to thirty seconds, respiration is arrested by spasm of the muscles of expiration and the muscles closing the glottis, so that cyanosis occurs and is sometimes extreme. The individual lies rigid, arms flexed, legs extended. This is followed by 3. the clonic stage, which may last for as long as three to four minutes and in which there is clonic jerking of the muscles which have hitherto been in tonic spasm. The jerking of the face muscles may cause the tongue or lips to be bitten. Froth often appears at the lips. Urine and faeces may be passed involuntarily. 4. There follows the stage of coma, during which the subject remains in a condition resembling sleep for a varying period of time, usually not more than an hour or two. In some patients the stage of coma is replaced or followed by a stage of (post-ictal) automatism.

During the seizure the plantar responses are extensor, the corneal reflexes absent. At first the pupils are usually small; then they dilate widely, and remain rigid until the attack ceases. Babinski's sign may be present for some hours. Usually there is no recurrence of the fit for some time, but occasionally fits succeed one another without intermission: this status epilepticus, if not treated, may go on to exhaustion and death. Major fits may be nocturnal or diurnal only, or occur at any time in the twenty-four hours. When the fits are nocturnal, suspicion of their presence may be aroused by the fact that the patient awakes in the morning feeling unduly tired, or because he finds that he has wet the bed, or that the bed-sheets have been torn.

After a fit, and recovery from the coma, the patient is usually transiently confused, and complains of headache and fatigue. In this phase of only partial consciousness and some bewilderment, he may perform acts which are semi-automatic: he may, for example, undress, or wander off, and if opposed may respond with violence. The automatic acts performed under these circumstances lack motive and no attempt is made at concealment.

After a major fit the patient's mental condition is usually temporarily improved —he is less irritable, and may even be unusually affable and pleasant for a time, in comparison often with his behaviour before the paroxysm.

Petit Mal. The typical seizure ('true *petit mal*') consists in a momentary loss of consciousness with which are associated few or no convulsive phenomena. There is no aura, and the subject may or may not be aware of the attack. He turns pale, suddenly becomes silent or halts in what he is doing, may drop what he is holding, seems to stare blankly and may exhibit some slight twitching of his facial muscles. The attack is over in 5 to 30 seconds, and he resumes his previous activity as if no interruption had occurred. He may have other types of epileptic seizure.

Petit mal commonly starts in childhood or early adolescence, and rarely continues into adult life; though *grand mal* may develop later in these subjects. The fits may be very frequent, up to 100 or so in the day. *Petit mal* status may develop, the child remaining confused and inattentive even for hours.

The associated bilaterally synchronous spike-and-wave discharge in the E.E.G. is very characteristic. The site of the origin of the discharge is probably in the thalamic reticular system.

Psychomotor Seizures. Various other names have been given to this rather common group of seizures, in which psychological symptoms predominate— 'psychic epilepsy', 'psychic equivalents' or 'epileptic equivalents': but the term equivalent is particularly inappropriate, since the disturbance is indubitably an epileptic seizure. These psychomotor fits are episodic disturbances (not losses) of consciousness, usually without detectable convulsive phenomena, but commonly associated with automatic motor acts. The clouding of consciousness may last for seconds, minutes, hours or, exceptionally, days.

A typical but rare form of psychomotor seizure is the so-called 'uncinate' fit, in which the focus of the epileptic discharge is in a temporal lobe. This variety of epilepsy was first described by Hughlings Jackson in 1888. In 1898 he and Colman published further details of the case of a medical man who, after death, was found to have a small patch of softening in the left uncinate gyrus. This patient's seizures were in the nature of 'dreamy states', during which he had vivid *déjà vu* experiences and a slight feeling of dread; he would act for a minute or two in a semipurposive, confused way, and on occasion he smacked his tongue and moved his lower jaw; and afterwards he would behave apparently normally for a period for which he subsequently had amnesia.

The automatic behaviour which occurs in these clouded states is co-ordinated and may appear to the observer to be purposeful. The patient may become immobile, dazed and retarded, or be impelled to violent action: he may wander away in a fugue. Illusions and vivid hallucinations, auditory or visual, may occur. The affective change may be extreme, the patient experiencing intense fear, depression, rage or ecstasy. Disturbances of the experience of self are also characteristic—feelings of unreality or of familiarity (*déjà vu*). Further symptoms include disorders of time perception, so-called panoramic memory (in which the patient feels that he remembers forgotten stretches of his life) and forced thinking or 'crowding thoughts'. If the mental clouding is prolonged, as it may be, it is often described as a twilight state.

The individual who has psychomotor seizures commonly also has *grand mal* seizures.

Temporal lobe epilepsy, so called, is a serviceable clinical concept: but neither clinically nor pathologically is the syndrome clear cut. There is a close relationship, but not identity, between psychomotor seizures and temporal lobe discharges. Psychomotor seizures are not due exclusively to disturbances of function within the temporal lobes, but may arise from foci outside this lobe and the limbic system. The diagnosis of temporal lobe epilepsy, often too loosely made and in too sharp differentiation from other types of epilepsy, should be reserved for cases in which there are epileptic seizures of psychomotor type and an E.E.G. focus or demonstrable lesion in one or other or both temporal lobes.

Sustained behavioural automatism suggests the probability that the seizures originate in the temporal lobe; and the description of a typical aura of sensations in the epigastrium, substernal region or throat, or of vertigo increases the probability. In the E.E.G., in the large majority of cases, there is a spike or sharp wave focus in the anterior or middle temporal region, unilaterally or bilaterally.

The incidence of temporal lobe epilepsy among epileptics admitted to hospital primarily on account of their epilepsy and becoming long-stay patients, is high. It ranges from 34 to 78 per cent., depending upon the diagnostic criteria employed (Margerison and Liddell, 1961): the higher figure being derived from diagnoses made on clinical grounds alone, the lower from cases where there was concordance between clinical and E.E.G. findings. Also, temporal lobe epilepsy is closely associated with epileptic disorders of personality and epileptic psychoses. Gibbs and his colleagues (1948) estimated that of those with temporal lobe lesions 50 per cent. develop a personality disorder and 25 per cent. an epileptic psychosis. In most cases of epileptic psychosis the locus of the seizures is in the temporal lobe.

Epileptic Emotions. Denis Williams (1956) has studied the emotions aroused by the epileptic process itself, in cases with focal abnormalities in the temporal lobe. Usually these ictal emotions are preceded or accompanied by abnormal sensations such as vertigo or by hallucinations or by both; and the patient's consciousness is usually clouded. The emotions themselves, simple rather than complex, are more often unpleasant than pleasant. They are vivid and un-related to the environment and the patient's current situation: arising thus autochthonously, they seem to the patient to be imposed upon him. In 100 epileptics who experienced such ictal emotions, Williams found that 61 reported anxiety, 21 depression, 9 a pleasant feeling and 9 an unpleasant one. Anger and suspicion may also occur.

Anxiety, the commonest of the ictal emotions and varying in intensity from apprehension to terror, occurs, according to Williams, only when the epileptic discharge involves the anterior half of a temporal lobe. In half of these cases the emotion is accompanied by visceral sensations or movements; and while experiencing it the patient may look afraid, call out or run to another for comfort. Ictal depression tends to last longer than fear: its causal lesions are not confined to any particular part of the lobe. Feelings of euphoria or elation, and the even less common feelings of distress or intense dislike, are most often associated with posterior temporal lesions.

Emotional changes closely related to his seizures may of course be experienced by the epileptic at other times, pre- or post-ictally. As he becomes increasingly tense and 'works up' to a fit, the epileptic may feel depressed; and depression is common in the period of malaise after a *grand mal* seizure.

Epileptic Psychoses. The clinical features of these psychotic reactions have been described in detail by Slater, Beard and Glithero (1963). They tend to chronicity, and are characterized particularly by recurrent confusional episodes and paranoid delusions. Beard, correlating clinical and E.E.G. data in a series of 69 patients, found evidence of temporal lobe epilepsy in 80 per cent. The most common lesion was an atrophic process.

The previous personality may or may not be epileptic in type, but there is always a history of fits over many years. The mean duration of the epilepsy at the time of onset of the psychosis was 14 years in Slater's series, and the mean age of onset 30. The onset may be insidious: the course of the illness is usually fluctuating, often stormy. In addition to disturbances of consciousness, which may take the form of prolonged twilight states, delusions, hallucinations and affective disturbances are prominent: in other words the symptomatology would resemble that seen in psychomotor seizures, if these were greatly prolonged. The delusions are usually paranoid: they may also be religious with a mystical trend. The hallucinations, which may arise in apparently clear consciousness as well as when the patient is clouded, are most often auditory and visual: olfactory and gustatory hallucinations are also recorded. Interest and activity are usually reduced, and there may be odd, repetitive or impulsive behaviour. There is a wide range of affective disturbances, ranging from depression to ecstasy. The ability to co-operate with others and to respond emotionally is better preserved than in cases of schizophrenia of similar duration.

Many of these cases end in an epileptic dementia. In a follow-up of 64 cases at a mean interval of 8 years after the onset of psychotic symptoms, Glithero and Slater found that 29 showed an organic dementia. Paranoid or 'schizophrenia-like' symptoms constituted the main continuing disability in a further 34.

Slater has emphasized the symptomatic similarities between epileptic and schizophrenic psychoses, has described the epileptic psychoses as schizophrenic in form and has discussed them under the heading 'symptomatic schizophrenias'. His description of the correspondences between these two conditions is illuminating: but to term the epileptic psychoses symptomatic schizophrenias is to go beyond the clinical facts and may hinder the differentiation between epilepsy and schizophrenia upon which effective treatment depends. It is only in cross-section that the two conditions may seem to resemble one another: but here too there are differences, the epileptic showing recurrent periods of confusion and relative lucidity and a retention of affect and rapport which are quite unlike the features of chronic schizophrenic states. When one studies the life-history, together with the E.E.G. and other physical findings, the dissimilarities are obvious: the E.E.G. foci and the pathological changes in the temporal lobes and elsewhere in cases of epileptic psychosis, have no parallels in schizophrenia. The epileptic psychoses show no links with schizophrenia in the family history and in the type of previous personality involved, the age of their onset is on the average later, there is no preponderance of males, and the end state is often a dementia which is clearly organic in type. Furthermore, the type of schizophrenic reaction which it is held that epileptic psychoses most resemble, namely paranoid schizophrenia, is the variety whose classification with the hebephrenic and catatonic reactions is already doubtful [see p. 304].

Case No. 35

A case which is of considerable medico-legal interest is that of a young man, 26 years old, who was convicted on a charge of murdering his mother, and also his nephew and niece, aged respectively 12 years and 2 years and 11 months, by cutting their throats with a razor. This crime was committed on the day on which he had been discharged from a general hospital where he had been a patient for seven months, during which time he had had a foot amputated. His history showed that ever since infancy he had a deformed leg, for which he had had considerable treatment. When a child he had been in a Home for crippled children, and while there he had caused trouble by turning younger children out of their cots, by reversing the pictures on the walls and so on. When about 16 years old he was a patient in a colony for mental defectives, but ran away. On one occasion, in his adolescence, he had attempted to commit suicide by throwing himself into the canal, from which he was rescued with great difficulty. During his adult life he had frequently been in trouble, and had served terms of imprisonment for assault and for theft. On one occasion he set the house on fire.

He stated that ever since the age of 14 years he had suffered from 'turns' of a peculiar nature, during which he felt strange. These 'turns' were accompanied by headache, and occasionally vomiting. After he lay down, the attack would gradually wear away, and he would feel better. In these attacks he was not completely conscious. During the seven months he had been in hospital previous to the commitment of his crime, he had two such attacks. In one of these the sister in charge of the ward stated that he had behaved in a strange way, tearing his bedclothes, and strewing cigarettes all round in great disorder. On another occasion, when on leave from the hospital, he was overcome by a feeling of dread, hurried home, asked his mother if he looked peculiar and, after having vomited, came to himself and realized that he had had a 'peculiar turn'. After the crime with which he was charged had been committed, he gave himself up to the police. He knew that something dreadful had happened, but he denied knowledge of the actual details. During the time he was in prison he behaved in a perfectly normal, rational way. His general intelligence was well up to the level of one of his social class.

His history indicated clearly that he was an unstable, irritable, impulsive man, who had been subject to peculiar episodes which he himself described as 'turns'. His physical deformity had no doubt helped to accentuate his character traits. It seemed reasonable to suggest, since the crime was committed without motive, and there was no attempt at concealment, that his condition was one of psychomotor epilepsy. The plea of epilepsy was not sustained in bar of trial, but his sentence was modified to one of penal servitude. In the course of a few months he made an unprovoked assault on a warder, and was certified as insane.

Other Types of Seizure. Most seizures can be categorized as belonging to one or other of the three main types whose characteristics have been outlined above. This classification cannot, however, be claimed as entirely satisfactory, and it is certainly not comprehensive though it is useful enough in practice. There are various forms of motor and sensory seizures which we have not described.

Hypsarrhythmia (see Jeavons and Bower, 1961) is not an aetiological entity. Infantile spasms begin usually in the first year of life, major and minor seizures are numerous and mental development is arrested. These children often become hyperkinetic. The fits usually stop after a few years but the mental defect remains.

Diencephalic autonomic seizures are rare and complicated fits, in which the manifestations are autonomic. They are characterized by vasodilatation, lachrymation, sweating, salivation, pupillary alteration, slowing of pulse rate and respiration, and hiccoughing. They may be elicited by electrical stimulation or tumour formation in the diencephalon.

Interparoxysmal

Everything that has been described in association with the fits may appear in an individual who shows no detectable abnormality between the attacks. In those cases where a more persistent abnormality is present at the outset or develops later, the clinical features are usually described under the headings of the 'epileptic personality' and 'epileptic dementia'.

The Epileptic Personality. It has been held by some that there is a characteristic epileptic make-up in which the disorder called epilepsy develops. Thus certain traits have been described as constituting the 'epileptic character' or 'epileptic personality': rigidity and egocentricity; moodiness and irritability, with a proneness to explosive reactions of rage and resentment; pedantry, circumstantiality, argumentativeness and religiosity. The egocentricity is said to lead to shallow professions of interest in others, and to a selfish kind of religious devotion, so that 'they are considerate without being kind, and are religious without zeal, and . . . they will work for praise but not for love' (MacCurdy, 1916). Clearly these particular traits are not peculiar to epileptics: and while it is true that in a proportion of persons developing idiopathic epilepsy an unusual degree of egocentricity and sensitiveness can be demonstrated, it is certainly not usually possible to demonstrate this type of make-up.

Since these traits were most commonly observed in individuals who had been epileptic for some years, the epileptic character was for long looked upon as secondary to 'the disease', *i.e.* to the fits: and indeed it could in many ways be considered the result of comprehensible responses to the frustration, insecurity and social ostracism which so often has been the lot of the epileptic. It is now recognized that the epileptic character can sometimes be shown to have existed before the fits began; and evidence is accumulating that in many of these instances the personality traits have been the first evidence, the earliest symptoms of temporal lobe epilepsy. It is particularly in temporal lobe epilepsy (though not confined to it) that transitory disturbances, especially of mood, are frequent in the interparoxysmal period. The patient becomes excessively irritable, and picks quarrels with great facility. Depression occasionally reaches such a pitch that suicide is attempted. Paranoid trends are common.

Epileptic Deterioration and Dementia. This is a state of very gradual mental decline and enfeeblement found most often in those cases where the epilepsy has begun in childhood or at an early age and has been very severe, leading to institutional care becoming necessary. It is therefore encountered only in a small minority of epileptics, and particularly amongst those with frequent fits whose condition has not responded to treatment..

The affected individual becomes more self-centred as he loses interest in his environment. In the earlier stages this slump in interest may be interrupted by special efforts at arousing the epileptic's attention, but spontaneously he pays less and less regard to what is going on around him. Hence his mental content becomes very limited, and his memory poor both for recent and for remote events —for recent ones because passing events are not registered, and for remote events ultimately for the same reason, and also because, in the absence of interest, associative thinking is reduced to a minimum. The defect of remote memory is not so great as at first appears, since special effort at recollection often improves it remarkably. Some patients have insight for their memory defect, but others fabricate to fill the gaps. Related to the effort of recall in memory, there develops sooner or later in many cases a functional aphasia—words are brought up and used with increasing difficulty, while in extreme instances there is mutism. In contradistinction to organic aphasias, reading, writing and spelling may be surprisingly well done. Composition is rambling and pedantic. Speech and thinking become slower, and perseveration is sometimes present in excessive degree. Speech may lose its normal inflections—the so-called 'plateau speech' resulting.

Pari passu with this intellectual deterioration, which is secondary to the affective defect—the loss of interest—there occur other changes also directly referable to the increased egocentricity. The patient becomes more susceptible to flattery; he indulges more and more in boasting, the childishness of which is in direct proportion to the degree to which insight and judgement in general have deteriorated; his vanity increases, and yet his care of his personal appearance decreases; he becomes less amenable to discipline; and he is increasingly inactive and lazy. His interest becomes exclusively centred on his body (hypochondriasis).

In the final stage of epileptic dementia the patient leads a vegetative existence, reminiscent of the helpless infant, but displaying much less spontaneity. He has to be fed, clothed and cleaned, is unable to control his sphincters, does not utter a word and has a vacuous expression.

The cause of the cerebral damage which underlies this terminal state is not certainly known, but recurrent anoxia due to frequent fits or status epilepticus is probably an important factor. Deterioration of interests and habits may also be produced by prolonged, excessive medication with drugs. The milder early symptoms of deterioration may be organically determined, but they are not necessarily so. The epileptic may lose contact with his environment because it fails to stimulate or has rejected him: without a job or confined to an institution he may become oppressed by a settled hopelessness about his future, and his pessimistic inertia may then be misinterpreted as an organic deterioration in his behaviour due to his disease.

ELECTROENCEPHALOGRAPHY

The interpretation of E.E.G. tracings requires specialized training and knowledge, and no attempt will be made here to explore the complexities of the subject. Reference may be made to the texts by Hill and Parr (1963) and by Kiloh and Osselton (1966). There are two main aspects of the examination: 1. assessment of the types of wave form, and their frequency, occurring during seizures and in the interparoxysmal period; and 2. their localization in the brain.

Gibbs, Gibbs and Lennox (1938) described the electrical discharges in the three main clinical types of epilepsy as follows: ' Grand mal is characterized by extreme acceleration of the electrical activity of the cortex, psychomotor attacks by extreme slowing of this activity, and petit mal by the alternation of fast and slow activity. With these disorders of frequency, there are associated abnormally high amplitudes.' This early classification, made in terms of wave form and frequency, was soon found inadequate: it failed to take account of the importance of the place of origin in the brain of the epileptic discharge. Jasper and Kershman (1949) then suggested a classification based on the importance of location: 1. focal cortical discharges; 2. projected subcortical discharges (centrencephalic epilepsy); and 3. diffuse dysrhythmias. Each of these groups can be further subdivided into subgroups based upon differences of wave form and frequency.

The E.E.G. is usually only of confirmatory value in the diagnosis of epilepsy, and rarely does the E.E.G. record alone provide a reliable diagnosis. About 10 per cent. of the normal population show anomalies in their E.E.G. tracings, mild irregularities of unknown origin and debatable significance: while about 20 per cent. of epileptics are said to have normal tracings. This latter figure can be reduced somewhat by supplementing recordings from the scalp with special electrode placements, pharyngeal or sphenoidal; and if methods of eliciting seizures are employed (*e.g.* voluntary overbreathing, barbiturate sleep, photic stimulation): but a remainder still show normal tracings, and a normal E.E.G. does not, therefore, rule out the diagnosis of epilepsy.

An unequivocally epileptic type of record will clinch a clinical diagnosis of epilepsy, and assist the differential diagnosis in cases of supposedly hysterical attacks and other episodic disturbances of consciousness. Some so-called faints and some fugues are revealed as epileptic by the E.E.G.

E.E.G. records are of particular value in assisting the localization of acquired cerebral lesions in cases of symptomatic epilepsy.

COURSE AND PROGNOSIS

The prognosis depends considerably on the stage at which the patient seeks treatment, and of course on the efficacy of the treatment he receives. If treatment is begun early there is considerable hope that the fits may at least be made very infrequent, if they are not stopped altogether. Fits may disappear for a long period of time, and sometimes cease entirely.

The great majority of epileptics never display mental symptoms; and amongst those who do, many never require institutional care and remain at their occupations throughout their lives. Mental deterioration is more common and more severe in symptomatic epilepsy following brain injuries than in idiopathic epilepsy, and is more commonly associated with psychomotor than with other types of seizure. It is only a very small minority of epileptics who have to be admitted to mental hospitals, and the average course in these cases is steadily downhill.

DIAGNOSIS

One must determine first if the patient's symptoms are due to epilepsy: and, if they are, the cause of the epilepsy must then be sought.

Epilepsy is characterized by a set of phenomena which in most cases differentiate it clearly from hysteria—the onset in many cases in early childhood, the tonic and clonic succession in the convulsion, the unconsciousness and the other symptoms of the *grand mal* attacks (often nocturnal, the sphincter incontinence, extensor plantar reflexes) are characteristic. Other typical features are the occurrence of the attack when the patient is alone, or in a position of danger (*e.g.* on a bicycle or driving a car), actual self-injury in the fall, the performance of some stereotyped action, drowsiness, headache and prolonged sleep afterwards. Hysterical fits are diurnal, there is always an audience, and if attempts are made to restrain the patient he responds with wild struggling: self-injury is unusual. Other hysterical symptoms may resemble epilepsy—hysterical amnesias and disturbances of consciousness, including fugues, stupors and so-called twilight states: but a search for personal emotional factors will reveal an adequate cause for the condition, which is then seen as purposive from the point of view of the patient's personality. The epileptic attack is not often seen by the physician and he has to rely much on the history obtained from the patient and from his relatives, on witnesses' descriptions of the attacks, on an assessment of the individual's make-up and recent circumstances, and on the results of both mental and physical examinations (including the E.E.G.). The typical hysterical personality differs considerably from that of the epileptic, but the latter is often not demonstrable. A history of mental stress immediately preceding the first attack is not necessarily in favour of hysteria, since epileptic seizures can also be precipitated by obvious psychological causes. In any instances where there is doubt, prolonged observation is desirable. When the description of the attack is not typical of major epilepsy or of *petit mal*, it is a good working rule to accept nothing as idiopathic epilepsy until a very thorough search has been made for psychological and for physical causes.

Where automatic acts follow an obvious seizure (are post-ictal, in Penfield's terminology) as a release phenomenon, the diagnosis is much easier than in the instances where the automatic acts are the seizure (ictal automatisms). When an epileptic clouded state is prolonged, the condition may be described as an epileptic psychosis, and may be mistaken for schizophrenia. The diagnosis may be for some time in doubt, and then revealed by the re-establishment of clear consciousness, without evidence of residual schizophrenic disorder. The occurrence of major seizures may also clarify the situation.

There is a close clinical resemblance between certain cases of psychomotor epilepsy and certain aggressive psychopathic states. In both conditions there occur explosions of disturbed behaviour, which may come suddenly or be prefaced by a period of increasing tension and irritability; which may be precipitated by emotional frustration, alcoholism or fatigue; and which may be accompanied by some clouding of consciousness and followed by a rapid recovery of equilibrium. The differential diagnosis often depends on the E.E.G. findings.

Some cases of migraine resemble epilepsy in having a well-marked sensory aura with a slow and distinctive 'march', *e.g.* from the finger up the arm; but the aura is much more prolonged than in epilepsy, and there is usually no consequent loss of consciousness.

When the diagnosis is in doubt, it is sometimes possible to induce a seizure for the purpose of immediate inspection, by voluntary over-breathing. In two or three minutes afterwards in some cases, the epileptic attack occurs, instead of the tetany which would occur in the non-epileptic person in the same circumstances. Other ways of inducing epileptic activity have been mentioned in the discussion of electroencephalography.

When a diagnosis of epilepsy has been established, the cause of the epilepsy must be sought: at least, it must be determined whether or not it is symptomatic. A careful general physical examination is as necessary in every case as a meticulous clinical examination of the nervous system. Where there is any doubt the blood Wassermann reaction, lumbar puncture, skull X-rays and E.E.G. must be carried out. Epilepsy occurring for the first time after the age of 30 years should be assumed to be symptomatic, until this has been disproved. Epilepsy in adult life is commonly associated with brain tumour and cerebral arterio-sclerosis, and there are many other causes, both general and local (cerebral). Advances in surgery make the early diagnosis of focal brain lesions a major responsibility for the clinician.

TREATMENT

The epileptic should not have his life made dull and miserable by unnecessary restrictions and a social stigma which belongs to a superstitious past. The great majority of epileptics are capable of living normal lives with the exception of driving motor-cars and the like, swimming in deep water, or indulging in any other occupation or recreation in which a fit would definitely endanger the lives of others or of themselves. The mortality of epileptics from accidents arising during fits is, in fact, exceedingly small. Wherever possible the epileptic should be gainfully employed: but excessive fatigue should be avoided since it tends to precipitate fits. The more stable, the less frustrating, the individual's emotional environment, the better.

Attention to the individual's general physical health and hygiene are impor-tant. Physical disease, major and minor, should, of course, be promptly treated: and Lennox and Cobb have drawn attention to the need for eliminating any nasal obstruction. Meals should be regular. Bowels should be kept open. Alcohol should not be taken in any circumstances.

Since we know little as yet about the hereditary transmission of epilepsy, it is difficult to give satisfactory advice about marriage. The hereditary factor is of considerably more significance in idiopathic than in symptomatic cases. From the eugenic point of view it is evident that one epileptic should not marry another; and it is probable that an epileptic should not marry an individual who has an abnormal E.E.G. The presence or absence of a positive family history is also important on both sides. Each case must be considered on its merits, and present evidence indicates that one is not justified in most cases in being too rigorous in prohibition of marriage and child-bearing.

The chief indications for the treatment of an epileptic in an institution (colony or mental hospital) are pronounced irritability, or frequent and prolonged psy-chomotor seizures, tending to violent assaults; and general mental deterioration. The settled régime of an institution is in itself helpful—the sources of irritation are lessened, meals, etc., are regular, and the patient is among people who are accustomed to dealing with epileptics. It is of particular importance that the epileptic in a clouded state should not be treated in an arbitrary, excited or aggressive way: he will only respond with greater violence to such clumsy handling. Further, in an institution suitable outlets can easily be provided for the development of the epileptic's interests, and this retards the progress of deterioration as well as lessening the frequency of the fits. Occupation should be a main part of the treatment from the beginning.

The drugs which have been tried are legion, and year by year more, and more effective, anticonvulsants are becoming available. Whatever drug is used the doses should be arranged so that a maximum saturation with the drug will be produced during the hours at which the fits most regularly occur; for example, if the fits occur during the night, the patient should have the largest dose in the evening. The patient should not be rendered retarded, stupid or drowsy with drugs. Often anticonvulsant treatment has to be continued for life: it should certainly be maintained until the individual has been without fits for at least three years. Sudden cessation of anticonvulsant treatment must always be avoided, since status epilepticus may be precipitated and the individual's life thus be put in danger.

Phenobarbitone (*Luminal*) has replaced bromide as the sheet anchor of treatment in the average case, and especially when the seizures are *grand mal* in type. The commencing dose should be 30 mg. twice a day. If control of the fits is not obtained with 120 to 180 mg. phenobarbitone daily, a combination of a smaller dose of phenobarbitone with one of the hydantoins should be tried.

The most commonly used of the hydantoins is sodium diphenylhydantoin (phenytoin sodium, B.P., *Epanutin*) 200 mg. daily, may be given initially and the dose raised gradually as required to 600 mg. daily or until intolerance develops. Toxic symptoms are fairly frequent in the skin, gastro-intestinal tract and nervous system: namely, skin rashes, anorexia, indigestion, nystagmus, ataxia, and (if dosage is prolonged, in some cases) hypertrophic gingivitis and hirsutism.

Primidone (*Mysoline*) is also a valuable anticonvulsant: 0·5 to 1·5 G. may be given daily in tablet form. Toxic effects, commonly drowsiness and ataxia, are usually mild and transient. This drug is of particular value in cases with *grand mal* attacks.

Petit mal seizures usually respond to trimethyloxazolidine dione (*Tridione*). An initial dose of 0·3 G. thrice daily may be raised to 2 G. daily. Toxic effects include rashes, nausea, visual glare and agranulocytosis. The latter, most serious complication is better guarded against by warning the patient to cease taking the drug immediately if he develops fever, malaise and a sore throat, than by carrying out routine blood counts at monthly intervals. Ethosuximide is also an effective, and toxic, drug.

When satisfactory control has not been gained by the use of the above drugs, alone or in various combinations, and in cases where there have been toxic or allergic reactions to these drugs, bromides may be tried. Potassium bromide is given in a commencing dose of 1 G. twice daily and the dose increased up to 6 G. in twenty-four hours. Acneiform rashes and mental dulling, which may develop into a delirious reaction if the blood bromide passes a figure around 150 mg. per 100 ml., limit the usefulness of this drug, which is probably most effective in cases with *grand mal*.

Psychomotor seizures are the most difficult to control with drugs. During a seizure the patient should if possible be coaxed to go to bed: and if he is violent, thiopentone, B.P., or amylobarbitone sodium, B.P.C., may be given intravenously. A prolonged clouded or twilight state may be interrupted by inducing a major fit electrically (E.C.T.). Phenobarbitone often makes patients suffering from temporal lobe epilepsy worse. Phenytoin, primidone or sulthiame (*Ospolot*) are likely to be more effective. Sulthiame can be a useful drug in cases of intractable epilepsy, but it may have serious toxic effects, which include drowsiness, paraesthesiae of face and limbs, disturbances of respiration and speech, and mental confusion.

Status epilepticus always endangers life and must be treated urgently. The series of convulsions can usually be interrupted successfully by giving 0·2 G. sodium phenobarbitone, B.P., intramuscularly, or 5 to 10 ml. sterile paraldehyde intramuscularly, or 0·5 G. amylobarbitone sodium intravenously. Further injections of sodium phenobarbitone, B.P., or paraldehyde may be required if there is relapse.

To all these drugs the individual response varies, and to a large extent the physician must proceed by trial and error until he finds the most suitable drug or combination of drugs. Apparently each of the major anticonvulsant drugs may cause folate deficiency [see p. 366]. Furthermore, it must always be remembered that drug treatment is symptomatic treatment only. In every case, if it is possible, one should seek to attack the cause rather than the symptom.

The appropriate treatment of cases of symptomatic epilepsy depends, of course, on the nature of the causal disease or lesion. The discovery and surgical treatment of focal brain lesions has of recent years assumed an increasing importance in this field. Following upon pioneering researches by Penfield and his colleagues in Montreal, anterior temporal lobectomy has become a standard treatment for temporal lobe epilepsy, where a macroscopic lesion or unilateral E.E.G. focus can be demonstrated. The results are most satisfactory when a structural lesion can be found, *e.g.* a vascular anomaly or tumour: but even in cases where the damage is hypoxic and presumably more widely spread, the operation may be successful, probably by breaking a vicious circle of epileptic activity. Seizures are usually reduced if not eliminated, and disturbed behaviour and intellectual performance may both be improved. The operation can be carried out only on one side, since bilateral temporal lobectomy profoundly impairs memory. In the usual operative procedure (Falconer and Serafetinides, 1963) the anterior part of the temporal lobe, together with the amygdala and hippocampus, is removed. The complications of this operation include a small upper quadrantic defect in the opposite visual field, transient dysphasia and diplopia, and rarely hemiparesis. When the ablation is in the dominant hemisphere, the subsequent defect of auditory learning may constitute a severe disability.

REFERENCES

Ascroft, P. B. (1941) *Brit. med. J.*, **1**, 739.
Conrad, K. (1935) *Z. ges. Neurol. Psychiat.*, **153**, 271.
Falconer, M. A., and Serafetinides, E. A. (1963) *J. Neurol. Neurosurg. Psychiat.*, **26**, 151.
Gibbs, E. L., Gibbs, F. A., and Fuster, B. (1948) *Arch. Neurol. Psychiat.*, **60**, 331.

Gibbs, F. A., Gibbs, E. L., and Lennox, W. G. (1938) *Arch. Neurol. Psychiat. (Chic.).* **39**, 298.

Hill, D., and Parr, G., ed. (1963) *Electro-encephalography,* 2nd ed., London.

Jasper, H. H., and Kershman, J. (1949) *Electroenceph. clin. Neurophysiol.,* Suppl. 2., 123.

Jeavons, P. M., and Bower, B. D. (1961) *Arch. Dis. Childh.,* **36,** 17.

Jennett, W. B. (1961) *Ann. roy. Coll. Surg. Engl.,* **29,** 370.

Kiloh, L. G., and Osselton, J. W. (1966) *Clinical Encephalography,* London.

Lennox, W. G., (1951) *J. Amer. med. Ass.,* **146,** 529.

Lennox, W. G., Gibbs, E. L., and Gibbs, F. A. (1940) *Arch. Neurol. Psychiat. (Chic.),* **44,** 1155.

Lennox, W. G., and Jolly, D. H. (1954) *Res. Publ. Ass. nerv. ment. Dis.,* **33,** 325.

MacCurdy, J. T. (1916) *Psychiat. Bull. N.Y. St. Hosp.,* **9,** 187.

Margerison, J. H., and Corsellis, J. A. N. (1966) *Brain,* **89,** 499.

Margerison, J. H., and Liddell, D. W. (1961) *J. ment. Sci.,* **107,** 909.

Mulder, D. W., Daly, B. and Bailey, A. A. (1954) *Arch. intern. Med.,* **93,** 481.

Penfield, W., and Baldwin, M. (1952) *Ann. Surg.,* **136,** 625.

Penfield, W., and Jasper, H. (1954) *Epilepsy and the Functional Anatomy of the Human Brain,* Boston.

Rosanoff, J. A., Handy, L. M., and Rosanoff, I. A. (1934) *Arch. Neurol. Psychiat. (Chic.),* **31,** 1165.

Slater, E., Beard, A. W., and Glithero, E. (1963) *Brit. J. Psychiat.,* **109,** 95.

Williams, D. (1956) *Brain,* **79,** 29.

18

PSYCHIATRIC EMERGENCIES

The psychiatric emergencies to which a doctor is most often summoned are: suicidal threats or attempts; acute schizophrenic or manic excitement; acute intoxication with alcohol or drugs; and acute anxiety or panic reactions. In cases of suicidal behaviour and panic usually only the patient is at risk. Where there is psychotic excitement or intoxication assaultive or destructive behaviour may be directed against inanimate objects, against the individual himself or against other people.

SUICIDAL THREATS AND ATTEMPTS

Suicidal threats, gestures or attempts are now the commonest kinds of psychiatric emergency.

A suicidal threat should never be dismissed or ignored in the belief that those who threaten suicide do not commit it. In fact many, both of those who attempt and of those who commit suicide, give more or less overt and even repeated warnings of their intention to do so. These warnings may be phrased as feelings of despair or failure, of having an incurable illness, of being a burden to others, of being sinful or unworthy or unloved and lonely. They are both calls for help and danger signals, to which the relatives and the family doctor should respond at once by safeguarding the individual until the circumstances of his distress have been fully explored and the relevant preventive action taken. In all situations of threatened or attempted suicide one's first duty is to preserve the patient's life.

When a suicidal attempt has been made, whether or not the injuries sustained appear to be slight, it is usually advisable to admit the patient forthwith to hospital: preferably to a general hospital which has a psychiatric unit. There the patient will receive the appropriate medical or surgical treatment, and the whole circumstances of his attempt, psychological, physical and social, can be reviewed. There too it is far easier to safeguard the patient against further self-injury, to ensure a calm and conflict-free atmosphere and to promote the sleep which is a sovereign healing agent after exposure to any emergency. Relatives must be interviewed, and a medical or psychiatric social worker's help may be needed in dealing with family relationships, financial and other social problems. A full assessment of a suicidal attempt may take a few days: it rarely need take longer, and the majority of these cases may then be discharged home reasonably safely within about ten days. Follow-up supervision by the family doctor or by a social worker, or out-patient psychiatric treatment, is often required. Much depends on the quality of the rapport which can be achieved with the patient, and it is inadvisable to hurry a decision, unless the family circumstances

or the patient's attitude necessitates this. Many of those given out-patient
appointments after suicidal attempts do not keep them, so that this form of
follow-up cannot be relied upon heavily. Still less can trust be placed upon an
assurance extracted from the patient that he will never attempt suicide again.
Such a promise, which should never be asked for, is as easily elicited as it is
futile as a safeguard.

There is no sharp dividing line between suicidal gestures and genuine suicidal
attempts. At one extreme the individual is wilfully using the threat of taking
his life as a means of getting his own way in something else: at the other, he
meant to kill himself and his intention has miscarried. In the past decade there
has been a sharply rising number of those who poison themselves; and amongst
these, predominantly young people, the number of suicidal gestures has markedly
increased. While recognizing that many drug overdoses are the product of
relatively superficial reactions and carry little risk to life, it is unwise to generalize
about these situations and to treat them too lightly. That the incident can be
seen as a call for help or as an attempt selfishly to manipulate the social environment, does not exclude the presence of a serious suicidal drive. The determination that lies behind a suicidal act is indeed often very difficult to measure, there
are few absolutely secure criteria for judging it, and the individual himself may
be unable to gauge the intensity of tendencies of which he has little conscious
awareness or clear memory. Insight is often lacking. Each act must be assessed
on its own.

What the individual himself or herself says about his suicidal act is important,
but may be misleading. A frank admission of suicidal intent can usually be
relied upon: denial cannot be, particularly if the person has obviously been
depressed in his spirits for some time prior to the incident and continues to be
so after it. He may insist that he had just wanted to get a good sleep, and that
it had been an accident that after his usual night sedative he had taken a further
dose and then when drowsy more tablets still. An overdose taken in this way is
rarely accidental, though relatives and others are only too ready and relieved to
believe that it has been. A farewell note or letter nearly always indicates a serious
intention: its contents may throw much light on the psychodynamics of the act,
and such notes, which are often destroyed or not reported upon by relatives
(who may be arraigned in them), should if possible be obtained by the doctor.
Attempts made when the individual has been under the influence of alcohol
are more than usually difficult to assess: probably most such attempts are to be
considered as serious if they have occurred in a setting either of persistent
alcoholism or of recent and unexpected recourse to alcohol.

The method of self-injury employed may throw a clear light upon the individual's wishes, but it is more frequently equivocal as evidence. If he has
attempted to hang, shoot or drown himself, or has thrown himself from a height,
if he has not only turned on the gas but has closed or sealed windows and doors,
if he has adopted more than one method of self-injury, if he has made sure that
he will be alone and uninterrupted, then one may conclude that he has been in
earnest. On the other hand a small dose of drugs or superficial cuts on wrists

or throat are not certain indications of slight suicidal intent. The psychotic patient may be too agitated, retarded or perplexed to effect his will. Amongst those who take barbiturate overdoses at home, the commonest category, is found the whole gamut of intent. The older the patient in general the more serious the suicidal act. Gestures, rare after middle life, are hardly ever made by the old. If in doubt, consider a gesture at any age to have been an attempt at suicide.

One does not of course confine one's attention to the suicidal act. If it has been unsuccessful, it is of less importance than the actor, his state of mind and the whole surrounding circumstances. Almost any mental disorder may eventuate in a suicidal attempt. There are two large groups which have to be distinguished clinically: the mentally ill on the one hand, and the temperamentally unstable on the other. Amongst the former, a depressive psychosis is the most common reaction; chronic alcoholism probably next most common. The young schizophrenic may make an impulsive and very violent attempt; the cerebral arteriosclerotic who realizes his increasing limitations may decide to terminate his life rather than be a mental or physical cripple; the paranoid patient, if he becomes depressed, may no longer be protected from self-injury by his outgoing aggression. The second group, the temperamentally unstable, are mainly young people, in their teens or early adult life, hysterical, psychopathic or exhibiting some other allied type of personality disorder. A very much smaller group than either of the two already mentioned is comprised of those who have appeared previously to be stable people, but who have reacted catastrophically to some sudden grave stress, such as bereavement or financial ruin or a summons to a Court of Law.

It will fall often to the non-specialist to distinguish the mentally ill from the temperamentally unstable. This may be a difficult task, and sometimes the two conditions coexist: but if a good clinical history has been obtained, a differential diagnosis can usually be reached with fair confidence. One must obtain, from the patient and from his relatives, a clear account of whether or not, prior to the emergency, this person had given evidence of having become nervously or mentally ill. Had there been a recent change in the individual's mental state, and if so, of what nature? Especially, have there been symptoms or signs of depression of mood which have persisted for more than a few days? Is there a family history or previous personal history of mental illness, and particularly of depression or suicide? If there has been a previous suicidal attempt, either in this or an earlier illness, there will be no doubt about the gravity of this further attempt. All depressive psychoses carry a suicidal risk, whether or not the illness has had obvious precipitants.

If there is evidence of mental illness, it will be advisable to refer the patient to a psychiatrist for further assessment, and to keep the patient in hospital until this has been done. Though a suicidal attempt occasionally seems to initiate the rapid clearing of a depressive illness, the great majority of those who are both mentally ill and suicidal will require specialized psychiatric in-patient treatment, at least for some weeks.

The previous histories of the second group, the temperamentally unstable, are different: these people have typically been a problem to themselves and others—for years often, they usually have poor work records, they are restless, headstrong, turbulent or feckless, the domestic situation is one of chronic conflict or turmoil, and there may be a background of crime and police charges. In these cases the suicidal gesture or attempt is most commonly triggered off by a quarrel: it is an acute frustration reaction, done on the spur of the moment and the individual frequently does not clearly visualize the results of his action: he is thwarted and is furious or sorry for himself, he wants sympathy or intends that others should suffer, he wishes to get away from it all. Often he or she has been drinking that evening, and the quarrel has quickly followed the return home. This sort of case usually settles very soon after admission to hospital, the individual may regain his poise even within a few hours, and the immediately continuing suicidal risk is very slight: but these wilful acts may be repeated, and with repetition the risk of suicide rises. Those who repeat such acts should be referred for specialist psychiatric assessment: but many of these situations are isolated and transient reactions, which have to be dealt with quickly by those into whose hands these impulsive people come. On the day after the crisis suicidal intent is usually denied and it is not long before the individual is demanding to be allowed home. He rarely considers himself abnormal and rarely wants to co-operate in psychiatric treatment: he is bent on having his own way and looks for changes in others but not in himself.

ACUTE PSYCHOTIC EXCITEMENT

Apart from the effects of drug or alcohol overdosage, acute psychiatric excitement occurs most frequently in cases of schizophrenia and mania. It is rarely the first evidence of schizophrenia. Usually the patient is known to be suffering from schizophrenia: and frequently nowadays he has been treated in a mental hospital or other psychiatric unit with tranquillizing drugs and has been discharged from hospital on a drug regime. Many of these patients fail to take their drugs when at home, and relapse consequently is a frequent occurrence: it may be acute, florid and dangerous both to the patient and to others. If there is a serious relapse, readmission to a psychiatric unit should be arranged without delay.

Acute mania, with its excessive activity and elated mood, is not difficult to diagnose. Here encouragement to talk and prolonged discussion of the situation just excites the patient further. It is no use spending time in trying to persuade the manic patient to enter hospital as a fully pondered act. Proceed firmly and without palaver to make arrangements, and it may be possible to admit the patient to hospital without having to take compulsory powers.

The agitation and delusions of a depressive psychosis may lead to a crisis at home, apart from the suicidal risk, since they may hinder or prevent the patient's admission to hospital informally for treatment. The patient may be so unable to concentrate, so indecisive and guilt-ridden, that he or she cannot resolve to follow the urgent recommendations of the family doctor and relatives. In these circumstances, the admission of the patient to a psychiatric unit as an emergency should be arranged without more ado.

ACUTE INTOXICATION

Cases of acute excitement due to drugs are probably in the majority of cases diagnosed retrospectively. The individual may not have the obvious symptoms of a delirium. He may not be mentally clouded and confused, and his speech may not be slurred. Acute intoxication with amphetamines may be misdiagnosed as paranoid schizophrenia, and understandably so. The patient, a young man usually, becomes acutely mentally ill, excited with paranoid delusions and hallucinations, in a state of apparently clear consciousness. It is only later that the history is obtained that he has been taking more than 50 mg. of amphetamines daily.

Even when the patient is delirious, the cause of the intoxication may not be immediately evident. Many a case of delirium tremens is recognized to be a delirium before it is known to be alcoholic. Delirium is easily diagnosed, the patient is very restless and confused, delusions and visual hallucinations are typically present and fear is the predominant affect. Treatment of these acute and serious symptoms and investigation of their cause is usually best carried out in a general hospital.

Individuals when under the influence of alcohol, but neither incapable nor delirious, often become noisy, threatening and assaultive, and their behaviour may require immediate control for the safety of others or of themselves. The rôles of the police, the general public and the medical profession are not clearly defined in this area; and perhaps they neither can nor should be. Alcoholics themselves seem increasingly to look to hospitals for succour when they are drunk and frequently present themselves at casualty departments, especially at week-ends. They may demand admission to hospital on the grounds that they feel depressed or homicidal or suicidal. Many of them are unemployed men, estranged from their families, they may have no fixed abode and they may not have a general practitioner to whom they can be referred. Usually also there is a history of previous admissions to general and mental hospitals, and of poor co-operation in treatment. The decision about whether or not to admit to a hospital bed is frequently an awkward one, having to be made late at night with little information and under pressure. When there is a previous psychiatric history or hint of violence, it is usually advisable to admit such an individual, at least overnight: and beds adjoining casualty departments should be available to meet this need. The brunt of dealing with these demanding individuals falls usually upon those with the least experience, the most junior housemen and casualty officers: and they should be given by their seniors more guidance than is now usual about how to act in these circumstances.

ACUTE ANXIETY AND PANIC ATTACKS

Panic attacks, which are overwhelming feelings of impending catastrophe, occur both in neurotic and psychotic illnesses.

Neurotic panics, which are episodes of acute anxiety arising in a setting of more persistently increased emotional tension, are much more often and obviously emergencies for the patient than for the doctor. Not only is the experience of them largely subjective; the doctor, who is summoned hurriedly on many of these occasions, usually arrives after the crisis has passed. An attack may last for a few minutes or up to half an hour or so. The patient usually feels that he is going to faint or to die, though he may be ashamed afterwards to admit to the latter fear, unless specifically asked about it. The attacks tend to occur most frequently when the patient is away from home, in a crowded place or when travelling, so that the sufferer becomes afraid to go out: they may also happen at home and are most likely to do so when the individual is left alone. The problem here is sometimes one of diagnosis: these patients may report their attacks as episodes of shaking or giddiness or faintness: they may not mention their emotional reactions at all, wishing to hide the fact that their fear has overwhelmed them. Sometimes the development of a coronary thrombosis is suspected by the doctor as well as by the patient.

During such an attack the presence of someone who is maintaining his own calm is of great reassurance to the patient. The most effective drug is amylobarbitone sodium, 120–180 mg., taken as soon as the patient feels that an attack is coming on or on entering a situation which is known to be liable to precipitate an attack.

Panic may also be of psychotic intensity and this is not sufficiently well recognized. Here the fear is accompanied by bewilderment and misinterpretations; there is extreme insecurity and suspiciousness; the individual may rapidly become both delusional and hallucinated and his behaviour very disorganized. He may be dangerous both to himself and to others.

One encounters psychotic panics in the wards of general hospitals. Following a surgical operation perhaps or coronary thrombosis or an episode of congestive cardiac failure, a patient becomes acutely disturbed, deluded and hallucinated, believes he hears other patients and the staff talking of and against him, declares that his relatives are being kept away, that the bed has been wired with electricity, that he himself is doomed and will shortly be done away with. There may or may not be mental clouding: if there is, one can describe the reaction properly as a delirium. Frequently there is little or no clouding: and whether or not there is clouding of consciousness, the most prominent symptom is the affect of fear. It is fear that lies behind the suspiciousness: fear of the illness and its possible fatal outcome, fear of investigative and treatment procedures, fear of what is going to happen (and the patient may not have been told much about that), fear of the unfamiliar and the unknown. If one gives these patients large doses of drugs, particularly barbiturates, in an effort to control their panic one risks increasing the mental confusion and aggravating the whole situation. The patient should not be put behind screens, his relatives should be allowed to sit by him, and if his physical condition permits it, he should be allowed to go home. A change of ward may help. It is nearly always a transiently paranoid reaction: but it is often very acute, and very disturbing in a general medical or surgical ward. It may also be dangerous: the patient demands to be allowed to get out of the ward where he feels trapped and may even go through a window to escape.

There is another psychiatric reaction which is known as homosexual panic, which is uncommon but which it is important to recognize: its diagnosis is certainly sometimes missed. Usually the patient, a youngish man, has for some time been in a state of insecurity and tension, complaining of anxiety or other apparently neurotic symptoms and probably for that reason receiving drugs from his family doctor. Then suddenly he believes that he has discovered in himself, or that others have detected in him, homosexual tendencies. He becomes panic-stricken. He may seek medical advice urgently and clamour for reassurance. He may become suspicious and aggressive, may rush about bewildered. He feels that people are looking at him: he hears himself called a 'poof' or other opprobrious names. Such a man should be brought under psychiatric care as soon as it is possible, since the suicidal risk is a very serious one. More rarely a similar condition may develop in a young man following the sudden irruption into consciousness of incestuous thoughts or wishes.

EMERGENCIES IN CHILDHOOD AND ADOLESCENCE

Though psychiatric emergencies are uncommon in childhood, they do occur: acute anxiety or panic attacks may develop, suicidal threats or attempts may be made (and must be taken seriously), temper tantrums may get beyond control, a very unhappy or maladjusted child may attack seriously another child or commit such a dangerous act against property as fire-raising. School refusal (separation anxiety) also may be seen by the family as an emergency, when the child finally digs his or her toes in and, in floods of tears and protesting loudly, refuses to be budged from home.

Emergencies in adolescence, adolescent crises, eruptions of aggressive, strange or bizarre behaviour, are much more demanding. A schizophrenic illness may come on acutely: depressive reactions are considerably commoner, many of them situationally determined. Very uninhibited behaviour at this age does not by any means always signify that the individual is psychotic. Suicidal gestures, attempts and suicide itself are becoming much commoner in adolescence (the suicide rate in males aged 14–20 has almost doubled in the past two decades). Acting out takes many forms—crime, promiscuity, drunkenness, drug taking, gross unreliability at home and at work. These young people are often very turbulent, uncooperative and difficult to influence, and in their bewilderment, anger and feelings of frustration they may thrash about wildly. Compulsory powers may have to be taken in an emergency to detain them and to bring them under psychiatric treatment. To enlist the adolescent's voluntary co-operation is of course greatly preferable to this. Since it is not certain that the older adolescents are best cared for in separate, segregated units, there should not be too much hesitation about admitting them to an adult psychiatric service.

THE GENERAL MANAGEMENT OF EMERGENCIES

The initial care of a psychiatric emergency has traditionally been the responsibility of the general practitioner: the police and other lay organizations such as the Salvation Army, Alcoholics Anonymous and Telephone Samaritans are also frequently called upon. Recently there has been an increasing tendency for such cases to be self-referred to general hospital casualty departments.

It is usually advisable first of all to hear what the source of the disturbance has to say about it, and to interview the individual alone at some length. This allows him to talk freely and gives a feeling of confidence that the examiner's judgement will be unhurried and independent: and unless he is wildly excited, the interview itself commonly lowers the patient's tension considerably and rapidly. In assessing the situation there are two objectives: to diagnose the patient's mental state, and to ascertain what has precipitated the upset, what its psychological and social setting may be. The crisis may have arisen more or less out of the blue: more commonly there are causal factors external to the patient, in his social environment. Many psychiatric crises, neurotic and psychotic, are precipitated by disordered domestic situations, by marital conflict, desertion, quarrels and frictions of many different kinds. These social stresses, where they are operative, must as soon as possible be identified and it is at a time of acute upheaval that they may be most obvious. They must be identified since they will have to be taken into account and, if it is practicable, dealt with. Commonly too, whatever the diagnosis, alcohol or drugs have released the brakes on self-control.

With regard to what the doctor should say on these occasions, there are two requirements: it should be brief, and it must be direct, open and unequivocal. If the patient does not know you, you must tell him who you are and why you are present: and if you think that admission to a psychiatric unit or mental hospital is necessary you must tell the patient so. Never pretend to the patient that he is going to be sent or taken somewhere else, for some other reason than his mental illness. Sometimes it is thought that the disturbed patient will go more quietly to hospital if he is not informed about his destination: he may indeed do so, but he is liable later bitterly to resent the deception practised upon him. Nor is it ever a necessary deception.

If the situation can be relieved without the use of drugs and particularly without recourse having to be made to giving the patient an injection, so much the better. Probably the three most useful drugs are: chlorpromazine in tablets of 25 mg. and 50 mg., and in ampoules of 50 mg. for intramuscular injection; amylobarbitone sodium in 60 mg. capsules; and pentobarbitone in capsules of 100 mg. According to the severity of his upset, the patient may be given, for example, amylobarbitone sodium 120–180 mg. by mouth, or pentobarbitone 200–300 mg. by mouth, or chlorpromazine 100–150 mg. intramuscularly.

If the strongest of these drugs is not sufficient to calm the patient, it is usually a situation which calls for his immediate admission to a mental hospital, on an emergency application: and in arranging this and carrying it out the doctor can enlist the assistance of a mental welfare (health) officer of the local authority and if need be of nurses from the nearest mental hospital. If there has been violence or there are indications of probable serious violence, or if the individual has barricaded himself in, one should not hesitate to summon the police. The presence of a policeman is seldom other than helpful and reassuring.

Psychiatric emergencies seldom persist for more than a day or two. First aid of the kind described above is of course only the initial step in dealing with them. It should lead on to more definitive treatment and where possible prevention. If first aid only is given the emergency is more liable to recur, to the disturbance and distress of everyone concerned and with perhaps an enhanced risk of serious or even fatal injury.

19

SUBNORMALITY AND SEVERE SUBNORMALITY (MENTAL DEFECT)[1]

In the Mental Health Act, 1959, 'mental defect' was renamed 'subnormality' and conditions of arrested or incomplete development of mind were divided into two newly designated groups, the 'subnormal' and the 'severely subnormal'. The subnormal group corresponds to what was previously termed 'feeble-mindedness' or high-grade mental defect. The severely subnormal group includes those who were previously named 'idiots' and 'imbeciles', and replaces the category of low-grade mental defect. The main distinction still lies between the slighter degrees of mental subnormality manifest by the dullest members of the general population, and the more gross syndromes often associated with the stigmata of frank physical abnormalities, which render the affected individuals childishly or helplessly dependent on others.

The Mental Health Act's definitions are as follows: '"Severe subnormality" means a state of arrested or incomplete development of mind which includes subnormality of intelligence and is of such a nature or degree that the patient is incapable of living an independent life or of guarding himself against serious exploitation, or will be so incapable when of an age to do so.'

'"Subnormality" means a state of arrested or incomplete development of mind (not amounting to severe subnormality) which includes subnormality of intelligence and is of a nature or degree which requires or is susceptible to medical treatment or other special care or training of the patient.'

With regard to the phrasing of these legal definitions, it may be pointed out that the term subnormal is clearly more applicable to those cases which border the normal, and it is difficult to see why care, training and medical treatment should be mentioned in relation to only one of the two main categories of subnormality. It may also be objected that these definitions are for clinical purposes rather lacking in specification.

The use of the terms subnormality and severe subnormality should be confined to those cases in which there is clear evidence of intellectual defect. Emotional instability, with or without social maladjustment or antisocial trends, may complicate the clinical picture, being either products of the same physical causes as have determined the intellectual defect or secondary developments, traits acquired by a limited individual in failing to come to acceptable terms with his environment. The diagnosis of intellectual subnormality can of course be made without the use of intelligence tests, but it must be able to stand up to and be confirmed by detailed testing. For medical purposes intelligence may be taken to mean the ability to understand one's environment and to make use of one's understanding

[1] In the Mental Health (Scotland) Act, 1960, the term mental deficiency is retained, but the terms idiot, imbecile and feeble-minded are abandoned. The category of Mental Deficiency in Scotland comprises Subnormality and Severe Subnormality.

to earn a living or manage a home. The individual's social failure may be so gross, childish and persistent that the diagnosis is never in doubt. In other cases, where the subnormality is of slight degree and particularly where emotional instability is in the foreground or neurological defects disturb the individual's performance, detailed psychological testing is necessary to determine accurately the patient's intellectual resources. In general, mental testing in cases of subnormality is of more importance in helping to gauge what the individual may be capable of and in pin-pointing special disabilities in the mental sphere, than in coming to the diagnosis itself. What the individual can achieve as a social being is of greater importance than his test scores.

Subnormality is most conspicuous during the school age period, when the individual's intellectual performance first comes under really close scrutiny. Technical difficulties in the accurate measurement of mental abilities, differing views of what should be considered a state of subnormality, and the considerable problems involved in making a full tally of the cases in any community, have made the prevalence of subnormality a matter of some dispute. In Great Britain probably a little less than one per cent. of the population are mentally subnormal. Lewis in a most painstaking and accurate investigation of a population of 600,000 individuals in England and Wales in 1929, reached the figure of 0·86 per cent. He found, as have others, that the incidence was considerably higher in rural than in urban areas. Similar results were obtained in Baltimore in 1942 by Lemkau and his colleagues, and have been reported from Scandinavia. In all these countries subnormality preponderates over severe subnormality. The most recent evidence suggests that in Britain the mildly subnormal constitute about 15 per 1000 of the general population. The prevalence rates for severe subnormality can be more accurately obtained. In Middlesex the prevalence per 1000 population of those with an I.Q. under 50 in the age group 10–14 years was 3·61 (Goodman and Tizard, 1962): in the Wessex Region in the age group 15–19 it was 3·75 (Kushlick, 1965). In North-East Scotland the case rate is 3·7 per 1000 population (Kidd et al., 1967).

'Moral defectiveness' and 'moral imbecility' are terms which have been applied to individuals who have shown antisocial conduct from an early age. They should not be perpetuated since classifications arrived at by moral judgements, which tend to be subjective, relative and changeable, cannot be securely translated into medical categories. If the delinquent individual is intellectually defective, we class him as a case of subnormality: if he is not intellectually defective, he may be suffering from a psychopathic state [see Chapter 13].

In Britain 'amentia' has been a synonym for subnormality. In drawing a distinction between amentia and dementia, Esquirol said, 'The demented man is deprived of the good that he formerly enjoyed: he is a rich man become poor. The ament has always lived in misfortune and poverty.' In other words, the ament lacks something, while the dement suffers from a disorder of that which he possesses. In Europe the term amentia has been applied to confusional states on a toxic-infective basis. Where there is risk of muddle, the term is best avoided: it is anyway *de trop*.

THE AETIOLOGY OF SUBNORMALITY

This is complex, varies very much from case to case and is probably often multiple, an admixture of genetic and environmental factors. In our present state of knowledge the aetiology in the majority of individual cases cannot be ascertained. This ignorance challenges us and points to the necessity for far more research than has so far been done in this field of medicine, where there has been often too fatalistic an acceptance of the facts of disability and too little curiosity about their antecedents.

There are broad and important differences between subnormality and severe subnormality. In the former there is usually a familial concentration of cases; in the latter much less markedly and infrequently so, and usually only in the proportions which might be expected from single-gene inheritance. The subnormal group, which cannot be sharply distinguished from the general population, have also been called the 'sub-cultural' and 'aclinical'. Most of the severely subnormal group suffer from clearly pathological syndromes, and have considerably damaged brains.

Probably at least three-quarters of the subnormal belong essentially to the normal population, though they are the dullest members of that population. Intelligence in the general population shows a normal or Gaussian distribution, a smooth bell-shaped curve: the subnormal constitute the lower end of this curve, down to about I.Q. 50. This quantitative variation of intelligence is largely genetically determined, it is thought, by numerous genes (polygenes) of small individual effect. Many of the parents and relatives of these subnormal individuals are themselves mentally dull or subnormal: about one-quarter of their siblings are said to be so. In the aetiology of these familial cases of subnormality it should be noted that adverse environments, which are very common, also play a part. The mentally poorly endowed tend to provide for their children not only a defective genetic inheritance, but also an environment which is neither intellectually stimulating nor educative: the term 'sub-cultural' could be applied as well to their homes as to their intelligence.

A significant number of cases of subnormality, perhaps as many as one-quarter of the total, are due to pathological causes, either genetic or environmental. This is also the situation with nearly all the cases of severe subnormality; the possible exceptions here occurring at the borderland between severe subnormality and subnormality.

For purposes of description it is convenient to distinguish between genetic (intrinsic) and environmental (extrinsic) aetiological factors, but we should not be misled into thinking that they are separated in nature. Though the genetic factors are present at conception, it is also important to recognize that their presence may not be obvious at birth: in every child, subnormal as well as normal, genetic and environmental factors continue to interact to produce the characteristics and complexity of the developing personality.

Both polygene (as explained above) and single-gene inheritance occur in the aetiology of subnormality, the former in the subnormal cases, the latter mainly in the severely subnormal. Syndromes due to dominant and recessive (single gene) types of inheritance will be described: and the recently discovered associations between subnormality and chromosome abnormalities.

The environmental factors producing mental subnormality are numerous, distributed in time from conception through the intra-uterine period of gestation, and continuing past birth and infancy to childhood itself. The clinical outcome depends not only on the nature and location of the injury to the brain, but also significantly on the time and period of development at which the injury is done.

Amongst the environmental factors acting during the intra-uterine period, which may cause mental subnormality, maternal infections are important: particularly rubella, syphilis and (much less commonly) toxoplasmosis. Radiation of the mother may also do profound damage to the developing embryo, causing microcephaly. Eclampsia and dietary deficiencies in the mother may possibly cause subnormality. Other traumata to the mother, physical and possibly psychological, may be considered speculatively.

At the time of birth, traumata due to obstetrical complications which may do most damage by causing intracranial haemorrhage and asphyxia, are important causes of subnormality as they are of cerebral palsy. The premature infant is especially at risk. The dangers also in these cases of giving oxygen in excess, and of thus producing retrolental fibroplasia (fibroplastic overgrowth of vascular tissue in the eyes) and possibly also serious brain damage, are now well recognized.

After birth, hazards of course continue to crop up but they are different. Severe neonatal jaundice with kernicterus may cause subnormality as well as other serious permanent neurological damage. Some endocrine disorders, which may have had their origins at an earlier time, become important aetiologically, notably hypothyroidism. An attack of encephalitis lethargica, or one of the other encephalitides (complicating, for example, measles or mumps), may so permanently damage the brain that the child becomes subnormal: so may a meningitis, tuberculous or septic. Lead poisoning is the classical instance of a metallic poisoning of aetiological importance in this field. Head injury is much more often claimed by parents to be the cause of a child's subnormality than the facts warrant, and in infancy and childhood is probably an uncommon cause.

THE DEGREES AND SYMPTOMS OF SUBNORMALITY

Severe Subnormality

This category spans a wide range of mental incapacity, extending from those who cannot guard themselves even against common physical dangers to those who, though capable of a certain amount of constructive work, are yet unable to earn a living independently. These intellectually very limited individuals do not at best have an I.Q. of more than about 49, or a mental age of more than 7 years. They number about one-quarter of the whole subnormal population and about three-quarters of those under care in mental deficiency institutions. In only about one-third of these cases of severe subnormality is the aetiology known.

At its most severe, severe subnormality represents the lowest form of mental development and is readily recognizable from a very early age. Physical deformities, paralyses and fits are very common. The affected individuals can do almost nothing for themselves. Their incapacity ranges from bedridden helplessness, to walking imperfectly and speaking a few monosyllables. If the child can feed himself, it is only clumsily: he cannot care for himself in the way of washing, dressing or keeping himself clean. His incontinence is a major problem in his nursing care. Most of these cripples die before reaching adult life.

The least disabled in this category can do a simple routine job, and simple tasks and cleanliness can be expected of the majority of those whose I.Q. ranges from 20 to 49. Some learn to write and read a few monosyllabic words, but further scholastic attainments are beyond them. Neurological defects and other physical stigmata are common, and they are characteristically ungainly. Often suggestible and easily exploited, they cannot manage their own affairs or be taught to do so. Their life span is below average.

Subnormality

Those who fall into this group do not usually exhibit the physical stigmata or the evidence of brain damage which are so common amongst the severely subnormal. In scholastic attainments they may not be any worse than the more poorly educated type of constitutionally normal child: and a considerable proportion of those who are educationally subnormal prove capable of supporting themselves socially on leaving school. Indeed, in routine and menial jobs they often prove industrious workers and as stable citizens as their fellows. But more often than is the case with the population of average intelligence, the subnormal are unstable in their aims and occupations, impulsive and lacking in common sense. This instability may be revealed in a poor work record, criminality or sexual promiscuity. Those amongst them that become criminal are responsible for many petty offences and indiscriminate violence: some, too readily suggestible, become the dupes of more practised criminals. The unstable subnormal woman may become illegitimately pregnant or drift into prostitution: as a mother she is usually incompetent and as a housewife slatternly. But it must be emphasized that gross social failure is the fate of only the minority of the subnormal.

The subnormal child cannot derive benefit from instruction in ordinary schools and requires special educational care and training.

The subnormal constitute about three-quarters of the whole defective population. Their I.Q.s range from about 50 to 69, their mental ages from 8 to 11 years.

SOME PHYSICAL ABNORMALITIES COMMONLY ACCOMPANYING SUBNORMALITY

Many different varieties of nervous system lesion, of cerebral developmental malformations, and of congenital abnormalities in other systems of the body are found in the subnormal, and naturally most frequently in those who are severely subnormal. The severely subnormal have usually, in fact, a constitution defective in many respects. Impairment of vision and hearing, aphasia of various types and specific reading disabilities may all complicate subnormality: and these disabilities, in the normal child, may occasionally lead to a misdiagnosis of subnormality. No attempt will be made here to give a comprehensive account of all the pathological conditions which may occur, but a brief review will be made of the commoner and more important varieties.

Cerebral Palsy

This is a relatively common condition, occurring in 1 to 2 per thousand of the school population. It is frequently associated with some degree of subnormality, and particularly with severe subnormality. Kirman (1956) reported that in the Fountain Hospital, which cares mostly for severely subnormal cases, 23 per cent. of the patients were affected.

The physical symptoms range from clumsiness and speech difficulties to such severe motor involvement that the child is helpless. Various clinical types and admixtures of types occur: they include spastic diplegia, hemiplegia, choreoathetosis and ataxia, the first of these being the commonest. Epilepsy is a common accompaniment of cerebral palsy and is said to be found in as many as half the hemiplegic cases.

Many varieties of pathological damage and aberrant brain development produce cerebral palsy. Some forms of spastic diplegia are inherited as recessive defects: damage early in intra-uterine life may lead to atrophy of both cerebral hemispheres: porencephaly, hemiatrophy or microgyria may result in hemiplegia: haemorrhage and asphyxia at birth are well-recognized causes: and in a much smaller number of cases the damage is sustained in early childhood. Cerebellar atrophy may be found in the ataxic varieties, and the commonest antecedent of choreo-athetosis is kernicterus with its lesions in the basal ganglia.

Epilepsy

Epilepsy is not a cause of subnormality but a symptom which commonly accompanies it, and which may be an expression of the same pathology as has determined the mental retardation. Both idiopathic and symptomatic types occur. In the former group genetic factors are important: in the latter some structural or metabolic abnormality disturbs brain function, and understandably epilepsy is most common in cases of severe subnormality with neurological deficits. Epilepsy is, for example, frequently associated with cerebral palsy. 10 to 15 per cent. of the subnormal in institutions are epileptic. All types of seizure are manifest—*grand mal*, *petit mal*, psychomotor and myoclonic.

Epileptic fits may aggravate a child's mental backwardness by interfering with his schooling: so may the dulling effect of anticonvulsant drugs, particularly if these are prescribed in excess.

2 G

Microcephaly

Microcephalic is a descriptive term for those subnormal individuals who have abnormally small heads. Microcephaly is not a clinical nor a pathological nor an aetiological entity: primary (genetic) cannot be separated from secondary (environmental) types. In a comprehensive and valuable review of the topic Brandon and his colleagues (1959) proposed that microcephaly should be defined as 'cases with a cranial circumference smaller than three standard deviations below the mean for the age and sex'. Fairly satisfactory norms are available.

Microcephaly is found in about one-fifth of the severely subnormal. The individual's skull is characteristically dolichocephalic, *i.e.* the breadth of the skull is less than four-fifths of the length: and the vertical measurements are also much reduced. In the most severe cases the microcephalic's appearance is most odd and bird-like. The forehead and chin are sharply receding, the nose appears like a beak, and the ears are out of proportion. The scalp may lie loosely, in longitudinal furrows.

The brain in these cases is also abnormally small, and light, and many other abnormalities of brain structure are common, *e.g.* microgyria, porencephaly. Other gross physical defects are frequent: dwarfism, cerebral palsy, epilepsy, cardiac and ophthalmic lesions: and the prognosis for life depends not only on the development of the brain but also largely on these other defects. Microcephalics tend to die earlier than those with larger heads. About one-third of mongols are microcephalic: so also are many phenylketonurics.

The degree of subnormality is as variable as the size of the head, and is not directly correlated with head size. The majority of microcephalics are severely subnormal. There is no characteristic temperamental type.

The aetiology is very various. Familial cases occur, and the risk of a sib being affected was estimated by Brandon from his series to be 6 per cent. Cases due to single gene (recessive) inheritance are probably very much in the minority, and not clearly separable from those of different aetiology. Traumatic environmental factors probably operate most commonly early in intra-uterine life: only two of these extrinsic factors so far are known—irradiation of the mother during pregnancy, and maternal rubella.

Hydrocephalus

This is a common finding in cases of subnormality, especially among the severely subnormal: like microcephaly, it is not a disease entity but a symptom of various pathologies. Its immediate cause is a disturbance of the formation, circulation or absorption of cerebrospinal fluid. In the congenital cases obstruction is the commonest cause, in the Sylvian aqueduct or at the foramina of Magendie and Luschka or elsewhere in the circulation pathway; and the abnormality of structure probably originates in the first three months of intra-uterine life. Obstetrical difficulties are likely then to be produced by the over-large head and such children may die during birth. In most congenital cases the subnormality is severe and other physical abnormalities are common: the hydrocephalus, for example, may be associated with spina bifida and lumbosacral meningocele. In infancy a meningitis, especially of the meningococcal variety, may produce hydrocephalus. Later causes such as tuberculous meningitis may lead to hydrocephalus without gross enlargement of the head.

In severe early cases the head becomes enormous, globular, the forehead bulging, the veins of the scalp visibly congested, the eyes pushed forward and downwards: cranial circumferences of 25 to 30 inches have been recorded. The cerebrospinal fluid pressure is increased, the ventricles are greatly dilated, the cortex stretched, thinned and deformed, and the skull itself may become very thin, with gaping sutures and greatly enlarged fontanelles. The inadequately protected brain is of course also vulnerable to external trauma: and the large head itself incapacitates the child, unbalancing it. Not only subnormality usually results: blindness, epilepsy and paralyses are common, and deafness only less so.

Hydrocephalus may be rapidly progressive, producing early death: or it may be self-arrested at any stage. The various surgical operations which have been devised to alleviate it have been of limited value.

Much more rarely, an abnormally large head in a subnormal individual may be due to megalencephaly or Paget's disease of the skull.

INHERITED SYNDROMES

Cases of single gene inheritance, dominant, recessive, and sex-linked, are rare. There is greater variability of the clinical picture in the case of the dominant defects. All these syndromes are associated usually with severe subnormality.

Dominant Syndromes

Tuberous Sclerosis (Epiloia). Tuberous sclerosis is inherited as a dominant, and sporadic cases seem to be evidence of a rather high mutation rate. Its incidence is probably lower than that of phenylketonuria; about 1 in 30,000 of the population (England and Wales). Incomplete forms of the syndrome occur, and it is found associated with all degrees of subnormality; occasionally even with mental normality. The pathological lesions are numerous. Most characteristic is the adenoma sebaceum—a brownish red, acneiform rash in a butterfly distribution on the cheeks and adjoining parts of the face, which develops usually about the time the child reaches school age.

In the brain there are multiple gliotic nodules with giant cells (tuberous sclerosis), which may become calcified and demonstrable radiologically. Similarly benign tumours occur in many other organs, including the retina (phakomata), heart (rhabdomyomata) and kidneys (hamartomata). All these tumours are prone to become malignant.

The affected individual is usually epileptic, his mental condition commonly deteriorates, and he has a reduced expectancy of life.

Neurofibromatosis (von Recklinghausen's Disease). This is another syndrome probably due to an irregularly dominant gene, which has similarities to tuberous sclerosis, and may be related. It is less common and it is not necessarily associated with subnormality. At least 10 per cent. of the cases are, however, subnormal. Skin lesions of two types are seen—*café au lait* patches of pigmentation, and subcutaneous neurofibromata. As in tuberous sclerosis, tumours of the retina (phakomata) also occur.

Naevoid Amentia (Sturge-Weber Syndrome). Naevoid amentia occurs in families and is thought to be a dominant defect. It is characterized by the concurrence of subnormality and angiomatous developments. Typically there is a large port-wine coloured naevus on one side of the face in the distribution of the trigeminal nerve, and an intracranial haemangioma on the same side which may become calcified. The affected individual is usually both severely subnormal and epileptic: he may also have a hemiplegia on the side opposite to the intracranial angioma.

Von Hippel-Lindau's Disease. This shows a similar association of subnormality and naevi.

Recessive Syndromes

Clear-cut syndromes are to be found in this group of the subnormal. A single gene appears typically in these syndromes to produce its effect by dislocating an enzyme system (an enzyme normally present may be absent): an 'inborn error of metabolism' results.

Already more than two dozen familial metabolic disorders associated with mental retardation have been described, and doubtless many others await discovery. Typical examples will be briefly delineated: disorders of amino acid metabolism—phenylketonuria and maple syrup urine disease; disorders of lipoid metabolism—amaurotic idiocy and gargoylism; disorder of carbohydrate metabolism—galactosaemia; disorder of copper metabolism—hepatolenticular degeneration.

It is with the study of the biochemical abnormalities manifest in these cases that a new era in psychiatric genetics opened. Though the group is still a small one numerically, comprising only 1–2 per cent. of the mental deficiency hospital population, we are reaching with them such fundamental understanding of the pathological mechanisms underlying the mental retardation that rational control and treatment have become possible. The paradigm is phenylketonuria.

Phenylketonuria. This condition was discovered in 1934 by Fölling, a Norwegian biochemist. The essential feature is excretion daily in the urine of about one gramme of phenylpyruvic acid. Due to the absence of an enzyme phenylalanine hydroxylase, phenylalanine is not converted to tyrosine, phenylalanine accumulates in the blood, and phenylpyruvic acid, phenyllactic acid and phenylacetic acid are voided in the urine. It is uncertain precisely how the subnormality is caused and what the neuropathological changes are. In this country and in the U.S.A. the incidence of the condition is probably between 1 in 10,000 and 1 in 20,000 births.

The affected individual is usually severely subnormal: rarely he is mentally normal or near normal. The diagnosis may be suspected on clinical grounds but the clinical features are not pathognomonic and the urine and blood must be tested to confirm the diagnosis. The subjects usually have fair hair, fair skin and blue eyes. The head measurements are slightly reduced and the incisor teeth are widely spaced. The posture is usually stooping and flexed, the gait stiff, the limbs hypertonic with very brisk tendon reflexes. These children tend to be hyperkinetic, to show digital mannerisms (such as flicking, twiddling, pill-rolling), and to suffer from epilepsy particularly in their earlier years. They also seem to be unusually prone to eczema and dermatitis.

The original method of diagnosing phenylketonuria was by adding to a sample of urine which had been acidified a few drops of 5 per cent. ferric chloride solution: a characteristic light green reaction quickly develops and darkens to a deep bluish green. It is of course difficult to obtain a sample of urine from an infant and to facilitate the diagnosis in babies a quick stick test for phenylketonuria (Phenistix) was introduced: the stick is pressed against a wet nappy, and if the test is positive a grey or grey-green colour appears on the stick within 30 seconds. This Phenistix test is not reliable until the baby is at least 3 weeks old and further experience has shown that it is insufficiently sensitive. Currently there are considered to be two suitable tests: the Guthrie test for blood phenylalanine, for which a drop of blood dried on filter paper is sent for examination to a central laboratory; and chromatography of the urine for o-hydroxyphenylacetic acid, for which the mother can collect a specimen from the baby on filter paper. The diagnosis must be confirmed by estimation of the serum phenylalanine. Recently it has been found that rarely a child who is not a phenylketonuric may show a temporary phenylalanine hydroxylase deficiency, and Stephenson and McBean (1967) have therefore suggested that in children under dietary treatment the diagnosis of phenylketonuria should be questioned if a serum phenylalanine concentration of 3 mg./100 ml. is difficult to sustain or where the genotype of one of the parents is in doubt.

After the pioneer work of Bickle, Woolf, Moncrieff, Coates and others, treatment of this most serious condition by feeding the infant with a diet low in phenylalanine is now well established. For treatment to be fully effective the diagnosis of phenylketonuria should be made before mental subnormality is detected and certainly before the age of 6 months. All infants should be routinely screened so as to ensure the earliest possible diagnosis. Phenylalanine-free casein hydrolysates are used, supplemented by milk. Dietary control must be checked by serial estimations of serum phenylalanine levels. The diet is expensive and unappetizing, and it is not yet known if it has to be continued indefinitely.

Clayton and her colleagues (1967) have reviewed the results of the dietetic treatment of 57 children suffering from phenylketonuria. The best results have been obtained when treatment has been started in early infancy. Surprisingly good results have also sometimes been obtained in older children. Twelve of the children attend a normal school, and a further 10 may be able to do so when they become of school age.

The discovery of a child with phenylketonuria indicates that the siblings must be investigated. Hsia (1966) and his colleagues found that the heterozygous, clinically normal, carriers of phenylketonuria can be detected by phenylalanine tolerance tests. Known carriers should be advised not to intermarry and have children. Now that the condition is treatable, some of the heterozygotes will bear children, and there will then be a rise in the gene frequency in the population.

Maple Syrup Urine Disease. This was first described by Menkes and his colleagues (1954). The amino acids valine, leucine and isoleucine accumulate in the blood and urine. It is because of the odour of the urine that the syndrome was given its present name. Mental defect is associated with generalized spasticity and epileptic seizures.

Amaurotic Idiocy (Cerebromacular Degeneration). Infantile (Tay-Sachs disease), late infantile (Bielschowsky-Jansky disease), and juvenile (Vogt-Spielmeyer disease) forms of this very rare condition have been described. It is not known what biochemical anomaly leads to the infiltration and distension of the brain cells with lipoid, which is mostly ganglioside. There is no effective treatment.

In the infantile form the onset is usually in the latter half of the first year of life, severe subnormality results, and death occurs in a year or two. The progress of the disease is marked by nystagmus, optic atrophy, epileptic fits and paralyses. In the retina, a cherry-red spot develops in the region of the macula where the choroid vessels become visible. The late infantile form, as its name indicates, begins later and develops more slowly; the macular spot may be absent. The juvenile form starts at the age of about 6 years and may run a course of 10 years or so, before it too is fatal.

Gargoylism (Lipochondrodystrophy, Hunter's or Hurler's Disease). The term gargoylism, though neatly descriptive, should perhaps be abandoned as likely to cause distress to relatives. About three-quarters of the cases have an autosomal recessive inheritance. The precise nature of the metabolic fault has not yet been defined. There appears to be a disturbance in the metabolism of lipopolysaccharides, and the brain and many other organs become the site of abnormal intracellular deposits of lipoids and polysaccharides. Subnormality does not always result but severe retardation is usual. There is no known treatment.

The appearance of these children is striking. The face is coarse, craggy and un-childlike. The head and face look heavy, bony prominences are large, the bridge of the nose is sunk, the eyebrows and lips are thick. The cornea may be misty or opaque. Deafness is common. The skeletal abnormalities include dwarfing, thoracic or lumbar kyphosis, and limitation of joint movements. The abdomen is swollen due to severe enlargement of the liver and spleen. There may be hypertension and cardiac enlargement: and early death from respiratory infection is common.

Galactosaemia. In these rare cases there is an inability to metabolize galactose, due to the absence of an enzyme, phospho-galactose-uridyl transferase: hence galactose accumulates in the body in toxic amounts, and appears in the urine in excess. Symptoms usually begin in early infancy, with vomiting and jaundice. Progressive wasting, enlargement of the liver, cataract and brain damage follow: and there is a high mortality.

All cases of severe subnormality associated with cataract should be investigated for galactosuria. Treatment will arrest the damage and the clinical signs may recede. Lactose and galactose must be eliminated from the diet: that is, the child must not be given milk, and other sugars must be substituted.

Hepatolenticular Degeneration (Wilson's Disease). Kinnier Wilson in 1911 first described this very rare condition, in which retardation is associated with lesions of the liver and corpus striatum.

There is in these cases a complex disturbance of copper metabolism. Copper is excreted in large amounts in the urine, and it is deposited in many organs, especially in the basal ganglia and in the liver: the blood copper is low. These changes appear to be due to a genetically determined deficiency of a plasma copper protein, ceruloplasmin, which normally binds 90 per cent. of the copper in the blood.

The onset of the disease may be in childhood, but more usually it is in adolescence: it may also be delayed until adult life. There is then a progressive development of extrapyramidal symptoms and dementia over the usually few years of remaining life. Tremor is often the earliest symptom, preceding the generalized development of a rigidity of Parkinsonian type, with progressive limitation of voluntary movement and interference with speech and swallowing. Choreoathetoid movements are also typical, and there may be torsion spasms. The dementia is of a non-specific type, with emotional lability. In some cases the cornea shows a characteristic change, due to the deposition there of copper: this is the Kayser-Fleischer ring, a golden-brownish staining of the periphery of the cornea which can best be seen with the aid of a slit-lamp. There are the usual systemic symptoms of cirrhosis.

The lesions in the brain, which consist of degeneration of ganglion cells, neuroglial overgrowth and deposition of copper, are found in the basal ganglia, the cortex and elsewhere: they are concentrated in the corpus striatum and particularly in the lenticular nucleus. The liver shows a multilobular cirrhosis.

Treatment with dimercaprol (B.A.L.), which aims to eliminate the excess copper in the body, has had uncertain results: but here again we have a disease the aetiology of which we are beginning to understand, and we may reasonably hope for more definitive treatment.

Sex-linked Syndromes

These are very rare. Only males are affected. The syndrome is transmitted by unaffected heterozygous female carriers.

Nephrogenic Diabetes Insipidus. The patient has polyuria from infancy, and if his fluid intake is not increased sufficiently death or severe subnormality commonly results. The polyuria is resistant to vasopressin. The carrier state can be identified in female relatives by a simple urine concentration test (Carter and Simpkiss, 1956).

Gargoylism. Possibly one-quarter of the cases of gargoylism are sex-linked (Penrose, 1963). They are distinguished from the others clinically by the absence of corneal opacities.

Glucose-6-phosphate Dehydrogenase Deficiency. There is a disorder both of the storage and of the liberation of glycogen, due to the deficiency of a specific glycolytic enzyme. Glycogen accumulates in various bodily organs, usually particularly in the liver and in some cases particularly in the heart. The child fails to grow and develop normally, the liver is grossly enlarged (its cells being distended with glycogen), and there is a low fasting blood sugar, with ketonuria. There is no splenomegaly.

Hydrocephaly. Edwards (1961) has suggested that in about 5 per cent. of male cases a sex-linked gene is responsible.

SUBNORMALITY ASSOCIATED WITH CHROMOSOME ABNORMALITIES

Only in the past decade has it become technically possible to count accurately human chromosomes, to identify individual pairs of chromosomes, and to ascertain the nuclear sex. In normal men and women the diploid number of chromosomes is 46:22 pairs of autosomes and one sex chromosome pair. Males and females have different numbers of X chromosomes, and the male has a Y chromosome which is absent in the female. In man this Y chromosome appears to be the male determinant: males are XY, females, XX. The nuclei of chromosomal females possess sex chromatin (are chromatin-positive), those of chromosomal males lack it.

Chromosome abnormalities associated with the autosomes are generally accompanied by mental subnormality. Sex chromosome abnormalities tend to produce deviations from the normal in temperament and behaviour, and the intellectual loss, if there is any, is much slighter.

Of the autosomal chromosome aberrations, Down's syndrome (mongolism) and the *cri-du-chat* syndrome will be described. Of the sex chromosome abnormalities an increased complement of X chromosomes seems to be most often associated with subnormality. Klinefelter's syndrome in males is typical of this and is the commonest. Maclean and his colleagues (1962) found that 37 out of 4514 patients in mental deficiency institutions had an abnormal sex-chromosome complement. The frequency of abnormal males was 10·7 per 1000, of XXX females 4·2 per 1000, and of XO females 0·5 per 1000.

Down's Syndrome (Mongolism)

This variety of subnormality was designated mongolism by Langdon Down in 1886 because of the resemblance of the physical characteristics of the patients to those of members of the Mongolian race. The resemblance is, however, superficial, and the physiognomy of the mongol can still be recognized when the individual is Mongolian by race.

Down's syndrome is a common type of subnormality, occurring in 1·4 per 1000 live births (Penrose and Smith, 1966). In a survey in the North-East region of Scotland Ross and his colleagues (1967) found that 8·4 per cent. of subnormal patients had Down's syndrome and that the prevalence was 0·5 per 1000 of the general population. There is a low familial incidence, though familial cases do occur, two or more affected sibs or other near relatives then being found in a family. According to Penrose, pairs of affected sibs occur about once for every 100 single cases randomly collected. The frequency of mongolism in twins is similar to that in other children, and there is commonly a concurrence of normal and mongoloid babies in the same twin pregnancy (Allen and Baroff, 1956).

Aetiology. Down's syndrome has been demonstrated to be associated usually with, and presumably to be due to, trisomy of one of the smallest chromosomes —No. 21 in the Denver classification (Lejeune *et al.*, 1959). There is a small extra chromosome, giving three No. 21 chromosomes and a total of 47 chromosomes. This extra chromosome is an acrocentric chromosome in the smallest size range: it belongs to one of the two short autosome pairs which resemble the Y, and it is probably the result of tripling of one of these normal pairs.

The risk of giving birth to a mongol child is closely related to increasing maternal age, the incidence of the syndrome rising rapidly in women over 30. Penrose (1951) and others have reported that the mean age of the mother at the birth of a mongol averages about 37 years, compared with a mean age of 29 years for all births. Between the maternal ages of 45 and 49, the incidence rises to 2–3 per cent. Probably usually the primary disorder lies in oogenesis, the trisomy being the result of 'non-disjunction' at one of the meiotic divisions of parental gametogenesis producing a gamete with 24 chromosomes instead of 23—a defect which apparently becomes more frequent as the gonad ages.

About 95 per cent. of cases of mongolism are due to trisomy 21 (trisomy G). The remainder are either mongol mosaics, where only some cells have the extra chromosome 21; or show translocations, in that the extra chromosome is fused to another autosome. These translocations may be of the 13–15 : 21 or 21–22 : 21 types. Maternal age does not influence these translocations, but a significant increase in paternal age has been noted in fusions of the 21 : 22 type (Penrose, 1962).

Clinical Features. Down's syndrome is characterized by a number of physical anomalies which when found together give an unmistakable clinical picture: these are found especially in the skull, eyes, tongue and hands. The skull is small, rounded and so diminished in its anteroposterior diameter (brachycephalic) that the anteroposterior and lateral measurements are nearly equal: both the face and the occiput are flattened. The small rounded ears may show an angular overlapping helix and prominent antihelix. The tongue is large, with hypertrophied papillae and transverse fissures (the 'scrotal tongue' of French writers), the mouth is often slightly open and the lower lip commonly protrudes. The palpebral fissures of the eyes are oblique, narrowed and slit-like, often there is a marked epicanthic fold, and other abnormalities are frequently found, *e.g.* strabismus, cataract, speckled irides (Brushfield's spots) and blepharitis. There are abnormalities of the creases and dermal ridges of the palms and soles: typically a single transverse palmar crease and a single crease on the fifth finger, while the dermal ridges also tend to be more transversely arranged than normal. The fifth finger commonly curves inwards, the terminal phalanx being atrophied and the middle phalanx shortened: and the joint ligaments are very lax, giving a greatly increased range of movement to the fingers and toes. The individual is dwarfed in stature, with generally scanty, dry and straight hair, congenital cardiac abnormalities are

462 TEXTBOOK OF PSYCHIATRY

common, there is some degree of generalized hypotonia and he is prone to catarrhal infections. Unlike many other subnormal individuals, mongols are not unduly prone to epilepsy: but they have a raised mortality from leukaemia. Mongols have thyroid auto-antibodies in their sera more commonly than controls, but the significance of this is uncertain (Mellon *et al.*, 1963).

Mentally, the mongol is usually severely subnormal. The majority have a mental age of between 4 and 7 years. Many observers have described the mongol as usually good-natured and easily amused, and as giving the appearance of being more alert and bright than he or she really is, because of a quick imitativeness and mischievousness: other authorities have denied that there is a characteristic personality. The brain is usually smaller and the convolutions simpler than normal.

Many mongols die during the first few months of life, but the mortality rate is decreasing and at birth the expectation of life is now about 16 years. Acute respiratory infection is the commonest cause of death.

The classical account is that given by Penrose and Smith (1966).

Cri-du-chat Syndrome (Partial Monosomy 5 Disease)

In this very rare syndrome, first described by Lejeune and his colleagues in 1963, mental subnormality occurs in association with partial deletion of the short arm of one of the No. 5 chromosome pair. There has been some variation in the clinical features of the two dozen or so cases recorded (Berg *et al.*, 1965). The mental defect is severe, the facies is abnormal and the infant or child has a peculiar cry resembling the mewing of a cat. Other signs noted have been poor physical development; microcephaly; and a round face with low-set ears, broad nasal bridge, hypertelorism, epicanthus and oblique palpebral fissures (an 'anti-mongol' slant).

Klinefelter's Syndrome

This type of male hypogonadism is characterized clinically by leg lengthening without corresponding lengthening of the arms, testes much smaller than normal, reduced facial and abdominal hair, and enlarged breasts (Stewart *et al.*, 1959). Most cases are chromatin-positive and have an extra sex chromosome, *i.e.* 47 chromosomes and an XXY sex chromosome complex (Jacobs and Strong, 1959). Some of these men are mentally dull or mildly subnormal. The incidence in the general population has been reported as 0·26 per cent.: in a mental deficiency hospital population Shapiro and Ridler (1960) found an incidence of 0·66 per cent.

Multiple X Syndromes

Of these syndromes in women, XXX (triplo-X) is fairly common. The presenting symptom is secondary amenorrhoea, and the individual tends to be mentally dull or subnormal.

Turner's Syndrome

A state of gonadal dysgenesis in women with 45 chromosomes and an XO sex chromosome complex is not definitely commoner in mental-defective populations.

ENDOCRINE DISEASE AND SUBNORMALITY

Of the endocrine disorders which may cause mental subnormality, cretinism is the commonest (though not itself common) and most important. Much less common causes are idiopathic hypoglycaemia and idiopathic hypoparathyroidism.

Cretinism. There are several distinct types, of different aetiologies. McGirr and Hutchison (1956 and subsequently) in Glasgow have contributed much to their understanding.

Endemic cretinism is almost always associated with endemic goitre which is due to iodine deficiency in the diet. It is found in certain goitrous regions of the world, but very rarely now in Britain or the U.S.A., and it has in recent years also become rare in Switzerland which used to be an affected area: mass prophylaxis with iodized salt has proved very effective.

Sporadic cretinism may occur with or without goitre. Where there is no goitre, there is a deficiency of thyroid tissue: some thyroid tissue is however usually present, though ectopic or undescended owing to some defect in the development of the thyroid gland. In sporadic goitrous cretinism, a rare condition, there is apparently usually some intrathyroid enzyme deficiency causing a block somewhere along the pathway of the synthesis of thyroid hormone. The condition may be inherited as a recessive disease and it is probably another of the inborn errors of metabolism.

Cretinism may be associated with any degree of subnormality: it also produces characteristically traits of placidity and unaggressiveness. It is upon the physical signs that the diagnosis is based. The body is dwarfed, the neck short and thick, the abdomen protuberant, the limbs short, podgy and often clumsy. The skin is dry, the hair coarse. The head is large, with swollen eyelids, pug nose, thick lips and protruding tongue. Ossification and dentition are delayed. The basal metabolic rate is low.

It is of the greatest importance to make the diagnosis as soon as possible and attention must therefore be directed to the earliest symptoms. Lowrey and his colleagues (1958) have given a helpful description of 49 cases, from this point of view. They state that in 50 per cent. of their cases, three or more of the following cardinal symptoms were present during the first month of life: lethargy with absence of crying; constipation; feeding problems due to somnolence and the large tongue; and respiratory difficulties (30 per cent. showed respiratory distress with cyanosis). The infant is shorter than it should be, and often has an umbilical hernia.

The diagnosis can be confirmed by laboratory tests. The serum protein-bound iodine is below normal, and hypercholesterolaemia is usual though the serum cholesterol may be normal. It may be helpful also to make a radiographic estimation of the bone age.

Early and fully adequate treatment may be curative. The child will need thyroid regularly for years, and must be given the optimum dose to ensure mental and physical growth. In the first year of life the dose of thyroid may begin at 7·5–30 mg. daily, but it must be raised soon to a level which is just below that which produces symptoms of toxicity. If treatment is delayed or intermittent, some degree of subnormality is inevitable.

Idiopathic Spontaneous Hypoglycamia. This, in children, is probably not a clinical entity and it is not the only syndrome in this age group of which hypoglycaemia is a symptom: hypoglycaemia in an infant may also, for example, be due to adrenocortical insufficiency, glycogen disease or islet cell adenoma. The syndrome has been reviewed by Haworth and Coodin (1960). Symptoms begin in the first two years of life, and in 60 per cent. of cases under the age of 6 months. Generalized convulsions are associated with pallor, sweating, limpness or stupor: the fasting blood sugar is usually below 45 mg. per 100 ml. Half of those children who develop the syndrome in the first six months of life become mentally retarded as a result of hypoglycaemic brain damage; paralyses and athetosis may be other neurological sequelae. Some cases respond to treatment with ACTH or adrenocorticosteroids; others which have resisted medical treatment have been cured by partial pancreatectomy; more than 10 per cent. die. The aetiology of these cases, as the name given to them implies, is still unknown. This is another syndrome the early recognition and treatment of which may forestall the development of subnormality.

Idiopathic Hypoparathyroidism. This, a rare disease in children, is due to the congenital absence or destruction of the parathyroid glands. Tetany is the characteristic symptom, presenting at first as paraesthesiae or cramps of the limbs: other features are weakness, epileptic seizures, defective skin, hair, nails and teeth, cataract and occasionally cerebral calcification, in addition to mental retardation. The plasma calcium is lowered, the plasma phosphorus raised. Treatment is based on calciferol (vitamin D_2) or dihydrotachysterol (*A.T.10*).

SOME OTHER CLINICAL SYNDROMES

Subnormality due to Rubella. Rubella infection of the pregnant mother during the first twelve weeks of her pregnancy may cause profound damage to the developing foetus; a situation which was first reported by Gregg from Australia in 1941. The risk of death for the baby *in utero* and up to 2 years of age is about doubled. In those that survive, subnormality, blindness due to cataract, nerve deafness, pyloric stenosis and congenital heart lesions may all result. Of these congenital defects, deafness is the commonest, affecting about 19 per cent.: subnormality occurs in 1·8 per cent. against 0·4 per cent. in controls (Manson *et al.*, 1960).

Congenital Syphilis. This is now an uncommon condition in this country, because of scrupulous antenatal care. In cases where the infection is transmitted by the mother before birth, the child shows usually subnormality and specific serological abnormalities, with or without other neurological signs of meningovascular lesions such as paralyses. The classical stigmata of congenital syphilis, the frontal bosses, keratitis, saddle nose, perioral scars and malformed teeth, may not be present. Later in childhood a congenital syphilitic infection may produce juvenile general paralysis (juvenile G.P.I.).

Subnormality due to Blood Incompatibility. Rhesus factor incompatibility is the commonest variety, though the minority of Rhesus-positive children of Rhesus-negative mothers develop these complications. Severe neonatal jaundice in this syndrome is associated with kernicterus and lesions of the basal ganglia, especially the caudate and lenticular nuclei. Convulsions and coma occur early, and many of the affected infants die: later spasticity and choreo-athetosis are associated with subnormality and often epilepsy to form a rather distinctive clinical picture.

Diffuse Sclerosis (Schilder's Disease and Allied Syndromes). Both familial and sporadic cases of these demyelinating diseases occur: their aetiology is unknown. The disease process begins usually in the white matter of both the occipital lobes symmetrically and spreads forwards: in the affected areas myelin sheaths and axis cylinders degenerate and are replaced by gliosis. In nearly half the cases, symptoms begin in the first ten years. Visual impairment, inco-ordination, bi-lateral spastic paralysis, and dementia are progressive. The child becomes helpless and blind, with spastic diplegia and fits, and dies within a few months or years. The cerebrospinal fluid shows usually no abnormality.

NEUROSES AND PSYCHOSES IN ASSOCIATION WITH SUBNORMALITY

This is a subject which would repay further investigation. We should know more than we do about symptomatology and response to treatment. The general situation seems to be that subnormal individuals are subject to the same abnormal reaction-types as intellectually normal individuals: but their abnormal reactions tend to be more easily precipitated by the environment and to be more transient. There is also some difficulty, particularly in the case of subnormal children, in classifying these reactions in terms of the classical psychiatric syndromes of adult life.

THE DIAGNOSIS OF SUBNORMALITY

In coming to a diagnosis, the doctor should seek more than a short answer to the simple question, 'is this child or adult subnormal?' He should try to determine also the degree of the subnormality, the mental fields in which the patient is subnormal, and the cause or causes of his subnormality. Both the patient and his environment will have to be carefully reviewed.

In the case of the severely subnormal the diagnosis of subnormality may be easy, one may have only to look at the individual's odd appearance or silly expression to come to the right conclusion. In cases of borderline subnormality, on the contrary, and in infancy and early childhood, the correct diagnosis may be much harder to reach. The subnormal child may be blamed and criticized for failures in performance for which he is in no way to blame, and the recidivist be given repeated prison sentences for crimes which are symptoms of his unrecognized subnormality.

The earlier in life the diagnosis can be made the better: and in the case of certain syndromes of severe subnormality, such as cretinism or hypoglycaemia, which are susceptible to treatment, early diagnosis is of critical importance.

A detailed history must be obtained from the patient's near relatives: this will include a family history of subnormality or other relevant illnesses; a detailed account of the mother's health during her pregnancy with this child, and of any obstetrical difficulties; and a comprehensive description of the child's development and total behaviour from infancy. Inquiry must be made about the times at which this child developed various skills, in comparison with the progress of the average child: as a baby at what age could he sit up unsupported, when did he begin to stand, walk and talk, when could he use a spoon, dress himself, gain control over his bladder and bowels, and when did his teeth erupt. Various 'developmental scales' have been devised for assessing the normality of mental and physical growth in the pre-school child, of which Gesell's and Griffith's are perhaps the best known, and these may be of some service: but a knowledge of what may be expected of the average pre-school child, critically applied in appraisal of the possibly subnormal child's performance, is usually a reasonably reliable guide to the doctor. The doctor must always keep in mind that the small child's mental growth is often uneven and that normal children show very wide individual differences in their modes and rates of maturation. Repeated examinations of the child, at intervals of some months, may be necessary when the diagnosis is doubtful.

When the child goes to school he is inevitably critically assessed: his intelligence is usually formally tested, his capacities are further revealed in his classroom work, and his normality or backwardness become more apparent as he mixes and competes in various ways with other children. In gauging the mental status of a child of school age, it is of great assistance to have a report from his head- or class-master. An educational psychologist's report, if available, should of course also be obtained: the results of mental tests given by an expert are much more reliable than the amateur's.

Intelligence tests are of great value in the diagnosis and assessment of mental defect. In most cases their results serve to refine the diagnosis rather than to establish it. They must be used critically always, with knowledge of their limitations. Below the age of three years intelligence tests are grossly unreliable. From school age their reliability is established.

The most commonly employed quantitative measure of intelligence is the Intelligence Quotient (I.Q.). The individual's Mental Age (M.A.) is the age at which the average child would have passed the tests the examinee has passed. The individual's I.Q. is the ratio of his Mental Age to his Chronological Age (C.A.), expressed as a percentage: that is, $I.Q. = \dfrac{M.A.}{C.A.} \times 100$. For adults, the C.A. is taken to be 15 or 16 years. The I.Q. is only one of the possible measures of intelligence, and though the best known it is perhaps not the most satisfactory. Many authorities would prefer to use percentile scores, as the indices of intellectual brightness or dullness.

The intelligence tests most commonly used are the Terman-Merrill revision of the Binet-Simon tests, and the Wechsler Intelligence Scales for Adults and for Children. The Terman-Merrill is probably the most useful test for the severely subnormal child and *faute de mieux* for the severely subnormal adult also. The Progressive Matrices is a valuable non-verbal test which is easily given and scored: it assesses the subject's capacity to reason by analogy. Various performance tests are also available, which do not depend on verbal or symbolic material: these are psychomotor tests of such special abilities as speed of manipulation, spatial ability and manual dexterity. While intelligence and manual dexterity are usually fairly closely allied and are alike necessary for any manual work which requires skill, their measurement alone cannot be used to predict success at such work. The temperamental qualities of the individual, his behaviour and emotional stability, are always of paramount importance. Further details of tests should be sought in such a textbook as Cronbach's (1960).

It is important to recognize that the I.Q. is by no means a constant like the individual's finger-prints. It is only relatively constant, and the reliability of its assessment depends on the skill of the tester. It may change even by 20 points or more, revealing fluctuations in the individual's performance not due to any change in his native capacity. It may show a marked and permanent improvement in cases where the mental retardation has been due considerably to an adverse upbringing and deprivation of education.

If intelligence tests are to produce the fullest and most reliable information, they should be administered by an expert; a psychologist's advice should certainly be sought in any difficult or marginal case. Mental testing should be used to reveal not only the patient's general intellectual level, but also his more specific aptitudes and disabilities, since knowing these we can then plan much more effectively an educational programme or give vocational guidance. It is deplorable that so many hospitals for the subnormal in this country are without psychologists on their staff.

In addition to the assessment and measurement of his intelligence, the subnormal child's or adult's personality must be appraised. His temperamental traits, his emotional stability, his persistence and reliability, his capacity to come to terms socially with normal children or adults, all these qualities must be elicited. These aspects of his make-up are often of major importance in gauging how best he can be helped, stimulated or cared for. And the subnormal individual must be seen in his family or social setting, his environment's normality, inadequacy or detrimental aspects must be known: in this part of the investigation of the case, the social worker who can visit and report on the family situation has a key rôle.

The doctor must in every case carry out a detailed physical examination, paying attention to abnormalities of physical constitution and development, to congenital lesions and stigmata, and particularly, of course, to the state of the nervous system. The child is often handicapped in more ways than intellectually, and these additional handicaps must be defined. Examination of the urine should be carried out routinely; blood samples may be required for laboratory examination if, for example, syphilitic infection or hypoglycaemia are suspected; X-rays and other specialized investigations may be indicated. The correct diagnosis of a subnormal child's clinical syndrome will often test the doctor's knowledge of general medicine at many points.

The biochemist has now an important and rapidly growing part to play in the diagnosis of syndromes of subnormality. Moncrieff (1960), in a valuable survey of the biochemistry of subnormality, has calculated that between 2500 and 4500 of the 126,000 ascertained subnormal individuals in England and Wales may have a biochemical factor in their aetiology; and he suggests that this may be an underestimate. Furthermore, if the subnormal individual is found to have a bio-chemical abnormality, study of this abnormality may necessitate laboratory examination of his relatives.

In conclusion, it must be emphasized that the diagnosis and evaluation of subnormality frequently requires the collaboration of all those concerned with the child's health and education, if it is to be made in a way which will facilitate constructive planning for the individual's future. And when the diagnosis has been made, the facts and their implications must be placed before the parents or guardians with great tact and sympathy, to elicit their co-operation and to minimize any feelings of family stigma or of personal failure which the diagnosis may have caused.

DIFFERENTIAL DIAGNOSIS

It is of course a most serious error, fraught with grave complications for the child's future, to diagnose a child as subnormal when he is not. Such a mistake is fortunately rare. Much more often the diagnosis of subnormality is missed, or for social or other reasons is rejected or glossed over.

Two groups of conditions may be wrongly diagnosed as subnormality: sensory, perceptual or aphasic defects, and psychoses. The deaf or deaf-mute child, the child with impaired vision or with some motor defect involving speech, the child seriously limited by a specific reading or calculating disability, may be mis-diagnosed as intellectually backward and the true reason for his poor perfor-mance may not be recognized. The only way to avoid such errors is to make examination in every case meticulous, with attention both to the medical and the psychological status of the child.

A schizophreniform psychosis or early infantile autism may be misdiagnosed as subnormality. There are of course symptomatic differences [see p. 502]: and the history of a more or less normal beginning to life with subsequent deteriora-tion would strongly suggest psychosis, if a state of subnormality due to an extrinsic cause such as encephalitis could be ruled out. Frequently cases of subnormality have been wrongly labelled 'childhood schizophrenia' by psychia-trists ignorant of the syndromes of subnormality.

PREVENTION AND TREATMENT

Preventive measures which are rational and effective can be based on a know-ledge of aetiology and as our understanding of the aetiology of subnormality grows more opportunities for mental hygiene therefore present themselves. Much can be done, and is being done, to diminish some of the causes of subnormality. This is effected most directly through control of environmental factors which may injure the child before, during and after birth. The maintenance of high standards of antenatal care, the avoidance of irradiation and possibly harmful drugs during pregnancy, skilled attention during childbirth, satisfactory nutrition and vastly improved control of infection in the infant, all these have been and will continue to be of great importance; and the medical services have been supported in these advances by a public better educated in health matters than its forebears. One of the most important of recent advances in medicine which is immediately relevant, is the prevention of rhesus haemolytic disease (Clarke, 1967), by the intramuscular injection into the mother within 48 hours of delivery of anti-D gamma globulin. Not all cases of Rh-haemolytic disease can be prevented in this way, since some women are already immunized; but nearly all cases can be prevented and the incidence of kernicterus thus reduced. Also, the biochemical screening of babies should be developed, so that metabolic abnormalities which may be treatable are detected as early in life as is possible.

Negative eugenic measures are harder to apply and are at present of slight practical importance; though our increasing knowledge of the genetics of subnormality provides data which can be used in genetic counselling, at least in connection with some of the clear-cut syndromes of subnormality. In cases of single gene inheritance and of chromosome abnormalities, where the mode of inheritance of the clinical entity is known, intelligent and inquiring adults may be given the facts about the expectation of abnormality in their offspring which will enable them to decide for themselves about marriage and birth control. Our ability to reduce the incidence of recessively inherited syndromes depends on the identification of carriers of the abnormal genes, and here progress has been slow. The important work already referred to on the carrier-states in phenylketonuria and nephrogenic diabetes insipidus should be followed up.

Early medical treatment is of prime importance in those syndromes where treatment is possible; for instance in cretinism, galactosaemia, phenylketonuria, diabetes insipidus, syphilitic infection. It is interesting that the specific treatment consists in several syndromes simply in giving a special diet, but unfortunately the control here is often still a matter of considerable technical difficulty. Once significant cerebral damage has been done it is usually irreversible; though one must note that hemispherectomy has sometimes proved a successful operation in carefully selected cases of subnormality which have been associated with hemiplegia and epilepsy. For programmes of immunization which will reduce the incidence of infectious diseases which may cause cerebral damage, and for early diagnosis upon which effective treatment so often depends, the maternal and child health services carry a particular responsibility.

Many educational, social and medical agencies are available to help the subnormal: special schools and special classes, occupation centres, sheltered workshops, out-patient psychiatric clinics for children and adults, hostels and colonies and hospitals for those who need in-patient care and treatment. Specialist

2 H

psychological testing and vocational guidance are available to orientate the treatment and management. We have developed the services, but all too often we lack the staff to make full use of them. The most serious shortage is perhaps in teachers for the educationally subnormal: it is impossible in over-large and insufficiently differentiated classes to give to backward children the individual attention they need and to which they will respond rewardingly. This is all the more deplorable since there has been much research and very significant advances have been made in methods of educating and training the subnormal (Clarke and Clarke, 1966). Doctors, teachers, psychologists, social workers, health visitors and voluntary associations of lay people all have their parts to play. But it must be said that the activities of those who seek to help the subnormal have not always been well co-ordinated: and the medical contribution to the problems of subnormality has been impaired by the inability of the specialist services to attract many of the best medical talents. In the last year or two, however, there has been a most welcome resurgence of interest and enthusiasm: biochemical and genetic researches in this field have aroused widespread medical interest, and there has been a much more optimistic attitude towards the rehabilitation of the subnormal. Both paediatrics and neurology have major contributions to make, and specialists in these disciplines should be encouraged to work in the health services for the subnormal.

Many of the severely subnormal children require admission to hospital. About 30 per cent. are non-ambulant and incontinent: many are both mentally and physically severely handicapped. Those with a mental age of less than 3 years demand above all skilled nursing care in their management, and this is probably the only group of the subnormal who should be considered ineducable. Much attention has been paid recently in this country to the training of the severely subnormal. Many will respond to patient and encouraging guidance: and some can be trained in repetitive mechanical tasks in Training Centres and sheltered workshops to such a degree of competence that they can contribute financially to their keep. They are, of course, much slower and less dexterous than the normal.

Subnormal children and adults should if possible be retained in the community. The great majority of the parents of subnormal children want to keep them at home, and most of these children do not impose intolerable burdens upon their families (Tizard and Grad, 1961). Many never need any medical care on account of their subnormality. If they are failing to adapt themselves socially many agencies are at hand to give them support, and full use of these should be made before hospitalization is decided upon. Admission to hospital cuts into the child's schooling, breaks the loving ties that exist in nearly all but the very worst homes, and marks the child off from his fellows: it should therefore be recommended only after careful consideration and for positive reasons, never as the easy way out. Some unstable subnormal adolescents and adults, who by reason of their delinquency or sexual promiscuity have become serious social problems, have, of course, to be segregated in hospital for prolonged periods: but hospital should for most of the subnormal be considered not as a place of segregation from the community but of preparation for it. It is with the mildly subnormal that the greatest progress can be made; naturally so, since they are at, or not far from, the borderland of normality: and the fact that about half of the patients in mental deficiency hospitals in this country fall into this group, presents a great challenge to the medical profession in whose care they have been placed. Major contributions to the rehabilitation of the subnormal have recently been made by psychologists, and this work has been reviewed by O'Connor and Tizard (1956): the authors themselves have been pioneers in the research they describe. A detailed account of their work will not be attempted here. We will only say in brief that subnormal patients in hospital must get, not only a kindly discipline which will inculcate regular habits and acceptable social attitudes, but also a schooling that will attempt to teach them at least reading, writing and simple calculation and a realistic training in work which will fit them to take jobs in the community. And when they leave hospital, subnormal patients must never be allowed to drop unsupported into a social void. They may be helped to progress to community life via a hostel. Finally, the homes to which they will return will often need the supervision and assistance of the local social services if further break-down is to be prevented.

Amongst those whose subnormality has been determined to a considerable degree by an adverse, subcultural upbringing in poor social circumstances, much improvement can usually be expected as they grow older. They are slower learners than normal children, but given time they do learn: and they mature emotionally more slowly. The result is that there may be a substantial rise in the I.Q. in adolescence and early adult life, and the educationally subnormal child may become a dull normal adult (Clarke and Clarke, 1966), at a much better level of personal and social stability. In a society where there is full employment, the majority of educationally subnormal school leavers can find work of the unskilled or semi-skilled type suited to them, provided that they do not have serious physical handicaps and are not seriously temperamentally unstable.

REFERENCES

Allen, G., and Baroff, G. S. (1956) *Acta genet. (Basel)*, **5**, 294.

Berg, J. M., Delhanty, J. D. A., Faunch, J. A., and Ridler, M. A. C. (1965) *J. ment. Defic. Res.*, **9**, 219.

Brandon, M. W. G., Kirman, B. H., and Williams, C. E. (1959) *J. ment. Sci.*, **105**, 721.

Carter, C., and Simpkiss, M. (1956) *Lancet*, ii, 1069.

Clarke, A. M., and Clarke, A. D. B. (1966) *Mental Deficiency: The Changing Outlook*, London.

Clarke, C. A. (1967) *Brit. med. J.*, **4**, 7.

Clayton, B., Moncrieff, A., and Roberts, G. E. (1967) *Brit. med. J.*, **2**, 133.

Cronbach, L. J. (1960) *Essentials of Psychological Testing*, 2nd ed., New York.

Edwards, J. H. (1961) *Arch. Dis. Childh.*, **36**, 486.

Goodman, N. and Tizard, J. (1962) *Brit. med. J.*, **1**, 216.

Haworth, J. C., and Coodin, F. J. (1960) *Pediatrics*, **25**, 748.

Hsia, D. Y. (1966) *Pediatrics*, **38**, 173.

Jacobs, P. A., and Strong, J. A. (1959) *Nature (Lond.)*, **183**, 302.

Kidd, C. B., Innes, G., and Ross, H. S. (1967) *Ulster med. J.*, **36**, 139.

Kirman, B. H. (1956) *Arch. Dis. Childh.*, **31**, 1.

Kushlick, A. (1965) *Proc. roy. Soc. Med.*, **58**, 374.

Lejeune, J., Gautier, M., and Turpin, R. (1959) *C. R. Acad. Sci. (Paris)*, **248**, 1721.

Lewis, E. O. (1929) Report of the Mental Deficiency Committee, London. H.M.S.O.

Lowrey, G. H., Aster, R. H., Carr, E. A., Ramon, G., Beierwaltes, W. H., and Spafford, N. R. (1958) *Amer. J. Dis. Child.*, **96**, 131.

Maclean, N., Mitchell, J. M., Harnden, D. G., Jacobs, P. A., Baikie, A. G., Williams, J., Buckton, K. A., Brown, W. M. C., McBride, J. A., Strong, J. A., Close, H. G., and Jones, D. C. (1962) *Lancet*, i, 293.

Manson, M. M., Logan, W. P. D., and Loy, R. M. (1960) Rubella and Other Virus Infections during Pregnancy, London, H.M.S.O.

McGirr, E. M., and Hutchison, J. H. (1956) *Lancet*, i, 106.

Mellon, J. P., Pay, B. Y., and Green, D. M. (1963) *J. ment. Defic. Res.*, **7**, 31.

Menkes, J. H., Hurst, P. L., and Craig, J. M. (1954) *Pediatrics*, **14**, 462.

Moncrieff, A. (1960) *Lancet*, ii, 273.

Moncrieff, E. M., and Hutchison, J. H. (1956) *Lancet*, i, 106.

O'Connor, N., and Tizard, J. (1956) *The Social Problem of Mental Deficiency*, London.

Penrose, L. S. (1951) *J. ment. Sci.*, **97**, 738.

Penrose, L. S. (1962) *Lancet*, i, 1101.

Penrose, L. S. (1963) *The Biology of Mental Defect*, London.

Penrose, L. S., and Smith, G. F. (1966) *Down's Anomaly*, London.

Ross, H. S., Innes, G., and Kidd, C. (1967) *Scot. med. J.*, **12**, 260.

Shapiro, A., and Ridler, M. A. C. (1960) *J. ment. Defic. Res.*, **4**, 48.

Stephenson, J. B. P., and McBean, M. S. (1967) *Brit. med. J.*, **2**, 579.

Stewart, J. S. S., Mack, W. S., Govan, A. D. T., Ferguson-Smith, M. A., and Lennox, B. (1959) *Quart. J. Med.*, **28**, 561.

Tizard, J., and Grad, J. C. (1961) *The Mentally Handicapped and their Families*, London.

20

THE PSYCHIATRY OF CHILDHOOD

PRINCIPAL CHARACTERISTICS OF CHILD PSYCHOPATHOLOGY

Three cardinal points exist for discussion in the psychology of children, in distinction from adults, as far as a distinction in this field can be drawn. They are: first, the enormous influence of environment on the child's mental processes; second, the plasticity of the latter; and third, the prominence of egoistic tendencies—their substitution and frustration—in the production of symptoms.

Influence of Environment

Environment means, of course, the personal environment of parents, brothers, sisters, teachers and companions; and an important reflection occurs here, that when signs of morbidity appear, they arise at the surface of contact, so to speak, of the child's environment with his aims and desires, rather than at some locus of conflict deeply within the psyche. It is far more often a question of some direct frustration than of an intrapsychic conflict.

This is a generalization which admits exceptions, but it is of sufficient importance in theory, and especially in practice, to warrant expansive discussion. For instance, it connotes that relatively simple adjustments of the environment, after careful consideration of the tendencies whose frustration or misdirection are indicated by the symptoms, will cause the latter to disappear, and that intensive intrapsychic exploration of the child's mind is usually unnecessary. Hence the psychiatrist's method of exploring the problem principally through interviews with parents and other adults more than with the child has its justification. There is, however, a small residue of cases in which intensive exploration is desirable.

Plasticity

The second point, the plasticity of the attitude and behaviour of children, is another aspect of the first, and is of immense practical and theoretical importance, although the plasticity is limited to some degree by inborn disposition and temperament. In the adult the problem of adjustment is complicated by the existence of a long accumulation of habits and attitudes, of the origin of most of which the subject is unconscious at the time the causal factors operate. In the child this accumulation is naturally much less, and even those attributes with the longest history are comparatively unfixed. The practical importance of the consequent plasticity lies not only in the management of nervous children, but in the prevention of neurotic and psychotic disorders in later life. There are two principal psychopathological views of the aetiology of adult mental illnesses. Both of them place the primary focus in the formative influences of childhood; but one view to which much attention has been paid in this book regards the adult illness as the cumulative result of mental habits acquired and ingrained throughout childhood and adolescence; while the other regards it as a regression to particular emotional fixations or attachments of an erotic kind at the same period. The apparent divergence of views lies perhaps more in emphasis and terminology; but they certainly agree in acknowledging the importance of early factors. It seems to us, however, that in its insistence on a set pattern, the Oedipus pattern in the infantile foundation of neuroses, the second view does less justice than the first to the almost infinite plasticity of the young organism's mental and emotional equipment, the wide variety of the influences that impinge upon it, and the multiplicity of its responses. This belief receives support from an unexpected quarter—so experienced a child analyst as Anna Freud has to confess that she has failed to observe directly in the children she has treated the developmental situations in the first two years of life classically considered by psychoanalysis as at the root of adult neuroses. She meets this by saying that the material presented by the child furnishes 'clear and unequivocal clues to the foundation of the infantile neurosis', but that the absence of the reaction-formations and cover-memories of the latency period deprives the child analyst of the material which alone furnishes the psychoanalytic data. The pre-speech period remains inaccessible—the analysts would say, not because the material was not there, but because in children it has not had time to be formulated. It would also be possible to suppose that the psychoanalytic situations were not commonly important at that age, and that the memories in most instances were relevant only to later neuroses.

Whatever view be taken, the plastic trend of childhood remains highly significant for the prophylaxis of adult neuroses, but the more immediate practical importance of the plasticity lies in the improvement that follows treatment in 'nervous children' generally. This therapeutic response is so marked and so invariable where it can be expected that the reflection readily arises that so-called 'nervous children' would usually get better of themselves without the aid of the clinic. Indeed, while giving proper weight to the immense effect of the child's environment in producing psychological disturbances in him, it is necessary to remember that all children are subjected to innumerable traumata, and the wonder is, not how many nervous and unstable children there are, but what a large proportion grow to be reasonably normal men and women.

Rôle of Innate Factors

But just as too much optimism may lead to a policy of *laissez faire* on the ground of the self-adjustment of the majority of psychopathological phenomena in children, so, on the other hand, may a pessimism preconceived on the score of the importance and immutability of inborn temperament and disposition lead to a failure to grasp numerous possibilities of modification, for the limitations produced by inborn factors are much less than is usually believed. It is a sound working rule to attribute nothing morbid, whether of behaviour, mood or thought, to congenital and therefore, presumably, less modifiable causes until a complete investigation has revealed nothing in the history of environmental influences and personal events that will reasonably account for the symptoms, and until the latter have proved but little modifiable by any known therapy; and even then the matter may not have been congenitally engraved.

A further point is the profound interconnection between mental and physical factors in the child. Even more than in the adult, the emotions influence bodily processes and vice versa. Not only do the various bodily functions have a lower threshold of irritability than in the adult, but the autonomic nervous system in particular appears to be less stable. Thus 'psychosomatic' reactions and disorders of various kinds are common, especially in children of sensitive, excitable disposition and often of above average intelligence. In addition to the same kinds of psychosomatic syndromes as one encounters in the adult, more superficial and transient reactions are commonly found, such as the vomiting which may precede parties or examinations.

With these general reflections we may proceed to a brief discussion of psychopathology as it applies to children. The intrinsic psychological factors are conveniently discussed first.

The Egoistic Tendencies

It is customary to designate the thinking of the young child as essentially egocentric. Quoting Piaget's example, we would say that for the child the sun or the moon appears to follow him wherever he goes; at first there is no thought of reconciling this relationship with the sun's possible appearance to other persons. But this is merely the more intellectual aspect of the general tendency and orientation of the child—he is not merely egocentric but egoistic. Growing up, psychologically, consists in a progressive diminution in egoism, and a corresponding socialization of derivatives of the instinctive tendencies, egoistic and other.

This egoism implies many things—a drive towards self-assertion in all regions of living, including therefore a desire for affection and approbation, a tendency towards self-display, a craving for personal prominence, rivalry with others and jealousy of them; and, on the other hand, a persistent awareness, dimly or not at all consciously formulated, of a lack of personal security. It is a cardinal principle of treatment that this many-sided egoism must have outlets, but they must be healthy, and such as are socially acceptable and adapted to the chronological stage of development. Mental growth is one long conflict between the demands of natural egoism and the conditions of the environment; but it need not be a painful conflict except at intervals. A very large proportion of children, and the grown-up children we call adults, who are brought for treatment are, however, suffering from the pains of this strife. Very often the pains are far more acute than is needful, since the parents, for reasons later to be explained, have begun by indulging the egoism. Hence the child finds on entering school or going among his coevals in any way, that the contrast is too sharp for him to bear, and so he develops truancy, or anxiety, or outbursts of temper, or hypochondriacal aches or pains. Along with egoism, and as an example of that bipolarity which is characteristic of so many aspects of the mind, there goes a feeling of helplessness and insignificance, the famous 'feeling of inferiority' which colours so many of the child's reactions as well as of the adult's.

The egoistic trends, like so many of the other childish characteristics, have a high degree of plasticity. It is usual to speak of this plasticity in its relationships to persons as suggestibility, and where an element of conscious volition enters as 'imitation'. The suggestibility can appear in relation to anyone in the environment, but especially towards those with whom bonds of affection exist, and towards those who are older or who for some reason possess prestige. Naturally the parents and their substitutes, as the most ordinary objects in the environment, and the mother especially as the most intimate, are potentially the mightiest factors of this kind. The nervous disorders of childhood, which are not dependent considerably or entirely on errors in parental example or attitude, and which cannot be greatly improved by modifying that attitude or example, are in the minority. The point is also usefully considered, however, from the aspect of abnormalities in the parents, which will be summarily discussed later. In the meantime, let us recall that the automatically suggested example of the parents and elders and companions becomes gradually embedded in the child's mind sometimes reaching conscious expression as the ideal ego, but more often operating quietly and unconsciously to modify the conduct (the super-ego or the unconscious conscience, see Chapter 7). Not all, however, of parental example and precept is incorporated in this way. Some of it is rejected, and may even provoke the opposite reaction to that desired (negativism or counter suggestibility), the result of egoistic aims coming into too direct collision with environmental demands. Negativism is apt to grow and flourish upon increase in the environmental resistance, on the principle, as it were, that every action produces an equal and opposite reaction; and, like many mental reactions, negativism may continue to operate automatically as a habit, in apparent independence of any connection with its original stimulus. Hence it comes about that the most rigid disciplinarian among parents may produce the most stubborn children. This general tendency towards conflict between egoism and the environment naturally has its foci of special concentration. The regulation of any special manifestation of the self-assertive tendencies along a social channel, or the relinquishing of any form of pleasure not socially permissible, can form such a focus. In accordance with his general theory, Freud attached importance principally to the conflict produced by enforced relinquishment, especially, of activities of a sensuous or, in the Freudian sense, erotic kind. Hence weaning and the education of the bladder, and especially the bowel function, become, on this theory, the critical points of development of temperament and character, and so also in the determination of the pattern of future reactions. Thus an unusual difficulty round the relinquishment of 'anal pleasure' (either from accidental accentuation of the latter, or from innate factors) is held to lead by 'reaction-formation' to traits of obstinacy (persistent negativism) This view differs from that encouraged by observation of the reactions of children, in attributing obstinacy specially to anal erotism instead of regarding it, as we do, as a reaction which may arise and persist as the result of mismanagement of any phase of development, of egoism generally or of its specific manifestations.

Negativistic conduct, being the outcome of aroused egoism, can naturally minister to egoism in a high degree. Temper tantrums, for example, serve the double purpose of avoiding some duty of accommodation of one's wishes to others, and of self-display. Some investigators consider that there is a definite crisis in the adjustment of the infantile egoism to society between the ages of three and five, and that if this stage is not properly managed, obstinacy may persist as an unusually prominent personal characteristic.

It has been a favourite phantasy of mankind that the original state was one of happiness and universal love. Mythology and religion alike tell of a 'Golden Age' when the world was young. English men of letters of the eighteenth century and later were fond of referring to the 'noble savage'. There are not wanting psychopathological grounds for seeing in this an unconscious desire for a return, on the part of those who advocate these views, to the 'Golden Age' of their own childhood, when all was (as they now believe) as they wished, and only ties of affection governed their relations to other men. It is a fact that affection is the readiest response of the infant and young child to other individuals; but as the latter do not always minister to his needs, and may even frustrate them, it is not difficult for the corresponding opposite to appear, namely, hatred or some degree of it. This may lead to a cordial death wish towards the obnoxious person. Death does not mean very much to a child; it represents disappearance as far as he is concerned; the antagonist is no longer in the path. Such feelings of hate, however, appear much more readily in relation to rivals, or, in other words, as jealousy, with results which have been exemplified above. In a wider circle than the family we find hatred combined with negativism to produce an attitude of hostility to the social group in which the child finds himself—especially his or her companions at school and the neighbouring children. Not infrequently a child is sent to a clinic with the label from school, 'Dangerous to others': we have known such a label to be attached to a six-year-old. The child had been sticking pins in others, or 'going for' their eyes or hitting them with slight or no apparent provocation. Usually such a child comes of a bad home, and is often reproducing the attitude to the world of school which it found meted out to it by its parents— hatred showing itself in verbal or corporal chastisement or in other ways. Some-times, of course, it is a direct retaliation for attitudes assumed by school-mates towards someone recognized as not belonging to their particular herd—children coming from some other country or another race; or some personal peculiarity, especially of such a type as Fröhlich's syndrome, may produce ridicule which stings the child to retaliation. As the majority of children are timid in face of much show of physical aggression by their comrades, another factor begins to act; the aggressor finds that he can dominate in this way, and so compensates doubly for his own felt inferiority. More often than is usually suspected a desire to dominate other children shows itself also in subtle ways, as in a girl of twelve who managed to impress and frighten a class-mate and competitor in such a way that the latter was miserable and consequently did her work badly, so allowing the tormentor to bear the palm.

In vindictive behaviour such as this there sometimes enters a definite element of cruelty. There is no doubt that all children possess a capacity for cruelty, but it is not commonly shown to any marked degree, and then only transiently as a rule. There is equally no doubt that behind such manifestations of cruelty lies a certain feeling of pleasure. Cruelty, however, except in cases of certain subnormal (mentally defective) and psychopathic children, nearly always yields to kindly deprecation and provision of other outlets.

The inner development of egoistic feeling determines, almost independently of outside influences, phantasies of power and importance. The upbringing of most young children favours this, for at first the baby is usually the centre of his little world and he does not readily relinquish the feeling so engendered. The couplet,

> 'I do not love the human race,
> I do not like its ugly face',

covers the survival in many adults of the results of the clash of reality which is felt to interfere unpleasantly with the infantile omnipotence (the Jehovah-complex, or God-complex, of the Freudians; the 'almightiness' of Adlerian usage, and the root of many phantasies and mannerisms of everyday life). But in children it is not a 'complex' in the morbid sense, but a normal state of affairs. The feeling of importance usually undergoes correction in the light of experience, as long as no close rival appears on the scene. But let a younger brother or sister appear before the elder child has outgrown the phase of wanting everything in his environment for his own delectation; then the signs of jealousy readily appear. One small girl was found to have banged her baby brother's head on the gas stove and at another time to have emptied him from his pram into the roadway, while yet another was discovered pulling the baby sister's hair and spitting on her face as the baby lay in her cot. Instances of that sort, less pronounced as a rule, are numberless.

The notion of power and omnipotence is closely linked with the unreality feelings, which are far more common in children than is usually realized. The latter present in a way the reverse side of the picture, and result from the contrast of a small being, suddenly aware of his own comparative insignificance, with the overwhelming immensity of the external world of space and time. The more intense the notion of power has been, the more intensely this contrast is felt, and the greater the resulting anxiety, reinforced, sometimes at least, by feelings of remorse for having provoked the external forces, often regarded at this age implicitly, if not explicitly, in a demoniacal light.

The Sexual Instinct and its Ramifications

Of the tendency of children to develop affectionate attachments to persons of either sex, everyone is aware, but it is difficult to differentiate their attitude to persons of the same sex from that shown towards persons of the opposite sex. The same elements of interest and regard and affectionate dependence are evident in either case, but what sex the choice is focused on seems to be a matter of circumstance. Much has been said of the tendency of a boy to prefer his mother, and a girl her father, but from infancy a strong preference for the parent of the same sex is not infrequently observed. This can sometimes depend on the attitude of the parents eliciting a differential response in the child. Similar factors can determine to some extent the attachments formed outside the family; thus males are chosen by small girls as substitutes for unaffectionate fathers.

To say, however, that any considerable proportion of the relationships just discussed have a sexual aspect, conscious or unconscious, in the sense of adult sexuality is still a large assumption; and to say further that such attachments, or the repression of these attachments upon a sexual basis, is the root cause of the symptoms of many of the persistent nervous disturbances in children is not yet justifiable. No one can deny the existence of infantile and childish sex manifestations, but their place in the psychopathology of childhood is another matter.

Parent-Child Relationships

It is a commonplace that the relationship of parent to child is of maximal importance for the shaping of character; it is of no less weight in the production of psychopathological deviations in childhood. The factors of dependence, imitation and suggestion already mentioned, with their complication in action and reaction, are of primary importance. There are two parental attitudes that are specially common, the over-anxious mother and the domineering father over-keen for the progress and advancement of his son. The father who expects his son to conform closely to his own desires and aspirations, and shows it, often succeeds in producing either a weak-kneed creature lacking in initiative, readily depressed and filled with morbid fears, or an unstable truant, or a sullen, defiant and sometimes furtive individual, who steals and goes with 'rough boys'.

The 'babying parent' is a caricature of the over-anxious one and may produce either the same namby-pamby type, or, in turn, frank rebellion. It is not very uncommon to find mothers who help at their son's bath until he is 16 or 17, and we have even encountered a father who was frequently present at the same function with his daughter of 16. A father of this type dandled his daughter on his knee and wrote poetry about her and with her, from her childhood into adolescence; her subsequent schizophrenic psychosis was strongly tinged with feelings of guilt towards him. 'Babying' of this kind has obvious sexual connotations, but at an earlier age these connotations do not usually enter. A mother's insistence on having her child sleep in the same room as the parents after the period of infancy can heighten a child's feeling of insecurity, increase his fears and fill him with an uncomfortable curiosity. It can also foster a close attachment of the child to the mother which can seriously hinder adaptation to marriage in later life.

'Spoiling' in the sense of indulgence and lack of discipline is a commonplace as a cause of childish misbehaviour, as well as of difficulty in after life. Of it are born temper tantrums, food fads, ostentation, mannerisms, tearfulness, jealousy and the like.

At the opposite extreme of these instances is that of the parent of an unwanted child, which, in consequence of the lack of love or actual spitefulness of its parent, displays similar traits in itself.

Parental dissatisfactions have, however, subtler consequences than this. A parent dissatisfied with his or her own life wants to see his or her own unfulfilled longings gratified in the children. A father expects his son to excel at games, and is annoyed, and the boy correspondingly depressed, when the expectations are not fulfilled; and at a later stage choice of occupation may be unfortunately regulated from the same motive. A young woman who has had an unhappy experience in relation to her own mother, tries to make her companionship with her offspring 'perfect', and so blocks out the possibility of her child making the fullest use of friendships with coevals. Or she may be unhappy in her marriage and seek emotional compensation in excessive devotion from her child, with a resulting conflict in the latter, and its consequences in fears or compulsions. Parental rejection, no matter how carefully disguised, is felt by the child as a lack of the affection it craves, and it is a frequent factor in producing psychological disturbances.

The grandparents (and over-indulgent uncles and aunts) can also have important formative, or, rather, deformative, influences on a child's life—especially if parents and grandparents happen to live together, as occurs fairly often in the houses of the poor. It is possible for a grandparent to be on more friendly terms with a child than its own parents, and it is equally possible for a grandparent to appear as a destructive kind of ogre and spoil-sport. It is not uncommon to find parents and grandparents differing openly in their attitude to the child, from personal prejudice and from the result of old-standing conflicts between them, with the result that the child's training and standards are impaired, and he learns to play off one generation against the other.

Difficulties found Primarily at School

Of these the most common, but even yet sometimes undetected, is scholastic backwardness, of all degrees from mere dullness to obvious subnormality (mental defect). Naturally, cases of severe subnormality announce themselves early, and if they appear in school at all are not long left there. But not infrequently with the dull and backward, or the subnormal, the first sign of anything amiss is some form of misbehaviour. Naturally, the child who is not capable of the average school work for his years becomes either uninterested, anxious and humiliated, or openly rebellious. Rarer and more localized forms of congenital handicap, like word-deafness and word-blindness, are still more readily missed, being mistaken for subnormality.

When intelligence testing first became popular, much was made of the idea of the possible discovery by this means of hidden talent, and even of genius. Expectations of this kind are only rarely borne out, but occasional instances of persistent ill-behaviour, or even apparent scholastic backwardness, are found, which depend on a child's being included in a class where the work is far below the level of his intelligence.

Emotional factors count no less than intellectual ones in the production of symptoms of unrest at school. Naturally, emotional conflicts at home may disturb the attitude at school, but much more rarely than would be expected. The school itself affords emotional difficulties *sui generis*.' Differential behaviour', *i.e.* a good report from school as compared with a bad one from home, or vice versa, is a valuable diagnostic aid. The child has to adapt to school-fellows as well as teachers—from both he begins by expecting the same kind of attitude as he experienced from members of the family. Disappointment in some degree is inevitable and may intensify a previous feeling of uncertainty and inferiority. But this will rarely reach pathological dimensions unless the soil has been prepared by unhappy relationships at home, or unless the teachers themselves adopt a mistaken attitude. The latter is not uncommon, but should never be inevitable. Large classes, while valuable in one way in reducing the chance of perpetuating 'spoiled' and similar reactions, operate against individual understanding when any preliminary difficulties have already appeared. It is not an uncommon experience to find a child given a bad name by schoolmasters, which in itself serves the worst possible purpose.

As with parents, so with teachers—dissatisfactions and morbid attitudes of their own may produce morbid reactions in the children under their care. A love of power, or sometimes actually sadistic trends, show themselves in teasing, bullying and stupid forms of punishment. Such minor manifestations of lack of the proper relationship between teacher and pupil as impatience, frequent criticism and heavy reproof in front of others and the like, can have a considerable effect in producing difficulties both of scholarship and behaviour. An attitude of a too affectionate kind on the part of the child depends for its results on the response of the teacher, who, if wise, may turn it to good account. Such attitudes frequently have, consciously or unconsciously, an erotic basis, and more is heard of them when this basis is of a homosexual kind; but heterosexual attachments, limited naturally by the arrangements of things in schools to preferences of female teachers for certain pupils, are commoner than is supposed, and account for some instances of favouritism, which is the equivalent in school of spoiling at home. Naturally such attitudes have a specious maternal look, and the ill-effect on the child is simply the ill-effect of most-favoured-nation treatment. All these possible variants of the relationship between child and school are fraught with greater importance in boarding-school than in day-school. A general observation is opportune: that just as the usual type of scholastic education suits one child far better than another, so does boarding-school vary in its value in comparison with day-school with various types of children. The choice of a suitable school is of enormous importance for the nervous child.

METHODS OF INVESTIGATION

These differ considerably in some respects from the methods used in adult mental and nervous illness, for two principal reasons, that the average child is even less conscious of his own mental processes than the average adult, and for this reason does not readily communicate material that is of value; and secondly, that since in practice it is found that so much can be done principally by manipulation of the environment, it is not necessary as a rule to attempt to probe the child's mental life too closely or in too great detail. The general principle is to make the lines of inquiry as broad as possible, by including school reports and (in clinic practice) a report from a social worker, visiting both home and school, as well as the evidence obtained from parents and from the child himself.

Since a child practically never seeks advice of its own accord, it is from the parent or guardian, or from the school, that the information about the 'complaints' or symptoms is obtained. This should be recorded in detail, and inquiries extended to all the fields of possible unrest mentioned in the subjoined classification. A history of the child from its earliest days is then taken, both with regard to physical development and physical illnesses, and with special reference to landmarks in mental and nervous development. The times of beginning to walk and talk are of great importance, and, of a very young child, of beginning to support its head, to sit up and to crawl. Of lesser importance is the date when bladder control in the day-time was obtained. Normally a child holds up its head at four months, can sit up unsupported at six months, can walk and talk by not later than two years, and can control the bladder sphincter by day and night at the latest at three years of age. In some exceptional cases talking has been delayed even as late as five years, without subsequent intellectual retardation, but usually a very considerable proportionate retardation in any of these functions beyond the times mentioned is evidence of subnormality. The dates of more educational and less intrinsic significance are those of sleeping alone, of first being allowed out to play with other children, and of going to school.

Then follows an inquiry directed to the family relationships—the number of brothers and sisters, their personalities and the place of the child in the family—whether eldest, youngest or what. Attempts have been made to demonstrate statistically that eldest and youngest children are more prone to maladjustment than children in other positions in the family series. Levy has shown that eldest children are slightly more liable to suffer generally; while only children are more likely to be victims of parental over-solicitude and ambition.

The actual sleeping arrangements (hours of sleep and whether alone or with brothers or sisters or with parents) and the history of these is to be ascertained, and behind any peculiarities the reasons for them (accommodation or parental wishes).

It is necessary to have particulars about play—whether the child is allowed to play with other children, at home or outside; whether he prefers to play alone; and the types of play he prefers (e.g. a girl, aged 6, preferred to amuse herself by shooting and killing tin soldiers, which was on a par with her behaviour to others).

Information about the parents themselves is naturally one of the most important lines of inquiry. They should be interviewed alone, as well as together (if possible), and a kindly attitude will usually prompt confidences about their own lives which may throw considerable light on the symptoms of the child. Tact is very necessary, since they are often naturally sensitive about their failures with the child. It may be possible to discover whether the child was wanted, whether the parents co-operate in training it and in their discipline, and what place the child is occupying in the mind of each parent with regard to the other. The grandparents are also of importance, not only because they had so much to do with forming the parents' character, but because they frequently intervene, deliberately or not, in the upbringing of the grandchildren. Not uncommonly a relationship which is more pleasing to the child can be found with its grand-parents than with its own immediate parents.

Stepchildren seem, from experience, more likely to come under the psychiatrist's care than when the parents still survive and live together; and the children of 'broken homes' are also more prone to do so.

The economic status of the family, the size of house and other facts of this order are often of much importance.

In all these fields of investigation the services of a social worker are invaluable, and for carrying out parts of the treatment, in hospitals and clinics at least, indispensable. She can arrange either to do this herself or by co-operation with some social agency outside the hospital or clinic, always of course under the psychiatrist's ultimate direction.

Not least in all this routine, and in spite of the reservation made at the beginning, is contact with the child himself. We say 'contact' advisedly, because we do not plunge into an investigation of the child, but rather seek to establish a friendly relationship. After that has been accomplished, and it can be done remarkably quickly with most children, since they are naturally friendly, it is possible with surprising frequency to get the patient to talk about his difficulties. This talk may not be very free, or, if it is free, it is usually superficial, but it is often illuminating. Even when deception enters, the fact of deception itself is of great interest; its evaluation can follow in the light of discoveries from other sources. In younger children it has to be remembered that denial has the rank of phantasy—the child readily believes his own statement, once made.

A child, however, cannot stand prolonged conversations. They are boring for him after a short time, unless something else is introduced. The natural thing to introduce is play. It is also the easiest way to study the child, as he is off his guard, at least to some extent, even if it is with a doctor or a member of the clinic staff that he plays. Strictly speaking, it is not necessary to institute observation during play for the investigation of the majority of problem children, but as we desire to know as much about the children as possible, we arrange play-time with a member of the clinic staff, if not with the psychiatrist himself, wherever possible. Organized play can be of three types—games with other children, where the social reactions can be studied; games of the solitary type, such as building bricks, Meccano and the like, cutting out shapes, plasticine modelling, dolls, toy soldiers; and aesthetic and intellectual pursuits—drawing, painting and story-telling (oral and written). All these give additional sidelights on a child's character and problems, as well as providing him with outlets and modes of expression, untrammelled by criticism.

For cases not yielding to these methods, and for those not likely to be satisfactorily treated by them, such as neurotic anxiety states not dependent on environmental influences, obsessive compulsive neuroses, and some behaviour disorders (*e.g.* cases of truancy, and stealing not resolvable in environmental terms or in terms of personality organization), play technique, either interpretative or non-interpretative, is indicated. It is in many cases, even of the apparently obscure kind, worth trying the simpler methods first, since often they are capable of subsiding in a surprising way in response to simple measures, *e.g.* physical or psychological alteration of the environment.

Play Technique

The method of studying the child when he is playing, and of making use of well-controlled interpretations based on his play, is the method of choice in any case requiring intensive study rather than environmental manipulation. For example, if a child of a family consisting of father, mother and two daughters is supplied with dolls to represent each of these, the child may proceed to a play in which the dolls clearly represent its own attitude to its parents. For example, one little girl who was very jealous of her younger brother, when given two dolls of different ages, used invariably to smack the face of the smaller one within a few minutes. In this case the interpretation told us nothing new, but the principle involved may lead to interesting discoveries in more complicated settings.

In brief, we should always remember to take account both of environmental factors and inner mental processes, and welcome any method, however indirect, of getting at the latter; for in a child this is a specially difficult task and a direct approach is of very limited value, being handicapped in many ways by the child's reserve and his lack of verbal formulation of his problems.

Materials. The materials for a more extended use of play as a means of discovering the contents of a child's mind include such primitive materials as sand and water; plasticine for modelling into objects of interest or curiosity; articles capable of functioning as power symbols such as toy motor-cars and engines; others such as toy guns or animals capable of symbolizing aggressive impulses; objects with direct or indirect reference to excretory functions such as toy lavatories, watering-cans, etc.; and pencil and paper. Such materials give a wide range of opportunity for the expression of aggressive, excretory and sexual impulses, and together are capable of expressing most of the child's interests.

Interpretative Technique. The degree to which the use made of these materials by the child can be utilized for the understanding of his or her inner interests and conflicts, is a matter of dispute. Melanie Klein considered that the play of children is comparable with the free association of adults and that interpretation to the child can and should be made accordingly. Apart from the dubiousness of some such interpretations and the impossibility in many cases of satisfactory confirmation, the objective value of the therapist's subsequent observations is diminished by the suggestive effect on the child of such interpretations.

Relationship to Therapist. Anna Freud believes that the relationship of the child to the analyst has something essentially different from the relationship of the adult in analysis and that the classical transference situation does not exist since the parents, the original love-objects, are still important in the patient's life and are not phantasies with which the adult can be clothed. As a corollary, she considers that the super-ego of the child is still attached to the external objects (persons) from whom it is derived, and that re-education is therefore possible and important.

As Rogerson pointed out, 'again and again one finds evidence that it is not the interpretation of a difficulty that causes it to vanish. On the contrary, the important things are the expression of it, and the reception of it without hostile criticism.' He also considered that the relationship with the therapist can be a very simple one, similar to what occurs in the shorter forms of psychotherapy in adults, but that it can be sufficient to enable the child to feel enough protection to discuss the jealousies, for example, that had been producing anxiety (Rogerson, 1939).

Modification According to Age. Play therapy in some form is the only medium of approach to the younger children. With older children, story telling, story writing, drawing and painting, the invention of and participation in little plays, and the use of a toy theatre. have all been found useful in one case or another. With groups puppet shows may be given and the children tend to pick out the episodes that stimulate their inner phantasies. They are asked at critical points in the play what the persons should do and are asked to retell the story in their own words. With young adolescents discussions become possible, and for deeper investigation, free association may, in a few instances, be found practicable. It is often helpful for the therapist to study the child in his immediate relationship to the therapist while playing and talking with him. By showing him how to deal with the mistakes in his attitude and behaviour which arise during the session, he helps the child to manage similar emotional problems occurring in the wider setting of his ordinary life.

Therapeutic Effect of Play Technique. The fact that in many instances the child improves without any interpretation being given to his play, suggests that it is the feeling of security that the child gets from expressing thoughts and impulses of which he is otherwise afraid, in the presence of a non-critical and kindly adult, that is the important medium of therapy. Rogerson instanced a child with obsessive thoughts about killing people who said to him, 'You know, it's funny I don't have these thoughts when you are here', and later she played violently aggressive games of killing and stabbing. It is not always aggressive impulses of which the patient has been afraid; sometimes it is the rebuffs that he would have experienced had he expressed his thoughts to anyone else.

Nature of Impulses Recorded in Play. In the course of play aggressive impulses may be displayed towards the therapist, and the child then oscillates between affection and antagonism. This may represent a reactivation of earlier and contemporary attitudes towards the parents. Rogerson pointed out that after an outburst of jealousy the child would call the therapist 'Daddy'. The expression of such contradictory feelings in the presence of an adult not reacting critically towards them evidently enables the child not only to get rid of the tension produced by them, but to accept them as part of himself.

Even general aggressiveness, without specific object, can lose its disturbing quality when expressed in play under the eye of the therapist. The timid child with underlying aggressive impulses which he is afraid to exhibit, derives lasting benefit from this release.

Relationship of Play Trends to Symptoms. The appearance of excretory and sexual phantasies in the play of children, does not mean that they are causally related to the symptoms. Curiosity, rivalry with the opposite sex, the difference

21

between the sexes, and anxiety about the absence of a penis or its possible loss, all may appear without apparent relevance to the symptoms: but this is not to say that a castration fear, founded on the observation of sex differences, may not play a part in the genesis of a chronic state of anxiety later on. But Rogerson noticed in practice that anxiety connected with birth phantasies as revealed in play (*e.g.* building a hollow house in which babies were found) tended not to disappear till an explanation was given to the child.

We have quoted Rogerson's work at some length as it was conducted with a deliberate avoidance of interpretation (except in the last instance quoted) and seemed to demonstrate that great improvement and recovery can occur without interference by actual interpretations; and that the child's acceptance of its own impulses and interests under the protection of an older person was the potent therapeutic factor.

Melanie Klein, on the other hand, declared that she had 'never seen any advantage follow from a policy of non-interpretation'. Nevertheless interpretation is certainly not necessary in a fair proportion even of those cases in which play technique is the only likely method of approach.

We have ourselves been impressed with the relative infrequency with which specifically sexual interests are causally associated with the problems of childhood. This is a judgement based on an examination of symptoms, of the circumstances apparently producing them, and of the results of treatment devised from our observations. On the other hand—and there is no seeming contradiction here—it is equally certain that children exhibit sexual interest of some sort, in some cases from their earliest days. Masturbation, presumably with pleasurable sensation, is found even in infants, and even as early as 4 years we have known it associated with conscious thoughts of the other sex, although there had been no known precocity of education in these matters. Curiosity as to the genitalia and excretory functions of children of both sexes, exhibited in looking or in actual mutual sexual play, is usually felt as wrong at the time because of the general social prohibition that is felt to surround them. Later they may become coloured with a greater feeling of guilt, from their conscious association with more adult forms of sexuality. Such associations may lead to anxiety or to obsessive-compulsive preoccupations in children, but not by any means necessarily; nor need anxiety or obsession necessarily or usually be related to erotic trends. Naturally, if as the result of unwise parental attitudes and actions, such as wlil be illustrated later, erotic feeling has been aroused in relation to the parents, the conflict will be more intense and the likelihood of a neurosis greater; but instances of nervousness dependent on such definitely sexual interests are much in the minority in children, and only begin to appear with any frequency in adolescents.

CLASSIFICATION

We have found the following classification useful for nervous disorders in children in general. Only the first three are additional to the syndromes, described in previous chapters, in adults.

1. Disorders of personality: Timidity, obstinacy, irritability, sensitiveness, shyness, day-dreaming, lack of sociability, emotional disturbances, etc.
2. Behaviour disorders: Truancy, wandering, temper tantrums, lying, stealing, begging, cruelty, sex misdemeanours, food fads, refusal of food, etc.
3. Habit disorders: Nail-biting, thumb-sucking, incontinence (nocturnal and diurnal), constipation, vomiting, stammering, etc.
4. Psychosomatic disorders: Migraine, asthma, cyclical vomiting, etc.
5. Neuroses: Anxiety, hysteria, obsessional states (including phobias, compulsions and some tics).
6. Psychoses: Schizophrenia, manic-depressive psychoses, early infantile autism, etc.
7. Epilepsy.
8. Subnormality (mental defect).
9. Mental disorders occurring with, and probably dependent on, some physical disease: *e.g.* chorea, encephalitis, trauma.

This grouping is for convenience of description only. The same patient may manifest disorders in several of the above categories. The following is a brief systematic description of the various categories.

Personality Deviations

Personality traits are the outcome of the interplay of inborn and environmental factors, and it is from the beginning difficult to distinguish how much each of these types of factor shares in the production of the traits which ultimately distinguish the individual. There is no doubt that temperament, which plays so large a part in the development of the personality, is largely an inborn affair. Infants a week old, living in the same environment, present to trained observers differences of a temperamental kind. The observation of twins gives some means of estimating the relative importance of environment and inheritance. Identical twins, even if reared apart, show a remarkable similarity in their traits of temperament, while dissimilar twins, brought up together, show obvious divergences from the earliest age.

The post-natal development of traits of temperament and character proceeds as a result of friction arising from within and without, and whatever views may be held with regard to the share of inheritance, there is no doubt of the modifiability of this development by changes in the external factors.

Some characteristics are the more or less direct expression of innate qualities —as, for example, energetic activity, impulsiveness, cheerfulness, persistence and pugnacity. They naturally undergo a progressive socialization in the course of time. Where the environment enters unusually early or forcibly the trait may be regarded as either imitative of the environment, *e.g.* vanity in the child of a doting mother (the mother dotes on the child and the child dotes on himself) or, as a reaction against it, *e.g.* sullenness in response to a nagging parent. Some traits, however, have a more complicated origin, of the same form as a neurotic symptom—they are reactions against certain inner tendencies and attitudes, which may of course themselves be largely determined by environmental influences.

Such in many instances are shyness and over-conscientiousness.

In any case, an attempt should be made from the main facts to surmise at least what may have been the exact cause of any trait so disadvantageous as to bring the child for treatment.

Paranoid and schizoid personalities can be discerned occasionally among children, especially from about twelve years onwards. Their occurrence is of particular importance, of course, for the topic of predisposition to and prevention of a psychosis in later life; and they deserve much more attention than they have yet received, both as to cause and treatment.

The following example illustrates many such points. The patient had already from the beginning of our observation been regarded as a psychopathic personality. He represents one of many possible varieties.

CASE No. 36

Solitariness, temper tantrums and a fanatical interest in religious ritual were the principal marks of a boy, age $12\frac{1}{2}$. His mother added that he was 'difficult', slept badly and was easily frightened. He went to bed at 9 p.m. but did not fall asleep till midnight, and insisted on one of his parents remaining by his bedside the while. At meal-times he frequently refused to stay at table, alleging as his reason for this that his mother 'did not eat right' or 'was not dressed right'. He had 'church on the brain'—his main topics of conversation were ecclesiastical, and his principal recreation out of school hours was rehearsing church services. His knowledge of these matters was said by his mother to be astonishingly detailed, and when he went to church he would find fault with the minutiae of the service.

He played ordinary boys' games very little. Football he only took part in when compelled to do so by other boys. He had no friends of his own age and said that he did not want any. If his parents invited another boy to the home he 'sat and talked quite nice to him', but he would not accept invitations in return.

From his mother it was discovered in addition that he swore, even in front of his father (who never punished him). He was not cleanly in his bodily habits. His mother bathed him, to the accompaniment of screaming and fighting. At night in his bedroom when his mother sat with him, he terrified her with his restlessness, throwing his arms about and talking incessantly. He had the habit of harping on one theme to the intense and frequently expressed annoyance of his parents—for example, he would talk for hours to his cat, saying 'nice boy' over and over again, *ad nauseam*.

He was in a private school, and the school report said:

'I have pleasure in stating that he has never given us the slightest trouble. The boy is obedient, quiet and inoffensive; in fact, the one thing that strikes us is that he is apathetic, dreamy and slow on the "up-take". In some subjects—English and drawing —he is in advance of his years; in others—arithmetic—he is slow and backward. When he first came here he kept somewhat aloof, but he is now mixing gradually with the other boys.

'Judging from his behaviour here I cannot understand the trouble over this boy. Here he is perfectly docile, without vice or troublesome tendencies.'

This divergence in the reports from school and home furnishes an example of the differentiation of behaviour which is so frequent in children, and is one of the evidences of environmental influences.

Family History. The father was quiet and retiring, sensitive and gentle in manner. He never cared to play with other boys when he was a child, and when he first went to work had a 'stiff' time, as he could not hold his own in the company of others. He neither smoked nor drank and had no hobbies. He took little interest in Peter, but took his part against the grandmother in a negative way—refusing to scold him at her demand.

The mother herself, who gave much of the above information when she came up to hospital and afterwards added considerably to it, was obviously greatly perturbed by her child's conduct. She confessed her entire helplessness to alter it. She admitted that she herself was of a worrying disposition. Since childhood she had thought worry the 'right thing to do'. She had been taken to a doctor at the age of 14 as she was 'all shaky'. Being afraid of her mother, who was ill-tempered and often thrashed her, she would wander about the streets at night afraid to go home.

The grandmother had now resided with the parents for the past three years, and entertained a violent dislike for the boy with whom she frequently quarrelled, while, on the other hand, she took his part against his mother on any question of discipline.

Home Conditions. The family occupied a good-sized house which they were buying by instalments. The situation was somewhat complicated, as they borrowed the capital for this venture from the maternal grandmother, and instead of paying her interest they kept her. They used four rooms—well-furnished sitting-room and kitchen, a bedroom for the old lady and one for themselves. The home gave the impression of real comfort and prosperity. There was a garden, and the neighbourhood was a good one. Part of the house was let.

Previous History. Birth was normal and the child appeared perfectly normal during his infancy. When he was one year old his father went into the Army and his mother went out to work. Peter was left to the care of his maternal grandmother until the age of 5, when his father returned. From 5 to 10 years of age Peter went to an elementary school. He did not get on well with the other boys, and his parents were anxious for him to mix with a good type of boy. Also, when he was about 10, he began to be difficult and moody, and the parents decided to make a great sacrifice to meet the expense of sending him to a private school.

Mental Status. In appearance he was a well-grown but thin and sallow-complexioned boy, who carried himself in slovenly fashion, with rather bent shoulders, and looked older than his years. He had a glum expression, and he did not talk spontaneously at the interview but only in answer to questions, and then rather briefly. He did not look his interlocutor in the eye, but usually looked at the ground instead. The general impression gained from his demeanour was of a rather surly reluctance.

He denied being unhappy and gave no evidence of realizing that his conduct and interests were abnormal, or of any desire to change them. In reply to questions, he admitted his interest in religious ritual. His reading, besides the Bible, consisted almost exclusively of Shakespeare and Mark Twain. He was not interested, he said, in comics or in tales of adventure.

A psychological rating a year later, at 13½, gave him an I.Q. of only 77 on the Binet-Simon scale and of 87 on a scale of performance tests. The report on the tests in general was as follows:

'Peter's school work is probably up to the level of his power. He is quite unsuited to prolonged education of a school type or to advanced work.'

These tests did not corroborate the schoolmaster's report in several important points. Part of the explanation lay in the lower general standard of pupils in certain private schools; but, from the subsequent history, it seems probable that the results of the tests were vitiated by temperamental factors.

Summary. It is clear that in this boy symptoms in the ordinary sense played an insignificant part. He was slow in going to sleep at nights and he had certain compulsions, but the preponderating abnormalities were in his conduct and in his trend of interests. The latter were unusual at his age—the Church and Shakespeare—and would be unusually one-sided at any age. He was preoccupied, like so many children of his type, with the problems of the hardship of life and the unkindness of fate. His predilection for the ritualistic aspect of religion perhaps reflected his own shrinking attitude to life, which was shown also in his shunning companions and their boisterous games. If we considered only these more subjective aspects we would conclude that we were dealing with a temperamentally abnormal boy, shy, timorous and tender-minded, weltering in difficulties of inner origin, partly perhaps hereditary, in the light of his father's history. But the more objective aspects of his behaviour were equally striking, and although they were the more immediate cause of his being brought for advice, they were much more suggestive of possibilities of treatment than the subjective characteristics which we have just considered. Evidently the boy had some inventiveness; his interests may have been perverse but they were strong, according to his mother's account, and they did not seem to derive anything directly from the parental example except some of the strength that springs from rebellion.

It was clear that the father was a minor factor in every sense; he had done little positive harm, but had erred rather in what he had failed to do, in not exerting some discipline. The mother was of much greater importance. She had been badly brought up by her own mother, knew no discipline except that of fear, and no attitude to difficulties except anxiety. The son unwittingly copied her timidity, and at the same time, not so unwittingly perhaps, took advantage of it, and of his father's feeble attitude. Also it was apparent that the follies of the parents were visited on the offspring in more subtle ways. The boy made use of the antagonism of mother and grandmother to play them off against each other, while he went himself unpunished. He saw that to defy his mother gave the grandmother opportunities for homilies to her daughter, and for maliciously gloomy forebodings that he was a little maniac and would end in an asylum; while, when he called his grandmother 'old cat', he earned but a mild reproof from his mother, whose inmost feelings to her own mother he was expressing only too well.

From the school report and from the results of psychological testing it was clear that the parents' ambition had placed the boy in an atmosphere too rare for his intellectual capacity. Probably also, their delicacy about allowing him to mix with rougher companions at his elementary school had something to do with his withdrawal from all companions later.

Treatment. 1. In view of the mismanagement at home and his mother's emotional condition, it was decided to send him for a time to a holiday home at the seaside. He remained there only two days, as he cried the whole time and was sent home.

2. Change of school. He was removed from the private secondary school he was attending and placed in an elementary school. This was followed by an immediate improvement in his behaviour; and he approximated much more closely to the normal in school.

3. Instruction was given to the parents, accompanied by reassurance and explanation of the nature of the boy's condition.

4. The boy himself was encouraged to join some social bodies like the Scouts and a Church Club.

Results. Besides the appearance of normal behaviour in school and the improvement of his work there, he gained in several ways. He was no longer morbidly interested in Church. He bathed himself. At home he was no longer omnipotent. Outside of school he remained solitary, however.

Twenty months later the mother reported that she had found him a post in making artificial teeth. He had proved efficient at it but 'did not like having to do clearing up', so he had left of his own accord. After being unemployed for about fourteen days he had found a good job for himself in a stockbroker's office, which he still held. He had entirely dropped his interest in Church, and now went every week to a theatre or music hall. He had made only one friend, who dropped him, 'as Peter was so rude'. He attended hospital again after nearly two years. He was then a grand young man in a bowler hat, and appeared to be happily settled in the stockbroker's office. He spoke with much feeling and bitterness against the grandmother, who, he said, was getting old and silly and was the cause of much friction at home. Peter had one friend, and was strongly advised to make more and if possible join a club. (It is an interesting and significant fact that this boy was at least three years retarded when given Intelligence Tests and had an I.Q. of 77, and yet apparently managed to pass muster as a clerk.)

The subsequent history of this youth, in spite of all that has been done with him, has not been encouraging. He is solitary, seldom goes out, except after dark, and has been back to Church again. In fact he appears to be heading for a schizophrenic psychosis.

Behaviour Disorders

These include such complicated actions as truancy from school, wandering, lying, stealing, refusal of food and refusal to speak, cruelty and temper outbursts.

These are positive acts, isolated or habitual, of the child as a whole, *i.e.* in relation to the society in which he finds himself. More uniformly and definitely than any of the previously described symptoms, they betoken a conflict of his urges with what his environment allows or requires. The point of outbreak, so to speak, of the abnormal behaviour does not necessarily represent the point of conflict. There is frequently a displacement from the real source of friction, and the large part of the psychiatric diagnosis and therapeutic task depends on detecting the true cause of the discontent.

It is important to realize that none of the disorders enumerated are themselves 'abnormal' in the strict sense. Ask any group of normal adults whether they have ever stolen anything in their lives and they will almost to a man answer 'yes'. Few people have not in their childhood secretly admired the boy who had the courage to play truant. Lying is a universal tendency. Cruelty, being less useful, is much more readily discarded and is a common enough trait in any child.

But when any of these reactions occur flagrantly or persistently, inquiry is indicated, lest the tendency become a habit and worse things befall.

Truancy may be a negative or avoidance phenomenon, as when a child funks going back to school in face of a threatened punishment or disgrace, or it may be a more primitive phenomenon, as the expression of the boy's urge for adventure and variety. Wandering is only a prolonged truancy, usually with a similar basis and in older children who have left school. Lying may be done for defence or prestige. Sometimes it depends on simple confusion of phantasy with fact. In the latter instance it is usually elaborate and based on egoistic phantasy. Stealing may be a simple matter of opportunity having presented itself, or it may also be done for prestige, as when a child spends the proceeds on gifts to his friends. It may, on the other hand, be a rebellion against discipline, directly as in deprivation of pocket-money, or indirectly against some other form of frustration. More rarely stealing represents a neurotic symptom, a compulsion being felt to steal because of the similarity of the guilty feeling aroused by the deed to that attaching to sexual curiosity which had been repressed. Some habitual stealing comes from the child's urge to compensate for what he feels to have been denied him, namely the love of his parents or their substitutes. Acts of cruelty express either an innate tendency, common to everyone but usually soon brought under discipline (except in places where it is tacitly encouraged, as it used to be in certain public schools), or as a response in kind to an unfriendly environment, as jealousy and revenge. Temper outbursts are either negativistic in origin or matters of egoistic self-display, or more usually composed of both, and refusal to eat or speak has similar origins.

Behaviour disorders are often of such a nature as to bring the child under the notice of the law; they then constitute the delinquencies which crowd the children's courts.

The following is an example, principally of temper tantrums:

CASE NO. 37
Stealing as rebellion was well shown by a boy of 13 who was brought by his mother, who was in great distress. He was the eldest child and only boy in the family, and had been the apple of his parents' eye, but two years previously he had begun to steal anything of value that he could find lying about the house. He stole his mother's money, his father's cigars and his sister's sweets. He was incorrigible; no punishment was of any avail. This hardened young delinquent, when interviewed, rapidly dissolved into tears. It came out bit by bit that after day-school, which ended about 4 o'clock, he was expected by his mother to do two hours' lessons; thereafter to practise the violin (which he loathed) for half an hour, and after that to help his mother in the garden. If any leisure remained before bedtime he was allowed to play with his sister in the garden; the village boys were considered 'too rough'. Nominally he had ample pocket-money for one of his years—but half of this he gave (under duress) to foreign missions, and the other half he placed in his bank against the purchase of Christmas and birthday presents for the rest of the family. A reasonable rearrangement of pocket-money and of the other conditions of his life led to an immediate cessation of stealing.

There is another kind of dog which is apt to be given a bad name and hanged in consequence, and that is the child who is labelled spiteful and cruel, and whom the doctor is sometimes asked in consequence to exclude from school.

CASE NO. 38
A small child called Gladys, age 6, was reported to scratch, kick and bite other children, to be disobedient and unmanageable at home and to be beyond control at school.
Family Circumstances. The father was a labourer, age 40, and the mother about the same age. They got on well together and had five children, of whom Gladys was the youngest but one. The second oldest child, also a girl, was reported to have been disobedient and unruly at one time, but by 'severe discipline', that is, by whipping, she was said to have been made into a normal child. The whole family of seven people lived in two rooms and they all slept in one of these rooms. The other room was very clean and tidy, and was kept so in case anyone called. Gladys and the other children were not allowed to play in anything but the bedroom.
Personal History. Until she was about 4 years of age Gladys was a perfectly normal and very affectionate, attractive child. Until the same age she was never allowed to play with her older brothers and sisters, but was kept altogether with the mother. The reason alleged for this was that the grandmother, who lived downstairs, complained of the noise that the children made in the yard, and it was felt that Gladys would be the last straw which would break the grandmother's back, and so Gladys was sacrificed.
At 4 she went to school and the mother began to allow her out to play, but the elder children regarded her as a nuisance, and as a rule made her stay in a corner. If she

emerged from this she was set on by the other children, and made to go back to what they considered was a place of safety for her. In the meantime, her restless liveliness in the confined precincts of the narrow space of the home became more than the mother could stand and she tried to repress it. If the child would not keep quiet she was smacked, and this happened often—so frequently in fact that ultimately it had no effect. Threats were tried, but Gladys screamed if deprived of her weekly pocket-money, and found that by this means she could always get it back. Putting her to bed was of no use, as the mother did all the housework in the room where the child slept. Thus repressive discipline completely broke down with the triumph of Gladys, but at the expense of a feeling of defeat and exasperation on the part of the mother.

Furthermore, the child followed instinctively the rule of doing as she was done by, through lack of being taught the other rule, to love one's neighbour as oneself. For example, Gladys had begun by being fond of the baby, but, just before she came to hospital, there had been an occasion on which, after being punished by her mother, she went and stuck pins into the baby.

Psychiatric Examination. When Gladys was first seen by the doctor she screamed and wept. The mother explained that she was always being punished and so was afraid. Later after playing with toys, she came happily to the examination room and talked quite freely. It was interesting that her favourite toys were soldiers, and she loved shooting them, and when she played with a doll she confessed quite blithely that she enjoyed sticking pins into it. She asserted without any sign of rancour that everybody hit her, as though this were the normal order of things. Our impression was that she lacked not moral sense but simply moral teaching, and that her spitefulness and cruelty were direct reactions to her environment. They could hardly be innate tendencies, as until she was 4 she was regarded as a pleasant and affectionate child.

An *intelligence test* showed that she was one year backward. This was by no means sufficient to account for her behaviour.

Treatment consisted in stopping all physical punishment forthwith and removing her to a different environment. We do not like removing a child from its environment when it is giving difficulty, but prefer to adjust the environment, so that the child need no longer be ill-behaved in order to assert itself in some way. In this instance, however, the conditions were so cramped, and it seemed so difficult to make a complete alteration in the attitude of the family without at least a preliminary absence of the child from home, that we decided to place her in a foster home.

Soon after her arrival in the foster home we received the following report: 'This child is not at all difficult to manage here. She has at times attacked other children, but not often, and lately she has been perfectly good. She takes very little real interest in any occupation; she only wants to rush about and give vent to her enormous activity.'

Finally, after some months, she returned home, and the report was that she was a happy child at home and there was seldom any difficulty. The school report was that Gladys was less given to kicking and unruly behaviour and seemed to be forgetting to do nasty and unkind things.

Some months later it was said that she was no bother unless she was kept indoors too long. The school report said that kicking was not unknown but was comparatively rare.

Delinquency

An outline of the causes of delinquency will be found in Chapter 22. The majority of juvenile delinquents are normal boys and girls. Probably most individuals pass through a period of delinquent behaviour as they grow up and the great majority are not caught and so do not come before the Courts. Of those who are caught and charged, the majority do not offend again.

Delinquent behaviour of a more severe and persistent kind has many deter-minants—in the individual's inherited make-up, in his home and in the social milieu; and it takes many forms. Even in those more seriously involved in anti-social acts, while a faulty development of the personality can often be detected, gross psychiatric disorder is rare. Scott (1964), investigating boys aged 13–15 in an Approved School, found that the incidence of frank mental disorder and subnormality was very low: but 60 per cent. of these boys showed marked disorders of personality.

Healy and Bronner (1936) suggested that a delinquent act may represent:

1. An attempt to avoid, even as a temporary measure, the unpleasant situation by escape or flight from it.
2. An attempt to achieve substitutive compensatory satisfactions, by adven-tures or through notoriety.
3. An attempt to strengthen or bolster up the ego wounded by feelings of inadequacy or inferiority—by obtaining status with the delinquent crowd, or, in a solitary individual, by proving his courage and worth to himself.
4. An attempt to get certain satisfactions through direct and conscious or even unconscious expression of revengeful attitudes, perhaps through a hidden desire to punish parents or others by conduct that will make life difficult for them.
5. An attempt to gain a maximum of self-satisfaction, to inflate the ego, by generally aggressive, antisocial attitudes.
6. A response to instinctual urges felt to be thwarted—sometimes in the form of sexual misbehaviour, but more often of attempts at emancipation.
7. A wish for punishment which is always a response to a conscious or uncon-scious sense of guilt.

The above outline gives some indication of the complexity of the psychogenesis of juvenile delinquent behaviour, which has now rightly become a subject of specialized study. The reader is referred to reviews by Scott (1965) and West (1967).

Both in Scotland (Kilbrandon Committee Reports Cmnd. 2306, 1964) and in England and Wales (Cmnd. 3601, 1968) Government White Papers have pro-posed major changes in the handling of cases of juvenile delinquency. The influ-ence of child psychiatry has been strongly felt in promoting these liberal and humane plans. Efforts to promote the child's welfare and social readjustment are to replace conviction and punishment, and will be related closely to the educa-tional and health services. Children of school age will so far as it is possible be removed from the jurisdiction of the criminal courts, and special measures of education, training and treatment will be arranged according to the child's needs and the family setting. New legislation is likely to be introduced soon (1968) to implement these proposals, of which only the briefest outline has been given here.

Habit Disorders

Habit disorders include thumb-sucking, nail-biting, head-rolling, masturba-tion, enuresis (nocturnal and diurnal), faecal incontinence, stammering (some cases) and other speech disorders. These, for the most part, are either primarily auto-erotic in basis or represent a regression to infantile sources of satisfaction in face of environmental frustration. They readily become associated secondarily with defiance (negativism).

Treatment again consists in analysing the situation in each case and making appropriate readjustments. Frustration in any direction, 'babying' by the parents, erotic stimulation by the parents (usually unrealized by them), jealousy of another child in the family and defiance of the parents from lack of their affection, or mismanagement in other ways, are the commonest causes.

It is particularly in this group that successes are obtained in young children by encouraging the child to keep a diary in which a star is marked on each successful day, and the dates of failure are left blank, and the child is mildly praised or rewarded in some small material way for successes.

CASE No. 39

Simon J., aged 5, was brought by his mother on account of a 'nervous habit' of a curious kind. On going to bed he would put his arm up to and round his head (without actually touching it) and rock his head and arm at increasing speed until he was 'hysterical', to use the mother's phrase. By this she meant that he seemed not to be able to hear when at the height of the habit, and could only be stopped by placing one's hand on him. The habit occurred every time he lay down and was also repeated if he woke up in the night.

Family History. The father was a professional man of an intelligent, stable type. The mother was a highly intelligent woman, and the married life was happy and marital relations normal. There was one younger child, a girl aged $2\frac{1}{2}$, of whom the patient was very fond. He displayed little jealousy of her, and would himself place her on his mother's knee.

History of Patient. His birth was two months premature and the labour was induced for obstetric reasons. His habit of head and arm rocking began at about 18 months, just after circumcision. He had an anaesthetic for the operation, but he screamed a good deal for three weeks after. He touched his penis so much that it was difficult to procure healing. Walking did not occur till 2 years of age, and he was still later in talking (3 years). The mother brought him up very strictly on Truby King methods. The régime was relaxed, however, when the baby sister arrived.

He had recently gone to school in the mornings from 9.30 till 12.30. He slept at midday and was in bed by 6.30. No food was given after 4.30. He now slept in the same room as his sister. Formerly he had talked a little about the 'dark coming in at the door', but less was heard of this after his sister had been put to sleep in the same room. He bit his nails for a time, but his mother's old nurse succeeded in stopping this. During a visit to his grandmother, who thought she could cure his head-rocking, the latter became worse.

His mother declared that his pleasure in his habit was obvious.

Psychiatric Examination. The boy was a bright-looking, lively youngster, with intelligence above the average. He had a very definite ambivalent reaction to the habit, a· look of pleasure passing over his face when it was mentioned, while at the same time he flatly denied indulging in it.

The inference was that his habit was an auto-erotic phenomenon. His mother had let him feel that it was 'naughty' on the basis that it was against her wishes. This, combined with the pleasure obtained, probably accounted for his abnormal attitude. The mother's opinion that she had been unduly severe in her discipline in the first three years of his life was of interest, especially in view of the fact that among his leading characteristics already were obstinacy and persistence.

Treatment. The mother was advised that the habit could not hurt him physically unless he banged himself against some hard object, and it was pointed out that the physical damage would be limited to that. An attempt was also made to reassure her on the whole subject, by explaining that while the form of the tic was unusual the motive behind it was not. The importance was stressed of trying to remove it. She was advised to talk to him about it and to give him a small diary, asking him to keep it himself and to put a cross against the days when he managed not to do it, and to give him little rewards for slight improvement.

Three months later the habit was reported to have ceased.

Enuresis and Encopresis. By the age of 3 most children have attained control of the sphincter of the bladder both by night and by day. The term nocturnal enuresis is applied to bed-wetting occurring after that stage. In an individual case it may occur every night, or nearly every night, or at intervals of days or weeks or months. It is one of the commonest disorders of childhood, occurring predominantly in males. There are two main clinical groups: those in whom it is a developmental disorder, the enuresis persisting from infancy, and those on the other hand who have attained control of the bladder and later relapse into enuresis. As a general rule no gross physical disorder is to be found which has any relevance: abnormalities of the lumbosacral spine such as fusion defects, lumbarization and sacralization are so common in ordinary life that they probably have no special relation to enuresis.

The findings of Stalker and Band (1946) were of much importance in advancing our knowledge of the constitutional aspects of this disorder. They described enuresis as an autonomic symptom complex assuming a variety of forms, *e.g.* nocturnal enuresis, rising at night, diurnal enuresis, diurnal frequency and urgency and encopresis; and associated often with deep sleep. The majority of enuretic patients have cystometrograms of the uninhibited neurogenic type showing a lack of cerebral inhibition similar to that present in certain organic cerebral diseases. Timid and anxious, and psychopathic, personality types predominate. Commonly there is a family history of psychosomatic disorders and of enuresis. In this type of case persistent enuresis may be seen as an aspect of delayed maturation, which may in part at least be hereditarily determined: and it does not often persist after adolescence has been passed.

Other cases in which bladder control is achieved late are due to defective habit training in the home. Subnormality (mental defect), and the impaired educability which goes with it, is another important cause of persistent enuresis; but the function of nocturnal control establishes itself sooner or later, except in those of the lowest grades.

In the other main clinical group, bladder control is achieved and later lost— usually only transiently. The enuresis is then attributable to regression or negativism, and some current cause of stress or unhappiness in the home or at school should be sought and appropriately treated.

Many drugs have been tried in the treatment of persistent enuresis—ephedrine and amphetamines (to combat too deep sleep), and more recently imipramine and amitriptyline: but all with little effect. A much more useful method is the aversive conditioning therapy given by the technique of using a buzzer-and-pad. Sphincter relaxation is the conditioned stimulus which becomes linked with the aversive stimulus which follows it—the buzzer that awakes the patient, which in turn the patient learns to avoid by sphincter contraction (Lovibond, 1964). A cure rate of as high as 74 per cent. with 9 per cent. greatly improved, is recorded (Wickes, 1963): relapses can be treated by further courses of conditioning therapy. Patience, encouragement and suggestion are also important elements in the treatment and management.

Encopresis (faecal incontinence) in any but the severely abnormal is so much more amenable to treatment than nocturnal enuresis that its origin must be very close to consciousness. Sheer unhappiness is often an important factor. Negativism is the basis in other cases: and in some the aspect of sensuous pleasure suggests itself, associated with erotic phantasies. It usually clears up when the child is made to discover disadvantages associated with it—not of the repressive type, but such disadvantages as the deprivation of some treat that would otherwise have been shared with companions.

Sleep-walking. This is a fairly common phenomenon, which usually occurs only on a few occasions in the child and does not persist, except in rare instances, into adult life. It must depend on an extensive dissociation of cortical function, and, like similar dissociations in waking life, can result from either psychological or physiological factors. It is, very rarely, an epileptic symptom. Sometimes it is found in several members of the family, *e.g.* mother, son and daughter, and may then be a peculiar physiological anomaly. It occurs, however, principally in children of emotionally labile, excitable disposition, and in children with definite discoverable conflicts, where the somnambulism is the equivalent of an hysterical symptom. In the hysterical group the goal of the sleep-walking may in itself suggest the psychological interpretation. For example, a boy of 10, very much attached to his mother, who had until recently slept in the same room with her, walked frequently in his sleep to his mother's bedroom, saying, 'You know about it', 'What is it?' 'Tell me the secret'. Talk of this kind is rarely recorded, but the apparent setting of a definite objective, especially the parent's room, is not rare.

It is not unknown, although it is very unusual, for a somnambulist to injure himself and even another person.

Treatment consists in adjusting psychological difficulties and prescribing a sedative at night.

Stammering (or Stuttering). The prevalence of stammering in the population is thought to be about 1 per cent. There are broadly two types of stammering: that acquired for the first time in adolescent or adult life in relation to some emotional problem, and stammering originating in childhood.

The first, of recent origin, and commonly of short duration, is a form of speech disorder that is easily and obviously imitatable by voluntary effort, and is, in effect, an hysterical symptom. The more usual type of stammering, commencing in the first five years of life and much commoner in boys, is not so susceptible of close imitation and can often attain considerable complication in the form of tonic or clonic spasm of the articulatory muscles and associated facial and bodily movements. The former is entirely psychogenic; the latter type is mainly due to physiological instability in the neuromuscular organization, although it may be provoked or increased by emotional causes. In many instances it induces a secondary shyness, but some stammerers of this type are remarkably unembarrassed by their disability.

The evidence for a physiological basis of some sort lies in a family history of stammering, which is fairly often elicited, or of some speech defect which may not always amount to stammering, but may consist in lisping, or of mere slowness in enunciation. Andrews and Harris (1964) found stammering to be associated with late talking, poor talking and mild intellectual deficit; and from family studies also reported much evidence of the operation of constitutional factors of genetic origin, though they were unable to determine whether the mode of inheritance was incompletely dominant or multifactorial. They found too that social pathology occurred more frequently in the home of the stammerers than amongst controls: the mothers were more often inadequate and somewhat feckless, or (less commonly) neurotic and making excessive demands on their children. A few cases of stammering are clearly organically determined by brain damage: amongst children with cerebral diplegia Ingram (1963) found its frequency to be 15 per cent.

The treatment of the constitutional type of stammering must obviously depend on re-education, in addition, of course, to removal of any emotional factors which may reinforce the stammering. There are many varieties of re-educational method, but they all depend on a mixture of suggestion and a mechanical trick of articulation. Attempts at a deeper psychotherapy of stammering of this type have usually been unsuccessful, but it is nevertheless possible that some stammers originating in the first few years of speech development may be mainly or preponderantly of psychological origin. It has been shown in some cases that stammering can originate around infantile conflicts even as early as the suckling phase (Despert, 1943). Any threat to the mouth area at a time when phantasies are apt to centre round it, especially those concerned with aggressive impulses and fears of retribution, is liable to elicit stammering as a neurotic symptom (Orton, 1937).

The prognosis for a stammer of early origin is usually of spontaneous disappearance in the course of later adolescence. Naturally, a previous habit of stammering may be re-aroused under emotional stress.

Night Terrors. Night terrors are distinct from nightmares. In the latter, a dreamer, who may be child or adult, wakes from the dream in fear, with recollection as a rule of part of the dream content. In night terrors, which are almost confined to childhood, the child sits up in bed in fright, but evidently unconscious of his surroundings. He does not wake spontaneously, and in the morning has rarely any recollection of the occurrence. Where recollection does occur it is of a terrifying but indescribable and unformed visual hallucination.

Night terrors are physiological disturbances on an emotional basis and are not susceptible to treatment by psychological symbolic interpretation. They are practically confined to the over-active, intelligent, anxious type of child, and they tend to be transient phenomena.

Neuroses

Hysteria. Hysterical symptoms in children appear to be determined largely by the influence of suggestion, coupled with the desire for self-assertion or sympathy, or for evasion. Hysterical symptoms of the type of somatic complaints (headache, bodily aches and pains and nausea) are frequent enough.

The influence of environmental example in determining the nature of the symptoms, not only in the hysterical type of reactions but in the anxiety type as well, was demonstrated by E. Richards, who pointed out that 'their symptom-pictures of distress are strangely similar to those of the adult invalid types—palpitation; shaking in stomach; headaches; pain in chest, abdomen and legs; giddy spells; fullness in the epigastrium; 'I feel all played out'; 'Sometimes I vomit a lot, too'. Here we see children who expressed complaints that they had absorbed from an atmosphere charged with hypochondriacal utterance and fear of disease, objectively reinforced by numerous prescriptions, patent medicines and the medical folk-lore of neighbourhood gossip. With the pattern of these reactions well established through the daily contact of actual behaviour, it needed but the catalysing agent of some unusual circumstance or emotional strain to produce a symptom-picture quite baffling to the ordinary approaches of clinical procedure.

Disregard of the symptom and care that nothing merely 'invalidish' is gained by the child in having it, coupled with the means already advocated for the treatment of the expression of psychological distress in children, are the necessary therapeutic methods in the hysteria of childhood.

In addition to hysterical symptoms it is possible to find in some children all the makings of a so-called hysterical personality. It is only necessary to encounter such a case to realize how wrong it is to regard the hysterical type of personality as 'child-like'. 'Childish' it is, but not 'child-like'.

Anxiety States. Neurotic anxiety states are frequently the result of conscious or unconscious imitation of an atmosphere of anxiety in the home. The anxious mother especially is apt to produce an anxious child, and later an anxious adult. But whereas the treatment of an adult of this kind is a long process of investigation and recapitulation of a life history, too frequently with a final result that is still unsatisfactory, in children the re-education of the parents, together with the provision of healthy contacts and outlets for the child, can result in a product that is robustly happy and promises well for future stability. If resort is made to the (in some ways feeble) expedient of removing the child from the home, the symptoms are apt to disappear with characteristic rapidity and finality. The symptoms are the same as in adults and the causes are in part identical. Parental over-solicitude, motivated not infrequently by dissatisfactions in the parents' own love-life, is by far the commonest cause. The exceptionally strong attachment of the child to the parent that usually results is not invariably to the parent of the opposite sex. Worrying fathers can produce anxious sons.

Some of these anxiety states may be dependent on an Oedipus situation in the Freudian sense. So far, such children's neuroses as we have treated have not suggested that the proportion so determined is high, and the effect of such treatment suggests that such an explanation is not by any means always the most far-reaching or practical. It might, of course, be assumed that in treatment of this kind the external readjustments, which are made automatically, bring about a redirection of libido within the patient, but we prefer to work with the ascertainable facts and to reserve interpretations of a Freudian kind for the rare cases that do not respond to our usual measures.

Phobias are much more difficult to treat than the other symptoms of neurotic anxiety. The special origin of the more usual phobias, such as fear of the dark, often remains undetermined. Probably some will never be further analysable and may be regarded as primitive or instinctive fears. Others can probably be produced in the manner of conditioned reflexes, by some accidental association, after the pattern of Watson's experiments on the effect of noise on infants. Some are produced by parental example, like the other symptoms of neurotic anxiety, while a residuum have the symbolic value of a symptom in the Freudian sense.

School Refusal (School Phobia). This is distinct from truanting, and from non-attendance at school because the parents are indifferent or deliberately withhold the child: it is a refusal by the child to go to school, for neurotic or other abnormal psychological reasons. While the truant is usually dissatisfied and rebellious, the child who refuses to go to school is most often afraid. Kahn and Nursten (1962), who have given a good account of this type of reaction, state that it accounts for 2–8 per cent. of the total referrals to child guidance clinics in this country. It is apparently an increasing problem.

There may or may not be prodromal symptoms. The child may be obviously emotionally upset, withdrawn, depressed or complaining of other fears: and in the mornings before the hour at which he is due to go to school there may be protests that he feels physically unwell, with abdominal pain or headache or cough or sore throat, and he may vomit or have diarrhoea. Finally, his anxiety mounting to a panic, and it may be crying, shouting and struggling, he refuses to go to school despite bribes, threats and punishment. This may occur at any age, but it is perhaps pre-adolescent girls who are most often affected. Only children, and children who are much younger than their siblings, are more than averagely vulnerable.

The child may be having difficulties at school, at work or at games, in mixing with other boys and girls, or because of bullying or teasing: but the major problem is at home. The refusal to go to school is a symptom of a disturbed parent-child relationship, usually a type of neurotic separation anxiety, the fear being more of leaving the mother than facing the school. The child, who is usually sensitive, timid and lacking in confidence, in striving to achieve independence feels alone and insecure. The mother too is usually insecure and mother and child are too dependent upon one another. The mother, who may not have reached a mature relationship with her own mother, is commonly over anxious, indulgent and protective; she has limited personality resources and interests and she needs to keep her child at home and dependent upon her. There may be other determinants, other neurotic conflicts involving mother and child. Less commonly school refusal is evidence of a personality disorder in the child, herald of the conflicts with society which may increase as he grows older; and rarely it may be a symptom of a childhood psychosis.

Treatment should be initiated as soon as possible, since the longer the child is away from school the greater become the resistances to his return. Crude attempts to force the child back to school are unavailing. It is the conflicts and the disturbed personal relationships which lie behind the symptom of school refusal towards which the treatment, which must be psychotherapeutic, should be directed. Frequently it is both the parents and the child who have to be brought into the treatment. The child's return to school depends considerably upon how quickly the mother gains insight and becomes able to be less over-protective and possessive. Anything which will increase the child's self-confidence is helpful. The father and the family doctor have key roles in encouraging mother and child to reach a better relationship. If the child is off school for more than a week or two, specialist advice should be sought. However inconvenient it may be administratively, it must be recognized that certain children cannot fit happily into the normal pattern of schooling and special, more flexible, arrangements may have to be made for their education.

Obsessional Neuroses. Obsessive-compulsive symptoms as they occur in children have been discussed briefly in the chapter on adult neuroses. It is only necessary to add here that in children they seldom by themselves constitute a condition that is brought for treatment.

Some *delinquent acts* appear to be produced in a way precisely analogous with the mode of production of neurotic symptoms. They are then the outcome of conflict, a substitute or compromise between opposing tendencies and symbolic of these repressed and unresolved drives. The delinquent is unaware of their real source, and may suffer from neurotic symptoms in the ordinary sense at the same time. In these cases the child is much more likely to be shy, timid, withdrawn and anxious, than aggressive and rebellious.

Psychoses

Compared with their prevalence in adult life, psychoses in childhood are relatively rare. Parents commonly fear that any oddity of behaviour in their children may be a sign of mental illness, particularly if there is a family history of it; but it is very unusual for the psychiatrist to have to confirm their fears. It is axiomatic that behaviour which would be considered psychotic in an adult may be normal in a child. This does not mean, however, that certain trends of behaviour in childhood, if left uncorrected, may not be factors in the development of a psychosis in adult life.

Though the numbers involved are small, these illnesses are important, not only

2 K

on account of the great suffering that they cause to the children themselves and
to their parents, but because of the possibility that an understanding of the psychoses of childhood may throw light on the aetiology of the much more numerous
psychoses of adult life. Clinical differentiation is still at an elementary stage: it has
been hindered by the reluctance of some child psychiatrists to give any diagnosis
to mental illnesses in childhood, and the tendency of others to attach the label of
'childhood schizophrenia' much too readily.

Early Infantile Autism. Kanner first described this condition in 1943. The
prevalence is probably about 2 per 10,000 (Lotter), and it is four times commoner in males than in females. The abnormalities, if not present from early
infancy, become manifest in the first two years of life. There is no evidence that
it is related to schizophrenia.

Children suffering from early infantile autism are commonly first suspected of
being deaf or subnormal (mentally defective). But these children, though they
are inaccessible to formal intelligence testing, do not look unintelligent. What is
most characteristic is their 'extreme autistic aloneness', and this may be apparent
from the first year of life, the child not stretching out its arms, for example, to be
picked up. They are abnormally self-sufficient, interested in things (and able to
manipulate them skilfully) but apparently not in people, with whom they seem
quite unable to form normal emotional relationships. In their behaviour they
show an obsessive need for the maintenance of the exact *status quo* in their
environment. Speech is grossly disturbed: about one third are mute, the others
have great difficulties in various ways—they cannot form sentences, or use personal pronouns easily, or understand the concept 'Yes', and they may exhibit
echolalia: rote memory on the other hand is often excellent. To these features,
described by Kanner, Rutter and Lockyer (1967) add a lack of response to
auditory stimuli, various ritualistic and compulsive phenomena, stereotyped
repetitive mannerisms, short attention span on given tasks together with non-
distractibility, and a tendency to self-injury.

The aetiology of this condition is unknown and the prognosis generally poor.
Autistic children appear to come usually from notably intelligent middle-class
families: many of the parents are university or college graduates. Kanner (1954)
described the majority of the parents as detached, humourless perfectionists,
'more at home in the world of abstractions than in the world of people. . . . They
treat their children about as meticulously and impersonally as they treat their
automobiles. . . . It is possible to speak of them as successfully autistic adults.'
Kanner thought that the autistic children of these parents had suffered 'emotional
refrigeration'. This may be true of some families: but it is most unlikely that
deviant parental attitudes alone could result in such a striking and fairly uniform
clinical picture. It is more likely that the condition is predominantly, if not
wholly, organically determined, though evidence about brain damage and genetic
factors is still inconclusive. Rutter, Greenfeld and Lockyer (1967) describe the
prognosis as follows: 'Only a minority of psychotic children reach a good level of
social adjustment by the time of adolescence, and very few enter paid employment. About half remain incapable of any kind of independent existence and

most of these are cared for in mental subnormality hospitals.' Ten of the 63 children followed up by these workers developed fits in adolescence—which strongly suggests the importance of organic neurological factors in the aetiology. For a comprehensive account, reference may be made to Wing (1966).

Dementia Infantilis. Heller (1908) described a condition, with onset usually in the third or fourth year, characterized by a specially rapid and profound disturbance of speech, leading to its almost complete loss, by extreme restlessness, and by a uniformly unfavourable outcome (only one case has been reported as improving) in a state of dementia, which is reached in a few months. Stereotyped and tic-like movements, episodes of anxiety, apparently hallucinatory experiences, and cruel and aggressive behaviour have also been described. The deterioration has been said to differ from a schizophrenic one in that there is retention of the emotional response to joy or shock, and of anxiety at an elementary level. The facial expression remains intelligent, the physical health is relatively well maintained, and there are no gross neurological signs or fits. Various quite different pathological changes in the brain have been reported, including inflammation and diffuse sclerosis.

This is probably not a clinical entity, but further research is required.

Schizophrenia. This is very uncommon in childhood, and probably does not occur before the age of 8 or 9 years. Understandably, the older the child the more nearly the clinical picture resembles that of adult schizophrenia, but differentiation into adult sub-types is very difficult. Kanner (1957) drew attention to the following features. The child's scholastic ability begins to deteriorate, concentration becomes impaired, interest in and contact with others begins to be lost. There is day-dreaming, seclusiveness, lack of rapport, irritability, and in some cases hypochondriasis. Speech and general behaviour become disordered, the latter in the direction either of great restlessness and impulsiveness, or immobility with catatonic features. Delusions tend to be simple and symbolization naïve.

Manic-Depressive Psychosis. Both manic and depressive psychotic reactions can occur in childhood, but mania is very rare. Depression is probably a good deal commoner than is usually suspected. Occasionally in the history of a manic-depressive psychosis in an adult, one finds indubitable evidence of a depressive phase having occurred within the first ten years of life. States of depression of a transient kind are common enough in childhood, and are recognized as such: but depressive illness may be both prolonged and unrecognized. Frommer (1967) has described 41 such cases in children between the ages of 9 and 15 years, mostly prepubertal. One-third of their parents had had depressions. The presenting symptoms were often misleading, being those apparently of anxiety or physical in origin or a behaviour disorder. The child who had symptoms of tension and phobias might deny that he felt depressed. Complaints of abdominal pain and headache were common. Irritability, outbursts of temper, social withdrawal or aggression, and failure at school might suggest the diagnosis of behaviour disorder. The mother-child relationship may become disturbed, owing to the illness of the child. Clues to the correct diagnosis may be found in unaccountable tearfulness, insomnia, talk of suicide and the response to antidepressive drugs.

Though these depressions had often a precipitant, the family history suggests that the constitutional factor is often strong.

Suicidal Acts in Childhood. Though relatively not nearly so common in childhood as in adult life, suicidal acts in childhood are probably not so rare as is usually supposed. They have been studied recently by Toolan (1962) and Connell (1965). Connell estimates that there are probably considerably more than 1600 suicidal attempts by children aged 16 or under in Great Britain each year. The incidence of attempted suicide rises through the 10–14 age group to become a very significant problem in adolescence. More girls than boys attempt suicide. Probably some actual suicides in the very young are explained away as accidents, and potentially dangerous suicidal threats and attempts are undoubtedly much too often dismissed lightly by parents and doctors. Connell rightly emphasizes the relationship between 'depression' and suicidal threats and attempts. Some of these children have been suffering from depressive psychoses which have not been recognized: many more may be diagnosed as evincing situationally determined depressive reactions, having become acutely unhappy at home—the home is often very disturbed, sometimes chaotic, the mother ill, the father absent; or at school, owing to academic pressures or inability to mix successfully with their peers. A suicidal attempt may be made quite unexpectedly by a child previously thought stable. The motives are complex: feelings of loneliness and of being unloved and unwanted, the feeling that the problems of life are too great to be borne or solved, the wish to die and to escape from it all, attempts to gain attention from others, hostility, revenge and guilt. Always such reactions call for a comprehensive investigation of the child and his environment, and help should be sought in most cases from the staff of a child psychiatric unit in assessing the situation and in providing the skilled treatment and management which is usually required.

The Brain-damaged Child

A child may sustain cerebral injury *in utero*, at birth or in the first few years after birth; as a result of anoxia, trauma, infection or other cause. It is well recognized that such an injury, if severe, may result in mental defect, cerebral palsy or epilepsy: and it has been suspected that, if slighter, it might in some cases be the cause of the behaviour disturbances and learning difficulties which are commonly encountered in childhood. But the symptoms often attributed to brain damage are not specific to it, and there is in many cases little more than a history of a difficult birth to suggest that there has been early brain damage and that the effects of it are continuing. The clinical concept of the brain-damaged child is therefore in many respects vague and uncertain: able reviews of it have been made by Eisenberg (1957) and Pond (1961).

There are often no frank neurological signs in cases which have been called brain-damaged, and the results of E.E.G. studies are more often than not equivocal. Some motor clumsiness is not uncommon. More definitely suggestive of early brain damage are perceptual and agnosic-apraxic difficulties, impaired visuo-motor capacity and (in some instances) specific dyslexia and dysgraphia.

The intelligence level is usually below what would be expected from the family setting, attention tends to be fleeting, the child is unusually distractible and learning is retarded. Irritability, temper tantrums, aggression and hyperkinesis are also thought to be typical features; so are mood swings and erratic, unpredictable behaviour.

The effects of cerebral trauma depend upon many factors—the locus and extent of the cerebral damage, the age at which it was sustained, the child's genetic inheritance and personality, parental attitudes and influences, the home and school environments in all their aspects. This means that there are many ways in which it may be possible to mitigate the effects of early brain damage. Parents and others can be helped in their understanding and management of the emotional problems of these children. Special educational difficulties can be defined by psychological testing and individual remedial teaching arranged. In some cases drug treatment may be useful. Always it is right to be patient and optimistic, since the child's potential for improvement and readjustment as he grows older is great.

Further research is required to clarify the diagnosis of children who may be brain-damaged and to elucidate the prognosis about which we still know very little. Meantime the concept of brain damage should be used sparingly in the explanation of phenomena in childhood which we do not fully understand. Where there has been undoubted brain trauma, sometimes of a severe kind, the prolonged after-effects in children are often surprisingly few and slight. Head trauma of some kind has almost invariably occurred: we should not be too influenced by the great weight commonly laid upon it by parents, so that of all incidents in the history it is likely to be singled out for special attention by them, nor too ready ourselves to attribute to the effects of birth trauma symptoms which can have other determinants.

Epilepsy in Childhood

Psychological difficulties have been found in about a quarter of the epileptic children studied in general practice. Behaviour disorders are not uncommon and may be severe. Many factors apart from the fits influence these situations: the presence, distribution and degree of cerebral damage, the child's personality and his response to the recurrent stress of having attacks, parental attitudes, the adequacy of drug treatment, the social environment generally and particularly the adjustment at school. Much disturbance in childhood bodes ill for adaptation in adult life.

Pond (1961) has delineated clearly the two forms of continuing epilepsy which are of most psychiatric importance in childhood—the centrencephalic variety and temporal lobe epilepsy. Febrile convulsions in the first three years appear to have a very low incidence of associated psychological problems.

Centrencephalic or primary subcortical epilepsy, of genetic origin, is expressed clinically in *petit mal* seizures and in the E.E.G. by bilaterally synchronous 3 per second spike and wave discharges. It does not occur before the age of 3 years, and is commonest between the age of 6 and puberty. The seizures may be precipitated by sudden unpleasurable emotions, such as embarrassment or surprise. Occasionally, in a very small group, they are self-induced for pleasure or to escape from tension, by inducing flicker with the fingers while looking at a bright light.

Temporal lobe epilepsy, arising from lesions in or near the rhinencephalon, rarely begins before the age of 5 years. Here too the seizures may be precipitated by emotional stress: but the period of stress is more prolonged. The clinical concomitants are in general much more serious than those of *petit mal*. Half the cases develop personality disorders, and there is the risk of an epileptic psychosis developing in adult life.

Both types of epilepsy may interfere with the child's learning of new material.

In *petit mal* the disturbances of consciousness, though very brief, may be very frequent. *Petit mal status* may occur, causing confusion for hours. These children appear inattentive, may become timid and withdrawn, may suffer from nightmares and develop other neurotic symptoms. Their intelligence is usually not impaired.

In temporal lobe epilepsy moodiness and aggression are particularly manifest, as in the adult. The hyperkinetic syndrome is a common complication, and in these cases intellectual development is usually seriously retarded. It is the associated brain damage, not the epilepsy, which is the major factor causing intellectual loss in this form of epilepsy.

It is of course of the utmost importance to prevent, if possible, the development of continuing epilepsy in childhood. Ounsted, Lindsay and Norman (1966), in their monograph on temporal lobe epilepsy, have discussed the possibilities of prophylaxis. They produce considerable evidence that severe febrile convulsions or *grand mal status* in infancy or early childhood, causing cerebral circulatory disturbances and anoxia, may result in severe and lasting brain damage. The avoidance of birth injury by better obstetric care, the effective treatment of intracranial infections with both antibiotics and anticonvulsants, and the prompt control of febrile convulsions in infective fevers (especially whooping cough) with phenytoin sodium or amylobarbitone, are ways in which the incidence of this most disabling condition may be reduced.

The Hyperkinetic Syndrome

The hyperkinetic syndrome in children may occur with or without epilepsy: it is a common but not invariable complication of temporal lobe epilepsy in childhood. Its clinical features have been well described in a series of 70 cases by Ounsted (1955).

Apparently only about 8 per cent. of epileptic children attending general hospitals are so affected, males predominate (79 per cent.) and the epilepsy has developed within the first five years of life. The seizures may be of any variety, excepting *petit mal.* and the underlying brain damage has many possible origins. The ceaseless energy and activity of these children who are 'on the go' day in day out, and their destructive outbursts, present serious problems of control and management. Though their hyperkinesis is in many ways an exaggeration of what is normal at this period of development, its intensity may make it impossible for the child to attend an ordinary school or to live at home, and it may persist for months or years.

The hyperkinesis is constant, at perhaps double the speed and energy output of the normal child. Attention is grossly impaired, being both narrowed and transient. Shyness and fear are absent, a shallow euphoria predominates. Frustration is very poorly tolerated and outbursts of rage or violence, directed against other people or against inanimate objects, may frighten adult bystanders by their suddenness and ferocity. Sleep is profound. The gross failure to concentrate impairs learning. Intellectual retardation or defect is common but not invariable: half the cases have an I.Q. below 70.

Relationships in the home are usually greatly strained. This sort of childhood disorder understandably monopolizes a mother's attention and exhausts her patience. She may need considerable support from the family doctor and from social agencies. Admission of the child to hospital, at least during the most disturbed or domestically exhausting periods, is usually in the best interests of the child and of his family.

Some of these cases are said to respond to some extent to treatment with dextro-amphetamine sulphate. Tranquillizing drugs, such as chlorpromazine or haloperidol, are usually required. Primidone is the most useful anticonvulsant: phenobarbitone often aggravates this condition.

In part this syndrome is a phenomenon of immaturity, ageing helps and considerable improvement can confidently be expected. Some of these children, followed up to puberty, are found then unexpectedly to have become abnormally slow.

Subnormality (Mental Defect)

Subnormality has been described in Chapter 19. Reference may be made here to the large numbers of the dull and backward group—those who are intellectually below average but not sufficiently so to be regarded as subnormal (mentally defective). They furnish many of the problems seen at psychiatric clinics for children. The disturbances they exhibit are not, however, different in kind from those described elsewhere in this chapter.

It is important to distinguish intrinsic from accidental retardation. A child may be backward at school and also score badly on intelligence tests as the result of emotional difficulties, or of faulty attitudes on the part of his teachers, or from lack of stimulation such as occurs in the institutionalized child, or from a defect such as word blindness with which some children struggle through school undiagnosed. We have known a child's intelligence quotient rise considerably in a few months when such difficulties have been dealt with along the lines indicated by the diagnostic conclusions. Ingram and Reid (1956) have shown how educational retardation and difficulties due to developmental aphasia, may lead to behaviour disorders of many different kinds. They presented a detailed account of 78 children of average intelligence referred to a department of child psychiatry, who were found to have specific dyslexia and dysgraphia due to developmental aphasia. Retarded speech development, expressive and receptive aphasia and speech defects were commonly also found in these children.

The relation between subnormality and psychosis in children is complicated. Some cases classed as subnormal are probably states of defect following a psychotic process such as infantile autism. Differentiation is often difficult clinically and depends a great deal on the history. As in the adult, a psychosis may be developed by one who is already subnormal.

REFERENCES

Andrews, G., and Harris, M. (1964) *The Syndrome of Stuttering*, London.
Children and Young Persons, Scotland (1964) Cmnd. 2306, London, H.M.S.O.
Children in Trouble (1968) Cmnd. 3601, London, H.M.S.O.
Connell, P. H. (1965) in *Modern Perspectives in Child Psychiatry*, ed. Howells, J. G., Edinburgh.
Despert, J. L. (1943) *Amer. J. Psychiat.*, 99, 881.
Eisenberg, L. (1957) *Psychiat. Quart.*, 31, 72.
Freud, A. (1928) *Introduction to the Technic of Child Analysis*, New York.
Frommer, E. A. (1967) *Brit. med. J.*, 1, 729.
Healy, W., and Bronner, A. F. (1936) *New Light on Delinquency and its Treatment*, London.
Heller, T. (1908) *Z. Erforsch. Jugendl. schwaehsinns*, 2, 17.
Ingram, T. T. S., and Reid, J. F. (1956) *Arch. Dis. Childh.*, 31, 161.
Ingram, T. T. (1963) *Proc. roy. Soc. Med.*, 56, 199.
Kahn, J. H. and Nursten, J. P. (1962) *Amer. J. Orthopsychiat.*, 32, 707.
Kanner, L. (1943) *Nerv. Child*, 2, 217.
Kanner, L. (1954) *Res. Publ. Ass. nerv. ment. Dis.*, 33, 378.
Kanner, L. (1957) *Child Psychiatry*, Springfield Ill.
Klein, M. (1932) *The Psycho-analysis of Children*, London.
Lovibond, S. H. (1964) *Conditioning and Enuresis*, Oxford.
Orton, S. T. (1937) *Reading, Writing and Speech Problems in Children*, New York.
Ounsted, C. (1955) *Lancet*, ii, 303.
Ounsted, C., Lindsay, J., and Norman, R. (1966) *Biological Factors in Temporal Lobe Epilepsy*, London.
Pond, D. A. (1961) *Brit. med. J.*, 2, 1377, 1454.
Rogerson, C. H. (1939) *Play Therapy in Childhood*, London.
Rutter, M., Greenfeld, D., and Lockyer, L. (1967) *Brit. J. Psychiat.*, 113, 1183.
Rutter, M., and Lockyer, L. (1967) *Brit. J. Psychiat.*, 113, 1169.
Scott, P. D. (1964) *Brit. J. Crim.*, 4, 525.
Scott, P. D. (1965) in *Modern Perspectives in Child Psychiatry*, ed. Howells, J. G., Edinburgh.
Stalker, H., and Band, D. (1946) *J. ment. Sci.*, 92, 324.
Toolan, J. M. (1962) *Amer. J. Psychiat.*, 118, 719.
West, D. J. (1967) *The Young Offender*, Harmondsworth.
Wickes, I. G. (1963) *Brit. med. J.*, 2, 1199.
Wing, J. K., ed. (1966) *Early Childhood Autism*, Oxford.

THERAPEUTIC COMMUNITIES, OCCUPATIONAL THERAPY AND REHABILITATION

There is a continuum of therapeutic opportunity and effort which extends from the psychiatric hospital or unit, through departments of occupational and industrial therapy, to day hospitals and the community with its family doctors, the after-care services of the local authorities and the facilities for rehabilitation provided by the Ministry of Labour. The main subject of this chapter is occupational therapy: but it must be placed in its setting, with at least brief reference to developments in the hospitals where departments of occupational therapy are situated and to complementary modes of rehabilitation.

Since the Second World War the psychiatric services in this country have undergone a transformation in their resources and efficiency. Many factors have contributed to this: a more enlightened public opinion, expressed in the Mental Health Acts of 1959–60; enhanced numbers and quality of staff; and finance for up-grading the fabric and facilities of the mental hospitals and for the provision of new psychiatric units in general hospitals. The mental hospitals have now a far more attractive appearance than they used to have, there is greater activity in the treatment and rehabilitation of their patients and the quality of life which patients in these hospitals can enjoy has been immensely improved. Contacts with relatives and with the outside world have multiplied, the patients have increased liberty of movement and scope for initiative, and their sense of personal responsibility is strengthened by their usually informal status as patients: their individuality can be expressed in wearing their own clothes, in taking part in entertainments, patient club functions and outings, in choosing their own menus and in many other ways. In conformity also with the climate of opinion in the community, and as a result of having more senior staff, medical and lay, who have had to be given their share in decision taking, a less hierarchical administrative structure has been evolved: and communications between all categories and grades of hospital staff, and between staff and patients, have been deliberately improved.

Another major factor in this changing scene has been the introduction of new methods of treatment and in particular the widespread use of potent tranquillizing and thymoleptic drugs. The control over impulsive, violent and dangerous behaviour which can be effected by means of drugs, has been of major importance in permitting a more liberal and humane hospital regime, with much less emphasis upon custodial care and restraint. The effectiveness of these drugs in bringing about at least symptomatic improvement, has encouraged also an optimism amongst staff and patients which has been contagious and therapeutically itself a powerful influence. Linn (1959) at St. Elizabeth's Hospital, Washington, attempted to separate the effects due to institutional changes from those of drug therapy, and studied what happened to those patients, aged 20–49 and predominantly schizophrenic, who were not treated with chlorpromazine or reserpine. He found that patients recently hospitalized for the first time, whether or not they were treated with tranquillizing drugs, were more likely to be discharged home than were patients hospitalized for the first time before the use of these drugs; and he concluded that the increasingly optimistic expectations of the staff that mental hospital patients would recover had increased the probability that, whether treated with drugs or not, they would in fact recover.

The mental hospitals in this country have undoubtedly in the past two decades had a good record: but that is no cause for complacency, and the impetus for improvement could easily be lost. The reasons for calling mental hospitals 'therapeutic communities', as it has become currently fashionable to do, should therefore be scrutinized. Are they hospitals or communities, essentially? From what activities comes their therapeutic potential? The answers to these questions should determine present policy and how these institutions will be constructed, equipped and staffed in the future. If one calls a mental hospital a therapeutic community because it has undergone the kind of changes which have been outlined already, is performing its functions well and is in fact a good hospital, the term therapeutic community is unexceptionable but hardly necessary. But if the term therapeutic community means that it is the community aspects of a mental hospital which contribute most to rehabilitation and cure, the claim is a most important one; and though it may possibly be true, it is still unproven. Certainly if these community and social aspects of hospital care are of central importance, they must be identified, refined and used as deliberately and critically as any other method of treatment. Unfortunately there has been relatively little research into these aspects of medical care, though there has been much anecdotal coverage of them and a considerable volume of propaganda.

SOCIAL THERAPY

This approach to treatment has been given various titles—social therapy, milieu therapy and the therapeutic community approach. It derives from psychoanalysis, group psychotherapy and sociology: but there has not yet been formulated for it a distinctive and coherent theory and its procedures are still ill defined. It originated from the experiences of psychiatrists during the Second World War, in the treatment of war neuroses, 'effort syndrome' and the rehabilitation of ex-prisoners of war. It has been developed notably in this country by Maxwell Jones (1952, 1962) at the Industrial Neurosis Unit at Belmont Hospital—later called the Henderson Hospital, by T. P. Rees at Warlingham Park, by T. M. Main at the Cassel Hospital and by D. V. Martin (1962) at Claybury. Sociologists have made valuable contributions: the reports of Stanton and Schwartz (1954), Dunham and Weinberg (1960) and Rapoport (1960) have been outstanding.

'Social therapy' rests on the well-founded observation that certain types of nervous and mental illness are directly the product of disturbances in personal relationships, and that many others lead to such disturbances. It operates in the belief that the culture of a hospital or ward can be used deliberately to assist the individual patient by group experiences and social influences.

Social therapy of this kind (it is not the only possible kind) consists mainly of the effects of frequent group meetings. Usually the patients of a ward and all the staff who are looking after them (doctors, nurses, occupational therapists, social workers, with or without the domestic staff) meet daily to discuss freely and informally ward happenings, grievances, personal relationships, tensions and rôles. Personal problems and misbehaviour occurring on the ward are treated as a communal responsibility, they are analysed and interpreted in psychodynamic terms and a consensus of opinion is sought so that they can be resolved by group influences. The way the affairs of the ward are conducted is determined largely at these group meetings: and they are the chief occasions of contact between the doctors and their patients.

These patient-staff meetings are supplemented by meetings of the staff: and much of the doctors' time is spent in trying to teach psychotherapeutic skills to various categories of staff and in helping them to deal with their anxieties. Doctors usually conduct both the ward and staff meetings: but it is upon the nurses that reliance is chiefly placed for transmission of the culture or 'group climate' of the unit.

Further principles are that all hospital doors should be opened, that both sexes of patient should be treated together, and that rôles should be blurred. Permissiveness and democratization are the order of the day. Mutual criticism (as well as support) is encouraged, and the 'pyramid of authority' is deliberately flattened: but the tip of the pyramid remains more visible than the theory allows for, and perhaps too little conscious recognition is given to how much depends upon the leader's personality, his enthusiasm, conviction and personal warmth.

This type of approach may be most relevant to those abnormal mental states which are known to derive from disordered personal and social relationships—namely, the neuroses, personality disorders and psychopathic states. It may, therefore, more successfully be applied in neurosis units than in the average mental hospital with its mixed population of which the largest groups consist of the dementias of old age and of the affective and schizophrenic psychoses. It has little relevance to the management of organic dementias; it upsets many of those suffering from affective psychoses (for whom there are other, more effective treatments); and it is doubtful if it is of value in the treatment of chronic schizophrenia. Letemendia and his colleagues (1967), who compared a group of long-term schizophrenic patients treated in an intensive therapeutic milieu of the Maxwell Jones type with a group treated by more conventional methods, found that neither programme had had much effect; and they concluded that for this very important clinical group the case for 'therapeutic community measures' rested on general humanitarian grounds rather than on therapeutic influences.

There has been a paucity of substantial studies with controls such as would permit a critical appraisal, and the effectiveness of social therapy is therefore still uncertain. It is even more difficult to assess than the more traditional methods of psychotherapy, being more diffuse, weaker in theory and vaguer in practice. It makes much use of unsophisticated personnel, without ensuring that they are suited and systematically trained for these tasks. The meetings upon which it depends are so numerous and time-consuming that detailed case-taking and examination, individual attention to patients and other forms of treatment are very liable to suffer. It may be objected also that a therapeutic community of this type is too self-conscious, too artificial and unlike the everyday world for which patients should be rehabilitated. Also, as a base for teaching and research in psychiatry, a hospital conducted entirely along such lines would be distinctly narrow.

Yet, when these criticisms have been made, it must be agreed that this approach has been a healthy challenge and that it has had a stimulating and leavening effect upon contemporary psychiatric practice. It should be the subject of further experiment and research. The over-all aim should not be too ambitious since it is very unlikely that the same kind of milieu therapy will be found applicable to many different kinds of illness.

OCCUPATIONAL THERAPY

We do not regard occupational therapy in a narrow sense as merely providing an agreeable craft for an idle moment while a patient is in hospital. Our horizon is far wider so that we regard habit formation and work therapy as the most important agents in preventing boredom and monotony, and in building up constructive useful lives which can be lived at a level of efficiency and consequent happiness.

Dr. Clarence B. Farrar has recorded that William James in his discussion on 'Habit' summed it up in the following epigram: 'Sow an action, and you reap a habit; sow a habit, and you reap a character; sow a character, and you reap a destiny.' The following extract by the same distinguished author may also be quoted: 'Nothing we ever do is, in strict scientific literalness, wiped out. Of course this has its good side as well as its bad one. As we become permanent drunkards by so many separate drinks, so we become saints in the moral, and authorities and experts in the practical and scientific spheres, by so many acts and hours of work. Let no youth have any anxiety about the upshot of his education, whatever the line of it may be. If he keeps faithfully busy each hour of the working day, he may safely leave the final result to itself. He can with perfect certainty count on waking up some fine morning, to find himself one of the competent ones of his generation, in whatever pursuit he may have singled out.' It is, we would suggest, such a philosophy of work that forms the core of healthy living.

An active, well-organized department of occupational therapy is an essential, integral part of every hospital dealing with the physical or psychological rehabilitation of those who are in need of such specialized help. It enlists the co-operation of the patients so that they themselves can form an estimate of their own progress and be encouraged to make further efforts. It adds to their resources and hastens a satisfactory and healthy adaptation to their bodily and psychological needs.

Furthermore the prescription of suitable occupation can attain its purpose: 1. through its own merit; 2. by being complementary to any other form of treatment; and 3. by its utilization not only during the course of the illness but after recovery has been effected. Its scope has been defined by a Committee of the American Occupational Therapy Association (1960), and its success, in a general way, is considered likely to depend on the activity undertaken, the atmosphere in which it is performed, and the relationship established with the professional staff.

The principles embodied in the above statement are by no means new. The acolytes, priests and other attendants who formed the staff at the 'healing temples' of Aesculapius, where it was believed that even the dead could be restored to life, were well aware of them. They did everything possible to promote the right atmosphere, the proper state of mind, so that the person might be more susceptible of cure. An attractive site was chosen for the temple, its natural beauties were enhanced, and everything possible was done to exteriorize the patient by employing his leisure in a purposeful, constructive manner, rather than by allowing him to sink into a state of contemplation which could so easily lead to apathy and stagnation. Unfortunately, however, the above healing methods were not followed up and organized as they might have been, and it was not until the 'humane period' of the treatment of the mentally disordered had been instituted that occupation as a form of therapy became recognized. The archives of many of our mental hospitals in Europe and Great Britain can verify these facts. The physician superintendents of those institutions in their annual reports invariably emphasized the value of suitable employment as a means of promoting efficiency, happiness, and a sense of accomplishment. Life in a mental hospital could be made constructive, the monotony of hospitalization could be alleviated, and the chance of improvement and recovery expedited. Congenial work was found to be an antidote to irritation, friction, gossip, boredom, introspection and bad habits. In a more positive way it bred interest, skill and orderly habits of mind and body. As an example reference may be made to the records of the Glasgow Royal Mental Hospital which date back to 1814. The evidence they provide is impressive. For instance in 1817 it is stated: 'Two looms and five spinning wheels are generally kept at work; clothes are made or mended, stockings and worsted gloves are knit, and occasionally a little muslin is flowered though, on the whole, this is the least profitable manufacture, because when any freak or wrangling occurs the figures are apt to rise on the wrong side. Every encouragement, however, is given to the exertions of industry, because nothing contributes so much to promote a cure, and prevent a relapse.'

Another excerpt from the enlightened report of 1820 is worthy of recording: 'Sociality has often been promoted, while the irksomeness of confinement has been alleviated by various occupations and amusements. Bowls and billiards have been favourite games, and reading, music and drawing have often served to arrest attention and to dispel illusion. Some write letters or poems, one solves mathematical problems, and another has been busily engaged in composing the history of a voyage round the world. . . . Some have laboured in the garden or shrubbery grounds; shoes have been made and cloth woven by various individuals, and one patient is at present very useful as a joiner. Some of the females have knitted and sewed diligently, and so many of them have been industriously employed in spinning that almost all the bed and table linen now used in the asylum is the product of their labour.'

A much wider aspect was also kept in mind because in 1821 we find the following: 'Our asylum, we believe, is the first establishment of the kind in which a sermon was ever preached. . . . We are not aware that divine service, as in Church, was ever performed in any lunatic establishment in this country until it was introduced into our asylum, and we are much gratified to find that our example in affording the benefit of religious instruction and consolation to the insane begins now to be generally followed.' The above innovation became so appreciated that one of the patients thanked the clergyman for his kind condescension and added that he was particularly gratified to be thought worthy of attending public worship.

The social side of hospital life was also developed. Weekly dances, ward parties, indoor games, *e.g.* billiards, cards, draughts, etc., outside activities such as cricket, hockey, curling, golf, tennis, all provided an opportunity for patients and staff to meet informally. Charitable organizations, by providing lectures, concerts, plays, did much to brighten the lives of all those patients whose illness might require continued treatment over many years. The so-called 'therapeutic communities', whose praises we sing to-day, were not unknown to our psychiatric forebears!

It must be admitted, however, that the institutional and economic needs of the hospital were probably given precedence over the more individual aspects which are the hall-mark of well organized occupational therapy. The criticism that good hard-working willing patients were exploited for the benefit of the institution would not be easy to refute. The patients were recommended, in a more or less haphazard way, to the laundry, kitchen, sewing-room, piggery, garden or artisan's department. They were sent where they were most needed, and they accepted hospital life uncomplainingly, so long as they received the extra privileges and perquisites which they were so well entitled to. But the withdrawn, listless, apathetic, depressed, delusional patients many of whom had never been accustomed to manual work were far too numerous, and came to be regarded as unemployable. It was only when it became more fully recognized that the success of an occupational therapy department could be measured by its ability to provide work for those who were thought to be unemployable that its organization was justified.

In Scotland (and perhaps in Great Britain) the earliest attempt to organize the employment of patients, on a specialized and systematic basis, was launched in 1880 when a far-sighted and charitably minded woman, Lady Brabazon, offered a grant of money to any workhouse or infirmary which developed a plan to employ their 'crippled and infirm inmates'. The challenge was taken up in 1895 by the managers of the Barnhill Poor House, Glasgow, and in 1898 Dr. Hamilton Marr at the Woodilee Mental Hospital, Glasgow, introduced a similar scheme.

It was arranged that, once a week, a group of ladies interested in handicrafts should visit the hospital so as to teach certain forms of handicraft. That particular day, subsequently known as 'Brabazon Day', became eagerly anticipated. In official circles, however, occupational therapy did not receive a very warm reception; it was regarded as a well-intentioned fad. In 1899 an editorial in the *Journal of Mental Science* commented as follows: 'Provided the work be carried on with the sympathy and accord of the asylum officials, as doubtless it would be, we see no objection to the Brabazon scheme in these institutions; at any rate for our pauper asylums it appears to be well worthy of an extended trial'. We need not be too severe in our criticism of that somewhat niggardly snobbish comment because government financial help was at a minimum, there were no adequate facilities and many mental hospitals were dependent for their existence on bequests and voluntary contributions. The maintenance of the institution was regarded as the first priority, and no surplus funds were available for necessary amenities which were regarded as luxuries. It is only in very recent years that we have witnessed the shift from rough-and-ready group methods to individualization, to the intensive study of the needs of each person. The majority of those who suffer from nervous and mental illness resent it, their pride and sense of prestige is hurt, they would love to exhibit an objective lesion to justify their apparent failure. They feel that they have been lacking in faith and determination, that they should have striven harder, that they are not suffering from an illness at all but merely sheer lack of will power. The truth is that they have struggled on for far too long, and have become exhausted bodily and mentally. It is our immediate duty to help them, and to supply them as speedily as possible with those physical and spiritual vitamins which they are so much in need of. Psyche responds to companionship, friends, attention and interest, congenial work and occupation, suitable literature and all those other things which a well-organized occupational department can supply. The programme must always be of an elastic nature, and so geared as likely to obtain a quick response.

When thinking along the above lines we were reminded of an address delivered in 1903 by that great philosopher-physician, Sir William Osler, to the undergraduates of Toronto University. Its title was the 'Master-Word in Medicine'. He said: 'Though a little one the master-word looms large in meaning. It is the open sesame to every portal, the great equalizer in the world, the true philosopher's stone which transmutes all the base metal of humanity into gold. The stupid man among you it will make bright, the bright man brilliant, and the brilliant student steady. With the magic word in your heart all things are possible, and without it all study is vanity and vexation. The miracles of life are with it; the blind see by touch, the deaf hear with eyes, the dumb speak with fingers. . . . The master-word is "Work" . . . a little one, as I have said . . . directly responsible for all advances in medicine during the past twenty-five centuries.' While those words were addressed as a principle, precept and injunction to medical students yet they appear peculiarly appropriate to the topic which concerns us here, and are not too great a digression from our chronological account of work as a healing agent.

Adolf Meyer in a paper entitled 'The Philosophy of Occupational Therapy' described how in 1893 he began to realize that 'the proper use of time in some helpful and gratifying activity appeared to be fundamental in the treatment of any neuro-psychiatric patient'. At a later date his interest was stimulated by Dr. W. R. Dunton, Jr., one of the founder members of the American Occupational Therapy Association. In 1902 at the Psychiatric Institute, Wards Island, New York, with the valuable help of Mrs. Meyer, and the enthusiastic support of Dr. Dent and Dr. Mabon the successive medical superintendents of the Manhattan State Hospital, an occupational therapy department with associated recreational activities was established. One of the staff nurses of the Manhattan State Hospital was chosen to attend a course of training under Miss Lathrop at the Chicago School of Civics and Philanthropy, and afterwards returned to the Manhattan State Hospital to organize occupational work. In this humble way organized occupational therapy took its rise to become, in due course, welded into the World Federation of Occupational Therapy which exercises great influence, and sets a high standard.

It seems appropriate enough that the Glasgow Royal Mental Hospital, whose archives have already given up some of their secrets, should have earned the distinction of being the first mental hospital in Scotland to organize an occupational therapy department. The occupational work we had seen and been able to take part in, in the United States, had impressed us so much that we were impelled to follow the example which had been set. In consequence, in 1919 a scheme was submitted to Dr. L. R. Oswald, the Physician Superintendent, and to the Managers of the Glasgow Royal Mental Hospital for their approval. Their support was most cordial, and with the co-operation of Miss Darney, the matron, and selected members of the nursing staff, and the patients themselves, classes of an occupational and recreational nature were arranged. In 1922 Miss Dorothea Robertson, a resourceful, intelligent and charming woman was appointed to be in charge of the department. Pavilions were erected apart from the main hospital buildings, and an attempt was made to make them as attractive as possible; a great variety of crafts were made available. In 1924 the Scottish Division of the Royal Medico-Psychological Association met at the hospital to discuss the value and importance of occupational therapy; that meeting constituted the first meeting ever devoted to that topic in Great Britain. It was the forerunner for the development of organized occupational departments in the mental hospitals throughout the British Isles. But to make such departments really effective it was soon realized that the establishment of training schools, for those wishing to adopt such work as a career, was an imperative necessity. Thus it was that in 1933 an occupational therapy department was opened at the Astley Ainslie Hospital, Edinburgh. In the first instance it was staffed by senior Canadian therapists recommended by the Canadian Medical Association. In 1937 the Training Centre was opened so that students could be prepared for occupational work both in the physical and psychiatric fields. The comprehensive course of instruction extends over a period of three years.

We have always been strongly of the opinion that the person in charge of such a department in a mental hospital should have been specially trained for the post. It has been argued that a trained mental hospital nurse would be more appropriate. That, however, is not our experience. The fact that the occupational therapist provides a different social and educational standard, and is not so concerned with the disciplinary side of hospital life as the nurse constitutes a great advantage. We believe, however, that the trained occupational therapists should have the ability to transmit their knowledge to others, and possess the sympathetic understanding whereby they can gain the co-operation both of patients and nursing staff. Jealousy and rivalry between hospital staff merely retards the improvement or recovery of the patients. There is much to be done to enable them to overcome their difficulties. While every effort must be made to produce work of a satisfying standard yet the work *per se* is not the main thing. The essential thing is to stimulate the patient to produce something, no matter how simple, so as to create a sense of accomplishment. A word or two of praise, a pat on the back, the individual touch can work wonders. Frequent discussions between the therapists and the medical and nursing staff regarding the progress of the patient are essential. Sometimes the doctor seems to think he has fulfilled his function by referring the patient to the occupational department, and may take no further interest in that part of the treatment. But occupational treatment should be prescribed with as much care and consideration as a drug, and should be altered or changed according to the progress, or lack of it, which is taking place. Those in charge of the occupational department can often make valuable contributions at the medical staff meetings when individual cases come up for discussion.

The accommodation provided for an occupational division should be quite simple, but it should be made attractive, well lit, with plenty of window-space, modern tools and appliances, and sufficient rooms so that, if necessary, certain crafts requiring quiet surroundings and special skill can be practised separately. It is of great advantage to provide a display room for completed articles. In addition to the work centre it is most advantageous to provide a play centre where games, physical exercises and dancing can be indulged in.

For the smooth and efficient working of the department it has seemed to us to be important to grade the patients into classes so that the less skilled do not feel over-awed by their more expert neighbours, and so that more individual attention can be given to those most in need of help. Some patients like to spend all their available time in the occupational department, but as a general rule the classes should not be longer than 1–2 hours, depending upon the patient's ability to maintain his interest and concentration. The work should never be allowed to become too monotonous and fatiguing.

Frequently we have been asked whether one type of work is more applicable to a particular form of mental or nervous disorder than to another. We have never found it to be so. The potential talent of each patient has to be considered anew apart altogether from the mental disorder from which he may be suffering. 'Familiarity breeds contempt' would seem to be the order of the day in an

2 L

occupational department for there it is not uncommon to see depressed patients who, if unoccupied, might be suicidal, using sharp tools and other lethal instruments with impunity. It is, however, important that such instruments should be carefully accounted for before the patient returns to his ward unit. When the patient goes to the department for the first time the work given should be able to yield quick results; the use of bright colours is preferred to something drab. Some patients adapt themselves easily to raffia and cane work, basket- and chair-making, weaving, joinery, toy making; others of a more aesthetic and artistic type may prefer china painting, drawing, embroidery, leather work, pottery, brass hammering, or a host of other crafts all of which may create a feeling of something well done. It should be possible to cater for every taste. Nor must the scope of employment be limited to the department alone. Our hospitals are usually situated in pleasant surroundings which provide ample opportunity for games, pleasant exercise, gardening and other out-door work. The house-keeping departments are always in need of good workers who prefer such employment to more exotic tasks.

The Purposes of the Department

1. It affords an additional outlet for a variety of interests and offers facilities for constructive work not only during the period of hospital treatment but also after the patient has returned home. For instance, a single man, 40 years old, who resented his admission to hospital, stated that he was unlawfully detained, that it was a 'frame-up'. He paced the floor continuously, was influenced by hallucinations of hearing, taste and smell, and resented being questioned. He thought the other patients were laughing at him, slept poorly, and looked ill both physically and mentally. He was persuaded, eventually, to visit the occupational division where he was amazed by the activity and happiness. He said that he would like to learn rug-making. He proved a diligent, capable worker who found great pleasure in working out his own designs. He became co-operative, his symptoms abated, and he made a satisfactory recovery. On returning to his own home he added considerably to his income by continuing his work at the craft which he had learned.

Another striking example of the curative value of an occupational department was instanced, in the case of a young man, 20 years old, who was sullen, perverse and antagonistic. He was determined to make things unpleasant for all who had to care for him. He refused to wash or shave, or dress himself. After much persuasion he was induced to visit the occupational department. There, fortunately, he soon found he was able to sublimate his feelings of antagonism and resentment. China painting proved an attraction, he expressed a wish to try it. He was given a bowl on which he drew his own design, and became so successful and talented that at a crafts exhibition, held in the city, he was awarded a first prize. The occupational department made his temporary hospital residence much more bearable, and indirectly helped him to tackle his problems in a better balanced frame of mind.

2. An occupational department creates new contacts. The trained teachers whose task it is to appeal to the patient's practical interests establish a relationship which is different from that of doctor or nurse. Patients who are antagonistic to the medical and nursing staff may, and often do, establish a most harmonious relationship with the occupational therapist. As an example we can report the case of a male schizophrenic patient who had been a 'wallflower' for over forty years. When it was suggested that he might be tried in the occupational department the nurses who were in charge of him shook their heads. They said that many attempts had been made to employ him but they had been useless. The result, however, which followed exceeded all expectations. He responded to the therapist and to the general activity of the department. He learned the art of cane-weaving so as to make seats for stools and chairs, and soon became a rug-maker as well. He acquired an interest which he never had had previously, life became pleasanter, and the monotony of his hospital residence was alleviated. He was weaned from his withdrawal into a constructive occupation.

3. An occupational department creates a work-atmosphere where there is a spirit of competition so that a healthy rivalry comes into play. The desire to be occupied becomes infectious.

All the above-mentioned factors work together to create a spirit of hope, faith and accomplishment. And these objects can be attained in every type of case from the subnormal child to the geriatric patient. It is only a matter of modifying techniques and of having the capacity to form a good personal relationship or rapport with the particular patient. Not every occupational therapist is suited for psychiatric work any more than every doctor is. It requires patience, understanding and a natural flair or aptitude for being able to get in touch with the nervous and mentally affected. The aim in view is to substitute good habits and thinking in place of bad ones, to establish a philosophy of life and work in place of fantasy thinking in terms of the unattainable. Through suitable work we can help the spark of light in the subnormal to burn a little brighter, the depressed anxious-minded patient can be made to feel that life has still something in store, the manic can direct his energy aright, the paranoid can be side-tracked from his supposed wrongs, and even those with organic brain disease and dwindling intellectual powers may be prevented from sinking into a more profound dementia.

Occupational Therapy at Home

Occupational therapy does not necessarily begin and end in hospital. What has been learned in hospital can often be continued at home, there is no reason why occupational therapists should not provide a home service analogous to that of the psychiatric social worker. There are many subnormal and geriatric patients who do not require hospital treatment but who would benefit from the imaginative advice of a skilled occupational therapist. The fascination of acquiring new knowledge, the recognition of a talent which had lain dormant, the ability to transform a hobby into a profitable vocation can all create intense satisfaction. The biggest incentive lies in the possibility of preserving one's general health, but if even a small financial reward is forthcoming it adds to one's enthusiasm and persistence of effort.

DAY HOSPITALS

Ewen Cameron (1947) in Montreal and Bierer in England pioneered the use of day hospitals, which are now considered by many to be elements of key importance in the development of 'community psychiatry'. A psychiatric day hospital may be located at a mental or general hospital but is most typically a detached physically independent unit, situated in a building adapted or built for this purpose and catering for the needs usually of less than 50 patients. The staff includes psychiatrists, nurses, social workers, occupational therapists and mental health officers of the local authority. The patients attend normally for five days a week and the aim is to provide the treatments available to psychiatric hospital in-patients, together with a varied programme of occupational, rehabilitative and diversional activities. Special transport may have to be arranged to bring patients from their homes to the unit; and transport is a factor of great importance in placing such units. Location, staffing, selection of patients, treatment and duration of care vary widely from one day hospital to another. (We except from this discussion geriatric day-care units, which are not concerned with active psychiatric treatment.)

The development of day hospitals has been advocated on three main grounds: that treatment there is less expensive than in-patient care; that the patient's links with his family and society are maintained; and that the adverse mental effects of hospitalization are avoided. The expense of such units depends of course largely upon how well they are staffed, staffing levels tend to be high (if they are not, the patients drift away), and there have been few claims in this country that they are very economical to run. The other claims advanced in their favour are also uncertain. The picture of patients 'incarcerated' in mental hospitals, cut off from their relatives and friends and demoralized by inactivity and forced dependence, has been tendentiously overdrawn in contrast with them. Further, though there is some evidence that the chronic schizophrenic may benefit most, there is no consensus of opinion about what type of psychiatric patient is most suited to day hospital care: and though the day hospital may bridge the gap between hospital and community for some patients discharged from hospital, no proof has so far been given that it is better than, for example, a period of living in a hostel.

Though there have been numerous descriptions of day hospitals and their activities, there have been regrettably very few critical studies of the results of psychiatric treatment in this setting. Amongst the few that have been published, that by Wilder and his colleagues (1966) is notable. Taking an unselected group of acute psychiatric admissions to the Bronx Municipal Hospital Center, they assigned the patients at random either to in-patient treatment or day hospital care. Of those thus allocated to day hospital care about two-thirds were accepted for it; about three-fifths of those accepted were treated throughout in this way; and if recourse had to be made to in-patient care, this occurred usually during the first two weeks of treatment and was a brief episode. Approximately 75 per cent. of patients in every non-organic diagnostic category were accepted, but cases of the acute and chronic organic reaction-types were not suitable for day care.

In this study both services used drugs and somatic treatments: in addition in the hospital there was individual psychotherapy, occupational therapy and recreation, while in the day hospital the orientation was of the 'therapeutic community' type, patients were treated in groups of 8–10, there were discussions, community meetings, group activities lead by a nurse and a 'patient government'. Follow-up showed that day hospital treatment was generally as effective as the traditional in-patient programme in the treatment of acutely mentally disturbed patients. Some, however, were found to be unsuitable for this type of care; and there seemed to be only one clinical group, cases of schizophrenia in women, for whom day treatment was perhaps preferable to hospitalization. In discussing these schizophrenic patients Wilder and his colleagues point out that day treatment, by enabling her to live at home, may help a mentally sick woman to preserve her self-image, her place in the family and her social skills. Day treatment seemed inappropriate for cases of acute schizophrenia in men and for severe depressions in older people; and for neurotic reactions and personality disorders out-patient care was thought to be preferable. These workers suggest that day hospital treatment may be more helpful to those who have been ill and are relapsing, than for the more acutely ill: and their conclusion is commendably cautious, that the day hospital is 'a feasible treatment, surprisingly well received by both patients and their families, and possibly with some therapeutic and economic advantages'.

If the establishment of day hospitals encourages patients to seek psychiatric treatment earlier, if it enables chronic schizophrenic or other patients whose adjustment is marginal to continue to live reasonably happily and effectively in the community, if it can aid the mentally ill woman who is a housewife and mother to retain her place in the home without disrupting it, if it can do these things more economically than the traditional in-patient psychiatric unit or otherwise substitute for in-patient care or assist materially to reduce its duration, then it is a development in psychiatric practice which should be encouraged and a necessary part of a comprehensive psychiatric service. But if day hospitals are not more economical, if they lead by the dispersal of skilled personnel to the less effective use of available resources, and above all if they encourage the part-time hospitalization of those who otherwise and as effectively would be cared for as out-patients, they are otiose. We consider that the case for the day hospital has not yet been established, and that further research is required before day hospitals are accepted as being more than just one of the possible ways in which psychiatric treatment and support may be provided in a community.

INDUSTRIAL REHABILITATION UNITS

Units in which psychiatric patients do work of an industrial nature have been a useful recent extension of occupational therapy and may be used as a bridge to industrial employment in the community.

Most of these units in Britain are situated in the mental hospitals and are engaged on contract work for outside firms: some hospital departments have marketed their own products. Various activities have been undertaken—making cement blocks, toys, cardboard boxes, wooden crates, fencing; and sorting, dismantling, assembling and packaging items ranging from screws to Christmas crackers. Much of this work is obviously of a simple, repetitive kind: but the patients learn habits of work, they may find some interest in it and they earn money for themselves. It is essential that therapeutic aims should be kept in the forefront of these endeavours and that as far as is possible the work should be geared to the individual needs of the patients. Continuity and variety of work should be ensured: and it should be closely supervised by occupational therapists or nurses. The success of these units must not be measured by their output and their financial returns. Quality is more important than quantity of work, and more important still is the process of resocialization which work with others promotes.

Industrial units which are situated in the community, to which the patient can go for training while still in hospital, are even more useful than hospital-based departments. They permit a more accurate assessment of the patient's potential for regular paid employment and of his ability to maintain himself outside hospital. Early (1960) in Bristol pioneered the setting up of an industrial therapy organization as a commercial concern, with the support of local industry and the trade unions and the approval of the Ministry of Labour; and similar town-based organizations with sheltered workshops, car washing units and other facilities have been developed elsewhere. Amongst the mentally ill, it is the male chronic schizophrenic patient who is apt to benefit most: but it is not so much the symptoms of his psychosis which are modified as the habits of withdrawal and inertia which are in part the products of a long period of hospitalization. It is therefore amongst the very long-stay hospital patients that the success rate may be highest, and Early and Magnus (1968) report a short-term success rate of 55 per cent. for patients in open industry or sheltered work after more than 20 years in hospital.

The Ministry of Labour's Industrial Rehabilitation Units have also a part to play in the rehabilitation of mental hospital patients. Wing, Bennett and Denham (1964) found that of 45 moderately handicapped schizophrenic patients, with a mean age of 39 and a mean length of hospital stay of $8\frac{1}{2}$ years who had attended an I.R.U., 24 were in employment one year after their discharge from the I.R.U. These patients had been carefully prepared by the hospital staff for transfer to the I.R.U., they had spent about 10 weeks there, and they were then closely supervised during the following year. All of them remained handicapped to some degree, being generally socially withdrawn, slow and lacking in initiative: but 'no patient was worse for having been to the I.R.U. and at least half benefited considerably'. Some of these schizophrenic patients obtained places in Remploy factories and were found there not to be more handicapped than physically disabled men who had started work at the same time.

The success of all these efforts towards rehabilitation depends greatly upon the local level of employment. If there is full employment, placing the mentally disabled in industry is easier. But it is never easy: and the majority of chronic schizophrenic patients will not at best become fit for employment except in sheltered workshops.

To carry out such a programme of rehabilitation effectively in a psychiatric service, it is necessary to have a senior psychiatrist in charge who has a special interest in rehabilitation, coupled with enthusiasm and drive. It is also necessary to have an active co-ordinating committee which will meet regularly and often, and upon which are represented all the groups which are professionally concerned—hospital doctors, nurses, occupational therapists and social workers; and from the community the family doctor, a representative of the local authority (doctor, mental health officer or health visitor) and a Disablement Resettlement Officer of the Ministry of Labour. Many long-term patients' problems will require individual attention from such a group of experts. Not only should the patient have vocational guidance if he needs it and be found appropriate employment, he will often require help also in finding suitable accommodation in a hostel or lodgings. His family may have to be advised and supported, his family doctor must be kept fully informed (if it has not been possible for him to attend the group's deliberations) and the help of voluntary associations may be usefully sought. And the therapeutic effort must not stop there. The quality of the after-care given to these patients will have a considerable influence upon whether or not they will be able to continue to live and work in the community.

Community care of a high standard is more of an aspiration than a reality in this country. General practitioners are not yet adequately trained in the treatment of mentally ill people, local authorities have few doctors with such specialized experience and few social workers, and hostel accommodation for the more chronically disabled is often lacking (and where provided, compares usually very unfavourably with the resources of a modern mental hospital). Grad and Sainsbury (1968), from an investigation of two psychiatric services with differing admission policies, report that the social cost of psychiatric care was higher in a service which favoured extramural treatment of patients than in a service which favoured their admission to hospital: and, very importantly, that the cost was higher in terms of the effects upon the mental health of family members. Their findings show the necessity of supplementing community care of the patient with adequate support to his family.

REFERENCES

American Occupational Therapy Association (1960) *Occupational Therapy Reference Manual for Physicians*, Dubuque, Iowa.
Cameron, D. E. (1947) *Mod. Hosp.*, **69**, 60.
Dunham, H. W., and Weinberg, S. K. (1960) *The Culture of the State Mental Hospital*, Detroit.
Dunton, W. R., and Licht, S., eds. (1957) *Occupational Therapy: Principles and Practice*, Springfield, Ill.
Early, D. F. (1960) *Lancet*, ii, 754.
Early, D. F., and Magnus, R. V. (1968) *Brit. J. Psychiat.*, **114**, 335.

Grad, J., and Sainsbury, P. (1968) *Brit. J. Psychiat.*, **114**, 265.
Henderson, D. K., and Thompson, A. G. W. (1925) *J. ment. Sci.*, **71**, 59.
James, W. (1890) *Psychology*, New York.
Jones, M. (1952) *Social Psychiatry*, London.
Jones, M. (1962) *Social Psychiatry, in the Community, in Hospitals, and in Prisons*, Springfield, Ill.
Letemendia, F. J. J., Harris, A. D., and Willems, P. J. A. (1967) *Brit. J. Psychiat.*, **113,** 959.
Le Vesconte, H. P. (1961) *Amer. J. Psychiat.*, **117**, 751.
Linn, E. L. (1959) *Arch. Neurol. Psychiat. (Chic.)*, **81**, 785.
Martin, D. V. (1962) *Adventure in Psychiatry*, Oxford.
Meyer, A. (1952) *Collected Papers*, Vol. IV, Baltimore.
Osler, W. (1910) *Aequanimitas*, Philadelphia.
Rapoport, R. N. (1960) *Community as Doctor*, London.
Stanton, A. H., and Schwartz, M. S. (1954) *The Mental Hospital*, New York.
Wilder, J. F., Levin, G., and Zwerling, I. (1966) *Amer. J. Psychiat.*, **122**, 1095.
Wing, J. K., Bennett, D. H., and Denham, J. (1964) *The Industrial Rehabilitation of Longstay Schizophrenic Patients*, London. H.M.S.O.

22

FORENSIC PSYCHIATRY

The register of crime is a long one. Indictable offences include larceny; breaking and entering; receiving, fraud and false pretences; violence against the person; and sexual offences. Amongst the non-indictable offences are common assaults; drunkenness; malicious damage; taking away cars; reckless, dangerous and drunken driving; exhibitionism and homosexual importuning.

Offences against property, theft and housebreaking, are much the commonest (80 per cent.) of indictable offences. The highest proportion of these offences occurs between the ages of 14 and 17 years. The highest proportion of cases of violence and hooliganism occurs between the ages of 17 and 20. Motoring offences, mainly adult, are very common and mostly minor: but motorists kill and injure ten times the number of those who are injured in the course of assaults or other intentional violence.

Such, in bare outline, are the offences and crimes with which the psychiatrist may be concerned. For an authoritative and comprehensive account of crime and punishment in Britain he is referred to Nigel Walker's (1965) excellent account. It provides the necessary background for what can only be the brief description in this book of one aspect of a complex field of human behaviour.

THE AETIOLOGY OF CRIMINAL BEHAVIOUR

Three factors are of undoubted importance in the aetiology of juvenile and adult delinquency and crime: age, sex and social background.

Age is a major factor. About one-half of those found guilty of indictable offences are aged 10–21 years. The peak age for conviction (mainly for minor larcencies) is 14 years: and the 17–21 age group has the highest incidence of convictions. In the past decade in this country, during which crime generally has been on the increase, convictions have risen faster among teenagers than amongst other age groups—especially for vandalism, assaults, alcoholism and drug offences. It is, however, the rare exception, not the rule, for a juvenile delinquent to become a recidivist. The majority of offenders are not convicted after the first occasion: and most juvenile delinquents, as they grow older and mature, grow out of crime. Even the delinquent careers of Borstal youths mainly end in their early twenties.

Sex is also a major factor. Delinquency and crime are largely male characteristics. Females commonly commit larceny and shoplifting; but are convicted rarely for breaking and entering, and much less often than males for sexual offences.

A nexus of social factors predisposes to delinquency and crime. They can be seen as indices of social deprivation and they include the following: low social class status (Class V); membership of a large family; irregular schooling—due often to lack of parental interest and leading to a poor academic record; and a broken or inadequate home. Contact with other delinquents in a slum neighbourhood is also of importance.

It is the 'broken home' situation which has received most attention from psychiatrists; and understandably so, since mentally disturbed offenders often give a history of a disturbed early home environment. It was Bowlby in this country and the Gluecks in the United States who first clearly associated broken homes, repeated changes of parental figures and emotional deprivation, with delinquency and crime.

Brown and Epps (1966), in an investigation of the backgrounds of 546 female and 168 male prisoners, found that, before they were aged 15, 18·2 per cent. of the women and 13·4 per cent. of the men had lost their fathers by death, and 13·2 per cent. and 8·6 per cent. their mothers. These were figures significantly higher than in the general population of the same age group. Brown and Epps concluded that both paternal and maternal orphanhood are significant factors in male and female criminality—particularly in the latter; and they suggested that it was probably not the bereavement itself, but the disorganization of upbringing following the loss of the parent which was the damaging situation. They noted further that many prisoners who had living parents had had as much disorganization of their childhood lives as if they had been parentless; 14·7 per cent. of the women prisoners had not known one or both parents. The conclusion drawn by these investigators is noteworthy: 'Though there are undoubtedly many factors in delinquency and crime, the consensus of evidence suggests that multiplicity of care and lack of stable parent figures in childhood are the most definite and perhaps the most preventable.'

Douglas (1968) has followed a cohort of 2300 boys born in 1946, of whom 288 have become delinquent. A significantly high proportion of these delinquent youths have come from homes broken by divorce or permanent separation of the parents. Early separation from the mother, removal to unfamiliar surroundings, and poor standards of maternal care have been more common in the delinquent group. Death of a parent or separation from the mother had no adverse effect if the child was kept in a familiar environment. Like Brown and Epps, Douglas concludes that bad family relationships are a most significant factor predisposing to delinquency.

So far we have described what is reasonably well established: but much remains obscure or unknown about the 'natural history' of criminal behaviour. Undoubtedly the aetiology of crime is multiple. It is quite insufficient to look for the causes of crime in general, more profitable to look for the causes of certain specific crimes, and essential to examine the individual criminal, his background, personality and motives. Amongst those who commit the same type of offence or crime, are to be found many different personalities, motives and circumstances.

Criminals are a very heterogeneous collection of people. Most of them are normal and their criminality is short-lived. A very small number become professional criminals. Those who are nervously or mentally ill also constitute a minority of the criminal population: and it is probably only in 10–20 per cent. of cases that the psychiatrist has undoubtedly a contribution to make to the understanding and 'treatment' of criminal behaviour. Nevertheless the psychiatrist's influence has been considerable in assisting the public and the Courts to come to a more humane and sensitive appreciation of the complexities of these situations. Sometimes it may seem that the criminal act was motiveless but there is always some reason—trivial though it may appear—which has set it in motion. Criminal behaviour is not a haphazard affair any more than mental disorder is; it is the expression of trends in the individual's personality which are more prominent or more easily evoked than in other people. The criminal is not simply a wicked person who with purpose and malice attempts to injure others, but like everyone else he may be the victim of emotional storms and distorted ideas which dominate his behaviour so that he may act, temporarily, in an uncontrollable manner. Dostoevsky has described in *Crime and Punishment* how nearly every criminal, at the moment of his crime, is subject to a collapse of reason and will power, exchanging them for an extraordinary childish heedlessness when judgement and caution are most indispensable. The emotionally determined situation which crystallizes out in action may have developed gradually; and it may be months or years before the individual comes to a full realization of his conduct. The power of the unconscious drives which may impel the individual to an emotional (catathymic) crisis and explosion of aggression, and the late development of insight, are very well described by Wertham in his book *Dark Legend* in which he tells the story of an Italian boy who committed matricide.

THE MENTALLY ABNORMAL OFFENDER

There is no psychiatric illness or abnormal mental state which is necessarily associated with criminality; and only one—the psychopathic state—in which perhaps the majority suffering from it are criminals. Nor is there any type of crime which is invariably the outcome of mental disease. The more abnormal the crime the more likely is it that the perpetrator will be found to be mentally abnormal; but even in one of the rarest and most abnormal of all crimes—murder, the murderer is found to be sane in about half the cases. In general, the distribution of types of crime is the same amongst 'normal' offenders and those found to be mentally disturbed.

Since minor mental disorders, character anomalies, psychopathic states and alcoholism may all be difficult to classify, there has been a good deal of uncertainty about how much mental abnormality is to be found in prison populations. Roper (1950, 1951) in Wakefield found 57 per cent. of the prisoners to be normal mentally, 23 per cent. to be dullards, 12 per cent. neurotic and 8 per cent. psychopathic. Bluglass (1967) in Perth prison found 11·6 per cent. to be dullards, 2·6 per cent. subnormal, 2·2 per cent. neurotic, 13·3 per cent. psychopathic and 1·9 per cent. psychotic. He diagnosed a further 11·2 per cent. as alcoholics and drug addicts, of whom one-third were chronic alcoholics. Other research workers have reported that about 10 per cent. of the prison population are psychopaths.

It is uncommon for individuals who are neurotically ill to become involved in criminal activities. The unconscious conflicts which may lead to delinquency (especially in juveniles) may be of much the same type as those which underlie neurotic reactions; the problems appear indeed often to be the same but the reaction is different, depending upon the constitutional make-up and personality structure of the individual. The neurotically ill individual is usually fully responsible for his actions; but in some cases it might be justifiable to enter a plea of diminished responsibility.

Not uncommonly a criminal will claim that he has an amnesia for the period of his crime. If this is the only nervous symptom complained of, it may be disregarded as significant of illness. If there are other neurotic symptoms, his amnesia must be carefully evaluated with reference to his previous personality, the history—if any, of neurotic illness earlier in life and particularly evidence which might confirm that he had had neurotic symptoms prior to the date of his alleged offence. It must be very rarely that a serious offence is committed in a state of hysterical dissociation—though such a dissociated state (*e.g.* a fugue) may follow the commission of a crime: and a Court of Law, even if an hysterical amnesia were to be proven, would not accept this as evidence of insanity.

Obsessional impulses which are antisocial are usually successfully resisted, unless a complicating factor such as depression has entered into the situation. Obsessional impulses may be to commit serious assaults or even murder, they may occur frequently and be intensely distressing, but the sufferer rejects them and maintains his self-control. We have never known a pure obsessive-compulsive state lead to a homicidal attack. Some sexual offences on the other hand, certain cases of exhibitionism for example, seem sometimes to have a compulsive quality: but it is doubtful if sexually deviant behaviour can be ranked properly as an obsessional symptom.

Both 'functional' and organic psychoses, the former more often than the latter, are of greater significance in relation to crime than the neuroses. Depressive psychoses are the cause not only of the majority of suicides but also of some murders. As a result of depressive delusions, convinced that he and his family are ruined or that he has transmitted to them insanity or venereal disease, a man may murder his wife and children: and a depressed woman, despairing in a similar way, may murder her children, within or without the puerperium. The murder is the first step in these cases to suicide, but the suicide is not always effected. A few serious assaults occur in similar circumstances. In the setting too of a depressive illness a man may be guilty of exhibitionism and a woman of shoplifting.

The disinhibition and lack of judgement and insight which are typical of hypomania may lead to delinquency and crime, but less commonly than does depression. The man who is hypomanic may be irritable and assaultive, may get involved in foolish, grandiose frauds and debt, or may drive a car recklessly.

A serious crime may be the first or almost the first evidence of schizophrenia—but this is rare. The young male schizophrenic is typically unpredictable and may be very dangerous. The schizophrenic murderer perhaps most typically kills his mother: but a sweetheart or complete stranger may be the victim, and a schizophrenic woman may kill her children. Some schizophrenics, unable to find and keep jobs, become vagrants and recidivists, involved usually in petty crimes.

The sufferer from a paranoid psychosis, if he thinks that he can identify his persecutor or persecutors, may go to law against them, attack their property or assault them personally. He may commit murder—and it is from a paranoiac that the *M'Naghten Rules* got their name. Such a man, though dominated by delusions of persecution, may otherwise be mentally very alert; and he may plan his crime carefully, carry it out cunningly and do his best to cover his tracks successfully. It has sometimes been said in Court that a crime committed thus, deliberately and maliciously, must be the work of a sane person: but it is typical also of the paranoiac who murders.

Organic psychoses, in which the dementing process results in a deterioration of the personality, lack of control and periods of confusion, may—though uncommonly—result in crimes being committed; assaults and sexual offences, even murder by an old man. Post-traumatic personality change and dementia, alcoholic dementia, cerebral arteriosclerosis, general paresis, post-leucotomy personality change, and Huntington's chorea are some of the reaction-types which occasionally have as symptoms behaviour which is antisocial and dangerous and usually out of keeping with the individual's previous personality.

The psychotically ill man or woman who commits a crime is not responsible for it, and if on a major charge he or she should be found insane and unfit to plead.

Of all the psychiatric reaction-types, the psychopathic state, in both its inadequate and its aggressive forms, is by far the most important in its close relationship to criminal behaviour of all degrees of severity. It has been fully described in Chapter 13.

The crime rate is not notably higher in epileptics than in the general population. If the epileptic has also an epileptic personality (as is not uncommon in cases of temporal lobe epilepsy), his personality traits of irritability and moodiness may lead him into conflict with other people and so into breaking the law. Of more importance is the association of epileptic clouding of consciousness with criminal behaviour. This is rare but may be very dangerous. It is the state of ictal (seizure) automatism which occurs in temporal lobe epilepsy and the clinically similar state of post-ictal automatism which may follow a *grand mal* fit, which may be associated with gross acts of violence against others. These acts lack any conscious motive, the individual makes no attempts to escape or to cover his tracks, and subsequently he has a partial or complete amnesia for what he has done. Under these circumstances the epileptic is not legally responsible, and may be found insane in bar of trial or of diminished responsibility. The epileptic, like anyone else, may of course commit crimes also in a setting of clear consciousness: but it may be impossible to refute, though one may doubt its validity, a plea by the defence that the individual's epilepsy may have been at least a contributory factor in his criminal behaviour.

There is no great difference between the average intelligence of delinquents and criminals and that of the general population. More criminals are however educationally subnormal, their schooling having been defective due to inattention, truancy, moves of home, institutional care or other causes. In the prison population one finds an excess of dullards and of those below average intellectually. Theft and housebreaking, assaults and sexual aggression require little intelligence and the stupid tend to get caught more easily: fraud on the other hand may be much more intellectually demanding.

The great majority of subnormal (mentally defective) individuals are law-abiding citizens, carrying out efficiently and happily menial tasks in the community. Amongst the delinquent subnormal, it is those who are least subnormal —the feebleminded, who constitute the problem. In most of these cases, the subnormality of intelligence is associated with temperamental or emotional instability. They may commit any kind of delinquent act, but especially minor offences against property and sexual misdemeanours and offences. Their crimes tend to be impulsive and elementary. A few unstable subnormal men are very dangerous and may be found guilty of serious assaults, rape and murder. Unstable subnormal women are incompetent housewives and mothers, and may be both neglectful and cruel to their children. Some feeble-minded women become prostitutes.

THE INFLUENCE OF ALCOHOL AND DRUGS

The importance of alcohol in predisposing to the commission of crimes, especially those of an aggressive or sexual nature, has on several previous occasions been alluded to; also the close relationship between chronic alcoholism and recidivism. The primary alcoholic offences are 'drunk and disorderly' and 'drunk and incapable'. Breaking and entering and thefts are often carried out by those in search of alcohol or drugs, or the money to buy them. It is however as a releasing, disinhibiting factor that alcohol is of major importance in aberrant, mischievous, antisocial and dangerous behaviour of many different sorts. How significant a factor it is has been demonstrated recently most clearly in the reduction in the number of road accidents and deaths on the roads of this country, following upon the introduction of 'breathalyser' tests by the police of the alcohol consumption of car drivers.

From their study of adolescent delinquents in London Remand Homes, amongst whom they found evidence of amphetamine-taking in 16–18 per cent., Scott and Willcox (1965) could not demonstrate a relationship between amphetamine taking and delinquency and concluded that in the majority of cases 'the taking of amphetamine appears to be incidental to delinquency, probably having similar roots in opportunity and predisposition'. No doubt the relationship between drug-taking and crime is usually a parallel one, and drug-taking rarely a major factor: but the taking of amphetamines may undoubtedly in some cases facilitate or precipitate criminal behaviour. Amphetamine's euphoriant effects, when the individual is 'high', may diminish self-control and social inhibitions in much the same way as alcohol does. Also, but probably much more rarely, in the paranoid psychosis which may result from intoxication or in the state of irritability and suspiciousness which may preface a state of frank intoxication an individual under the influence of amphetamines may commit a serious assault or murder. Scott and Willcox quote the case of a psychopathic youth aged 18 who committed murder impulsively after having taken 10 'purple hearts' (amphetamine plus amylobarbitone): he had been detected when about to break into a shop and killed the man who shone a torch at him. It is only supposition of course that in such a case the influence of the drug had tipped the balance fatally.

CRIMINALITY AND CHROMOSOME ABNORMALITIES

Jacobs and her colleagues (1965) were the first to report that men with an XYY chromosome complement (*i.e.* with an extra Y chromosome, which is strongly male determining) were unusually frequent in the criminal population of a State Hospital; and they found a frequency of 3 per cent. in the State Hospital at Carstairs in Scotland. Similar findings have been reported in England, from the Special Hospitals at Broadmoor, Rampton and Moss Side. Seven of the 9 XYY patients investigated by Price and Whatmore (1967) at Carstairs were regarded as mentally subnormal (I.Q. 60–80): the degree of intellectual retardation is apparently not usually severe, and an XYY man with an I.Q. of 118 has been reported elsewhere. The most striking effects of the XYY complement seem to be upon personality and behaviour rather than upon intelligence: but the caveat must be issued that little is known about XYY individuals in the community and in other kinds of hospitals, so that controls are lacking. These individuals are also unusually tall—on the average 6 inches taller than XY males similarly detained, and usually at least 5 ft. 10 in. in height. It has been stated that in the State Hospitals about one-quarter of the men 6 ft. or more in height have two Y chromosomes. Their physical appearance and development are otherwise normal.

This association between chromosome abnormality and crime is of the greatest interest, and it is apparently not uncommon. Further research is being undertaken, and the account of the XYY individual who is a criminal must at present be a provisional one. It seems clear that it is the individual's constitution, not the home background, which is abnormal in these cases and which predisposes to the criminal behaviour. The typical XYY offender is described by Price and Whatmore as being emotionally unstable, immature, impulsive, defective in personal relationships, without depth of feeling or remorse and liable to be an absconder: in short, he shows psychopathic traits. The average age at first conviction is 13 years, and the crimes are usually against property. In the Carstairs cases repeated and prolonged attempts at corrective training and treatment had been unsuccessful.

An XYY complement may not be the only genetic make-up which predisposes to criminal behaviour. There is evidence that XXY, XXYY and XY/XXY mosaics have constitutions which may be similarly handicapping.

OFFENDERS AND CRIMES WHICH REQUIRE PSYCHIATRIC INVESTIGATION

In any case in which the least suspicion of mental disorder has been aroused, it has become the almost routine practice to ask for a psychiatric examination and report: this refers not only to cases of serious crime, *e.g.* murder and dangerous assault, but also to minor crime, *e.g.* theft, housebreaking, fraud, sexual offences. This procedure has constituted a great advance, has stimulated research into causation and motivation, has led to greater differentiation in relation to treatment and punishment, and has shown the importance of effecting a correlation between the criminal act and the setting or background in which it occurs. If this is not done then the issue may become prejudiced and the judgement both of the Court and the public become distorted so that injustice may result.

Psychiatric disorder in the criminal may become manifest at the time of arrest, during prosecution and trial, and after conviction in a prison or other institution: and attention may be drawn to this aspect of the case by the police, by the prosecutor or by the defence.

Whereas the juvenile first offender is usually mentally normal, the senile first offender is usually mentally ill: and the first offender who is aged 60 or over should therefore be assumed to be mentally disturbed until it has been clearly demonstrated that some sort of senile deterioration or affective disorder is not present. At any age those with a history of previous psychiatric disorder, whether or not it has required treatment in hospital, should be referred for a psychiatric opinion, since the crime may be associated with a recrudescence or recurrence of the illness. Those who commit motiveless or bizarre crimes, or crimes quite out of keeping with their previous personalities, should also obviously be investigated psychiatrically.

Looking at forensic psychiatric problems from the aspect of the offences committed, the following are some of the crimes in connection with which psychiatric reports are commonly called for—recidivism, murder, arson, sexual offences, shoplifting. Before these crimes are discussed individually, one general statement should be made: the nature of his psychiatric illness or disorder is not often a major factor in influencing the individual's choice of offence. There are exceptions to this (*e.g.* the relationship between schizophrenia and matricide); but it follows that one can rarely deduce the mental state of the criminal from the circumstances and nature of his crime.

RECIDIVISM

Recidivists (persistent offenders who have been imprisoned on several occasions), though statistically-speaking not common, are the hard core of the forensic problem, from both the penal and the psychiatric points of view. Most of them are men. Less than half of them have commenced their criminal careers as juveniles. Between one-quarter and a half are mentally abnormal: in a survey of 100 recidivists West (1963) found that 10 per cent. were or had been psychotic, and a further 16 per cent. had been patients in mental hospitals or discharged on psychiatric grounds from the Armed Services.

Amongst the mentally more grossly abnormal recidivists are many inadequate and aggressive psychopaths and chronic alcoholics; and perhaps 10 per cent. who are suffering from schizophrenic or less commonly epileptic or other psychoses.

They are generally individuals with poor work records and an inability to make stable personal relationships: many are estranged from their families, solitary, friendless drifters of no fixed abode, the flotsam and jetsam of cheap lodging-houses. The majority are petty thieves and burglars: some are violent, recurrently assaultive, and a minority are sex offenders.

The characteristics of the psychopathic personality have been described in Chapter 13. Recidivism and a psychopathic state are not synonymous terms. All recidivists are not psychopaths nor are all psychopaths recidivists: but psychopathic states comprise the majority of those whose feckless and aggressive behaviour results in their being repeatedly committed to prison. Recidivism differs from a psychopathic state in that the latter typically begins at an early age or at least before adult life is reached: and it resembles a psychopathic state in that both conditions are comparatively rarely seen after the age of 50 years.

Gibbens (1963), observing the reconviction rate of 200 Borstal boys aged 17–21 over a period of ten years, found it much heavier in those 'assessed originally as helpless, unrealistic, lacking in energy, solitary, submissive, or with weak sex interest'. Those of passive, inadequate personality may break down and become recidivist when faced unsupported by the demands of adult life. The more aggressive may become delinquent at an earlier age, but their combativeness may also fit them better for later challenges and enable them to make a reasonable adjustment as adults.

The association between recidivism and alcoholism is also a close one. Alcoholism both facilitates crime by reducing the psychological inhibitions against it, and by the loss of social status, employment and earnings which it brings in its train, increases the temptation to acquire money and goods illegally.

The sexual deviants who are most liable to become recidivists are exhibitionists, homosexuals who frequent lavatories, and paedophiliacs; and over half these individuals have convictions also for other offences—usually larceny.

Amongst the mentally ill who become recidivists, schizophrenics are the commonest clinical group. Most of these unfortunates become involved in petty crime; but the schizophrenic is notably unpredictable, and he may also commit a serious assault or murder. Many of these schizophrenics have been patients in mental hospitals and have been discharged improved by drug treatment. But they are often not well enough to be employed, family, social and medical support may be inadequate, and they may cease to take their drugs. There is no doubt that many of these mental cripples would be better and happier cared for on a long-term basis in a mental hospital, than discharged to fend for themselves when so disabled.

MURDER

Murder is one of the rarest crimes in this country. In England and Wales during the period 1951–60 the average annual number of murders was 3·3 per million population. In the past year (1967), while there has been some evidence for the first time in several years of an over-all decrease of crime, violence and

2 M

murder have continued to increase: but there is little evidence yet of a significant long-term growth of this problem. Murders are of course a part of the much larger problem of crimes of violence against the person—woundings, assaults and rapes. Chance plays a considerable part in the outcome of all these attacks, particularly in those which arise in the course of drunken brawls. Whether the crime is grievous bodily harm or murder may depend upon whether the aggressor had a lethal weapon at hand and upon the ability of the victim to defend himself or to escape.

A statistical study of murder by a Home Office Research Unit (1961) gives a clear outline of the situation in England and Wales. There are social as well as individual determinants of this crime and the picture varies therefore from culture to culture: what is characteristic of England and Wales is not entirely typical even of a neighbouring and very similar culture such as Scotland's. In England and Wales 22 per cent. of murderers are found to be insane and a further 24 per cent. are found guilty of a reduced charge of manslaughter by reason of their diminished responsibility (usually on psychiatric grounds). Nearly one-third of murderers in England and Wales commit suicide: and there are other differences between the group who commit suicide and those who do not. The murder-suicide group are often insane or at least definitely mentally ill, 30–40 per cent. are women, and they murder usually members of their own families or close associates. In the majority of these cases a parent kills his or her own children, and the commonest method is gassing. About three-quarters of all the children who are murdered are killed by a parent or other older relative. Amongst those aged 16 or over who are killed, there are nearly twice as many women victims as men, because so many women are murdered by their husbands: over 40 per cent. of adult women victims are killed by their husbands, and most of the remainder are killed by relatives or associates. In contrast, about half the adult males are killed by strangers.

The murderers who do not commit suicide are as a group in several ways different: they are younger, they are almost all men, and the majority of those they kill are not their relatives. Sixty per cent. of these murderers have previous convictions, usually for larceny or breaking and entering but 25 per cent. also for offences against the person. Besides the quarrels and outbursts of rage which account for perhaps half of these acts, the criminal pursuit of financial gain, e.g. by robbery, is an important motive. The commonest methods of attack are by the use of a blunt instrument, or by hitting or kicking. Shooting is the least commonly used method: it is more often adopted by those who are mentally ill and by those who commit suicide.

Although nearly 50 per cent. of murderers are found on examination before trial to show no mental abnormality of significance, the remainder are either mentally ill or temperamentally so grossly unstable that their responsibility for their acts is diminished. This is of course what one would expect to find: where the crime is very abnormal, the criminal is likely to be abnormal also. Aggressive psychopathic states comprise the largest clinical group: the callous psychopath is probably the most dangerous of all aggressive individuals. Next commonest are the schizophrenic and paranoid psychoses: after these, depressions. A good deal less common than the foregoing are cases of mental defect (subnormality), epilepsy and organic dementia. Women who kill are more often mentally ill than men who do so. It is noteworthy that murder may be the first or almost the first sign of schizophrenia; and that the mother is particularly at risk. Gillies calls matricide 'the schizophrenic crime'.

Alcohol is an important factor in aggressive crimes, and this is exemplified by Gillies (1965) in an important paper from Glasgow in which he describes the features of 66 murderers who killed a total of 70 people in the West of Scotland. Gillies emphasizes 'the clumsy, chance and unpremeditated circumstances' of most of these killings. Fifty-two of these murderers came from Social Classes IV and V, 36 were affected by alcohol at the time of the offences, and Gillies estimated that alcohol was the commonest causal factor in the murders. The setting was most often a drunken quarrel. These murders were to a considerable extent an expression of the cultural pattern of life in an industrial city where heavy drinking, especially at weekends, is usual. The commonest psychiatric diagnoses were psychopathic personality (18 cases) and schizophrenia (10 cases). Only 10 men, all psychopaths, were considered to be menacingly antisocial.

In England and Wales, where about one-third of murderers commit suicide, nearly always the suicide immediately follows the murder; and many of these murders may be regarded as extended suicides. They are mainly family murders: and have been the subject of a valuable monograph by West (1965). Surprisingly, the murder-suicide group do not, according to West, seem to differ from ordinary murderers in the proportion—about one-half, who are considered insane or of diminished responsibility. But there is a substantial number of seriously mentally involved people in this group, particularly amongst the women. Very few of these people have had previous convictions of any kind: and the young thug whose aim is theft or robbery is not found amongst them.

In this murder-suicide group there is a large number of young married women who kill their children; only some of them are suffering from a puerperal illness. A depression is much the commonest diagnosis. These mothers are despairing and actively suicidal at the time of the killing. The method of both homicide and suicide is most often coal-gas.

Amongst the men there is a wider range of diagnoses and reactions. Many are psychopathic or of seriously unstable temperament, with a history of having a violent temper and of aggressive behaviour in personal relationships; and some of them have previously attempted suicide. As West says: 'At least some of the persons liable to commit murder-suicide crimes are individuals with a high level of aggression which may turn against others or against themselves according to circumstances.' There may be a long history of a turbulent, cat-and-dog relationship with a wife or paramour. Jealousy, resentment and vindictiveness are amongst the motives which fuse the culminating outburst. Other men in this group suffer from affective, schizophrenic and paranoid psychoses.

In contrast to the situation in England and Wales, in Scotland the incidence of suicide amongst those suspected of murder is much lower. Gillies recorded only

3 suicidal attempts in his 66 cases; and he commented, 'the low incidence of suicide and suicidal attempts is probably due to so many murders (in Scotland) being almost accidental and being brought about by drunken quarrels; in such circumstances the offender feels little guilt'.

Many motives underlie murderous attacks. Most commonly they arise from quarrels in which emotions of hate, rage and jealousy have been aroused: this applies both to the 'normal' and to the mentally ill murderer. By no means all murderers are vicious or aggressive people: some have been inhibited, docile and previously inoffensive. Desperation and despair in those who are depressed, and amongst other psychotic individuals the influence of delusional beliefs and auditory hallucinations, are also of much importance. Murders with a sexual motive are relatively uncommon—only about 8 of these occur per year in England and Wales. Nearly always the motives are identifiable, whether the murderer is sane or insane. In the case of the schizophrenic they may be bizarre.

Mowat (1966), investigating the motives of murderers found insane and admitted to Broadmoor, found that at least 12 per cent. of the male and 3 per cent. of the female psychotic murderers had killed for motives of morbid jealousy. In nearly half of these cases the diagnosis was either a schizophrenic or a paranoid psychosis: morbid jealousy was also found in depressive, alcoholic and organic illnesses. A common history was the development in a man, after six or more years of cohabiting, of suspicions of the infidelity of the spouse or mistress. The husband or paramour becomes progressively more jealous and suspicious; there are quarrels, blows, accusations, attempts to find evidence or extract confessions of guilt. As the psychosis becomes aggravated, delusions may be harboured that the wife has infected him with V.D., or is trying to poison him, or that his children are not his own. In middle age, often after he has been delusional for some years, the paranoid individual kills the wife or mistress in an access of rage, crudely, by strangulation or clubbing or bludgeoning to death. In one-third of such cases the murderer then attempts suicide. Frequently he confesses to the crime. Mowat rightly points to the danger which should be recognized and forestalled in such a development, and considers that where there is a morbidly jealous situation with aggressive attacks or threats to kill, legal separation or divorce of the married pair appears to be the only effective means of preventing such a murder.

Probably only a minority of murderous attacks succeed in their purpose, and many of those who are guilty of serious assaults have psychological characteristics similar to the murderers.

ARSON

The incidence of arson is rising in this country. In England and Wales in the quinquennium 1950–54 there were on an average 580 cases of arson annually; in 1955–59, 770 annually; and in 1964 alone 1442 cases. In the latter year, 443 people were convicted of arson. Nearly one-fifth of the damage by fire for which insurance claims are made, is known to be due to arson. The amount of material loss is often very great, and loss of life also occasionally results. It is surprising therefore that few studies of fire-raisers have been made and that we know comparatively little about the mental state of those involved. The most recent study has been an Australian one, an investigation of 21 children by Nurcombe (1964).

Males are much more commonly fire-raisers than females, at all ages. Both children and adults are involved. Nurcombe found the peak age of onset in his series of children was 6 years; and the deviant behaviour, begun in childhood, may be carried into adult life.

The children nearly all come from disturbed home environments: they have been emotionally deprived, rejected, moved from home to home or reared in institutions. Many are of below average intelligence and other delinquent behaviour is usual: a history of truancy, theft and bedwetting is common. The fire-raising may be seen as a product of a lack of parental love, education and control, and as the acting out of feelings of unhappiness, frustration and revenge. A few of the children have suffered brain damage, due to birth defects or later cerebral injuries or infections; and in these cases organic factors may contribute to the aetiology.

Amongst adults, there is no one type of fire-raiser: the 'normal', the psychopathic and the psychotic may all act in this way. In the more or less normal group may be included those who start fires in order to commit fraud on insurance companies, and some teenage hooligans. A sense of grievance and a wish for revenge may impel both the disgruntled, dismissed employee and the delusional sufferer from a paranoid psychosis. The persistent, malicious or thrill-seeking fire-setter is probably most often a psychopath. In a very few instances, a fire is raised to conceal a murder.

SEXUAL OFFENCES

Sexual anomalies have been described in Chapter 9. Some additional considerations will be mentioned here.

Alcoholism plays an important part in many sexual offences, of all types. That the individual was drunk at the time rarely reduces his responsibility in law for his actions, since for alcoholism to be pleaded as a defence the individual must have been rendered mentally ill by it (e.g. delirious).

The great majority of sexual offenders probably go undetected. Amongst those who are caught, though some are persistent offenders, the prognosis is on the whole good. In the Cambridge study of 2000 sex offenders (Radzinowicz and Turner, 1957), it was found that 82·7 per cent. had not previously been convicted of sex offences and that 84·5 per cent. were not reconvicted in the four years after their release. There is, however, a minority whose sexual abnormality is of a much more malignant kind. The 5 per cent. of sexual offenders who become recidivist includes exhibitionists, homosexuals and paedophiliacs: in the Cambridge series 27 per cent. of the men who had committed homosexual offences with boys were reconvicted.

Over half the males who commit sexual offences are accused of sexually deviant behaviour—exhibitionism, paedophilia and homosexuality. Youths and adult men are about equally responsible for homosexual offences (this is not so for other crimes, *e.g.* for theft or violence); and there is a wide variety of personality types. The offence may represent a failure to grow to sexual maturity, or a temporary lapse due to some intercurrent psychological stress or unhappiness, or it may be only one amongst many antisocial features of a psychopathic state. Obviously the psychodynamics, the treatment required and the prognosis vary from case to case. The man who commits an act of indecent exposure during a depressive illness may require only to be treated for that illness. Also, and this is relevant to many cases, there is a strong natural tendency for the immature to become with time more mature; and patience, understanding and sympathetic encouragement are obviously more beneficial than punishment in these circumstances.

The paedophiliac, the adult who becomes heterosexually or homosexually involved with children, is both detested and feared by the public, but he is in fact rarely dangerous. He has been the subject of a comprehensive study by Mohr, Turner and Jerry (1964) in Toronto. Few paedophiliacs are psychotic or mentally defective: but many are described as immature, inadequate and schizoid. They crop up in adolescence, in middle life and in old age. The adolescent offender is typically shy, timid, dependent; and for neurotic reasons retarded in his sexual and social development. The middle-aged paedophiliac is usually married but the marriage is seriously disturbed, and in this situation of stress his probably already precarious sexual adjustment has broken down. In old age, loneliness and organic mental deterioration are very significant factors. It is relatives and friends who mostly abuse children in this way, and many of the children are willing victims—perhaps as many as two-thirds of them (Gibbens and Prince, 1963). Sex murders of children are very rare: only about four occur in any year in this country. These murderers are almost always seriously disordered, psychotic, subnormal or grossly psychopathic.

It is amongst youths and young men aged 17–21 that convictions for indecent assaults upon women and rape are commonest. Most of these young men, though they may be aggressive, defiant and irresponsible, are mentally within the normal range. So are most of the men who commit incest with their daughters. Reconvictions for rape and incest are rare.

There is a relationship between subnormal intelligence and sexual offences. Walker (1965) compared the indictable offences of all male offenders aged 17 or more dealt with by English Courts in 1961 and the offences of 305 subnormal males of similar age, and found that the percentage of subnormal offenders dealt with for sexual offences was six times as high as that of all offenders. Walker rightly draws attention to the predisposing factors—their immaturity and gaucherie, their backwardness in learning social prohibitions, and their relative incompetence in rivalry with normal men in seeking heterosexual relationships. The subnormal are not unusually prone to violence.

Amongst women prostitutes one finds the mentally dull and backward, the psychopathic, and a few who are more neurotically unstable, with a marked hostility towards men and acting out a sort of moral suicide. Many teenagers and young women, especially those from broken or unhappy homes, go through a period of promiscuity, as a phase of rebellion or seeking affection or adventure: and most of them pass through it. It is a minority who seem to need psychiatric help, and certainly it is a minority who will accept it.

SHOPLIFTING

Shoplifting is a widespread and increasing social phenomenon, and is only in a minority of cases associated with mental illness. In Britain convictions for larceny from shops and stalls have almost doubled, compared with the years before the Second World War; with the steepest rise since 1956. This parallels the general rise in the crime rate. The increase in number of multiple stores and self-service shops has enhanced the opportunities and the temptations to theft. For a detailed study of shoplifting the reader is referred to the work of Gibbens and Prince (1962).

Shoplifting has rather different characteristics in juvenile and adult cases, and in men and women. The peak age of juvenile shoplifting for both sexes is 14 years. The large majority of juveniles steal in company. Most of them are normal boys and girls, acting in concert, for a thrill or in emulation of others or out of greed for what they could not at the moment afford to buy. But about 40 per cent., according to Gibbens and Prince, are emotionally disturbed, in rebellion against their parents, acting defiantly, or feeling depressed, guilty and worthless—and in this indirect way probably appealing for help. Shoplifting is not often a type of offence which is persisted with into adult life.

Twice as many women as men are convicted of shoplifting. It is men in their twenties who are mainly involved: half of them have previous convictions and shoplifting is only one activity in their criminal repertoire. It is the commonest crime in men over 60, and appears to be a favourite crime of elderly recidivists. The theft of books is the commonest type of shoplifting in men and it is confined to men. Like some other shoplifted goods and books acquired by more ordinary transactions, these acquisitions may not be made for use.

Amongst women, shoplifting occurs at all ages. Food and clothes are the usual targets. Only a small minority are professional thieves: but about one-quarter have previous and subsequent convictions. Amongst the younger women more are greedy than in need. Some are chronically poor, while others have incurred debts. Some are influenced by the low standards of behaviour of their neighbours. The material good fortune of the affluent is a provocation. A minority of those below middle-age are significantly disturbed psychologically, in conflict with parents or spouse, resentful, sexually frustrated, unhappy and seeking solace.

Shoplifting is particularly common amongst women over 40: and Gibbens and Prince reported that the peak age for the offence is 51–60. Many of these women are separated, divorced or widows. A few of them begin a recidivist career in shoplifting at this age. All social classes are involved. The majority have the money to buy what they steal. Probably about a quarter of these older women are mentally disordered in some way and depression is the commonest diagnosis. Feelings of loneliness and resentment are important in the aetiology: and in some cases feelings of guilt have clearly impelled the individual to get caught and to incur punishment. Some of these women are profoundly depressed in their spirits and are serious suicidal risks. Though they are confused and usually puzzled about their intentions and motives, they have been aware of what they were doing, and there is rarely any true clouding of consciousness.

The great majority of arrested shoplifters are to be considered normal people caught in wrong-doing. The minority who are mentally ill must be identified, they are much in need of help and likely to respond well to treatment. They are to be found most often amongst women of middle age or older, of previously good character, who are lonely or living alone: not only is there no history of a previous conviction in the great majority of such cases, the shoplifting has been behaviour quite foreign to the previous standards of the individual, who has often been of anxious or obsessional temperament. Occasionally shoplifting, occurring in the setting of a manic-depressive psychosis, is repeated during subsequent attacks of depression.

PSYCHIATRIC EXAMINATIONS AND REPORTS TO THE COURT

The individual who is accused of a crime may be remanded on bail or in custody for psychiatric examination. Under the Mental Health (Scotland) Act, 1960, an accused person can also be remanded in hospital, which permits a more detailed, less hurried assessment to be carried out: but it is doubtful if admission to hospital is often necessary in order to obtain a clear picture of the accused person's mental state. Wherever the person is seen the doctor may have to make more than one examination, and he should always do so if he is in any doubt about his findings. He is entitled to ask for all the relevant information and he should never omit to scrutinize it—information from the prosecution and from the defence, police reports, probation officers' reports, information from lawyers and friends, school record and anything else that may be pertinent. The examining doctor should also ask the accused's family doctor about the accused's previous health and evidence of recent illness; and interview if it is possible at least one member of the accused's family.

It is always most important for the doctor to explain to the accused who he is, why he has come to see him and who has instructed him.

In the first place the doctor must attempt to determine whether the accused's mental state is such that he is likely to understand the evidence, to be able to instruct counsel and to follow the procedure of the Court—in other words, whether he is or is not fit to plead. It is advisable to ask the accused what plea he is making. In those cases in which a person on account of his disordered mental state is unable to understand the charge against him or instruct his defence, he cannot be tried, is found 'insane in bar of trial' and will be transferred to an ordinary or State mental hospital. It should be noted that a Court will not accept subnormality (mental deficiency) as a plea in bar of trial.

The accused should be asked to tell his story and be allowed to do so with as little interruption as possible: leading questions are best avoided, and to make the account telling a verbatim record should be made of the most important of the accused's spontaneous statements.

Further general points which it may be helpful to keep in mind are the following:

1. A criminal act is rarely the first indication of a disordered mental state. If the person has managed his life satisfactorily up until the time of his criminal act, the presumption is that he is of sound mind.

2. Those prisoners who state that they have no memory of the criminal act of which they are accused should always be viewed with considerable suspicion especially when there is no previous history of amnesia; under such circumstances the excuse may be more an evasion than a reality.

3. The probability is that the accused may be suffering from some degree of mental disorder if he (a) reports the matter to the police and gives himself up, (b) attempts suicide, (c) commits the deed during daylight when he is sober, (d) attacks a person to whom he has been deeply devoted.

In formulating his report, the doctor should state the accused's full name and the charge made against him, where and on what date the examination has been made, and at whose instance he has been acting. He should then record his opinion as to whether or not the accused is fit to plead to the charge or charges made against him. What follows should also be couched in clear, concise and unambiguous language. It must be made clear what information is derived from the accused's statements alone and is unconfirmed. No information which points to the individual's guilt should be disclosed. What the Court requires is a statement of the medical facts ascertained during the examination of the accused and derived from other sources, which point to his being mentally ill or subnormal or of seriously disordered personality. The nature of his psychiatric abnormality should be stated in words which the layman can understand, and if technical terms are used these should be defined. A discussion of psychodynamics and theoretical issues should be avoided.

On the basis of his findings about the accused's mental state, the doctor recommends to the Court how best the accused might be dealt with. He should make it plain whether or not the accused requires, is likely to benefit from and will co-operate in psychiatric treatment, where he can have this treatment and why one possibility has been preferred to another. The doctor should never try to dictate to the Court: his responsibility is to advise.

If a careful and conscientious examination has been made in this way, the doctor need have no fear of appearing in Court and of being cross-examined upon his report. It is the duty of the medical witness to assist the Court to come to a fair judgement. He must be non-partisan, be able to speak as to the medical facts disclosed by his examination, and avoid hypothesis unless in answer to the Judge. He should be master of his facts, realistic in his recommendations, and tentative in all matters of prognosis. Where he is not sure of his ground, he should say so. Attempts by counsel to test or undermine the doctor's opinion (which is his business) should be met not with attitudes expressing chagrin or irritation but calmly and constructively. The presiding Judge will see to it that justice is done to the expert witness as well as to the accused.

In cases involving claims for compensation it may be particularly difficult to obtain from the claimant and his relatives accurate information about the family history, the individual's own previous medical history and his work record. It is essential therefore to ask the family doctor for background information. In making his report the doctor should record the sources from which further information has been sought, and the results even if negative of inquiries into the family and previous personal history of his claimant. If there is no evidence that, immediately prior to the accident or injury or at an earlier date, the individual has had a nervous or mental illness, any subsequent mental upset if it has begun soon afterwards is likely to be found attributable to the accident or injury—however uncertain on theoretical grounds the association between trauma and illness may be thought to be, and however strongly the doctor may feel that the claimant's personality has previously been unstable and that the motive of financial gain is currently paramount. It is of course always proper for the doctor to comment upon the efforts (or absence of them) which the claimant has made to obtain psychiatric help and treatment for the mental disabilities for which compensation is being claimed.

PUNISHMENT AND TREATMENT

In recent years the aims of penal systems have been under review in this and other countries. Denunciation of the criminal, threats and the demand for retribution have become less prominent. Concepts of responsibility and guilt get less attention than they did formerly, they seem less important, their dominance having been weakened by the influence of psychiatric thought and practice. What is seen to be necessary is to promote in the individual, by whatever means are effective, a greater degree of temperamental stability, so that he can fulfil his personal and social responsibilities more satisfactorily. Thus in the Courts, punishment and treatment are increasingly intermingled, and the Courts more frequently make hospital orders instead of sentencing offenders to prison. Increasing use is being made of social agencies, including most importantly the Probation Service. Probation and psychiatric treatment, and prison or other penal institutional detention and psychiatric treatment, are now often combined. These are all developments which can be warmly welcomed. What is most necessary now is to carry this process further in a more critical way, to learn far more than we know at present about prognosis and to make sentencing a less haphazard, more scientific procedure. We must get to know the efficacy of various sentences, and try to match them not so much to the crime but more to the individual criminal. The high rate of reconviction after short sentences, particularly in the case of those of dull or subnormal intelligence, points to the inadequacy of our present procedures.

The offender or criminal who is found to be mentally disturbed can be dealt with in a number of different ways, and this variety in the possible modes of 'disposal' enables justice to be done to the complexity of these situations. If the offence is not a serious one and the individual is obviously mentally ill, the charge may be dropped when it is known that psychiatric treatment is being undertaken. Under the Criminal Justice Act also a Court may suspend sentence if the offender accepts psychiatric treatment, and may later discharge the case if the individual has co-operated in medical care.

Under the Criminal Justice Act, psychiatric treatment for up to one year, either as an in-patient or as an out-patient, may be made a condition of probation. The patient's condition should not be such as would warrant compulsory detention.

Part V of the Mental Health Act, 1959[1] makes further provisions. Where the charge is a more serious one (excluding murder, for which the penalty is fixed by law), a Court may, after hearing medical evidence, order (Section 60) the offender to be detained in a specified mental hospital; or, and it happens much less often, the offender may be committed to guardianship. If the mental state of the individual is such that he is a grave danger to others, he may be committed to a State Hospital where there are special provisions for security. The age limits in relation to ordinary compulsory procedures do not apply in these cases.

The provision of psychiatric units in a number of English prisons, e.g. Holloway, Wormwood Scrubs and Wakefield, is a further important development. A psychiatric prison at Grendon, Buckinghamshire, was opened in 1962.

Under Section 65 of the Mental Health Act a Court can impose a restriction order on a mentally ill offender committed to a mental hospital: it can order that he be detained for a minimum period or indefinitely. The patient cannot then be discharged from hospital or given leave except with the consent of the Home Secretary. Restricting discharge in this way is done in the case of dangerous individuals who have been guilty of violence or sexual offences, and the object is of course to protect the public. It is a provision which has given rise to a good many difficulties. Most mental hospitals now have a liberal, more or less 'open door' policy of care and treatment, which is not suited to the detention of uncooperative and dangerous men. Nor would most mental hospitals wish to have areas of much greater security, since the introduction of such a prison element into a hospital will alter its therapeutic ethos. The ordinary mental hospital therefore finds it difficult to be responsible for the dangerous patient who is determined to abscond, and is understandably reluctant to undertake his care. Another source of medical frustration is that a Court can only guess for how long a period of detention should last and the psychiatrist may feel in some instances that the period imposed has been too long, restricting improperly his clinical freedom and militating against a good outcome from treatment. With some justice on each side, the Courts, the staff of the mental hospitals and the lay public are all to some extent dissatisfied with the present situation.

While one does not wish to foster more restrictive attitudes, it seems inappropriate in most instances to commit dangerous criminals to ordinary mental

---

[1] The corresponding Act in Scotland is the Mental Health (Scotland) Act, 1960.

hospitals. The need is for more places to be provided in the State (Special) hospitals; and for particular provision to be made for the violent criminal psychopath who constitutes the greatest problem.

In the case of the subnormal individual a prison sentence, long or short, has little deterrent or remedial effect and is apt to create an increased hostility. If he is too unstable to remain in the community, hospital care and further education and training in controlled and constructive conditions are required; and a return to the community should not be considered advisable until a sense of social responsibility has been consolidated. A very small number of subnormal men are so dangerous that they must be detained for an indefinite period in a State (Special) hospital.

CRIMINAL RESPONSIBILITY

The criminal responsibility of those offenders who are suffering from some degree of mental disorder has always been far from easy to assess, and has constituted a controversial problem which has led to much argument between doctors and lawyers. But the introduction of the Criminal Justice Act, 1949, the Homicide Act, 1957, and the Mental Health Act, 1959, has been instrumental in clarifying certain issues, and has led to greater unanimity of opinion. The result attained has been the development of a greater sense of social justice whereby more imaginativeness is being practised in relation to the rehabilitation and social adjustment of the individual; the reformatory aspect rather than the deterrent is in the ascendant. We know that behaviour disorders may stem from a vast variety of sources, and when they involve the young—as they so frequently do—are a matter of grave concern to parents, teachers, doctors, social workers and to organizations such as special schools, Approved Schools, Borstals and occupation centres. The aim of everyone dealing with such matters is to organize specific methods of treatment so as to counteract, or at least minimize, those faulty and unhygienic reactions which so often lead to frustration, defeatism and dangerous antisocial over-compensation mechanisms. We suggest that in dealing with all such matters the same tactics should be employed as in all other branches of medical and social work—to prevent criminal conduct, and any accompanying mental disorder from developing, rather than to attempt the somewhat futile task of remedying it after it has become fully established. If we are to be successful it is important that the laws which govern us should keep in step with our ever-increasing knowledge of medical, legal, and social practice. We have made considerable progress towards that goal, and the conformity of opinion between doctor and lawyer is much closer than it used to be. It may be that it will soon become unnecessary to stress the different attitudes between doctors and lawyers which previously existed. It was suggested that the doctor's interest was centred in the individual, the lawyer's in the criminal act; the doctor thinks in terms of illness and disease, the lawyer is concerned with the protection of the public; the medical concept is of functions actuated by emotion, and determined by intrinsic factors operating at a subconscious level, the legal concept is of mind dominated by reason and free-will operating at a conscious level. The above differences are not nearly so irreconcilable as they might appear. It is generally agreed that there is no sharp dividing line between sanity and insanity, or perhaps better expressed between normality and abnormality or some degree of unsoundness of mind—the two shade into one another by imperceptible gradations. The degree of individual responsibility varies equally widely; no clear boundary can be drawn between responsibility and irresponsibility.

In those cases in which a person on account of his disordered mental state is unable to understand the charge against him or instruct his defence, he cannot be tried. He is found insane 'in bar of trial'. Similarly, if the jury find that an accused person did the act charged but was insane at the time he may be 'acquitted because insane'. Under such circumstances he will be ordered to be detained in a State (Special) hospital or such other hospital as, exceptionally, the Court may specify; the sanction of the Secretary of State will be necessary to effect transfer to another hospital, leave of absence, or discharge.

The plea of insanity in bar of trial has been extended to summary proceedings in the Sheriff Court. If the accused person is found to be insane, the Sheriff may order his detention in a hospital without hearing evidence as to whether or not he committed the crime charged. It should be noted, however, that the Court does not accept mental deficiency as a plea in bar of trial.

The current law in relation to responsibility in cases of murder was formulated in 1843 and centred on the trial of a Glasgow man, M'Naghten, a paranoiac who was tried in London for the wilful murder of Mr. Edward Drummond, the private secretary to Sir Robert Peel. M'Naghten's history showed that, for many years, he had suffered from delusions of persecution as a result of which he had visited various countries in an attempt to escape from his persecutors. His complaints to his parents, and to public authorities, were unavailing, he became embittered, and so with the object of drawing attention to his case and of righting his supposed wrongs, he devised a plan to kill Sir Robert Peel. He kept a watch on his house, and when he saw a man come out he shot Mr. Drummond under the mistaken belief that he was shooting Sir Robert Peel. At his trial M'Naghten was most ably defended by Mr. Cockburn (afterwards Lord Chief Justice), who concluded his speech in the following terms: he did not bring forward this as a case of complete, but of partial insanity; of what a great French authority had denominated homicidal monomania. He trusted he had satisfied the jury, by the authorities he had quoted, that there existed such a disease as partial insanity, or homicidal monomania, in which the unhappy patient acting under the influence of instinct, was led on by delusion to commit a crime for which morally he could not be held responsible. Cockburn's plea was upheld and M'Naghten was certified as of unsound mind and detained in a lunatic asylum.

The verdict in the above case created a great sensation and much controversy ensued. A few days after the trial the case was debated in the House of Lords by a number of distinguished law lords, e.g. the Lord Chancellor (Lyndhurst)

Lord Brougham, Lord Cottenham and Lord Campbell. The opposing viewpoints were expressed by Lord Brougham and Lord Cottenham in the following extracts: Lord Brougham said: 'If the perpetrator knew what he was doing, if he had taken precautions to accomplish his purpose, if he knew at the time of doing the desperate act that it was forbidden by the law, that was his test of sanity; he cared not what judge gave another test, he should go to his grave in the belief that it was the real, sound and consistent test.'

On the other hand Lord Cottenham, with whose opinion the other judges concurred, 'thought it was impossible to listen to any doctrine which proposed to punish persons labouring under insane delusions. Their lordships could not mean to say that the man who was incapable of judging between right and wrong, of knowing whether an act were good or bad, ought to be made accountable for his actions. Such a man had not that within him which formed the foundation of accountability either from a moral or legal point of view. It appeared very strange that any persons should be labouring under a delusion and yet be aware that it was a delusion; in fact if they were aware of their state there could be no delusion.'

As a result of the difference of opinion which was expressed, the House of Lords put certain specific questions to the judges in the hope that the position might be clarified. These questions were as follows:

1. What is the law respecting alleged crimes committed by persons afflicted with insane delusions in respect of one or more particular subjects or persons; as, for instance, where at the time of commission of the alleged crime the accused knew he was acting contrary to law, but did the act complained of, with a view, under the influence of insane delusion, of redressing or revenging some supposed grievance or injury or of producing some supposed public benefit?

2. What are the proper questions to be submitted to a jury when a person afflicted with insane delusions respecting one or more particular subjects or persons is charged with the commission of a crime (murder, for instance) and insanity is set up as a defence?

3. In what terms ought the question to be left to the jury as to the prisoner's state of mind at the time when the act was committed?

4. If a person under an insane delusion as to existing facts commits an offence in consequence thereof, is he thereby excused?

There was also a fifth question, but it was essentially of a hypothetical nature and does not require to be discussed here.

The answers given, of which we shall state the gist, became known as the *M'Naghten Rules* and are still operative in our courts of law. They are as follows:

1. If the accused person did the act complained of under the influence of an insane delusion, but with a view to redress or revenge some supposed grievance or injury, or to produce some public benefit, he was nevertheless punishable according to the nature of the crime committed, if he knew at the time of committing such a crime that he was acting contrary to law.

2. and 3. These two questions are the crux of the matter and were answered in this way:

> Jurors ought to be told, in all cases, that every man is presumed to be sane, and to possess a sufficient degree of reason to be responsible for his crimes, until the contrary be proved to their satisfaction; and that to establish a defence on the ground of insanity it must be clearly proved that at the time of the committing of the act the accused party was labouring under such a defect of reason from disease of the mind as not to know the nature and quality of the act he was doing; or if he did know it, that he did not know that he was doing what was wrong.

4. The judges considered that if the delusion was only a partial delusion, and if otherwise the individual was not insane that he should be considered responsible for his act. They stated that if, under the influence of his delusion, he supposed another man to be attempting to take his life, and he killed that man, as he supposed in self-defence, he would be exempt from punishment. If, however, his delusion was that the deceased had inflicted a serious injury to his character and fortune, and he killed him in revenge, he would be liable to punishment.

Critical opinions expressed by distinguished legal authorities are illuminating. Lord Brougham stated: 'Nobody is hardly ever really mad enough to be within the definition of madness laid down in the judges' answers.' Lord Coleridge, the Lord Chief Justice of England, in 1888 said: 'the judicial decisions on questions of insanity are bound by an old authority which, by the law of modern science, is altogether unsound and wrong'. At a later date he added: 'It was said by a legal authority, when he was a young man, that if a person was found guilty of murder he should be hanged whether he was insane or not, for if he was sane he deserved it, and if he was mad it was to him no harm.' That seemed to him to be a horrible doctrine, and he was glad that it was no longer held. Lord Blackburn stated that he had never been able to find an accurate definition of responsibility. 'You must take it that in every individual case you must look at the circumstances, and do the best you can to say whether it was the disease of the mind which was the cause of the crime or the party's criminal will'. For another succinct statement we would refer to the charge to the jury made by Lord Justice Clerk Inglis in 1863 when he said that if they were satisfied that the murderer was suffering from insane delusions at the time of the offence they did not need to inquire whether he knew right from wrong, or whether he knew what was murder in the eyes of the law, or what was a punishable act. In a strictly legal sense there is no insane criminal. The act of the insane, which in the sane would be criminal, lacks every element of crime.

The *M'Naghten Rules* smack of the ancient and medically out-of-date doctrine of the mental faculties, the mind being regarded as divided up into a series of independent compartments, the cognitive faculty being one of the large subdivisions. With this doctrine there flourished almost inevitably the belief in the existence of partial insanities in which one mental compartment and faculty was affected, and not any other; monomania, for instance, was freely translated as 'being insane on only one subject'. Medicine has now come to recognize that the mind is a whole, one and indivisible. There is no mental disorder, however partial, that does not have its reverberations throughout the rest of the affected mind. Consequently the purely intellectual criterion of responsibility falls to the ground, for the intellect as intellect may be unimpaired, but an emotional disturbance will alter, or impede or nullify its effect on conduct. Conversely, intellectual defect means deficient emotional control. Allowance is now being made for all such well-known phenomena as the disordered ideation of the schizophrenic, epileptic automatisms and the overwhelming influence of affective disorder, which may, for example, cause a depressed person to murder his children whom he loves, and whom he knows full well it is morally wrong to kill.

The passing of the Homicide Act, 1957 with its partial abolition of the death penalty and the total abolition of the death penalty in 1965 have transformed the situation. Much less attention is paid now to the rigorous interpretation and application of the *M'Naghten Rules*. The murderer, if sane, is given a life sentence—with review of his sentence as it proceeds by the Home Secretary and his advisers; for some it may be a sentence for life, for others release after serving an average of about 9 years, and the judges have power to recommend a minimum period of imprisonment during a life sentence. The charge may be reduced to manslaughter on the grounds of diminished responsibility or provocation; and the judge has then full discretion with regard to the sentence imposed. While if the individual who has murdered is insane he is committed to a State (Special) hospital for the duration of Her Majesty's pleasure; or if psychotic and found guilty of manslaughter may be committed to a N.H.S. hospital under Section 60 of the Mental Health Act, with or without an order restricting discharge.

The most difficult problem now is that of the aggressive psychopathic murderer, who may plead successfully abnormality of mind and diminished responsibility, and who is then sentenced to a fixed term of imprisonment with the possibility of earning one-third remission of sentence for good conduct; so that he may be released while his behaviour is still unpredictable and potentially very dangerous. It is paradoxical that, had his plea of diminished responsibility failed, he would have been detained until the Home Secretary had satisfied himself that he was safe enough to be released.

DIMINISHED RESPONSIBILITY

The doctrine of diminished responsibility in cases of capital crime has for many years been accepted in the practice of the Scottish Courts. When such a plea is introduced the charge may be reduced from murder to manslaughter or (in Scotland) to culpable homicide. The Report of the Royal Commission on Capital Punishment (1949–53) referred to a memorandum submitted by the Crown Agent and Faculty of Advocates in which in 1867 in the case of Dingwall, Lord Deas directed the jury to take note of the fact that the mental state of the prisoner might constitute an extenuating circumstance and that it was not beyond their province to find a verdict of culpable homicide. In 1923 the matter was formulated more fully in the case of Rex v. Savage by Lord Alness as follows: 'Formerly there were only two classes of prisoner, those who were completely responsible, and those who were completely irresponsible. Our law has now come to recognize in murder cases a third class, those who, while they may not merit the description of being insane, are nevertheless in such a con- dition as to reduce the quality of their act from murder to culpable homicide . . . there must be aberration or weakness of mind; there must be some form of mental unsoundness; there must be a state of mind bordering on, though not amounting to insanity; there must be a mind so affected that responsibility is diminished from full responsibility to partial responsibility; the prisoner in question must be only partially responsible for his action.' The above doctrine is now accepted by the High Court of Justiciary as part of the Common Law of Scotland.

It is possible that the success of our Scottish practice was instrumental in effecting its applicability to England by its inclusion into the Homicide Act, 1957. According to that Act it is stated: 'Where a person kills or is party to the killing of another, he shall not be convicted of murder if he was suffering from such abnormality of mind (whether arising from a condition of arrested or retarded development of mind or any inherent causes or induced by disease or injury) as substantially impaired his mental responsibility for his acts and omissions in doing or being a party to the killing.' Under the above circum- stances the verdict will be one of manslaughter and not of murder.

The interpretation of the type of case which should be included under the category of diminished responsibility is still a matter of controversy. In the meantime we can only advise that each case must be determined on its individual merits irrespective of whether the predominating state is one of subnormality (mental deficiency), psychopathic personality, epilepsy, neurosis or other state in which a degree of abnormality of mind can be demonstrated. We would like to see the concept extended so that it might be made applicable, or at least be taken into careful consideration, not only in murder cases, but also in other offences, e.g. sexual offences, assault, fire-raising and so on. The enlargement of our outlook in such directions might lead to much greater research into the causes and motivation of criminal conduct, and in that way foster a closer alliance between lawyer and doctor whose mutual aim, as has been stated previously, is to do everything possible compatible with the safety of the lieges to rehabilitate the individual.

CIVIL RESPONSIBILITY

Evidence

Mental disorder is usually a bar to the ability to give evidence. There are, however, occasions on which a mentally disordered person has been adjudged able to do so. It is a matter for the Judge to determine whether the individual

2 N

in question understands the nature and obligations of an oath. Before he is sworn he may be examined, and evidence given of the state of his mind. If he is admitted as a witness it is for the jury to determine how much weight or importance should be given to his evidence. Before an affidavit (written evidence) is sworn there is a similar inquiry.

Contract

The general theory of contract is that there must be free and full consent of each of the contracting parties, and the consent must be an act of reason accompanied by due deliberation. A contract made by a person during a state of mental disorder is regarded as void. With the object, however, of preventing the mentally disordered person from benefiting from his act, he is required to make restitution to the other party if the latter has suffered. A contract made during a 'lucid' interval is as binding as if made by a person of sound mind. Patients compulsorily detained as a result of mental disorder are permitted to execute deeds and similar documents provided the responsible medical officer of the hospital in which they are certifies that the nature of the act is understood by the patient.

In the case of 'necessaries' there is an exception to the above general rule. 'Necessaries' are such articles as clothing, and whatever other articles the Court may decide in a particular case. They include, for instance, all expenses necessarily incurred in caring for the patient. An obligation rests upon the patient whether compulsorily detained or not, to repay a person who has supplied necessaries to him, if such necessaries are suitable to his position in life. The same rule holds in the case of a contract made by a person under the influence of alcohol.

Marriage. Marriage is a type of contract. Marriage with a person who is mentally disordered is null and void, when it is proved in a court of law that either contracting party was unable to comprehend the nature, or to fulfil the physical conditions of the marriage contract. The incapacity must be such that the party was, at the time of the marriage, incapable either of understanding the nature of the contract, and the duties and responsibilities it creates, or of taking care of his own person or property. Only a modest degree of understanding is necessary to comprehend the marriage contract. Hence impairment or weakness of mind, as distinguished from mental illness, does not invalidate a marriage unless fraud by the other party is proved. A person who marries during his mental disorder may sue for divorce on his recovery; while he is mentally disordered he may not sue, but his friends may do so on his behalf.

Contract of Insurance and Suicide. The Suicide Act, 1961, abrogates in England and Wales the law whereby it was a crime for a person to commit suicide. If a person who has insured his life while sane, commits suicide as a result of becoming mentally ill or disordered, a contract of life insurance will stand, unless the policy contained a special clause designed to meet the contingency of suicide.

Supervention of Mental Disorder. Mental disorder supervening after a contract has been made does not release either party from his obligations under the contract, unless the nature of the mental disorder makes fulfilment impossible. For instance, mental disorder supervening after marriage does not *per se* entitle either party to a divorce or to a judicial separation. On the other hand, it is not a sufficient defence to proceedings for divorce or separation by the partner of the marriage on the ground of cruelty or misconduct, unless it can be shown that the mental disorder was such as to render the mentally disordered person incapable of appreciating the character and consequences of the acts which led the partner to seek divorce or separation, and unless it can be shown that the mental disorder is persistent, and not merely transitory or intermittent.

Torts. Torts consist of wrongs done to the person, reputation or estate of an individual, and render the offender liable under the civil but not under the criminal law. The chief forms are trespass, libel, slander, fraud, nuisance and negligence. A mentally disordered person is considered as incapable of committing a tort unless it can be shown, to the satisfaction of the Court, that the mental disorder did not preclude the person from understanding the nature and probable consequence of the act complained of.

Receiver (England), Judicial Factor or Curator Bonis (Scotland)

A patient who has been compulsorily admitted to a mental hospital is deprived of his civil rights, and in consequence it is often of considerable importance to safeguard the management of his affairs. In England a 'receiver' may be appointed by a Judge in Lunacy upon application being made by the petitioner. In Scotland a curator bonis or judicial factor is appointed by petition to the Junior Lord Ordinary of the Court of Session. When the estate in question does not exceed £100 per annum the application may be made in the Sheriff Court. If the patient is not ill enough or is not so circumstanced as to require compulsory treatment and yet cannot or will not grant a Power of Attorney, then the above procedure may be carried out by a statement to the effect that by reason of mental infirmity arising from disease or age the patient is incapable of mangaing his affairs. The petition may be presented by:

1. The nearest relative, failing whom, any party having an interest.
2. In Scotland there is also a duty on the local health authority to petition the Court for such an appointment wherever it seems to them that it ought to be made, and no other person (a relative or creditor) is taking the necessary action.
3. The patient himself, if capable of understanding the effect of his doing so.

In the latter case the patient usually prefers to grant a Power of Attorney. Two medical certificates are required to support the application. The certificate is given on Soul and Conscience, and in Scotland it is sufficient to state that the patient's mental state is such as to render him incapable of managing his affairs or of giving instructions to others for their management. This petition must be served on the patient unless it is considered injurious to his interests to do so. In addition the petition is intimated on the walls and in the Minute Book of the Court, and any person wishing to oppose it must do so within a statutory period of eight days. The Curator makes an inventory of the estate, and renders annual accounts to the Accountant of Court under whose supervision he acts.

In England and Wales the medical certificates are much more detailed and explanations must be given as to why such a course is necessary.

Certificate of Sanity

A certificate of sanity may be required in a variety of cases; for instance, a patient who has been compulsorily admitted may believe that there is no justification for his detention in a mental hospital, and may demand an examination by two independent medical men, whom he is at liberty to name. If, after examination, medical certificates are granted stating that the patient has recovered and the Ministry of Health or Mental Health Review Tribunal (England) or the Mental Welfare Commission or Sheriff (Scotland) approves then the patient may be discharged. If the Tribunal or Mental Welfare Commission are satisfied by their own examination that the patient is recovered, then his discharge can be effected. Eight days' notice in writing is given to the person at whose instance the patient is detained, or failing such, to the nearest relative.

When a patient who has been compulsorily detained has been discharged either as relieved or recovered, a certificate of sanity may be required as presumptive evidence of his capacity to make a will, or sign a legal document. Furthermore, certificates of sanity are required to rescind a curatory, or receivership. The patient may require to be seen on several occasions before such a certificate is granted.

Testamentary Capacity

The point in this matter is to determine, not whether the testator is sane or mentally disordered, but whether his mental capacity is adequate to the testamentary act. This matter was put very clearly by Lord Chief Justice Cockburn in Banks v. Goodfellow, 1870, when he said:

'It is essential to the exercise of the powers of making a will that the testator shall understand the nature of the act and its effects; shall understand the extent of the property of which he is disposing; shall be able to comprehend and appreciate the claims to which he ought to give effect; and, with a view to the latter object, that no disorder of the mind shall poison the affections, pervert his sense of right, or prevent the exercise of his natural faculties; that no insane delusion shall influence his will in disposing of his property and bring about a disposal of it which, if the mind had been sound, would not have been made.'

He said further: 'No doubt when the fact that a testator has been subject to any insane delusion is established, a will should be regarded with great distrust, and every presumption should in the first instance be made against it. When an insane delusion has ever been shown to have existed it may be difficult to say whether the mental disorder may not possibly have extended beyond the particular form or instance in which it has manifested itself. It may be equally difficult to say how far the delusion may not have influenced the testator in the particular disposal of his property, and the presumption against a will made under such circumstances becomes additionally strong when the will is an inofficious one, that is to say, one in which natural affection and the claims of near relationship have been disregarded.'

It may be seen then that testamentary capacity can be interpreted within very wide limits, and that it may be consistent with mental disorder. Each case has to be decided on its merits, but there are certain points which the testator should be thoroughly cognizant of. He must be able at the time when he makes his will to recall and to keep clearly before his mind:

1. the nature and extent of his property;
2. the persons who will have claims upon his bounty; and
3. his judgement and will must be so unclouded and free as to enable him to determine the relative strength of these claims.

Furthermore, it is essential that a will, to maintain its validity, should be made by 'a person of full age and sound disposing mind, executed in due form'. 'A sound disposing mind' is not necessarily synonymous with perfect sanity, as there are persons who are mentally ill, who are compulsorily detained in a hospital, and yet are capable of making a satisfactory will. The most usual types of mental illness in which testamentary capacity may be questioned are those associated with the mental enfeeblement of old age, delusional states, delirium and other conditions in which the mind of the testator may be easily influenced, e.g. subnormality. In addition to any information and opinion we may have regarding the testator's appreciation of his act, the extent of his property, and the nature and effect of his act, it is advisable to inquire regarding the behaviour and conversation of the testator as known to his friends, relatives and business associates. His entire life history should be passed under review and especially his ability to transact business. The case of Thoms and Others v. Thoms' Trustee and Others (reported by Glaister) contains many instructive points; it shows how gross eccentricity may be combined with business acumen. The actual writing in the case of a holograph will, both from the point of view of expression and writing, may prove important. Spelling, tremors, ambiguous and involved statements have all to be taken into account. It should also be remembered that a person may be capable of making a simple will but not an involved one; it is only the actual will, however, which can be taken into account. In a case of physical disease it requires to be shown that there is a correlation between the physical and mental health leading to mental impairment. If the will can be proved not to be capricious or frivolous or venomous, even though it may appear so, but is really the expression of the person's real mind and intention, it should stand.

The same principles which govern the making of a will should also hold good to enable it to be revoked.

It should be noted that in the judgement in Banks v. Goodfellow, quoted above, it has been held that the clauses must be read conjunctively and not disjunctively, i.e. 'no disorder of the mind shall poison the affections (and) that no insane delusion shall influence his will' (Mr. Justice Langton in Bohrman v. Bohrman).

LEGAL ENACTMENTS

The Mental Health Acts

A Royal Commission was appointed in 1954, to inquire into the law in relation to mental illness and defect. The Mental Health Acts (1959, 1960) which have resulted are applicable to England and Wales, and Scotland. They reflect the progressive trends which have been taking place, not only in the general administration of our hospitals, but also in regard to the admission of patients and their care and treatment. The English Act differs from the Scottish one in certain minor particulars, which will be noted later, but they are in complete agreement on the broad principles on which the reforms have been based. These are:

1. To give the maximum encouragement to patients suffering from any form of mental illness or disability to seek treatment promptly and informally.
2. To ensure adequate restraint and safeguards where patients, in the interests of safety, must be compulsorily treated and detained.

It should be noted that the National Health Service Acts (1946, 1947) make the necessary provision for mental and nursing care and treatment whether carried out in hospital or at home. Every effort is being made to extend and improve the community services whereby the mentally ill or subnormal patient can be successfully cared for without recourse to hospital treatment, or if that becomes necessary, then the period of residence should be of as short duration as possible. The purpose and policy of the Mental Health Acts and the National Health Service Acts is to effect an integration so that harmonious working relationships can be established between them. The local health authority, in the case of mentally disordered persons, may—and, if so directed, should—carry out certain functions for the prevention of illness, and after-care:

1. the provision of residential accommodation, and the care of persons resident therein;
2. the exercise of functions in respect of persons under guardianship, and the supervision of subnormal patients not in hospital or subject to guardianship;
3. the ascertainment of subnormality in persons not of school age (education authorities have already a statutory duty in respect of children of school age);
4. the appointment of mental health officers to carry out duties relating to compulsory detention and guardianship; and
5. ancillary and supplementary services.

In addition to the above, it is the duty of the local authority to provide suitable training and occupation for children under 16 years of age who are unsuitable for education or training in a special school, and for subnormal persons over 16 years of age. Provisions are also incorporated whereby the local authority can arrange for visits to mentally disordered persons while in hospital. It is also laid down that there should be complete co-operation between education authorities and the local health authority. Such an arrangement is particularly necessary in the development of occupation centres some of which might be made residential.

The Mental Health Act (England and Wales), 1959, repeals the Lunacy and Mental Treatment Acts, 1890 to 1930, and the Mental Deficiency Acts, 1913 to 1938. It effects a completely new orientation in relation to the classification and care and treatment of mentally disordered persons. For instance the statutory designation of mental and mental deficiency hospitals is abolished, and any suitable hospital can admit mentally disordered patients. This, of course, does not mean that specialized psychiatric clinics and hospitals can be dispensed with, but it may lead to the quicker and more general development of psychiatric wards and clinics as part of general hospitals.

The English Act recognizes 4 groups of mentally disordered patients: 1. Mentally ill; 2. Severely subnormal; 3. Subnormal; 4. Psychopathic.

These categories have been defined as follows:

1. 'Mental disorder' means mental illness, arrested or incomplete development of mind, psychopathic disorder, and any other disorder or disability of mind; and 'mentally disordered' shall be construed accordingly.

2. 'Severe subnormality' means a state of arrested or incomplete development of mind which includes subnormality of intelligence and is of such a nature or degree that the patient is incapable of living an independent life, or will be so incapable when of an age to do so.

3. 'Subnormality' means a state of arrested or incomplete development of mind (not amounting to severe subnormality) which includes subnormality of intelligence and is of a nature or degree which requires or is susceptible to medical treatment or other special care or training of the patient.

4. 'Psychopathic disorder' means a persistent disorder of mind (whether or not accompanied by subnormality of intelligence) which results in abnormally aggressive or seriously irresponsible conduct on the part of the patient, and requires, or is susceptible to, medical treatment.

It is further laid down by the Act that subnormal and psychopathic patients should not be compulsorily admitted to hospital over the age of 21 years except for a short period of observation or after conviction in the Courts. They are, however, liable to compulsory admission under the age of 21 years, but unless admitted through the Courts or considered dangerous they should not be detained beyond the age of 25 years.

The above regulations may prove difficult to implement. There seems to be no particular point in attempting thus to differentiate between subnormality and severe subnormality—the one shades into the other, it is a matter of degree which, for administrative purposes, could safely be left to the decision of the medical specialist.

The definition of the term 'psychopathic disorder' might have been phrased much more in keeping with its clinical symptoms. We would suggest that it is not necessarily 'a persistent disorder of mind'. If it were so, then the last part of the definition suggesting that such a person 'requires or is susceptible to medical treatment' becomes superfluous. We have no accurate knowledge of how or why a psychopathic personality is determined, or how much is due to innate constitutional factors as compared with acquired characteristics of a multiple nature derived from a variety of personal, social and economic causes. In the absense of such knowledge it is perhaps a little presumptuous to speak in terms of 'persistence' or lack of it. From our own personal experience we can remember a considerable number of psychopathic persons who have made reasonably good readjustments. The definition also makes use of qualifying terms, e.g. 'abnormally aggressive' or 'seriously irresponsible'. Such qualifications are open to much argument and are likely to lead to difficulty, especially in the law courts. We prefer to think of psychopathic states as inclusive of persons who conform to a certain intellectual standard, sometimes high, sometimes approaching intellectual subnormality, but yet not amounting to it, who throughout their lives have exhibited disorders of conduct of an antisocial or asocial nature, usually of a recurrent or episodic type, which, in many instances, have proved difficult to influence by social, personal or medical measures.

Furthermore, the introduction of an age range during which the compulsory treatment of the subnormal and the psychopathic must be carried out—under 21 years and not beyond 25 years—is an assumption of knowledge and an attempt at certainty which is hardly justifiable.

The Board of Control of England and Wales which formerly was the responsible supervisory body concerned with mental illness and deficiency has been dissolved, and its duties have become merged in the work of the Ministry of Health, and in Mental Health Review Tribunals consisting of legal, medical and other members who consider applications from patients or their relatives, for release from hospital. There is one Tribunal for each of the fifteen Hospital Regions. The members in each region are drawn from three panels, one of legal members, one of medical members, and one of other members of relevant experience. We are inclined to think that the term 'Tribunal' is unfortunate—it smacks more of a court-martial or of criminal proceedings than of the beneficent purpose for which it has been introduced.

The drafters of the Mental Health (Scotland) Act, 1960, appear to have had the skill to evade some of the unnecessary complications of the English Act to which we have drawn attention. It repeals the Lunacy (Scotland) Acts 1913 to 1940. It provides that patients may be treated in hospitals or nursing homes for mental disorder without any formality, and makes new provision for those cases in which use of compulsory powers may be necessary, specifying the circumstances in which mentally disordered persons (including those involved in criminal proceedings) may be detained in hospital or placed under guardianship. It sets up a Mental Welfare Commission (in place of the General Board of Control) for Scotland to exercise protective functions in respect of mentally disordered persons who may be unable to protect themselves or their interests, and makes other provisions for the protection of patients and their property. The Commission includes, at least, two medical practitioners amongst its members of whom there are not fewer than five, and not more than seven. The Act makes minor amendments to the National Health Service (Scotland) Act, 1947, and other Acts relating to care and treatment and services that may be provided by local authorities for persons suffering from mental disorder. It provides for the registration of private hospitals and residential homes for persons suffering from mental disorder. For instance 'State Hospitals' replace the provision in the Mental Deficiency and Lunacy (Scotland) Act, 1913, for State institutions and in the Criminal Justice (Scotland) Act, 1949, for State Mental Hospitals. The 'State Hospitals' are for patients requiring treatment under conditions of special security on account of their dangerous, violent or criminal propensities.

Mental disorder is used in the Act as a general term to cover mental illness and subnormality however caused or manifested. These are the only categories referred to, and thus the questionable differentiations detailed in the English Act are avoided.

In those cases in which compulsion may be required for admission to hospital the application must receive the approval of the Sheriff as has heretofore been the case. In England the judicial authority has now been abrogated. The application must be supported by two medical recommendations—one by a doctor approved by the Regional Hospital Board who has had special experience in the diagnosis and treatment of mental disorder, the other by the patient's general practitioner, or by another doctor with previous acquaintance of the patient. Apart from the above-mentioned differences the regulations governing the care of patients and their interests follow an almost identical pattern to those in England. When compulsion is required, the application and medical recommendations must state the form of the patient's disorder which warrants the detention of the patient in a hospital, and that the interests of the patient's health and safety or the protection of other persons cannot be secured otherwise than by such detention. The application may be made by the nearest relative of the patient or by a mental welfare officer; in the latter case, the nearest relative should have been consulted, previously, by the mental welfare officer except in cases involving unreasonable delay in making arrangements. The patient should have been seen within the period of fourteen days ending with the date of the application; the medical recommendations are required to be given by practitioners who have personally seen the patient either together or at an interval of not more than seven days. The application shall be addressed to the managers of the hospital to which admission is sought, and shall specify the qualification of the applicant. In this respect certain statutory prohibitions must be complied with. For instance, a medical recommendation cannot be given by : 1. the applicant; 2. a partner of the applicant or of a practitioner by whom another medical recommendation is given for the purposes of the same application; 3. a person employed as an assistant by the applicant or by any such practitioner aforesaid; 4. a person who receives or has an interest in the receipt of any payments made on account of the maintenance of the patient; or 5. in the case of a private patient, by a practitioner on the staff of the hospital to which the patient is to be admitted.[1]

In cases of emergency the application may be made either by a mental welfare officer or by any relative of the patient. The patient can be detained for seven days in Scotland, and three days in England so as to provide time for the normal procedure to be effected.

Similar provision is made for application, founded on two medical recommendations, for reception of a patient into guardianship. The guardian may be a person or a local health authority. It is, however, specified that two classes of patient are not to be liable to admission to hospital or into guardianship under compulsion if they are over the age of 21 years. These are:

1. persons who, though mentally subnormal, are not so defective as to be unable to lead an independent life or to guard themselves against serious exploitation; and

2. mentally ill persons with a persistent disorder manifested only by abnormally aggressive or seriously irresponsible conduct. Such patients are to be discharged on reaching the age of 25 years, unless likely to act dangerously.

While, therefore, the Scottish Act does not mention psychopathic persons it subscribes to and adopts the definition given in the English Act which we have already criticized.

According to the English Act a patient who is compulsorily detained may apply to a Mental Health Review Tribunal within the period of six months since admission, or when he attains the age of 16 years, to have his case reconsidered. In Scotland the appeal may be made to the Sheriff of the County in which the patient resides, or to the Mental Welfare Commission which has a right to discharge a patient at any time, and a duty to do so in certain circumstances. The Commission will also be constantly available to hear and investigate any complaint of wrongful detention or improper treatment.

The foregoing is merely a general summary of the main changes which have been effected by the new Acts which now operate in Great Britain. For the detailed changes the respective Acts should be consulted.

In all cases in which a patient is advised to seek admission to a hospital or clinic either informally or under compulsion, the doctor has a highly important and serious responsibility. It is almost too easy to advise hospital care and treatment, and we strongly support the view that every other avenue should be explored before such a course is taken. No deception should ever be utilized: when admission to hospital is considered necessary the patient and his relatives should be fully informed regarding all the legal implications which may be involved. And it is advisable in cases of mental illness of whatsoever kind that the doctor should keep detailed notes of the circumstances which led him to the opinion that hospital treatment was necessary. There are a number of cases

[1] Here the provisions of the Mental Health Act, 1959, have been quoted.

who may prove to be uncooperative, and for whom compulsion might seem to be the only practicable method of providing adequate care and treatment, but social or economic or business circumstances may be such that attempts at compromise should be persevered with. There should, however, so as to avoid a disastrous occurrence, be no undue delay. The particular aims in employing compulsion are: 1. to protect the public from injury; 2. to protect the patient from self-injury; 3. to give treatment with a view to care or amelioration which cannot otherwise be given; and/or 4. to protect the patient from injury due to want of care. The prescribed forms require to be filled in with meticulous care, and with sufficient detail to satisfy the officials of the Ministry of Health (England and Wales) and the Sheriff of the County (Scotland) that all the regulations have been complied with, and that the patient's condition is such that hospital care is imperative.

A good general plan to follow is to describe the appearance of the patient, whether depressed, elated, excited, suspicious, antagonistic. Any abnormality of conduct should be noted, whether unduly talkative, restless, destructive, liable to self-injury; or mute, inactive, stereotyped in speech and action. It is important to describe any hallucinatory or delusional symptoms which may be present, and if possible to give a short verbatim statement of abnormal remarks uttered by the patient. If the patient's intellectual functions are involved, then attention should be drawn to memory impairment, facility, lack of insight and judgement, and the obvious necessity for hospital treatment. It is wiser to avoid a definite diagnosis; it may be wrong, or at least arguable, and is more an inference than a fact.

The reason for exercising so much care is because, at a later date, a person who has been compelled to accept hospital treatment may demand an examination by two independent medical men, and may seek compensation by an action of damages for unnecessary and wrongful treatment. The doctors, therefore, who have made the recommendation must be able to produce proof that they have acted in good faith, and with reasonable care.

The above-mentioned beneficial changes and improvements which have now been introduced into Great Britain were anticipated or forestalled by the Irish Acts, which also deserve consideration.

The Republic of Ireland

The Mental Treatment Act, 1945, may be said to have ushered in a new era in the care and treatment of mentally ill persons. It abolished judicial certification, and transferred complete responsibility for the care and treatment of mentally ill persons to the Minister of Health. That arrangement has proved eminently successful. The main provisions of the Act are as follows:

Reception Orders. An application for the reception and detention of a patient is made to an authorized medical practitioner. The applicant must be over the age of 21 years, and must have seen the patient within a period of fourteen days. The authorized medical practitioner shall, within twenty-four hours: 1. visit and examine the person to whom the application relates: and 2. shall either accept or reject the recommendation. If the patient is accepted for care and treatment then (a) the recommendation shall be dated and signed on the same day; (b) the recommendation shall contain a certificate stating that the person concerned is of unsound mind, is a proper person to be taken charge of and detained under care and treatment, and is unlikely to recover within six months from the date of such examination; (c) the facts as determined by the examiner, and as obtained from others require to be stated. The certificate should be acted on within fourteen days. When the resident medical superintendent or his deputy examines the patient at the local mental hospital he must decide whether the patient is suitable for care and treatment. If not suitable then a statement to that effect, with reasons for refusal, must be transmitted to the Minister of Health.

Temporary Reception Orders. A temporary reception order may be utilized in those cases in which the patient is likely to recover within six months or if he is an addict to drugs or intoxicants, and will require at least six months' preventive and curative treatment. Temporary orders may be extended for a period not exceeding eighteen months.

Voluntary Patients. The application for admission is directed to the medical officer in charge of the mental hospital, and must be supported by a recommendation from an authorized doctor.

Northern Ireland

The Mental Health Act (N.I.), 1948, has also effected many improvements, and has simplified and expedited the admission of mentally ill patients to hospital.

Judicial certification has been abolished and all admissions to a mental hospital are arranged on a voluntary or temporary basis.

Temporary Patients. In the case of temporary patients a written application is made to the medical superintendent of the mental hospital by a relative of the patient, or, when a relative is not available, by a welfare officer. The application requires the recommendation of one medical practitioner stating reasons why such treatment is considered necessary. The initial period of temporary treatment extends for not longer than twelve months. This period may be extended by application to the Northern Ireland Ministry of Health and Local Government by two further periods not exceeding six months each. In exceptional circumstances an additional extension may be obtained. When a person alleged to be suffering from mental illness is brought to a place of safety, or is not under proper control, or cruelly treated, a judicial order is required for his removal to a mental hospital, but the order requires the patient to be dealt with on a temporary basis. If the temporary patient is considered unlikely to recover, and if further care in the mental hospital is required, then a judicial order becomes necessary. But certification is effected while the patient is still in the mental hospital.

Addicts. Addicts can be dealt with on a temporary basis. They are defined as persons who: 1. by reason of their addiction to drugs or intoxicants are dangerous to themselves or others, or incapable of managing themselves, or their affairs, or of ordinary proper conduct; or 2. by reason of their addiction are in serious danger of mental disorder. The net appears to have been spread very wide; almost anyone might be caught in it.

Mentally Infirm. Elderly persons who are mentally unable to care for themselves or their affairs are specially provided for.

Mental Defectives. These patients are defined as persons requiring special care on account of arrested or incomplete development of mind whether arising from inherent causes or induced by disease or injury which renders them socially inefficient to such an extent that they require supervision, training or control in their own or the public interest. The responsibility for the ascertainment and community care of the mentally subnormal is vested in the Northern Ireland Hospital Authority.

Criminal Justice (Scotland) Act, 1949

The introduction of this Act, which was similar to the Criminal Justice Act (England and Wales) 1948, made many beneficial changes in dealing with offenders. Its provisions have been largely replaced by Part V of the Mental Health (Scotland) Act, and only one will be considered here.

Probation Orders requiring Treatment for Mental Condition. Where the Court is satisfied on the evidence of a medical practitioner who has knowledge and experience of mental disorders that the offender requires or is likely to benefit from treatment, it may make a probation order for a period not exceeding twelve months. The probationer may receive treatment as an in-patient or out-patient at an appropriate hospital, or under the direction of a registered medical practitioner. The necessary arrangements for the reception and treatment of the patient should be made before the probation order is sanctioned. The medical practitioner under whose direction the probationer is being treated is allowed considerable discretion if special circumstances arise, *e.g.* if a surgical operation should become necessary. A probationer retains his right to refuse surgical, electrical or other treatment if the Court, in view of all the circumstances, is satisfied that the refusal is reasonable.

The Matrimonial Causes Act, 1965

1. No petition for divorce shall be presented to the High Court unless at the date of presentation of the petition three years have passed since the date of the marriage.

A Judge of the High Court, however, may allow a petition to be presented before three years have passed on the ground that the case is one of exceptional hardship suffered by the petitioner, or of exceptional depravity on the part of the respondent.

2. A petition for divorce may be presented to the Court either by the husband or the wife on the ground that the respondent:

(*a*) has since the celebration of the marriage committed adultery; or
(*b*) has deserted the petitioner without cause for a period of at least three years immediately preceding the presentation of the petition; or

(c) has since the celebration of the marriage treated the petitioner with cruelty; or

(d) is incurably of unsound mind, and has been continually under care and treatment for a period of at least five years immediately preceding the presentation of the petition; and by the wife on the ground that her husband has since the celebration of the marriage, been guilty of rape, sodomy or bestiality.

3. It should be noted that no mention of subnormality is made in these divorce provisions.

4. On a petition for divorce it shall be the duty of the Court:

(a) to inquire, so far as it reasonably can, into the facts alleged and whether there has been any connivance or condonation on the part of the petitioner and whether any collusion exists between the parties and also to inquire into any countercharge which is made against the petitioner.

(b) If the Court is satisfied on the evidence that:

(i) the case for the petition has been proved; and

(ii) when the ground of the petition is adultery, the petitioner has not in any manner been accessory to, or connived at, or condoned the adultery, or where the ground of the petition is cruelty the petitioner has not in any manner condoned the cruelty; and

(iii) the petition is not presented or prosecuted in collusion with the respondent or either of the respondents;

the Court shall grant a decree of divorce, but if the Court is not satisfied with respect to any of the aforesaid matters, it shall dismiss the petition.

Provided that the Court shall not be bound to pronounce a decree of divorce it may dismiss the petition if it finds that the petitioner has during the marriage been guilty of adultery or if, in the opinion of the Court, the petitioner has been guilty:

(a) of unreasonable delay in presenting or prosecuting the petition; or

(b) of cruelty towards the other party to the marriage; or

(c) where the ground of the petition is adultery or cruelty, of having without reasonable excuse deserted, or having without reasonable excuse wilfully separated himself or herself from the other party before the the adultery or cruelty complained of; or

(d) where the ground of the petition is adultery or unsoundness of mind or desertion, or such wilful neglect or misconduct as has condoned to the adultery or unsoundness of mind or desertion.

5. In addition to any other grounds on which a marriage is by law void or voidable, a marriage shall be voidable on the ground:

(a) that the marriage has not been consummated owing to the wilful refusal of the respondent to consummate the marriage; or

(b) that either party to the marriage was at the time of the marriage of unsound mind or suffering from mental disorder or subject to recurrent attacks of insanity or epilepsy; or

(c) that the respondent was at the time of the marriage suffering from venereal disease in a communicable form; or

(d) that the respondent was at the time of the marriage pregnant by some person other than the petitioner.

Provided that, in the cases specified in paragraphs (b), (c) and (d) of this subsection, the Court shall not grant a decree unless it is satisfied:

(i) that the petitioner was at the time of the marriage ignorant of the facts alleged;

(ii) that proceedings were instituted within a year from the date of the marriage; and

(iii) that marital intercourse with the consent of the petitioner has not taken place since the discovery by the petitioner of the existence of the grounds for a decree.

It should be noted that subnormality is included in the provisions relating to nullity, though subnormality is not a ground for divorce.

'Of unsound mind' is not defined in the Act but is equivalent to the older terms 'insane' or 'lunatic'. An important legal point which arises is the meaning of 'incurably of unsound mind'. It means irrecoverable by any means whatever—whether in the course of nature, or in consequence of mental treatment.

'Recoverable' means that degree of recovery which would enable the patient (respondent) to undertake again the ordinary responsibilities of marriage. It does not mean capable of improvement to the extent merely of being able to live outside of a mental hospital, or of being released from compulsory detention while still being under some kind of supervision.

A very important point for the medical witness is what degree of certainty must attach to the statement that a patient is irrecoverable; must he be absolutely irrecoverable, as in the case of some of the organic dementias, or must recovery be only extremely improbable? Rulings in these cases have shown that the latter is the legal view. There must be a reasonable certainty that the patient will not recover, but it is not necessary to be able to say that recovery is utterly inconceivable. Thus where the case was one of a chronic schizophrenic type of reaction and the chances were stated to be at least 30 to 1 against recovery, a decree was granted.

The medical problem of the prognosis after five years' continuous mental illness is an interesting one, and one of which few statistical studies appear to have been made. In organic dementias, once the diagnosis is definitely established, the problem is usually simple. A patient with an alcoholic or syphilitic or arteriosclerotic dementia, who has been detained in hospital for that reason for five years or more, may safely be regarded as incurable. A very rare case of recovery from a long-standing epileptic type of dementia has been recorded, but this is so rare that for the purposes of this Act the knowledge of its occurrence could not influence the Judge.

The problem is more difficult with the chronic forms of manic-depressive and schizophrenic illness, especially the former. Of the 'late recoveries' that have been recorded in the literature, most cases have been designated 'chronic mania'.

The medical witness should therefore beware of emphasizing too greatly the impossibility of recovery in a case of this sort. Examples of recovery in chronic mania have been recorded after five or seven or even more years; but they are, of course, very rare, the aggregate of such cases being small anyhow. Recovery from chronic depression, whether manic-depressive or involutional in type, can be said to be very exceptional after five years; and this statement applies even more to the chronic schizophrenic reactions.

The other matters connected with these Acts are mainly of a legal kind.

In determining whether any period of care and treatment has been continuous, any interruption of the period for twenty-eight days or less is disregarded.

Infanticide Act, 1938

The Courts have invariably dealt with a woman who has been convicted of the murder of her child under one year old with the greatest kindness and consideration. In all such cases allowance is made for all the mitigating circumstances which may be present. The statute states that, when a woman causes the death of her child under the age of 12 months, and at the time of her act the balance of her mind was disturbed by reason of her not having fully recovered from the effect of giving birth, or by reason of the effect of lactation consequent upon the birth of her child, the verdict will be one of infanticide in lieu of murder.

The Infanticide Act does not apply to Scotland. In Scotland, under similar circumstances, the woman would be tried on a charge of culpable homicide.

As an indication of the leniency with which such cases are regarded the Royal Commission on Capital Punishment in its Report stated that during the years 1923 to 1948, 602 women were tried for infanticide of whom 512 were convicted. 'Of these 5 were sentenced to penal servitude, 167 were sentenced to imprisonment or Borstal detention, 161 were bound over with a probation order, 165 were bound over on their own recognizances, and 14 were dealt with under the Mental Deficiency Acts.'

REFERENCES

Bluglass, R. S. (1967) *M.D. Thesis*, University of St. Andrews.
Brown, F., and Epps, P. (1966) *Brit. J. Psychiat.*, **112**, 1043.
Douglas, J. W. B. (1968) *Genetics and Environmental Influences on Behaviour*, ed. Thoday, J. M., and Parkes, Sir A., Edinburgh.
Gibbens, T. C. N. (1963) *Psychiatric Studies of Borstal Lads*, London.
Gibbens, T. C. N., and Prince, J. (1962) *Shoplifting*, London.
Gibbens, T. C. N., and Prince, J. (1963) *Child Victims of Sex Offences*, Institute for the Study and Treatment of Delinquency, London.
Gillies, H. (1965) *Brit. J. Psychiat.*, **111**, 1087.
Jacobs, P. A., Brunton, M., Melville, M. M., Brittain, R. P., and McClemont, W. F. (1965) *Nature (Lond.)*, **208**, 1351.
Mohr, J. W., Turner, R. E., and Jerry, M. B. (1964) *Pedophilia and Exhibitionism*, Toronto.
Mowat, R. R. (1966) *Morbid Jealousy and Murder*, London.
Murder: A Home Office Research Unit Report (1961), London, H.M.S.O.
Nurcombe, B. (1964) *Med. J. Aust.*, **1**, 579.

Price, W. H., and Whatmore, P. B. (1967) *Brit. med. J.*, **1**, 533.
Radzinowicz, L., and Turner, J. W. C., eds. (1957) *Sexual Offences*, London.
Roper, W. F. (1950) *Brit. J. Delinq.*, **1**, 15.
Roper, W. F. (1951) *Brit. J. Delinq.*, **1**, 243.
Royal Commission on Capital Punishment, 1949–1953, London, H.M.S.O.
Scott, P. D., and Willcox, D. R. C. (1965) *Brit. J. Psychiat.*, **111**, 865.
Walker, N. (1965) *Crime and Punishment in Britain*, Edinburgh.
West, D. J. (1963) *The Habitual Prisoner*, London.
West, D. J. (1965) *Murder Followed by Suicide*, London.

INDEX